D0027998

JUNG CHANG

A TOUCHSTONE BOOK
Published by Simon & Schuster
New York London Toronto Sydney

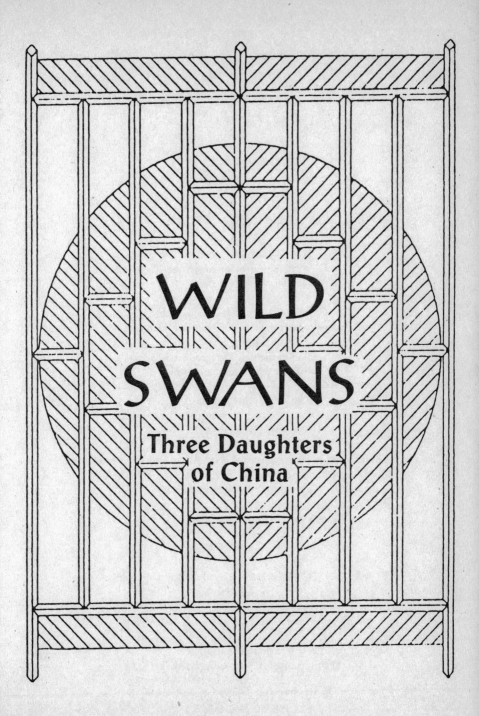

WILD SWANS

Three Daughters of China

Touchstone
Rockefeller Center
1230 Avenue of the Americas
New York, NY 10020

First Touchstone Edition 2003
TOUCHSTONE and colophon are registered trademarks
of Simon & Schuster, Inc.

For information regarding special discounts for bulk purchases,
please contact Simon & Schuster Special Sales at 1-800-456-6798
or business@simonandschuster.com

Manufactured in the United States of America

5 7 9 10 8 6

The Library of Congress has cataloged the hardcover edition
as follows:
Chang, Jung.
Wild swans : three daughters of China / Jung Chang.
p.   cm.
Includes index
1. Chang, Jung. 2. China—Biography. I. Title.
CT1828.C478 A3   1991
951.05'092 B—dc20   91-20696
ISBN 0-7432-4698-5

To my grandmother and my father
who did not live to see this book

Acknowledgments

Jon Halliday has helped me create *Wild Swans*. Of his many contributions, polishing my English was only the most obvious. Through our daily discussions, he forced me into greater clarification of both the stories and my thoughts, and helped me search the English language for the exact expressions. I felt safer under his historian's knowledgeable and meticulous scrutiny, and relied on his sound judgment.

Toby Eady is the best agent anyone could possibly hope for. He helped push me, gently, into taking up the pen in the first place.

I feel privileged to be associated with such outstanding professionals as Alice Mayhew, Charles Hayward, Jack McKeown and Victoria Meyer at Simon & Schuster in New York and Simon King, Carol O'Brien, and Helen Ellis at HarperCollins in London. To Alice Mayhew, my editor at Simon & Schuster, I owe special gratitude for her insightful comments and invaluable dynamism. Robert Lacey at HarperCollins did a superb job editing the manuscript, for which I am deeply indebted. Ari Hoogenboom's efficiency and warmth on the transatlantic phone have been energizing. I am also thankful to all those who have worked on this book.

The enthusiastic interest of my friends has been a perpetual source of encouragement. To all of them I am most grateful. I have received particular help from Peter Whitaker, I Fu En, Emma Tennant, Gavan McCormack, Herbert Bix, R. G. Tiedemann, Hugh Baker, Yan Jiaqi, Su Li-qun, Y. H. Zhao, Michael Fu, John Chow, Clare Peploe, André Deutsch, Peter Simpkin, Ron Sarkar, and Vanessa Green. Clive Lindley has played a special role through his valuable advice from the beginning.

My brothers and sister and my relatives and friends in China have generously allowed me to tell their stories, without which *Wild Swans* would not have been possible. I can never thank them sufficiently.

Much of the book is the story of my mother. I hope I have done her justice.

JUNG CHANG
May 1991
London, England

Contents

Introduction to the 2003 Edition

Wild Swans was first published in 1991. The event changed my life, because I finally became a writer.

I had always dreamed of being a writer. But when I was growing up in China, the idea of writing for publication seemed out of the question. In those years, the country was under Mao's tyranny, and most writers suffered appallingly in endless political persecutions. Many were denounced, some sent to labor camps, and some driven to suicide. In 1966 through 1967, during Mao's Great Purge misnamed the Cultural Revolution, the majority of books in people's homes were burned. My father, who had been a Communist official but had fallen victim, was forced to burn his beloved collection, and this was one of the main things that drove him to insanity. Even writing for oneself was extremely dangerous. I had to tear up the first poem I ever wrote, which was on my sixteenth birthday on 25 March 1968, and flush it down the toilet because my father's persecutors had come to raid our apartment.

But I had an urge to write, and kept on writing with an imaginary pen. In the next few years, I worked as a peasant and an electrician. While I was spreading manure in the paddy fields and checking power distribution at the top of electricity poles, I would polish long passages in my mind, or commit short poems to memory.

I came to Britain in September 1978. Mao had died two years earlier, and China was beginning to emerge from the stifling isolation he had imposed on the country. For the first time since the founding of Communist China, scholarships for studying abroad were awarded on academic, not political, grounds. I was able to leave the country after taking these exams, and was perhaps the first person from the land-locked province of Sichuan, which then had a population of about 90 million, to study in the West since 1949. With this incredible good fortune, at last I had the freedom to write, and to write what I wanted.

And yet it was at this moment that I lost the passion. In fact, the last thing I wished to do was write. To me, it would have meant turning inward and dwelling on a life and a time that I hated to think about. I was trying to forget China. Having landed in a place that felt like another planet, I was instantly smitten and had no desire but to spend every minute soaking in this new world.

Everything about London was exhilarating. My first letter to my mother was a gushing flourish about some window boxes and front gardens en route to 42 Maida Vale, a Chinese embassy property that was my accommodation. This was a time when flowers were yet to readorn most Chinese homes. In 1964, Mao had denounced cultivating flowers and grass as "feudal" and "bourgeois," and ordered, "Get rid of most gardeners." As a child, I had had to join others in removing the grass from the lawns at our school, and had seen flowerpots disappear from buildings. I had felt intensely sad, and had not only struggled to hide my feelings, but also blamed myself for having instincts that went against Mao's instructions, a mental activity I had been brainwashed to engage in like other children in China. Although by the time I left, one could express love for flowers without being condemned, China was still a bleak place where there were virtually no houseplants or flower vendors. Most parks were brutalized wastelands.

So it was with indescribable pleasure that I took a long walk in the great expanse of Hyde Park on the first day I was allowed out. There, under those majestic chestnut trees, every blade of grass and every flower petal made me mad with joy. One day I risked being sternly told off, or worse, by proposing to the political supervisor of the group to which I belonged that we should move our Saturday indoctrination sessions, called "political studies," to the lawns of the famed Kew Gardens.

At the time, weekly indoctrination sessions, which had bored me sick in China, were still compulsory, and in London we from the Mainland were still under prisonlike control. We were forbidden to go anywhere without permission, or on our own. Disobeying orders could mean being sent back to China in disgrace, to a life ruined. Feeling suffocated in the tantalizing freedom of London, I became obsessed with designing schemes to stretch or break the rules. And I succeeded sometimes, as when I went to Kew Gardens, because the political supervisor himself hankered after this even though he was very worried about trouble from the embassy. As a result, a group of young men and women in baggy blue uniform-like "Mao suits" sat incongruously—but happily—next to a splendidly colorful rose garden.

And there was no trouble. I was lucky because this was the very time when dramatic changes were sweeping China. At the end of 1978 came the turning point when the country rejected the essence of Maoism. In the following year, I was able to keep pushing the limits of restriction with risks but no repercussions. One place I particularly set my eyes on was the English pub opposite our college, because we were specifically told not to visit it. The Chinese translation for "pub," *jiu-ba*, in those days suggested somewhere indecent, with nude women gyrating. I was torn with curiosity. One day, I sneaked away and darted for the pub. I pushed the door open and stole in. I saw nothing sensational, only some old men sitting around drinking beer. I was rather disappointed.

I may well have been the first Mainland student abroad to have gone out on his or her own. A member of the staff at the college I was attending—now Thames Valley University—invited me to go to Greenwich with him. As per our rule, I asked him whether I could "bring a friend." He misunderstood me, and said, "You are safe with me." I was embarrassed, but could not explain. Our orders were that we must not tell anyone that it was a regulation to have a chaperon; we had to invent our own excuses. But I did not want to lie, and moreover, I desperately wanted to go without a minder. So I begged the embassy attaché in charge of the students to let me go; otherwise, I implored, the Englishman would think we Chinese did not trust him, or even suspected his motives, which would be bad for Anglo-Chinese friendship and for the reputation of our socialist motherland. At the end of this tosh the attaché said yes, and told me to be discreet. My hunch was that he did not much like the system himself. In fact, he had hinted at this by confiding in me one evening when we found ourselves alone in the building. He had loved a girl two decades before, and just when they were about to be married, she was condemned as a "Rightist" in a political campaign. To go ahead with the marriage would have meant the end of his own career, which was looking very bright. She insisted on breaking off their engagement. After much agonizing he agreed, and went on to become a successful diplomat. But he never got over her, or forgave himself. He was in tears while talking to me.

It did not seem strange that an embassy official who hardly knew me should bare his heart. In those years, people were so weighed down with tragedies in their lives that they were prone to unburdening themselves suddenly when they sensed a kindred spirit. The liberalization in China was loosening the locks on the floodgates of people's memory. It also made it possible for the attaché to risk giving me groundbreaking permission to step out of my living quarters alone.

I remember that outing to Greenwich vividly to this day. It was an unexceptional one: driving, walking, and photo-taking at the meridian with one foot in each hemisphere. But I was dizzy with tension. All the time, I was looking out for people who appeared Chinese, and making a quick judgment about whether they were from the Mainland based on their clothes; if I decided they were, which was irrationally often (there were very few Mainland Chinese in the West then), I would turn my head to avoid them, while straining to behave as naturally as possible to my companion. I was frightened that someone might spot me and report to the embassy, in which case I would be finished, and the nice attaché could be endangered as well. An exotic picnic with cheese sandwiches on a vast, serene lawn was the most nerve-racking moment of the day, as I was tied to the spot with nowhere to hide.

Fear did not stop me from trying other adventures—not out of love for the thrills of danger, but simply because I could not help it. As rules got looser and looser, I was out and about more and more on my own, and quickly made friends with people from different walks of life. To most I said I was from South Korea rather than China. Apart from the semiclandestine nature of my activities, I did not want people's curiosity to be focused on my country of origin, which in those days fascinated as if it were outer space, thanks to its hermetic isolation. I wanted to mingle unobtrusively, like a normal person in London. I was able to do this—and my first and most powerful impression was that Britain was a marvelously classless society. I was born into the Communist elite, and saw how class-ridden and hierarchical Mao's China was. Everyone was slotted into a rigid category. On every form, next to "date of birth" and "sex" was the inevitable column "family background." This determined one's career, relationships, and life. Many from the elite tended to be snooty, and those who happened to be born into a "bad" family were destined to lives wrecked. The upshot of this horrible reality was that we were all obsessed with who came from what family, and often people would ask the question outright in their first conversation with you. But meeting people in London, I sensed none of this pressure. Everyone seemed to be extraordinarily equal, and could not care less about one's background.

My views have been somewhat modified over the years, but I don't think I was entirely starry-eyed. In spite of its tradition of class differences, people in Britain have dignity, and the underprivileged are not abused or downtrodden as they were under Mao. And the fairness of the society, and the weight the nation places on this concept, is something today's China still cannot begin to match.

So it was with both reason and emotion that I fell in love with Britain. My first year here was a whirlwind of the most intoxicating time. I visited every museum and gallery marked on the tourist map, and saw show after show that charged next to nothing for students. I welcomed walking for hours across London to save on fares, because every building and every street was of interest. I poked my head into sleazy nightclubs and glanced at the wares of Soho sex shops. My first disco was delirious. Even an average cinema felt like an Aladdin's cave, where dimmed lights on old red upholstery and the odd gilding here and there suggested mystery and treasures. I asked what I later realized to be bizarre questions, and learned about people of different cultures. The last taboo to break was having foreign boyfriends, which I had to do secretly, still expecting catastrophe. A cautionary tale I had carried with me from China, and which I firmly believed, was that anyone who attempted to have a foreign lover would be drugged and carted back to China in a jute sack. When I was anywhere remotely near Portland Place, where the embassy is, my legs would turn to jelly, and if I was in a car I would shrink down in the seat so my head would disappear below the window. It was then that I put on make-up for the first time in my life—I thought this would provide satisfactory disguise from the embassy (which in fact was not then carrying out the kind of surveillance I imagined at this time). Daubed liberally with scarlet or purple lipstick and green-gold eye shadow, my face was hardly recognizable even to myself.

It was also fun to play with makeup while diving into a doctorate in linguistics. I was offered a scholarship by the University of York, a town which, even before I set eyes on it, had already exercised an incredible lure for me, with its legendary minster, city walls (the nearest thing, I had heard, to the Great Wall of China), and the Wars of the Roses. At the time, foreign scholarships had to be routed through the Chinese government and could not be accepted by individuals. But I was given yet another path-blazing go-ahead to take up the offer, thanks to people like the sympathetic attaché in the embassy and the growing relaxation in China. As a result, when I completed my degree in 1982, I became the first person from Communist China to receive a doctorate from a British university.

I learned far more than linguistic theories (which, I am ashamed to say, I have since largely forgotten). I remember the day I went to discuss the plan for my thesis with my supervisor, Professor Le Page, who, through his sensitive presence alone, had already begun to help dispel the perpetual anxiety and sudden panic that were embedded in me. His mildly ironic manner and understated authority constantly reassured me, as England did, that I had come to a just place, and that I had nothing to worry about. Feeling totally relaxed, I babbled on about my views on the linguistic theories I was supposed to survey. He listened, and at the end asked me, "Could you show me your thesis?" I was nonplussed, and exclaimed, "But I haven't started it yet!" He said, "But you have all the conclusions."

That single remark untied a strangling knot fastened on my brain by a totalitarian "education." We in China had been trained not to draw conclusions from facts, but to start with Marxist theories or Mao thoughts or the Party line and to deny, even condemn, the facts that did not suit them. I pondered over the new approach as I walked back to my campus room in a building on a corner of the beautiful lake. Water birds had formed a colony under my window and woke me with their singing every morning. They were now flying across the sky, a fitting image for my sensation of having found the right way of thinking. Keeping an open mind: so simple, and yet it had taken me so long to discover it.

It was at York that one night the thought of writing a book about my past life came to me. I was invited to a talk by a professor who had just been in China. He showed some slides of a school he had visited, where the pupils were having lessons on an obviously freezing winter day, in classrooms with no heating but roundly broken windows. "Are they not cold?" the kindly professor had asked. "No, they are not," the school had answered.

After the slide show there was a reception, and one woman, perhaps struggling to find something to say to me, began: "You must feel very hot here." This innocent remark hurt me so badly that I left the room abruptly and had my first cry since I came to Britain. It was not so much a feeling of being insulted, but an overwhelming pain for the people of my native land. We were not treated by our own government as proper human beings, and consequently some outsiders did not regard us as the same kind of humans as themselves. I thought of the old observation that Chinese lives were cheap, and one Englishman's amazement that his Chinese servant should find a toothache unbearable. I was infuriated once again by the many admiring comments of Westerners who had visited Mao's China that the Chinese were extraordinary people who seemed to enjoy being criticized, denounced, "reformed" in labor camps—all things that would seem sheer misery to Westerners.

With these thoughts churning in my head, I recalled my life in China, my family and all those people I knew, and at that moment I longed to tell the world our stories and how the Chinese really felt. My urge to write returned.

But it was years before I wrote *Wild Swans*. Subconsciously, I resisted the idea of writing. I was unable to dig deep into my memory. In the violent Cultural Revolution between 1966 and 1976, my family suffered atrociously. Both my father and my grandmother died painful deaths. I did not want to relive my grandmother's years of untreated illness, my father's imprisonment, and my mother's kneeling on broken glass. The few lines I produced were superficial and lifeless. I was not happy with them.

Then, in 1988, my mother came to London to stay with me. This was her first trip abroad. I wanted her to enjoy herself thoroughly, and spent much time taking her out. After a short while, I noticed she was not having the time of her life. Something was on her mind; she was restless. One day, she declined a shopping trip, and settled at my black dining table on which a bouquet of golden daffodils shone. Cupping a mug of jasmine tea in her hands, she told me that what she most wanted to do was to talk to me.

My mother talked every day for months. For the first time in our lives, she told me about herself and about my grandmother. My grandmother, I learned, had been the concubine of a warlord general, and my mother had joined the Communist underground at the age of fifteen. Both of them had eventful lives in a China that was tossed about by wars, foreign invasions, revolutions, and then a totalitarian tyranny. In the general maelstrom they were involved in poignant romances. I learned about my mother's ordeals, her close shaves with death, and her love for my father and emotional conflicts with him. I also came to know the agonizing details of my grandmother's footbinding: how her feet had been crushed under a big stone when she was two to satisfy the standards of beauty of the day.

Tourism became the backdrop of our conversations. As we traveled to the Isle of Skye in Scotland and Lake Lugano in Switzerland, my mother would talk in planes and cars, on boats, during walks, and halfway through the night. When I was out working, she would stay at home and speak into a tape recorder. By the time she left Britain, she had done sixty hours of recordings. Here, outside the social and political confines of China, she was able to do something she had not been able to do all her life: open her mind and her heart.

As I listened to my mother, I was overwhelmed by her longing to be understood by me. It also struck me that she would really love me to write. She seemed to know that writing was where my heart lay, and was encouraging me to fulfil my dreams. She did this not through making demands, which she never did, but by providing me with stories—and showing me how to face the past. Despite her having lived a life of suffering and torment, her stories were not unbearable or depressing. Underlying them was a fortitude that was all the time uplifting.

It was my mother who finally inspired me to write *Wild Swans*, the stories of my grandmother, my mother, and myself through the turbulence of twentieth-century China. For two years, I shed my fair share of tears, and tossed and turned through quite a few sleepless nights. I would not have persevered had it not been for the fact that by that time I had found a love that filled my life and cushioned me with a deep tranquillity. Jon Halliday, my knight without armor, for his inner strength under the softest exterior is enough to conquer, is the most priceless treasure I have taken from my adopted country, Britain. He was there, and everything would be all right—everything, including the writing of *Wild Swans*.

I relied a great deal on Jon in the creation of the book. English was a language I had only started learning properly when I was twenty-one, in an environment totally cut off from the outside world. The only foreigners I had spoken to before I came to Britain were some sailors in the south China port of Zhanjiang, a former French colony where my fellow students and I were sent to practice our English for a fortnight. When I arrived in London, although I could manage to read a lot—*Nineteen Eighty-four* was one of the first books I devoured, marveling constantly at how aptly Orwell's description fitted Mao's China—the idiomatic use of English was beyond me. My textbooks in China had been written by people who had never had any contact with foreigners themselves, and had mostly been direct translations from Chinese texts. The lesson "Greetings," for example, gave the exact equivalent of the expressions we used in China, which were, literally "Where are you going?" and "Have you eaten?" And this was how I used to greet people initially in Britain.

I needed Jon's help to write a book in English—and make it a good book, as I hoped it would be. A writer and historian himself, Jon was indispensable to what made *Wild Swans* work. I was totally dependent on his judgment and his infallible eye—his beautiful and gazelle-like eyes. It is also impossible to overstate what I have learned from him in writing.

So I was blessed with the support of the two most important people in my life, my mother and my husband, when *Wild Swans* was written. Just before it was published, my mother wrote to me and said that the book may not do well and people may not pay much attention to it, but I was not to be disheartened; I had made her a contented woman because writing the book had brought us closer. This alone, she said, was enough for her. My mother was right. I had come to a new degree of respect and love for her. But precisely because I now knew her better, I could see that her professed indifference to recognition was her typical effort to try to protect me from potential hurt. I was very moved.

With no pressure and only understanding from my mother, I was spared anxiety about what sort of reception *Wild Swans* might get. I hoped that readers would like it, but did not dwell on that dream. Jon was most encouraging. He said, "It's a great book," and I trusted him, as I had done in making all the decisions connected with the text, and do in everything else in my life.

Wild Swans turned out to be a success. Numerous people have expressed appreciation to me in person or through letters in the past twelve years, and this has made my life a flow of continuous waves of bliss. My mother, who still lives in Chengdu, China, is visited by people of many different nationalities, from diplomats to backpackers, from businessmen to tourists. She has been invited to countries as diverse as Holland and Thailand, Hungary and Brazil—not to mention Britain. In Japan, women stopped her with heartwarming words under high-rises and cherry blossoms, and once a silver tray carried over to us across a restaurant an exquisite kimono handkerchief for her to sign. At more than one airport, people helped her with her luggage before expressing admiration for her. She has found understanding not only in her daughter, but in millions of readers all over the world.

The sad thing in this otherwise perfect happy ending is that *Wild Swans* is not allowed to be published in Mainland China. The regime seems to regard the book as a threat to the Communist Party's power. *Wild Swans* is a personal story, but it reflects the history of twentieth-century China, from which the Party does not come out well. To justify its rule, the Party has dictated an official version of history, but *Wild Swans* does not toe that line. In particular, *Wild Swans* shows Mao to have criminally misruled the Chinese people, rather than being basically a good and great leader, as Peking decrees. Today, Mao's portrait still hangs on Tiananmen Square in the heart of the capital, and across the vast cement expanse lies his corpse as an object of worship. The current leadership still upholds the myth of Mao—because it projects itself as his heir, and claims legitimacy from him.

This is why publication of *Wild Swans* is banned in China. So is any mention of the book or of me in the media. Although over the years many Chinese journalists have interviewed me or written about *Wild Swans,* all write-ups except a couple have bitten the dust, as few editors dare to break the ban. The ban is particularly deterring because the toughly worded, top secret injunction was co-signed by the Foreign Ministry, which, for a book, is most unusual, if not unique. This frightens people, as they feel getting mixed up with *Wild Swans* could bring serious trouble. However, it also intrigues; as a result, quite a few people, including some working for the state censors, have sought out the book to read.

In China today, life is immeasurably better than within most people's living memory—a fact that never ceases to delight me. But although there is a large degree of personal freedom, the nation is far from at its freest. The press and publications are under much tighter control than in the pre-Communist decades. Before the ban on *Wild Swans* was enforced in 1994, a Chinese publisher had submitted a text to the censors that contained some cuts, especially my reflections on Mao. Because such comments were actually relatively few, I had agreed to the cuts on condition, which was accepted by the publisher, that it was stated on the page that "the following xxx words have been cut." This was a device that had been used under the censorship before the Communists. But it does not work with today's government. The version with the cuts eventually appeared—but only as a pirated edition. Even the pirates did not dare to publish a full version.

I am told there is another pirated edition, with an uncut text. This is probably a photocopy of the Chinese-language edition published in Taiwan as well as Hong Kong, where publication has not been affected by the takeover in 1997. Many copies have been taken into China (the customs officials rarely search travelers' luggage). I myself have brought in copies with no problem, but the ones posted have never arrived. One great Chinese film director whom I admire enormously has tried to make a film of the book, in vain, as he was told that this was not permitted, and that if he were to make it abroad, his other films and his crew would be adversely affected. As a result of the strangulation by the regime, relatively few people in China have ever heard of *Wild Swans.*

But the book does have a degree of fame in the country, since there is plenty of communication with the outside world. It is even an object of exploitation by sharp-eyed con men. One seems to be a small-time impostor in my home city, Chengdu. As was reported in the local newspaper on 6 May 2000, he hung around major hotels and sites, and speaking fluent English and a little French, German, and Japanese, would chat up foreign tourists with the claim that he was a good friend of mine. He would then take them to meals that would land the tourists with hefty bills, while he took a cut from the restaurants afterward.

There have also been touching gestures. Once, after Jon and I had dinner in a Peking restaurant, Jon was about to pay the bill when he was told it had already been settled by a young local who said he had learned about his own country "from your wife's book."

Although *Wild Swans* is banned, people are not persecuted for reading it or talking about it privately. I can travel in China quite freely, with no perceptible surveillance. Clearly, while the book is regarded as a threat, I am not, because I do not hold meetings, give speeches, or do any clandestine work. With the media ban on me, I am a mere individual without a public voice. The regime today is very focused with its repression: it only targets what it considers to be threats, which boils down to anything that might have public influence and the potential to lead to an organized opposition. This approach is a vast improvement on Mao's rule, under which millions of innocent people were victimized for no reason. But it also means that the Party is determined to keep its monopoly of power, and that 1.3 billion Chinese will have to continue to live at the mercy of a handful of secretly selected men. The world, too, has to rely on pure luck that the leaders of a major nuclear power are not evil.

Writing *Wild Swans* has deepened my feelings toward China. With the past exorcised, I no longer want to "forget all about" it. I feel restless if I am away from the country for any length of time. The place, so old and yet so energetically young, having experienced so much tragedy and yet remaining so raw and optimistic, is under my skin. I go back once or twice a year. It is not a home to relax in, and I often return to London feeling drained. Exaltation and excitement are exhausting; so are exasperation and outrage, all of which dog my every step there. What has made these journeys addictive is that I have been going there to research a biography of Mao, which Jon and I have been writing jointly for the past ten years, and will be published in 2004.

I decided to write about Mao because I was fascinated by this man who dominated my life in China, and who devastated the lives of my fellow countrymen, a quarter of the world's population. He was as evil as Hitler or Stalin, and did as much damage to mankind as they did. Yet the world knows astonishingly little about him. While those two

European despots have been condemned around the world, Mao has achieved the incredible feat of having had his name only mildly dented—far, far insufficiently compared to his crimes—even though he has been dead for nearly three decades. Jon and I relish the challenge of unraveling the labyrinth of myths about him.

The Chinese regime, as is to be expected, has put many obstacles in my way, but few are insurmountable, and most have only added to the fun, making the two authors more like a pair of detectives. A warning against talking to me has been issued to a number of key people in Peking. But it seems it is not a rigorous ban as that on writing about or publishing *Wild Swans*, but rather "Watch what you say." So, while some have opted to avoid trouble and not see me, most have talked. There are so many things people yearn to get off their chest, and the Chinese also have a deeply ingrained sense of duty to history. The warning itself helped: it became a kind of advertisement for the prestige of the biography, with a central message that it would not follow the Party line, which was a huge incentive for some to speak. Ultimately, it is *Wild Swans* that has smoothed my path. Most people I see have either read the book or heard about it, and seem to agree it is honest. They seem to believe that the Mao biography will also tell the truth.

Wild Swans has also opened doors to international statesmen and untapped sources around the globe. In these researches, I am reminded time and again how incredibly fortunate I am to have Jon as my coauthor, as he not only speaks many languages, but is also a walking encyclopedia on international politics, of which Mao was a part. The past ten years have given Jon and me the most fabulous time as we've traveled to many parts of the world in pursuit of information about Mao—and as we have been working, day after day, year after year, determined to take all the time that is needed, not to cut corners, but to produce a book of which we can be proud.

Every day when I am at home in Notting Hill in London, I sit at my desk writing. Jon is downstairs in his study, its door occasionally opening as he gets up, perhaps to make a cup of tea. At the sound, my mind wanders off briefly and pleasurably to our next meeting, a lunchtime exchange of discoveries or evening out with friends. Outside the sash window to the right of my desk is a huge plane tree that dominates the sky with its cascading branches. The sky is at its most ravishingly beautiful on a lightly showery day, when the sun smiles behind thin misty clouds, producing the subtlest sunshine. Under the tree there is a black lamppost, like those obligatory ones in all films about London. In the street beyond, equally classic red double-deckers sail by. Pedestrians stride under umbrellas. A most ordinary London scene. And yet I am never tired of gazing at it, just as I am never bored with writing. There have been moments of frustration in the years of hard work, and times I exclaim to myself and to friends "I'm fed up." But I am in seventh heaven.

Jung Chang
London, May 2003

Author's Note

My name "Jung" is pronounced "Yung."

The names of members of my family and public figures are real, and are spelled in the way by which they are usually known. Other personal names are disguised.

Two difficult phonetic symbols: X and Q are pronounced, respectively, as *sh* and *ch*.

In order to describe their functions accurately, I have translated the names of some Chinese organizations differently from the Chinese official versions. I use "the Department of Public Affairs" rather than "the Department of Propaganda" for *xuan-chuan-bu*, and "the Cultural Revolution Authority" rather than "the Cultural Revolution Group" for *zhong-yang-wen-ge*.

Family Tree

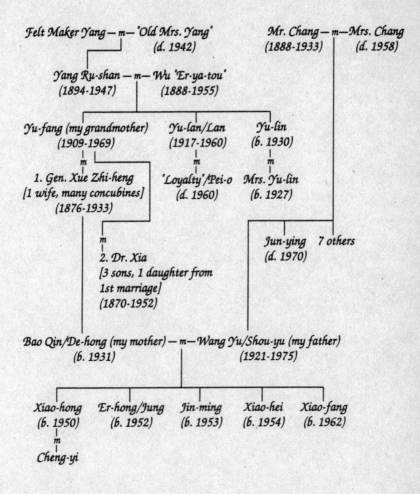

Chronology

Year	Family/Author	General
1870	Dr. Xia born.	Manchu empire (1644–1911).
1876	Xue Zhi-heng (grandfather) born.	
1909	Grandmother born.	
1911		Empire overthrown; republic; warlords.
1921	Father born.	
1922–24	General Xue chief of police in warlord government, Peking.	
1924	Grandmother becomes concubine of General Xue. General Xue loses power.	
1927		Kuomintang under Chiang Kai-shek unifies most of China.
1931	Mother born.	Japan invades Manchuria.
1932		Japanese occupy Yixian, Jinzhou. "Manchukuo" established under Pu Yi.
	Grandmother and mother to Lulong.	
1933	General Xue dies.	
1934–35		Long March: Communists to Yan'an.

Year	Family/Author	General
1935	Grandmother marries Dr. Xia.	
1936	Dr. Xia, grandmother, and mother move to Jinzhou.	
1937		Japan attacks deep into China. Communist-Kuomintang alliance.
1938	Father joins Communist Party.	
1940	Father walks to Yan'an.	
1945		Japanese surrender. Jinzhou occupied by Russians, Chinese Communists, and Kuomintang.
	Father to Chaoyang.	
1946–48	Father in guerrilla unit around Chaoyang. Mother becomes student leader, joins Communist underground.	Kuomintang-Communist Civil War (to 1949–50).
1948	Mother arrested.	
		Siege of Jinzhou.
	Father and mother meet.	
1949	Parents marry, leave Jinzhou, march to Nanjing. Mother's miscarriage.	
		People's Republic proclaimed.
	Father arrives in Yibin.	Communists take Sichuan. Chiang Kai-shek to Taiwan.
1950	Mother reaches Yibin; food-gathering, fighting bandits.	
		Land reform. China enters Korean War (to July 1953).
	Xiao-hong born.	

Year	Family/Author	General
1951		Campaign to "suppress counterrevolutionaries" (Hui-ge executed).
	Mother head of Yibin Youth League under Mrs. Ting; full Party membership. Grandmother and Dr. Xia to Yibin.	
		Three Antis Campaign.
1952	I am born. Dr. Xia dies. Father governor of Yibin.	Five Antis Campaign.
1953	Jin-ming born. Family moves to Chengdu. Mother head of Public Affairs Department for Eastern District.	
1954	Father deputy head of Public Affairs Department for Sichuan. Xiao-hei born.	
1955	Mother detained. Children into nurseries.	Campaign to "uncover hidden counter-revolutionaries" (Jinzhou friends branded). Nationalization.
1956	Mother released.	Hundred Flowers.
1957		Anti-Rightist Campaign.
1958		Great Leap Forward: backyard steel furnaces and communes.
	I start school.	
1959		Famine (to 1961). Peng Dehuai challenges Mao, condemned. Campaign to catch "rightist opportunists."
1962	Xiao-fang born.	

Year	Family/Author	General
1963		"Learn from Lei Feng"; cult of Mao escalates.
1966		Cultural Revolution starts.
	Father scapegoated and detained.	
	Mother to Peking to appeal.	
	Father released.	
	I join Red Guards; pilgrimage to Peking.	
	I leave Red Guards.	
1967	Parents tormented.	
		Marshals fail to stop Cultural Revolution.
		Tings in power in Sichuan.
	Father writes to Mao; arrested; mental breakdown.	
	Mother to Peking, sees Zhou Enlai.	
	Parents in on-off detention in Chengdu (to 1969).	
1968		Sichuan Revolutionary Committee formed.
	Family moved out of compound.	
1969	Father to Miyi camp.	
	I am exiled to Ningnan.	
		IX Congress formalizes Cultural Revolution.
	Grandmother dies.	
	I work as a peasant in Deyang.	
	Mother to Xichang camp.	
1970	Aunt Jun-ying dies.	
	I become a "barefoot doctor."	
		Tings fired.
1971	Mother very ill; to hospital in Chengdu.	
		Lin Biao dies.

Year	Family/Author	General
1971	Mother rehabilitated. I return to Chengdu, become steelworker and electrician.	
1972		Nixon visit.
	Father released.	
1973		Deng Xiaoping reappears.
	I enter Sichuan University.	
1975	Father dies.	
	I meet my first foreigners.	
1976		Zhou Enlai dies; Deng ousted. Demonstrations in Tiananmen Square. Mao dies; Gang of Four arrested.
1977	I become assistant lecturer; sent to village.	
		Deng back to power.
1978	I win scholarship to Britain.	

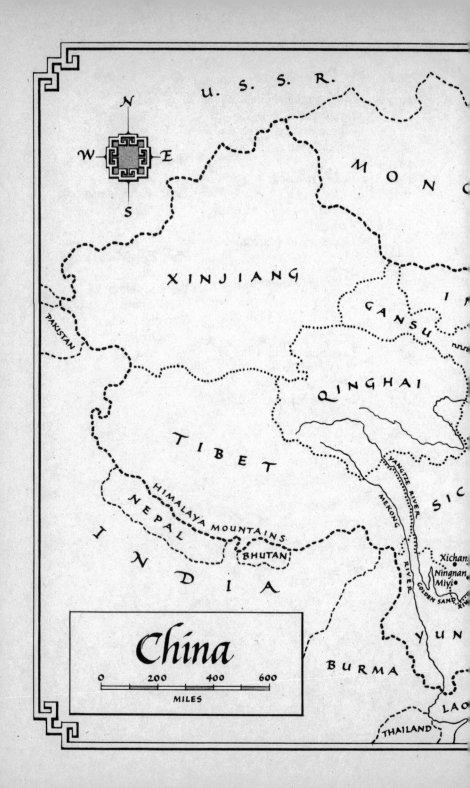

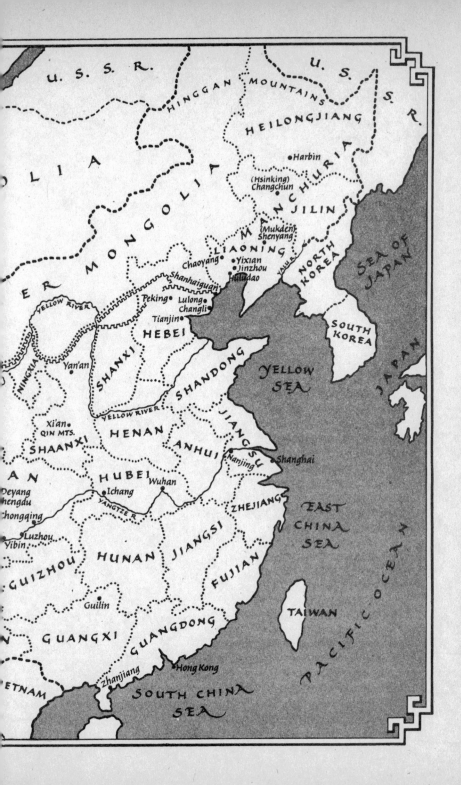

1. "Three-Inch Golden Lilies"—
Concubine to a Warlord General
(1909–1933)

At the age of fifteen my grandmother became the concubine of a warlord general, the police chief of a tenuous national government of China. The year was 1924 and China was in chaos. Much of it, including Manchuria, where my grandmother lived, was ruled by warlords. The liaison was arranged by her father, a police official in the provincial town of Yixian in southwest Manchuria, about a hundred miles north of the Great Wall and 250 miles northeast of Peking.

Like most towns in China, Yixian was built like a fortress. It was encircled by walls thirty feet high and twelve feet thick dating from the Tang dynasty (A.D. 618–907), surmounted by battlements, dotted with sixteen forts at regular intervals, and wide enough to ride a horse quite easily along the top. There were four gates into the city, one at each point of the compass, with outer protecting gates, and the fortifications were surrounded by a deep moat.

The town's most conspicuous feature was a tall, richly decorated bell tower of dark brown stone, which had originally been built in the sixth century when Buddhism had been introduced to the area. Every night the bell was rung to signal the time, and the tower also functioned as a fire and flood alarm. Yixian was a prosperous market town. The plains around produced cotton, maize, sorghum, soybeans, sesame, pears, apples, and grapes. In the grassland areas and in the hills to the west, farmers grazed sheep and cattle.

My great-grandfather, Yang Ru-shan, was born in 1894, when the whole of China was ruled by an emperor who resided in Peking. The imperial family were Manchus who had conquered China in 1644 from Manchuria, which was their base. The Yangs were Han, ethnic Chinese, and had ventured north of the Great Wall in search of opportunity.

My great-grandfather was the only son, which made him of supreme importance to his family. Only a son could perpetuate the family name—without him, the family line would stop, which, to the Chinese, amounted to the greatest possible betrayal of one's ancestors. He was sent to a good school. The goal was for him to pass the examinations to become a mandarin, an official, which was the aspiration of most Chinese males at the time. Being an official brought power, and power brought money. Without power or money, no Chinese could feel safe from the depredations of officialdom or random violence. There had never been a proper legal system. Justice was arbitrary, and cruelty was both institutionalized and capricious. An official with power *was* the law. Becoming a mandarin was the only way the child of a non-noble family could escape this cycle of injustice and fear. Yang's father had decided that his son should not follow him into the family business of felt-making, and sacrificed himself and his family to pay for his son's education. The women took in sewing for local tailors and dressmakers, toiling late into the night. To save money, they turned their oil lamps down to the absolute minimum, causing lasting damage to their eyes. The joints in their fingers became swollen from the long hours.

Following the custom, my great-grandfather was married young, at fourteen, to a woman six years his senior. It was considered one of the duties of a wife to help bring up her husband.

The story of his wife, my great-grandmother, was typical of millions of Chinese women of her time. She came from a family of tanners called Wu. Because her family was not an intellectual one and did not hold any official post, and because she was a girl, she was not given a name at all. Being the second daughter, she was simply called "Number Two Girl" (Er-ya-tou). Her father died when she was an infant, and she was brought up by an uncle. One day, when she was six years old, the uncle was dining with a friend whose wife was pregnant. Over dinner the two men agreed that if the baby was a boy he would be married to the six-year-old niece. The two young people never met before their wedding. In fact, falling in love was considered almost shameful, a family disgrace. Not because it was taboo—there was, after all, a venerable tradition of romantic love in China—but because young people were not supposed to be exposed to situations where such a thing could happen, partly because it was immoral for them to meet, and partly because marriage was seen above all as a duty, an arrangement between two families. With luck, one could fall in love after getting married.

At fourteen, and having lived a very sheltered life, my great-grand-father was little more than a boy at the time of his marriage. On the first night, he did not want to go into the wedding chamber. He went to bed in his mother's room and had to be carried in to his bride after he fell asleep. But, although he was a spoiled child and still needed help to get dressed, he knew how to "plant children," according to his wife. My grandmother was born within a year of the wedding, on the fifth day of the fifth moon, in early summer 1909. She was in a better position than her mother, for she was actually given a name: Yu-fang. Yu, meaning "jade," was her generation name, given to all the off-spring of the same generation, while *fang* means "fragrant flowers."

The world she was born into was one of total unpredictability. The Manchu empire, which had ruled China for over 260 years, was tottering. In 1894–95 Japan attacked China in Manchuria, with China suffering devastating defeats and loss of territory. In 1900 the nationalist Boxer Rebellion was put down by eight foreign armies, contingents of which had stayed on, some in Manchuria and some along the Great Wall. Then in 1904–5 Japan and Russia fought a major war on the plains of Manchuria. Japan's victory made it the dominant outside force in Manchuria. In 1911 the five-year-old emperor of China, Pu Yi, was overthrown and a republic was set up with the charismatic figure of Sun Yat-sen briefly at its head.

The new republican government soon collapsed and the country broke up into fiefs. Manchuria was particularly disaffected from the republic, since the Manchu dynasty had originated there. Foreign powers, especially Japan, intensified their attempts to encroach on the area. Under all these pressures, the old institutions collapsed, resulting in a vacuum of power, morality, and authority. Many people sought to get to the top by bribing local potentates with expensive gifts like gold, silver, and jewelry. My great-grandfather was not rich enough to buy himself a lucrative position in a big city, and by the time he was thirty he had risen no higher than an official in the police station of his native Yixian, a provincial backwater. But he had plans. And he had one valuable asset—his daughter.

My grandmother was a beauty. She had an oval face, with rosy cheeks and lustrous skin. Her long, shiny black hair was woven into a thick plait reaching down to her waist. She could be demure when the occasion demanded, which was most of the time, but underneath her composed exterior she was bursting with suppressed energy. She was petite, about five feet three inches, with a slender figure and sloping shoulders, which were considered the ideal.

But her greatest assets were her bound feet, called in Chinese "three-inch golden lilies" *(san-tsun-gin-lian)*. This meant she walked "like a tender young willow shoot in a spring breeze," as Chinese connoisseurs of women traditionally put it. The sight of a woman teetering on bound feet was supposed to have an erotic effect on men, partly because her vulnerability induced a feeling of protectiveness in the onlooker.

My grandmother's feet had been bound when she was two years old. Her mother, who herself had bound feet, first wound a piece of white cloth about twenty feet long round her feet, bending all the toes except the big toe inward and under the sole. Then she placed a large stone on top to crush the arch. My grandmother screamed in agony and begged her to stop. Her mother had to stick a cloth into her mouth to gag her. My grandmother passed out repeatedly from the pain.

The process lasted several years. Even after the bones had been broken, the feet had to be bound day and night in thick cloth because the moment they were released they would try to recover. For years my grandmother lived in relentless, excruciating pain. When she pleaded with her mother to untie the bindings, her mother would weep and tell her that unbound feet would ruin her entire life, and that she was doing it for her own future happiness.

In those days, when a woman was married, the first thing the bride-groom's family did was to examine her feet. Large feet, meaning normal feet, were considered to bring shame on the husband's household. The mother-in-law would lift the hem of the bride's long skirt, and if the feet were more than about four inches long, she would throw down the skirt in a demonstrative gesture of contempt and stalk off, leaving the bride to the critical gaze of the wedding guests, who would stare at her feet and insultingly mutter their disdain. Sometimes a mother would take pity on her daughter and remove the binding cloth; but when the child grew up and had to endure the contempt of her husband's family and the disapproval of society, she would blame her mother for having been too weak.

The practice of binding feet was originally introduced about a thousand years ago, allegedly by a concubine of the emperor. Not only was the sight of women hobbling on tiny feet considered erotic, men would also get excited playing with bound feet, which were always hidden in embroidered silk shoes. Women could not remove the binding cloths even when they were adults, as their feet would start growing again. The binding could only be loosened temporarily at night in bed, when they would put on soft-soled shoes. Men rarely saw naked bound feet, which were usually covered in rotting flesh and stank when the bindings were removed. As a child, I can remember my grandmother being in constant pain. When we came home from shopping, the first thing she would do was soak her feet in a bowl of hot water, sighing with relief as she did so. Then she would set about cutting off pieces of dead skin. The pain came not only from the broken bones, but also from her toenails, which grew into the balls of her feet.

In fact, my grandmother's feet were bound just at the moment when foot-binding was disappearing for good. By the time her sister was born in 1917, the practice had virtually been abandoned, so she escaped the torment.

However, when my grandmother was growing up, the prevailing attitude in a small town like Yixian was still that bound feet were essential for a good marriage—but they were only a start. Her father's plans were for her to be trained as either a perfect lady or a high-class courtesan. Scorning the received wisdom of the time—that it was virtuous for a lower class woman to be illiterate—he sent her to a girl's school that had been set up in the town in 1905. She also learned to play Chinese chess, mah-jongg, and go. She studied drawing and embroidery. Her favorite design was mandarin ducks (which symbolize love, because they always swim in pairs), and she used to embroider them onto the tiny shoes she made for herself. To crown her list of accomplishments, a tutor was hired to teach her to play the qin, a musical instrument like a zither.

My grandmother was considered the belle of the town. The locals said she stood out "like a crane among chickens." In 1924 she was fifteen, and her father was growing worried that time might be running out on his only real asset—and his only chance for a life of ease. In that year General Xue Zhi-heng, the inspector general of the Metropolitan Police of the warlord government in Peking, came to pay a visit.

Xue Zhi-heng was born in 1876 in the county of Lulong, about a hundred miles east of Peking, and just south of the Great Wall, where the vast North China plain runs up against the mountains. He was the eldest of four sons of a country schoolteacher.

He was handsome and had a powerful presence, which struck all who met him. Several blind fortune-tellers who felt his face predicted he would rise to a powerful position. He was a gifted calligrapher, a talent held in high esteem, and in 1908 a warlord named Wang Huai-qing, who was visiting Lulong, noticed the fine calligraphy on a plaque over the gate of the main temple and asked to meet the man who had done it. General Wang took to the thirty-two-year-old Xue and invited him to become his aide-de-camp.

He proved extremely efficient, and was soon promoted to quarter-master. This involved extensive traveling, and he started to acquire food shops of his own around Lulong and on the other side of the Great Wall, in Manchuria. His rapid rise was boosted when he helped General Wang to suppress an uprising in Inner Mongolia. In almost no time he had amassed a fortune, and he designed and built for himself an eighty-one-room mansion at Lulong.

In the decade after the end of the empire, no government established authority over the bulk of the country. Powerful warlords were soon fighting for control of the central government in Peking. Xue's faction, headed by a warlord called Wu Pei-fu, dominated the nominal government in Peking in the early 1920s. In 1922 Xue became inspector general of the Metropolitan Police and joint head of the Public Works Department in Peking. He commanded twenty regions on both sides of the Great Wall, and more than 10,000 mounted police and infantry. The police job gave him power; the public works post gave him patronage.

Allegiances were fickle. In May 1923 General Xue's faction decided to get rid of the president, Li Yuan-hong, whom it had installed in office only a year earlier. In league with a general called Feng Yu-xiang, a Christian warlord, who entered legend by baptizing his troops *en masse* with a firehose, Xue mobilized his 10,000 men and surrounded the main government buildings in Peking, demanding the back pay which the bankrupt government owed his men. His real aim was to humiliate President Li and force him out of office. Li refused to resign, so Xue ordered his men to cut off the water and electricity to the presidential palace. After a few days, conditions inside the building became unbearable, and on the night of 13 June President Li abandoned his malodorous residence and fled the capital for the port city of Tianjin, seventy miles to the southeast.

In China the authority of an office lay not only in its holder but in the official seals. No document was valid, even if it had the president's signature on it, unless it carried his seal. Knowing that no one could take over the presidency without them, President Li left the seals with one of his concubines, who was convalescing in a hospital in Peking run by French missionaries.

As President Li was nearing Tianjin his train was stopped by armed police, who told him to hand over the seals. At first he refused to say where he had hidden them, but after several hours he relented. At three in the morning General Xue went to the French hospital to collect the seals from the concubine. When he appeared by her bed-side, the concubine at first refused even to look at him: "How can I hand over the president's seals to a mere policeman?" she said haughtily. But General Xue, resplendent in his full uniform, looked so intimidating that she soon meekly placed the seals in his hands.

Over the next four months, Xue used his police to make sure that the man his faction wanted to see as president, Tsao Kun, would win what was billed as one of China's first elections. The 804 members of parliament had to be bribed. Xue and General Feng stationed guards on the parliament building and let it be known that there would be a handsome consideration for anyone who voted the right way, which brought many deputies scurrying back from the provinces. By the time everything was ready for the election there were 555 members of parliament in Peking. Four days before the election, after much bargaining, they were each given 5,000 silver yuan, a rather substantial sum. On 5 October 1923, Tsao Kun was elected president of China with 480 votes. Xue was rewarded with promotion to full general. Also promoted were seventeen "special advisers"—all favorite mistresses or concubines of various warlords and generals. This episode has entered Chinese history as a notorious example of how an election can be manipulated. People still cite it to argue that democracy will not work in China.

In early summer the following year General Xue visited Yixian. Though it was not a large town, it was strategically important. It was about here that the writ of the Peking government began to run out. Beyond, power was in the hands of the great warlord of the northeast, Chang Tso-lin, known as the Old Marshal. Officially, General Xue was on an inspection trip, but he also had some personal interests in the area. In Yixian he owned the main grain stores and the biggest shops, including a pawnshop which doubled as the bank and issued its own money, which circulated in the town and the surrounding area.

For my great-grandfather, this was a once-in-a-lifetime chance, the closest he was ever going to get to a real VIP. He schemed to get himself the job of escorting General Xue, and told his wife he was going to try to marry their daughter off to him. He did not ask his wife for her agreement; he merely informed her. Quite apart from this being the custom of the day, my great-grandfather despised his wife.

She wept, but said nothing. He told her she must not breathe a word to their daughter. There was no question of consulting his daughter. Marriage was a transaction, not a matter of feelings. She would be informed when the wedding was arranged.

My great-grandfather knew that his approach to General Xue had to be indirect. An explicit offer of his daughter's hand would lower her price, and there was also the possibility that he might be turned down. General Xue had to have a chance to see what he was being offered. In those days respectable women could not be introduced to strange men, so Yang had to create an opportunity for General Xue to see his daughter. The encounter had to seem accidental.

In Yixian there was a magnificent 900-year-old Buddhist temple made of precious wood and standing about a hundred feet high. It was set within an elegant precinct, with rows of cypress trees, which covered an area of almost a square mile. Inside was a brightly painted wooden statue of the Buddha, thirty feet high, and the interior of the temple was covered with delicate murals depicting his life. It was an obvious place for Yang to take the visiting VIP. And temples were among the few places women of good families could go on their own.

My grandmother was told to go to the temple on a certain day. To show her reverence for the Buddha, she took perfumed baths and spent long hours meditating in front of burning incense at a little shrine. To pray in the temple she was supposed to be in a state of maximum tranquillity, and to be free of all unsettling emotions. She set off in a rented horse-drawn carriage, accompanied by a maid. She wore a duck-egg-blue jacket, its edges embroidered in gold thread to show off its simple lines, with butterfly buttons up the right-hand side. With this she wore a pleated pink skirt, embroidered all over with tiny flowers. Her long black hair was woven into a single plait. Peeping out at the top was a silk black-green peony, the rarest kind. She wore no makeup, but was richly scented, as was considered appropriate for a visit to a temple. Once inside, she knelt before the giant statue of the Buddha. She kowtowed several times to the wooden image and then remained kneeling before it, her hands clasped in prayer.

As she was praying, her father arrived with General Xue. The two men watched from the dark aisle. My great-grandfather had planned well. The position in which my grandmother was kneeling revealed not only her silk trousers, which were edged in gold like her jacket, but also her tiny feet in their embroidered satin shoes.

When she finished praying, my grandmother kowtowed three times to the Buddha. As she stood up she slightly lost her balance, which was easy to do with bound feet. She reached out to steady herself on her maid's arm. General Xue and her father had just begun to move forward. She blushed and bent her head, then turned and started to walk away, which was the right thing to do. Her father stepped forward and introduced her to the general. She curtsied, keeping her head lowered all the time.

As was fitting for a man in his position, the general did not say much about the meeting to Yang, who was a rather lowly subordinate, but my great-grandfather could see he was fascinated. The next step was to engineer a more direct encounter. A couple of days later Yang, risking bankruptcy, rented the best theater in town and put on a local opera, inviting General Xue as the guest of honor. Like most Chinese theaters, it was built around a rectangular space open to the sky, with timber structures on three sides; the fourth side formed the stage, which was completely bare: it had no curtain and no sets. The seating area was more like a café than a theater in the West. The men sat at tables in the open square, eating, drinking, and talking loudly throughout the performance. To the side, higher up, was the dress circle, where the ladies sat more demurely at smaller tables, with their maids standing behind them. My great-grandfather had arranged things so that his daughter was in a place where General Xue could see her easily.

This time she was much more dressed up than in the temple. She wore a heavily embroidered satin dress and jewelry in her hair. She was also displaying her natural vivacity and energy, laughing and chatting with her women friends. General Xue hardly looked at the stage.

After the show there was a traditional Chinese game called lantern-riddles. This took place in two separate halls, one for the men and one for the women. In each room were dozens of elaborate paper lanterns, stuck on which were a number of riddles in verse. The person who guessed the most answers won a prize. Among the men General Xue was the winner, naturally. Among the women, it was my grandmother.

Yang had now given General Xue a chance to appreciate his daughter's beauty and her intelligence. The final qualification was artistic talent. Two nights later he invited the general to his house for dinner. It was a clear, warm night, with a full moon—a classic setting for listening to the *qin*. After dinner, the men sat on the veranda and my grandmother was summoned to play in the courtyard. Sitting under a trellis, with the scent of syringa in the air, her performance enchanted General Xue. Later he was to tell her that her playing that evening in the moonlight had captured his heart. When my mother was born, he gave her the name Bao Qin, which means "Precious Zither."

Before the evening was over he had proposed—not to my grand-mother, of course, but to her father. He did not offer marriage, only that my grandmother should become his concubine. But Yang had not expected anything else. The Xue family would have arranged a marriage for the general long before on the basis of social positions. In any case, the Yangs were too humble to provide a wife. But it was expected that a man like General Xue should take concubines. Wives were not for pleasure—that was what concubines were for. Concu-bines might acquire considerable power, but their social status was quite different from that of a wife. A concubine was a kind of institu-tionalized mistress, acquired and discarded at will.

The first my grandmother knew of her impending liaison was when her mother broke the news to her a few days before the event. My grandmother bent her head and wept. She hated the idea of being a concubine, but her father had already made the decision, and it was unthinkable to oppose one's parents. To question a parental decision was considered "unfilial"—and to be unfilial was tantamount to trea-son. Even if she refused to consent to her father's wishes, she would not be taken seriously; her action would be interpreted as indicating that she wanted to stay with her parents. The only way to say no and be taken seriously was to commit suicide. My grandmother bit her lip and said nothing. In fact, there was nothing she could say. Even to say yes would be considered unladylike, as it would be taken to imply that she was eager to leave her parents.

Seeing how unhappy she was, her mother started telling her that this was the best match possible. Her husband had told her about General Xue's power: "In Peking they say, 'When General Xue stamps his foot, the whole city shakes.'" In fact, my grandmother had been rather taken with the general's handsome, martial demeanor. And she had been flattered by all the admiring words he had said about her to her father, which were now elaborated and embroidered upon. None of the men in Yixian were as impressive as the warlord general. At fifteen, she had no idea what being a concubine really meant, and thought she could win General Xue's love and lead a happy life.

General Xue had said that she could stay in Yixian, in a house which he was going to buy especially for her. This meant she could be close to her own family, but, even more important, she would not have to live in his residence, where she would have to submit to the authority of his wife and the other concubines, who would all have precedence over her. In the house of a potentate like General Xue, the women were virtual prisoners, living in a state of permanent squabbling and bickering, largely induced by insecurity. The only security they had was their husband's favor. General Xue's offer of a house of her own meant a lot to my grandmother, as did his promise to solemnize the liaison with a full wedding ceremony. This meant that she and her family would have gained a considerable amount of face. And there was one final consideration which was very important to her: now that her father was satisfied, she hoped he would treat her mother better.

Mrs. Yang suffered from epilepsy, which made her feel undeserving towards her husband. She was always submissive to him, and he treated her like dirt, showing no concern for her health. For years, he found fault with her for not producing a son. My great-grandmother had a string of miscarriages after my grandmother was born, until a second child came along in 1917—but again, it was a girl.

My great-grandfather was obsessed with having enough money to be able to acquire concubines. The "wedding" allowed him to fulfill this wish, as General Xue lavished betrothal gifts on the family, and the chief beneficiary was my great-grandfather. The gifts were magnificent, in keeping with the general's station.

On the day of the wedding, a sedan chair draped with heavy, bright-red embroidered silk and satin appeared at the Yangs' house. In front came a procession carrying banners, plaques, and silk lanterns painted with images of a golden phoenix, the grandest symbol for a woman. The wedding ceremony took place in the evening, as was the tradition, with red lanterns glowing in the dusk. There was an orchestra with drums, cymbals, and piercing wind instruments playing joyful music. Making a lot of noise was considered essential for a good wedding, as keeping quiet would have been seen as suggesting that there was something shameful about the event. My grandmother was splendidly dressed in bright embroidery, with a red silk veil covering her head and face. She was carried in the sedan chair to her new home by eight men. Inside the sedan chair it was stuffy and boiling hot, and she discreetly pulled the curtain back a few inches. Peeping out from under her veil, she was delighted to see people in the streets watching her procession. This was very different from what a mere concubine would get—a small sedan chair draped in plain cotton of the unglamorous color of indigo, borne by two or at the most four people, and no procession or music. She was taken right around the town, visiting all four gates, as a full ritual demanded, with her expensive wedding gifts displayed on carts and in large wicker baskets carried behind her. After she had been shown off to the town, she reached her new home, a large, stylish residence. My grandmother was satisfied. The pomp and ceremony made her feel she had gained prestige and esteem. There had been nothing like this in Yixian in living memory.

When she reached the house General Xue, in full military dress, was waiting, surrounded by the local dignitaries. Red candles and dazzling gas lamps lit up the center of the house, the sitting room, where they performed a ceremonial kowtow to the tablets of Heaven and Earth. After this, they kowtowed to each other, then my grandmother went into the wedding chamber alone, in accordance with the custom, while General Xue went off to a lavish banquet with the men.

General Xue did not leave the house for three days. My grandmother was happy. She thought she loved him, and he showed her a kind of gruff affection. But he hardly spoke to her about serious matters, in keeping with the traditional saying: "Women have long hair and short intelligence." A Chinese man was supposed to remain reticent and grand, even within his family. So she kept quiet, just massaging his toes before they got up in the morning and playing the *qin* to him in the evening. After a week, he suddenly told her he was leaving. He did not say where he was going—and she knew it was not a good idea to ask. Her duty was to wait for him until he came back. She had to wait six years.

In September 1924, fighting erupted between the two main warlord factions in North China. General Xue was promoted to deputy commander of the Peking garrison, but within weeks his old ally General Feng, the Christian warlord, changed sides. On 3 November, Tsao Kun, whom General Xue and General Feng had helped install as president the previous year, was forced to resign. The same day the Peking garrison was dismissed, and two days later the Peking police office was disbanded. General Xue had to leave the capital in a hurry. He retired to a house he owned in Tianjin, in the French concession, which had extraterritorial immunity. This was the very place to which President Li had fled the year before when Xue had forced him out of the presidential palace.

In the meantime, my grandmother was caught up in the renewed fighting. Control of the northeast was vital in the struggle between the warlord armies, and towns on the railway, especially junctions like Yixian, were particular targets. Shortly after General Xue left, the fighting came right up to the walls of the town, with pitched battles just outside the gates. Looting was widespread. One Italian arms company appealed to the cash-strapped warlords by advertising that it would accept "lootable villages" as collateral. Rape was just as commonplace. Like many other women, my grandmother had to blacken her face with soot to make herself look filthy and ugly. Fortunately, this time Yixian emerged virtually unscathed. The fighting eventually moved south and life returned to normal.

For my grandmother, "normal" meant finding ways to kill time in her large house. The house was built in the typical North Chinese style, around three sides of a quadrangle, the south side of the courtyard being a wall about seven feet high, with a moon gate which opened onto an outer courtyard, which in turn was guarded by a double gate with a round brass knocker.

These houses were built to cope with the extremes of a brutally harsh climate, which lurched from freezing winters to scorching summers, with virtually no spring or autumn in between. In summer, the temperature could rise above 95°F, but in winter it fell to minus 20°F, with howling winds which roared down from Siberia across the plains. Dust tore into the eyes and bit into the skin for much of the year, and people often had to wear masks which covered their entire faces and heads. In the inner courtyard of the houses, all the windows in the main rooms opened to the south to let in as much sunshine as possible, while the walls on the north side took the brunt of the wind and the dust. The north side of the house contained a sitting room and my grandmother's chamber; the wings on the two sides were for the servants and for all other activities. The floors of the main rooms were tiled, while the wooden windows were covered with paper. The pitched roof was made of smooth black tiles.

The house was luxurious by local standards—and far superior to her parents' home—but my grandmother was lonely and miserable. There were several servants, including a doorkeeper, a cook, and two maids. Their task was not only to serve, but also to act as guards and spies. The doorkeeper was under instructions not to let my grandmother out alone under any circumstances. Before he left, General Xue told my grandmother a cautionary tale about one of his other concubines. He had found out that she had been having an affair with a male servant, so he had her tied to a bed and stuffed a gag into her mouth. Then raw alcohol was dripped onto the cloth, slowly choking her to death. "Of course, I could not give her the pleasure of dying speedily. For a woman to betray her husband is the vilest thing possible," he said. Where infidelity was involved, a man like General Xue would hate the woman far more than the man. "All I did with the lover was have him shot," he added casually. My grandmother never knew whether or not all this had really happened, but at the age of fifteen she was suitably petrified.

From that moment she lived in constant fear. Because she could hardly ever go out, she had to create a world for herself within the four walls. But even there she was not the real mistress of her home, and she had to spend a great deal of time buttering up the servants in case they invented stories against her—which was so common it was considered almost inevitable. She gave them plenty of presents, and also organized mah-jongg parties, because the winners would always have to tip the servants generously.

She was never short of money. General Xue sent her a regular allowance, which was delivered every month by the manager of his pawnshop, who also picked up the bills for her losses at the mah-jongg parties.

Throwing mah-jongg parties was a normal part of life for concubines all over China. So was smoking opium, which was widely available and was seen as a means of keeping people like her contented— by being doped—and dependent. Many concubines became addicted in their attempts to cope with their loneliness. General Xue encouraged my grandmother to take up the habit, but she ignored him.

Almost the only time she was allowed out of the house was to go to the opera. Otherwise, she had to sit at home all day, every day. She read a lot, mainly plays and novels, and tended her favorite flowers, garden balsam, hibiscus, common four-o'clock, and roses of Sharon in pots in the courtyard, where she also cultivated dwarf trees. Her other consolation in her gilded cage was a cat.

She was allowed to visit her parents, but even this was frowned upon, and she was not permitted to stay the night with them. Although they were the only people she could talk to, she found visiting them a trial. Her father had been promoted to deputy chief of the local police because of his connection to General Xue, and had acquired land and property. Every time she opened her mouth about how miserable she was, her father would start lecturing her, telling her that a virtuous woman should suppress her emotions and not desire anything beyond her duty to her husband. It was all right to miss her husband, that was virtuous, but a woman was not supposed to complain. In fact, a good woman was not supposed to have a point of view at all, and if she did, she certainly should not be so brazen as to talk about it. He would quote the Chinese saying, "If you are married to a chicken, obey the chicken; if you are married to a dog, obey the dog."

Six years passed. To begin with, there were a few letters, then total silence. Unable to burn off her nervous energy and sexual frustration, unable even to pace the floor with a full stride because of her bound feet, my grandmother was reduced to mincing around the house. At first, she hoped for some message, going over and over again in her mind her brief life with the general. Even her physical and psychological submission was mulled over nostalgically. She missed him very much, though she knew that she was only one of his many concubines, probably dotted around China, and she had never imagined that she would spend the rest of her life with him. Still she longed for him, as he represented her only chance to live a sort of life.

But as the weeks turned into months, and the months into years, her longing became dulled. She came to realize that for him she was a mere plaything, to be picked up again only when it was convenient for him. Her restlessness now had no object on which to focus. It became forced into a straitjacket. When occasionally it stretched its limbs she felt so agitated she did not know what to do with herself. Sometimes, she would fall to the floor unconscious. She was to have blackouts like these for the rest of her life.

Then one day, six years after he had walked casually out of the door, her "husband" reappeared. The meeting was very unlike what she had dreamed of at the beginning of their separation. Then she had fantasized that she would give herself totally and passionately to him, but now all she could find in herself was restrained dutifulness. She was also racked with anxiety in case she might have offended one of the servants, or that they might invent stories to ingratiate themselves with the general and ruin her life. But everything went smoothly. The general, now past fifty, seemed to have mellowed, and did not look nearly as majestic as before. As she expected, he did not say a word about where he had been, why he had left so suddenly, or why he was back, and she did not ask. Quite apart from not wanting to be scolded for being inquisitive, she did not care.

In fact, all this time the general had not been far away at all. He had been leading the quiet life of a wealthy retired dignitary, dividing his time between his house in Tianjin and his country mansion near Lulong. The world in which he had flourished was becoming a thing of the past. The warlords and their fief system had collapsed and most of China was now controlled by a single force, the Kuomintang, or Nationalists, headed by Chiang Kai-shek. To mark the break with the chaotic past, and to try to give the appearance of a new start and of stability, the Kuomintang moved the capital from Peking ("Northern Capital") to Nanjing ("Southern Capital"). In 1928, the ruler of Manchuria, Chang Tso-lin, the Old Marshal, was assassinated by the Japanese, who were becoming increasingly active in the area. The Old Marshal's son, Chang Hsueh-liang (known as the Young Marshal), joined up with the Kuomintang and formally integrated Manchuria with the rest of China—though Kuomintang rule was never effectively established in Manchuria.

General Xue's visit to my grandmother did not last long. Just like the first time, after a few days he suddenly announced he was leaving. The night before he was due to leave, he asked my grandmother to go and live with him at Lulong. Her heart missed a beat. If he ordered her to go, it would amount to a life sentence under the same roof as his wife and his other concubines. She was invaded by a wave of panic. As she massaged his feet, she quietly pleaded with him to let her stay in Yixian. She told him how kind he was to have promised her parents he would not take her away from them, and gently reminded him that her mother was not in good health: she had just had a third child, the longed-for son. She said that she would like to observe filial piety, while, of course, serving him, her husband and master, whenever he graced Yixian with his presence. The next day she packed his things and he left, alone. On his departure, as on his arrival, he showered jewels on my grandmother—gold, silver, jade, pearls, and emeralds. Like many men of his kind, he believed this was the way to a woman's heart. For women like my grandmother, jewelry was their only insurance.

A short time later, my grandmother realized she was pregnant. On the seventeenth day of the third moon, in spring 1931, she gave birth to a baby girl—my mother. She wrote to General Xue to let him know, and he wrote back telling her to call the girl Bao Qin and to bring her to Lulong as soon as they were strong enough to travel.

My grandmother was ecstatic at having a child. Now, she felt, her life had a purpose, and she poured all her love and energy into my mother. A happy year passed. General Xue wrote many times asking her to come to Lulong, but each time she managed to stall him. Then, one day in the middle of summer 1932, a telegram arrived saying that General Xue was seriously ill and ordering her to bring their daughter to see him at once. The tone made it clear that this time she should not refuse.

Lulong was about 200 miles away, and for my grandmother, who had never traveled, the journey was a major undertaking. It was also extremely difficult to travel with bound feet; it was almost impossible to carry luggage, especially with a young child in one's arms. My grandmother decided to take her fourteen-year-old sister, Yu-lan, whom she called "Lan," with her.

The journey was an adventure. The area had been convulsed yet again. In September 1931 Japan, which had been steadily expanding its power in the area, had launched a full-scale invasion of Manchuria, and Japanese troops had occupied Yixian on 6 January 1932. Two months later the Japanese proclaimed the founding of a new state, which they named Manchukuo ("Manchu Country"), covering most of northeast China (an area the size of France and Germany combined). The Japanese claimed that Manchukuo was independent, but in fact it was a puppet of Tokyo. As its head they installed Pu Yi, who as a child had been the last emperor of China. At first he was called Chief Executive; later, in 1934, he was made emperor of Manchukuo. All this meant little to my grandmother, who had had very little contact with the outside world. The general population were fatalistic about who their rulers were, since they had no choice in the matter. For many, Pu Yi was the natural ruler, a Manchu emperor and proper Son of Heaven. Twenty years after the republican revolution there was still no unified nation to replace the rule of the emperor, nor, in Manchuria, did the people have much concept of being citizens of something called "China."

One hot summer's day in 1932 my grandmother, her sister, and my mother took the train south from Yixian, passing out of Manchuria at the town of Shanhaiguan, where the Great Wall sweeps down from the mountains to the sea. As the train chugged along the coastal plain, they could see the landscape changing: instead of the bare, brown-yellow soil of the plains of Manchuria, here the earth was darker and the vegetation denser, almost lush compared with the northeast. Soon after it passed the Great Wall, the train turned inland, and about an hour later it stopped at a town called Changli where they disembarked at a green-roofed building which looked like a railway station in Siberia.

My grandmother hired a horse-drawn cart and drove north along a bumpy, dusty road to General Xue's mansion, which lay about twenty miles away, just outside the wall of a small town called Yanheying, which had once been a major military camp frequently visited by the Manchu emperors and their court. Hence the road had acquired the grand name of "the Imperial Way." It was lined with poplars, their light-green leaves shimmering in the sunlight. Beyond them were orchards of peach trees, which flourished in the sandy soil. But my grandmother scarcely enjoyed the scenery, as she was covered in dust and jolted badly by the rough road. Above all, she was worrying about what would greet her at the other end.

When she first saw the mansion, she was overwhelmed by its grandeur. The immense front gate was guarded by armed men, who stood stiffly at attention beside enormous statues of reclining lions. There was a row of eight stone statues for tying up horses: four were of elephants, and four of monkeys. These two animals were chosen for their lucky sounds: in Chinese the words "elephant" and "high office" have the same sound (*xiang*), as do "monkey" and "aristocracy" (*hou*).

As the cart passed through the outer gate into an inner yard my grandmother could see only a huge blank wall facing her; then, off to one side, she saw a second gate. This was a classic Chinese structure, a concealing wall so that strangers could not see into one's property, also making it impossible for assailants to shoot or charge directly through the front gate.

The moment they passed through the inner gate, a servant materialized at my grandmother's side and peremptorily took her child away. Another servant led my grandmother up the steps of the house and showed her into the sitting room of General Xue's wife.

As soon as she entered the room, my grandmother went down on her knees and kowtowed, saying, "I greet you, my mistress," as etiquette demanded. My grandmother's sister was not allowed into the room, but had to stand outside like a servant. This was nothing personal: the relatives of a concubine were not treated as part of the family. After my grandmother had kowtowed for a suitable length of time, the general's wife told her she could get up, using a form of address which immediately established my grandmother's place in the hierarchy of the household as a mere submistress, closer to a higher form of servant than to a wife.

The general's wife told her to sit down. My grandmother had to make a split-second decision. In a traditional Chinese household, where one sits automatically reflects one's status. General Xue's wife was sitting at the north end of the room, as befitted a person in her position. Next to her, separated by a side table, was another chair, also facing south: this was the general's seat. Down each side of the room was a row of chairs for people of different status. My grandmother shuffled backwards and sat on one of the chairs nearest the door, to show humility. The wife then asked her to come forward—just a little. She had to show some generosity.

When my grandmother was seated, the wife told her that from now on her daughter would be brought up as her (the wife's) own daughter and would call her, not my grandmother, "Mama"; my grandmother was to treat the child as the young mistress of the house, and was to behave accordingly.

A maid was summoned to lead my grandmother away. She felt her heart was breaking, but she forced back her sobs, only letting herself go when she reached her room. Her eyes were still red when she was taken to meet General Xue's number-two concubine, his favorite, who ran the household. She was pretty, with a delicate face, and to my grandmother's surprise she was quite sympathetic, but my grandmother restrained herself from having a good cry with her. In this strange new environment, she felt intuitively that the best policy was caution.

Later that day she was taken to see her "husband." She was allowed to take my mother with her. The general was lying on a *kang*, the type of bed used all over North China, a large, flat, rectangular surface about two and a half feet high heated from underneath by a brick stove. A pair of concubines or maids were kneeling round the prostrate general, massaging his legs and stomach. General Xue's eyes were closed, and he looked terribly sallow. My grandmother leaned over the edge of the bed, calling to him softly. He opened his eyes and managed a kind of a half-smile. My grandmother put my mother on the bed and said: "This is Bao Qin." With what seemed a great effort, General Xue feebly stroked my mother's head and said, "Bao Qin takes after you; she is very pretty." Then he closed his eyes.

My grandmother called out to him, but his eyes remained shut. She could see that he was gravely ill, perhaps dying. She picked my mother off the bed and hugged her tight. But she had only a second to cuddle her before the general's wife, who had been hovering alongside, tugged impatiently at her sleeve. Once outside, the wife warned my grandmother not to disturb the master too often, or indeed at all. In fact, she should stay in her room unless she was summoned.

My grandmother was terrified. As a concubine, her whole future and that of her daughter were in jeopardy, possibly even in mortal peril. She had no rights. If the general died, she would be at the mercy of the wife, who had the power of life and death over her. She could do anything she wanted—sell her to a rich man, or even into a brothel, which was quite common. Then my grandmother would never see her daughter again. She knew she and her daughter had to get away as fast as possible.

When she got back to her room, she made a tremendous effort to calm herself and begin planning her escape. But when she tried to think, she felt as though her head were flooding with blood. Her legs were so weak she could not walk without holding on to the furniture. She broke down and wept again—partly with rage, because she could see no way out. Worst of all was the thought that the general might die at any moment, leaving her trapped forever.

Gradually she managed to bring her nerves under control and force herself to think clearly. She started to look around the mansion systematically. It was divided into many different courtyards, set within a large compound, surrounded by high walls. Even the garden was designed with security rather than aesthetics in mind. There were a few cypress trees, some birches and winter plums, but none near the walls. To make doubly sure that any potential assassin would have no cover, there were not even any large shrubs. The two gates leading out from the garden were padlocked, and the front gate was guarded around the clock by armed retainers.

My grandmother was never allowed to leave the walled precincts. She was permitted to visit the general each day, but only on a sort of organized tour with some of the other women, when she would file past his bed and murmur, "I greet you, my lord."

Meanwhile, she began to get a clearer idea of the other personalities in the household. Apart from the general's wife, the woman who seemed to count most was the number-two concubine. My grandmother discovered that she had instructed the servants to treat her well, which made her situation much easier. In a household like this, the attitude of the servants was determined by the status of those they had to serve. They fawned on those in favor, and bullied those who had fallen from grace.

The number-two concubine had a daughter a little older than my mother. This was a further bond between the two women, as well as being a reason for the concubine's favor with General Xue, who had no other children apart from my mother.

After a month, during which the two concubines became quite friendly, my grandmother went to see the general's wife and told her she needed to go home to fetch some clothes. The wife gave permission, but when my grandmother asked if she could take her daughter to say goodbye to her grandparents, she refused. The Xue bloodline could not be taken out of the house.

And so my grandmother set off alone down the dusty road to Changli. After the coachman had dropped her off at the railway station, she started asking around among the people hanging about there. She found two horsemen who were prepared to provide her with the transportation she needed. She waited for nightfall, and then raced back to Lulong with them and their two horses by a shortcut. One of the men seated her on a saddle and ran in front, holding the horse by the rein.

When she reached the mansion, she made her way to a back gate and gave a prearranged signal. After a wait that felt like hours but was in fact only a few minutes, the door in the gate swung open and her sister emerged in the moonlight, holding my mother in her arms. The door had been unlocked by the friendly number-two concubine, who had then hit it with an axe to make it look as though it had been forced open.

There was hardly time for my grandmother to give my mother a quick hug—besides, she did not want to wake her, in case she made a noise and alerted the guards. She and her sister mounted the two horses while my mother was tied onto the back of one of the horse- men, and they headed off into the night. The horsemen had been paid well, and ran fast. By dawn they were at Changli, and before the alarm could be given, they had caught the train north. When the train finally drew into Yixian toward nightfall, my grandmother fell to the ground and lay there for a long time, unable to move.

She was comparatively safe, 200 miles from Lulong and effectively out of reach of the Xue household. She could not take my mother to her house, for fear of the servants, so she asked an old schoolfriend if she could hide my mother. The friend lived in the house of her father- in-law, a Manchu doctor called Dr. Xia, who was well known as a kindly man who would never turn anyone away or betray a friend.

The Xue household would not care enough about my grand- mother, a mere concubine, to pursue her. It was my mother, the blood descendant, who mattered. My grandmother sent a telegram to Lulong saying my mother had fallen ill on the train and had died. There followed an agonizing wait, during which my grandmother's moods oscillated wildly. Sometimes she felt that the family must have believed her story. But then she would torment herself with the thought that this might not be the case, and that they were sending thugs to drag her, or her daughter, back. Finally she consoled herself with the thought that the Xue family was far too preoccupied with the impending death of the patriarch to expend energy worrying about her, and that it was probably to the women's advantage not to have her daughter around.

Once she realized the Xue family was going to leave her alone, my grandmother settled back quietly into her house in Yixian with my mother. She did not even worry about the servants, since she knew that her "husband" would not be coming. The silence from Lulong lasted over a year, until one autumn day in 1933, when a telegram arrived informing her that General Xue had died, and that she was expected at Lulong immediately for the funeral.

The general had died in Tianjin in September. His body was brought back to Lulong in a lacquered coffin covered with red em- broidered silk. Accompanying him were two other coffins, one simi- larly lacquered and draped in the same red silk as his own, the other of plain wood with no covering. The first coffin contained the body of one of his concubines, who had swallowed opium to accompany him in death. This was considered the height of conjugal loyalty. Later a plaque inscribed by the famous warlord Wu Pei-fu was put up in her honor in General Xue's mansion. The second coffin contained the remains of another concubine, who had died of typhoid two years before. Her corpse had been exhumed for reburial alongside General Xue, as was the custom. Her coffin was of bare wood because, having died of a horrible illness, she was considered ill fortune. Mercury and charcoal had been placed inside each of the coffins to prevent the corpses rotting, and the bodies had pearls in their mouths.

General Xue and the two concubines were buried together in the same tomb; his wife and the other concubines would eventually be interred alongside them. At a funeral, the essential duty of holding a special flag for calling the spirit of the deceased had to be performed by the dead man's son. As the general had no son, his wife adopted his ten-year-old nephew so he could carry out the task. The boy also enacted another ritual—kneeling by the side of the coffin and calling out "Avoid the nails!" Tradition held that if this was not done, the dead person would be hurt by the nails.

The tomb site had been chosen by General Xue himself according to the principles of geomancy. It was in a beautiful, tranquil spot, backing onto distant mountains to the north, while the front faced a stream set among eucalyptus trees to the south. This location expressed the desire to have solid things behind on which to lean— mountains—and the reflection of the glorious sun, symbolizing rising prosperity, in front.

But my grandmother never saw the site: she had ignored her summons, and was not at the funeral. The next thing that happened was that the manager of the pawnshop failed to turn up with her allowance. About a week later, her parents received a letter from General Xue's wife. My grandfather's last words had been to give my grandmother her freedom. This, for its time, was exceptionally enlightened, and she could hardly believe her good fortune.

At the age of twenty-four, she was free.

2. "Even Plain Cold Water Is Sweet"— My Grandmother Marries a Manchu Doctor

(1933–1938)

The letter from General Xue's wife also asked my grandmother's parents to take her back. Though the point was couched in the traditional indirect manner, my grandmother knew that she was being ordered to move out.

Her father took her in, but with considerable reluctance. By now he had abandoned any pretense of being a family man. From the moment he had arranged the liaison with General Xue, he had risen in the world. As well as being promoted to deputy chief of the Yixian police and entering the ranks of the well-connected, he had become relatively rich, and had bought some land and taken up smoking opium.

No sooner had he been promoted than he acquired a concubine, a Mongolian woman who was presented to him by his immediate boss. Giving a concubine as a present to an up-and-coming colleague was a common practice, and the local police chief was happy to oblige a protégé of General Xue. But my great-grandfather soon began casting around for another concubine; it was good for a man in his position to have as many as possible—they showed a man's status. He did not have to look far: the concubine had a sister.

When my grandmother returned to her parents' house, the setup was quite different from when she had left almost a decade before. Instead of just her unhappy, downtrodden mother, there were now three spouses. One of the concubines had produced a daughter, who was the same age as my mother. My grandmother's sister, Lan, was still unmarried at the advanced age of sixteen, which was a cause of irritation to Yang.

My grandmother had moved from one cauldron of intrigue into another. Her father was resentful of both her and her mother. He resented his wife simply for being there, and he was even more unpleasant to her now that he had the two concubines, whom he favored over her. He took his meals with the concubines, leaving his wife to eat on her own. My grandmother he resented for returning to the house when he had successfully created a new world for himself.

He also regarded her as a jinx *(ke)*, because she had lost her husband. In those days, a woman whose husband had died was superstitiously held responsible for his death. My great-grandfather saw his daughter as bad luck, a threat to his good fortune, and he wanted her out of the house.

The two concubines egged him on. Before my grandmother came back, they had been having things very much their own way. My great-grandmother was a gentle, even weak person. Although she was theoretically the superior of the concubines, she lived at the mercy of their whims. In 1930 she gave birth to a son, Yu-lin. This deprived the concubines of their future security, as on my great-grandfather's death all his property would automatically go to his son. They would throw tantrums if Yang showed any affection at all to his son. From the moment Yu-lin was born, they stepped up their psychological warfare against my great-grandmother, freezing her out in her own house. They only spoke to her to nag and complain, and if they looked at her it was with cold stony faces. My great-grandmother got no support from her husband, whose contempt for her was not pacified by the fact that she had given him the son. He found new ways to find fault with her.

My grandmother was a stronger character than her mother, and the misery of the past decade had toughened her up. Even her father was a little in awe of her. She told herself that the days of her subservience to her father were over, and that she was going to fight for herself and for her mother. As long as she was in the house, the concubines had to restrain themselves, even presenting a toadying smile occasionally.

. . .

This was the atmosphere in which my mother lived the formative years from two to four. Though shielded by her mother's love, she could sense the tension which pervaded the household.

My grandmother was now a beautiful young woman in her mid-twenties. She was also highly accomplished, and several men asked her father for her hand. But because she had been a concubine, the only ones who offered to take her as a proper wife were poor and did not stand a chance with Mr. Yang.

My grandmother had had enough of the spitefulness and petty vengefulness of the concubine world, in which the only choice was between being a victim and victimizing others. There was no halfway house. All my grandmother wanted was to be left alone to bring up her daughter in peace.

Her father was constantly badgering her to remarry, sometimes by dropping unkind hints, at other times telling her outright she had to take herself off his hands. But there was nowhere for her to go. She had no place to live, and she was not allowed to get a job. After a time, unable to stand the pressure, she had a nervous breakdown.

A doctor was called in. It was Dr. Xia, in whose house my mother had been hidden three years before, after the escape from General Xue's mansion. Although she had been a friend of his daughter-in-law, Dr. Xia had never seen my grandmother—in keeping with the strict sexual segregation prevalent at the time. When he first walked into her room, he was so struck by her beauty that in his confusion he backed straight out again and mumbled to the servant that he felt unwell. Eventually, he recovered his composure and sat and talked to her at length. He was the first man she had ever met to whom she could say what she really felt, and she poured out her grief and her hopes to him—although with restraint, as befitted a woman talking to a man who was not her husband. The doctor was gentle and warm, and my grandmother had never felt so understood. Before long, the two fell in love, and Dr. Xia proposed. Moreover, he told my grandmother that he wanted her to be his proper wife, and to bring my mother up as his own daughter. My grandmother accepted, with tears of joy. Her father was also happy, although he was quick to point out to Dr. Xia that he would not be able to provide any dowry. Dr. Xia told him that was completely irrelevant.

Dr. Xia had built up a considerable practice in traditional medicine in Yixian, and enjoyed a very high professional reputation. He was not a Han Chinese, as were the Yangs and most people in China, but a Manchu, one of the original inhabitants of Manchuria. At one time his family had been court doctors for the Manchu emperors, and had been honored for their services.

Dr. Xia was well known not only as an excellent doctor, but also as a very kind man, who often treated poor people for nothing. He was a big man, over six feet tall, but he moved elegantly, in spite of his size. He always dressed in traditional long robes and jacket. He had gentle brown eyes, and a goatee and a long drooping mustache. His face and his whole posture exuded calm.

The doctor was already an elderly man when he proposed to my grandmother. He was sixty-five, and a widower, with three grown-up sons and one daughter, all of them married. The three sons lived in the house with him. The eldest looked after the household and managed the family farm, the second worked in his father's practice, and the third, who was married to my grandmother's schoolfriend, was a teacher. Between them the sons had eight children, one of whom was married and had a son himself.

Dr. Xia called his sons into his study and told them about his plans. They stole disbelieving, leaden glances at one another. There was a heavy silence. Then the eldest spoke: "I presume, Father, you mean she will be a concubine." Dr. Xia replied that he was going to take my grandmother as a proper wife. This had tremendous implications, as she would become their stepmother, and would have to be treated as a member of the older generation, with venerable status on a par with her husband. In an ordinary Chinese household the younger generations had to be subservient to the older, with suitable decorum to mark their relative positions, but Dr. Xia adhered to an even more complicated Manchu system of etiquette. The younger generations had to pay their respects to the older every morning and evening, the men kneeling and the women curtsying. At festivals, the men had to do a full kowtow. The fact that my grandmother had been a concubine, plus the age gap, which meant they would have to do obeisance to someone with an inferior status and much younger than themselves, was too much for the sons.

They got together with the rest of the family and worked themselves up into a state of outrage. Even the daughter-in-law who was my grandmother's old schoolfriend was upset, as her father-in-law's marriage would force her into a radically new relationship with someone who had been her classmate. She would not be able to eat at the same table as her old friend, or even sit down with her; she would have to wait on her hand and foot, and even kowtow to her.

Each member of the family—sons, daughters-in-law, grandchildren, even the great-grandson—went in turn to beg Dr. Xia to "consider the feelings" of his "own flesh and blood." They went down on their knees, they prostrated themselves in a full kowtow, they wept and screamed.

They begged Dr. Xia to consider the fact that he was a Manchu, and that according to ancient Manchu custom a man of his status should not marry a Han Chinese. Dr. Xia replied that the rule had been abolished a long time before. His children said that if he was a good Manchu, he should observe it anyway. They went on and on about the age gap. Dr. Xia was more than twice my grandmother's age. One of the family trotted out an ancient saying: "A young wife who has an old husband is really another man's woman."

What hurt Dr. Xia more was the emotional blackmail—especially the argument that taking an ex-concubine as a proper wife would affect his children's position in society. He knew his children *would* lose face, and he felt guilty about this. But Dr. Xia felt he had to put my grandmother's happiness first. If he took her as a concubine, she would not merely lose face, she would become the slave of the whole family. His love alone would not be enough to protect her if she was not his proper wife.

Dr. Xia implored his family to grant an old man's wish. But they—and society—took the attitude that an irresponsible wish should not be indulged. Some hinted that he was senile. Others told him: "You already have sons, grandsons, and even a great-grandson, a big and prosperous family. What more do you want? Why do you have to *marry* her?"

The arguments went on and on. More and more relatives and friends appeared on the scene, all invited by the sons. They unanimously pronounced the marriage to be an insane idea. Then they turned their venom against my grandmother. "Marrying again when her late husband's body and bones are not yet cold!" "That woman has it all worked out: she is refusing to accept concubine status so that she can become a proper wife. If she really loves you, why can't she be satisfied with being your concubine?" They attributed motives to my grandmother: she was scheming to get Dr. Xia to marry her, and would then take over the family and ill-treat his children and grandchildren.

They also insinuated that she was plotting to lay her hands on Dr. Xia's money. Underneath all their talk about propriety, morality, and Dr. Xia's own good, there was an unspoken calculation involving his assets. The relatives feared my grandmother might lay her hands on Dr. Xia's wealth, as she would automatically become the manageress of the household as his wife.

Dr. Xia was a rich man. He owned 2,000 acres of farmland dotted around the county of Yixian, and even had some land south of the Great Wall. His large house in the town was built of gray bricks stylishly outlined in white paint. Its ceilings were whitewashed and the rooms were wallpapered, so that the beams and joints were concealed, which was considered an important indicator of prosperity. He also owned a flourishing medical practice and a medicine shop.

When the family saw they were getting nowhere, they decided to work on my grandmother directly. One day the daughter-in-law who had been at school with her paid a call. After tea and social chitchat, the friend got around to her mission. My grandmother burst into tears, and took her by the hand in their usual intimate manner. What would she do if she were in her position, she asked. When she got no reply, she pressed on: "You know what being a concubine is like. You wouldn't like to be one, would you? You know, there is an expression of Confucius: 'Jiang-xin-bi-xin—Imagine my heart was yours'!" Appealing to someone's better instincts with a precept from the sage sometimes worked better than a direct no.

The friend went back to her family feeling quite guilty, and reported her failure. She hinted that she did not have the heart to push my grandmother anymore. She found an ally in De-gui, Dr. Xia's second son, who practiced medicine with his father, and was closer to him than his brothers. He said he thought they should let the marriage go ahead. The third son also began to weaken when he heard his wife describe my grandmother's distress.

The ones who were most indignant were the eldest son and his wife. When she saw that the other two sons were wavering, the eldest son's wife said to her husband: "Of course they don't care. They've got other jobs. That woman can't take those away from them. But what have you got? You are only the manager of the old man's estate —and it will all go to *her* and her daughter! What will become of poor me and our poor children? We have nothing to fall back on. Perhaps we should all die! Perhaps that is what your father really wants! Perhaps I should kill myself to make them all happy!" All this was accompanied by wailing and floods of tears. Her husband replied in an agitated manner: "Just give me till tomorrow."

When Dr. Xia woke the next morning he found his entire family, with the sole exception of De-gui, fifteen people in all, kneeling outside his bedchamber. The moment he emerged, his eldest son shouted "Kowtow!" and they all prostrated themselves in unison. Then, in a voice quaking with emotion, the son declaimed: "Father, your children and your entire family will stay here and kowtow to you till our deaths unless you start to think of us, your family—and, above all, your elderly self."

Dr. Xia was so angry his whole body shook. He asked his children to stand up, but before anyone could move the eldest son spoke again: "No, Father, we won't—not unless you call off the wedding!" Dr. Xia tried to reason with him, but the son continued to hector him in a quivering voice. Finally Dr. Xia said: "I know what is on your minds. I won't be in this world much longer. If you are worried about how your future stepmother will behave, I have not the slightest doubt that she will treat you all very well. I know she is a good person. Surely you can see there is no other reassurance I can give you except her character . . ."

At the mention of the word "character," the eldest son gave a loud snort: "How can you mention the word 'character' about a concubine! No good woman would have become a concubine in the first place!" He then started to abuse my grandmother. At this, Dr. Xia could not control himself. He lifted his walking stick and began thrashing his son.

All his life Dr. Xia had been the epitome of restraint and calm. The whole family, still on their knees, was stunned. The great-grandson started screaming hysterically. The eldest son was dumbstruck, but only for a second; then he raised his voice again, not only from physical hurt, but also for his wounded pride at being beaten in front of his family. Dr. Xia stopped, short of breath from anger and exertion. At once the son started bellowing more abuse against my grandmother. His father shouted at him to shut up, and struck him so hard his walking stick broke in two.

The son reflected on his humiliation and pain for a few seconds. Then he pulled out a pistol and looked Dr. Xia in the face. "A loyal subject uses his death to remonstrate with the emperor. A filial son should do the same with his father. All I have to remonstrate with you is my death!" A shot rang out. The son swayed, then keeled over onto the floor. He had fired a bullet into his abdomen.

A horse-drawn cart rushed him to a nearby hospital, where he died the next day. He probably had not intended to kill himself, just to make a dramatic gesture so the pressure on his father would be irresistible.

His son's death devastated Dr. Xia. Although outwardly he appeared calm as usual, people who knew him could see that his tranquillity had become scarred with a deep sadness. From then on he was subject to bouts of melancholy, very much out of character with his previous imperturbability.

Yixian was boiling with indignation, rumor, and accusations. Dr. Xia and particularly my grandmother were made to feel responsible for the death. Dr. Xia wanted to show he was not going to be deterred. Soon after the funeral of his son, he fixed a date for the wedding. He warned his children that they must pay due respect to their new mother, and sent out invitations to the leading townspeople. Custom dictated that they should attend and give presents. He also told my grandmother to prepare for a big ceremony. She was frightened by the accusations and their unforeseeable effect on Dr. Xia, and was desperately trying to convince herself that she was not guilty. But, above all, she felt defiant. She consented to a full ceremonial ritual. On the wedding day she left her father's house in an elaborate carriage accompanied by a procession of musicians. As was the Manchu custom, her own family hired the carriage to take her halfway to her new home, and the bridegroom sent another to carry her the second half of the way. At the handover point, her five-year-old brother, Yu-lin, waited at the foot of the carriage door with his back bent double, symbolizing the idea that he was carrying her on his back to Dr. Xia's carriage. He repeated the action when she arrived at Dr. Xia's house. A woman could not just walk into a man's house; this would imply a severe loss of status. She had to be seen to be taken, to denote the requisite reluctance.

Two bridesmaids led my grandmother into the room where the wedding ceremony was to take place. Dr. Xia was standing before a table draped with heavy red embroidered silk on which lay the tablets of Heaven, Earth, Emperor, Ancestors, and Teacher. He was wearing a decorated hat like a crown with a tail-like plumage at the back and a long, loose, embroidered gown with bell-shaped sleeves, a traditional Manchu garment, convenient for riding and archery, deriving from the Manchus' nomadic past. He knelt and kowtowed five times to the tablets and then walked into the wedding chamber alone.

Next my grandmother, still accompanied by her two attendants, curtsied five times, each time touching her hair with her right hand, in a gesture resembling a salute. She could not kowtow because of the mass of her elaborate headdress. She then followed Dr. Xia into the wedding chamber, where he removed the red cover from her head. The two bridesmaids presented each of them with an empty gourd-shaped vase, which they exchanged with each other, and then the bridesmaids left. Dr. Xia and my grandmother sat silently alone together for a while, and then Dr. Xia went out to greet the relatives and guests. My grandmother had to sit, motionless and alone, on the *kang*, facing the window on which was a huge red "double happiness" paper cut, for several hours. This was called "sitting happiness in," symbolizing the absence of restlessness that was deemed to be an essential quality for a woman. After all the guests had gone, a young male relative of Dr. Xia's came in and tugged her by the sleeve three times. Only then was she allowed to get down from the *kang*. With the help of her two attendants, she changed out of her heavily embroidered outfit into a simple red gown and red trousers. She removed the enormous headdress with all the clicking jewels and did her hair in two coils above her ears.

So in 1935 my mother, now age four, and my grandmother, age twenty-six, moved into Dr. Xia's comfortable house. It was really a compound all on its own, consisting of the house proper in the interior and the surgery, with the medicine shop, facing onto the street. It was customary for successful doctors to have their own shops. Here Dr. Xia sold traditional Chinese medicines, herbs and animal extracts, which were processed in a workshop by three apprentices.

The facade of the house was surmounted by highly decorated red-and-gold eaves. In the center was a rectangular plaque denoting the Xia residence in gilded characters. Behind the shop lay a small courtyard, with a number of rooms opening off it for the servants and cooks. Beyond that the compound opened out into several smaller courtyards, where the family lived. Farther back was a big garden with cypresses and winter plums. There was no grass in the courtyards—the climate was too harsh. They were just expanses of hard, bare, brown earth, which turned to dust in the summer and to mud in the brief spring when the snow melted. Dr. Xia loved birds and had a bird garden, and every morning, whatever the weather, he did *qigong*, a form of the slow, graceful Chinese exercises often called *t'ai chi*, while he listened to the birds singing and chirping.

After the death of his son, Dr. Xia had to endure the constant silent reproach of his family. He never talked to my grandmother about the pain this caused him. For Chinese men a stiff upper lip was mandatory. My grandmother knew what he was going through, of course, and suffered with him, in silence. She was very loving toward him, and attended to his needs with all her heart.

She always showed a smiling face to his family, although they generally treated her with disdain beneath a veneer of formal respect. Even the daughter-in-law who had been at school with her tried to avoid her. The knowledge that she was held responsible for the eldest son's death weighed on my grandmother.

Her entire lifestyle had to change to that of a Manchu. She slept in a room with my mother, and Dr. Xia slept in a separate room. Early every morning, long before she got up, her nerves would start to strain and jangle, anticipating the noise of the family members approaching. She had to wash hurriedly, and greet each of them in turn with a rigid set of salutations. In addition, she had to do her hair in an extremely complicated way so that it could support a huge headdress, under which she had to wear a wig. All she got was a sequence of icy "Good morning"s, virtually the only words the family ever spoke to her. As she watched them bowing and scraping, she knew they had hate in their hearts. The ritual grated all the more for its insincerity.

On festivals and other important occasions, the whole family had to kowtow and curtsy to her, and she would have to jump up from her chair and stand to one side to show that she had left the chair empty, which symbolized their late mother, to acknowledge their respect. Manchu custom conspired to keep her and Dr. Xia apart. They were not supposed even to eat together, and one of the daughters-in-law always stood behind my grandmother to serve her. But the woman would present such a cold face that my grandmother found it difficult to finish her meal, much less enjoy it.

Once, soon after they had moved into Dr. Xia's house, my mother had just settled down into what looked like a nice, comfortable, warm place on the *kang* when she saw Dr. Xia's face suddenly darken, and he stormed over and roughly pulled her off the seat. She had sat in his special place. This was the only time he ever hit her. According to Manchu custom, his seat was sacred.

The move to Dr. Xia's house brought my grandmother a real measure of freedom for the first time—but also a degree of entrapment. For my mother it was no less ambivalent. Dr. Xia was extremely kind to her and brought her up as his own daughter. She called him "Father," and he gave her his own name, Xia, which she carries to this day—and a new given name, "De-hong," which is made up of two characters: *Hong*, meaning "wild swan," and *De*, the generation name, meaning "virtue."

Dr. Xia's family did not dare insult my grandmother to her face— that would have been tantamount to treason to one's "mother." But her daughter was another matter. My mother's first memories, apart from being cuddled by her mother, are of being bullied by the younger members of Dr. Xia's family. She would try not to cry out, and to hide her bruises and cuts from her mother, but my grandmother knew what was going on. She never said anything to Dr. Xia, as she did not want to upset him or create more problems for him with his children. But my mother was miserable. She often begged to be taken back to her grandparents' house, or to the house General Xue had bought, where everyone had treated her like a princess. But she soon realized she should stop asking to "go home," as this only brought tears to her mother's eyes.

My mother's closest friends were her pets. She had an owl, a black myna bird which could say a few simple phrases, a hawk, a cat, white mice, and some grasshoppers and crickets which she kept in glass bottles. Apart from her mother, her only close human friend was Dr. Xia's coachman, "Big Old Lee." He was a tough, leathery-skinned man from the Hinggan mountains in the far north, where the borders of China, Mongolia, and the Soviet Union meet. He had very dark skin, coarse hair, thick lips, and an upturned nose, all of which are very unusual among Chinese. In fact, he did not look Chinese at all. He was tall, thin, and wiry. His father had brought him up as a hunter and trapper, digging out ginseng roots and hunting bears, foxes, and deer. For a time they had done very well selling the skins, but they had eventually been put out of business by bandits, the worst of whom worked for the Old Marshal, Chang Tso-lin. Big Old Lee referred to him as "that bandit bastard." Later, when my mother was told the Old Marshal had been a staunch anti-Japanese patriot, she remembered Big Old Lee's mockery of the "hero" of the northeast.

Big Old Lee looked after my mother's pets, and used to take her out on expeditions with him. That winter he taught her to skate. In the spring, as the snow and ice were melting, they watched people performing the important annual ritual of "sweeping the tombs" and planting flowers on the graves of their ancestors. In summer they went fishing and gathering mushrooms, and in the autumn they drove out to the edge of town to shoot hares.

In the long Manchurian evenings, when the wind howled across the plains and the ice froze on the inside of the windows, Big Old Lee would sit my mother on his knee on the warm *kang* and tell her fabulous stories about the mountains of the north. The images she took to bed were of mysterious tall trees, exotic flowers, colorful birds singing tuneful songs, and ginseng roots which were really little girls —after you dug them out you had to tie a red string around them, otherwise they would run away.

Big Old Lee also told my mother about animal lore. Tigers, which roamed the mountains of northern Manchuria, were kind-hearted and would not hurt human beings unless they felt threatened. He loved tigers. But bears were another matter: they were fierce and one should avoid them at all costs. If you did happen to meet one, you must stand still until it lowered its head. This was because the bear has a lock of hair on his forehead which falls over his eyes and blinds him when he drops his head. With a wolf you should not turn and run, because you could never outrun it. You should stand and face it head-on, looking as though you were not afraid. Then you should walk backwards very, very slowly. Many years later, Big Old Lee's advice was to save my mother's life.

One day when she was five years old my mother was in the garden talking to her pets when Dr. Xia's grandchildren crowded around her in a gang. They started jostling her and calling her names, and then began to hit her and shove her around more violently. They forced her into a corner of the garden where there was a dried-up well and pushed her in. The well was quite deep, and she fell hard on the rubble at the bottom. Eventually someone heard her screams and called Big Old Lee, who came running with a ladder; the cook held it steady while he climbed in. By now my grandmother had arrived, frantic with worry. After a few minutes, Big Old Lee resurfaced carrying my mother, who was half unconscious and covered with cuts and bruises. He put her in my grandmother's arms. My mother was taken inside, where Dr. Xia examined her. One hipbone was broken. For years afterward it sometimes became dislocated, and the accident left her with a permanent slight limp.

When Dr. Xia asked her what had happened, my mother said she had been pushed by "Number Six [Grandson]." My grandmother, ever attentive to Dr. Xia's moods, tried to shush her up because Number Six was his favorite. When Dr. Xia left the room, my grandmother told my mother not to complain about "Number Six" again, so as not to upset Dr. Xia. For some time my mother was confined to the house because of her hip. The other children ostracized her completely.

Immediately after this, Dr. Xia began to go away for several days at a time. He went to the provincial capital, Jinzhou, about twenty-five miles to the south, looking for a job. The atmosphere in the family was unbearable, and my mother's accident, which might easily have been fatal, convinced him that a move was essential.

This was no small decision. In China, to have several generations of a family living under one roof was considered a great honor. Streets even had names like "Five Generations Under One Roof" to commemorate such families. Breaking up the extended family was viewed as a tragedy to be avoided at all costs, but Dr. Xia tried to put on a cheerful face to my grandmother, saying he would be glad to have less responsibility.

My grandmother was vastly relieved, although she tried not to show it. In fact, she had been gently pushing Dr. Xia to move, especially after what happened to my mother. She had had enough of the extended family, always glacially present, icily willing her to be miserable, and in which she had neither privacy nor company.

Dr. Xia divided his property up among the members of his family. The only things he kept for himself were the gifts which had been bestowed on his ancestors by the Manchu emperors. To the widow of his eldest son he gave all his land. The second son inherited the medicine shop, and the house was left to his youngest son. He saw to it that Big Old Lee and the other servants were well taken care of. When he asked my grandmother if she would mind being poor, she said she would be happy just to have her daughter and himself: "If you have love, even plain cold water is sweet."

On a freezing December day in 1936 the family gathered outside the front gate to see them off. They were all dry-eyed except De-gui, the only son who had backed the marriage. Big Old Lee drove them in the horse-drawn carriage to the station, where my mother said a tearful goodbye to him. But she became excited when they got on the train. This was the first time she had been on a train since she was a year old and she was thrilled, jumping up and down as she looked out the window.

Jinzhou was a big city, with a population of almost 100,000, the capital of one of the nine provinces of Manchukuo. It lies about ten miles inland from the sea, where Manchuria approaches the Great Wall. Like Yixian, it was a walled town, but it was growing fast and had already spread well beyond its walls. It boasted a number of textile factories and two oil refineries; it was an important railroad junction, and even had its own airport.

The Japanese had occupied it in early January 1932, after heavy fighting. Jinzhou was in a highly strategic location, and had played a central role in the takeover of Manchuria, its seizure becoming the focus of a major diplomatic dispute between the United States and Japan and a key episode in the long chain of events which ultimately led to Pearl Harbor ten years later.

When the Japanese began their attack on Manchuria in September 1931, the Young Marshal, Chang Hsueh-liang, was forced to abandon his capital, Mukden, to the Japanese. He decamped to Jinzhou with some 200,000 troops and set up his headquarters there. In one of the first such attacks in history, the Japanese bombed the city from the air. When the Japanese troops entered Jinzhou they went on a rampage.

This was the town where Dr. Xia, now age sixty-six, had to start again from the bottom. He could only afford to rent a mud hut about ten by eight feet in size in a very poor part of town, a low-lying area by a river, under a levee. Most of the local shack owners were too poor to afford a proper roof: they laid pieces of corrugated iron over their four walls and put heavy stones on top to try to stop them from being blown away in the frequent high winds. The area was right on the edge of the town—on the other side of the river were sorghum fields. When they first arrived in December, the brown earth was frozen solid—and so was the river, which was about thirty yards wide at this point. In the spring, as the ice thawed, the ground around the hut turned to a quagmire, and the stench of sewage, kept down in winter because it immediately froze, permanently lodged in their nostrils. In the summer the area was infested with mosquitoes, and floods were a constant worry because the river rose well above the level of the houses and the embankments were poorly maintained.

My mother's overwhelming impression was of almost unbearable cold. Every activity, not just sleeping, had to take place on the *kang*, which took up most of the space in the hut, apart from a small stove in one corner. All three of them had to sleep together on the *kang*. There was no electricity or running water. The toilet was a mud shack with a communal pit.

Right opposite the house was a brightly painted temple dedicated to the God of Fire. People coming to pray in it would tie their horses up in front of the Xias' shack. When it got warmer, Dr. Xia would take my mother for walks along the riverbank in the evenings and recite classical poetry to her, against the background of the magnificent sunsets. My grandmother would not accompany them: there was no custom of husbands and wives taking walks together, and in any case, her bound feet meant that walking could never be a pleasure for her.

They were on the edge of starvation. In Yixian the family had had a supply of food from Dr. Xia's own land, which meant they always had some rice even after the Japanese had taken their cut. Now their income was sharply down—and the Japanese were appropriating a far greater proportion of the available food. Much of what was produced locally was forcibly exported to Japan, and the large Japanese army in Manchuria took most of the remaining rice and wheat for itself. The local population could occasionally get hold of some maize or sorghum, but even these were scarce. The main food was acorn meal, which tasted and smelled revolting.

My grandmother had never experienced such poverty, but this was the happiest time of her life. Dr. Xia loved her, and she had her daughter with her all the time. She was no longer forced to go through any of the tedious Manchu rituals, and the tiny mud hut was filled with laughter. She and Dr. Xia sometimes passed the long evenings playing cards. The rules were that if Dr. Xia lost, my grandmother would smack him three times, and if she lost, Dr. Xia would kiss her three times.

My grandmother had many women friends in the neighborhood, which was something new for her. As the wife of a doctor she was respected, even though he was not well off. After years of being humiliated and treated as chattel, she was now truly surrounded by freedom.

Every now and then she and her friends would put on an old Manchu performance for themselves, playing hand drums while they sang and danced. The tunes they played consisted of very simple, repetitive notes and rhythms, and the women made up the lyrics as they went along. The married women sang about their sex lives, and the virgins asked questions about sex. Being mostly illiterate, the women used this as a way to learn about the facts of life. Through their singing, they also talked to each other about their lives and their husbands, and passed on their gossip.

My grandmother loved these gatherings, and would often practice for them at home. She would sit on the *kang*, shaking the hand drum with her left hand and singing to the beat, composing the lyrics as she went along. Often Dr. Xia would suggest words. My mother was too young to be taken along to the gatherings, but she could watch my grandmother rehearsing. She was fascinated and particularly wanted to know what words Dr. Xia had suggested. She knew they must be great fun, because he and her mother laughed so much. But when her mother repeated them for her, she "fell into clouds and fog." She had no idea what they meant.

But life was tough. Every day was a battle just to survive. Rice and wheat were only available on the black market, so my grandmother began selling off some of the jewelry General Xue had given her. She ate almost nothing herself, saying she had already eaten, or that she was not hungry and would eat later. When Dr. Xia found out she was selling her jewelry, he insisted she stop: "I am an old man," he said. "Some day I will die, and you will have to rely on those jewels to survive."

Dr. Xia was working as a salaried doctor attached to another man's medicine shop, which did not give him much chance to display his skill. But he worked hard, and gradually his reputation began to grow. Soon he was invited to go on his first visit to a patient's home. When he came back that evening he was carrying a package wrapped in a cloth. He winked at my mother and his wife and asked them to guess what was inside the package. My mother's eyes were glued to the steaming bundle, and even before she could shout out "Steamed rolls!" she was already tearing the package open. As she was devouring the rolls, she looked up and met Dr. Xia's twinkling eyes. More than fifty years later she can still remember his look of happiness, and even today she says she cannot remember any food as delicious as those simple wheat rolls.

Home visits were important to doctors, because the families would pay the doctor who made the call rather than his employer. When the patients were happy, or rich, the doctors would often be given handsome rewards. Grateful patients would also give doctors valuable presents at New Year and on other special occasions. After a number of home visits, Dr. Xia's circumstances began to improve.

His reputation began to spread, too. One day the wife of the provincial governor fell into a coma, and he called in Dr. Xia, who managed to restore her to consciousness. This was considered almost the equivalent of bringing a person back from the grave. The governor ordered a plaque to be made on which he wrote in his own hand: "Dr. Xia, who gives life to people and society." He ordered the plaque to be carried through the town in procession.

Soon afterward the governor came to Dr. Xia for a different kind of help. He had one wife and twelve concubines, but not one of them had borne him a child. The governor had heard that Dr. Xia was particularly skilled in questions of fertility. Dr. Xia prescribed potions for the governor and his thirteen consorts, several of whom became pregnant. In fact, the problem had been the governor's, but the diplomatic Dr. Xia treated the wife and the concubines as well. The governor was overjoyed, and wrote an even larger plaque for Dr. Xia inscribed: "The reincarnation of Kuanyin" (the Buddhist goddess of fertility and kindness). The new plaque was carried to Dr. Xia's house with an even larger procession than the first one. After this, people came to see Dr. Xia from as far away as Harbin, 400 miles to the north. He became known as one of the "four famous doctors" of Manchukuo.

By the end of 1937, a year after they had arrived in Jinzhou, Dr. Xia was able to move to a bigger house just outside the old north gate of the city. It was far superior to the shack by the river. Instead of mud, it was made of red brick. Instead of one room, it had no fewer than three bedrooms. Dr. Xia was able to set up his own practice again, and used the sitting room as his surgery.

The house occupied the south side of a big courtyard which was shared with two other families, but only Dr. Xia's house had a door which opened directly into it. The other two houses faced out onto the street and had solid walls on the courtyard side, without even a window looking onto it. When they wanted to get into the courtyard they had to go around through a gate from the street. The north side of the courtyard was a solid wall. In the courtyard were cypresses and Chinese ilex trees on which the three families used to hang up clotheslines. There were also some roses of Sharon, which were tough enough to survive the harsh winters. During the summer my grandmother would put out her favorite annuals: white-edged morning glory, chrysanthemums, dahlias, and garden balsam.

My grandmother and Dr. Xia never had any children together. He subscribed to a theory that a man over the age of sixty-five should not ejaculate, so as to conserve his sperm, which was considered the essence of a man. Years later my grandmother told my mother, somewhat mysteriously, that through *qigong* Dr. Xia developed a technique which enabled him to have an orgasm without ejaculating. For a man of his age he enjoyed extraordinary health. He was never ill, and took a cold shower every day, even in temperatures of minus 10°F. He never touched alcohol or tobacco, in keeping with the injunctions of the quasi-religious sect to which he belonged, the *Zai-li-hui* (Society of Reason).

Although he was a doctor himself, Dr. Xia was not keen on taking medicine, insisting that the way to good health was a sound body. He adamantly opposed any treatment which in his opinion cured one part of the body while doing damage to another, and would not use strong medicines because of the side effects they might have. My mother and grandmother often had to take medicines behind his back. When they did fall ill, he would always bring in another doctor, who was a traditional Chinese doctor but also a shaman and believed that some ailments were caused by evil spirits, which had to be placated or exorcized by special religious techniques.

My mother was happy. For the first time in her life she felt warmth all around her. No longer did she feel tension, as she had for the two years at her grandparents', and there was none of the bullying she had undergone for a whole year from Dr. Xia's grandchildren.

She was particularly excited by the festivals which came around almost every month. There was no concept of the workweek among ordinary Chinese. Only government offices, schools, and Japanese factories had a day off on Sunday. For other people only festivals provided a break from the daily routine.

On the twenty-third day of the twelfth moon, seven days before the

Chinese New Year, the Winter Festival began. According to legend, this was the day when the Kitchen God, who had been living above the stove with his wife, in the form of their portraits, went up to Heaven to report on the behavior of the family to the Celestial Emperor. A good report would bring the family abundant food in the kitchen in the coming year. So on this day every household would busily kowtow to the portraits of Lord and Lady Kitchen God before they were set ablaze to signify their ascent to Heaven. Grandmother would always ask my mother to stick some honey on their lips. She would also burn lifelike miniature horses and figures of servants which she made out of sorghum plants so the royal couple would have extra-special service to make them happier and thus more inclined to say many nice things about the Xias to the Celestial Emperor.

The next few days were spent preparing all sorts of food. Meat was cut into special shapes, and rice and soybeans were ground into powder and made into buns, rolls, and dumplings. The food was put into the cellar to wait for the New Year. With the temperature as low as minus 20°F, the cellar was a natural refrigerator.

At midnight on Chinese New Year's Eve, a huge burst of fireworks was let off, to my mother's great excitement. She would follow her mother and Dr. Xia outside and kowtow in the direction from which the God of Fortune was supposed to be coming. All along the street, people were doing the same. Then they would greet each other with the words "May you run into good fortune."

At Chinese New Year people gave each other presents. When dawn lit up the white paper in the windows to the east, my mother would jump out of bed and hurry into her new finery: new jacket, new trousers, new socks, and new shoes. Then she and her mother called on neighbors and friends, kowtowing to all the adults. For every bang of her head on the floor, she got a "red wrapper" with money inside. These packets were to last her the whole year as pocket money.

For the next fifteen days, the adults went round paying visits and wishing each other good fortune. Good fortune, namely money, was an obsession with most ordinary Chinese. People were poor, and in the Xia household, like many others, the only time meat was in reasonably abundant supply was at festival time.

The festivities would culminate on the fifteenth day with a carnival procession followed by a lantern show after dark. The procession centered on an inspection visit by the God of Fire. The god would be carried around the neighborhood to warn people of the danger of fire; with most houses partly made of timber and the climate dry and windy, fire was a constant hazard and source of terror, and the statue of the god in the temple used to receive offerings all year round. The procession started at the temple of the God of Fire, in front of the mud hut where the Xias had lived when they first came to Jinzhou. A replica of the statue, a giant with red hair, beard, eyebrows, and cloak, was carried on an open sedan chair by eight young men. It was followed by writhing dragons and lions, each made up of several men, and by floats, stilts, and *yangge* dancers who waved the ends of a long piece of colorful silk tied around their waists. Fireworks, drums, and cymbals made a thundering noise. My mother skipped along behind the procession. Almost every household displayed tantalizing foods along the route as offerings to the deity, but she noticed that the deity jolted by rather quickly, not touching any of it. "Goodwill for the gods, offerings for the human stomachs!" her mother told her. In those days of scarcity my mother looked forward keenly to the festivals, when she could satisfy her stomach. She was quite indifferent to those occasions which had poetic rather than gastronomic associations, and would wait impatiently for her mother to guess the riddles stuck on the splendid lanterns hung at people's front doors during the Lantern Festival, or for her mother to tour the chrysanthemums in people's gardens on the ninth day of the ninth moon.

During the Fair of the Town God's Temple one year, my grandmother showed her a row of clay sculptures in the temple, all redecorated and painted for the occasion. They were scenes of Hell, showing people being punished for their sins. My grandmother pointed out a clay figure whose tongue was being pulled out at least a foot while simultaneously being cut up by two devils with spiky hair standing on end like hedgehogs and eyes bulging like frogs. The man being tortured had been a liar in his previous life, she said—and this was what would happen to my mother if she told lies.

There were about a dozen groups of statues, set amid the buzzing crowds and the mouth-watering food stalls, each one illustrating a moral lesson. My grandmother cheerfully showed my mother one horrible scene after another, but when they came to one group of figures she whisked her by without any explanation. Only some years later did my mother find out that it depicted a woman being sawed in half by two men. The woman was a widow who had remarried, and she was being sawed in half by her two husbands because she had been the property of both of them. In those days many widows were frightened by this prospect and remained loyal to their dead husbands, no matter how much misery that entailed. Some even killed themselves if they were forced by their families to remarry. My mother realized that her mother's decision to marry Dr. Xia had not been an easy one.

3. "They All Say What a Happy Place Manchukuo Is"— Life under the Japanese

(1938–1945)

Early in 1938, my mother was nearly seven. She was very bright, and very keen to study. Her parents thought she should begin school as soon as the new school year started, immediately after Chinese New Year.

Education was tightly controlled by the Japanese, especially the history and ethics courses. Japanese, not Chinese, was the official language in the schools. Above the fourth form in elementary school teaching was entirely in Japanese, and most of the teachers were Japanese.

On 11 September 1939, when my mother was in her second year in elementary school, the emperor of Manchukuo, Pu Yi, and his wife came to Jinzhou on an official visit. My mother was chosen to present flowers to the empress on her arrival. A large crowd stood on a gaily decorated dais, all holding yellow paper flags in the colors of Manchukuo. My mother was given a huge bouquet of flowers, and she was full of self-confidence as she stood next to the brass band and a group of VIPs in morning coats. A boy about the same age as my mother was standing stiffly near her with a bouquet of flowers to present to Pu Yi. As the royal couple appeared the band struck up the Manchukuo national anthem. Everyone sprang to attention. My mother stepped forward and curtsied, expertly balancing her bouquet. The empress was wearing a white dress and very fine long white gloves up to her elbows. My mother thought she looked extremely beautiful. She managed to snatch a glance at Pu Yi, who was in military uniform. Behind his thick spectacles she thought he had "piggy eyes."

Apart from the fact that she was a star pupil, one reason my mother was chosen to present flowers to the empress was that she always filled in her nationality on registration forms as "Manchu," like Dr. Xia, and Manchukuo was supposed to be the Manchus' own independent state. Pu Yi was particularly useful to the Japanese because, as far as most people were concerned, if they thought about it at all, they were still under the Manchu emperor. Dr. Xia considered himself a loyal subject, and my grandmother took the same view. Traditionally, an important way in which a woman expressed her love for her man was by agreeing with him in everything, and this came naturally to my grandmother. She was so contented with Dr. Xia that she did not want to turn her mind even slightly in the direction of disagreement.

At school my mother was taught that her country was Manchukuo, and that among its neighboring countries there were two republics of China—one hostile, led by Chiang Kai-shek; the other friendly, headed by Wang Jing-wei (Japan's puppet ruler of part of China). She was taught no concept of a "China" of which Manchuria was part.

The pupils were educated to be obedient subjects of Manchukuo. One of the first songs my mother learned was:

Red boys and green girls walk on the streets,
They all say what a happy place Manchukuo is.
You are happy and I am happy,
Everyone lives peacefully and works joyfully free of any worries.

The teachers said that Manchukuo was a paradise on earth. But even at her age my mother could see that if the place could be called a paradise it was only for the Japanese. Japanese children attended separate schools, which were well equipped and well heated, with shining floors and clean windows. The schools for the local children were in dilapidated temples and crumbling houses donated by private patrons. There was no heating. In winter the whole class often had to run around the block in the middle of a lesson or engage in collective foot-stamping to ward off the cold.

Not only were the teachers mainly Japanese, they also used Japanese methods, hitting the children as a matter of course. The slightest mistake or failure to observe the prescribed rules and etiquette, such as a girl having her hair half an inch below her earlobes, was punished with blows. Both girls and boys were slapped on the face, hard, and boys were frequently struck on the head with a wooden club. Another punishment was to be made to kneel for hours in the snow.

When local children passed a Japanese in the street, they had to bow and make way, even if the Japanese was younger than themselves. Japanese children would often stop local children and slap them for no reason at all. The pupils had to bow elaborately to their teachers every time they met them. My mother joked to her friends that a Japanese teacher passing by was like a whirlwind sweeping through a field of grass—you just saw the grass bending as the wind blew by.

Many adults bowed to the Japanese, too, for fear of offending them, but the Japanese presence did not impinge greatly on the Xias at first. Middle- and lower-echelon positions were held by locals, both Manchus and Han Chinese, like my great-grandfather, who kept his job as deputy police chief of Yixian. By 1940, there were about 15,000 Japanese in Jinzhou. The people living in the next house to the Xias were Japanese, and my grandmother was friendly with them. The husband was a government official. Every morning his wife would stand outside the gate with their three children and bow deeply to him as he got into a rickshaw to go to work. After that she would start her own work, kneading coal dust into balls for fuel. For reasons my grandmother and my mother never understood, she always wore white gloves, which became filthy in no time.

The Japanese woman often visited my grandmother. She was lonely, with her husband hardly ever at home. She would bring a little sake, and my grandmother would prepare some snacks, like soy-pickled vegetables. My grandmother spoke a little Japanese and the Japanese woman a little Chinese. They hummed songs to each other and shed tears together when they became emotional. They often helped in each other's gardens, too. The Japanese neighbor had very smart gardening tools, which my grandmother admired greatly, and my mother was often invited over to play in her garden.

But the Xias could not avoid hearing what the Japanese were doing. In the vast expanses of northern Manchuria villages were being burned and the surviving population herded into "strategic hamlets." Over five million people, about a sixth of the population, lost their homes, and tens of thousands died. Laborers were worked to death in mines under Japanese guards to produce exports to Japan—for Manchuria was particularly rich in natural resources. Many were deprived of salt and did not have the energy to run away.

Dr. Xia had argued for a long time that the emperor did not know about the evil things being done because he was a virtual prisoner of the Japanese. But when Pu Yi changed the way he referred to Japan from "our friendly neighbor country" to "the elder brother country" and finally to "parent country," Dr. Xia banged his fist on the table and called him "that fatuous coward." Even then, he said he was not sure how much responsibility the emperor should bear for the atrocities, until two traumatic events changed the Xias' world.

One day in late 1941 Dr. Xia was in his surgery when a man he had never seen came into the room. He was dressed in rags, and his emaciated body was bent almost double. The man explained that he was a railway coolie, and that he had been having agonizing stomach pains. His work involved carrying heavy loads from dawn to dusk, 365 days a year. He did not know how he could go on, but if he lost his job he would not be able to support his wife and newborn baby.

Dr. Xia told him his stomach could not digest the coarse food he had to eat. On 1 June 1939, the government had announced that henceforth rice was reserved for the Japanese and a small number of collaborators. Most of the local population had to subsist on a diet of acorn meal and sorghum, which were difficult to digest. Dr. Xia gave the man some medicine free of charge, and asked my grandmother to give him a small bag of rice which she had bought illegally on the black market.

Not long afterward, Dr. Xia heard that the man had died in a forced labor camp. After leaving the surgery he had eaten the rice, gone back to work, and then vomited at the railway yard. A Japanese guard had spotted rice in his vomit and he had been arrested as an "economic criminal" and hauled off to a camp. In his weakened state, he survived only a few days. When his wife heard what had happened to him, she drowned herself with their baby.

The incident plunged Dr. Xia and my grandmother into deep grief. They felt responsible for the man's death. Many times Dr. Xia would say: "Rice can murder as well as save! A small bagful, three lives!" He started to call Pu Yi "that tyrant."

Shortly after this, tragedy struck closer to home. Dr. Xia's youngest son was working as a schoolteacher in Yixian. As in every school in Manchukuo, there was a big portrait of Pu Yi in the office of the Japanese headmaster, which everyone had to salute when they entered the room. One day Dr. Xia's son forgot to bow to Pu Yi. The headmaster shouted at him to bow at once and slapped him so hard across the face he knocked him off balance. Dr. Xia's son was enraged: "Do I have to bend double every day? Can I not stand up straight even for a moment? I have just done my obeisance in morning assembly. . . ." The headmaster slapped him again and barked: "This is your emperor! You Manchurians need to be taught elementary propriety!" Dr. Xia's son shouted back: "Big deal! It's only a piece of paper!" At that moment two other teachers, both locals, came by and managed to stop him from saying anything more incriminating. He recovered his self-control and eventually forced himself to perform a bow of sorts to the portrait.

That evening a friend came to his house and told him that word was out that he had been branded a "thought criminal"—an offense which was punishable by imprisonment, and possibly death. He ran away, and his family never heard of him again. Probably he was caught and died in prison, or else in a labor camp. Dr. Xia never recovered from the blow, which turned him into a determined foe of Manchukuo and of Pu Yi.

This was not the end of the story. Because of his brother's "crime," local thugs began to harass De-gui, Dr. Xia's only surviving son, demanding protection money and claiming he had failed in his duty as the elder brother. He paid up, but the gangsters only demanded more. In the end, he had to sell the medicine shop and leave Yixian for Mukden, where he opened a new shop.

By now, Dr. Xia was becoming more and more successful. He treated Japanese as well as locals. Sometimes after treating a senior Japanese officer or a collaborator he would say, "I wish he were dead," but his personal views never affected his professional attitude. "A patient is a human being," he used to say. "That is all a doctor should think about. He should not mind what kind of a human being he is."

My grandmother had meanwhile brought her mother to Jinzhou. When she left home to marry Dr. Xia, her mother had been left alone in the house with her husband, who despised her, and the two Mongolian concubines, who hated her. She began to suspect that the concubines wanted to poison her and her small son, Yu-lin. She always used silver chopsticks, as the Chinese believe that silver will turn black if it comes into contact with poison, and she never touched her food or let Yu-lin touch it until she had tested it out on her dog. One day, a few months after my grandmother had left the house, the dog dropped dead. For the first time in her life, she had a big row with her husband; and with the support of her mother-in-law, old Mrs. Yang, she moved out with Yu-lin into rented accommodation. Old Mrs. Yang was so disgusted with her son that she left home with them, and never saw her son again—except at her deathbed.

In the first three years, Mr. Yang reluctantly sent them a monthly allowance, but at the beginning of 1939 this stopped, and Dr. Xia and my grandmother had to support the three of them. In those days there was no maintenance law, as there was no proper legal system, so a wife was entirely at the mercy of her husband. When old Mrs. Yang died in 1942 my great-grandmother and Yu-lin moved to Jinzhou, and went to live in Dr. Xia's house. She considered herself and her son to be second-class citizens, living on charity. She spent her time washing the family's clothes and cleaning up obsessively, nervously obsequious toward her daughter and Dr. Xia. She was a pious Buddhist and every day in her prayers asked Buddha not to reincarnate her as a woman. "Let me become a cat or a dog, but not a woman," was her constant murmur as she shuffled around the house, oozing apology with every step.

My grandmother had also brought her sister, Lan, whom she loved dearly, to Jinzhou. Lan had married a man in Yixian who turned out to be a homosexual. He had offered her to a rich uncle, for whom he worked and who owned a vegetable-oil factory. The uncle had raped several female members of the household, including his young granddaughter. Because he was the head of the family, wielding immense power over all its members, Lan did not dare resist him. But when her husband offered her to his uncle's business partner she refused. My grandmother had to pay the husband to disown her (*xiu*), as a woman could not ask for a divorce. My grandmother brought her to Jinzhou, where she was remarried, to a man called Pei-o.

Pei-o was a warder in the prison, and the couple often visited my grandmother. Pei-o's stories made my mother's hair stand on end. The prison was crammed with political prisoners. Pei-o often said how brave they were, and how they would curse the Japanese even as they were being tortured. Torture was standard practice, and the prisoners received no medical treatment. Their wounds were just left to rot.

Dr. Xia offered to go and treat the prisoners. On one of his first visits he was introduced by Pei-o to a friend of his called Dong, an executioner, who operated the garrote. The prisoner was tied to a chair with a rope around his neck. The rope was then slowly tightened. Death was excruciatingly slow.

Dr. Xia knew from his brother-in-law that Dong's conscience was troubled, and that whenever he was due to garrote someone, he had to get himself drunk beforehand. Dr. Xia invited Dong to his house. He offered him gifts and suggested that perhaps he could avoid tightening the rope all the way. Dong said he would see what he could do. There was usually a Japanese guard or a trusted collaborator present, but sometimes, if the victim was not important enough, the Japanese did not bother to show up. At other times, they left before the prisoner was actually dead. On such occasions, Dong hinted, he could stop the garrote before the prisoner died.

After prisoners were garroted, their bodies were put into thin wooden boxes and taken on a cart to a stretch of barren land on the outskirts of town called South Hill, where they were tipped into a shallow pit. The place was infested with wild dogs, who lived on the corpses. Baby girls who had been killed by their families, which was common in those days, were also often dumped in the pit.

Dr. Xia struck up a relationship with the old cart driver, and gave him money from time to time. Occasionally the driver would come into the surgery and start rambling on about life, in an apparently incoherent way, but eventually he would begin talking about the graveyard: "I told the dead souls it was not my fault they had ended up there. I told them that, for my part, I wished them well. 'Come back next year for your anniversary, dead souls. But in the meantime, if you wish to fly away to look for better bodies to be reincarnated in, go in the direction your head is pointed. That is a good path for you.' " Dong and the cart driver never spoke to each other about what they were doing, and Dr. Xia never knew how many people they had saved. After the war the rescued "corpses" chipped in and raised money for Dong to buy a house and some land. The cart driver had died.

One man whose life they helped save was a distant cousin of my grandmother's called Han-chen, who had been an important figure in the resistance movement. Because Jinzhou was the main railway junction north of the Great Wall, it became the assembly point for the Japanese in their assault on China proper, which started in July 1937. Security was extremely tight, and Han-chen's organization was infiltrated by a spy, and the entire group was arrested. They were all tortured. First water with hot chiles was forced down their noses; then their faces were slapped with a shoe which had sharp nails sticking out of the sole. Then most of them were executed. For a long time the Xias thought Han-chen was dead, until one day Uncle Pei-o told them that he was still alive—but about to be executed. Dr. Xia immediately contacted Dong.

On the night of the execution Dr. Xia and my grandmother went to South Hill with a carriage. They parked behind a clump of trees and waited. They could hear the wild dogs rummaging around by the pit, from which rose the sickly stench of decomposing flesh. At last a cart appeared. Through the darkness they could dimly see the old driver climbing down and tipping some bodies out of wooden boxes. They waited for him to drive off and then went over to the pit. After groping among the corpses they found Han-chen, but could not tell if he was dead or alive. Eventually they realized he was still breathing.

He had been so badly tortured he could not walk, so with great effort they lifted him into the carriage and drove him back to their house.

They hid him in a tiny room in the innermost corner of the house. Its one door led into my mother's room, to which the only other access was from her parents' bedroom. No one would ever go into the room by chance. As the house was the only one which had direct access to the courtyard, Han-chen could exercise there in safety, as long as someone kept watch.

There was the danger of a raid by the police or the local neighborhood committees. Early on in the occupation the Japanese had set up a system of neighborhood control. They made the local big shots the heads of these units, and these neighborhood bosses helped collect taxes and kept a round-the-clock watch for "lawless elements." It was a form of institutionalized gangsterism, in which "protection" and informing were the keys to power. The Japanese also offered large rewards for turning people in. The Manchukuo police were less of a threat than ordinary civilians. In fact, many of the police were quite anti-Japanese. One of their main jobs was to check people's registration, and they used to carry out frequent house-to-house searches. But they would announce their arrival by shouting out "Checking registrations! Checking registrations!" so that anyone who wanted to hide had plenty of time. Whenever Han-chen or my grandmother heard this shout she would hide him in a pile of dried sorghum stacked in the end room for fuel. The police would saunter into the house and sit down and have a cup of tea, telling my grandmother rather apologetically, "All this is just a formality, you know. . . ."

At the time my mother was eleven. Even though her parents did not tell her what was going on, she knew she must not talk about Han-chen being in the house. She learned discretion from childhood.

Slowly, my grandmother nursed Han-chen back to health, and after three months he was well enough to move on. It was an emotional farewell. "Elder sister and elder brother-in-law," he said, "I will never forget that I owe my life to you. As soon as I have the chance, I will repay my great debt to you both." Three years later he came back and was as good as his word.

As part of their education, my mother and her classmates had to watch newsreels of Japan's progress in the war. Far from being ashamed of their brutality, the Japanese vaunted it as a way to inculcate fear. The films showed Japanese soldiers cutting people in half and prisoners tied to stakes being torn to pieces by dogs. There were lingering close-ups of the victims' terror-stricken eyes as their attackers came at them. The Japanese watched the eleven- and twelve-year-old schoolgirls to make sure they did not shut their eyes or try to stick a handkerchief in their mouths to stifle their screams. My mother had nightmares for years to come.

During 1942, with their army stretched out across China, Southeast Asia, and the Pacific Ocean, the Japanese found themselves running short of labor. My mother's whole class was conscripted to work in a textile factory, as were the Japanese children. The local girls had to walk about four miles each way; the Japanese children went by truck. The local girls got a thin gruel made from moldy maize with dead worms floating in it; the Japanese girls had packed lunches with meat, vegetables, and fruit.

The Japanese girls had easy jobs, like cleaning windows. But the local girls had to operate complex spinning machines, which were highly demanding and dangerous even for adults. Their main job was to reconnect broken threads while the machines were running at speed. If they did not spot the broken thread, or reconnect it fast enough, they would be savagely beaten by the Japanese supervisor.

The girls were terrified. The combination of nervousness, cold, hunger, and fatigue led to many accidents. Over half of my mother's fellow pupils suffered injuries. One day my mother saw a shuttle spin out of a machine and knock out the eye of the girl next to her. All the way to the hospital the Japanese supervisor scolded the girl for not being careful enough.

After the stint in the factory, my mother moved up into junior high school. Times had changed since my grandmother's youth, and young women were no longer confined to the four walls of their home. It was socially acceptable for women to get a high school education. However, boys and girls received different educations. For girls the aim was to turn them into "gracious wives and good mothers," as the school motto put it. They learned what the Japanese called "the way of a woman"—looking after a household, cooking and sewing, the tea ceremony, flower arrangement, embroidery, drawing, and the appreciation of art. The single most important thing imparted was how to please one's husband. This included how to dress, how to do one's hair, how to bow, and, above all, how to obey, without question. As my grandmother put it, my mother seemed to have "rebellious bones," and learned almost none of these skills, even cooking.

Some exams took the form of practical assignments, such as preparing a particular dish or arranging flowers. The examination board was made up of local officials, both Japanese and Chinese, and as well as assessing the exams, they also sized up the girls. Photos of them wearing pretty aprons they had designed themselves were put up on the notice board with their assignments. Japanese officials often picked fiancées from among the girls, as intermarriage between Japanese men and local women was encouraged. Some girls were also selected to go to Japan to be married to men they had not met. Quite often the girls—or rather their families—were willing. Toward the end of the occupation one of my mother's friends was chosen to go to Japan, but she missed the ship and was still in Jinzhou when the Japanese surrendered. My mother looked askance at her.

In contrast with their Chinese Mandarin predecessors, who shunned physical activity, the Japanese were keen on sports, which my mother loved. She had recovered from her hip injury, and was a good runner. Once she was selected to run in an important race. She trained for weeks, and was all keyed up for the big day, but a few days before the race the coach, who was Chinese, took her aside and asked her not to try to win. He said he could not explain why. My mother understood. She knew the Japanese did not like to be beaten by the Chinese at anything. There was one other local girl in the race, and the coach asked my mother to pass on the same advice to her, but not to tell her that it came from him. On the day of the race my mother did not even finish in the first six. Her friends could tell she was not trying. But the other local girl could not bear to hold back, and came in first.

The Japanese soon took their revenge. Every morning there was an assembly, presided over by the headmaster, who was nicknamed "Donkey" because his name when read in the Chinese way *(Mao-li)* sounded like the word for donkey *(mao-lü)*. He would bark out orders in harsh, guttural tones for the four low bows toward the four designated points. First, "Distant worship of the imperial capital!" in the direction of Tokyo. Then, "Distant worship of the national capital!" toward Hsinking, the capital of Manchukuo. Next, "Devoted worship of the Celestial Emperor!"—meaning the emperor of Japan. Finally, "Devoted worship of the imperial portrait!"—this time to the portrait of Pu Yi. After this came a shallower bow to the teachers.

On this particular morning, after the bowing was completed, the girl who had won the race the day before was suddenly dragged out of her row by "Donkey," who claimed that her bow to Pu Yi had been less than ninety degrees. He slapped and kicked her and announced that she was being expelled. This was a catastrophe for her and her family.

Her parents hurriedly married her off to a petty government official. After Japan's defeat her husband was branded as a collaborator, and as a result the only job his wife could get was in a chemical plant.

There were no pollution controls, and when my mother went back to Jinzhou in 1984 and tracked her down she had gone almost blind from the chemicals. She was wry about the ironies of her life: having beaten the Japanese in a race, she had ended up being treated as a kind of collaborator. Even so, she said she had no regrets about winning the race.

It was difficult for people in Manchukuo to get much idea of what was happening in the rest of the world, or of how Japan was faring in the war. The fighting was a long way away, news was strictly censored, and the radio churned out nothing but propaganda. But they got a sense that Japan was in trouble from a number of signs, especially the worsening food situation.

The first real news came in summer 1943, when the newspapers reported that one of Japan's allies, Italy, had surrendered. By the middle of 1944 some Japanese civilians staffing government offices in Manchukuo were being conscripted. Then, on 29 July 1944, American B-29s appeared in the sky over Jinzhou for the first time, though they did not bomb the city. The Japanese ordered every household to dig air-raid shelters, and there was a compulsory air-raid drill every day at school. One day a girl in my mother's class picked up a fire extinguisher and squirted it at a Japanese teacher whom she particularly loathed. Previously, this would have brought dire retribution, but now she was allowed to get away with it. The tide was turning.

There had been a long-standing campaign to catch flies and rats. The pupils had to chop off the rats' tails, put them in envelopes, and hand them in to the police. The flies had to be put in glass bottles. The police counted every rat tail and every dead fly. One day in 1944 when my mother handed in a glass bottle full to the brim with flies, the Manchukuo policeman said to her: "Not enough for a meal." When he saw the surprised look on her face, he said: "Don't you know? The Nips like dead flies. They fry them and eat them!" My mother could see from the cynical gleam in his eye that he no longer regarded the Japanese as awesome.

My mother was excited and full of anticipation, but during the autumn of 1944 a dark cloud had appeared: her home did not seem to be as happy as before. She sensed there was discord between her parents.

The fifteenth night of the eighth moon of the Chinese year was the Mid-Autumn Festival, the festival of family union. On that night my grandmother would place a table with melons, round cakes, and buns outside in the moonlight, in accordance with the custom. The reason this date was the festival of family union is that the Chinese word for "union" *(yuan)* is the same as that for "round" or "unbroken"; the full autumn moon was supposed to look especially, splendidly, round at this time. All the items of food eaten on that day had to be round too.

In the silky moonlight, my grandmother would tell my mother stories about the moon: the largest shadow in it was a giant cassia tree which a certain lord, Wu Gang, was spending his entire life trying to cut down. But the tree was enchanted and he was doomed to repeated failure. My mother would stare up into the sky and listen, fascinated. The full moon was mesmerizingly beautiful to her, but on that night she was not allowed to describe it, because she was forbidden by her mother to utter the word "round," as Dr. Xia's family had been broken up. Dr. Xia would be downcast for the whole day, and for several days before and after the festival. My grandmother would even lose her usual flair for storytelling.

On the night of the festival in 1944, my mother and my grandmother were sitting under a trellis covered with winter melons and beans, gazing through the gaps in the shadowy leaves into the vast, cloudless sky. My mother started to say, "The moon is particularly round tonight," but my grandmother interrupted her sharply, then suddenly burst into tears. She rushed into the house, and my mother heard her sobbing and shrieking: "Go back to your son and grandsons! Leave me and my daughter and go your own way!" Then, in gasps between sobs, she said: "Was it my fault—or yours—that your son killed himself? Why should we have to bear the burden year after year? It isn't me who is stopping you seeing your children. It is they who have refused to come and see you. . . ." Since they had left Yixian, only De-gui, Dr. Xia's second son, had visited them. My mother did not hear a sound from Dr. Xia.

From then on my mother felt there was something wrong. Dr. Xia became increasingly taciturn, and she instinctively avoided him. Every now and then my grandmother would become tearful, and murmur to herself that she and Dr. Xia could never be completely happy with the heavy price they had paid for their love. She would hug my mother close and tell her that she was the only thing she had in her life.

My mother was in an uncharacteristically melancholy mood as winter descended on Jinzhou. Even the appearance of a second flight of American B-29s in the clear, cold December sky failed to lift her spirits.

The Japanese were becoming more and more edgy. One day one of my mother's schoolfriends got hold of a book by a banned Chinese writer. Looking for somewhere quiet to read, she went off into the countryside, where she found a cavern which she thought was an empty air-raid shelter. Groping around in the dark, her hand touched what felt like a light switch. A piercing noise erupted. What she had touched was an alarm. She had stumbled into an arms depot. Her legs turned to jelly. She tried to run, but got only a couple of hundred yards before some Japanese soldiers caught her and dragged her away.

Two days later the whole school was marched to a barren, snow-covered stretch of ground outside the west gate, in a bend of the Xiao-ling River. Local residents had also been summoned there by the neighborhood chiefs. The children were told they were to witness "the punishment of an evil person who disobeys Great Japan." Suddenly my mother saw her friend being hauled by Japanese guards to a spot right in front of her. The girl was in chains and could hardly walk. She had been tortured, and her face was so swollen that my mother could barely recognize her. Then the Japanese soldiers lifted their rifles and pointed them at the girl, who seemed to be trying to say something, but no sound came out. There was a crack of bullets, and the girl's body slumped as her blood began to drip onto the snow. "Donkey," the Japanese headmaster, was scanning the rows of his pupils. With a tremendous effort, my mother tried to hide her emotions. She forced herself to look at the body of her friend, which by now was lying in a glistening red patch in the white snow.

She heard someone trying to suppress sobs. It was Miss Tanaka, a young Japanese woman teacher whom she liked. In an instant "Donkey" was on Miss Tanaka, slapping and kicking her. She fell to the ground, and tried to roll out of the way of his boots, but he went on kicking her ferociously. She had betrayed the Japanese race, he bawled. Eventually "Donkey" stopped, looked up at the pupils, and barked the order to march off.

My mother took one last look at the crooked body of her teacher and the corpse of her friend and forced down her hate.

4. "Slaves Who Have No Country of Your Own"— Ruled by Different Masters

(1945–1947)

In May 1945 the news spread around Jinzhou that Germany had surrendered and that the war in Europe was over. U.S. planes were flying over the area much more often: B-29s were bombing other cities in Manchuria, though Jinzhou was not attacked. The feeling that Japan would soon be defeated swept through the city.

On 8 August my mother's school was ordered to go to a shrine to pray for the victory of Japan. The following day, Soviet and Mongolian troops entered Manchukuo. News came through that the Americans had dropped two atom bombs on Japan: the locals cheered the news. The following days were punctuated by air-raid scares, and school stopped. My mother stayed at home helping to dig an air-raid shelter.

On 13 August the Xias heard that Japan was suing for peace. Two days later a Chinese neighbor who worked in the government rushed into their house to tell them there was going to be an important announcement on the radio. Dr. Xia stopped work and came and sat with my grandmother in the courtyard. The announcer said that the Japanese emperor had surrendered. Immediately afterward came the news that Pu Yi had abdicated as emperor of Manchukuo. People crowded into the streets in a state of high excitement. My mother went to her school to see what was happening there. The place seemed dead, except for a faint noise coming from one of the offices. She crept up to have a look: through the window she could see the Japanese teachers huddled together weeping.

She hardly slept a wink that night and was up at the crack of dawn. When she opened the front door in the morning she saw a small crowd in the street. The bodies of a Japanese woman and two children were lying in the road. A Japanese officer had committed *hara-kiri*; his family had been lynched.

One morning a few days after the surrender, the Xias' Japanese neighbors were found dead. Some said they had poisoned themselves. All over Jinzhou Japanese were committing suicide or being lynched. Japanese houses were looted and my mother noticed that one of her poor neighbors suddenly had quite a lot of valuable items for sale. Schoolchildren revenged themselves on their Japanese teachers and beat them up ferociously. Some Japanese left their babies on the doorsteps of local families in the hope that they would be saved. A number of Japanese women were raped; many shaved their heads to try to pass as men.

My mother was worried about Miss Tanaka, who was the only teacher at her school who never slapped the pupils and the only Japanese who had shown distress when my mother's schoolfriend had been executed. She asked her parents if she could hide her in their house. My grandmother looked anxious, but said nothing. Dr. Xia just nodded.

My mother borrowed a set of clothes from her aunt Lan, who was about the teacher's size, then went and found Miss Tanaka, who was barricaded in her apartment. The clothes fit her well. She was taller than the average Japanese woman, and could easily pass for a Chinese. In case anybody asked, they would say she was my mother's cousin. The Chinese have so many cousins no one can keep track of them. She moved into the end room, which had once been Han-chen's refuge.

In the vacuum left by the Japanese surrender and the collapse of the Manchukuo regime the victims were not just Japanese. The city was in chaos. At night there were gunshots and frequent screams for help. The male members of the household, including my grandmother's fifteen-year-old brother Yu-lin and Dr. Xia's apprentices, took turns keeping guard on the roof every night, armed with stones, axes, and cleavers. Unlike my grandmother, my mother was not scared at all. My grandmother was amazed: "You have your father's blood in your veins," she used to say to her.

The looting, raping, and killing continued until eight days after the

Japanese surrender, when the population was informed that a new army would be arriving—the Soviet Red Army. On 23 August the neighborhood chiefs told residents to go to the railway station the next day to welcome the Russians. Dr. Xia and my grandmother stayed at home, but my mother joined the large, high-spirited crowd of young people holding colorful triangle-shaped paper flags. As the train pulled in, the crowd started waving their flags and shouting "*Wula*" (the Chinese approximation of *Ura*, the Russian word for "Hurrah"). My mother had imagined the Soviet soldiers as victorious heroes with impressive beards, riding on large horses. What she saw was a group of shabbily dressed, pale-skinned youths. Apart from the occasional fleeting glimpse of some mysterious figure in a passing car, these were the first white people my mother had ever seen.

About a thousand Soviet troops were stationed in Jinzhou, and when they first arrived people felt grateful to them for helping to get rid of the Japanese. But the Russians brought new problems. Schools had closed down when the Japanese surrendered, and my mother was getting private lessons. One day on her way home from the tutor's, she saw a truck parked by the side of the road: some Russian soldiers were standing beside it handing out bolts of textiles. Under the Japanese, cloth had been strictly rationed. She went over to have a look; it turned out the cloth was from the factory where she had worked when she was in primary school. The Russians were swapping it for watches, clocks, and knickknacks. My mother remembered that there was an old clock buried somewhere at the bottom of a chest at home. She rushed back and dug it out. She was a bit disappointed to find it was broken, but the Russian soldiers were overjoyed and gave her a bolt of beautiful white cloth with a delicate pink flower pattern on it. Over supper, the family sat shaking their heads in disbelief at these strange foreigners who were so keen on useless old broken clocks and baubles.

Not only were the Russians distributing goods from the factories, they were also dismantling entire factories, including Jinzhou's two oil refineries, and shipping the equipment back to the Soviet Union. They said these were "reparations," but for the locals what this meant was that industry was crippled.

Russian soldiers would walk into people's homes and simply take anything they fancied—watches and clothes in particular. Stories about Russians raping local women swept Jinzhou like wildfire. Many women went into hiding for fear of their "liberators." Very soon the city was seething with anger and anxiety.

The Xias' house was outside the city walls, and was very poorly protected. A friend of my mother's offered to lend them a house inside the city gates, surrounded by high stone walls. The family decamped immediately, taking my mother's Japanese teacher with them. The move meant that my mother had to walk much farther—about thirty minutes each way—to her tutor's. Dr. Xia insisted on taking her there and collecting her in the afternoon. My mother did not want him to walk so far, so she would walk part of the way back on her own and he would meet her. One day a jeep-load of laughing Russian soldiers skidded to a halt near her and the Russians jumped out and started running in her direction. She ran as fast as she could, with the Russians pounding after her. After a few hundred yards she caught sight of her stepfather in the distance, brandishing his walking stick. The Russians were close behind, and my mother turned into a deserted kindergarten she knew well, which was like a labyrinth. She hid there for over an hour and then sneaked out the back door and got home safely. Dr. Xia had seen the Russians chasing my mother into the building; to his immense relief they soon came out again, obviously baffled by the layout.

Just over a week after the Russians arrived, my mother was told by the chief of her neighborhood committee to attend a meeting the following evening. When she got there she saw a number of shabby Chinese men—and a few women—making speeches about how they had fought eight years to defeat the Japanese so that ordinary people could be the masters of a new China. These were Communists— Chinese Communists. They had entered the city the previous day, without fanfare or warning. The women Communists at the meeting wore shapeless clothes exactly like the men. My mother thought to herself: How could you claim to have defeated the Japanese? You haven't even got decent guns or clothes. To her, the Communists looked poorer and scruffier than beggars.

She was disappointed because she had imagined them as big and handsome, and superhuman. Her uncle Pei-o, the prison warder, and Dong, the executioner, had told her that the Communists were the bravest prisoners: "They have the strongest bones," her uncle often said. "They sang and shouted slogans and cursed the Japanese until the very last minute before they were strangled," said Dong.

The Communists put up notices calling on the population to keep order, and started arresting collaborators and people who had worked for the Japanese security forces. Among those arrested was Yang, my grandmother's father, still deputy police chief of Yixian. He was imprisoned in his own jail and his boss, the police chief, was executed. The Communists soon restored order and got the economy going again. The food situation, which had been desperate, improved markedly. Dr. Xia was able to start seeing patients again, and my mother's school reopened.

The Communists were billeted in the houses of local people. They seemed honest and unpretentious, and would chat with the families: "We don't have enough educated people," they used to say to one friend of my mother's. "Come and join us and you can become a county chief."

They needed recruits. At the time of the Japanese surrender, both Communists and Kuomintang had tried to occupy as much territory as they could, but the Kuomintang had a much larger and better-equipped army. Both were maneuvering for position in preparation for renewing the civil war which had been partly suspended for the previous eight years in order to fight the Japanese. In fact, fighting between Communists and Kuomintang had already broken out. Manchuria was the crucial battleground because of its economic assets. Because they were nearby, the Communists had got their forces into Manchuria first, with virtually no assistance from the Russians. But the Americans were helping Chiang Kai-shek establish himself in the area by ferrying tens of thousands of Kuomintang troops to North China. At one point the Americans tried to land some of them at Huludao, the port about thirty miles from Jinzhou, but had to withdraw under fire from Chinese Communists. The Kuomintang troops were forced to land south of the Great Wall and make their way north by train. The United States gave them air cover. Altogether, over 50,000 U.S. Marines landed in North China, occupying Peking and Tianjin.

The Russians formally recognized Chiang Kai-shek's Kuomintang as the government of China. By 11 November, the Soviet Red Army had left the Jinzhou area and pulled back to northern Manchuria, as part of a commitment by Stalin to withdraw from the area within three months of victory. This left the Chinese Communists alone in control of the city. One evening in late November my mother was walking home from school when she saw large numbers of soldiers hurriedly gathering their weapons and equipment and moving in the direction of the south gate. She knew there had been heavy fighting in the surrounding countryside and guessed the Communists must be leaving.

This withdrawal was in line with the strategy of the Communist leader Mao Zedong not to try to hold cities, where the Kuomintang would have the military advantage, but to retreat to the rural areas. "To surround the cities with our countryside and eventually take the cities" was Mao's guideline for the new phase.

On the day after the Chinese Communists withdrew from Jinzhou, a new army entered the city—the fourth in as many months. This army had clean uniforms and gleaming new American weapons. It was the Kuomintang. People ran out of their houses and gathered in the narrow mud streets, clapping and cheering. My mother squeezed her way to the front of the excited crowd. Suddenly she found she was waving her arms and cheering loudly. These soldiers really look like the army which beat the Japanese, she thought to herself. She ran home in a state of high excitement to tell her parents about the smart new soldiers.

There was a festival atmosphere in Jinzhou. People competed to invite troops to stay in their homes. One officer came to live with the Xias. He behaved extremely respectfully, and the family all liked him. My grandmother and Dr. Xia felt that the Kuomintang would maintain law and order and ensure peace at last.

But the goodwill people had felt toward the Kuomintang soon turned to bitter disappointment. Most of the officials came from other parts of China, and talked down to the local people, addressing them as *Wang-guo-nu* ("Slaves who have no country of your own") and lecturing them about how they ought to be grateful to the Kuomintang for liberating them from the Japanese. One evening there was a party at my mother's school for the students and Kuomintang officers. The three-year-old daughter of one official recited a speech which began: "We, the Kuomintang, have been fighting the Japanese for eight years and have now saved you, who were the slaves of Japan. . . ." My mother and her friends walked out.

My mother was also disgusted by the way the Kuomintang rushed to grab concubines. By early 1946 Jinzhou was filling up with troops. My mother's school was the only girls' school in town, and officers and officials descended on it in droves in search of concubines or, occasionally, wives. Some of the girls got married willingly, while others were unable to say no to their families, who thought that marrying an officer would give them a good start in life.

At fifteen, my mother was highly marriageable. She had grown into a very attractive and popular young woman, and she was the star pupil at her school. Several officers had already proposed, but she told her parents she did not want any of them. One, who was chief of staff of a general, threatened to send a sedan chair to carry her off after his gold bars had been refused. My mother was eavesdropping outside the door as he put this proposal to her parents. She burst in and told him to his face that she would kill herself in the sedan chair. Fortunately, not long afterward his unit was ordered out of the city.

My mother had made up her mind to choose her own husband. She was disenchanted with the treatment of women, and hated the whole system of concubinage. Her parents supported her, but they were harassed by offers, and had to deploy intricate, nerve-racking diplomacy to find ways of saying no without unleashing reprisals.

One of my mother's teachers was a young woman called Miss Liu, who liked her very much. In China, if people are fond of you, they often try to make you an honorary member of their family. At this time, although they were not so segregated as in my grandmother's days, there were not many opportunities for boys and girls to mix, so being introduced to the brother or sister of a friend was a common way for young people who did not like the idea of arranged marriages to get to know each other. Miss Liu introduced my mother to her brother. But first Mr. and Mrs. Liu had to approve the relationship.

Early in 1946, my mother was invited to spend the Chinese New Year at the Lius' house, which was quite grand. Mr. Liu was one of the biggest shopowners in Jinzhou. The son, who was about nineteen, seemed to be a man of the world; he was wearing a dark-green suit with a handkerchief sticking out of his breast pocket, which was tremendously sophisticated and dashing for a provincial town like Jinzhou. He was enrolled in a university in Peking, where he was reading Russian language and literature. My mother was very impressed with him, and his family approved of her. They soon sent a go-between to Dr. Xia to ask for her hand, without, of course, saying a word to her.

Dr. Xia was more liberal than most men of his time, and asked my mother how she felt about the matter. She agreed to be a "friend" to young Mr. Liu. At that time, if a boy and a girl were seen talking to each other in public, they had to be engaged, at the minimum. My mother was longing to have some fun and freedom, and to be able to make friends with men without committing herself to marriage. Dr. Xia and my grandmother, knowing my mother, were cautious with the Lius, and declined all the customary presents. In the Chinese tradition, a woman's family often did not consent to a marriage proposal immediately, as they should not appear too keen. If they accepted presents, this implicitly indicated consent. Dr. Xia and my grandmother were worried about a misunderstanding.

My mother went out with young Liu for a while. She was rather taken with his urbanity, and all her relatives, friends, and neighbors said she had made a good match. Dr. Xia and my grandmother thought they were a handsome couple, and had privately settled on him as their son-in-law. But my mother felt he was shallow. She noticed that he never went to Peking, but lounged around at home enjoying the life of a dilettante. One day she discovered he had not even read *The Dream of the Red Chamber*, the famous eighteenth-century Chinese classic, with which every literate Chinese was familiar. When she showed how disappointed she felt, young Liu said airily that the Chinese classics were not his forte, and that what he actually liked most was foreign literature. To try to reassert his superiority, he added: "Now, have you read *Madame Bovary?* That's my all-time favorite. I consider it the greatest of Maupassant's works."

My mother had read *Madame Bovary*—and she knew it was by Flaubert, not Maupassant. This vain sally put her off Liu in a big way, but she refrained from confronting him there and then—to do so would have been considered "shrewish."

Liu loved gambling, particularly mah-jongg, which bored my mother to death. One evening soon afterward, in the middle of a game, a female servant came in and asked: "Which maid would Master Liu like to serve him in bed?" In a very casual way, Liu said "So-and-so." My mother was shaking with anger, but all Liu did was to raise his eyebrow as though he was surprised at her reaction. Then he said in a supercilious way: "This is a perfectly common custom in Japan. Everybody does it. It's called *si-qin* ('bed with service')." He was trying to make my mother feel she was being provincial and jealous, which was traditionally regarded in China as one of the worst vices in a woman, and grounds for a husband to disown his wife. Once again my mother said nothing, even though she was boiling with rage inside.

My mother decided she could not be happy with a husband who regarded flirtations and extramarital sex as essential aspects of "being a man." She wanted someone who loved her, who would not want to hurt her by doing this sort of thing. That evening she made up her mind to end the relationship.

A few days later, Mr. Liu senior suddenly died. In those days a spectacular funeral was very important, particularly if the dead person had been the head of the family. A funeral which failed to meet the expectations of the relatives and of society would bring disapproval on the family. The Lius wanted an elaborate ceremony, not simply a procession from the house to the cemetery. Monks were brought in to read the Buddhist sutra of "putting the head down" in the presence of the whole family. Immediately after this, the family members burst out crying. From then to the day of the burial, on the forty-ninth day after the death, the sound of weeping and wailing was supposed to be heard nonstop from early morning until midnight, accompanied by the constant burning of artificial money for the deceased to use in the other world. Many families could not keep up this marathon, and hired professionals to do the job for them. The Lius were too filial to do this, and did all the keening themselves, with the help of relatives, of whom there were many.

On the forty-second day after his death, the corpse, which had been put in a beautifully carved sandalwood coffin, was placed in a marquee in the courtyard. On each of the last seven nights before his interment the dead man was supposed to ascend a high mountain in the other world and look down on his whole family; he would only be happy if he saw that every member of his family was present and taken care of. Otherwise, it was believed, he would never find rest. The family wanted my mother to be there as the intended daughter-in-law.

She refused. She felt sad for old Mr. Liu, who had been kind to her, but if she attended, she would never be able to get out of marrying his son. Relays of messengers from the Liu family came to the Xia house.

Dr. Xia told my mother that breaking her relationship at this moment was tantamount to letting Mr. Liu senior down, and that this was dishonorable. Although he would not have objected to my mother breaking up with young Mr. Liu normally, he felt that under the circumstances her wishes should be subordinated to a higher imperative. My grandmother also thought she should go. In addition she said, "Who ever heard of a girl rejecting a man because he got the name of some foreign writer wrong, or because he had affairs? All rich young men like to have fun and sow their wild oats. Besides, you have no need to worry about concubines and maids. You're a strong character; you can keep your husband under control."

This was not my mother's idea of the life she wanted, and she said so. In her heart, my grandmother agreed. But she was frightened about keeping my mother at home because of the persistent proposals from Kuomintang officers. "We can say no to one, but not to all of them," she told my mother. "If you don't marry Zhang, you will have to accept Lee. Think it over: isn't Liu much better than the others? If you marry him, no officer will be able to bother you anymore. I worry day and night about what may happen to you. I won't be able to rest until you leave the house." But my mother said she would rather die than marry someone who could not give her happiness—and love.

The Lius were furious with my mother, and so were Dr. Xia and my grandmother. For days they argued, pleaded, cajoled, shouted, and wept, to no avail. Finally, for the first time since he had hit her as a child for sitting in his seat on the *kang*, Dr. Xia flew into a rage with my mother. "What you are doing is bringing shame on the name of Xia. I don't want a daughter like you!" My mother stood up and flung back the words: "All right, then, you won't have a daughter like me. I'm leaving!" She stormed out of the room, packed her things, and left the house.

In my grandmother's time, leaving home like this would have been out of the question. There were no jobs for women, except as servants, and even they had to have references. But things had changed. In 1946 women could live on their own and find work, like teaching or medicine, although working was still regarded as the last resort by most families. In my mother's school was a teacher training department which offered free board and tuition for girls who had completed three years in the school. Apart from an exam, the only condition for entry was that the graduates had to become teachers. Most pupils in the department were either from poor families who could not afford to pay for an education or people who did not think they had a chance to get into a university, and therefore did not want to stay on at the normal high school. It was only since 1945 that women could contemplate getting into a university; under the Japanese, they could not go beyond high school, where they were mainly taught how to run a family.

Up till now my mother had never considered going to this department, which was generally looked down on as second best. She had always thought of herself as university material. The department was a little surprised when she applied, but she persuaded them of her fervent wish to join the teaching profession. She had not yet finished her obligatory three years in the school, but she was known as a star pupil. The department gladly took her after giving her an exam which she passed with little difficulty. She went to live in the school. It was not long before my grandmother rushed over to beg her to come home. My mother was glad to have a reconciliation; she promised she would go home and stay often. But she insisted on keeping her bed on the campus; she was determined not to be dependent on anyone, however much they loved her. For her, the department was ideal. It guaranteed her a job after graduation, whereas university graduates often could not find jobs. Another advantage was that it was free— and Dr. Xia was already beginning to suffer the effects of the mismanagement of the economy.

The Kuomintang personnel put in charge of the factories—those that had not been dismantled by the Russians—were conspicuously unsuccessful at getting the economy moving again. They got a few factories working at well below full capacity, but pocketed most of the revenue themselves.

Kuomintang carpetbaggers were moving into the smart houses

which the Japanese had vacated. The house next door to the Xias' old house, where the Japanese official had lived, was now occupied by an official and one of his newly acquired concubines. The mayor of Jinzhou, a Mr. Han, was a local nobody. Suddenly he was rich—from the proceeds of property confiscated from the Japanese and collaborators. He acquired several concubines, and the locals began to call the city government "the Han household," as it was bulging with his relatives and friends.

When the Kuomintang took Yixian they released my great-grandfather, Yang, from prison—or he bought his way out. The locals believed, with good reason, that Kuomintang officials made fortunes out of the ex-collaborators. Yang tried to protect himself by marrying off his remaining daughter, whom he had had with one of his concubines, to a Kuomintang officer. But this man was only a captain, not powerful enough to give him any real protection. Yang's property was confiscated and he was reduced to living as a beggar—"squatting by open drains," as the locals called it. When she heard about this, his wife told her children not to give him any money or do anything to help him.

In 1947, a little more than a year after his release from jail, he developed a cancerous goiter on his neck. He realized he was dying and sent word to Jinzhou begging to see his children. My great-grandmother refused, but he kept sending messages entreating them to come. In the end his wife relented. My grandmother, Lan and Yu-lin set off for Yixian by train. It was ten years since my grandmother had seen her father, and he was a crumpled shadow of his former self. Tears streamed down his cheeks when he saw his children. They found it hard to forgive him for the way he had treated their mother —and themselves—and they spoke to him using rather distant forms of address. He pleaded with Yu-lin to call him Father, but Yu-lin refused. Yang's ravaged face was a mask of despair. My grandmother begged her brother to call him Father, just once. Finally he did, through gritted teeth. His father took his hand and said: "Try to be a scholar, or run a small business. Never try to be an official. It will ruin you, the way it has ruined me." These were his last words to his family.

He died with only one of his concubines at his side. He was so poor he could not even afford a coffin. His corpse was put in a battered old suitcase and buried without ceremony. Not one member of his family was there.

Corruption was so widespread that Chiang Kai-shek set up a special organization to combat it. It was called the "Tiger-Beating Squad," because people compared corrupt officials to fearsome tigers, and it invited citizens to send in their complaints. But it soon became apparent that this was a means for the really powerful to extort money from the rich. "Tiger-beating" was a lucrative job.

Much worse than this was the blatant looting. Dr. Xia was visited every now and then by soldiers who would salute punctiliously and then say in an exaggeratedly cringing voice: "Your honor Dr. Xia, some of our colleagues are very short of money. Could you perhaps lend us some?" It was unwise to refuse. Anyone who crossed the Kuomintang was likely to be accused of being a Communist, which usually meant arrest, and frequently torture. Soldiers would also swagger into the surgery and demand treatment and medicine without paying a penny. Dr. Xia did not particularly mind giving them free medical treatment—he regarded it as a doctor's duty to treat anyone —but the soldiers would sometimes just take the medicine without asking, and sell it on the black market. Medicines were in desperately short supply.

As the civil war intensified the number of soldiers in Jinzhou rose. The troops of the central command, which came directly under Chiang Kai-shek, were relatively well disciplined, but the others received no pay from the central government and had to "live off the land."

At the teacher training department my mother struck up a close friendship with a beautiful, vivacious seventeen-year-old girl called Bai. My mother admired her and looked up to her. When she told Bai about her disenchantment with the Kuomintang, Bai told her to "look at the forest, not the individual trees": any force was bound to have some shortcomings, she said. Bai was passionately pro-Kuomintang, so much so that she had joined one of the intelligence services. In a training course it was made clear to her that she was expected to report on her fellow students. She refused. A few nights later her colleagues in the course heard a shot from her bedroom. When they opened the door, they saw her lying on her bed, gasping, her face deathly white. There was blood on her pillow. She died without being able to say a word. The newspapers published the story as what was called a "peach-colored case," meaning a crime of passion. They claimed she had been murdered by a jealous lover. But nobody believed this. Bai had behaved in a very demure manner where men were concerned. My mother heard that she had been killed because she had tried to pull out.

The tragedy did not end there. Bai's mother was working as a live-in servant in the house of a wealthy family which owned a small gold shop. She was heartbroken at the death of her only daughter, and incensed by the scurrilous suggestions in the papers that her daughter had had several lovers who had fought over her and eventually killed her. A woman's most sacred possession was her chastity, which she was supposed to defend to the death. Several days after Bai's death, her mother hanged herself. Her employer was visited by thugs who accused him of being responsible for her death. It was a good pretext to extort money, and it did not take long for the man to lose his gold shop.

One day there was a knock on the Xias' door and a man in his late thirties, dressed in Kuomintang uniform, came in and bowed to my grandmother, addressing her as "elder sister" and Dr. Xia as "elder brother-in-law." It took them a moment to realize that this smartly dressed, healthy, well-fed man was Han-chen, who had been tortured and saved from the garrote, and whom they had hidden in their old house for three months and nursed back to health. With him, also in uniform, was a tall, slender young man who looked more like a college student than a soldier. Han-chen introduced him as his friend Zhu-ge. My mother immediately took to him.

Since their last encounter Han-chen had become a senior official in Kuomintang intelligence, and was in charge of one of its branches for the whole of Jinzhou. As he left, he said: "Elder sister, I was given back my life by your family. If you ever need anything, anything at all, all you have to do is say the word and it will be done."

Han-chen and Zhu-ge came to visit often, and Han-chen soon found jobs in the intelligence apparatus for both Dong, the former executioner who had saved his life, and my grandmother's brother-in-law Pei-o, the former prison warder.

Zhu-ge became very friendly with the family. He had been studying science at university in Tianjin and had fled to join the Kuomintang when the city had fallen into Japanese hands. On one of his visits my mother introduced him to Miss Tanaka, who had been living with the Xias. They hit it off, got married, and went to live in rented rooms. One day Zhu-ge was cleaning his gun when he accidentally touched the trigger and the gun went off. The bullet passed straight through the floor and killed the landlord's youngest son, who was in bed downstairs. The family did not dare to bring a charge against Zhu-ge because they were frightened of intelligence men, who could accuse anyone they chose to of being a Communist. Their word was law, and they had the power of life and death. Zhu-ge's mother gave the family a large sum of money as compensation. Zhu-ge was distraught, but the family did not even dare show any anger toward him. Instead, they showed exaggerated gratitude, out of fear that he might anticipate that they would be angry, and harm them. He found this hard to bear, and soon moved out.

Lan's husband, Uncle Pei-o, prospered in the intelligence system and was so delighted with his new employers that he changed his name to "Xiao-shek" ("Loyalty to Chiang Kai-shek"). He was a member of a three-man group under Zhu-ge. Initially their job was to purge anyone who had been pro-Japanese, but very soon this slid into watching out for students showing pro-Communist sympathies. For a while, "Loyalty" Pei-o did what was asked of him, but his conscience soon began to trouble him; he did not want to be responsible for sending people to prison or choosing victims for extortion. He asked for a transfer and was given a job as a watchman at one of the city checkpoints. The Communists had left the city of Jinzhou but had not gone very far. They were engaged in constant battles with the Kuomintang in the surrounding countryside. The Jinzhou authorities were trying to keep tight control over the most vital commodities to stop the Communists from getting hold of them.

Being in intelligence gave "Loyalty" power, which brought him money. Gradually he began to change. He started smoking opium, drinking heavily, gambling, and frequenting brothels, and soon contracted a venereal disease. My grandmother offered him money to try to get him to behave, but he carried on as before. However, he could see that food was becoming increasingly scarce for the Xias, and often invited them to good meals at his house. Dr. Xia would not let my grandmother go. "Those are ill-gotten gains and we don't want to touch them," he said. But the thought of some decent food was sometimes too strong a temptation for my grandmother and occasionally she would sneak off to the Pei-o house with Yu-lin and my mother for a square meal.

When the Kuomintang first came to Jinzhou Yu-lin was fifteen years old. He had been studying medicine with Dr. Xia, who thought he had a promising future as a doctor. By now my grandmother had taken on the position of the female head of the family as her mother, sister, and brother were all dependent on her husband for a living, and she felt it was time Yu-lin got married. She soon settled on a woman who was three years older than him and came from a poor family, which meant she would be hard-working and capable. My mother went with my grandmother to see the prospective bride; when she came in to bow to the visitors in the sitting room, she was wearing a green velvet gown which she had had to borrow for the occasion.

The couple were married in a registry office in 1946, the bride wearing a rented Western-style white silk veil. Yu-lin was sixteen and his wife was nineteen.

My grandmother asked Han-chen to find Yu-lin a job. One of the vital commodities was salt, and the authorities had forbidden selling it to the countryside. Of course, they were running a salt racket themselves. Han-chen got Yu-lin a job as a salt guard, and several times he was almost involved in serious skirmishes with Communist guerrillas and other Kuomintang factions who were trying to capture the salt. Many people were being killed in the fighting. Yu-lin found the job frightening, and was also tormented by his conscience. Within a few months he quit.

By this time, the Kuomintang was gradually losing control of the countryside, and was finding it harder and harder to get recruits. Young men were increasingly unwilling to become "bomb ashes" (*pao-hui*). The civil war had become much more bloody, with enormous casualties, and the danger of being conscripted or simply impressed into the army was growing. The only way to keep Yu-lin out of uniform was to buy him some form of insurance, so my grandmother asked Han-chen to find him a job in intelligence. To her surprise, he refused, telling her it was no place for a decent young man.

My grandmother did not realize that Han-chen was in deep despair about his work. Like "Loyalty" Pei-o he had become an opium addict, and was drinking heavily and visiting prostitutes. He was visibly wasting away. Han-chen had always been a self-disciplined man, with a strong sense of morality, and it was most unlike him to let himself go in this way. My grandmother thought that the ancient remedy of marriage might pull him around, but when she put this to him he said he could not take a wife, because he did not want to live. My grandmother was shocked, and pressed him to tell her why, but Han-chen only started weeping and said bitterly that he was not free to tell her, and that she could not help anyway.

Han-chen had joined the Kuomintang because he hated the Japanese. But things had turned out differently from what he had envisaged. Being involved in the intelligence system meant that he could hardly avoid having innocent blood—of his fellow Chinese—on his hands. But he could not get out. What had happened to my mother's college friend Bai was what happened to anyone who tried to quit. Han-chen probably felt that the only way out was to kill himself, but suicide was a traditional gesture of protest and might bring trouble to his family. Han-chen must have come to the conclusion that the only thing he could do was to die a "natural" death, which was why he was going to such wild extremes in abusing his body and why he refused to take any treatment.

On the eve of Chinese New Year 1947 he returned to his family home in Yixian to spend the festival period with his brother and his elderly father. As if he felt that this was to be their last meeting, he stayed on. He fell gravely ill, and died in the summer. He had told my grandmother that the only regret he would have in dying was not being able to fulfill his filial duty and hold a grand funeral for his father.

But he did not die without fulfilling his obligation to my grandmother and her family. Even though he refused to take Yu-lin into intelligence work, he acquired an identity card for him which said he was a Kuomintang intelligence official. Yu-lin never did any work for the intelligence system, but his membership guaranteed him against being conscripted, and he was able to stay and help Dr. Xia in the medicine shop.

One of the teachers at my mother's school was a young man named Kang, who taught Chinese literature. He was very bright and knowledgeable, and my mother respected him tremendously. He told her and some other girls that he had been involved in anti-Kuomintang activities in the city of Kunming in southwest China, and that his girlfriend had been killed by a hand grenade during a demonstration. His lectures were clearly pro-Communist, and made a strong impression on my mother.

One morning in early 1947 my mother was stopped at the school gate by the old porter. He handed her a note and told her that Kang had gone. What my mother did not know was that Kang had been tipped off, as some of the Kuomintang intelligence agents were secretly working for the Communists. At the time my mother did not know much about the Communists, or that Kang was one of them. All she knew was that the teacher she most admired had had to flee because he was about to be arrested.

The note was from Kang, and consisted of only one word: "Silence." My mother saw two possible meanings in this word. It could refer to a line from a poem Kang had written in memory of his girlfriend, "Silence—in which our strength is gathering," in which case it might be an appeal not to lose heart. But the note could also be a warning against doing something impetuous. My mother had by then established quite a reputation for fearlessness, and she commanded support among the students.

The next thing she knew a new headmistress arrived. She was a delegate to the National Congress of the Kuomintang, reputedly with ties to the secret services. She brought with her a number of intelligence men, including one called Yao-han, who became the political supervisor, with the special task of keeping a watch on the students. The academic supervisor was the district party secretary of the Kuomintang.

My mother's closest friend at this time was a distant male cousin called Hu. His father owned a chain of department stores in Jinzhou, Mukden, and Harbin, and had a wife and two concubines. His wife had produced a son, Cousin Hu, while the concubines had not. Cousin Hu's mother therefore became the object of intense jealousy on their part. One night when her husband was out of the house the concubines drugged her food and that of a young male servant, then put them into the same bed. When Mr. Hu came back and found his wife, apparently blind drunk, in bed with the servant, he went berserk; he locked his wife up in a tiny room in a remote corner of the house, and forbade his son to see her again. He had a sneaking suspicion that the whole thing might have been a plot by his concubines, so he did not disown his wife and throw her out, which would have been the ultimate disgrace (to himself as well as to her). He was worried that the concubines might harm his son, so he sent him away to boarding school in Jinzhou, which is how my mother met him, when she was seven and he was twelve. His mother soon went mad in her solitary confinement.

Cousin Hu grew up to be a sensitive boy who kept to himself. He never got over what had happened, and occasionally talked to my mother about it. The story made my mother reflect on the blighted lives of women in her own family and on the numerous tragedies that had happened to so many other mothers, daughters, wives, and concubines. The powerlessness of women, the barbarity of the age-old customs, cloaked in "tradition" and even "morality," enraged her. Although there had been changes, they were buried by the still overwhelming prejudice. My mother was impatient for something more radical.

In her school she learned that one political force had openly promised change—the Communists. The information came from a close friend of hers, an eighteen-year-old girl called Shu who had broken with her family and was staying in the school because her father had tried to force her into an arranged marriage with a boy of twelve. One day Shu bade farewell to my mother: she and the man she was secretly in love with were running away to join the Communists. "They are our hope," were her parting words.

It was about this time that my mother became very close to Cousin

Hu, who had realized that he was in love with her when he found that he was very jealous of young Mr. Liu, whom he regarded as a dandy. He was delighted when she broke up with Liu, and came to see my mother almost every day.

One evening in March 1947 they went to the cinema together. There were two kinds of tickets: one for a seat; the other, which was much cheaper, for standing only. Cousin Hu bought my mother a seat, but a standing ticket for himself, saying he did not have enough money on him. My mother thought this was a bit odd, and so she stole a glance in his direction every now and then. Halfway through the film she saw a smartly dressed young woman approach him, slide by him slowly, and then, for a split second, their hands touched. She got up at once and insisted on leaving. When they got outside she demanded an explanation. At first Cousin Hu tried to deny that anything had happened; when my mother made it clear she was not going to swallow this, he said he would explain later. There were things my mother could not understand, he said, because she was too young. When they reached her house, she refused to let him in. Over the next few days he called repeatedly, but my mother would not see him.

After a while, she was ready for an apology and a reconciliation, and would keep looking out toward the gate to see if he was there. One evening, when it was snowing hard, she saw him coming into the courtyard accompanied by another man. He did not make for her part of the house, but went straight to where the Xias' tenant, a man called Yu-wu, was living. After a short time Hu reemerged and walked briskly over to her room. With an urgent edge to his voice, he told her he had to leave Jinzhou immediately, as the police were after him. When she asked him why, all he said was, "I am a Communist," and disappeared into the snowy night.

It dawned on my mother that the incident in the cinema must have been a clandestine mission of Cousin Hu's. She was heartbroken, as there was now no time to make up with him. She realized that their tenant, Yu-wu, must also be an underground Communist. The reason Cousin Hu had been brought to Yu-wu's quarters was to hide there. Cousin Hu and Yu-wu had not known each other's identity until this evening. Both of them realized it was out of the question for Cousin Hu to stay there, as his relationship with my mother was too well known, and if the Kuomintang came to the house to look for him Yu-wu would be discovered as well. That same night Cousin Hu tried to make for the Communist-controlled area, which lay about twenty miles beyond the city boundaries. Some time later, as the first buds of spring were bursting out, Yu-wu received news that Hu had been captured as he left the city. His escort had been shot dead. A later report said Hu had been executed.

My mother had been turning more and more strongly against the Kuomintang for some time. The only alternative she knew was the Communists, and she had been particularly attracted by their promises to put an end to injustices against women. Up to now, at the age of fifteen, she had not felt ready to commit herself fully. The news of Cousin Hu's death made her mind up. She decided to join the Communists.

5. "Daughter for Sale for 10 Kilos of Rice"— In Battle for a New China
(1947–1948)

Yu-wu had first appeared at the house some months earlier, bearing an introduction from a mutual friend. The Xias had just moved from their borrowed residence into a big house inside the walls near the north gate, and had been looking for a rich tenant to help with the rent. Yu-wu arrived wearing the uniform of a Kuomintang officer, accompanied by a woman whom he presented as his wife and a young baby. In fact, the woman was not his wife but his assistant. The baby was hers, and her real husband was somewhere far away in the regular Communist army. Gradually this "family" became a real one. They later had two children together and their original spouses remarried.

Yu-wu had joined the Communist Party in 1938. He had been sent to Jinzhou from the Communists' wartime headquarters, Yan'an, shortly after the Japanese surrender, and was responsible for collecting and delivering information to the Communist forces outside the city. He operated under the identity of a Kuomintang military bureau chief for one of the districts of Jinzhou, a position the Communists had bought for him. At the time, posts in the Kuomintang, even in the intelligence system, were virtually for sale to the highest bidder. Some people bought posts to protect their families from being forced into the army and from harassment by thugs, others to be able to extort money. Because of its strategic importance, there were a great many officers in Jinzhou, which facilitated the Communist infiltration of the system.

Yu-wu played his part to perfection. He gave a lot of gambling and dinner parties, partly to make connections and partly to weave a protective web around himself. Mingled with the constant comings and goings of Kuomintang officers and intelligence officials was an unending stream of "cousins" and "friends." They were always different people, but nobody asked any questions.

Yu-wu had another layer of cover for these frequent visitors. Dr. Xia's surgery was always open, and Yu-wu's "friends" could walk in off the street without attracting attention, and then go through the surgery to the inner courtyard. Dr. Xia tolerated Yu-wu's rowdy parties without demur, even though his sect, the Society of Reason, forbade gambling and drinking. My mother was puzzled, but put it down to her stepfather's tolerant nature. It was only years later when she thought back that she felt certain that Dr. Xia had known, or guessed, Yu-wu's real identity.

When my mother heard that her cousin Hu had been killed by the Kuomintang she approached Yu-wu about working for the Communists. He turned her down, on the grounds that she was too young.

My mother had become quite prominent at her school and she was hoping that the Communists would approach her. They did, but they took their time checking her out. In fact, before leaving for the Communist-controlled area, her friend Shu had told her own Communist contact about my mother, and had introduced him to her as "a friend." One day, this man came to her and told her out of the blue to go on a certain day to a railway tunnel halfway between the Jinzhou south station and the north station. There, he said, a good-looking man in his mid-twenties with a Shanghai accent would contact her. This man, whose name she later discovered was Liang, became her controller.

Her first job was to distribute literature like Mao Zedong's *On Coalition Government*, and pamphlets on land reform and other Communist policies. These had to be smuggled into the city, usually hidden in big bundles of sorghum stalks which were to be used for fuel. The pamphlets were then repacked, often rolled up inside big green peppers.

Sometimes Yu-lin's wife would buy the peppers and keep a lookout in the street when my mother's associates came to collect the literature. She also helped hide the pamphlets in the ashes of various stoves, heaps of Chinese medicines, or piles of fuel. The students had to read this literature in secret, though left-wing novels could be read more or less openly: among the favorites was Maksim Gorky's *Mother*.

One day a copy of one of the pamphlets my mother had been distributing, Mao's *On New Democracy*, ended up with a rather absent-minded schoolfriend of hers, who put it in her bag and forgot about it. When she went to the market she opened her bag to get some money and the pamphlet dropped out. Two intelligence men happened to be there and identified it from its flimsy yellow paper. The girl was taken off and interrogated. She died under torture.

Many people had died at the hands of Kuomintang intelligence, and my mother knew that she risked torture if she was caught. This incident, far from daunting her, only made her feel more defiant. Her morale was also boosted enormously by the fact that she now felt herself part of the Communist movement.

Manchuria was the key battleground in the civil war, and what happened in Jinzhou was becoming more and more critical to the outcome of the whole struggle for China. There was no fixed front, in the sense of a single battle line. The Communists held the northern part of Manchuria and much of the countryside; the Kuomintang held the main cities, except for Harbin in the north, plus the seaports and most of the railway lines. By the end of 1947, for the first time, the Communist armies in the area outnumbered those of their opponents; during that year they had put over 300,000 Kuomintang troops out of action. Many peasants were joining the Communist army, or swinging their support behind the Communists. The single most important reason was that the Communists had carried out a land-to-the-tiller reform and the peasants felt that backing them was the way to keep their land.

At the time, the Communists controlled much of the area around Jinzhou. Peasants were reluctant to enter the city to sell their produce because they had to go through Kuomintang checkpoints where they were harassed: exorbitant fees were extorted, or they simply had their products confiscated. The grain price in the city was rocketing upwards almost day by day, made worse by the manipulation of greedy merchants and corrupt officials.

When the Kuomintang first arrived, they had issued a new currency known as the "Law money." But they proved unable to control inflation. Dr. Xia had always been worried about what would happen to my grandmother and my mother when he died—and he was now nearly eighty. He had been putting his savings into the new money because he had faith in the government. After a time the Law money was replaced by another currency, the Golden Yuan, which soon became worth so little that when my mother wanted to pay her school fees she had to hire a rickshaw to carry the huge pile of notes (to "save face" Chiang Kai-shek refused to print any note bigger than 10,000 yuan). Dr. Xia's entire savings were gone.

The economic situation deteriorated steadily through the winter of 1947–48. Protests against food shortages and price gouging multiplied. Jinzhou was the key supply base for the large Kuomintang armies farther north, and in mid-December 1947 a crowd of 20,000 people raided two well-stocked grain stores.

One trade was prospering: trafficking in young girls for brothels and as slave-servants to rich men. The city was littered with beggars offering their children in exchange for food. For days outside her school my mother saw an emaciated, desperate-looking woman in rags slumped on the frozen ground. Next to her stood a girl of about ten with an expression of numb misery on her face. A stick was poking up out of the back of her collar and on it was a poorly written sign saying "Daughter for sale for 10 kilos of rice."

Among those who could not make ends meet were the teachers. They had been demanding a pay rise, to which the government responded by increasing tuition fees. This had little effect, because the parents could not afford to pay more. A teacher at my mother's school died of food poisoning after eating a piece of meat he had picked up off the street. He knew the meat was rotten, but he was so hungry he thought he would take a chance.

By now my mother had become the president of the students' union. Her Party controller, Liang, had given her instructions to try to win over the teachers as well as the students, and she set about organizing a campaign to get people to donate money for the teaching staff. She and some other girls would go to cinemas and theaters and before the performances started they would appeal for donations. They also put on song-and-dance shows and ran rummage sales, but the returns were paltry—people were either too poor or too mean.

One day she bumped into a friend of hers who was the granddaughter of a brigade commander and was married to a Kuomintang officer. The friend told her there was going to be a banquet that evening for about fifty officers and their wives in a smart restaurant in town. In those days there was a lot of entertaining going on among Kuomintang officials. My mother raced off to her school and contacted as many people as she could. She told them to gather at 5 P.M. in front of the city's most prominent landmark, the sixty-foot-high eleventh-century stone drum tower. When she got there, at the head of a sizable contingent, there were over a hundred girls waiting for her orders. She told them her plan. At around six o'clock they saw large numbers of officers arriving in carriages and rickshaws. The women were dressed to the nines, wearing silk and satin and jingling with jewelry.

When my mother judged that the diners would be well into their food and drink, she and some of the girls filed into the restaurant. Kuomintang decadence was such that security was unbelievably lax. My mother climbed onto a chair, her simple dark-blue cotton gown making her the image of austerity among the brightly embroidered silks and jewels. She made a brief speech about how hard up the teachers were, and finished with the words: "We all know you are generous people. You must be very pleased to have this opportunity to open your pockets and show your generosity."

The officers were in a spot. None of them wanted to look mean. In fact, they more or less had to try to show off. And, of course, they wanted to get rid of the unwelcome intruders. The girls went round the heavily laden tables and made a note of each officer's contribution. Then, first thing next morning, they went round to the officers' homes and collected their pledges. The teachers were enormously grateful to the girls, who delivered the money to them right away, so it could be used before its value was wiped out, which would be within hours.

There was no retribution against my mother, perhaps because the diners were ashamed of being caught like this, and did not want to bring further embarrassment on themselves—although, of course, the whole town knew about it at once. My mother had successfully turned the rules of the game against them. She was appalled by the casual extravagance of the Kuomintang elite while people were starving to death in the streets—and this made her even more committed to the Communists.

As food was the problem inside the city, so clothing was in desperately short supply outside, as the Kuomintang had placed a ban on selling textiles to the countryside. As a watchman on the gates, "Loyalty" Pei-o's main job was to stop textiles being smuggled out of the city and sold to the Communists. The smugglers were a mixture of black marketeers, men working for Kuomintang officials, and underground Communists.

The usual procedure was that "Loyalty" and his colleagues would stop the carts and confiscate the cloth, then release the smuggler in the hope that he would come back with another load which they could also seize. Sometimes they had a deal with the smugglers for a percentage. Whether they had a deal or not, the guards would sell the cloth to the Communist-controlled areas anyway. "Loyalty" and his colleagues waxed fat.

One night a dirty, nondescript cart rolled up at the gate where "Loyalty" was on duty. He performed his customary charade, poking the pile of cloth on the back while he swaggered around, hoping to intimidate the driver and soften him up for an advantageous deal. As he sized up the value of the load and the likely resistance of the driver, he was also hoping to engage him in conversation and find out who his employer was. "Loyalty" took his time because this was a big consignment, more than he could get out of the city before dawn.

He got up beside the driver and ordered him to turn around and take the consignment back into the city. The driver, accustomed to being on the receiving end of arbitrary instructions, did as he was told.

My grandmother was sound asleep in bed when she heard banging on the door at about 1 A.M. When she opened it, she found "Loyalty" standing there. He said he wanted to leave the cartload at the house for the night. My grandmother had to agree, because the Chinese tradition made it virtually impossible to say no to a relation. The obligation to one's family and relatives always took precedence over one's own moral judgment. She did not tell Dr. Xia who was still asleep.

Well before daybreak "Loyalty" reappeared with two carts; he transferred the consignment onto them and drove off just as dawn was beginning to light up the sky. Less than half an hour later armed police appeared and cordoned off the house. The cart driver, who had been working for another intelligence system, had informed his patrons. Naturally, they wanted their merchandise back.

Dr. Xia and my grandmother were quite put out, but at least the goods had disappeared. For my mother, though, the raid was almost a catastrophe. She had some Communist leaflets hidden in the house, and as soon as the police appeared, she grabbed the leaflets and raced to the toilet, where she pushed them down her padded trousers which were tightened round the ankles to conserve heat, and put on a heavy winter coat. Then she sauntered out as nonchalantly as she could, pretending she was on her way to school. The policemen stopped her and said they were going to search her. She screamed at them that she would tell her "Uncle" Zhu-ge how they had treated her.

Up to that moment the policemen had had no idea about the family's intelligence connections. Nor had they any idea who had confiscated the textiles. The administration of Jinzhou was in utter confusion because of the enormous number of different Kuomintang units stationed in the city and because anyone with a gun and some sort of protection enjoyed arbitrary power. When "Loyalty" and his men had appropriated this load the driver did not ask them who they were working for.

The moment my mother mentioned Zhu-ge's name, there was a

change in the attitude of the officer. Zhu-ge was a friend of his boss. At a signal, his subordinates lowered their guns and dropped their insolently challenging manner. The officer bowed stiffly and muttered profuse apologies for disturbing such an august family. The rank-and-file police looked even more disappointed than their commander—no booty meant no money, and no money meant no food. They shambled off sullenly, dragging their feet as they went.

At the time there was a new university, the Northeast Exile University, in Jinzhou, formed around students and teachers who had fled Communist-occupied northern Manchuria. Communist policies there had often been harsh: many landowners had been killed. In the towns, even small factory owners and shopkeepers were denounced and their property was confiscated. Most intellectuals came from relatively well-to-do families, and many had seen their families suffer under Communist rule or been denounced themselves.

There was a medical college in the Exile University, and my mother wanted to get into it. It had always been her ambition to be a doctor. This was partly Dr. Xia's influence and partly because the medical profession offered a woman the best chance of independence. Liang endorsed the idea enthusiastically. The Party had plans for her. She enrolled in the medical college on a part-time basis in February 1948.

The Exile University was a battleground where the Kuomintang and the Communists competed fiercely for influence. The Kuomintang could see how badly it was doing in Manchuria, and was actively encouraging students and intellectuals to flee farther south. The Communists did not want to lose these educated people. They modified their land reform program, and issued an order that urban capitalists were to be well treated and intellectuals from well-to-do families protected. Armed with these more moderate policies, the Jinzhou underground set out to persuade the students and teachers to stay on. This became my mother's main activity.

In spite of the Communists' policy switch, some students and teachers decided it was safer to flee. One shipload of students sailed to the city of Tianjin, about 250 miles to the southwest, at the end of June. When they arrived there they found that there was no food and nowhere for them to stay. The local Kuomintang urged them to join the army. "Fight back to your homeland!" they were told. This was not what they had fled Manchuria for. Some Communist underground workers who had sailed with them encouraged them to take a stand, and on 5 July the students demonstrated in the center of Tianjin for food and accommodations. Troops opened fire and scores of students were injured, some seriously, and a number were killed.

When the news reached Jinzhou, my mother immediately decided to organize support for the students who had gone to Tianjin. She called a meeting of the heads of the student unions of all the seven high and technical schools, which voted to set up the Jinzhou Federation of Student Unions. My mother was elected to the chair. They decided to send a telegram of solidarity to the students in Tianjin and to stage a march to the headquarters of General Chiu, the martial law commander, to present a petition.

My mother's friends were waiting anxiously at school for instructions. It was a gray, rainy day and the ground had turned to sticky mud. Darkness fell and there was still no sign of my mother and the other six student leaders. Then the news came that the police had raided the meeting and taken them away. They had been informed on by Yao-han, the political supervisor at my mother's school.

They were marched to the martial law headquarters. After a while, General Chiu strode into the room. He faced them across a table and started to talk to them in a patient, paternalistic tone of voice, apparently more in sorrow than in anger. They were young and liable to do rash things, he said. But what did they know about politics? Did they realize they were being used by the Communists? They should stick to their books. He said he would release them if they would sign a confession admitting their mistakes and identifying the Communists behind them. Then he paused to watch the effect of his words.

My mother found his lecturing and his whole attitude insufferable. She stepped forward and said in a loud voice: "Tell us, Commander, what mistake have we made?" The general became irritated: "You were used by the Communist bandits to stir up trouble. Isn't that mistake enough?" My mother shouted back: "What Communist bandits? Our friends died in Tianjin because they had run away from the Communists, on your advice. Do they deserve to be shot by you? Have we done anything unreasonable?" After some fierce exchanges the general banged his fist on the table and bellowed for his guards. "Show her around," he said, and then, turning to my mother, "You need to realize where you are!" Before the soldiers could seize her, my mother leaped forward and banged her fist on the table: "Wherever I may be, I have not done anything wrong!"

The next thing my mother knew she was held tight by both arms and dragged away from the table. She was pulled along a corridor and down some stairs into a dark room. On the far side she could see a man dressed in rags. He seemed to be sitting on a bench and leaning against a pillar. His head was lolling to one side. Then my mother realized that he was tied to the pillar and his thighs were tied to the bench. Two men were pushing bricks under his heels. Each additional brick brought forth a deep, stifled groan. My mother felt her head was filled with blood, and she thought she heard the cracking of bones. The next thing she knew she was looking into another room. Her guide, an officer, drew her attention to a man almost next to where they were standing. He was hanging from a wooden beam by his wrists and was naked from the waist upward. His hair hung down in a tangled mess, so that my mother could not see his face. On the floor was a brazier, with a man sitting beside it casually smoking a cigarette. As my mother watched, he lifted an iron bar out of the fire; the tip was the size of a man's fist and was glowing red-hot. With a grin, he plunged it into the chest of the man hanging from the beam. My mother heard a sharp scream of pain and a horrible sizzling sound, saw smoke coming from the wound, and could smell the heavy odor of burned flesh. But she did not scream or faint. The horror had aroused in her a powerful, passionate rage which gave her enormous strength and overrode any fear.

The officer asked her if she would now write a confession. She refused, repeating that she knew of no Communists behind her. She was bundled into a small room which contained a bed and some sheets. There she spent several long days, listening to the screams of people being tortured in rooms nearby, and refusing repeated demands to name names.

Then one day she was taken to a yard at the back of the building, covered with weeds and rubble, and ordered to stand against a high wall. Next to her a man who had obviously been tortured and could barely stand was propped up. Several soldiers lazily took their positions. A man blindfolded her. Even though she could not see, she closed her eyes. She was ready to die, proud that she was giving her life for a great cause.

She heard shots, but felt nothing. After a minute or so her blindfold was removed and she looked around, blinking. The man who had been standing next to her was lying on the ground. The officer who had taken her down to the dungeons came over, grinning. One eyebrow was raised in surprise that this seventeen-year-old girl was not a gibbering wreck. My mother told him calmly that she had nothing to confess.

She was taken back to her cell. Nobody bothered her, and she was not tortured. After a few more days she was set free. During the previous week the Communist underground had been busy pulling strings. My grandmother had been to the martial law headquarters every day, weeping, pleading, and threatening suicide. Dr. Xia had visited his most powerful patients, bearing expensive gifts. The family's intelligence connections were also mobilized. Many people had vouched for my mother in writing, saying that she was not a Communist, she was just young and impetuous.

What had happened to her did not daunt her in the slightest. The moment she came out of prison she set about organizing a memorial service for the dead students in Tianjin. The authorities gave permission for the service. There was great anger in Jinzhou about what had happened to the young people who had, after all, left on the government's advice. At the same time, the schools hurriedly announced an early end to the term, scrapping examinations, in the hope that the students would go home and disband.

At this point the underground advised its members to leave for the Communist-controlled areas. Those who did not want to, or could not leave, were ordered to suspend their clandestine work. The Kuomintang was clamping down fiercely, and too many operatives were being arrested and executed. Liang was leaving, and he asked my mother to go too, but my grandmother would not allow it. My mother was not suspected of being a Communist, she said, but if she left with the Communists she would be. And what about all the people who had vouched for her? If she went now they would all be in trouble.

So she stayed. But she was longing for action. She turned to Yu-wu, the only person left in the city who she knew was working for the Communists. Yu-wu did not know Liang or my mother's other contacts. They belonged to different underground systems, which operated completely separately, so that if anyone was caught and could not withstand torture they could only reveal a limited number of names.

Jinzhou was the key supply and logistic center for all the Kuomintang armies in the northeast. They numbered over half a million men, strung out along vulnerable railway lines and concentrated in a few shrinking areas around the main cities. By the summer of 1948 there were about 200,000 Kuomintang troops in Jinzhou, under several different commands. Chiang Kai-shek had been squabbling with many of his top generals, juggling the commands, which created severe demoralization. The different forces were badly coordinated and often distrusted one another. Many strategists, including his senior American advisers, thought that Chiang should abandon Manchuria completely. The key to any pullout, "voluntary" or forced, by sea or by rail, was the retention of Jinzhou. The city was only a hundred miles north of the Great Wall, quite near to China proper, where the Kuo-

mintang position still seemed relatively secure, and it was easily reinforced from the sea—Huludao was only about thirty miles to the
south, and was linked by a seemingly secure railway.

In spring 1948 the Kuomintang had begun to construct a new defense system around Jinzhou, made of cement blocks encased in steel
frames. The Communists, they thought, had no tanks and poor artillery, and no experience attacking heavily fortified positions. The idea
was to ring the city with self-contained fortresses, each of which could
operate as an independent unit even if it was surrounded. The fortresses were to be connected by trenches six feet wide and six feet
deep, protected by a continuous fence of barbed wire. The supreme
commander in Manchuria, General Wei Li-huang, came on an inspection visit and declared the system impregnable.

But the project was never finished, partly due to lack of materials
and poor planning, but mainly because of corruption. The man in
charge of the construction work siphoned off building materials and
sold them on the black market; the workers were not paid enough to
eat. By September, when the Communist forces began to cut the city
off, only a third of the system had been completed, much of it small,
unconnected cement forts. Other parts had been hastily assembled
from mud taken from the old city wall.

It was vital for the Communists to know about this system and
about the disposition of the Kuomintang troops. The Communists
were building up enormous forces—about a quarter of a million men
—for a decisive battle. The commander in chief of all the Communist
armies, Zhu De, cabled the commander on the spot, Lin Biao: "Take
Jinzhou . . . and the whole Chinese situation is in our hands." Yu-
wu's group was asked to provide up-to-date information before the
final attack. He urgently needed more hands, and when my mother
approached him asking for work, he and his superiors were delighted.

The Communists had sent some officers into the city in disguise to
reconnoiter, but a man wandering around the outskirts alone would
immediately attract attention. An amorous couple would be much less
conspicuous. By then, Kuomintang rule had made it quite acceptable
for young men and women to be seen together in public. Because the
reconnaissance officers were male, my mother would be ideal as a
"girlfriend."

Yu-wu told her to be at an appointed place at a particular time. She
was to wear a pale-blue gown and a red silk flower in her hair. The
Communist officer would be carrying a copy of the Kuomintang newspaper, the *Central Daily*, folded into a triangle, and would identify

himself by wiping sweat three times off the left side of his face and then three times off the right.

On the appointed day, my mother went to a small temple just outside the old north wall but within the defense perimeter. A man carrying the triangular newspaper came up to her and gave the correct signals. My mother stroked his right cheek three times with her right hand, then he stroked her left cheek three times with his left hand. Then my mother took his arm, and they walked off.

My mother did not understand fully what he was doing, and she did not ask. Most of the time they walked in silence, only talking when they passed someone. The mission passed off without incident.

There were to be more, around the city outskirts and to the railway, the vital communications artery.

It was one thing to obtain the information, but it was another to get it out of the city. By the end of July the checkpoints were firmly shut, and anyone trying to enter or leave was thoroughly searched. Yu-wu consulted my mother, whose ability and courage he had grown to trust. The vehicles of senior officers could go in and out without being searched, and my mother thought of a contact she might be able to use. One of her fellow students was the granddaughter of a local army commander, General Ji, and the girl's brother was a colonel in their grandfather's brigade.

The Jis were a Jinzhou family, with considerable influence. They occupied a whole street, nicknamed "Ji Street," where they had a large compound with an extensive, well-groomed garden. My mother had often strolled in the garden with her friend, and was quite friendly with her brother, Hui-ge.

Hui-ge was a handsome young man in his mid-twenties who had a university degree in engineering. Unlike many young men from wealthy, powerful families, he was not a dandy. My mother liked him, and the feeling was mutual. He began to pay social calls on the Xias and to invite my mother to tea parties. My grandmother liked him a lot; he was extremely courteous, and she considered him highly eligible.

Soon Hui-ge started to invite my mother out on her own. At first his sister accompanied him, pretending to be a chaperone, but soon she would disappear with some flimsy excuse. She praised her brother to my mother, adding that he was their grandfather's favorite. She must also have told her brother about my mother, because my mother discovered that he knew a lot about her, including the fact that she had been arrested for her radical activities. They found they had much in common. Hui-ge was very frank about the Kuomintang.

Once or twice he tugged at his colonel's uniform and sighed that he hoped the war would end soon so he could go back to his engineering. He told my mother he thought the Kuomintang's days were num- bered, and she had the feeling that he was baring his innermost thoughts.

She was certain he was fond of her, but she wondered if there might be political motives behind his actions. She deduced that he must be trying to get a message across to her, and through her to the Com- munists. The message had to be: I don't like the Kuomintang, and I am willing to help you.

They became tacit conspirators. One day my mother suggested that he might surrender to the Communists with some troops (which was a fairly common occurrence). He said he was only a staff officer and did not command any troops. My mother asked him to try to persuade his grandfather to go over, but he replied sadly that the old man would probably have him shot if he even suggested it.

My mother kept Yu-wu informed, and he told her to cultivate Hui-ge. Soon Yu-wu told her to ask Hui-ge to take her for a trip outside the city in his jeep. They went on such trips three or four times, and each time, when they reached a primitive mud toilet, she said she had to use it. She got out and hid a message in a hole in the toilet wall while he waited in his jeep. He never asked any questions. His conversations became more and more centered on his worries about his family and himself. In a roundabout way, he hinted that the Communists might execute him: "I'm afraid I'll soon just be a disem- bodied soul outside the western gate!" (The Western Heaven was sup- posed to be the destination of the dead, because it was the site of eternal peace. So the execution ground in Jinzhou, like most places in China, was outside the western gate.) When he said this, he would look questioningly into my mother's eyes, clearly inviting contradic- tion.

My mother felt certain that because of what he had done for them the Communists would spare him. Although everything had been implicit, she would say confidently: "Don't think such gloomy thoughts!" or "I'm sure that won't happen to you!"

The Kuomintang position continued to deteriorate through the late summer—and not only because of military action. Corruption wreaked havoc. Inflation had risen to the unimaginable figure of just over 100,000 percent by the end of 1947—and it was to go to 2,870,000 percent by the end of 1948 in the Kuomintang areas. The price of sorghum, the main grain available, increased seventyfold overnight in

Jinzhou. For the civilian population the situation was becoming more desperate every day, as increasingly more food went to the army, much of which was sold by local commanders on the black market.

The Kuomintang high command was divided over strategy. Chiang Kai-shek recommended abandoning Mukden, the largest city in Manchuria, and concentrating on holding Jinzhou, but he was unable to impose a coherent strategy on his top generals. He seemed to place all his hope on greater American intervention. Defeatism permeated his top staff.

By September the Kuomintang held only three strongholds in Manchuria—Mukden, Changchun (the old capital of Manchukuo, Hsinking), and Jinzhou—and the 300 miles of railway track linking them. The Communists were encircling all three cities simultaneously, and the Kuomintang did not know where the main attack would come. In fact it was to be Jinzhou, the most southerly of the three and the strategic key, because once it fell the other two would be cut off from their supplies. The Communists were able to move large numbers of troops around undetected, but the Kuomintang were dependent on the railway, which was under constant attack, and, to a lesser extent, on air transport.

The assault on Jinzhou began on 12 September 1948. An American diplomat, John F. Melby, flying to Mukden, recorded in his diary on 23 September: "North along the corridor to Manchuria the Communist artillery was systematically making rubble out of the airfield at Chinchow [Jinzhou]." The next day, 24 September, the Communist forces moved closer. Twenty-four hours later Chiang Kai-shek ordered General Wei Li-huang to break out of Mukden with fifteen divisions and relieve Jinzhou. General Wei dithered, and by 26 September the Communists had virtually isolated Jinzhou.

By 1 October the encirclement of Jinzhou was completed. Yixian, my grandmother's hometown twenty-five miles to the north, fell that day. Chiang Kai-shek flew to Mukden to take personal command. He ordered seven extra divisions to be thrown into the Jinzhou battle, but he was unable even to get General Wei to move out of Mukden until 9 October, two weeks after the order had been given—and even then with only eleven divisions, not fifteen. On 6 October Chiang Kai-shek flew to Huludao and ordered troops there to move up to relieve Jinzhou. Some did, but piecemeal, and they were soon isolated and destroyed.

The Communists were getting ready to turn the assault on Jinzhou into a siege. Yu-wu approached my mother and asked her to undertake a critical mission: to smuggle detonators into one of the ammunition depots—the one supplying Hui-ge's own division. The ammunition was stored in a big courtyard, the walls of which were topped with barbed wire which was reputed to be electrified. Everyone who went in and out was searched. The soldiers living inside the complex spent most of their time gambling and drinking. Sometimes prostitutes were brought in and the officers would hold a dance in a makeshift club. My mother told Hui-ge she wanted to go and have a look at the dancing, and he agreed without asking any questions.

The detonators were handed to my mother the next day by a man she had never seen. She put them into her bag and drove into the depot with Hui-ge. They were not searched. When they got inside, she asked Hui-ge to show her around, leaving her bag in the car, as she had been instructed. Once they were out of sight, underground operatives were supposed to remove the detonators. My mother strolled at a deliberately leisurely pace to give the men more time. Hui-ge was happy to oblige.

That night, the city was rocked by a gigantic explosion. Detonations went off in chain reactions and the dynamite and shells lit up the sky like a spectacular fireworks display. The street where the depot had been was in flames. Windows were shattered within a radius of about fifty yards. The next morning, Hui-ge invited my mother over to the Ji mansion. His eyes were hollow and he was unshaven. He had obviously not slept a wink. He greeted her a little more guardedly than usual.

After a heavy silence, he asked her whether she had heard the news. Her expression must have confirmed his worst fears—that he had helped to cripple his own division. He said there was going to be an investigation. "I wonder whether the explosion will sweep my head from my shoulders," he sighed, "or blow a reward my way?" My mother, who was feeling sorry for him, said reassuringly: "I am sure you are beyond suspicion. I'm certain you will be rewarded." At this, Hui-ge stood up and saluted her in formal fashion. "Thank you for your promise!" he said.

By now, Communist artillery shells had begun to crash into the city. When my mother first heard the whine of the shells flying over, she was a little frightened. But later, when the shelling became heavier, she got used to it. It became like permanent thunder. A kind of fatalistic indifference deadened fear for most people. The siege also broke down Dr. Xia's rigid Manchu ritual; for the first time the whole household ate together, men and women, masters and servants. Previously, they had been eating in no less than eight groups, all having different food. One day, as they were sitting around the table preparing to have dinner, a shell came bursting through the window over the *kang*, where Yu-lin's one-year-old son was playing, and thudded to a halt under the dining table. Fortunately, like many of the shells, it was a dud.

Once the siege started there was no food to be had, even on the black market. A hundred million Kuomintang dollars could barely buy a pound of sorghum. Like most families who could afford to do so, my grandmother had stored some sorghum and soybeans, and her sister's husband, "Loyalty" Pei-o, used his connections to get some extra supplies. During the siege the family's donkey was killed by a piece of shrapnel, so they ate it.

On 8 October the Communists moved almost a quarter of a million troops into attack positions. The shelling became much more intense. It was also very accurate. The top Kuomintang commander, General Fan Han-jie, said that it seemed to follow him wherever he went. Many artillery positions were knocked out, and the fortresses in the uncompleted defense system came under heavy fire, as did the road and railway links. Telephone and cable lines were cut, and the electricity system broke down.

On 13 October the outer defenses collapsed. More than 100,000 Kuomintang troops retreated pell-mell into the center of the city. That night a band of about a dozen disheveled soldiers stormed into the Xias' house and demanded food. They had not eaten for two days. Dr. Xia greeted them courteously and Yu-lin's wife immediately started cooking a huge saucepan of sorghum noodles. When they were ready, she put them on the kitchen table and went into the next room to tell the soldiers. As she turned her back, a shell landed in the saucepan and exploded, spattering the noodles all over the kitchen. She dived under a narrow table in front of the *kang*. A soldier was ahead of her, but she grabbed him by the leg and pulled him out. My grandmother was terrified. "What if he had turned around and pulled the trigger?" she hissed once he was out of earshot.

Until the very final stage of the siege the shelling was amazingly accurate; few ordinary houses were hit, but the population suffered from the terrible fires which the shelling ignited, and there was no water to douse the flames. The sky was completely obscured by thick, dark smoke and it was impossible to see more than a few yards, even in daytime. The noise of the artillery was deafening. My mother could hear people wailing, but could never tell where they were or what was happening.

On 14 October, the final offensive started. Nine hundred artillery pieces bombarded the city nonstop. Most of the family hid in an improvised air-raid shelter which they had dug earlier, but Dr. Xia refused to leave the house. He sat calmly on the *kang* in the corner of his room by the window and prayed silently to the Buddha. At one point fourteen kittens ran into the room. He was delighted: "A place a cat tries to hide in is a lucky place," he said. Not a single bullet came into his room—and all the kittens survived. The only other person who would not go down into the shelter was my great-grandmother, who just curled up under the oak table next to the *kang* in her room. When the battle ended the thick quilts and blankets covering the table looked like a sieve.

In the middle of one bombardment, Yu-lin's baby son, who was down in the shelter, wanted to have a wee-wee. His mother took him outside, and a few seconds later the side of the shelter where she had been sitting collapsed. My mother and grandmother had to come up and take cover in the house. My mother crouched next to the *kang* in the kitchen, but soon pieces of shrapnel started hitting the brick side of the *kang* and the house began to shake. She ran out into the back garden. The sky was black with smoke. Bullets were flying through the air and ricocheting all over the place, spattering against the walls; the sound was like mighty rain pelting down, mixed with screams and yells.

In the small hours of the next day a group of Kuomintang soldiers burst into the house, dragging about twenty terrified civilians of all ages with them—the residents of the three neighboring courtyards. The troops were almost hysterical. They had come from an artillery post in a temple across the street, which had just been shelled with pinpoint accuracy, and were shouting at the civilians that one of them must have given away their position. They kept yelling that they wanted to know who had given the signal. When no one spoke up, they grabbed my mother and shoved her against a wall, accusing her. My grandmother was terrified, and hurriedly dug out some small gold pieces and pressed them into the soldiers' hands. She and Dr. Xia went down on their knees and begged the soldiers to let my mother go. Yu-lin's wife said this was the only time she ever saw Dr. Xia looking really frightened. He pleaded with the soldiers: "She's my little girl. Please believe me that she did not do it. . . ."

The soldiers took the gold and let my mother go, but they forced everyone into two rooms at bayonet point and shut them in—so they would not send any more signals, they said. It was pitch-dark inside the rooms, and very frightening. But quite soon my mother noticed that the shelling was decreasing. The noises outside changed. Mixed with the whine of bullets were sounds of hand grenades exploding and the clash of bayonets. Voices were yelling, "Put down your weapons and we'll spare your life!"—there were blood-curdling shrieks and screams of anger and pain. Then the shots and the shouts came closer and closer, and she heard the sound of boots clattering on the cobblestones as the Kuomintang soldiers ran away down the street.

Eventually the din subsided a bit and the Xias could hear banging on the side gate of the house. Dr. Xia went warily to the door of the room and eased it open: the Kuomintang soldiers had gone. Then he went to the side gate of the house and asked who was there. A voice answered: "We are the people's army. We have come to liberate you." Dr. Xia opened the gate and several men in baggy uniforms entered swiftly. In the darkness, my mother could see that they were wearing white towels wrapped around their left sleeves like armbands and held their guns at the ready, with fixed bayonets. "Don't be afraid," they said. "We won't harm you. We are *your* army, the people's army." They said they wanted to check the house for Kuomintang soldiers. It was not a request, though it was put politely. The soldiers did not turn the place upside down, nor did they ask for food or steal anything. After the search they left, bidding the family a courteous farewell.

It was only when the soldiers entered the house that it sank in that the Communists had really taken the city. My mother was overjoyed. This time she did not feel let down by the Communist soldiers' dust-covered, torn uniforms.

All the people who had been sheltering in the Xias' house were anxious to get back to their houses to see if they had been damaged or looted. One house had in fact been leveled, and a pregnant woman who had remained there was killed.

Shortly after the neighbors left there was another knock on the side gate. My mother opened it: half a dozen terrified Kuomintang soldiers stood there. They were in a pitiable state and their eyes were gnawed by fear. They kowtowed to Dr. Xia and my grandmother and begged for civilian clothes. The Xias felt sorry for them and gave them some old clothes which they hurriedly put on over their uniforms and left.

At first light Yu-lin's wife opened the front gate. Several corpses were lying right outside. She let out a terrified yell and ran back into the house. My mother heard her shriek and went outside to have a look. Corpses were lying all over the street, many of them with their heads and limbs missing, others with their intestines pouring out. Some were just bloody messes. Chunks of flesh and arms and legs were hanging from the telegraph poles. The open sewers were clogged with bloody water, human flesh, and rubble.

The battle for Jinzhou had been herculean. The final attack had lasted thirty-one hours, and in many ways it was the turning point of the civil war. Twenty thousand Kuomintang soldiers were killed and over 80,000 captured. No fewer than eighteen generals were taken prisoner, among them the supreme commander of the Kuomintang forces in Jinzhou, General Fan Han-jie, who had tried to escape disguised as a civilian. As the prisoners of war thronged the streets on their way to the temporary camps, my mother saw a friend of hers with her Kuomintang officer husband, both of them wrapped in blankets against the morning chill.

It was Communist policy not to execute anyone who laid down their arms, and to treat all prisoners well. This would help win over the ordinary soldiers, most of whom came from poor peasant families. The Communists did not run prison camps. They kept only middle- and high-ranking officers, and dispersed the rest almost immediately. They would hold "speak bitterness" meetings for the soldiers, at which they were encouraged to speak up about their hard lives as landless peasants. The revolution, the Communists said, was all about giving them land. The soldiers were given a choice: either they could go home, in which case they would be given their fare, or they could stay with the Communists to help wipe out the Kuomintang so that nobody would ever take their land away again. Most willingly stayed and joined the Communist army. Some, of course, could not physically reach their homes with a war going on. Mao had learned from ancient Chinese warfare that the most effective way of conquering the people was to conquer their hearts and minds. The policy toward prisoners proved enormously successful. Particularly after Jinzhou, more and more Kuomintang soldiers simply let themselves be captured. Over 1.75 million Kuomintang troops surrendered and crossed over to the Communists during the civil war. In the last year of the civil war, battle casualties accounted for less than 20 percent of all the troops the Kuomintang lost.

One of the top commanders who had been caught had his daughter with him; she was in an advanced stage of pregnancy. He asked the Communist commanding officer if he could stay in Jinzhou with her. The Communist officer said it was not convenient for a father to help his daughter deliver a baby, and that he would send a "woman comrade" to help her. The Kuomintang officer thought he was only saying this to get him to move on. Later on he learned that his daughter had been very well treated, and the "woman comrade" turned out to be the wife of the Communist officer. Policy toward prisoners was an intricate combination of political calculation and humanitarian consideration, and this was one of the crucial factors in the Communists' victory. Their goal was not just to crush the opposing army but, if possible, to bring about its disintegration. The Kuomintang was defeated as much by demoralization as by firepower.

The first priority after the battle was cleaning up, most of which was done by Communist soldiers. The locals were also keen to help, as they wanted to get rid of the bodies and the debris around their homes as quickly as possible. For days, long convoys of carts loaded with corpses and lines of people carrying baskets on their shoulders could be seen wending their way out of the city. As it became possible to move around again, my mother found that many people she knew had been killed; some from direct hits, others buried under rubble when their houses had collapsed.

The morning after the siege ended the Communists put up notices asking the townspeople to resume normal life as quickly as possible. Dr. Xia hung out his gaily decorated shingle to show that his medicine shop was open—and was later told by the Communist administration that he was the first doctor in the city to do so. Most shops reopened on 20 October even though the streets were not yet cleared of bodies. Two days later, schools reopened and offices began working normal hours.

The most immediate problem was food. The new government urged the peasants to come and sell food in the city and encouraged them to do so by setting prices at twice what they were in the countryside. The price of sorghum fell rapidly, from 100 million Kuomintang dollars for a pound to 2,200 dollars. An ordinary worker could soon buy four pounds of sorghum with what he could earn in a day. Fear of starvation abated. The Communists issued relief grain, salt, and coal to the destitute. The Kuomintang had never done anything like this, and people were hugely impressed.

Another thing that captured the goodwill of the locals was the discipline of the Communist soldiers. Not only was there no looting or rape, but many went out of their way to demonstrate exemplary behavior. This was in sharp contrast with the Kuomintang troops.

The city remained in a state of high alert. American planes flew over threateningly. On 23 October sizable Kuomintang forces tried unsuccessfully to retake Jinzhou with a pincer movement from Huludao and the northeast. With the loss of Jinzhou, the huge armies around Mukden and Changchun quickly collapsed or surrendered, and by 2 November the whole of Manchuria was in Communist hands.

The Communists proved extremely efficient at restoring order and getting the economy going again. Banks in Jinzhou reopened on 3

December, and the electricity supply resumed the next day. On 29 December a notice went up announcing a new street administration system, with residents' committees in place of the old neighborhood committees. These were to be a key institution in the Communist system of administration and control. The next day running water resumed and on the 31st the railway reopened.

The Communists even managed to put an end to inflation, setting a favorable exchange rate for converting the worthless Kuomintang money into Communist "Great Wall" currency.

From the moment the Communist forces arrived, my mother had been longing to throw herself into working for the revolution. She felt herself to be very much a part of the Communist cause. After some days of waiting impatiently, she was approached by a Party representative who gave her an appointment to see the man in charge of youth work in Jinzhou, a Comrade Wang Yu.

6. "Talking about Love"—
A Revolutionary Marriage
(1948-1949)

My mother set off to see Comrade Wang one morning on a mild autumn day, the best time of year in Jinzhou. The summer heat had gone and the air had begun to grow cooler, but it was still warm enough to wear summer clothes. The wind and dust which plague the town for much of the year were deliciously absent.

She was wearing a traditional loose pale-blue gown and a pale-blue silk scarf. Her hair had just been cut short in keeping with the new revolutionary fashion. As she walked into the courtyard of the new provincial government headquarters she saw a man standing under a tree with his back to her, brushing his teeth at the edge of a flowerbed. She waited for him to finish, and when he lifted his head she saw that he was in his late twenties, with a very dark face and big, wistful eyes. Under his baggy uniform she could see that he was thin, and she thought he looked a little shorter than herself. There was something dreamy about him. My mother thought he looked like a poet. "Comrade Wang, I am Xia De-hong from the students' association," she said. "I am here to report on our work."

"Wang" was the *nom de guerre* of the man who was to become my father. He had entered Jinzhou with the Communist forces a few days earlier. Since late 1945 he had been a commander with the guerrillas in the area. He was now head of the Secretariat and a member of the Communist Party Committee governing Jinzhou, and was soon to be appointed head of the Public Affairs Department of the city, which looked after education, the literacy drive, health, the press, entertainment, sports, youth, and sounding out public opinion. It was an important post.

He was born in 1921 in Yibin in the southwestern province of Sichuan, about 1,200 miles from Jinzhou. Yibin, which then had a population of about 30,000, lies at the spot where the Min River joins the Golden Sand River to form the Yangtze, the longest river in China. The area around Yibin is one of the very fertile parts of Sichuan, which is known as "Heaven's Granary," and the warm, misty climate in Yibin makes it an ideal place for growing tea. Much of the black tea consumed in Britain today comes from there.

My father was the seventh of nine children. His father had worked as an apprentice for a textile manufacturer since the age of twelve. When he became an adult he and his brother, who worked in the same factory, decided to start their own business. Within a few years they were prospering, and were able to buy a large house.

But their old boss was jealous of their success, and brought a lawsuit against them, accusing them of stealing money from him to start their business. The case lasted seven years, and the brothers were forced to spend all their assets trying to clear themselves. Everyone connected with the court extorted money from them, and the greed of the officials was insatiable. My grandfather was thrown into prison. The only way his brother could get him out was to get the ex-boss to drop the suit. To do this he had to raise 1,000 pieces of silver. This destroyed them, and my great-uncle died soon afterward at the age of thirty-four from worry and exhaustion.

My grandfather found himself looking after two families, with fifteen dependents. He started up his business again, and by the late 1920s was beginning to do well. But it was a time of widespread fighting among warlords, who all levied heavy taxes. This, combined with the effects of the Great Depression, made it an extremely difficult time to run a textile factory. In 1933 my grandfather died of overwork and strain, at age forty-five. The business was sold to pay off the debts, and the family was scattered. Some became soldiers, which was considered pretty much a last resort; with all the fighting going on, it was easy for a soldier to get killed. Other brothers and cousins found odd jobs and the girls married as best they could. One of my father's cousins, who was fifteen years old and to whom he was very attached, had to marry an opium addict several decades her senior. When the sedan chair came to carry her away, my father ran after her, not knowing if he would ever see her again.

My father loved books, and began to learn to read classical prose at the age of three, which was quite exceptional. The year after my grandfather died he had to abandon school. He was only thirteen and hated having to give up his studies. He had to find a job, so the following year, 1935, he left Yibin and went down the Yangtze to Chongqing, a much bigger city. He found a job as an apprentice in a grocery store working twelve hours a day. One of his jobs was to carry his boss's enormous water pipe as he moved around the city reclining on a bamboo chair carried on the shoulders of two men. The sole purpose of this was for his boss to flaunt the fact that he could afford a servant to carry his water pipe, which could easily have been put in the chair. My father received no pay, just a bed and two meager meals a day. He got no supper, and went to bed every night with cramps from an empty stomach; he was obsessed by hunger.

His eldest sister was also living in Chongqing. She had married a schoolteacher, and their mother had come to live with them after her husband died. One day my father was so hungry he went into their kitchen and ate a cold sweet potato. When his sister found out she turned on him and yelled: "It's difficult enough for me to support our mother. I can't afford to feed a brother as well." My father was so hurt he ran out of the house and never returned.

He asked his boss to give him supper. His boss not only refused, but started to abuse him. In anger, my father left and went back to Yibin and lived doing odd jobs as an apprentice in one store after another. He encountered suffering not only in his own life, but all around him. Every day as he walked to work he passed an old man selling baked rolls. The old man, who shuffled along with great difficulty, bent double, was blind. To attract the attention of passersby, he sang a heart-rending tune. Every time my father heard the song he said to himself that the society must change.

He began to cast around for some way out. He had always remembered the first time he heard the word "communism": it was when he was seven years old, in 1928. He was playing near his home when he saw that a big crowd had gathered at a crossroads nearby. He squeezed his way to the front: there he saw a young man sitting cross-legged on the ground. His hands were tied behind his back; standing over him was a stout man with an enormous broadsword. The young man, strangely, was allowed to talk for a time about his ideals and about something called communism. Then the executioner brought the sword down on the back of his neck. My father screamed and covered his eyes. He was shaken to the core, but he was also hugely impressed by the man's courage and calmness in the face of death.

By the second half of the 1930s, even in the remote backwater of

Yibin, the Communists were beginning to organize a sizable underground. Their main plank was resisting the Japanese. Chiang Kai-shek had adopted a policy of nonresistance in the face of the Japanese seizure of Manchuria and increasing encroachments on China proper and had concentrated on trying to annihilate the Communists. The Communists launched a slogan, "Chinese must not fight Chinese," and put pressure on Chiang Kai-shek to focus on fighting the Japanese. In December 1936 Chiang was kidnapped by two of his own generals, one of them the Young Marshal, Chang Hsueh-liang, from Manchuria. He was saved partly by the Communists, who helped get him released in return for his agreement to form a united front against Japan. Chiang Kai-shek had to consent, albeit half-heartedly, since he knew this would allow the Communists to survive and develop. "The Japanese are a disease of the skin," he said, "the Communists are a disease of the heart." Though the Communists and the Kuomintang were supposed to be allies, the Communists still had to work underground in most areas.

In July 1937 the Japanese began their all-out invasion of China proper. My father, like many others, felt appalled and desperate about what was happening to his country. At about this time he started working in a bookshop which sold left-wing publications. He devoured book after book at night in the shop, where he functioned as a kind of night watchman.

He supplemented his earnings from the bookshop with an evening job as an "explainer" in a cinema. Many of the films were American silents. His job was to stand beside the screen and explain what was going on, as the films were neither dubbed nor subtitled. He also joined an anti-Japanese theater group, and as he was a slender young man with delicate features, he acted women's roles.

My father loved the theater group. It was through the friends he made there that he first entered into contact with the Communist underground. The Communist stance about fighting the Japanese and about creating a just society fired his imagination and he joined the Party in 1938, when he was seventeen. It was a time when the Kuomintang was being extremely vigilant about Communist activities in Sichuan. Nanjing, the capital, had fallen to the Japanese in December 1937, and Chiang Kai-shek subsequently moved his government to Chongqing. The move precipitated a flurry of police activity in Sichuan, and my father's theater group was forcibly disbanded. Some of his friends were arrested. Others had to flee. My father felt frustrated that he could not do anything for his country.

A few years before, Communist forces had passed through remote parts of Sichuan on their 6,000-mile Long March, which ultimately took them to the small town of Yan'an in the northwest. People in the theater group had talked a lot about Yan'an as a place of camaraderie, uncorrupt and efficient—my father's dream. At the beginning of 1940 he set out on his own long march to Yan'an. He first went to Chong-qing, where one of his brothers-in-law, who was an officer in Chiang Kai-shek's army, wrote a letter to help him cross Kuomintang-occu-pied areas and get through the blockade that Chiang Kai-shek had thrown up around Yan'an. The journey took him almost four months. By the time he arrived it was April 1940.

Yan'an lay on the Yellow Earth Plateau, in a remote and barren part of northwest China. Dominated by a nine-tiered pagoda, much of the town consisted of rows of caves cut into the yellow cliffs. My father was to make these caves his home for over five years. Mao Zedong and his much-depleted forces had arrived there at different times in 1935–1936, at the end of the Long March, and subsequently made it the capital of their republic. Yan'an was surrounded by hostile territory; its chief advantage was its remoteness, which made it diffi-cult to attack.

After a short spell at a Party school, my father applied to join one of the Party's most prestigious institutions, the Academy of Marxist-Leninist Studies. The entrance exam was quite stiff, but he took first place, as a result of his reading deep into the night in the loft of the bookshop in Yibin. His fellow candidates were amazed. Most of them had come from the big cities like Shanghai, and had looked down on him as a bit of a yokel. My father became the youngest research fellow in the Academy.

My father loved Yan'an. He found the people there full of enthu-siasm, optimism, and purpose. The Party leaders lived simply, like everyone else, in striking contrast with Kuomintang officials. Yan'an was no democracy, but compared with where he had come from it seemed to be a paradise of fairness.

In 1942 Mao started a "Rectification" campaign, and invited criti-cisms about the way things were being run in Yan'an. A group of young research fellows from the Academy, led by Wang Shi-wei and includ-ing my father, put up wall posters criticizing their leaders and demand-ing more freedom and the right to greater individual expression. Their action caused a storm, and Mao himself came to read the posters.

Mao did not like what he saw, and turned his campaign into a witch-hunt. Wang Shi-wei was accused of being a Trotskyite and a spy. My father, as the youngest person in the Academy, was said by Ai Si-qi, the chief exponent of Marxism in China and one of the leaders of the Academy, to have "committed a very naive mistake." Earlier, Ai Si-qi had often praised my father as a "brilliant and sharp mind." My father and his friends were subjected to relentless criticisms and obliged to undertake self-criticisms at intensive meetings for months. They were told that they had caused chaos in Yan'an and weakened the Party's unity and discipline, which could damage the great cause of saving China from the Japanese—and from poverty and injustice. Over and over again, the Party leaders inculcated into them the absolute necessity for complete submission to the Party, for the good of the cause.

The Academy was shut down, and my father was sent to teach ancient Chinese history to semi-literate peasants-turned-officials at the Central Party School. But the ordeal had turned him into a convert. Like so many other young people, he had invested his life and faith in Yan'an. He could not let himself be easily disappointed. He regarded his harsh treatment as not only justified, but even a noble experience—soul-cleansing for the mission to save China. He believed that the only way this could be done was through disciplined, perhaps drastic, measures, including immense personal sacrifice and the total subordination of the self.

There were less demanding activities as well. He toured the surrounding areas collecting folk poetry, and learned to be a graceful and elegant dancer in Western-style ballroom dancing, which was very popular in Yan'an—many of the Communist leaders, including the future prime minister, Zhou Enlai, enjoyed it. At the foot of the dry, dusty hills was the meandering, dark-yellow, silt-filled Yan River, one of the scores which join the majestic Yellow River, and here my father often went swimming; he loved to do the backstroke while looking up at the simple solid pagoda.

Life in Yan'an was hard but exhilarating. In 1942, Chiang Kai-shek tightened his blockade. Supplies of food, clothing, and other necessities became drastically curtailed. Mao called on everyone to take up hoes and spinning wheels and produce essential goods themselves. My father became an excellent spinner.

He stayed in Yan'an for the whole of the war. In spite of the blockade, the Communists strengthened their control over large areas, particularly in northern China, behind the Japanese lines. Mao had calculated well: the Communists had won vital breathing space. By the end of the war they claimed some sort of control over ninety-five million people, about 20 percent of the population, in eighteen "base areas." Equally important, they gained experience at running a government and an economy under tough conditions. This stood them in good stead: their organizational ability and their system of control were always phenomenal.

On 9 August 1945, Soviet troops swept into northeast China. Two days later the Chinese Communists offered them military cooperation against the Japanese, but they were turned down: Stalin was supporting Chiang Kai-shek. That same day the Chinese Communists started to order armed units and political advisers into Manchuria, which everyone realized was going to be of critical importance.

A month after the Japanese surrender my father was ordered to leave Yan'an and head for a place called Chaoyang in southwest Manchuria, about 700 miles to the east, near the border with Inner Mongolia.

In November, after walking for two months, my father and his small group reached Chaoyang. Most of the territory was barren hills and mountains, almost as poor as Yan'an. The area had been part of Manchukuo until three months before. A small group of local Communists had proclaimed its own "government." The Kuomintang underground then did the same. Communist troops came racing over from Jinzhou, about fifty miles away, arrested the Kuomintang governor, and executed him—for "conspiring to overthrow the Communist government."

My father's group took over, with the authority of Yan'an, and within a month a proper administration began to function for the whole area of Chaoyang, which had a population of about 100,000. My father became its deputy chief. One of the first acts of the new government was to put up posters announcing its policies: the release of all prisoners; the closure of all pawnshops—pawned goods could be recovered free of charge; brothels were to be closed and prostitutes given six months' living allowance by their owners; all grain stores were to be opened and the grain distributed to those most in need; all property belonging to Japanese and collaborators was to be confiscated; and Chinese-owned industry and commerce was to be protected.

These policies were enormously popular. They benefited the poor, who formed the vast majority of the population. Chaoyang had never known even moderately good government; it had been ransacked by different armies in the warlord period, and then occupied and bled white by the Japanese for over a decade.

A few weeks after my father had started his new job, Mao issued an order to his forces to withdraw from all vulnerable cities and major communication routes and to pull back into the countryside—"leaving the high road alone and seizing the land on both sides" and "surrounding the cities from the countryside." My father's unit withdrew from Chaoyang into the mountains. It was an area almost devoid of vegetation, except for wild grass and the occasional hazelnut tree and wild fruits. The temperatures fell at night to around minus 30°F with icy gales. Anyone caught outside at night without cover froze to death. There was practically no food. From the exhilaration of seeing Japan's defeat and their own sudden expansion into large tracts of the northeast, the Communists' apparent victory was seemingly turning to ashes within weeks. As my father and his men hunkered down in caves and poor peasant huts, they were in a somber mood.

The Communists and the Kuomintang were both maneuvering for advantage in preparation for a resumption of full-scale civil war. Chiang Kai-shek had moved his capital back to Nanjing, and with American help, had transported large numbers of troops to North China, issuing secret orders for them to occupy all strategic places as fast as possible. The Americans sent a leading general, George Marshall, to China to try to persuade Chiang to form a coalition government with the Communists as junior partners. A truce was signed on 10 January 1946, to go into effect on 13 January. On the 14th the Kuomintang entered Chaoyang and immediately started setting up a large armed police force and an intelligence network and arming local landlords' squads. Altogether, they put together a force of over 4,000 men to annihilate the Communists in the area. By February my father and his unit were on the run, retreating deeper and deeper into more and more inhospitable terrain. Most of the time they had to hide with the poorest peasants. By April there was nowhere left to run, and they had to break up into smaller groups. Guerrilla warfare was the only way to survive. Eventually my father set up his base at a place called Six Household Village, in hilly country where the Xiaoling River starts, about sixty-five miles west of Jinzhou.

The guerrillas had very few arms; they had to obtain most of their guns from the local police or "borrow" them from landlord forces. The other main source was former members of the Manchukuo army and police, to whom the Communists made a particular pitch because of their weapons and fighting experience. In my father's area, the main thrust of the Communists' policy was to reduce the rent and interest on loans the peasants had to pay to the landlords. They also confiscated grain and clothing from landlords and distributed them to the poor peasants.

At first progress was slow, but by July, when the sorghum had grown to its full height ready for harvesting, and was high enough to conceal them, the different guerrilla units were able to come together for a meeting in Six Household Village, under a huge tree which stood guard over the temple. My father opened by referring to the Chinese Robin Hood story, *The Water Margin:* "This is our 'Hall of Justice.' We are here to discuss how to 'rid the people of evil and uphold justice on behalf of Heaven.' "

At this point my father's guerrillas were fighting mainly westward, and the areas they took included many villages inhabited by Mongolians. In November 1946, as winter closed in, the Kuomintang stepped up their attacks. One day my father was almost captured in an ambush. After a fierce firefight, he just managed to break out. His clothes were torn to shreds and his penis was dangling out of his trousers, to the amusement of his comrades.

They rarely slept in the same place two nights running, and often had to move several times in one night. They could never take their clothes off to sleep, and their life was an uninterrupted succession of ambushes, encirclements, and breakouts. There were a number of women in the unit, and my father decided to move them and the wounded and unfit to a more secure area to the south, near the Great Wall. This involved a long and hazardous journey through Kuomintang-held areas. Any noise might be fatal, so my father ordered all babies to be left behind with local peasants. One woman could not bring herself to abandon her child, and in the end my father told her she would have to choose between leaving the baby behind or being court-martialed. She left the baby.

In the following months, my father's unit moved eastward toward Jinzhou and the key railway line from Manchuria to China proper. They fought in the hills west of Jinzhou before the regular Communist army arrived. The Kuomintang launched a number of unsuccessful "annihilation campaigns" against them. The unit's actions began to have an impact. My father, now twenty-five, was so well known that there was a price on his head and "Wanted" notices up all over the Jinzhou area. My mother saw these notices, and began to hear a lot about him and his guerrillas from her relatives in Kuomintang intelligence.

When my father's unit was forced to withdraw, Kuomintang forces returned and took back from the peasants the food and clothing which the Communists had confiscated from the landlords. In many cases peasants were tortured, and some were killed, particularly those who had eaten the food—which they had often done because they were starving—and could not now hand it back.

In Six Household Village the man who had owned the most land, one Jin Ting-quan, had also been the police chief, and had brutally raped many local women. He had run away with the Kuomintang, and my father's unit had presided over the meeting which opened his house and his grain store. When Jin came back with the Kuomintang the peasants were made to grovel in front of him and return all the goods they had been given by the Communists. Those who had eaten the food were tortured and their homes smashed. One man who refused to kowtow or return the food was slowly burned to death.

In spring 1947 the tide began to turn, and in March my father's group was able to retake the town of Chaoyang. Soon the whole surrounding area was in their hands. To celebrate their victory, there was a feast followed by entertainment. My father was brilliant at inventing riddles out of people's names, which made him a great hit with his comrades.

The Communists carried out a land reform, confiscating land which had hitherto been owned by a small number of landlords and redistributing it equally among the peasants. In Six Household Village the peasants at first refused to take Jin Ting-quan's land, even though he had now been arrested. Although he was under guard, they bowed and scraped to him. My father visited many peasant families, and gradually learned the horrible truth about him. The Chaoyang government sentenced Jin to death by shooting, but the family of the man who had been burned to death, with the support of the families of other victims, determined to kill him the same way. As the flames began to lick around his body Jin clenched his teeth, and did not utter even a moan until the moment the fire surrounded his heart. The Communist officials sent to carry out the execution did not prevent the villagers from doing this. Although the Communists were opposed to torture in theory and on principle, officials were told that they should not intervene if the peasants wished to vent their anger in passionate acts of revenge.

People such as Jin were not just wealthy owners of land, but had wielded absolute and arbitrary power, which they indulged willfully, over the lives of the local population. They were called e-ba ("ferocious despots").

In some areas the killing extended to ordinary landlords, who were called "stones"—obstacles to the revolution. Policy toward the "stones" was: "When in doubt, kill." My father thought this was wrong and told his subordinates, and the people at public meetings, that only those who unquestionably had blood on their hands should be sentenced to death. In his reports to his superiors he repeatedly said that the Party should be careful with human lives, and that excessive executions would only harm the revolution. It was partly because many people like my father spoke up that in February 1948 the Communist leadership issued urgent instructions to stop violent excesses.

All the time, the main forces of the Communist army were coming nearer. In early 1948 my father's guerrillas joined up with the regular army. He was put in charge of an intelligence-gathering system covering the Jinzhou-Huludao area; his job was to track the deployment of Kuomintang forces and monitor their food situation. Much of his information came from agents inside the Kuomintang, including Yu-wu. From these reports he heard of my mother for the first time.

The thin, dreamy-looking man my mother saw brushing his teeth in the courtyard that October morning was known among his fellow guerrillas for his fastidiousness. He brushed his teeth every day, which was a novelty to the other guerrillas and to the peasants in the villages he had fought through. Unlike everyone else, who simply blew their noses onto the ground, he used a handkerchief, which he washed whenever he could. He never dipped his face towel in the public washbasin like the other soldiers, as eye diseases were widespread. He was also known as scholarly and bookish and always carried some volumes of classical poetry with him, even in battle.

When she had first seen the "Wanted" posters and heard about this dangerous "bandit" from her relatives, my mother could tell that they admired as well as feared him. Now she was not a bit disappointed that the legendary guerrilla did not look at all warriorlike.

My father also knew of my mother's courage and, most unusual of all, the fact that she, a seventeen-year-old girl, was giving orders to men. An admirable and emancipated woman, he had thought, although he had also imagined her as a fierce dragon. To his delight he found her pretty and feminine, even rather coquettish. She was both soft-spoken and persuasive, and also, something rare in China, precise. This was an extremely important quality for him, as he hated the traditional florid, irresponsible, and vague way of talking.

She noticed that he laughed a lot, and that he had shiny white teeth, unlike most other guerrillas, whose teeth were often brown and rotting. She was also attracted by his conversation. He struck her as learned and knowledgeable—definitely not the sort of man who would mix up Flaubert and Maupassant.

When my mother told him she was there to report on the work of her students' union, he asked her what books the students were reading. My mother gave him a list and asked if he would come and give them some lectures on Marxist philosophy and history. He agreed, and asked her how many people there were at her school. She gave him an exact figure at once. Then he asked her what proportion of them backed the Communists; again she immediately gave him a careful estimate.

A few days later he turned up to start his course of lectures. He also took the students through Mao's works and explained what some of Mao's basic theories were. He was an excellent speaker, and the girls, including my mother, were bowled over.

One day, he told the students that the Party was organizing a trip to Harbin, the Communists' temporary capital in the north of Manchuria. Harbin was largely built by Russians and was known as "the Paris of the East" because of its broad boulevards, ornate buildings, smart shops, and European-style cafés. The trip was presented as a sight-seeing tour, but the real reason for it was that the Party was worried that the Kuomintang was going to try to retake Jinzhou, and they wanted to get the pro-Communist teachers and students, as well as the professional elite like doctors, out in case the city was reoccupied—but they did not want to set off alarm bells by saying so. My mother and a number of her friends were among the 170 people chosen to go.

In late November my mother set off by train for the north in a state of high excitement. It was in snow-covered Harbin, with its romantic old buildings and its Russian mood of lingering pensiveness and poetry, that my parents fell in love. My father wrote some beautiful poems for my mother there. Not only were they in very elegant classical style, which was a considerable accomplishment, but she discovered that he was a good calligrapher, which raised him even higher in her esteem.

On New Year's Eve he invited my mother and a girlfriend of hers to his quarters. He was living in an old Russian hotel, which was like something out of a fairy tale, with a brightly colored roof, ornate gables, and delicate plasterwork around the windows and on the veranda. When my mother came in, she saw a bottle sitting on a rococo table; it had foreign lettering on it—champagne. My father had never actually drunk champagne before; he had only read about it in foreign books.

By this time it was well known among my mother's fellow students that the two were in love. My mother, being the student leader, often went to give long reports to my father, and it was noticed that she did not come back until the small hours. My father had several other admirers, including the friend who was with my mother that night, but she could see from how he looked at my mother, his teasing remarks and the way they seized every chance to be physically close to each other, that he was in love with her. When the friend left toward midnight, she knew my mother was going to stay behind. My father found a note under the empty champagne bottle: "Alas! I shall have no more reason to drink champagne! I hope the champagne bottle is always full for you!"

That night, my father asked my mother whether she was committed to anyone else. She told him about her previous relationships, and said the only man she had really loved was her cousin Hu, but that he had been executed by the Kuomintang. Then, in line with the new Communist moral code which, in a radical departure from the past, enjoined that men and women should be equal, he told her about his previous relationships. He said he had been in love with a woman in Yibin, but that that had ended when he left for Yan'an. He had had a few girlfriends in Yan'an, and in his guerrilla days, but the war had made it impossible even to contemplate the idea of marriage. One of his former girlfriends was to marry Chen Boda, the head of my father's section of the Academy in Yan'an, who later rose to enormous power as Mao's secretary.

After hearing each other's frank accounts of their past lives, my father said he was going to write to the Jinzhou City Party Committee asking for permission to "talk about love" *(tan-nian-ai)* with my mother, with a view to marriage. This was the obligatory procedure. My mother supposed it was a bit like asking permission from the head of the family, and in fact that is exactly what it was: the Communist Party was the new patriarch. That night, after their talk, my mother received her first present from my father, a romantic Russian novel called *It's Only Love.*

The next day my mother wrote home saying she had met a man she liked very much. The immediate reaction of her mother and Dr. Xia was not enthusiasm but concern, because my father was an official, and officials had always had a bad name among ordinary Chinese. Apart from their other vices, their arbitrary power meant they were thought unlikely to treat women decently. My grandmother's immediate assumption was that my father was married already and wanted my mother as a concubine. After all, he was well beyond the marrying age for men in Manchuria.

After about a month it was judged safe for the Harbin group to return to Jinzhou. The Party told my father that he had permission to "talk about love" with my mother. Two other men had also applied, but their applications came too late. One of them was Liang, who had been her controller in the underground. In his disappointment he asked to be transferred away from Jinzhou. Neither he nor the other man had breathed a word of their intentions to my mother.

My father got back to be told he had been appointed head of the

Public Affairs Department of Jinzhou. A few days later my mother took him home to introduce him to her family. The moment he came in the door my grandmother turned her back on him, and when he tried to greet her she refused to answer. My father was dark and terribly thin—the result of the hardships he had been through in the guerrilla days, and my grandmother was convinced he was well over forty, and therefore that it was impossible he had not been married before. Dr. Xia treated him politely, if formally.

My father did not stay long. When he left, my grandmother was in floods of tears. No official could be any good, she cried. But Dr. Xia already realized, through meeting my father and from my mother's explanations, that the Communists exercised such tight control over their people that an official like my father would not be able to cheat. My grandmother was only half reassured: "But he is from Sichuan. How can the Communists find out when he comes from so far away?"

She kept up her barrage of doubts and criticism, but the rest of the family took to my father. Dr. Xia got on very well with him, and they would talk together for hours. Yu-lin and his wife also liked him very much. Yu-lin's wife had come from a very poor family. Her mother had been forced into an unhappy marriage after her grandfather had staked her in a card game and lost. Her brother had been caught in a roundup by the Japanese and had had to do three years of forced labor, which destroyed his body.

From the day she married Yu-lin, she had to get up at three o'clock every morning to start preparing the various different meals demanded by the complicated Manchu tradition. My grandmother was running the house and, although they were in theory members of the same generation, Yu-lin's wife felt that she was the inferior because she and her husband were dependent on the Xias. My father was the first person to make a point of treating her as an equal, which in China was a considerable departure from the past, and several times he gave the couple film tickets, which for them was a big treat. He was the first official they had ever met who did not put on airs, and Yu-lin's wife certainly felt that the Communists were a big improvement.

Less than two months after returning from Harbin my mother and father filed their application. Marriage had traditionally been a contract between families, and there had never been civil registration or a marriage certificate. Now, for those who had "joined the revolution," the Party functioned as the family head. Its criteria were "28-7-regiment-1"—which meant that the man had to be at least twenty-eight years old, a Party member for at least seven years, and with a rank equivalent to that of a regimental commander; the "1" referred to the only qualification the woman had to meet, to have worked for the Party for a minimum of one year. My father was twenty-eight according to the Chinese way of counting age (one year old at birth), he had been a Party member for over ten years, and he held a position equivalent to that of a deputy division commander. Although my mother was not a member of the Party, her work for the underground was accepted as meeting the "1" criterion, and since she had come back from Harbin she had been working full time for an organization called the Women's Federation, which dealt with women's affairs: it supervised the freeing of concubines and shutting down brothels, mobilized women to make shoes for the army, organized their education and their employment, informed them of their rights, and helped ensure that women were not entering into marriages against their wishes.

The Women's Federation was now my mother's "work unit" (*danwei*), an institution wholly under the control of the Party, to which everyone in the urban areas had to belong and which regulated virtually every aspect of an employee's life like in an army. My mother was supposed to live on the premises of the Federation, and had to obtain its permission to marry. The Federation left it up to my father's work unit, as he was a higher official. The Jinzhou City Party Committee speedily gave its written permission, but because of my father's position, clearance also had to come from the Party Committee for the province of West Liaoning. Assuming there would be no problem, my parents set the wedding day for 4 May, my mother's eighteenth birthday.

On that day my mother wrapped up her bedroll and her clothes and got ready to move into my father's quarters. She wore her favorite pale-blue gown and a pale-blue silk scarf. My grandmother was appalled. It was unheard of for a bride to walk to the bridegroom's house. The man had to get a sedan chair to carry her over. For a woman to walk was a sign that she was worthless and that the man did not really want her. "Who cares about all that stuff now?" said my mother as she tied up her bedroll. But my grandmother was more dismayed at the thought that her daughter was not going to have a magnificent traditional wedding. From the moment a baby girl was born, her mother would start putting things aside for her dowry. Following the custom, my mother's trousseau contained a dozen satin-covered quilts and pillows with embroidered mandarin ducks, as well as curtains and a decorated pelmet for a four-poster bed. But my mother regarded a traditional ceremony as old-fashioned and redundant. Both she and my father wanted to get rid of rituals like that, which they felt had nothing to do with their feelings. Love was the only thing that mattered to these two revolutionaries.

My mother walked, carrying her bedroll, to my father's quarters. Like all officials, he was living in the building where he worked, the City Party Committee; the employees were housed in rows of bungalows with sliding doors situated around a big courtyard. As dusk fell, and they were on the point of going to bed for the night, my mother was kneeling down to take off my father's slippers when there was a knock on the door. A man was standing there, and he handed my father a message from the Provincial Party Committee. It said they could not get married yet. Only the tightening of my mother's lips showed how unhappy she was. She just bent her head, silently gathered up her bedroll, and left with a simple "See you later." There were no tears, no scene, not even any visible anger. The moment was etched indelibly into my father's mind. When I was a child he used to say: "Your mother was so graceful." Then, jokingly, "How times have changed! You're not like your mother! You wouldn't do something like that—kneel down to take off a man's shoes!"

What had caused the delay was that the Provincial Committee was suspicious of my mother because of her family connections. They questioned her in great detail about how her family had come to be connected with Kuomintang intelligence. They told her she must be completely truthful. It was like giving evidence in court.

She also had to explain how each of the Kuomintang officers had sought her hand, and why she was friends with so many Kuomintang Youth League members. She pointed out that her friends were the most anti-Japanese and the most socially conscious people; and that when the Kuomintang had come to Jinzhou in 1945, they had seen it as the government of China. She herself might well have joined, but at fourteen she was too young. In fact, most of her friends had soon switched to the Communists.

The Party was divided: the City Committee took the view that my mother's friends had acted out of patriotic motives; but some of the provincial leaders treated them with open-ended suspicion. My mother was asked to "draw a line" between herself and her friends. "Drawing a line" between people was a key mechanism the Communists introduced to increase the gap between those who were "in" and those who were "out." Nothing, even personal relationships, was left to chance, or allowed to be fluid. If she wanted to get married, she had to stop seeing her friends.

But the most painful thing for my mother was what was happening to Hui-ge, the young Kuomintang colonel. The moment the siege was over, after her initial exhilaration that the Communists had won, her strongest urge had been to see whether he was all right. She ran all the way through the blood-soaked streets to the Jis' mansion. There was nothing there—no street, no houses, only a gigantic pile of rubble. Hui-ge had disappeared.

In the spring, just as she was preparing to get married, she found out that he was alive, a prisoner—and in Jinzhou. At the time of the siege he had managed to escape south and had ended up at Tianjin; when the Communists took Tianjin in January 1949, he was captured and brought back.

Hui-ge was not regarded as an ordinary prisoner of war. Because of his family's influence in Jinzhou, he fell into the category of "snakes in their old haunts," meaning established powerful local figures. They were especially dangerous for the Communists because they commanded loyalty from the local population, and their anti-Communist inclinations posed a threat to the new regime.

My mother felt confident that Hui-ge would be fairly treated after it was known what he had done, and she immediately started to appeal on his behalf. As was the procedure, she had to talk first to her immediate boss in her unit, the Women's Federation, which forwarded the appeal to a higher authority. My mother did not know who had the final say. She went to Yu-wu, who knew about, and indeed had instructed, her contact with Hui-ge, and asked him to vouch for the colonel. Yu-wu wrote a report describing what Hui-ge had done, but added that he had perhaps acted out of love for my mother, and that he might not even have known he was helping the Communists because he was blinded by love.

My mother went to another underground leader who knew what the colonel had done. He too refused to say that Hui-ge had been helping the Communists. In fact he was not willing to mention the colonel's role in getting information out to the Communists at all, so that he could take full credit for it himself. My mother said that she and the colonel had not been in love, but she could not produce any proof. She cited the veiled requests and promises that had passed between them, but these were regarded only as evidence that the colonel was trying to buy "insurance," something about which the Party was particularly chary.

All this was going on at the time that my mother and father were preparing to get married, and it cast a dark shadow over their relationship. However, my father sympathized with my mother's quandary, and thought Hui-ge should be treated fairly. He did not let the fact that my grandmother had favored the colonel as her son-in-law influence his judgment.

In late May, permission finally arrived for the wedding to go ahead. My mother was at a meeting of the Women's Federation when someone came in and slipped a note into her hand. The note was from the city Party chief, Lin Xiao-xia, who was a nephew of the top general who had led the Communist forces in Manchuria, Lin Biao. It was in verse, and said simply: "The provincial authorities have given the okay. You can't possibly want to be stuck in a meeting. Come quickly and get married!"

My mother tried to look calm as she walked up and gave the note to the woman presiding over the meeting, who nodded approval for her to leave. She ran all the way to my father's quarters, still wearing her blue "Lenin suit," a uniform for government employees that had a double-breasted jacket tucked in at the waist and worn over baggy trousers. When she opened the door, she saw Lin Xiao-xia and the other Party leaders and their bodyguards, who had just arrived. My father said a carriage had been sent for Dr. Xia. Lin asked: "What about your mother-in-law?" My father said nothing. "That's not right," Lin said, and ordered a carriage to be sent for her. My mother felt very hurt, but attributed my father's action to his loathing of my grandmother's Kuomintang intelligence connections. Still, she thought, was that her mother's fault? It did not occur to her that my father's behavior might have been a reaction to the way her mother had treated him.

There was no wedding ceremony of any kind, only a small gathering. Dr. Xia came up to congratulate the couple. Everyone sat around for a while eating fresh crabs which the City Party Committee had provided as a special treat. The Communists were trying to institute a frugal approach to weddings, which had traditionally been the occasion for huge expenditure, far out of proportion to what people could afford. It was not at all unusual for families to bankrupt themselves to put on a lavish wedding. My parents had dates and peanuts, which had been served at weddings in Yan'an, and dried fruit called *longan*, which traditionally symbolizes a happy union and sons. After a short time, Dr. Xia and most of the guests left. A group from the Women's Federation turned up later, after their meeting was over.

Dr. Xia and my grandmother had had no idea about the wedding, nor did the first carriage driver tell them. My grandmother only heard that her daughter was about to be married when the second carriage came. As she hurried up the path and came into view through the window, the women from the Federation started whispering to each other and then scuttled out the back door. My father left as well. My mother was on the verge of tears. She knew the women from her group despised my grandmother not only because of her Kuomintang connections but also because she had been a concubine. Far from being emancipated on these issues, many Communist women from uneducated peasant backgrounds were set in their traditional ways. For them, no good girl would have become a concubine—even though the Communists had stipulated that a concubine enjoyed the same status as a wife, and could dissolve the "marriage" unilaterally. These women from the Federation were the very ones supposed to be implementing the Party's policies of emancipation.

My mother covered up, telling her mother that her bridegroom had had to go back to work: "It is not the Communist custom to give people leave for a wedding. In fact, I am about to go back to work myself." My grandmother thought that the offhand way in which the Communists treated a big thing like a wedding was absolutely extraordinary, but they had broken so many rules relating to traditional values, maybe this was just one more.

At the time one of my mother's jobs was teaching reading and writing to the women in the textile factory where she had worked under the Japanese, and informing them about women's equality with men. The factory was still privately owned, and one of the foremen was still beating women employees whenever he felt like it. My mother was instrumental in getting him sacked, and helped the women workers elect their own forewoman. But any credit she might have received for achieving this was obscured by the Federation's dissatisfaction about another matter.

One major task of the Women's Federation was to make cotton shoes for the army. My mother did not know how to make shoes, so she got her mother and aunts to do it. They had been brought up making elaborate embroidered shoes, and my mother proudly presented the Women's Federation with a large number of beautifully made shoes, far exceeding her quota. To her surprise, instead of being praised for her ingenuity, she was scolded like a child. The peasant women in the Federation could not conceive that there could be a woman on the face of the earth who did not know how to make shoes. It was like saying someone did not know how to eat. She was criticized at the Federation meetings for her "bourgeois decadence."

My mother did not get on with some of her bosses in the Women's Federation. They were older, and conservative, peasant women who had slogged for years with the guerrillas, and they resented pretty, educated city girls like my mother who immediately attracted the Communist men. My mother had applied to join the Party, but they said that she was unworthy.

Every time she went home she found herself being criticized. She was accused of being "too attached to her family," which was condemned as a "bourgeois habit," and had to see less and less of her own mother.

At the time there was an unwritten rule that no revolutionary could spend the night away from his or her office except on Saturdays. My mother's assigned sleeping place was in the Women's Federation, which was separated from my father's quarters by a low mud wall. At night she would clamber over the wall and cross a small garden to my father's room, returning to her own room before dawn. She was soon found out, and she and my father were criticized at Party meetings. The Communists had embarked on a radical reorganization not just of institutions, but of people's lives, especially the lives of those who had "joined the revolution." The idea was that everything personal was political; in fact, henceforth nothing was supposed to be regarded as "personal" or private. Pettiness was validated by being labeled "political," and meetings became the forum by which the Communists channeled all sorts of personal animosities.

My father had to make a verbal self-criticism, and my mother a written one. She was said to have "put love first," when revolution should have had priority. She felt very wronged. What harm could it do the revolution if she spent the night with her husband? She could understand the rationale for such a rule in the guerrilla days, but not now. She did not want to write a self-criticism, and told my father so. To her dismay he admonished her, saying: "The revolution is not won. The war is still going on. We have broken the rules, and we should admit mistakes. A revolution needs steel-like discipline. You have to obey the Party even if you do not understand it or agree with it."

Soon after this disaster struck out of the blue. A poet called Bian, who had been in the delegation to Harbin and who had become a close friend of my mother, tried to kill himself. Bian was a follower of the "New Moon" school of poetry, a leading exponent of which was Hu Shi, who became Kuomintang ambassador to the United States. It concentrated on aesthetics and form and was particularly influenced by Keats. Bian had joined the Communists during the war, but then found that his poetry was deemed not to be in harmony with the revolution, which wanted propaganda, not self-expression. He accepted this with part of his mind, but he was also very torn and depressed. He began to feel that he would never be able to write again, and yet, he said, he could not live without his poetry.

His attempted suicide shocked the Party. It was bad for its image for people to think that anyone might be so disillusioned with Liberation that they would try to kill themselves. Bian was working in Jinzhou as a teacher at the school for Party officials, many of whom were illiterate. The Party organization at the school conducted an investigation and leapt to the conclusion that Bian had tried to kill himself because of unrequited love—for my mother. In its criticism meetings the Women's Federation suggested that my mother had led Bian on and then ditched him for a bigger prize, my father. My mother was furious, and demanded to see the evidence for the accusation. Of course, none was ever produced.

In this case, my father stood by my mother. He knew that on the trip to Harbin, when my mother was supposed to have been having trysts with Bian, she had been in love with him, not the poet. He had seen Bian reading his poems to my mother and knew that my mother admired him, and did not think there was anything wrong with it. But neither he nor my mother could stop the flood of gossip. The women in the Federation were particularly virulent.

At the height of this whispering campaign my mother heard that her appeal for Hui-ge had been turned down. She was beside herself with anguish. She had made a promise to Hui-ge, and now she felt that she had somehow misled him. She had been visiting him regularly in prison, bringing him news of her efforts to get his case reviewed, and she had felt it was inconceivable that the Communists would not spare him. She had been genuinely optimistic and had tried to cheer him up. But this time when he saw her face, red-eyed and distorted from the effort of hiding her despair, he knew there was no hope. They wept together, sitting in full view of the guards with a table between them on which they had to place their hands. Hui-ge took my mother's hands in his; she did not pull back.

My father was informed of my mother's visits to the prison. At first he said nothing. He sympathized with her predicament. But gradually he became angry. The scandal about Bian's attempted suicide was at its height, and now it was alleged that his wife had had a relationship with a Kuomintang colonel—and they were still supposed to be on their honeymoon! He was furious, but his personal feelings were not the decisive factor in his acceptance of the Party's attitude toward the colonel. He told my mother that if the Kuomintang came back people like Hui-ge would be the first to use their authority to help restore it to power. The Communists, he said, could not afford that risk: "Our revolution is a matter of life and death." When my mother tried to tell him how Hui-ge had helped the Communists he responded that her visits to the prison had done Hui-ge no good, particularly their holding hands. Since the time of Confucius, men and women had to be married, or at least lovers, to touch in public, and even under these circumstances it was extremely rare. The fact that my mother and Hui-ge had been seen holding hands was taken as proof that they had been in love, and that Hui-ge's service to the Communists had not been motivated by "correct" reasons. My mother found it hard to disagree with him, but this did not make her feel any less desolate.

Her sense of being caught up in impossible dilemmas was heightened by what was happening to several of her relatives and many people close to her. When the Communists arrived, they had announced that anybody who had worked for Kuomintang intelligence had to report to them at once. Her uncle Yu-lin had never worked in intelligence, but he had an intelligence card, and felt he should report to the new authorities. His wife and my grandmother tried to dissuade him, but he thought it best to tell the truth. He was in a difficult situation. If he had not turned himself in and the Communists had discovered the facts about him, which was highly likely, given their formidable organization, he would have been in dire trouble. But by coming forward, he himself had given them grounds to suspect him.

The Party's verdict was: "Has a political blemish in his past. No punishment, but can only be employed under control." This verdict, like almost all others, was not delivered by a court, but by a Party body. There was no clear definition of what it meant, but as a result of it, for three decades Yu-lin's life would depend on the political climate and on his Party bosses. In those days Jinzhou had a relatively relaxed City Party Committee, and he was allowed to go on helping Dr. Xia in the shop.

My grandmother's brother-in-law, "Loyalty" Pei-o, was exiled to the country to do manual labor. Because he had no blood on his hands, he was given a sentence called "under surveillance." Instead of being imprisoned, this meant being guarded (just as effectively) in society. His family chose to go to the country with him, but before they could leave, "Loyalty" had to enter a hospital. He had contracted venereal disease. The Communists had launched a major campaign to wipe out VD, and anyone who had it was obliged to undergo treatment.

His work "under surveillance" lasted three years. It was rather like assigned labor under parole. People under surveillance enjoyed a measure of freedom, but they had to report to the police at regular intervals with a detailed account of everything they had done, or even thought, since their last visit, and they were openly watched by the police.

When they finished their term of formal surveillance, they would join people like Yu-lin in a looser category of "quiet" surveillance.

One common form of this was the "sandwich"—being kept under close watch by two neighbors who had been specifically assigned this task, often called "two reds sandwiching a black." Of course, other neighbors, through the residents' committees, were also entitled—and encouraged—to report and inform on the unreliable "black." The "people's justice" was watertight, and was a central instrument of rule because it enlisted so many citizens in active collusion with the state.

Zhu-ge, the scholarly looking intelligence officer who had married Miss Tanaka, my mother's Japanese teacher, was sentenced to forced labor for life and exiled to a remote border area (along with many former Kuomintang officials, he was released in an amnesty in 1959). His wife was sent back to Japan. As in the Soviet Union, almost all of those sentenced to detention did not go to prison but into labor camps, often working in dangerous jobs or highly polluted areas.

Some important Kuomintang figures, including intelligence men, went unpunished. The academic supervisor at my mother's school had been district secretary of the Kuomintang, but there was evidence that he had helped to save the lives of many Communists and Communist sympathizers, including my mother, so he was spared.

The headmistress and two teachers who had worked for intelligence managed to hide, and eventually escaped to Taiwan. So did Yao-han, the political supervisor who had been responsible for my mother's arrest.

The Communists also spared big shots like the "last emperor," Pu Yi, and top generals—because they were "useful." Mao's stated policy was: "We kill small Chiang Kai-sheks. We don't kill big Chiang Kai-sheks." Keeping people like Pu Yi alive, he reasoned, would "be well received abroad." No one could complain openly about this policy, but it was a cause of much discontent in private.

It was a time of great anxiety for my mother's family. Her uncle Yu-lin and her aunt Lan, whose fate was hitched inexorably to that of her husband, "Loyalty," were in a state of acute uncertainty about their futures, and suffering ostracism. But the Women's Federation ordered my mother to write one self-criticism after another, as her grief indicated she had "a soft spot for the Kuomintang."

She was also sniped at for visiting a prisoner, Hui-ge, without asking for permission from the Federation first. Nobody had told her she was supposed to do this. The Federation said that they had not stopped her before because they made allowances for someone who was "new to the revolution"; they were waiting to see how long it would take her to reach her own sense of discipline and ask the Party for instructions. "But what are the things for which I need to apply for instructions?"

she asked. "Anything," was the answer. The need to obtain authorization for an unspecified "anything" was to become a fundamental element in Chinese Communist rule. It also meant that people learned not to take any action on their own initiative.

My mother became ostracized within the Federation, which was her whole world. There were whispers that she had been used by Hui-ge to help him prepare for a comeback. "What a mess she got herself into," exclaimed the women, "all because she was 'loose.' Look at all these involvements with men! And what kind of men!" My mother felt surrounded by accusing fingers, and that the people who were supposed to be her comrades in a glorious new and liberating movement were questioning her character and her commitment, for which she had risked her life. She was even criticized for having left the meeting of the Women's Federation to go and get married—a sin termed "putting love first." My mother said that the city chief had asked her to go. To this the chairwoman retorted: "But it was up to you to show your correct attitude by putting the meeting first."

Just eighteen, recently married, and full of hope for a new life, my mother felt miserably confused and isolated. She had always trusted her own strong sense of right and wrong, but this now seemed to be in conflict with the views of her "cause" and, often, the judgment of her husband, whom she loved. She began to doubt herself for the first time.

She did not blame the Party, or the revolution. Nor could she blame the women in the Federation, because they were her comrades and seemed to be the voice of the Party. Her resentment turned against my father. She felt that his loyalty was not primarily to her and that he always seemed to side with his comrades against her. She understood that it might be difficult for him to express his support in public, but she wanted it in private—and she did not get it. From the very beginning of their marriage, there was a fundamental difference between my parents. My father's devotion to communism was absolute: he felt he had to speak the same language in private, even to his wife, that he did in public. My mother was much more flexible; her commitment was tempered by both reason and emotion. She gave a space to the private; my father did not.

My mother was finding Jinzhou unbearable. She told my father she wanted to leave, right away. He agreed, in spite of the fact that he was just about to receive a promotion. He applied to the City Party Committee for a transfer, giving as the reason that he wanted to go back to his hometown, Yibin. The Committee was surprised, as he had just told them this was exactly what he did not want to do. Throughout

Chinese history, it had been a rule that officials were stationed away from their hometowns to avoid problems of nepotism.

In the summer of 1949 the Communists were advancing southward with unstoppable momentum: they had captured Chiang Kai-shek's capital, Nanjing, and seemed certain to reach Sichuan soon. Their experience in Manchuria had shown them that they badly needed administrators who were local—and loyal.

The Party endorsed my father's transfer. Two months after their marriage—and less than one year after Liberation—they were being driven out of my mother's hometown by gossip and spite. My mother's joy at Liberation had turned to an anxious melancholy. Under the Kuomintang she had been able to discharge her tension in action—and it had been easy to feel she was doing the right thing, which gave her courage. Now she just felt in the wrong all the time. When she tried to talk it over with my father he would tell her that becoming a Communist was an agonizing process. That was the way it had to be.

7. "Going through the Five Mountain Passes"— My Mother's Long March

(1949–1950)

Just before my parents left Jinzhou, my mother was granted provisional membership in the Party, thanks to the deputy mayor who oversaw the Women's Federation, who argued that she needed it because she was going to a new place. The decision meant she could become a full member in one year's time, if she was deemed to have proved herself worthy.

My parents were to join a group of over a hundred people traveling to the southwest, most of them to Sichuan. The bulk of the group were men, Communist officials from the southwest. The few women were Manchurians who had married Sichuanese. For the journey they were organized into units and given green army uniforms. The civil war was still raging in their path.

On 27 July 1949 my grandmother, Dr. Xia, and my mother's closest friends, most of whom were under suspicion from the Communists, came to the station to see them off. As they stood on the platform saying goodbye, my mother felt torn by contradictory feelings. With one part of her heart she felt like a bird which was now going to burst out of its cage and fly to the sky. With the other part she wondered when—or if—she would ever see these people she loved, particularly her mother, again. The journey was fraught with danger, and Sichuan was still in the hands of the Kuomintang. It was also 1,000 miles away, inconceivably far, and she had no idea if she would ever be able to get back to Jinzhou. She felt an overwhelming desire to cry, but she held back her tears because she did not want to make her mother sadder than she already was. As the platform slipped out of sight my father tried to comfort her. He told her that she must be strong, and that as a young student "joining the revolution" she needed to "go through the five mountain passes"—which meant adopting a completely new attitude to family, profession, love, life-style, and manual labor, through embracing hardship and trauma. The Party's theory was that educated people like her needed to stop being "bourgeois" and become closer to the peasants, who formed over 80 percent of the population. My mother had heard these theories a hundred times. She accepted the need to reform oneself for a new China; in fact she had just written a poem about meeting the challenge of "the storm of sand" in her future. But she also wanted more tenderness and personal under-standing, and she resented the fact that she did not get them from my father.

When the train reached Tianjin, about 250 miles to the southwest, they had to stop because the line ended. My father said he would like to take her around the city. Tianjin was a huge port where the United States, Japan, and a number of European states had until recently had "concessions," extraterritorial enclaves (General Xue had died in the French concession in Tianjin, although my mother did not know this). There were whole quarters built in different foreign styles, with grandiose buildings: elegant turn-of-the-century French palaces; light Italian palazzi; overblown, late rococo Austro-Hungarian townhouses. It was an extraordinary condensation of display by eight different na-tions, all of whom had been trying to impress one another and the Chinese. Apart from the squat, heavy, gray Japanese banks, familiar from Manchuria, and the green-roofed Russian banks, with their del-icate pink-and-yellow walls, it was the first time my mother had ever seen buildings like these. My father had read a lot of foreign literature, and the descriptions of European buildings had always fascinated him. This was the first time he had seen them with his own eyes. My mother could tell he was going to a lot of trouble to try to fire her with his enthusiasm, but she was still down in the dumps as they strolled along the streets, which were lined with heavily scented Chinese scholar trees. She was already missing her mother, and she could not rid herself of her anger against my father for not saying anything sympa-thetic, and for his stiffness, although she knew he was trying, awk-wardly, to help her out of her mood.

The broken railway line was only the beginning. They had to continue their journey on foot, and the route was peppered with local landlords' forces, bandits, and units of Kuomintang soldiers who had been left behind as the Communists advanced. There were only three rifles in the entire group, one of which my father had, but at each stage along the route the local authorities sent a squad of soldiers as an escort, usually with a couple of machine guns.

They had to walk long distances every day, often on rough paths, carrying their bedrolls and other belongings on their backs. Those who had been in the guerrillas were used to this, but after one day the soles of my mother's feet were covered with blisters. There was no way she could stop for a rest. Her colleagues advised her to soak her feet in hot water at the end of the day and to let the fluid out by piercing the blisters with a needle and a hair. This brought instant relief, but the next day it was laceratingly painful when she had to start walking again. Each morning she gritted her teeth and struggled on.

Much of the way there were no roads. The going was appalling, especially when it rained: the earth became a mass of slippery mud, and my mother fell down more times than she could count. At the end of the day she would be covered with mud. When they reached their destination for the night, she would collapse on the ground and just lie there, unable to move.

One day they had to walk over thirty miles in heavy rain. The temperature was well over 90°F, and my mother was soaked to the skin with rain and sweat. They had to climb a mountain—not a particularly high one, only about 3,000 feet, but my mother was completely exhausted. She felt her bedroll weighing on her like a huge stone. Her eyes were clogged with sweat pouring from her forehead. When she opened her mouth to gasp for air, she felt she could not get enough into her lungs to breathe. Thousands of stars were dancing before her eyes and she could hardly drag one foot in front of the other. When she got to the top she thought her misery was over, but going downhill was almost as difficult. Her calf muscles seemed to have turned to jelly. It was wild country, and the steep, narrow path ran along the edge of a cliff, with a drop of hundreds of feet. Her legs were trembling and she felt sure she was going to fall into the abyss. Several times she had to cling to trees to keep from toppling over the cliff.

After they had crossed the mountain there were several deep, fast-flowing rivers in their path. The water level rose to her waist and she found it almost impossible to keep her footing. In the middle of one river she stumbled and felt she was about to be swept away when a man leaned over and caught hold of her. She almost broke down and wept, particularly since at this very moment she spotted a friend of hers whose husband was carrying her across the river. Although the husband was a senior official, and had the right to use a car, he had waived his privilege in order to walk with his wife.

My father was not carrying my mother. He was being driven along· in a jeep, with his bodyguard. His rank entitled him to transportation —either a jeep or a horse, whichever was available. My mother had often hoped that he would give her a lift, or at least carry her bedroll in his jeep, but he never offered. The evening after she almost drowned in the river, she decided to have it out with him. She had had a terrible day. What was more, she was vomiting all the time. Could he not let her travel in his jeep occasionally? He said he could not, because it would be taken as favoritism since my mother was not entitled to the car. He felt he had to fight against the age-old Chinese tradition of nepotism. Furthermore, my mother was supposed to ex- perience hardship. When she mentioned that her friend was being carried by her husband, my father replied that that was completely different: the friend was a veteran Communist. In the 1930s she had commanded a guerrilla unit jointly with Kim Il Sung, who later be- came president of North Korea, fighting the Japanese under appalling conditions in the northeast. Among the long list of sufferings in her revolutionary career was the loss of her first husband, who had been executed on orders from Stalin. My mother could not compare herself to this woman, my father said. She was only a young student. If other people thought she was being pampered she would be in trouble. "It's for your own good," he added, reminding her that her application for full Party membership was pending. "You have a choice: you can either get into the car, or get into the Party, but not both."

He had a point. The revolution was fundamentally a peasant revo- lution, and the peasants had an unrelentingly harsh life. They were particularly sensitive about other people enjoying or seeking comfort. Anyone who took part in the revolution was supposed to toughen themselves to the point where they became inured to hardship. My father had done this at Yan'an and as a guerrilla.

My mother understood the theory, but that did not stop her think- ing about the fact that my father was giving her no sympathy while she was sick and exhausted the whole time, trudging along, carrying her bedroll, sweating, vomiting, her legs like lead.

One night she could not stand it anymore, and burst into tears for the first time. The group usually stayed overnight in places like empty storerooms, or classrooms. That night they were all sleeping in a temple, packed close together on the ground. My father was lying next to her. When she first started crying, she turned her face away from him and buried it in her sleeve, trying to muffle her sobs. My father woke up at once and hurriedly clapped his hand over her mouth. Through her tears she heard him whispering into her ear: "Don't cry out loud! If people hear you, you will be criticized." To be criticized was serious. It meant her comrades would say she was not worthy of "being in the revolution," even a coward. She felt him urgently pushing a handkerchief into her hand so that she could stifle her sobs.

The next day my mother's unit head, the man who had saved her from falling over in the river, took her aside and told her he had received complaints about her crying. People were saying she had behaved like "a precious lady from the exploiting classes." He was not unsympathetic, but he had to reflect what other people were saying. It was disgraceful to cry after walking a few steps, he said. She was not behaving like a proper revolutionary. From then on, though she often felt like it, my mother never cried once.

She slogged on. The most dangerous area they had to go through was the province of Shandong, which had fallen to the Communists only a couple of months previously. On one occasion they were walking through a deep valley when bullets started pouring down on them from above. My mother took cover behind a rock. The shooting went on for about ten minutes, and when it died down they found that one of their group had been killed trying to get around behind the assailants, who turned out to be bandits. Several others were injured. They buried the dead man by the roadside. My father and the other officials gave up their horses to the injured.

After forty days of marching and more skirmishes they reached the city of Nanjing, about 700 miles due south of Jinzhou, which had been the capital of the Kuomintang government. It is known as "the Furnace of China," and in mid-September it was still like an oven. The group was housed in a barracks. The bamboo mattress on my mother's bed had a dark human figure imprinted on it by the sweat of those who had slept there before her. The group had to do military training in the sweltering heat, learning how to tie up a bedroll, puttees, and knapsack on the double, and practicing quick marching carrying their kits. As part of the army, they had to observe strict discipline. They wore khaki uniforms and rough cotton shirts and underwear. Their uniforms had to be buttoned right up to the neck and they were never allowed to unbutton the collar. My mother found it hard to breathe, and like everyone she had a huge dark patch of sweat covering her back. They also wore a double-thickness cotton cap, which had to fit tightly around the head so that it did not show any hair. This made my mother perspire profusely, and the edge of her cap was permanently soaked in sweat.

Occasionally they were allowed out, and the first thing she did was to devour several ice lollipops. Many of the people in the group had never been in a big city, apart from their brief stop at Tianjin. They were tremendously excited by the ice lollipops, and bought some to take back to their comrades in the barracks, wrapping them up carefully in their white hand towels and putting them in their bags. They were amazed when they got back to find that all that was left was water.

At Nanjing they had to attend political lectures, some of which were given by Deng Xiaoping, the future leader of China, and General Chen Yi, the future foreign minister. My mother and her colleagues sat on the lawn at the Central University, in the shade, while the lecturers stood in the blazing sun for two or three hours at a stretch. In spite of the heat, the lecturers mesmerized their audience.

One day my mother and her unit had to run several miles on the double, fully laden, to the tomb of the founding father of the republic, Sun Yat-sen. When they returned, my mother felt an ache in her lower abdomen. There was a performance of the Peking Opera that night in another part of the city, with one of China's most famous stars in the lead. My mother had inherited her mother's passion for the Peking Opera and was looking forward eagerly to the performance.

That evening she walked with her comrades in file to the opera, which was about five miles away. My father went in his car. On the way, my mother felt more pain in her abdomen, and contemplated turning back, but decided against it. Halfway through the performance the pain became unbearable. She went over to where my father was sitting and asked him to take her home in his car. She did not tell him about the pain. He looked round to where his driver was sitting and saw him glued to his seat, open-mouthed. He turned back to my mother and said: "How can I interrupt his enjoyment just because my wife wants to leave?" My mother lost any desire to explain that she was in agony and turned abruptly away.

She walked all the way back to the barracks in excruciating pain. Everything in front of her eyes was spinning. She saw blackness with sharp stars and felt as though she were plodding through cotton wool. She could not see the road and lost track of how long she had been walking. It seemed like a lifetime. When she got back, the barracks was deserted. Everybody except the guards had gone to the opera. She managed to drag herself to her bed, and by the light of a lamp she saw that her trousers were soaked with blood. She fainted as soon as her head hit the bed. She had lost her first child. And there was nobody near her.

A little later my father returned. Being in a car, he got back before most of the others. He found my mother sprawled on the bed. At first he thought she was just exhausted, but then he saw the blood and realized that she was unconscious. He rushed off to find a doctor, who thought she must have had a miscarriage. Being an army doctor he had no experience of what to do, so he telephoned a hospital in the city and asked them to send an ambulance. The hospital agreed—but only on condition that they were paid in silver dollars for the ambulance and the emergency operation. Even though he had no money of his own, my father agreed without hesitation. Being "with the revolution" brought automatic health insurance.

My mother had very nearly died. She had to have a blood transfusion and her womb scraped. When she opened her eyes after the operation she saw my father sitting by her bedside. The first thing she said was: "I want a divorce." My father apologized profusely. He had had no idea she had been pregnant—nor, in fact, had she. She knew that she had missed her period, but had thought it was probably the result of the unrelenting exertion of the march. My father said he had not known what a miscarriage was. He promised to be much more considerate in future, and said over and over again he loved her and would reform.

While my mother was in a coma, he had washed her blood-soaked clothes, which was very unusual for a Chinese man. Eventually my mother agreed not to ask for a divorce, but she said she wanted to go back to Manchuria to resume her medical studies. She told my father she could never please the revolution, no matter how hard she tried; all she ever got was criticism. "I might as well leave," she said. "You mustn't!" my father said, anxiously. "That will be interpreted as meaning you are afraid of hardship. You will be regarded as a deserter and you will have no future. Even if the college accepted you, you would never be able to get a good job. You would be discriminated against for the rest of your life." My mother was not yet aware that there was an unbreakable ban on opting out of the system, because, typically, it was unwritten. But she caught the tone of extreme urgency in his voice. Once you were "with the revolution" you could never leave.

My mother was in the hospital when, on 1 October, she and her comrades were alerted to expect a special broadcast, which would come over loudspeakers that had been rigged up around the hospital. They gathered to listen to Mao proclaiming the founding of the People's Republic from the top of the Gate of Heavenly Peace in Peking. My mother cried like a child. The China she had dreamed of, fought for, and hoped for was here at last, she thought, the country to which she could devote herself heart and soul. As she listened to Mao's voice announcing that "the Chinese people have stood up," she chided herself for ever having wavered. Her suffering was trivial compared to the great cause of saving China. She felt intensely proud and full of nationalistic feeling, and pledged to herself that she would stick with the revolution forever. When Mao's short proclamation was over, she and her comrades burst into cheers and threw their caps in the air—a gesture the Chinese Communists had learned from the Russians. Then, after drying their tears, they had a little feast to celebrate.

A few days before the miscarriage, my parents had their first formal photograph taken together. It shows them both in army uniform, staring pensively and rather wistfully into the camera. The photograph was taken to commemorate their entry into the former Kuomintang capital. My mother immediately sent a print to her mother.

On 3 October my father's unit was moved out. Communist forces were nearing Sichuan. My mother had to stay in the hospital another month, and was then allowed some time to recuperate in a magnificent mansion which had belonged to the main financier of the Kuomintang, Chiang Kai-shek's brother-in-law H. H. Kung. One day her unit was told they were going to be extras in a documentary film about the liberation of Nanjing. They were given civilian clothes and dressed up as ordinary citizens welcoming the Communists. This reconstruction, which was not inaccurate, was shown all over China as a "documentary"—a common practice.

My mother stayed on in Nanjing for nearly two more months. Every now and then she would get a telegram or a bunch of letters from my father. He wrote every day and sent the letters whenever he could find a post office that was working. In every one, he told her how much he loved her, promised to reform, and insisted that she must not go back to Jinzhou and "desert the revolution."

Toward the end of December, my mother was told there was a place for her on a steamer with some other people who had been left behind because of illness. They were to assemble on the dock at nightfall—Kuomintang bombing made it too dangerous during daylight. The quay was shrouded in a chilly fog. The few lights had been turned out as a precaution against air raids. A bitter north wind was sweeping snow across the river. My mother had to wait for hours on the dock, desperately stamping her numb feet, which were clad only in the standard-issue thin cotton shoes known as "liberation shoes," some of which had slogans such as "Beat Chiang Kai-shek" and "Safeguard Our Land" painted on their soles.

The steamer carried them west along the Yangtze. For about the first 200 miles, as far as the town of Anqing, it moved only at night, tying up during the day among reeds on the north bank of the river to hide from Kuomintang planes. The ship carried a contingent of soldiers, who set up machine guns on the deck, and a large amount of military equipment and ammunition. There were occasional skirmishes with Kuomintang forces and landowners' gangs. Once, as they were edging into the reeds to anchor for the day, they came under heavy fire and some Kuomintang troops tried to board the ship. My mother and the other women hid belowdecks while the guards fought them off. The ship had to sail off and anchor farther on.

When they reached the Yangtze Gorges, where Sichuan begins and the river becomes dramatically narrower, they had to change into two smaller boats which had come from Chongqing. The military cargo and some guards were transferred to one boat, while the rest of the group took the second boat.

The Yangtze Gorges were known as "the Gates of Hell." One afternoon the bright winter sun suddenly disappeared. My mother rushed on deck to see what had happened. On both sides huge perpendicular cliffs towered over the river, leaning toward the boat as though they were about to crush it. The cliffs were covered with thick vegetation and were so high that they almost obscured the sky. Every cliff seemed steeper than the last, and they looked as though some mighty sword had smashed down from heaven and cleaved its way through them.

The small boat battled for days against the currents, whirlpools, rapids, and submerged rocks. Sometimes the force of the current swept it backwards, and it felt as though it was going to capsize at any moment. Often my mother thought they were going to be dashed into a cliff, but each time the helmsman managed to steer away at the last second.

The Communists had taken most of Sichuan only within the last month. It was still infested with Kuomintang troops, who had been stranded there when Chiang Kai-shek had abandoned his resistance on the mainland and fled to Taiwan. The worst moment came when a band of these Kuomintang soldiers shelled the first boat, which was carrying the ammunition. One round hit it square on. My mother was standing on deck when it blew up about a hundred yards ahead of her. It seemed as though the whole river suddenly burst into fire. Flaming chunks of timber rushed toward my mother's boat, and it looked as if there was no way they could avoid colliding with the burning wreckage. But just as a collision seemed inevitable, it floated past, missing them by inches. Nobody showed any signs of fear, or elation. They all seemed to have grown numb to death. Most of the guards on the first boat were killed.

My mother was entering a whole new world of climate and nature. The precipices along the gorges were covered with gigantic rattan creepers which made the eerie atmosphere even more exotic. Monkeys were jumping from branch to branch in the luxuriant foliage. The endless, magnificent, precipitous mountains were a stunning novelty after the flat plains around Jinzhou.

Sometimes the boat would moor at the foot of a narrow flight of black stone stairs, which seemed to climb endlessly up the side of a mountain with its peak hidden in the clouds. Often there was a small town at the top of the mountain. Because of the permanent thick mist, the inhabitants had to burn rapeseed-oil lamps even in the daytime. It was chilly, with damp winds blowing off the mountains and the river. To my mother, the local peasants seemed horribly dark, bony, and tiny, with much sharper features and much bigger and rounder eyes than the people she was used to. They wore a kind of turban made of long white cloth wound around their foreheads. White being the color of mourning in China, my mother at first thought they were wearing mourning.

By the middle of January they had reached Chongqing, which had been the Kuomintang's capital during the war against Japan, where my mother had to move to a smaller boat for the next stage to the town of Luzhou, about a hundred miles farther upriver. There she received a message from my father that a sampan had been sent to meet her and that she could come to Yibin right away. This was the first she knew that he had arrived at his destination alive. By now her resentment against him had evaporated. It was four months since she had seen him, and she missed him. She had imagined the excitement he must have felt along the way at seeing so many sites described by the ancient poets, and she felt a glow of warmth in the sure knowledge that he would have composed poems for her on the journey.

She was able to leave that same evening. Next morning when she woke, she could feel the warmth of the sun coming through the soft mist. The hills along the river were green and gentle, and she was able to lie back and relax and listen to the water lapping against the prow of the sampan. She got to Yibin that afternoon, the eve of Chinese New Year. Her first sight of the town was like an apparition—a delicate image of a city floating in the clouds. As the boat approached the quay, she looked about for my father. Eventually, through the mist, she could make out his hazy image: he was standing in an unbuttoned army greatcoat, his bodyguard behind him. The riverbank was wide and covered with sand and cobblestones. She could see the city climbing up to the top of the hill. Some of the houses were built on long, thin, wooden stilts and seemed to be swaying in the wind as though they might collapse at any minute.

The boat tied up at a dock on the promontory at the tip of the city. A boatman laid down a plank of wood and my father's bodyguard came across and took my mother's bedroll. She bounced down the gangway, and my father stretched out his arms to help her off. It was not the proper thing to embrace in public, though my mother could tell he was as excited as she, and she felt very happy.

8. "Returning Home Robed in Embroidered Silk"— To Family and Bandits

(1949–1951)

All the way, my mother had been wondering what Yibin would be like. Would there be electricity? Would the mountains be as high as those along the Yangtze? Would there be theaters? As she climbed up the hill with my father, she was thrilled to see she had come to a beautiful place. Yibin stands on a hill overlooking a promontory at the confluence of two rivers, one clear, the other muddy. She could see electric lights shining in the rows of cottages. Their walls were made of mud and bamboo, and to her eyes the thin, curved tiles on the roofs seemed delicate, almost lacelike compared to the heavy ones needed to cope with the winds and snow of Manchuria. In the distance, through the mist, she could see little houses of bamboo and earth set in the midst of dark-green mountains covered in camphor trees, metasequoia, and tea bushes. She felt unburdened at last, not least because my father was letting his bodyguard carry her bedroll. Having passed through scores of war-torn towns and villages, she was delighted to see that here there was no war damage at all. The 7,000-man Kuomintang garrison had surrendered without a fight.

My father was living in an elegant mansion which had been taken over by the new government as combined offices and living quarters, and my mother moved in with him. It had a garden full of plants she had never seen: phoebe nanmu, papayas, and bananas, on grounds covered with green moss. Goldfish swam in a tank, and there was even a turtle. My father's bedroom had a double sofa bed, the softest thing she had ever slept on, having previously known only brick *kangs*. Even in winter, all one needed in Yibin was a quilt. There was no biting wind or all-pervasive dust like in Manchuria. You did not have to wear a gauze scarf over your face to be able to breathe. The well was not covered with a lid; there was a bamboo pole sticking out, with a bucket tied to the other end for drawing water. People washed their clothes on slabs of smooth shiny stones propped up at a slight angle, and used palm-fiber brushes to clean them. These operations would have been impossible in Manchuria, where the clothes would immediately have been either covered in dust or frozen solid. For the first time in her life, my mother could eat rice and fresh vegetables every day.

The following weeks were my parents' real honeymoon. For the first time my mother could live with my father without being criticized for "putting love first." The general atmosphere was relaxed; the Communists were elated at their sweeping victories and my father's colleagues did not insist on married couples staying together only on Saturday nights.

Yibin had fallen less than two months earlier, on 11 December 1949. My father had arrived six days later, and had been appointed head of the county of Yibin, which had a population of over a million people, about 100,000 of whom lived in the city of Yibin. He had arrived by boat with a group of more than a hundred students who had "joined the revolution" in Nanjing. When the boat came up the Yangtze, it stopped first at the Yibin power station on the riverbank opposite the city, which had been a stronghold of the underground. Several hundred workers came out to greet my father's party on the quay, waving little red paper flags with five stars—the new flag of Communist China—and shouting welcoming slogans. The flags had the stars in the wrong place—the local Communists did not know the right place to put them. My father went ashore with another officer to address the workers, who were delighted when they heard him speaking in Yibin dialect. Instead of the ordinary army cap which everyone else was wearing he wore an old eight-cornered cap of the type which the Communist army used to wear in the 1920s and early 1930s, which struck the locals as unusual and rather stylish.

Then the boat took them across the river to the city. My father had been away ten years. He had been very fond of his family, especially his youngest sister, to whom he had written enthusiastically from Yan'an about his new life and how he wanted her to join him there someday. The letters had stopped coming as the Kuomintang tightened its blockade, and the first the family had heard from my father for many years was when they received the photo of him and my mother taken in Nanjing. For the previous seven years they had not even known if he was alive. They had missed him, cried at the thought of him, and prayed to the Buddha for his safe return. With the photograph he had sent a note saying he would soon be in Yibin, and that he had changed his name. While in Yan'an, like many others, he had taken a *nom de guerre*, Wang Yu. *Yu* meant "Selfless to the point of being considered foolish." As soon as he arrived my father reverted to his real surname, Chang, but he incorporated his *nom de guerre* and called himself Chang Shou-yu, meaning "Keep *Yu*."

Ten years before, my father had left as a poor, hungry, and put-upon apprentice; now he had returned, not yet thirty, as a powerful man. This was a traditional Chinese dream, which has entered the language as *yi-jin-huan-xiang*, "returning home robed in embroidered silk." His family was tremendously proud of him, and they were longing to see what he was like after ten years, as they had heard all sorts of strange things about the Communists. And of course his mother, especially, wanted to know about his new wife.

My father talked and laughed loudly and heartily. He was the picture of unrestrained, almost boyish excitement. He has not changed after all, his mother thought with a sigh of relief and happiness. Through their traditional, deep-rooted reserve, the family showed their joy in their eager, tear-filled eyes. Only his youngest sister was more animated. She talked vividly while playing with her long plaits, which every now and then she threw back over her shoulder when she tilted her head to emphasize what she was saying. My father smiled as he recognized the traditional Sichuan gesture of feminine playfulness. He had almost forgotten it in his ten years of austerity in the North.

There was a lot of catching up to do. My father's mother was well into her account of what had happened to the family since he had left when she said there was one thing worrying her: what was going to happen to her eldest daughter, who had looked after her in Chongqing. This daughter's husband had died and left her some land, which she had hired a few laborers to work. There were a lot of rumors flying around about the Communists' land reform, and the family was worried that she would be classified as a landlord and have her land taken away. The women became emotional, their worries shading into recriminations: "What is going to happen to her? How is she going to live? How can the Communists do a thing like this?"

My father was hurt and exasperated. He burst out: "I have looked forward so much to this day, to share our victory with you. All injustice is going to be a thing of the past. It is a time to be positive, to rejoice. But you are so distrustful, so critical. You only want to find fault . . ." Whereupon he burst into tears like a little boy. The women all cried too. For him, they were tears of disappointment and frustration. For them, the feelings must have been more complex; among them were doubt and uncertainty.

My father's mother was living in the old family home just outside the city, which had been left to her by her husband when he died. It was a modestly luxurious country house—low-lying, made of wood and brick, and walled off from the road. It had a big garden at the front, and at the back was a field of winter plums, which gave off a delicious perfume, and thick bamboo groves, which lent it the atmosphere of an enchanted garden. It was spotlessly clean. All the windows were gleaming, and there was not a speck of dust anywhere. The furniture was made of beautiful shiny padauk wood, which is a deep red, sometimes almost shading into black. My mother fell in love with the house from her first visit, on the day after she arrived in Yibin.

This was an important occasion. In Chinese tradition the person with the most power over a married woman was always her mother-in-law, to whom she had to be completely obedient and who would tyrannize her. When she in turn became a mother-in-law, she would bully her own daughter-in-law in the same way. Liberating daughters-in-law was an important Communist policy, and rumors abounded that Communist daughters-in-law were arrogant dragons, ready to boss their mothers-in-law around. Everyone was on tenterhooks waiting to see how my mother would behave.

My father had a very large extended family, and they all gathered in the house that day. As my mother approached the front gate, she heard people whispering, "She's coming, she's coming!" Adults were shushing their children, who were jumping around trying to catch a glimpse of the strange Communist daughter-in-law from the far north.

When my mother entered the sitting room with my father, her mother-in-law was seated at the far end on a formal, carved square padauk chair. Leading up to her on both sides of the room, enhancing the formality, were two symmetrical rows of square, exquisitely carved padauk chairs. A small table with a vase or some other ornament on it stood between every two chairs. Walking up the middle, my mother saw that her mother-in-law had a very calm face, with high cheekbones (which my father had inherited), small eyes, a sharp chin, and thin lips which drooped slightly at the corners. She was tiny, and her eyes seemed to be half closed, almost as though she were meditating.

My mother walked slowly up to her with my father, and stopped in front of her chair. Then she knelt and kowtowed three times. This was the correct thing to do according to the traditional ritual, but everyone had been wondering if the young Communist would go through with it. The room burst into relieved sighs. My father's cousins and sisters whispered to his obviously delighted mother: "What a lovely daughter-in-law! So gentle, so pretty, and so respectful! Mother, you are really in good fortune!"

My mother was quite proud of her little conquest. She and my father had spent some time discussing what to do. The Communists had said they were going to get rid of kowtowing, which they considered an insult to human dignity, but my mother wanted to make an exception, just this once. My father agreed. He did not want to hurt his mother, or offend his wife—not after the miscarriage; and besides, this kowtow was different. It was to make a point for the Communists. But he would not kowtow himself, although it was expected of him.

All the women in my father's family were Buddhists, and one of his sisters, Jun-ying, who was unmarried, was particularly devout. She took my mother to kowtow to a statue of the Buddha, to the shrines of the family ancestors which were set up on Chinese New Year, and even to the groves of winter plums and bamboo in the back garden. Aunt Jun-ying believed that every flower and every tree had a spirit. She would ask my mother to do a dozen kowtows to the bamboos to beg them not to flower, which the Chinese believed portended disaster. My mother found all this great fun. It reminded her of her childhood and gave her a chance to indulge her sense of playfulness. My father did not approve, but she mollified him by saying it was just a performance to help the Communists' image. The Kuomintang had said the Communists would wipe out all traditional customs, and she said it was important for people to see that this was not happening.

My father's family was very kind to my mother. In spite of her initial formality, my grandmother was in fact extremely easygoing. She seldom passed judgment, and was never critical. Aunt Jun-ying's round face was marked by smallpox, but her eyes were so gentle that anyone could see that she was a kind woman, with whom they could feel safe and relaxed. My mother could not help comparing her new in-laws with her own mother. They did not exude her energy and sprightliness, but their ease and serenity made my mother feel completely at home. Aunt Jun-ying cooked delicious spicy Sichuan food, which is quite different from the bland northern food. The dishes had exotic names which my mother loved: "tiger fights the dragon," "imperial concubine chicken," "hot saucy duck," "suckling golden cock crows to the dawn." My mother went to the house often, and would eat with the family, looking out into the orchard of plums, almonds, and peaches which made a sea of pink and white blossoms in early spring. She found a warm, welcoming atmosphere among the women in the Chang family, and felt very much loved by them.

My mother was soon assigned a job in the Public Affairs Department of the government of Yibin County. She spent very little time in the office. The first priority was to feed the population—and this was beginning to be difficult.

The southwest was the last holdout of the Kuomintang leadership, and a quarter of a million soldiers had been stranded in Sichuan when Chiang Kai-shek fled the province for Taiwan in December 1949. Sichuan was, moreover, one of the few places where the Communists had not occupied the countryside before they took the cities. Kuomintang units, disorganized but often well armed, still controlled much of the countryside in southern Sichuan, and most of the food supply was in the hands of landlords who were pro-Kuomintang. The Communists urgently needed to secure supplies to feed the cities, as well as their own forces and the large numbers of Kuomintang troops who had surrendered.

At first they sent people out to try to buy food. Many of the big landlords had traditionally had their own private armies, which now joined up with the bands of Kuomintang soldiers. A few days after my mother reached Yibin, these forces launched a full-scale uprising in south Sichuan. Yibin was in danger of starvation.

The Communists started sending out armed teams made up of officials escorted by army guards to collect food. Almost everyone was mobilized. Government offices were empty. In the whole of the Yibin county government only two women were left behind: one was a receptionist and the other had a newborn baby.

My mother went on a number of these expeditions, which lasted many days at a time. There were thirteen people in her team: seven civilians and six soldiers. My mother's gear consisted of a bedroll, a bag of rice, and a heavy umbrella made of tung-oil-painted canvas, all of which she had to carry on her back. The team had to trek for days through wild country and over what the Chinese call "sheep's-intestine trails"—treacherous narrow mountain paths winding around steep precipices and gullies. When they came to a village they would go to the shabbiest hovel and try to form a rapport with the very poor peasants, telling them that the Communists would give people like them their own land and a happy life, and then asking them which landowners had rice hoarded. Most of the peasants had inherited a traditional fear and suspicion of any officials. Many had only vaguely heard of the Communists, and everything they had heard was bad; but my mother, having quickly modified her northern dialect with a local accent, was highly articulate and persuasive. Explaining the new policy turned out to be her forte. If the team succeeded in getting information about the landlords, they would go and try to persuade them to sell at designated collection points, where they would be paid on delivery. Some were scared and disgorged without much fuss. Others informed on the team's whereabouts to one of the armed gangs. My mother and her comrades were often fired at, and spent every night on the alert, sometimes having to move from place to place to avoid attack.

At first they would stay with poor peasants. But if the bandits found out someone had helped them, they would kill the entire household. After a number of killings, the team decided they could not jeopardize innocent people's lives. So they slept in the open, or in abandoned temples.

On her third expedition, my mother started vomiting and suffering from dizzy spells. She was pregnant again. She got back to Yibin exhausted and desperate for a rest, but her team had to set off on another expedition at once. It had been left vague what a pregnant woman should do, and she was torn about whether to go or not. She wanted to go, and the mood at the time was very much one of self-sacrifice; it was considered shameful to complain about anything. But she was frightened by the memory of her miscarriage only five months before, and by the thought of having another one in the midst of the wilderness, where there were no doctors or transportation. Moreover, the expeditions involved almost daily battles with the bandits, and it was important to be able to run—and run fast. Even walking made her dizzy.

Still, she decided to go. There was one other woman going, who was also pregnant. One afternoon the team was settling down for lunch in a deserted courtyard. They assumed the owner had fled, probably from them. The shoulder-high mud walls which ran around the weed-covered yard had collapsed in several places. The wooden gate was unlocked and was creaking in the spring breeze. The team's rice was being prepared in the abandoned kitchen by their cook, when a middle-aged man appeared. He had the appearance of a peasant: he was wearing straw sandals and loose trousers, with a big apronlike piece of cloth tucked up on one side into a cotton cummerbund, and he had a dirty white turban on his head. He told them that a gang of men belonging to a notorious group of bandits known as the Broadsword Brigade was headed their way and that they were especially keen to capture my mother and the other woman in the team, because they knew they were the wives of high Communist officials.

This man was not an ordinary peasant. Under the Kuomintang, he had been the chieftain of the local township, which governed a number of villages, including the one the team was in. The Broadsword Brigade had tried to win his cooperation, as they did with all former Kuomintang men and landlords. He had joined the brigade, but he wanted to keep his options open, and he was tipping off the Communists to buy insurance. He told them the best way to escape.

The team immediately jumped up and ran. But my mother and the other pregnant woman could not move very fast, so the chieftain led them out through a gap in the wall and helped them hide in a haystack nearby. The cook lingered in the kitchen to wrap up the cooked rice and pour cold water onto the wok to cool it down so that he could take it with him. The rice and the wok were too precious to be abandoned; an iron wok was hard to obtain, especially in wartime. Two of the soldiers stayed in the kitchen helping him and trying to hurry him up. At last the cook grabbed the rice and the wok and the three of them raced for the back door. But the bandits were already coming through the front door, and caught up with them after a few yards. They fell on them and knifed them to death. The gang was short of guns and did not have enough ammunition to shoot at the rest of the team, whom they could see not far away. They did not discover my mother and the other woman in the haystack.

Not long afterward the gang was captured, along with the chieftain. He was both a leader of the gang and one of the "snakes in their old haunts," which made him eligible for execution. But he had tipped off the team and saved the lives of the two women. At the time, death sentences had to be endorsed by a three-man review board. It happened that the head of the tribunal was my father. The second member was the husband of the other pregnant woman, and the third was the local police chief.

The tribunal split two to one. The husband of the other woman voted to spare the chieftain's life. My father and the police chief voted to uphold the death sentence. My mother pleaded with the tribunal to let the man live, but my father was adamant. This was exactly what the man had been banking on, he told my mother: he had chosen this particular team to tip off precisely because he knew it contained the wives of two important officials. "He has a lot of blood on his hands," my father said. The husband of the other woman disagreed vehe-. mently. "But," my father retorted, banging his fist on the table, "we cannot be lenient, precisely *because* our wives are involved. If we let personal feelings influence our judgment, what would be the differ- ence between the new China and the old?" The chieftain was exe- cuted.

My mother could not forgive my father for this. She felt that the man should not die, because he had saved so many lives, and my father, in particular, "owed" him a life. The way she looked at it, which was how most Chinese would have seen it, my father's behavior meant he did not treasure her, unlike the husband of the other woman.

No sooner was the trial over than my mother's team was sent off to the countryside again. She was still feeling very sick from her preg- nancy, vomiting a lot and exhausted all the time. She had had pains in her abdomen ever since the violent rush to the haystack. The husband of the other pregnant woman decided he was not going to let his wife go again. "I will protect my pregnant wife," he said. "And I will protect any wives who are pregnant. No pregnant woman should have to undergo such dangers." But he met fierce opposition from my mother's boss, Mrs. Mi, a peasant woman who had been a guerrilla. It was unthinkable for a peasant woman to take a rest if she was pregnant. She worked right up to the moment of delivery, and there were innumerable stories about women cutting the umbilical cord with a sickle and carrying on. Mrs. Mi had borne her own baby on a battlefield and had had to abandon it on the spot—a baby's cry could have endangered the whole unit. After losing her child, she seemed to want others to suffer a similar fate. She insisted on sending my mother off again, producing a very effective argument. At the time, no Party members were allowed to marry except relatively senior offi- cials (those who qualified as "28-7-regiment-1"). Any woman who was pregnant, therefore, was virtually bound to be a member of the elite. And if they did not go, how could the Party hope to persuade other people to go? My father agreed with her, and told my mother she ought to go.

My mother accepted this, in spite of her fears of another miscar- riage. She was prepared to die, but she had hoped that my father would be against her going—and would say so; that way she would have felt he put her safety first. But she could see that my father's first loyalty was to the revolution, and she was bitterly disappointed.

She spent several painful and exhausting weeks traipsing around the hills and mountains. The skirmishes were intensifying. Almost every day came news of members of other teams being tortured and murdered by bandits. They were particularly sadistic to women. One day the corpse of one of my father's nieces was dumped just outside the city gate: she had been raped and knifed, and her vagina was a bloody mess. Another young woman was caught by the Broadsword Brigade during a skirmish. They were surrounded by armed Communists, so they tied the woman up and told her to shout out to her comrades to let them escape. Instead she shouted, "Go ahead, don't worry about me!" Every time she called out one of the bandits cut a hunk out of her flesh with a knife. She died horribly mutilated. After several such incidents, it was decided that women would not be sent on food-collecting expeditions anymore.

Meanwhile, in Jinzhou my grandmother had been worrying constantly about her daughter. As soon as she got a letter from her saying she had arrived in Yibin, she decided to go and make sure she was all right. In March 1950 she set off on her own long march across China, alone.

She knew nothing about the rest of the huge country, and imagined that Sichuan was not only mountainous and cut off, but also lacking in the daily necessities of life. Her first instinct was to take a large supply of basic goods with her. But the country was still in a state of upheaval, and fighting was still going on along her intended route; she realized she was going to have to carry her own luggage, and probably walk a good deal of the way, which was extremely difficult on bound feet. In the end she settled on one small bundle, which she could carry herself.

Her feet had grown bigger since she had married Dr. Xia. By tradition, the Manchus did not practice foot-binding, so my grandmother had taken off the binding cloths and her feet gradually grew a little. This process was almost as painful as the original binding. The broken bones could not mend, of course, so the feet did not go back to their original shape, but remained crippled and shrunken. My grandmother wanted her feet to look normal, so she used to stuff cotton wool into her shoes.

Before she left, Lin Xiao-xia, the man who had brought her to my parents' wedding, gave her a document which said she was the mother of a revolutionary; with this, Party organizations along the way would provide her with food, accommodations, and money. She followed almost the same route as my parents, taking the train part of the way, sometimes traveling in trucks, and walking when there was no other transportation. Once she was on an open truck with some women and children who all belonged to families of Communists. The truck stopped for some of the children to have a pee. The moment it did so bullets ripped into the wooden planks around the side. My grandmother hunkered down in the back while bullets zinged by inches above her head. The guards fired back with machine guns and managed to silence the attackers, who turned out to be Kuomintang stragglers. My grandmother emerged unscathed, but several of the children and some of the guards were killed.

When she got to Wuhan, a big city in central China, which was about two-thirds of the way, she was told that the next stretch, by boat up the Yangtze, was unsafe because of bandits. She had to wait a month until things quieted down—even so, her ship was attacked several times from the shore. The boat, which was rather ancient, had a flat, open deck, so the guards built a wall of sandbags about four feet high down both sides of it, with slits for their guns. It looked like a floating fortress. Whenever it was fired on, the captain would put it on full steam ahead and try to race through the fusillade, while the guards shot back from behind their sandbagged embrasures. My grandmother would go belowdecks and wait until the shooting was over.

She changed to a smaller boat at Yichang and passed through the Yangtze Gorges, and by May she was near Yibin, sitting in a boat covered with palm fronds, sailing quietly among crystal-clear ripples, the breeze scented with orange blossom.

The boat was rowed upstream by a dozen oarsmen. As they rowed they sang traditional Sichuan opera arias and improvised songs about the names of the villages they were passing, the legends of the hills, and the spirits of the bamboo groves. They sang about their moods too. My grandmother was most amused by the flirtatious songs they sang to one of the female passengers, with a twinkle in their eye. She could not understand most of the expressions they used, because they were in Sichuan dialect, but she could tell they were sexually suggestive by the way the passengers gave out low laughs betraying both pleasure and embarrassment. She had heard about the Sichuan character, which was supposed to be as saucy and spicy as the food. My grandmother was in a happy mood. She did not know that my mother had had several close shaves with death, nor had my mother said anything about her miscarriage.

It was mid-May when she arrived. The journey had taken over two months. My mother, who had been feeling sick and miserable, was ecstatic at seeing her again. My father was not so pleased. Yibin was the first time he had been alone with my mother in an even semi-stable situation. He had only just gotten away from his mother-in-law, and now here she was again, when he had hoped she was a thousand miles away. He was well aware that he was no match for the bonds between mother and daughter.

My mother was seething with resentment against my father. Since the bandit threat had become more acute, the quasi-military life-style had been reinstated. And because they were both away so much, my mother rarely spent the night with my father. He was traveling around the country most of the time, investigating conditions in the rural areas, hearing the peasants' complaints, and dealing with every kind of problem, particularly ensuring the food supply. Even when he was in Yibin, my father would work late at the office. My parents were seeing less and less of each other, and were drifting apart again.

The arrival of my grandmother reopened old wounds. She was allotted a room in the courtyard where my parents were living. At the time, all officials were living on a comprehensive allowance system called *gong-ji-zhi*. They received no salary, but the state provided them with housing, food, clothing, and daily necessities, plus a tiny amount of pocket money—as in an army. Everyone had to eat in canteens, where the food was meager and unappetizing. You were not allowed to cook at home, even if you had cash from some other source.

When my grandmother arrived she started selling some of her jewelry to buy food in the market; she was especially keen to cook for my mother because it was traditionally thought vital for pregnant women to eat well. But soon complaints started pouring in via Mrs. Mi about my mother being "bourgeois"—getting privileged treatment and using up precious fuel which, like food, had to be collected from the countryside. She was also criticized for being "pampered"; having her mother there was bad for her reeducation. My father made a self-criticism to his Party organization and ordered my grandmother to stop cooking at home. My mother resented this, and so did my grandmother. "Can't you stand up for me just once?" my mother said bitterly. "The baby I am carrying is yours as well as mine, and it needs nourishment!" Eventually my father conceded a little: my grandmother could cook at home twice a week, but no more. Even this was breaking the rules, he said.

It turned out that my grandmother was breaking a more important rule. Only officials of a certain rank were entitled to have their parents staying with them, and my mother did not qualify. Because officials did not receive salaries, the state was responsible for looking after their dependents, and wanted to keep the numbers down. Even though my father was senior enough, he let his own mother continue to be supported by Aunt Jun-ying. My mother pointed out that her mother would not be a burden on the state, because she had enough jewelry to support herself, and she had been invited to stay with Aunt Jun-ying. Mrs. Mi said my grandmother should not be there at all and would have to go back to Manchuria. My father agreed.

My mother argued vehemently with him, but he said that a rule was a rule—and he would not fight to have it bent. In old China one of the major vices was that anyone with power was above the rules, and an important component of the Communist revolution was that officials, like everyone else, should be subject to rules. My mother was in tears. She was afraid of having another miscarriage. Perhaps my father could consider her safety and let her mother stay until the birth? Still he said no. "Corruption always starts with little things like this. This is the sort of thing that will erode our revolution." My mother could not find any argument to win him over. He has no feelings, she thought. He does not put my interests first. He does not love me.

My grandmother had to go, and my mother was never to forgive my father for this. My grandmother had been with her daughter for little more than a month, having spent over two months traveling across China, at the risk of her life. She was afraid my mother might have another miscarriage, and she did not trust the medical services in Yibin. Before she left she went to see my aunt Jun-ying and solemnly kowtowed to her, saying she was leaving my mother in her care. My aunt was sad, too. She was worried about my mother, and wanted my grandmother to be there for the birth. She went to plead with her brother, but he would not budge.

With a heavy heart, and amid bitter tears, my grandmother hobbled down to the quay with my mother to take the little boat back down the Yangtze on the start of the long and uncertain journey back to Manchuria. My mother stood on the riverbank, waving as the boat disappeared into the mist, and wondering if she would ever see her mother again.

It was July 1950. My mother's one-year provisional membership in the Party was due to end, and her Party cell was grilling her intensively. It had only three members: my mother, my father's bodyguard, and my mother's boss, Mrs. Mi. There were so few Party members in Yibin that these three had been thrown together rather incongruously. The other two, who were both full members, were leaning toward turning down my mother's application, but they did not give a straightforward no. They just kept grilling her and forcing her to make endless self-criticisms.

For each self-criticism, there were many criticisms. My mother's two comrades insisted that she had behaved in a "bourgeois" manner. They said she had not wanted to go to the country to help collect food; when she pointed out that she had gone, in line with the Party's wishes, they retorted: "Ah, but you didn't really want to go." Then they accused her of having enjoyed privileged food—cooked, moreover, by her mother at home—and of succumbing to illness more than most pregnant women. Mrs. Mi also criticized her because her mother had made clothes for the baby. "Who ever heard of a baby wearing new clothes?" she said. "Such a bourgeois waste! Why can't she just wrap the baby up in old clothes like everyone else?" The fact that my mother had shown her sadness that my grandmother had to leave was singled out as definitive proof that she "put family first," a serious offense.

The summer of 1950 was the hottest in living memory, with high humidity and temperatures above 100°F. My mother had been washing every day, and she was attacked for this, too. Peasants, especially in the North where Mrs. Mi came from, washed very rarely, because of the shortage of water. In the guerrillas, men and women used to compete to see who had the most "revolutionary insects" (lice). Cleanliness was regarded as unproletarian. When the steamy summer turned into cool autumn my father's bodyguard weighed in with a new accusation: my mother was "behaving like a Kuomintang official's grand lady" because she had used my father's leftover hot water. At the time, in order to save fuel, there was a rule that only officials above a certain rank were entitled to wash with hot water. My father fell into this group, but my mother did not. She had been strongly advised by the women in my father's family not to touch cold water when she came near to delivery time. After the bodyguard's criticism, my father would not let my mother use his water. My mother felt like screaming at him for not taking her side against the endless intrusions into the most irrelevant recesses of her life.

The Party's all-around intrusion into people's lives was the very point of the process known as "thought reform." Mao wanted not only external discipline, but the total subjection of all thoughts, large or small. Every week a meeting for "thought examination" was held for those "in the revolution." Everyone had both to criticize themselves for incorrect thoughts and be subjected to the criticism of others. The meetings tended to be dominated by self-righteous and petty-minded people, who used them to vent their envy and frustration; people of peasant origin used them to attack those from "bourgeois" backgrounds. The idea was that people should be reformed to be more like peasants, because the Communist revolution was in essence a peasant revolution. This process appealed to the guilt feelings of the educated; they had been living better than the peasants, and self-criticism tapped into this.

Meetings were an important means of Communist control. They left people no free time, and eliminated the private sphere. The pettiness which dominated them was justified on the grounds that prying into personal details was a way of ensuring thorough soul-cleansing. In fact, pettiness was a fundamental characteristic of a revolution in which intrusiveness and ignorance were celebrated, and envy was incorporated into the system of control. My mother's cell grilled her week after week, month after month, forcing her to produce endless self-criticisms.

She had to consent to this agonizing process. Life for a revolutionary was meaningless if they were rejected by the Party. It was like excommunication for a Catholic. Besides, it was standard procedure. My father had gone through it and had accepted it as part of "joining the revolution." In fact, he was still going through it. The Party had never hidden the fact that it was a painful process. He told my mother her anguish was normal.

At the end of all this, my mother's two comrades voted against full Party membership for her. She fell into a deep depression. She had been devoted to the revolution, and could not accept the idea that it did not want her; it was particularly galling to think she might not get in for completely petty and irrelevant reasons, decided by two people whose way of thinking seemed light years away from what she had conceived the Party's ideology to be. She was being kept out of a progressive organization by backward people, and yet the revolution seemed to be telling her that it was she who was in the wrong. At the back of her mind was another, more practical point which she did not even spell out to herself: it was vital to get into the Party, because if she failed she would be stigmatized and ostracized.

With these thoughts churning through her mind, my mother came to feel the world was against her. She dreaded seeing people and spent as much time as possible alone, crying to herself. Even this she had to conceal, as it would have been considered as showing lack of faith in the revolution. She found she could not blame the Party, which seemed to her to be in the right, so she blamed my father, first for making her pregnant and then for not standing by her when she was attacked and rejected. Many times she wandered along the quay, gazing down into the muddy waters of the Yangtze, and thought of committing suicide to punish him, picturing to herself how he would be filled with remorse when he found she had killed herself.

The recommendation of her cell had to be approved by a higher authority, which consisted of three open-minded intellectuals. They thought my mother had been treated unfairly, but the Party rules made it difficult for them to overturn the recommendation of her cell. So they procrastinated. This was relatively easy because the three were seldom in one place at the same time. Like my father and the other male officials, they were usually away in different parts of the countryside foraging for food and fighting bandits. Knowing that Yibin was almost undefended, and driven to desperation by the fact that all their escape routes—both to Taiwan and through Yunnan to Indochina and Burma—had been cut, a sizable army of Kuomintang stragglers, landlords, and bandits laid siege to the city, and for a time it looked as though it was going to fall. My father raced back from the countryside as soon as he heard about the attack.

The fields started just outside the city walls and there was vegetation to within a few yards of the gates. Using this for cover, the attackers managed to get right up to the walls and began to pound the north gate with huge battering rams. In the vanguard was the Broadsword Brigade, consisting largely of unarmed peasants who had drunk "holy water" which, they believed, made them immune to bullets. The Kuomintang soldiers were behind them. At first the Communist army commander tried to aim his fire at the Kuomintang, not at the peasants, whom he hoped to scare into retreating.

Even though my mother was seven months pregnant, she joined the other women in taking food and water to the defenders on the walls and carrying the wounded to the rear. Thanks to the training she had had at school, she was good at first aid. She was also brave. After about a week, the attackers abandoned the siege and the Communists counterattacked, mopping up virtually all armed resistance in the area for good.

Immediately after this, land reform started in the Yibin area. The Communists had passed an agrarian reform law that summer, which was the key to their program for transforming China. The basic concept, which they called "the land returning home," was to redistribute all farmland, as well as draft animals and houses, so that every farmer owned a more or less equal amount of land. Landowners were to be allowed to keep a plot, on the same basis as everyone else. My father was one of the people running the program. My mother was excused from going to the villages because of her advanced pregnancy.

Yibin was a rich place. A local saying has it that with one year's work, peasants could live at ease for two. But decades of incessant warfare had devastated the land; on top of this had come heavy taxes to pay for the fighting and for the eight-year war against Japan. Depredations had escalated when Chiang Kai-shek moved his wartime capital to Sichuan, and corrupt officials and carpetbaggers had descended on the province. The last straw came when the Kuomintang made Sichuan their final redoubt in 1949 and levied exorbitant taxes just before the Communists arrived. All this, plus greedy landlords, had combined to produce appalling poverty in the rich province. Eighty percent of the peasants did not have enough to feed their families. If the crops failed, many were reduced to eating herbs and the leaves of sweet potatoes, which were normally fed to pigs. Starvation was widespread, and life expectancy was only about forty years. The poverty in such a rich land was one of the reasons my father had been attracted to communism in the first place.

In Yibin the land reform drive was on the whole nonviolent, partly because the fiercer landlords had been involved in the rebellions during the first nine months of Communist rule and had already been killed in battle or executed. But there was some violence. In one case a Party member raped the female members of a landowner's family and then mutilated them by cutting off their breasts. My father ordered that the man be executed.

One bandit gang had captured a young Communist, a university graduate, while he was out in the country looking for food. The bandit chief ordered him to be cut in half. The chief was later caught, and beaten to death by the Communist land reform team leader, who had been a friend of the man who had been killed. The team leader then cut out the chief's heart and ate it to demonstrate his revenge. My father ordered the team leader to be dismissed from his job, but not shot. He reasoned that while he had engaged in a form of brutality, it was not against an innocent person but a murderer, and a cruel one at that.

The land reform took over a year to complete. In the majority of cases, the worst the landlords suffered was the loss of most of their land and their homes. So-called open-minded landlords, those who had not joined the armed rebellion, or who had actually helped the Communist underground, were treated well. My parents had friends whose families were local landlords, and had been to dinner at their grand old houses before they were confiscated and divided up among the peasants.

My father was completely wrapped up in his work, and was not in town when my mother gave birth to her first child, a girl, on 8 November. Because Dr. Xia had given my mother the name De-hong, which incorporates the character for "wild swan" *(Hong)* with a generation name *(De)*, my father named my sister Xiao-hong, which means "to be like" *(Xiao)* my mother. Seven days after my sister's birth Aunt Jun-ying had my mother brought home from the hospital to the Chang house on a bamboo litter carried by two men. When my father got back a few weeks later, he said to my mother that, as a Communist, she should not have allowed herself to be carried by other human beings. She said she had done it because, according to traditional wisdom, women were not supposed to walk for a while after a birth. To this my father replied: what about the peasant women who have to carry on working in the fields immediately after they give birth?

My mother was still in a deep depression, uncertain whether she could stay in the Party or not. Unable to let her rage out on my father or the Party, she blamed her baby daughter for her misery. Four days after they came out of the hospital, my sister cried all through the night. My mother was at the end of her tether, and screamed at her and smacked her quite hard. Aunt Jun-ying, who was sleeping in the next room, rushed in and said: "You're exhausted. Let me look after her." From then on my aunt looked after my sister. When my mother went back to her own place a few weeks later my sister stayed on with Aunt Jun-ying in the family house.

To this day my mother remembers with grief and remorse the night she hit my sister. When my mother went to see her, Xiao-hong used to hide, and—in a tragic reversal of what had happened to her as a young child at General Xue's mansion—my mother would not allow Xiao-hong to call her "Mother."

My aunt found a wet-nurse for my sister. Under the allowance system the state paid for a wet-nurse for every newborn baby in an official's family, and also provided free physical checkups for the wet-nurses, who were treated as state employees. They were not servants, and did not even have to wash diapers. The state could afford to pay for them since, according to the Party's rules governing people "in the revolution," the only ones who were allowed to marry were senior officials, and they produced relatively few babies.

The wet-nurse was in her late teens, and her own baby had been stillborn. She had married into a landlord family who had now lost their income from the land. She did not want to work as a peasant, but wanted to be with her husband, who taught and lived in Yibin City. Through mutual friends she was put in touch with my aunt and went to live in the Chang family house with her husband.

Gradually my mother began to pull out of her depression. After the birth she was allowed thirty days' statutory leave, which she spent with her mother-in-law and Aunt Jun-ying. When she went back to work she moved to a new job in the Communist Youth League of Yibin City, in connection with a complete reorganization of the region. The region of Yibin, covering an area of about 7,500 square miles and with a population of over two million, was redivided into nine rural counties and one city, Yibin. My father became a member of the four-man committee which governed the whole of the region and the head of the Department of Public Affairs for the region.

This reorganization transferred Mrs. Mi and brought my mother a new boss: the head of the Department of Public Affairs for the city of Yibin, which controlled the Youth League. In Communist China, in spite of the formal rules, the personality of one's immediate boss was far more important than in the West. The boss's attitude is the Party's. Having a nice boss makes all the difference to one's life.

My mother's new chief was a woman called Zhang Xi-ting. She and her husband had been in an army unit which was part of the force earmarked to take Tibet in 1950. Sichuan was the staging post for Tibet, which was considered the back of beyond by Han Chinese. The couple had asked to be discharged and were sent to Yibin instead. Her husband was called Liu Jie-ting. He had changed his name to Jie-ting ("Linked to Ting") to show how much he admired his wife. The couple became known as "the two Tings."

In the spring my mother was promoted to head of the Youth League, an important job for a woman not yet twenty. She had recovered her equilibrium and much of her old bounce. It was in this atmosphere that I was conceived, in June 1951.

9. "When a Man Gets Power, Even His Chickens and Dogs Rise to Heaven"— Living with an Incorruptible Man

(1951–1953)

My mother was now in a new Party cell, made up of herself, Mrs. Ting, and a third woman who had been in the Yibin underground, with whom my mother got on very well. The nonstop intrusion and demands for self-criticisms came to an immediate halt. Her new cell quickly voted for her to become a full Party member, and in July she was given Party membership.

Her new boss, Mrs. Ting, was no beauty, but her slender figure, sensuous mouth, freckled face, lively eyes, and sharp repartee all exuded energy and showed she was a character. My mother warmed to her at once.

Instead of sniping at her like Mrs. Mi, Mrs. Ting let my mother do all sorts of things she wanted, like reading novels; before, reading a book without a Marxist cover would bring down a rain of criticism about being a bourgeois intellectual. Mrs. Ting allowed my mother to go to the cinema on her own, which was a great privilege, as at the time those "with the revolution" were allowed to see only Soviet films—and even then only in organized groups—whereas the public cinemas, which were privately owned, were still showing old American films, such as Charlie Chaplin's. Another thing which meant a lot to my mother was that she could now have a bath every other day.

One day my mother went to the market with Mrs. Ting and bought two yards of fine pink flower-patterned cotton from Poland. She had seen the cloth before, but had not dared to buy it for fear of being criticized for being frivolous. Soon after she had reached Yibin, she had had to hand in her army uniform and return to her "Lenin suit." Under that she wore a shapeless, undyed, rough cotton shirt. There was no rule saying it was compulsory to wear this garb, but anyone who did not do the same as everybody else would come in for criticism. My mother had been longing to wear a dash of color. She and Mrs. Ting rushed over to the Changs' house with the cloth in a state of high excitement. In no time, four pretty blouses were ready, two for each of them. Next day they wore them under their Lenin jackets. My mother turned her pink collar out and spent the whole day feeling terribly excited and nervous. Mrs. Ting was even more daring; she not only turned her collar outside her uniform, but rolled up her sleeves so that a broad band of pink showed on each arm.

My mother was staggered, almost awestruck, at this defiance. As expected, there were plenty of disapproving glances. But Mrs. Ting held her chin up: "Who cares?" she said to my mother. My mother was tremendously relieved; with the sanction of her boss, she could ignore any criticisms, verbal or wordless.

One reason Mrs. Ting was not frightened of bending the rules a bit was that she had a powerful husband, who was less scrupulous in exercising his power. A sharp-nosed, sharp-chinned, and slightly hunched man of my father's age, Mr. Ting was head of the Party Organization Department for the region of Yibin, which was a very important position, as this department was in charge of promotions, demotions, and punishments. It also kept the files of Party members. In addition, Mr. Ting, like my father, was a member of the four-man committee governing the region of Yibin.

In the Youth League my mother was working with people her own age. They were better educated, more carefree, and more ready to see the humorous side of things than the older, self-righteous, peasant-turned-Party-official women she had been working with before. Her new colleagues liked dancing, they went on picnics together, and they enjoyed talking about books and ideas.

Having a responsible job also meant my mother was treated with more respect, and this increased as people realized that she was extremely capable as well as dynamic. As she grew to be more confident and to rely less on my father, she felt less disappointed with him.

Besides, she was getting used to his attitudes; she had stopped expecting him always to put her first, and was much more at peace with the world.

Another bonus of my mother's promotion was that it qualified her to bring her mother to Yibin on a permanent basis. At the end of August 1951, after an exhausting journey, my grandmother and Dr. Xia arrived; the transportation system was working properly again and they had traveled the whole way by regular train and boat. As dependents of a government official, they were assigned lodgings at the state's expense, a three-room house in a guesthouse compound. They received a free ration of basic goods, like rice and fuel, which were delivered to them by the manager of the compound, and they were also given a small allowance to buy other food. My sister and her wet-nurse went to live with them, and my mother spent most of her brief spare time there, enjoying my grandmother's delicious cooking.

My mother was delighted to have her mother—and Dr. Xia, whom she loved—with her. She was particularly glad that they had gotten away from Jinzhou, as war had recently broken out in Korea, on the doorstep of Manchuria; at one point in late 1950 American troops had stood on the banks of the Yalu River, on the border between Korea and China, and American planes had bombed and strafed towns in Manchuria.

One of the first things my mother wanted to know was what had happened to Hui-ge, the young colonel. She was devastated to hear that he had been executed by firing squad, by the bend in the river outside the western gate of Jinzhou.

For the Chinese, one of the most terrible things that could happen was not to have a proper burial. They believed that only when the body was covered and placed deep in the earth could the dead find peace. This was a religious feeling, but it also had a practical side: if the body was not buried, it would be torn to pieces by wild dogs and picked to the bone by birds. In the past, the bodies of people who had been executed had traditionally been exposed for three days as a lesson to the population; only then were the corpses collected and given a sort of burial. Now the Communists issued an order that the family should immediately bury an executed relative; if they could not do it, the task was carried out by gravediggers hired by the government.

My grandmother had gone herself to the execution ground. Hui-ge's body had been left lying on the ground, riddled with bullets, one of a row of corpses. He had been shot along with fifteen other people. Their blood had stained the snow dark red. There was no one from his family left in the city, so my grandmother had hired professional undertakers to give him a decent burial. She herself brought a long piece of red silk in which to wrap his body. My mother asked if there were other people she knew there. Yes, there had been. My grandmother had bumped into a woman she knew who was collecting the corpses of her husband and her brother. Both had been Kuomintang district chiefs.

My mother was also horrified to hear that my grandmother had been denounced—by her own sister-in-law, Yu-lin's wife. She had long felt put-upon by my grandmother, as she had to do the hard work around the house, while my grandmother ran it as its mistress. The Communists had urged everyone to speak up about "oppression and exploitation," so Mrs. Yu-lin's grudges were given a political framework. When my grandmother collected Hui-ge's corpse Mrs. Yu-lin denounced her for being well-disposed toward a criminal. The neighborhood gathered to hold a "struggle meeting" to "help" my grandmother understand her "faults." My grandmother had to attend, but wisely decided to say nothing and appear meekly to accept the criticism. Inwardly, she was fuming against her sister-in-law and the Communists.

The episode did not help relations between my grandmother and my father. When he found out what she had done, he was enraged, saying she was more in sympathy with the Kuomintang than with the Communists. But it was obvious that he also felt a twinge of jealousy. While she hardly spoke to my father, my grandmother had been very fond of Hui-ge and had considered him a good match for my mother.

My mother was caught in the middle—between her mother and her husband; and between her personal feelings, her grief over Hui-ge's death, and her political feelings, her commitment to the Communists.

The execution of the colonel was part of a campaign to "suppress counterrevolutionaries." Its goal was to eliminate all supporters of the Kuomintang who had had power or influence, and it was triggered by the Korean War, which had started in June 1950. When U.S. troops had come right up to the Manchurian border Mao had feared the United States might attack China, or unleash Chiang Kai-shek's army against the mainland, or both. He sent over a million men into Korea to fight on the side of the North Koreans against the Americans.

Although Chiang Kai-shek's army never left Taiwan, the United States did organize an invasion into southwest China by Kuomintang forces from Burma; raids were also frequent in the coastal areas, many agents were landed, and acts of sabotage increased. Large numbers of Kuomintang soldiers and bandits were still at large and there were sizable rebellions in parts of the hinterland. The Communists worried that supporters of the Kuomintang might try to topple their newly established order, and that if Chiang Kai-shek tried to stage a comeback they would rise up as a fifth column. They also wanted to show people that they were there to stay, and getting rid of their opponents was one way to impress the concept of stability on the population, who had traditionally yearned for it. However, opinions were divided about the degree of ruthlessness necessary. The new government decided not to be fainthearted. As one official document put it: "If we do not kill them they will come back and kill us."

My mother was not convinced by the argument, but she decided there was not much point trying to talk to my father about it. In fact she rarely saw him, as he spent much of the time away in the countryside, troubleshooting. Even when he was in town, she did not see much of him. Officials were supposed to work from 8 A.M. until 11 P.M., seven days a week, and one or both of them usually came home so late they hardly had time to talk to each other. Their baby daughter did not live with them, and they ate in the canteen, so there was almost nothing one could call a home life.

Once the land reform was completed, my father was off again, supervising the construction of the first proper road through the region. Formerly, the only link between Yibin and the outside world had been by river. The government decided to build a road south to the province of Yunnan. In only one year, using no machinery at all, they built over eighty miles through a very hilly area, with numerous rivers. The labor force was made up of peasants, who worked in exchange for food.

During the digging, the peasants hit the skeleton of a dinosaur, which got slightly damaged. My father made a self-criticism and ensured it was excavated carefully and shipped to a museum in Peking. He also sent soldiers to guard some tombs dating from about A.D. 200 from which the peasants had been taking bricks to improve their pigsties.

One day two peasants were killed by a rock slide. My father walked through the night along mountain paths to the scene of the accident. This was the first time in their lives the local peasants had set eyes on an official of my father's rank, and they were moved to see that he was concerned about their well-being. In the past it had been assumed that all officials were only out to line their pockets. After what my father did, the locals thought the Communists were marvelous.

Meanwhile, one of my mother's main jobs was to galvanize support for the new government, particularly among factory workers. From the beginning of 1951 she had been visiting factories, making speeches, listening to complaints, and sorting out problems. Her job included explaining to the young workers what communism was and encouraging them to join the Youth League and the Party. She lived for long periods in a couple of factories: Communists were supposed to "live and work among the workers and peasants," as my father was doing, and to know their needs.

One factory just outside the city made insulating circuits. Living conditions there, as in every other factory, were appalling, with scores of women sleeping in a huge shack built of straw and bamboo. The food was woefully inadequate: the workers got meat only about twice a month, even though they were doing exhausting work. Many of the women had to stand in cold water for eight hours at a stretch washing the porcelain insulators. Tuberculosis, from malnutrition and lack of hygiene, was common. The eating bowls and chopsticks were never properly washed and were all mixed up together.

In March my mother began to cough up a little blood. She knew at once that she had TB, but she kept on working. She was happy because no one was intruding on her life. She believed in what she was doing, and she was excited by the results of her work: conditions in the factory were improving, the young workers liked her, and many pledged their allegiance to the Communist cause as the result of her. She genuinely felt that the revolution needed her devotion and self-sacrifice, and she worked flat out, all day, seven days a week. But after working without a break for months, it became obvious that she was extremely ill. Four cavities had developed in her lungs. By the summer she was also pregnant with me.

One day in late November my mother fainted on the factory floor. She was rushed to a small hospital in the city which had originally been set up by foreign missionaries. There she was looked after by Chinese Catholics. There was still one European priest there, and a few European nuns wearing religious habits. Mrs. Ting encouraged my grandmother to bring her food, and my mother ate an enormous amount—a whole chicken, ten eggs, and a pound of meat a day sometimes. As a result, I became gigantic in her womb—and she put on thirty pounds.

The hospital had a small amount of American medicine for TB. Mrs. Ting charged in and got hold of the whole lot for my mother. When my father found out he asked Mrs. Ting to take at least half of it back, but she snapped at him: "What sense does that make? As it is, this is not enough for one person. If you don't believe me, you can go and ask the doctor. Besides, your wife works under me and I am making the decisions about her." My mother was enormously grateful to Mrs. Ting for standing up to my father. He did not insist. He was obviously torn between concern for my mother's health and his principles, according to which his wife's interest must not override that of the ordinary people, and at least some of the medicine ought to be saved for others.

Because of my huge size and the way I grew upward, the cavities in her lungs were compressed and started to close. The doctors told her this was a compliment to her baby, but my mother thought the credit should probably go to the American medicine she had been able to take, thanks to Mrs. Ting. My mother stayed in the hospital three months, until February 1952, when she was eight months pregnant. One day she was suddenly asked to leave, "for her own safety." An official told her that some guns had been found in the residence of a foreign priest in Peking, and all foreign priests and nuns had fallen under extreme suspicion.

She did not want to leave. The hospital was set in a pretty garden with beautiful water lilies, and she found the professional care and the clean environment, which were rare in China at that time, extremely soothing. But she had no choice, and was moved to the Number One People's Hospital. The director of this hospital had never delivered a baby before. He had been a doctor with the Kuomintang army until his unit had mutinied and gone over to the Communists. He was worried that if my mother died giving birth, he would be in dire trouble because of his background and because my father was a high official.

Near the date when I was due to appear, the director suggested to my father that my mother should be moved to a hospital in a larger city, where there were better facilities and specialist obstetricians. He was afraid that when I emerged, the sudden removal of pressure might cause the cavities in my mother's lung to reopen and produce a hemorrhage. But my father refused; he said his wife had to be treated like anyone else, as the Communists had pledged themselves to combat privilege. When my mother heard this she thought bitterly that he always seemed to act against her interest and that he did not care whether she lived or died.

I was born on 25 March 1952. Because of the complexity of the case, a second surgeon was invited in from another hospital. Several other doctors were present, along with staff with extra oxygen and blood transfusion equipment, and Mrs. Ting. Chinese men traditionally did not attend births, but the director asked my father to stand by outside the delivery room because it was a special case—and to protect himself in case anything went wrong. It was a very difficult delivery. When my head came out, my shoulders, which were unusually broad, got caught. And I was too fat. The nurses pulled my head with their hands, and I came out squeezed blue and purple, and half strangled. The doctors placed me first in hot water, then in cold water, and lifted me up by my feet and smacked me hard. Eventually I started crying, very loudly, too. They all laughed with relief. I weighed just over ten pounds. My mother's lungs were undamaged.

A woman doctor picked me up and showed me to my father, whose first words were: "Oh dear, this child has bulging eyes!" My mother was very upset at this remark. Aunt Jun-ying said, "No, she just has beautiful big eyes!"

As for every occasion and condition in China, there was a particular dish considered just right for a woman immediately after she had given birth: poached eggs in raw sugar juice with fermented glutinous rice. My grandmother prepared these in the hospital, which, like all hospitals, had kitchens where patients and their families could cook their own food, and had them ready the minute my mother was able to eat.

When the news of my birth reached Dr. Xia, he said: "Ah, another wild swan is born." I was given the name Er-hong, which means "Second Wild Swan."

Giving me my name was almost the last act in Dr. Xia's long life. Four days after I was born he died, at the age of eighty-two. He was leaning back in bed drinking a glass of milk. My grandmother went out of the room for a minute and when she came back to get the glass she saw the milk had spilled and the glass had fallen to the floor. He had died instantly and painlessly.

Funerals were very important events in China. Ordinary people would often bankrupt themselves to lay on a grand ceremony—and my grandmother loved Dr. Xia and wanted to do him proud. There were three things she absolutely insisted on: first, a good coffin; second, that the coffin must be carried by pallbearers and not pulled on a cart; and third, to have Buddhist monks to chant the sutras for the dead and musicians to play the *suona*, a piercing woodwind instrument traditionally used at funerals. My father agreed to the first and second requests, but vetoed the third. The Communists regarded any extravagant ceremony as wasteful and "feudal." Traditionally, only very lowly people were buried quietly. Noise-making was considered important at a funeral to make it a public affair: this brought "face" and also showed respect for the dead. My father insisted there could be no *suona* or monks. My grandmother had a blazing row with him. For her, these were essentials which she just had to have. In the middle of the altercation she fainted from anger and grief. She was also wrought up because she was all alone at the saddest moment of her life. She had not told my mother what had happened, for fear of upsetting her, and the fact that my mother was in the hospital meant that my grandmother had to deal directly with my father. After the funeral she had a nervous breakdown and had to be hospitalized for almost two months.

Dr. Xia was buried in a cemetery on top of a hill on the edge of Yibin, overlooking the Yangtze. His grave was shaded by pines, cypresses, and camphor trees. In his short time in Yibin Dr. Xia had won the love and respect of all who knew him. When he died, the manager of the guesthouse where he had been living arranged everything for my grandmother and led his staff in the silent funeral procession.

Dr. Xia had been happy in his old age. He loved Yibin and took tremendous pleasure in all the exotic flowers which flourished in the subtropical climate, so different from Manchuria. Right up until the very end he enjoyed extraordinarily good health. He had had a good life in Yibin, with his own house and courtyard rent free; he and my grandmother were well looked after, with abundant supplies of food delivered to their home. It was the dream of every Chinese, in a society without any social security, to be cared for in old age. Dr. Xia was able to enjoy this, and it was no small thing.

Dr. Xia had got on very well with everybody, including my father, who respected him enormously as a man of principle. Dr. Xia considered my father a very knowledgeable man. He used to say he had seen many officials in the past, but never one like my father. Common wisdom had it that "there is no official who is not corrupt," but my father never abused his position, not even to look after the interests of his own family.

The two men would talk together for hours. They shared many ethical values, but whereas my father's were dressed in the garb of an ideology, Dr. Xia's rested on a humanitarian foundation. Once Dr. Xia said to my father: "I think the Communists have done many good things. But you have killed too many people. People who should not have been killed." "Like who?" my father asked. "Those masters in the Society of Reason," which was the quasi-religious sect to which Dr. Xia had belonged. Its leaders had been executed as part of the campaign to "suppress counterrevolutionaries." The new regime suppressed all secret societies, because they commanded loyalties, and the Communists did not want divided loyalties. "They were not bad people, and you should have let the Society be," Dr. Xia said. There was a long pause. My father tried to defend the Communists, saying that the struggle with the Kuomintang was a matter of life and death. Dr. Xia could tell that my father was not fully convinced himself, but felt he had to defend the Party.

When my grandmother left the hospital she came to live with my parents. My sister and her wet-nurse also moved in. I shared a room with my wet-nurse, who had had her own baby twelve days before I was born and had taken the job because she desperately needed money. Her husband, a manual worker, was in jail for gambling and dealing in opium, both of which had been outlawed by the Communists. Yibin had been a major center of the opium trade, with an estimated 25,000 addicts, and opium had previously circulated as money. Opium dealing had been closely linked to gangsters and provided a substantial portion of the Kuomintang's budget. Within two years of coming to Yibin the Communists wiped out opium smoking.

There was no social security or unemployment benefit for someone in the position of my wet-nurse. But when she came to us the state paid her salary, which she sent to her mother-in-law, who was looking after her baby. My nurse was a tiny woman with fine skin, unusually big round eyes, and long exuberant hair, which she kept in a bun. She was a very kind woman, and treated me like her own daughter.

Traditionally, square shoulders were regarded as unbecoming for girls, so my shoulders were bound tightly to make them grow into the required slopy shape. This made me bawl so loudly that my nurse would release my arms and shoulders, allowing me to wave at people who came to the house, and clutch them, which I liked doing from an early age. My mother always attributed my outgoing character to the fact that she was happy when she was pregnant with me.

We were living in the old landlord's mansion where my father had his office; it had a big garden with Chinese pepper trees, banana groves, and lots of sweet-smelling flowers and subtropical plants, which were looked after by a gardener provided by the government. My father grew his own tomatoes and chiles. He enjoyed this work, but it was also one of his principles that a Communist official should perform physical labor, which had traditionally been looked down on by mandarins.

My father was very affectionate to me. When I began to crawl, he would lie on his stomach to be my "mountains," and I would climb up and down him.

Soon after I was born my father was promoted to become the governor of the Yibin region, the number-two man in the area, below only the first secretary of the Party. (The Party and the government were formally distinct, but actually inseparable.)

When he had first returned to Yibin, his family and old friends all expected him to help them. In China it was assumed that anyone in a powerful position would look after their relatives. There was a well-known saying: "When a man gets power, even his chickens and dogs rise to heaven." But my father felt that nepotism and favoritism were the slippery slope to corruption, which was the root of all the evils of the old China. He also knew that the local people were watching him to see how the Communists would behave, and that what he did would influence how they regarded communism.

His strictness had already estranged him from his family. One of his cousins had asked him for a recommendation for a job in the box office at a local cinema. My father told him to go through the official channels. Such behavior was unheard of, and after this no one ever asked him for a favor again. Then something else happened soon after he was appointed governor. One of his older brothers was a tea expert who worked in a tea marketing office. The economy was doing well in the early 1950s, production was expanding, and the local tea board wanted to promote him to manager. All promotions above a certain level had to be cleared by my father. When the recommendation landed on his desk, he vetoed it. His family was incensed, and so was my mother. "It's not you who is promoting him, it's his management!" she exploded. "You don't have to help him, but you don't have to block him either!" My father said that his brother was not capable enough and that he would not have been put forward for promotion if he had not been the governor's brother. There was a long tradition of anticipating the wishes of one's superiors, he pointed out. The tea management board was indignant because my father's action implied that their recommendation had ulterior motives. My father ended up offending everyone, and his brother never spoke to him again.

But my father was unrepentant. He was fighting his own crusade against the old ways, and he insisted on treating everyone by the same criteria. But there was no objective standard for fairness, so he relied on his own instincts, bending over backward to be fair. He did not consult his colleagues, partly because he knew that none of them would ever tell him that a relative of his was undeserving.

His personal moral crusade reached its zenith in 1953 when a civil service ranking system was instituted. All officials and government employees were divided into twenty-six grades. The pay of the lowest grade, Grade 26, was one-twentieth of that of the highest grade. But the real difference lay in the subsidies and perks. The system determined almost everything: from whether one's coat was made of expensive wool or cheap cotton to the size of one's apartment and whether it had an indoor toilet or not.

The grading also determined every official's access to information. A very important part of the Chinese Communist system was that all information was not only very tightly controlled, but highly compartmentalized and rationed, not only to the general public—who were told very little—but also within the Party.

Although its eventual significance was not apparent, even at the time civil servants could feel that the grading system was going to be crucial to their lives, and they were all nervous about what grade they would get. My father, whose grade had already been set at 11 by higher authorities, was in charge of vetting the rankings proposed for everyone in the Yibin region. These included the husband of his youngest sister, who was his favorite. He demoted him two grades. My mother's department had recommended my mother to be Grade 15; he relegated her to Grade 17.

This grade system is not directly linked to a person's position in the civil service. Individuals could be promoted without necessarily being upgraded. In nearly four decades, my mother was upgraded only twice, in 1962 and 1982; each time she moved up only one grade, and by 1990 she was still Grade 15. With this ranking, in the 1980s, she was not entitled to buy a plane ticket or a "soft seat" on a train: these can be bought only by officials of Grade 14 and above. So, thanks to my father's actions in 1953, almost forty years later she was one rung too low on the ladder to travel in comfort in her own country. She could not stay in a hotel room which had a private bath, as these were for Grade 13 and above. When she applied to change the electric meter in her apartment to one with a larger capacity, the management of the block told her that only officials of Grade 13 and above were entitled to a bigger meter.

The very acts which infuriated my father's family were deeply appreciated by the local population, and his reputation has endured to this day. One day in 1952 the headmaster of the Number One Middle School mentioned to my father that he was having difficulty finding accommodations for his teachers. "In that case, take my family's house—it's too big for only three people," my father said instantly, in spite of the fact that the three people were his mother, his sister Junying, and a brother who was retarded, and that they all adored the beautiful house with its enchanted garden. The school was delighted; his family less so, although he found them a small house in the middle of town. His mother was not too pleased, but being a gracious and understanding woman, she said nothing.

Not every official was as incorruptible as my father. Quite soon after taking power, the Communists found themselves facing a crisis. They had attracted the support of millions of people by promising clean government, but some officials began taking bribes or bestowing favors on their families and friends. Others threw extravagant banquets, which is a traditional Chinese indulgence, almost a disease, and a way of both entertaining and showing off—all at the expense, and in the name, of the state, at a time when the government was extremely short of funds; it was trying to reconstruct the shattered economy and also fight a major war in Korea, which was eating up about 50 percent of the budget.

Some officials started embezzling on a large scale. The regime was worried. It sensed that the goodwill which had swept it into power and the discipline and dedication which had ensured its success were eroding. In late 1951 it decided to launch a movement against corruption, waste, and bureaucracy. It was called the "Three Antis Campaign." The government executed some corrupt officials, imprisoned quite a number, and dismissed many others. Even some veterans of the Communist army who had been involved in large-scale bribery or embezzlement were executed, to set an example. Henceforth, corruption was severely punished, and it became rare among officials for the next couple of decades.

My father was in charge of the campaign in his region. There were no corrupt senior officials in his area, but he felt it was important to demonstrate that the Communists were keeping their promise to provide clean government. Every official had to make a self-criticism about any infraction, however minor: for example, if they had used an office telephone to make a personal call, or a piece of official notepaper to write a private letter. Officials became so scrupulous about using state property that most of them would not even use the ink in their office to write anything except official communications. When they switched from official business to something personal they changed pens.

There was a puritanical zeal about sticking to these prescriptions. My father felt that through these minutiae they were creating a new attitude among the Chinese: public property would, for the first time, be strictly separate from private; officials would no longer treat the people's money as their own, or abuse their positions. Most of the people who worked with my father took this position, and genuinely believed that their painstaking efforts were directly linked to the noble cause of creating a new China.

The Three Antis Campaign was aimed at people in the Party. But it takes two to make a corrupt transaction, and the corrupters were often outside the Party, especially "capitalists," factory owners and merchants, who had still hardly been touched. Old habits were deeply entrenched. In spring 1952, soon after the Three Antis Campaign got going, another, overlapping campaign was started. This was called the "Five Antis" and was aimed at capitalists. The five targets were bribery, tax evasion, fraud, theft of state property, and obtaining economic information through corruption. Most capitalists were found to have committed one or more of these offenses, and the punishment was usually a fine. The Communists used this campaign to coax and (more often) cow the capitalists, but in such a way as to maximize their usefulness to the economy. Not many were imprisoned.

These two linked campaigns consolidated mechanisms of control, originally developed in the early days of communism, which were unique to China. The most important was the "mass campaign" (*qiun-zhong yun-dong*), which was conducted by bodies known as "work teams" (*gong-zuo-zu*).

Work teams were *ad hoc* bodies, made up mainly of employees from government offices and headed by senior Party officials. The central government in Peking would send teams to the provinces to vet the provincial officials and employees. These, in turn, formed teams which checked up on the next level, where the process was repeated, all the way down to the grass roots. Normally, no one could become a member of a work team who had not already been vetted in that particular campaign.

Teams were sent to all organizations where the campaign was to be conducted "to mobilize the people." There were compulsory meetings most evenings to study instructions issued by the top authorities. Team members would talk, lecture, and try to persuade people to stand up and expose suspects. People were encouraged to place anonymous complaints in boxes provided for the purpose. The work team would investigate each case. If the investigation confirmed the charge, or revealed grounds for suspicion, the team would formulate a verdict which was sent up to the next level of authority for approval.

There was no genuine appeal system, although a person who came under suspicion could ask to see the evidence and would usually be allowed to make some sort of defense. Work teams could impose a range of sentences including public criticism, dismissal from one's job, and various forms of surveillance; the maximum sentence they could give was to send a person to the countryside to do physical labor. Only the most serious cases went to the formal judicial system, which was under the Party's control. For each of the campaigns, a set of guidelines was issued from the very top, and the work teams had to abide strictly by these. But when it came down to individual cases, the judgment—and even the temperament—of the specific work team could also be important.

In each campaign everyone in the category which had been designated as the target by Peking came under some degree of scrutiny, mostly from their workmates and neighbors rather than the police. This was a key invention of Mao's—to involve the entire population in the machinery of control. Few wrongdoers, according to the regime's criteria, could escape the watchful eyes of the people, especially in a society with an age-old concierge mentality. But the "efficiency" was acquired at a tremendous price: because the campaigns operated on very vague criteria, and because of personal vendettas, and even gossip, many innocent people were condemned.

Aunt Jun-ying had been working as a weaver to help support her mother, her retarded brother, and herself. Every night she worked into the small hours, and her eyes became quite badly damaged from the dim light. By 1952 she had saved and borrowed enough money to buy two more weaving machines, and had two friends working with her. Although they divided the income, in theory my aunt was paying them because she owned the machines. In the Five Antis Campaign anyone employing other people fell under some sort of suspicion. Even very small businesses like Aunt Jun-ying's, which were in effect cooperatives, came under investigation. She wanted to ask her friends to leave, but did not want them to feel she was giving them the sack. But then the two friends told her it would be best if they left. They were worried that if someone else threw mud at her, she might think it was them.

By the middle of 1953 the Three Antis and Five Antis campaigns had wound down; the capitalists had been brought to heel, and the Kuomintang had been eradicated. Mass meetings were coming to an end, as officials had come to recognize that much of the information which emerged at them was unreliable. Cases were being examined on an individual basis.

In May 1953 my mother went into hospital to have her third child, who was born on 23 May: a boy called Jin-ming. It was the missionary hospital where she had stayed when she was pregnant with me, but the missionaries had now been expelled, as had happened all over China. My mother had just been given a promotion to head of the Public Affairs Department for the city of Yibin, still working under Mrs. Ting, who had risen to be Party secretary for the city. At the time my grandmother was also in the hospital with severe asthma.

And so was I, with a navel infection; my wet-nurse was staying with me in the hospital. We were being given good treatment, which was free, as we belonged to a family "in the revolution." Doctors tended to give the very scarce hospital beds to officials and their families. There was no public health service for the majority of the population: peasants, for example, had to pay.

My sister and my aunt Jun-ying were staying with friends in the country, so my father was alone at home. One day Mrs. Ting came to report on her work. Afterward she said she had a headache and wanted to lie down. My father helped her onto one of the beds, and as he did so she pulled him down toward her and tried to kiss and stroke him. My father backed away at once. "You must be very exhausted," he said, and immediately left the room. A few moments later he returned, in a very agitated state. He was carrying a glass of water which he put on the bedside table. "You must know that I love my wife," he said, and then, before Mrs. Ting had a chance to do anything, he went to the door and closed it behind him. Under the glass of water he had left a piece of paper with the words "Communist morality."

A few days later my mother left the hospital. As she and her baby son crossed the threshold of the house, my father said: "We're leaving Yibin the minute we can, for good." My mother could not imagine what had got into him. He told her what had happened, and said Mrs. Ting had been eyeing him for some time. My mother was more shocked than angry. "But why do you want to leave so urgently?" she asked. "She's a determined woman," my father said. "I'm afraid she might try again. And she is also a vindictive woman. What I am most worried about is that she might try to harm you. That would be easy, because you work under her." "Is she that bad?" my mother replied. "I did hear some gossip that when she was in jail under the Kuomintang she seduced the warder, that sort of thing. But some people like to spread rumors. Anyway, I'm not surprised she should fancy you," she smiled. "But do you think she would really turn nasty on me? She is my best friend here."

"You don't understand—there is something called 'rage out of being shamed' [*nao-xiu-cheng-nu*]. I know that is how she is feeling. I wasn't very tactful. I must have shamed her. I'm sorry. On the spur of the moment I acted on impulse, I'm afraid. She is a woman who will take revenge."

My mother could visualize exactly how my father might have abruptly rebuffed Mrs. Ting. But she could not imagine Mrs. Ting would be that malicious, nor could she see what disaster Mrs. Ting could bring down on them. So my father told her about his predecessor as governor of Yibin, Mr. Shu.

Mr. Shu had been a poor peasant who had joined the Red Army on the Long March. He did not like Mrs. Ting, and criticized her for being flirtatious. He also objected to the way she wound her hair into many tiny plaits, which verged on the outrageous for the time. Several times he said that she should cut her plaits. She refused, telling him to mind his own business, which only made him redouble his criticisms, making her even more hostile to him. She decided to take revenge on him, with the help of her husband.

There was a woman working in Mr. Shu's office who had been the concubine of a Kuomintang official who had fled to Taiwan. She had been seen trying her charms on Mr. Shu, who was married, and there was gossip about them having an affair. Mrs. Ting got this woman to sign a statement saying that Mr. Shu had made advances to her and had forced her to have sex with him. Even though he was the governor, the woman decided the Tings were more fearsome. Mr. Shu was charged with using his position to have relations with a former Kuomintang concubine, which was considered inexcusable for a Communist veteran.

A standard technique in China to bring a person down was to draw together several different charges to make the case appear more substantial. The Tings found another "offense" with which to charge Mr. Shu. He had once disagreed with a policy put forward by Peking and had written to the top Party leaders stating his views. According to the Party charter, this was his right; moreover, as a veteran of the Long March, he was in a privileged position, so he felt confident that he could be quite open with his complaints. The Tings used this to claim that he was opposed to the Party.

Stringing the two charges together, Mr. Ting proposed expelling Mr. Shu from the Party and sacking him. Mr. Shu denied the charges vigorously. The first, he said, was simply untrue. He had never made a pass at the woman; all he had done was to be civil to her. As for the second, he had done nothing wrong and had no intention of opposing the Party. The Party Committee that governed the region was composed of four people: Mr. Shu himself, Mr. Ting, my father, and the first secretary. Now Mr. Shu was judged by the other three. My father defended him. He felt sure Mr. Shu was innocent, and he regarded writing the letter as completely legitimate.

When it came to the vote, my father lost, and Mr. Shu was dismissed. The first secretary of the Party supported Mr. Ting. One reason he did so was that Mr. Shu had been in the "wrong" branch of the Red Army. He had been a senior officer in what was called the Fourth Front in Sichuan in the early 1930s. This army had joined forces with the branch of the Red Army led by Mao on the Long March in 1935. Its commander, a flamboyant figure called Zhang Guo-tao, challenged Mao for the leadership of the Red Army and lost. He then left the Long March with his troops. Eventually, after suffering heavy casualties, he was forced to rejoin Mao. But in 1938, after the Communists reached Yan'an, he went over to the Kuomintang. Because of this, anyone who had been in the Fourth Front bore a stigma, and their allegiance to Mao was considered suspect. This issue was particularly touchy, as many of the people in the Fourth Front had come from Sichuan.

After the Communists took power this type of unspoken stigma was attached to any part of the revolution which Mao had not directly controlled, including the underground, which included many of the bravest, most dedicated—and best educated—Communists. In Yibin, all the former members of the underground felt under some sort of pressure. Among the added complications was the fact that many of the people in the local underground had come from well-to-do backgrounds, and their families had suffered at the hands of the Communists. Moreover, because they were usually better educated than the people who had arrived with the Communist army, who were mainly from peasant backgrounds and often illiterate, they became the object of envy.

Though himself a guerrilla fighter, my father was instinctively much closer to the underground people. In any case, he refused to go along with the insidious ostracism, and spoke out for the former members of the underground. "It is ridiculous to divide Communists into 'underground' and 'overground,' " he often said. In fact, most of the people he picked to work with him had been in the underground, because they were the most able.

My father thought that to consider Fourth Front men like Mr. Shu as suspect was unacceptable, and he fought to have him rehabilitated. First, he advised him to leave Yibin to avoid further trouble, which he did, taking his last meal with my family. He was transferred to Chengdu, the capital of Sichuan province, where he was given a job as a clerk in the Provincial Forestry Bureau. From there he wrote appeals to the Central Committee in Peking, naming my father as his reference. My father wrote supporting his appeal. Much later, Mr. Shu was cleared of "opposing the Party," but the lesser charge of "having extramarital affairs" stood. The former concubine who had lodged the accusation dared not retract it, but she gave a patently feeble and incoherent account of the alleged advances, which was clearly designed to signal to the investigating group that the accusations were untrue. Mr. Shu was given a fairly senior post in the Forestry Ministry in Peking, but he did not get his old position back.

The point my father was trying to get across to my mother was that the Tings would stop at nothing to settle old scores. He gave more examples and repeated that they had to leave at once. The very next day he traveled to Chengdu, one day's journey to the north. There he went straight to the governor of the province, whom he knew well, and asked to be transferred, saying that it was very difficult to work in his hometown and to cope with the expectations of his many relatives. He kept his real reasons to himself, as he had no hard evidence about the Tings.

The governor, Lee Da-zhang, was the man who had originally sponsored the application by Mao's wife, Jiang Qing, to join the Party. He expressed sympathy with my father's position and said he would help him get a transfer, but he did not want him to move immediately: all the suitable posts in Chengdu had been filled. My father said he could not wait, and would accept anything. After trying hard to dissuade him, the governor finally gave up and told him he could have the job of head of the Arts and Education Office. But he warned, "This is much below your ability." My father said he did not mind as long as there was a job to do.

My father was so worried that he did not go back to Yibin at all, but sent a message to my mother telling her to join him as soon as possible. The women in his family said it was out of the question for my mother to move so soon after giving birth, but my father was terrified about what Mrs. Ting might do, and as soon as the traditional month's postnatal convalescence was over, he sent his bodyguard to Yibin to collect us.

It was decided that my brother Jin-ming would stay behind, as he was considered too young to travel. Both his wet-nurse and my sister's wanted to stay, to be near their families. Jin-ming's wet-nurse was very fond of him, and she asked my mother if she could keep him with her. My mother agreed. She had complete confidence in her.

My mother, my grandmother, my sister, and I, with my wet-nurse and the bodyguard, left Yibin before dawn one night at the end of June. We all crammed into a jeep with our meager luggage, just a couple of suitcases. At the time, officials like my parents did not own any property at all—only a few articles of basic clothing. We drove over potholed dirt roads until we reached the town of Neijiang in the morning. It was a sweltering day, and we had to wait there for hours for the train.

Just as it was finally coming into the station, I suddenly decided I had to relieve myself and my nurse picked me up and carried me to the edge of the platform. My mother was afraid that the train might suddenly leave and tried to stop her. My nurse, who had never seen a train before and had no concept of a timetable, rounded on her and said rather grandly: "Can't you tell the driver to wait? Er-hong has to have a pee." She thought everyone would, like her, automatically put my needs first.

Because of our different status, we had to split up when we got on the train. My mother was in a second-class sleeper with my sister, my grandmother had a soft seat in another carriage, and my nurse and I were in what was called the "mothers' and children's compartment," where she had a hard seat and I had a cot. The bodyguard was in a fourth carriage, with a hard seat.

As the train chugged slowly along my mother gazed out at the rice paddies and sugarcane. The occasional peasants walking on the mud ridges seemed to be half asleep under their broad-brimmed straw hats, the men naked to the waist. The network of streams flowed haltingly, obstructed by tiny mud dams which channeled the water into the numerous individual rice paddies.

My mother was in a pensive mood. For the second time within four years, she and her husband and family were having to decamp from a place to which they were deeply attached. First from her hometown, Jinzhou, and now from my father's, Yibin. The revolution had not, it seemed, brought a solution to their problems. Indeed, it had caused new ones. For the first time she vaguely reflected on the fact that, as the revolution was made by human beings, it was burdened with their failings. But it did not occur to her that the revolution was doing very little to deal with these failings, and actually relied on some of them, often the worst.

As the train approached Chengdu in the early afternoon, she found herself increasingly looking forward to a new life there. She had heard a lot about Chengdu, which had been the capital of an ancient kingdom and was known as "the City of Silk" after its most famous product. It was also called "the City of Hibiscus," which was said to bury the city with its petals after a summer storm. She was twenty-two. At the same age, some twenty years before, her mother had been living as a virtual prisoner in Manchuria in a house belonging to her absent warlord "husband," under the watchful eyes of his servants; she was the plaything and the property of men. My mother, at least, was an independent human being. Whatever her misery, she was sure it bore no comparison with the plight of her mother as a woman in old China. She told herself she had a lot to thank the Communist revolution for. As the train pulled into Chengdu station, she was full of determination to throw herself into the great cause again.

10. "Suffering Will Make You a Better Communist"— My Mother Falls under Suspicion

(1953–1956)

My father met us at the station. The air was motionless and oppressive, and my mother and my grandmother were exhausted from the jolting car journey the night before and the burning heat which had blown through the train all the way. We were taken to a guesthouse belonging to the Sichuan provincial government, which was to be our temporary lodging. My mother's transfer had happened so quickly that she had not been assigned a job, and there had been no time to make proper arrangements about a place for us to live.

Chengdu was the capital of Sichuan, which was the most populous province in China, with some sixty-five million people then. It was a large city, with a population of over half a million, and had been founded in the fifth century B.C. Marco Polo visited it in the thirteenth century and was enormously impressed by its prosperity. It was laid out on the same plan as Peking, with ancient palaces and major gates all on a north-south axis which divided the city neatly into two parts, western and eastern. By 1953 it had outgrown its original neat plan and was divided into three administrative districts—eastern, western, and the outskirts.

Within a few weeks of arriving my mother was given a job. My father was consulted about it, but, in the good old tradition of China, not my mother herself. My father said anything would do, as long as she was not working directly under him, so she was made head of the Public Affairs Department for the Eastern District of the city. As one's work unit was responsible for one's accommodations, she was assigned rooms which belonged to her department, in a traditional courtyard. We moved into these rooms, while my father stayed on in his office suite.

Our living quarters were in the same compound as the Eastern District administration. Government offices were mostly housed in large mansions which had been confiscated from Kuomintang officials and wealthy landlords. All government employees, even senior officials, lived at their office. They were not allowed to cook at home, and all ate in canteens. The canteen was also where everyone got their boiled water, which was fetched in thermos flasks.

Saturday was the only day married couples were allowed to spend together. Among officials, the euphemism for making love was "spending a Saturday." Gradually, this regimented life-style relaxed a bit and married couples were able to spend more time together, but almost all still lived and spent most of their time in their office compounds.

My mother's department ran a very broad field of activities, including primary education, health, entertainment, and sounding out public opinion. At the age of twenty-two, my mother was in charge of all these activities for about a quarter of a million people. She was so busy we hardly ever saw her. The government wanted to establish a monopoly (known as "unified purchasing and marketing") over trade in the basic commodities—grain, cotton, edible oil, and meat. The idea was to get the peasants to sell these exclusively to the government, which would then ration them out to the urban population and to parts of the country where they were in short supply.

When the Chinese Communist Party launched a new policy, they accompanied it with a propaganda drive to help put the new policy across. It was part of my mother's job to try to convince people that the change was for the good. The core of the message this time was that China had a huge population and that the problem of feeding and clothing it had never been solved; now the government wanted to make sure the basic necessities were fairly distributed and that nobody starved while others hoarded grain or other essentials. My mother set about her job with gusto, rushing around on her bicycle, talking at endless meetings every day, even when she was in the last months of pregnancy with her fourth child. She enjoyed her work, and believed in it.

She only went into the hospital at the last minute to have her next child, a son, who was born on 15 September 1954. It was a dangerous delivery again. The doctor was getting ready to go home when my mother stopped him. She was bleeding abnormally, and knew there was something wrong. She insisted on the doctor staying and giving her a checkup. A fragment of her placenta was missing. Finding it was considered a major operation, so the doctor had her placed under a general anesthetic and searched her womb again. They found the fragment, which probably saved her life.

My father was in the countryside trying to galvanize support for the state monopoly program. He had just been upgraded to Grade 10 and promoted to deputy director of the Public Affairs Department for the whole of Sichuan. One of its major functions was to keep a running check on public opinion: How did the people feel about a particular policy? What complaints did they have? Since peasants formed the overwhelming majority of the population, he was often in the countryside finding out their views and feelings. Like my mother, he believed passionately in his work, which was to keep the Party and the government in touch with the people.

On the seventh day after my mother gave birth, one of his colleagues sent a car to the hospital to bring her home. It was accepted that, if the husband was away, the Party organization was responsible for taking care of his wife. My mother gratefully accepted the lift, as "home" was half an hour's walk away. When my father came back a few days later, he reprimanded his colleague. The rules stipulated that my mother could ride in an official car only when my father was in it. Using a car when he was not there would be seen as nepotism, he said. My father's colleague said he had authorized the car because my mother had just been through a serious operation which had left her extremely weak. But a rule is a rule, replied my father. My mother found it hard to take this puritanical rigidity once again. This was the second time my father had attacked her immediately after a difficult birth. Why was he not there to take her home, she asked, so they would not have to break the rules? He had been tied up with his work, he said, which was important. My mother understood his dedication —she was dedicated herself. But she was also bitterly disappointed.

Two days after he was born my new brother, Xiao-hei, developed eczema. My mother thought this was because she had not eaten any boiled green olives during the summer, when she was too busy working. The Chinese believe that olives get rid of body heat that otherwise comes out in heat bumps. For several months Xiao-hei's hands had to be tied to the railings of his cot to prevent him from scratching himself. When he was six months old he was sent to a dermatology hospital. At this point my grandmother had to rush to Jinzhou as her mother was ill.

Xiao-hei's nurse was a country girl from Yibin, with luxuriant long black hair and flirtatious eyes. She had accidentally killed her own baby—she had been breast-feeding it lying down, had fallen asleep, and had smothered it. She had gone to see my aunt Jun-ying via a family connection and begged her to give her a recommendation to my family. She wanted to go to a big city and have fun. My aunt gave her a reference, in spite of the opposition of some local women who said she only wanted to get to Chengdu to be rid of her husband. Jun-ying, though unmarried, was far from being jealous of other people's pleasure, especially sexual pleasure; in fact, she was always delighted for them. She was full of understanding and tolerant of human foibles, and quite unjudgmental.

Within a few months the nurse was alleged to be having an affair with an undertaker in the compound. My parents considered such things private matters, and turned a blind eye.

When my brother went into the skin hospital, the wet-nurse went with him. The Communists had largely eliminated venereal disease, but there were still some VD patients in one of the wards, and one day the wet-nurse was spotted in bed with a patient in that ward. The hospital told my mother and suggested it would be unsafe for the nurse to continue breastfeeding Xiao-hei. My mother asked her to leave. After that, Xiao-hei was cared for by my wet-nurse and the wet-nurse who looked after my other brother, Jin-ming, who had now joined us from Yibin.

At the end of 1954 Jin-ming's nurse had written to my mother saying she would like to come and live with us, as she had been having trouble with her husband, who had become a heavy drinker and was beating her up. My mother had not seen Jin-ming for eighteen months, since he was a month old. But his arrival was terribly distressing. For a long time he would not let her touch him, and the only person he would call "Mother" was his nurse.

My father also found it difficult to strike up a close relationship with Jin-ming, but he was very close to me. He would crawl on the floor and let me ride on his back. Usually he put some flowers in his collar for me to smell. If he forgot, I would point at the garden and make commanding noises, indicating that some should be brought instantly. He would often kiss me on the cheek. Once, when he had not shaved, I wrinkled up my face and complained, "Old beard, old beard!" at the top of my voice. I called him Old Beard (lao hu-zi) for months. He kissed me more gingerly after that. I loved to toddle in and out of offices and play with the officials. I used to chase after them and call them by special names I invented for them, and recite nursery rhymes to them. Before I was three I was known as "Little Diplomat."

I think my popularity was really due to the fact that the officials welcomed a break and a bit of fun, which I provided with my childish chattiness. I was very plump, too, and they all liked sitting me on their laps and pinching and squeezing me.

When I was a little over three years old my siblings and I were all sent away to different boarding nurseries. I could not understand why I was being taken away from home, and kicked and tore the ribbon in my hair in protest. In the nursery I deliberately created trouble for the teachers and used to pour my milk into my desk every day, following it with my cod-liver-oil capsules. We had to take a long siesta after lunch, during which I would tell frightening stories, which I had made up, to the other children in the big dormitory. I was soon found out and punished by being made to sit on the doorstep.

The reason we were in the nurseries was that there was no one to look after us. One day in July 1955, my mother and the 800 employees in the Eastern District were all told they had to stay on the premises until further notice. A new political campaign had started—this time to uncover "hidden counterrevolutionaries." Everyone was to be thoroughly checked.

My mother and her colleagues accepted the order without question. They had been leading a regimented life anyway. Besides, it seemed natural for the Party to want to check on its members in order to ensure that the new society was stable. Like most of her comrades, my mother's desire to devote herself to the cause overrode any wish to grumble about the strictness of the measure.

After a week, almost all her colleagues were cleared and allowed to go out freely. My mother was one of the few exceptions. She was told that certain things in her past were not yet clarified. She had to move out of her own bedroom and sleep in a room in a different part of the office building. Before that she was allowed a few days at home to make arrangements for her family as, she was told, she might be confined for quite a long time.

The new campaign had been triggered by Mao's reaction to the behavior of some Communist writers, notably the prominent author Hu Feng. They did not necessarily disagree with Mao ideologically, but they betrayed an element of independence and an ability to think for themselves which he found unacceptable. He feared that any independent thinking might lead to less than total obedience to him. He insisted that the new China had to act and think as one, and that stringent measures were needed to hold the country together, or it might disintegrate. He had a number of leading writers arrested and labeled them a "counterrevolutionary conspiracy," a terrifying accusation, as "counterrevolutionary" activity carried the harshest punishment, including the death sentence.

This signaled the beginning of the end of individual expression in China. All the media had been taken over by the Party when the Communists came to power. From now on it was the minds of the entire nation that were placed under ever tighter control.

Mao asserted that the people he was looking for were "spies for the imperialist countries and the Kuomintang, Trotskyists, ex-Kuomintang officers, and traitors among the Communists." He claimed that they were working for a comeback by the Kuomintang and the "U.S. imperialists," who were refusing to recognize Peking and were surrounding China with a ring of hostility. Whereas the earlier campaign to suppress counterrevolutionaries, in which my mother's friend Hui-ge had been executed, had been directed at actual Kuomintang people, the targets now were people in the Party, or working in the government, who had Kuomintang connections in their backgrounds.

Compiling detailed files on people's backgrounds had been a crucial part of the Communists' system of control even before they came to power. The files on Party members were kept by the Organization Department of the Party. The dossier on anyone working for the state who was not a Party member was assembled by the authorities in their work unit and kept by its personnel management. Every year a report was written about every employee by their boss, and this was put into their file. No one was allowed to read their own file, and only specially authorized people could read other people's.

To be targeted in this new campaign it was enough to have some sort of Kuomintang connection in one's past, however tenuous or vague. The investigations were carried out by work teams made up of officials who were known to have no Kuomintang connections. My mother became a prime suspect. Our nurses also became targets because of their family ties.

There was a work team responsible for investigating the servants and staff of the provincial government—chauffeurs, gardeners, maids, cooks, and caretakers. My nurse's husband was in jail for gambling and smuggling opium, which made her an "undesirable." Jinming's nurse had married into a landlord's family and her husband had been a minor Kuomintang official. Because wet-nurses were not in positions of importance, the Party did not delve into their cases very vigorously. But they had to stop working for our family.

My mother was informed of this when she was home briefly before her detention. When she broke the news to the two nurses, they were distraught. They loved Jin-ming and me. My nurse was also worried about losing her income if she had to go back to Yibin, so my mother wrote to the governor there asking him to find her a job, which he did. She went to work on a tea plantation and was able to take her young daughter to live with her.

Jin-ming's nurse did not want to go back to her husband. She had acquired a new boyfriend, a caretaker in Chengdu, and wanted to marry him. In floods of tears, she begged my mother to help her get a divorce so she could marry him. Divorce was exceedingly difficult, but she knew that a word from my parents, particularly my father, could assist greatly. My mother liked the nurse very much and wanted to help her. If she could get a divorce and marry the caretaker she would automatically move from the "landlord" category into the working class—and then she would not have to leave my family after all. My mother talked to my father, but he was against it: "How can you arrange a divorce? People would say the Communists were breaking up families." "But what about our children?" my mother said. "Who will look after them if the nurses both have to go?" My father had an answer to that, too: "Send them to nurseries."

When my mother told Jin-ming's nurse that she would have to leave, she almost collapsed. Jin-ming's first ever memory is of her departure. One evening at dusk someone carried him to the front door. His nurse was standing there, wearing a countrywoman's outfit, a plain top with cotton butterfly buttons on the side, and carrying a cotton bundle. He wanted her to take him in her arms, but she stood just out of reach as he stretched out his hands toward her. Tears were streaming down her face. Then she walked down the steps toward the gate on the far side of the courtyard. Someone he did not know was with her. She was about to pass through the gate when she stopped and turned around. He screamed and bawled and kicked, but he was not carried any nearer. She stood for a long time framed in the arch of the courtyard gate, gazing at him. Then she turned quickly and disappeared. Jin-ming never saw her again.

My grandmother was still in Manchuria. My great-grandmother had just died of tuberculosis. Before being "confined to barracks," my mother had to pack us four children off to nurseries. Because it was so sudden, none of the municipal nurseries could take more than one of us, so we had to be split up among four different institutions.

As my mother was leaving for detention, my father advised her: "Be completely honest with the Party, and have complete trust in it. It will give you the right verdict." A wave of aversion swept over her. She wanted something warmer and more personal. Still feeling resentful against my father, she reported one steamy summer day for her second bout of detention—this time under her own Party.

Being under investigation did not in itself carry the stigma of guilt. It just meant there were things in one's background which had to be cleared up. Still, she was grieved to be subjected to such a humiliating experience after all her sacrifices and her manifest loyalty to the Communist cause. But part of her was full of optimism that the dark cloud of suspicion which had been hanging over her for almost seven years would finally be swept away forever. She had nothing to be ashamed of, nothing to hide. She was a devoted Communist and she felt sure the Party would recognize this.

A special team of three people was put together to investigate her. The head of it was a Mr. Kuang, who was in charge of Public Affairs for the city of Chengdu, which meant he was below my father and above my mother. His family knew my family well. Now, though he was still kindly to my mother, his attitude was more formal and reserved.

Like other detainees, my mother was assigned various women "companions" who followed her everywhere, even to the toilet, and slept in the same bed with her. She was told that this was for her protection. She understood implicitly that she was being "protected" from committing suicide, or trying to collude with anyone else.

Several women rotated in shifts as her companion. One of them was relieved of her duties because she had to go into detention herself to be investigated. Each companion had to file a report on my mother every day. They were all people my mother knew because they worked in the district offices, though not in her department. They were friendly and, except for the lack of freedom, my mother was treated well.

The interrogators, plus her companion, conducted the sessions like friendly conversations, although the subject of these conversations was extremely unpleasant. The presumption was not exactly of guilt, but it was not of innocence, either. And because there were no proper legal procedures, there was little opportunity to defend oneself against insinuations.

My mother's file contained detailed reports about every stage of her life—as a student working for the underground, in the Women's Federation in Jinzhou, and at her jobs in Yibin. These had been written by her bosses at the time. The first issue that came up was her release from prison under the Kuomintang in 1948. How had her family been able to get her out, considering that her offense had been so serious?

She had not even been tortured! Could the arrest actually have been a hoax, designed to establish her credentials with the Communists so that she could worm her way into a trusted position as an agent for the Kuomintang?

Then there was her friendship with Hui-ge. It became obvious that her bosses in the Women's Federation in Jinzhou had put disparaging comments into her file about this. Since Hui-ge had been trying to buy insurance from the Communists through her, they alleged, was she not perhaps trying to acquire similar insurance from the Kuomintang in case it won?

The same question was asked about her Kuomintang suitors. Did she not encourage them as insurance for herself? And then back to the same grave suspicion: Had any of them instructed her to lie low inside the Communist Party and work for the Kuomintang?

My mother was put in the impossible position of having to prove her innocence. All the people she was being asked about either had been executed or were in Taiwan, or she did not know where. In any case, they were Kuomintang people—and their word was not going to be trusted. How can I convince you? she sometimes thought with exasperation, as she went over the same incidents again and again.

She was also asked about her uncles' Kuomintang connections, and about her relationship with every one of her schoolfriends who, as teenagers, had joined the Kuomintang's Youth League in the period before the Communists took Jinzhou. The guidelines for the campaign classified anyone who had been appointed a branch chief of the Kuomintang Youth League after the Japanese surrender as a "counterrevolutionary." My mother tried to argue that Manchuria was a special case: the Kuomintang had been seen as representing China, the motherland, after the Japanese occupation. Mao himself had been a senior official in the Kuomintang once, though she did not mention this. Besides, her friends had switched their allegiance to the Communists within a couple of years. But she was told that these old friends of hers were now all designated counterrevolutionaries. My mother did not belong to any condemned category, but she was asked the impossible question: Why was it that you had so many connections with Kuomintang people?

She was kept in detention for six months. During this period she had to attend several mass rallies at which "enemy agents" were paraded, denounced, sentenced, handcuffed, and led away to prison—amidst thunderous shouting of slogans and raising of fists by tens of thousands of people. There were also "counterrevolutionaries" who had "confessed" and therefore been given "lenient punishment"—

which meant not being sent to prison. Among these was a friend of my mother's. After the rally she committed suicide because, under interrogation, in despair, she had made a false confession. Seven years later the Party acknowledged that she had been innocent all along.

My mother was taken to these rallies "to receive a lesson." But, being a strong character, she was not crushed by fear, like so many, or confused by the deceptive logic and coaxing of the interrogations. She kept a clear head and wrote the story of her life truthfully.

There were long nights when she lay awake, unable to stifle her bitterness at her unfair treatment. As she listened to the whining mosquitoes outside the net over her bed in the airless heat of the summer, then the autumn rain pattering on the window, and the damp silence of winter, she chewed over the unfairness of the suspicions against her—particularly the doubts about her arrest by the Kuomintang. She was proud of the way she had behaved then, and had never dreamed it would become the reason for her becoming alienated from the revolution.

But then she began to persuade herself that she should not resent the Party for trying to maintain its purity. In China, one was accustomed to a certain amount of injustice. Now, at least, it was for a worthy cause. She also repeated to herself the Party's words when it demanded sacrifice from its members: "You are going through a test, and suffering will make you a better Communist."

She contemplated the possibility of being classified as a "counter-revolutionary." If that happened, her children would also be contaminated, and our entire lives ruined. The only way she could avoid this would be to divorce my father and "disown" herself as our mother. At night, thinking about these grim prospects, she learned not to shed tears. She could not even toss and turn, as her "companion" was sleeping in the bed with her, and no matter how friendly they were, they had to report every scrap of information about how she behaved. Tears would be interpreted as meaning she was feeling wounded by the Party or losing confidence in it. Both were unacceptable, and could have a negative effect on the final verdict.

My mother gritted her teeth and told herself to put her faith in the Party. Even so, she found it very hard being totally cut off from her family, and missed her children terribly. My father did not write or visit her once—letters and meetings were forbidden. What she needed more than anything else at the time was a shoulder on which to rest her head, or at least a loving word.

But she did get phone calls. From the other end of the line would come jokes and words of trust which cheered her up enormously. The only phone in the whole department was on the desk of the woman who was in charge of secret documents. When a call came for my mother, her "companions" would stand in the room while she was on the line, but because they liked her and wanted her to get some comfort, they would show they were not listening. The woman in charge of secret documents was not part of the team investigating my mother, so she was not entitled to listen to or report on her. My mother's companions made sure that she never got into trouble for these phone calls. They would simply report: "Director Chang telephoned. Discussed family matters." Word went around about what a considerate husband my father was, so concerned about my mother and so affectionate. One of my mother's young companions told her she wanted to find a husband as nice as my father.

No one knew that the caller was not my father, but another high official who had come over to the Communists from the Kuomintang during the war against Japan. Having once been a Kuomintang officer, he had come under suspicion and had been imprisoned by the Communists in 1947, although he was eventually cleared. He cited his experience to reassure my mother, and in fact remained a lifelong friend of hers. My father never phoned once in the six long months. He knew from his years of being a Communist that the Party preferred the person under investigation to have no contact with the outside world, not even with their spouse. As he saw it, to comfort my mother would imply some kind of distrust of the Party. My mother could never forgive him for deserting her at a time when she needed love and support more than anything. Once again he had proved that he put the Party first.

One January morning, as she was staring at the clumps of shivering grass being battered by the dismal rain under the jasmine on the trellis with its masses of intertwined green shoots, my mother was summoned to see Mr. Kuang, the head of the investigating team. He told her she was being allowed to go back to work—and to go out. But she had to report in every night. The Party had not reached a final conclusion about her.

What had happened, my mother realized, was that the investigations had bogged down. Most of the suspicions could not be either proved or disproved. Although this was unsatisfactory for her, she pushed it to the back of her mind in her excitement at the thought of seeing her children for the first time in six months.

In our different boarding nurseries, we seldom saw our father, either. He was constantly away in the countryside. On the rare occasions when he was back in Chengdu, he would send his bodyguard to bring my sister and me home on Saturdays. He never had the two boys fetched because he felt he could not cope with them, they were too young. "Home" was his office. When we got there he would always have to go off to some meeting, so his bodyguard would lock us up in the office, where there was nothing to do, apart from competing at blowing soap bubbles. Once I got so bored I drank a lot of soapy water and was ill for days.

When my mother was told she could go out, the first thing she did was jump on her bicycle and speed off to our nurseries. She was particularly worried about Jin-ming, now two and a half, whom she had hardly had any time to get to know. But, after sitting around unused for six months, her bicycle's tires were flat, and she was barely out of the gate when she had to stop and get some air put in them. She had never felt so impatient in her life, as she paced around the shop while the man pumped up her tires in what seemed to her a very lackadaisical manner.

She went to see Jin-ming first. When she arrived, the teacher looked at her coldly. Jin-ming, the teacher said, was one of the very few children who had been left behind on weekends. My father had hardly ever come to see him, and had never taken him home. At first, Jin-ming had asked for "Mother Chen," the teacher said. "That's not you, is it?" she asked. My mother acknowledged that "Mother Chen" was his wet-nurse. Later, Jin-ming would hide in a corner room when it was time for the other parents to come and collect their offspring. "You must be a stepmother," the teacher said accusingly. My mother could not explain.

When Jin-ming was brought in, he remained at the far end of the room and would not go near my mother. He just stood there silently, resentfully refusing to look at her. My mother produced some peaches and asked him to come over and eat them while she peeled them. But Jin-ming would not move. She had to put the peaches on her handkerchief and push them along the table. He waited for her to withdraw her hand before he grabbed one peach and devoured it. Then he took another one. In no time the three peaches were gone. For the first time since she had been taken into detention, my mother let her tears fall.

I remember the evening she came to see me. I was nearly four, and was in my wooden bed which had bars like a cage. One side of the railing was let down so she could sit and hold my hand while I fell asleep. But I wanted to tell her about all my adventures and mischief. I was worried that once I fell asleep she would disappear again forever.

Whenever she thought I was asleep and tried to slip her hand away, I gripped it and started to cry. She stayed until around midnight. I screamed when she started to leave, but she pulled herself away. I did not know that "parole" time was up.

11. "After the Anti-Rightist Campaign No One Opens Their Mouth"— China Silenced

(1956–1958)

Because we now had no nurses and my mother had to check in for her "parole" report every evening, we children had to stay on in our nurseries. My mother could not have looked after us anyway. She was too busy "racing toward socialism"—as a propaganda song went— with the rest of Chinese society.

While she had been in detention Mao had accelerated his attempt to change the face of China. In July 1955 he had called for a speeding up of collective farming, and in November he abruptly announced that all industry and commerce, which had so far remained in private hands, were to be nationalized.

My mother was thrown straight into this movement. In theory, the state was supposed to own enterprises jointly with the former owners, who were to draw 5 percent of the value of their business for twenty years. Since there was officially no inflation, this was supposed to represent full payment of the total value. The former owners were to stay on as managers and be paid a relatively high wage, but there would be a Party boss over them.

My mother was put in charge of a work team supervising the na- tionalization of over a hundred food factories, bakeries, and restaurants in her district. Although she was still on "parole," and had to report in every evening, and could not even sleep in her own bed, she was entrusted with this important job.

The Party had attached a stigmatic label to her—*kong-zhi shi-yong*, which meant "employed but under control and surveillance." This was not made public, but was known to her and the people in charge of her case. The members of her work team knew she had been detained for six months, but did not know she was still under surveillance.

When my mother was put in detention, she had written to my grandmother asking her to stay on in Manchuria for the time being. She had concocted an excuse, as she did not want my grandmother to know she was being detained, which would have worried her terribly.

My grandmother was still in Jinzhou when the nationalization program started, and she found herself caught up in it. After she had left Jinzhou with Dr. Xia in 1951 his medicine business had been run by her brother, Yu-lin. When Dr. Xia died in 1952 ownership of the medicine shop passed to her. Now the state was planning to buy it out. In every business a group, made up of work team members and representatives of both employees and management, was set up to value its assets so the state could pay a "fair price." They would often suggest a very low figure—to please the authorities. The value placed on Dr. Xia's shop was ridiculously low, but there was an advantage to this for my grandmother: it meant that she was classified only as a "minor capitalist," which made it easier for her to keep a low profile. She was not happy about being quasi-expropriated, but she kept her own counsel.

As part of the nationalization campaign, the regime organized processions with drums and gongs—and endless meetings, some of them for the capitalists. My grandmother saw that all of them were expressing willingness to be bought out, even gratitude. Many said that what was happening to them was much better than they had feared. In the Soviet Union, they had heard, businesses were confiscated outright. Here in China the owners were being indemnified, and what was more, the state did not just order them to hand over their businesses. They had to be willing. Of course, everyone was.

My grandmother was confused about how she should feel—resentful toward the cause her daughter was engaged in, or happy with her lot, as she was told she should be. The medicine business had been built up by Dr. Xia's hard work, and her livelihood and that of her daughter had depended on it. She was reluctant to see it go just like that.

Four years earlier, during the Korean War, the government had encouraged people to donate their valuables to help buy fighter planes. My grandmother did not want to give up her jewelry, which had been given to her by General Xue and Dr. Xia, and had at times been her only source of income. It also had strong sentimental value. But my mother added her voice to that of the government. She felt that jewelry was connected with an outdated past, and shared the Party's view that it was the fruit of "the exploitation of the people"— and should therefore be returned to them. She also produced the standard line about protecting China from being invaded by the "U.S. imperialists," which did not mean very much to my grandmother. Her clinching arguments were: "Mother, what do you still want these things for? Nobody wears this sort of thing nowadays. And you don't have to rely on them to live. Now that we have the Communist Party, China is no longer going to be poor. What have you got to be worried about? In any case, you have me. I will look after you. You never have to worry again. I have to persuade other people to donate. It's part of my work. How can I ask them if my own mother doesn't do it?" My grandmother gave up. She would do anything for her daughter. She surrendered all her jewelry except a couple of bracelets, a pair of gold earrings, and a gold ring, which were wedding presents from Dr. Xia. She got a receipt from the government and much praise for her "patriotic zeal.."

But she was never happy about losing her jewelry, though she hid her feelings. Apart from sentimental attachment, there was a very practical consideration. My grandmother had lived through constant insecurity. Could one really trust the Communist Party to look after everyone? Forever?

Now, four years later, she was again in the situation of having to hand over to the state something she wanted to keep, in fact the last possession she had. This time, she did not really have any choice. But she was also positively cooperative. She did not want to let her daughter down, and wanted to make sure her daughter would not be even slightly embarrassed by her.

The nationalization of the shop was a long process, and my grandmother stayed on in Manchuria while it dragged on. My mother did not want her to come back to Sichuan anyway until she herself had her full freedom of movement restored and was able to live in her own quarters. It was not until summer 1956 that my mother recovered freedom of movement and the "parole" restrictions were lifted. However, even then there was no definitive decision on her case.

It was finally brought to a conclusion at the end of that year. The verdict, which was issued by the Chengdu Party authorities, said in effect that they believed her account, and that she had no political connection with the Kuomintang. This was a clear-cut decision which exonerated her completely. She was tremendously relieved, as she knew her case could well have been left open "for lack of satisfactory evidence," like many other similar cases. Then a stigma would have stuck with her for life. Now the chapter was closed, she thought. She was very grateful to the chief of the investigation team, Mr. Kuang. Usually officials tended to err on the side of overzealousness in order to protect themselves. It needed courage on the part of Mr. Kuang to decide to accept what she had said.

After eighteen months of intense anxiety, my mother was in the clear again. She was lucky. As a result of the campaign over 160,000 men and women were labeled "counterrevolutionaries," and their lives were ruined for three decades. Among these were some of my mother's friends in Jinzhou who had been the Kuomintang Youth League cadres. They were summarily branded "counterrevolutionaries," sacked from their jobs, and sent to do manual labor.

This campaign to root out the last vestiges of the Kuomintang past pushed family background and connections to the forefront. Throughout Chinese history, when one person was condemned sometimes the entire clan—men, women, and children, even newborn babies—was executed. Execution could extend to cousins nine times removed (*zhu-lian jiu-zu*). Someone being accused of a crime could endanger the lives of a whole neighborhood.

Hitherto the Communists had included people with "undesirable" backgrounds in their ranks. Many sons and daughters of their enemies rose to high positions. In fact, most early Communist leaders had come from "bad" backgrounds themselves. But after 1955 family origins became increasingly important. As the years went by and Mao launched one witch-hunt after another, the number of victims snowballed, and each victim brought down many others, including, first and foremost, his or her immediate family.

In spite of these personal tragedies, or perhaps partly because of the steely control, China was more stable in 1956 than at any time this century. Foreign occupation, civil war, widespread death from starvation, bandits, inflation—all seemed to be things of the past. Stability, the dream of the Chinese, sustained the faith of people like my mother in their sufferings.

In the summer of 1956 my grandmother returned to Chengdu. The first thing she did was to rush to the nurseries and take us back to my mother's place. My grandmother had a fundamental dislike of nurseries. She said children could not be properly looked after in a group. My sister and I looked all right, but as soon as we spotted her, we screamed and demanded to go home. The two boys were another matter: Jin-ming's teacher complained that he was terribly withdrawn, and would not let any adult touch him. He only asked, quietly but obstinately, for his old nurse. My grandmother burst into tears when she saw Xiao-hei. He looked like a wooden puppet, with a meaningless grin on his face. Wherever he was put, whether sitting or standing, he would just remain there, motionless. He did not know how to ask to go to the lavatory, and did not even seem to be able to cry. My grandmother swept him up into her arms and he instantly became her favorite.

Back at my mother's apartment, my grandmother gave vent to her anger and incomprehension. In between her tears she called my father and my mother "heartless parents." She did not know that my mother had no choice.

Because my grandmother could not look after all four of us, the two older ones, my sister and I, had to go to a nursery during the week. Every Monday morning, my father and his bodyguard would lift us onto their shoulders and carry us off howling, kicking, and tearing their hair.

This went on for some time. Then, subconsciously, I developed a way of protesting. I began to fall ill at the nursery, with high fevers which alarmed the doctors. As soon as I was back home, my illness miraculously evaporated. Eventually, my sister and I were allowed to stay at home.

For my grandmother, all flowers and trees, the clouds and the rain were living beings with a heart and tears and a moral sense. We would be safe if we followed the old Chinese rule for children, *ting-hua* ("heeding the words," being obedient). Otherwise all sorts of things would happen to us. When we ate oranges my grandmother would warn us against swallowing the seeds. "If you don't listen to me, one day you won't be able to get into the house. Every little seed is a baby orange tree, and he wants to grow up, just like you. He'll grow quietly inside your tummy, up and up, and then one day, *Ai-ya!* There he is, out from the top of your head! He'll grow leaves, and bear more oranges, and he'll become taller than our door . . ."

The thought of carrying an orange tree on my head fascinated me so much that one day I deliberately swallowed a seed—one, no more. I did not want an orchard on my head: that would be too heavy. For the whole day, I anxiously felt my skull every other minute to see whether it was still in one piece. Several times I almost asked my grandmother whether I would be allowed to eat the oranges on my head, but I checked myself so that she would not know I had been disobedient. I decided to pretend it was an accident when she saw the tree. I slept very badly that night. I felt something was pushing up against my skull.

But usually my grandmother's stories sent me happily to sleep. She had a wealth of them from classical Chinese opera. We also had a lot of books about animals and birds and myths and fairy tales. We had foreign children's stories, too, including Hans Christian Andersen and Aesop's fables. *Little Red Riding Hood, Snow White and the Seven Dwarfs*, and *Cinderella* were among my childhood companions.

Along with the stories, I loved nursery rhymes. They were my earliest encounters with poetry. Because the Chinese language is based on tones, its poetry has a particularly musical quality to it. I was mesmerized by my grandmother's chanting of classical poems, whose meaning I did not understand. She read them in traditional style, producing singsong, lingering sounds, rising and falling in cadence. One day my mother overheard her reciting to us some poems written in about 500 B.C. My mother thought they were far too difficult for us and tried to stop her. But my grandmother insisted, saying we did not have to understand the meaning, just get the feel for the musicality of the sounds. She often said she regretted losing her zither when she left Yixian twenty years before.

My two brothers were not so interested in bedtime stories, or in being read to. But my sister, who shared a room with me, was just like me: she loved these stories. And she had an extraordinary memory. She had impressed everyone by reciting Pushkin's long ballad "The Fisherman and the Goldfish" flawlessly at the age of three.

My family life was tranquil and loving. Whatever resentment my mother felt for my father, she seldom had rows with him, at least not in front of the children. My father's love for us was rarely shown through physical contact now that we were older. It was not customary for a father to hold his children in his arms, or to show affection by kissing them or embracing them. He would often give the boys piggyback rides, and would pat their shoulders or stroke their hair, which he rarely did to us girls. When we got beyond the age of three he would lift us carefully with his hands under our armpits, strictly adhering to Chinese convention, which prescribed avoiding intimacy with one's daughters. He would not come into the room where my sister and I slept without our permission.

My mother did not have as much physical contact with us as she would have liked. This was because she fell under another set of rules: those of the Communists' puritanical life-style. In the early 1950s, a Communist was supposed to give herself so completely to the revolution and the people that any demonstration of affection for her children was frowned on as a sign of divided loyalties. Every single hour apart from eating or sleeping belonged to the revolution, and was supposed to be spent working. Anything that was regarded as not to do with the revolution, like carrying your children in your arms, had to be dispatched with as speedily as possible.

At first, my mother found this hard to get used to. "Putting family first" was a criticism constantly leveled at her by her Party colleagues. Eventually, she became drilled into the habit of working nonstop. By the time she came home in the evening, we had long since gone to sleep. She would sit by our bedsides watching our faces as we slept and listening to our peaceful breathing. It was the happiest moment in her day.

Whenever she had time she would cuddle us, gently scratching or tickling us, especially on our elbows, which was intensely pleasurable. Pure heaven for me was putting my head on her lap and having the inside of my ears tickled. Ear-picking was a traditional form of pleasure for the Chinese. As a child, 1 remember seeing professionals carrying a stand with a bamboo chair on one end and scores of tiny fluffy picks dangling from the other.

Starting in 1956 officials started to have Sundays off. My parents would take us to parks and playgrounds where we played on the swings and merry-go-rounds or rolled down the grass-covered slopes. I have a memory of somersaulting dangerously but thrillingly downhill, meaning to career into my parents' arms, but instead crashing into two hibiscus trees, one after the other.

My grandmother was still appalled at how often my parents were absent. "What sort of parents are these?" she would sigh, shaking her head. To make up for them, she gave all her heart and energy to us. But she could not cope with four children on her own, so my mother invited Aunt Jun-ying to come and live with us. She and my grandmother got on very well, and this harmony continued when they were joined in early 1957 by a live-in maid. This coincided with our move to new quarters, in a former Christian vicarage. My father came with us, and so, for the first time ever, the whole family was living together under one roof.

The maid was eighteen. When she first arrived she was wearing a flower-patterned cotton top and slacks, which city dwellers, who wore quiet colors in keeping with both urban snobbery and Communist puritanism, would have regarded as rather garish. City ladies also had their clothes cut like Russian women's, but our maid wore traditional peasant-style garb, buttoned at the side, with cotton buttons instead of the new plastic ones. Instead of a belt, she used a cotton string to tie up her trousers. Many peasant women coming to town would have changed their attire so as not to look like country bumpkins. But she was completely unselfconscious about her clothes, which showed her strength of character. She had big, rough hands and a shy, honest smile on her dark, suntanned face, with two permanent dimples in her rosy cheeks. Everyone in our family liked her immediately. She ate with us and did the housework with my grandmother and my aunt. My grandmother was delighted to have two close friends and confidantes, as my mother was never there.

Our maid came from a landlord's family, and had been desperate to get away from the countryside and the constant discrimination she faced there. In 1957 it had again become possible to employ people from a "bad" family background. The 1955 campaign was over, and the atmosphere was generally more relaxed.

The Communists had instituted a system under which everyone had to register their place of residence *(hu-kou)*. Only those registered as urban dwellers were entitled to food rations. Our maid had a country registration so she had no source of food when she was with us, but the rations for my family were more than enough to feed her too. One year later, my mother helped her to move her registration into Chengdu.

My family also paid her wages. The system of state allowances had been abolished in late 1956, when my father also lost his bodyguard, who was replaced by a shared manservant who did chores for him in his office, like serving him tea and arranging cars. My parents were now earning salaries fixed according to their civil service grades. My mother was Grade 17, and my father was Grade 10, which meant he earned twice as much as she did. Because basics were cheap, and there was no concept of a consumer society, their combined income was more than adequate. My father was a member of a special category known as *gao-gan*, "high officials," a term applied to people of Grade 13 and above, of whom there were about 200 in Sichuan. There were fewer than twenty people of Grade 10 and above in the whole province, which had a population of about seventy-two million now.

In the spring of 1956 Mao announced a policy known as the Hundred Flowers, from the phrase "let a hundred flowers bloom" *(bai-hua qi-fang)*, which in theory meant greater freedom for the arts, literature, and scientific research. The Party wanted to enlist the support of China's educated citizens, which the country needed, as it was entering a stage of "post-recovery" industrialization.

The general educational level of the country had always been very low. The population was huge—over 600 million by then—and the vast majority had never enjoyed anything like a decent standard of living. The country had always had a dictatorship which operated by keeping the public ignorant and thus obedient. There was also the problem of the language: the Chinese script is exceedingly difficult; it is based on tens of thousands of individual characters which are not related to sounds, and each has complicated strokes and needs to be remembered separately. Hundreds of millions of people were completely illiterate.

Anybody with any education at all was referred to as an "intellectual." Under the Communists, who based their policies on class categories, "intellectuals" became a specific, if vague, category, which included nurses, students, and actors as well as engineers, technicians, writers, teachers, doctors, and scientists.

Under the Hundred Flowers policy, the country enjoyed about a year of relative relaxation. Then, in spring 1957, the Party urged intellectuals to criticize officials all the way to the top. My mother thought this was to encourage further liberalization. After a speech by Mao on the subject, which was gradually relayed down to her level, she was so moved she could not sleep all night. She felt that China was really going to have a modern and democratic party, a party that would welcome criticism to revitalize itself. She felt proud of being a Communist.

When my mother's level was told about Mao's speech soliciting criticism of officials, they were not informed about some other remarks he had made around the same time, about enticing snakes out of their lairs—to uncover anyone who dared to oppose him or his regime. One year before, the Soviet leader, Khrushchev, had denounced Stalin in his "secret speech," and this had devastated Mao, who identified himself with Stalin. Mao was further rattled by the Hungarian uprising that autumn, the first successful—if short-lived—attempt to overthrow an established Communist regime. Mao knew that a large proportion of China's educated people favored moderation and liberalization. He wanted to prevent a "Chinese Hungarian uprising." In fact, later, he effectively told the Hungarian leaders that his solicitation of criticism had been a trap, which he had prolonged after his colleagues suggested bringing it to a halt, in order to make sure he had smoked out every single potential dissident.

He was not worried about the workers or the peasants, as he was confident they were grateful to the Communists for bringing them full stomachs and stable lives. He also had a fundamental contempt for them—he did not believe they had the mental capacity to challenge his rule. But Mao had always distrusted intellectuals. They had played a big role in Hungary, and were more likely than others to think for themselves.

Unaware of Mao's secret maneuvers, officials and intellectuals alike engaged in soliciting and offering criticisms. According to Mao, they were to "say whatever they want to say, and to the full." My mother enthusiastically repeated this in the schools, hospitals, and entertainment groups she looked after. All kinds of opinions were aired at organized seminars and on wall posters. Well-known people set an example by making criticisms in the newspapers.

My mother, like almost everyone, came in for some criticism. The main one from the schools was that she showed favoritism toward "key" *(zhong-dian)* schools. In China there were a number of officially designated schools and universities on which the state concentrated its limited resources. These got better teachers and facilities, and selected the brightest pupils, which guaranteed that they had a high entrance rate into institutions of higher education, especially the "key" universities. Some teachers from ordinary schools complained that my mother had been paying too much attention to the "key" schools at their expense.

Teachers were also graded. Good teachers were given honorary grades which entitled them to much higher salaries, special food supplies when there was a shortage, better housing, and complimentary theater tickets. Most graded teachers under my mother seemed to have come from "undesirable" family backgrounds, and some of the ungraded teachers complained that my mother placed too much importance on professional merit rather than "class background." My mother made self-criticisms about her lack of evenhandedness regarding the "key" schools, but she insisted that she was not wrong in using professional merit as the criterion for promotion.

There was one criticism to which my mother turned a deaf ear in disgust. The headmistress of one primary school had joined the Communists in 1945—earlier than my mother—and was unhappy at having to take orders from her. This woman attacked my mother on the grounds that she had got her job solely on the strength of my father's status.

There were other complaints: the headmasters wanted the right to choose their own teachers, instead of having them assigned by a higher authority. Hospital directors wanted to be able to buy herbs and other medicines themselves, because the state supply did not meet their needs. Surgeons wanted larger food rations: they considered their job to be as demanding as that of a kung-fu player in a traditional opera, but their ration was a quarter less. A junior official lamented the disappearance from Chengdu markets of some famous traditional items like "Pockmark Wong scissors" and "Beards Hu brushes," which had been replaced by inferior mass-produced substitutes. My mother agreed with many of these views, but there was nothing she could do about them, as they involved state policies. All she could do was report them to higher authorities.

The outburst of criticisms, which were often personal grouses or practical, nonpolitical suggestions for improvements, blossomed for about a month in the early summer of 1957. At the beginning of June, Mao's speech about "enticing snakes out of their lairs" was relayed down orally to my mother's level.

In this talk, Mao said that "rightists" had gone on a rampage attacking the Communist Party and China's socialist system. He said these rightists made up between 1 percent and 10 percent of all intellectuals —and that they must be smashed. To simplify things, a figure of 5 percent, halfway between Mao's two extremes, had been established as the quota for the number of rightists who had to be caught. To meet it, my mother was expected to find over a hundred rightists in the organizations under her.

She had not been very happy about some of the criticisms made to her. But few of them could even remotely be considered "anti-Communist" or "anti-socialist." Judging from what she had read in the newspapers, it seemed there had been some attacks on the Communists' monopoly of power and on the socialist system. But in her schools and hospitals, there were no such grand calls. Where on earth could she find the rightists?

Besides, she thought, it was unfair to penalize people who had spoken up after they had been invited, indeed urged, to do so. Moreover, Mao had explicitly guaranteed that there would be no reprisals for speaking up. She herself had called enthusiastically on people to voice their criticisms.

Her dilemma was typical of that facing millions of officials across China. In Chengdu, the Anti-Rightist Campaign had a slow and painful start. The provincial authorities decided to make an example of one man, a Mr. Hau, who was the Party secretary of a research institute staffed by top scientists from all over Sichuan. He was expected to catch a considerable number of rightists, but he reported that there was not a single one in his institute. "How is that possible?" his boss said. Some of the scientists had studied abroad, in the West. "They must have been contaminated by Western society. How can you expect them to be happy under communism? How can there be no rightists among them?" Mr. Hau said that the fact that they were in China by choice proved they were not opposed to the Communists, and went so far as to give a personal guarantee for them. He was warned several times to mend his ways. In the end he was declared a rightist himself, expelled from the Party, and sacked from his job. His civil service grade was drastically reduced, which meant his salary was slashed, and he was put to work sweeping the floors of the laboratories in the institute he had formerly been running.

My mother knew Mr. Hau, and admired him for sticking to his guns. She developed a great friendship with him which has lasted till today. She spent many evenings with him, giving vent to her anxieties. But in his fate she saw her own if she did not fill her quota.

Every day, after the usual endless meetings, my mother had to report to the municipal Party authorities on how the campaign was going. The person in charge of the campaign in Chengdu was a Mr. Ying, a lean, tall, rather arrogant man. My mother was supposed to produce figures for him showing how many rightists had been nailed. There did not have to be any names. It was numbers that mattered.

But where could she find her 100-plus "anti-Communist, anti-socialist rightists"? Eventually one of her deputies, a Mr. Kong, who was in charge of education for the Eastern District, announced that the headmistresses of a couple of schools had identified some teachers in their schools. One was a teacher in a primary school whose husband, a Kuomintang officer, had been killed in the civil war. She had said something to the effect that "China today is worse off than in the past." One day she got into a row with the headmistress, who had criticized her for slacking off. She flew into a rage and hit the headmistress. A couple of other teachers tried to stop her, one telling her to be careful because the headmistress was pregnant. She was reported to have screamed that she wanted to "get rid of that Communist bastard" (meaning the baby in the woman's womb).

In another case, a teacher whose husband had fled to Taiwan with the Kuomintang was reported to have shown off to other young women teachers some jewelry her husband had given her, trying to make them envious of her life under the Kuomintang. These young women also said she told them it was a pity the Americans had not won the war in Korea and advanced into China.

Mr. Kong said he had checked the facts. It was not up to my mother to investigate. Caution would be seen as trying to protect the rightists and questioning her colleagues' integrity.

The hospital chiefs and the deputy who was running the health bureau did not name any rightists themselves, but several doctors were labeled rightists by the higher authorities of the Chengdu municipality for their criticisms made at earlier meetings organized by the city authorities.

All these rightists together came to fewer than ten, far short of the quota. By now Mr. Ying was fed up with the lack of zeal displayed by my mother and her colleagues, and he told her that the fact that she could not spot rightists showed she was "rightist material" herself. To be labeled a rightist not only meant becoming a political outcast and losing one's job, but, most important, one's children and family would suffer discrimination and their future would be in jeopardy. The children would be ostracized at school and in the street where they lived. The residents' committee would spy on the family to see who was visiting them. If a rightist was sent to the countryside, the peasants would give the hardest jobs to him and his family. But no one knew the exact impact, and this uncertainty was itself a powerful cause of fear.

This was the dilemma facing my mother. If she was labeled a rightist, she would either have to renounce her children or ruin their future. My father would probably be forced to divorce her, or he too would be blacklisted and under permanent suspicion. Even if my mother sacrificed herself and divorced him, the whole family would still be marked as suspects, forever. But the cost of saving herself and her family was the well-being of more than a hundred innocent people and their families.

My mother did not talk to my father about this. What solution could he have come up with? She felt resentful because his high position meant he did not have to deal with specific cases. It was the lower- and middle-rank officials like Mr. Ying, my mother, her deputies, the headmistresses, and hospital directors who had to make these agonizing decisions.

One of the institutions in my mother's district was the Chengdu Number Two Teacher Training College. Students in teacher training colleges were given scholarships which covered their fees and living expenses, and these institutions naturally attracted people from poor families. The first railway linking Sichuan, "Heaven's Granary," with the rest of China had recently been completed. As a result, a lot of food was suddenly transported out of Sichuan to other parts of China, and the prices of many items doubled or even tripled almost overnight. The students at the college found their standard of living practically halved, and staged a demonstration calling for higher grants. This action was compared by Mr. Ying to those of the Petőfi Circle in the

1956 Hungarian uprising, and he called the students "kindred spirits of the Hungarian intellectuals." He ordered that every student who had participated in the demonstration should be classified as a rightist. There were about 300 students at the college, of whom 130 had taken part in the demonstration. All of them were labeled rightists by Mr. Ying. Although the college was not under my mother, as she looked after primary schools only, it was located in her district, and the city authorities arbitrarily counted the students as her quota.

My mother was not forgiven for her lack of initiative. Mr. Ying put her name down for further investigation as a rightist suspect. But before he could do anything, he was condemned as a rightist himself.

In March 1957 he had gone to Peking for a conference of the heads of provincial and municipal Public Affairs departments from the whole of China. In the group discussions, delegates were encouraged to voice their complaints about the way things were run in their areas. Mr. Ying aired some fairly innocuous grumbles against the first secretary of the Sichuan Party Committee, Li Jing-quan, who was always known as Commissar Li. My father was the head of the Sichuan delegation at the conference, so it fell to him to write the routine report when they came back. When the Anti-Rightist Campaign started, Commissar Li decided he did not like what Mr. Ying had said. He checked with the deputy head of the delegation, but this man had adroitly absented himself in the toilet when Mr. Ying started his criticism. In the later stage of the campaign, Commissar Li labeled Mr. Ying a rightist. When he heard this, my father became desperately upset, tormenting himself with the thought that he was partly responsible for Mr. Ying's downfall. My mother tried to convince him this was not the case: "It's not your fault!" she told him. But he never stopped agonizing about it.

Many officials used the campaign to settle personal scores. Some found that one easy way to fill their quota was to offer up their enemies. Others acted out of sheer vindictiveness. In Yibin, the Tings purged many talented people with whom they did not get on, or of whom they were jealous. Almost all of my father's assistants there, whom he had picked out and promoted, were condemned as rightists. One former assistant whom my father liked very much was branded an "extreme rightist." His crime was a single remark to the effect that China's reliance on the Soviet Union should not be "absolute." At the time the Party was proclaiming that it should be. He was sentenced to three years in one of China's gulags and worked on building a road in a wild, mountainous area, where many of his fellow prisoners died.

The Anti-Rightist Campaign did not affect society at large. Peasants and workers carried on with their lives. When the campaign ended after a year, at least 550,000 people had been labeled as rightists—students, teachers, writers, artists, scientists, and other professionals. Most of them were sacked from their jobs and became manual laborers in factories or on farms. Some were sent to do hard labor in gulags. They and their families became second-class citizens. The lesson was harsh and clear: criticism of any kind was not going to be tolerated. From that point on people stopped complaining, or speaking up at all. A popular saying summed up the atmosphere: "After the Three Antis no one wants to be in charge of money; after the Anti-Rightist Campaign no one opens their mouth."

But the tragedy of 1957 was more than that of reducing people to silence. The possibility of falling into the abyss now became unpredictable. The quota system combined with personal vendettas meant that anyone could be persecuted, for nothing.

The vernacular caught the mood. Among the categories of rightists were "lots-drawing rightists" (*chou-qian you-pai*), people who drew lots to decide who should be named as rightists, and "toilet rightists" (*cesuo you-pai*), people who found they had been nominated in their absence after they could not restrain themselves from going to the toilet during the many long, drawn-out meetings. There were also rightists who were said to "have poison but not released it" (*you-du bu-fang*); these were people who were named as rightists without having said anything against anyone. When a boss did not like someone, he could say: "He doesn't look right," or "His father was executed by the Communists, how can he not feel resentful? He just won't say it openly." A kindhearted unit leader sometimes did the opposite: "Whom should I nail? I can't do that to anyone. Say it's me." He was popularly called a "self-acknowledged rightist" (*zi-ren you-pai*).

For many people 1957 was a watershed. My mother was still devoted to the Communist cause, but doubts crept in about its practice. She talked about these doubts with her friend Mr. Hau, the purged director of the research institute, but she never revealed them to my father—not because he had no doubts, but because he would not discuss them with her. Party rules, like military orders, forbade members from talking about Party policies among themselves. It was stipulated in the Party charter that every member must unconditionally obey his Party organization, that a lower-rank official must obey a higher-rank one. If you had any disagreement, you could mention it only to a higher-rank official, who was deemed to be an incarnation of the Party organization. This regimental discipline, which the Communists had insisted on since the Yan'an days and earlier, was crucial to their success. It was a formidable instrument of power, as it needed to be in a society where personal relationships overrode any other rules. My father adhered to this discipline totally. He believed that the revolution could not be preserved and sustained if it were challenged openly. In a revolution you had to fight for your side even if it was not perfect—as long as you believed it was better than the other side. Unity was the categorical imperative.

My mother could see that as far as my father's relationship with the Party was concerned, she was an outsider. One day, when she ventured some critical comments about the situation and got no response from him, she said bitterly, "You are a good Communist, but a rotten husband!" My father nodded. He said he knew.

Fourteen years later, my father told us children what had almost happened to him in 1957. Since his early days in Yan'an, when he was a young man of twenty, he had been close friends with a well-known woman writer called Ding Ling. In March 1957, when he was in Peking leading the Sichuan delegation at a Public Affairs conference, she sent him a message inviting him to visit her in Tianjin, near Peking. My father wanted to go, but decided against it because he was in a hurry to get home. Several months later Ding Ling was labeled as the number-one rightist in China. "If I had gone to see her," my father told us, "I would have been done for too."

12. "Capable Women Can Make a Meal without Food"— Famine

(1958–1962)

In the autumn of 1958, when I was six, I started going to a primary school about twenty minutes' walk from home, mostly along muddy cobbled back alleys. Every day on my way to and from school, I screwed up my eyes to search every inch of ground for broken nails, rusty cogs, and any other metal objects that had been trodden into the mud between the cobbles. These were for feeding into furnaces to produce steel, which was my major occupation. Yes, at the age of six, I was involved in steel production, and had to compete with my schoolmates at handing in the most scrap iron. All around me uplifting music blared from loudspeakers, and there were banners, posters, and huge slogans painted on the walls proclaiming "Long Live the Great Leap Forward!" and "Everybody, Make Steel!" Although I did not fully understand why, I knew that Chairman Mao had ordered the nation to make a lot of steel. In my school, cruciblelike vats had replaced some of our cooking woks and were sitting on the giant stoves in the kitchen. All our scrap iron was fed into them, including the old woks, which had now been broken to bits. The stoves were kept permanently lit—until they melted down. Our teachers took turns feeding firewood into them around-the-clock, and stirring the scraps in the vats with a huge spoon. We did not have many lessons, as the teachers were too preoccupied with the vats. So were the older, teenage children. The rest of us were organized to clean the teachers' apartments and babysit for them.

I remember visiting a hospital once with some other children to see one of our teachers who had been seriously burned when molten iron had splashed onto her arms. Doctors and nurses in white coats were rushing around frantically. There was a furnace on the hospital grounds, and they had to feed logs into it all the time, even when they were performing operations, and right through the night.

Shortly before I started going to school, my family had moved from the old vicarage into a special compound, which was the center of government for the province. It enclosed several streets, with blocks of apartments and offices and a number of mansions; a high wall blocked it off from the outside world. Inside the main gate was what had been the U.S. Servicemen's Club during the Second World War. Ernest Hemingway had stayed there in 1941. The club building was in traditional Chinese style, with the ends of its yellow tiled roof turning upward, and heavy dark red pillars. It was now the office of the secretariat of the Sichuan government.

A huge furnace was erected in the parking lot where the chauffeurs used to wait. At night the sky was lit up, and the noise of the crowds around the furnace could be heard 300 yards away in my room. My family's woks went into this furnace, together with all our cast-iron cooking utensils. We did not suffer from their loss, as we did not need them anymore. No private cooking was allowed now, and everybody had to eat in the canteen. The furnaces were insatiable. Gone was my parents' bed, a soft, comfortable one with iron springs. Gone also were the iron railings from the city pavements, and anything else that was iron. I hardly saw my parents for months. They often did not come home at all, as they had to make sure the temperature in their office furnaces never dropped.

It was at this time that Mao gave full vent to his half-baked dream of turning China into a first-class modern power. He called steel the "marshal" of industry, and ordered steel output to be doubled in one year—from 5.35 million tons in 1957 to 10.7 million in 1958. But instead of trying to expand the proper steel industry with skilled workers, he decided to get the whole population to take part. There was a steel quota for every unit, and for months people stopped their normal work in order to meet it. The country's economic development was reduced to the simplistic question of how many tons of steel could be produced, and the entire nation was thrown into this single act. It was officially estimated that nearly 100 million peasants were pulled out of agricultural work and into steel production. They had been the labor force producing much of the country's food. Mountains were stripped bare of trees for fuel. But the output of this mass production amounted only to what people called "cattle droppings" (niu-shi-ge-da), meaning useless turds.

This absurd situation reflected not only Mao's ignorance of how an economy worked, but also an almost metaphysical disregard for reality, which might have been interesting in a poet, but in a political leader with absolute power was quite another matter. One of its main components was a deep-seated contempt for human life. Not long before this he had told the Finnish ambassador, "Even if the United States had more powerful atom bombs and used them on China, blasted a hole in the earth, or blew it to pieces, while this might be a matter of great significance to the solar system, it would still be an insignificant matter as far as the universe as a whole is concerned."

Mao's voluntarism had been fueled by his recent experience in Russia. Increasingly disillusioned with Khrushchev after his denunciation of Stalin in 1956, Mao went to Moscow in late 1957 to attend a world Communist summit. He returned convinced that Russia and its allies were abandoning socialism and turning "revisionist." He saw China as the only true believer. It had to blaze a new path. Megalomania and voluntarism meshed easily in Mao's mind.

Mao's fixation on steel went largely unquestioned, as did his other obsessions. He took a dislike to sparrows—they devour grain. So every household was mobilized. We sat outside ferociously beating any metal object, from cymbals to saucepans, to scare the sparrows off the trees so they would eventually drop dead from exhaustion. Even today I can vividly hear the din made by my siblings and me, as well as by the government officials, sitting under a mammoth wolfberry tree in our courtyard.

There were also fantastic economic goals. Mao claimed that China's industrial output could overtake that of the United States and Britain within fifteen years. For the Chinese, these countries represented the capitalist world. Overtaking them would be seen as a triumph over their enemies. This appealed to people's pride, and boosted their enthusiasm enormously. They had felt humiliated by the refusal of the United States and most major Western countries to grant diplomatic recognition, and were so keen to show the world that they could make it on their own that they wanted to believe in miracles. Mao provided the inspiration. The energy of the population had been eager to find an outlet. And here it was. The gung-ho spirit overrode caution, as ignorance triumphed over reason.

In early 1958, shortly after returning from Moscow, Mao visited

Chengdu for about a month. He was fired up with the idea that China could do anything, especially seize the leadership of socialism from the Russians. It was in Chengdu that he outlined his "Great Leap Forward." The city organized a big parade for him, but the participants had no idea that Mao was there. He lurked out of sight. At this parade a slogan was put forward, "Capable women can make a meal without food," a reversal of a pragmatic ancient Chinese saying, "No matter how capable, a woman cannot make a meal without food." Exaggerated rhetoric had become concrete demands. Impossible fantasies were supposed to become reality.

It was a gorgeous spring that year. One day Mao went for an outing to a park called the Thatched Cottage of Du Fu, the eighth-century Tang poet. My mother's Eastern District office was responsible for the security of one area of the park, and she and her colleagues patrolled it, pretending to be tourists. Mao rarely kept to a schedule, or let people know his precise movements, so for hours and hours my mother sat sipping tea in the teahouse, trying to keep on the alert. She finally grew restless and told her colleagues she was going for a walk. She strayed into the security area of the Western District, whose staff did not know her, and was immediately followed. When the Party secretary of the Western District received reports about a "suspicious woman" and came to see for himself, he laughed: "Why, this is old Comrade Xia from the Eastern District!" Afterward my mother was criticized by her boss, district chief Guo, for "running around without discipline."

Mao also visited a number of farms in the Chengdu Plain. Thus far, peasant cooperatives had been small. It was here that Mao ordered them all to be merged into bigger institutions, which were later called "people's communes."

That summer, all of China was organized into these new units, each containing between 2,000 and 20,000 households. One of the forerunners of this drive was an area called Xushui, in Hebei province in North China, to which Mao took a shine. In his eagerness to prove that they deserved Mao's attention, the local boss there claimed they were going to produce over ten times as much grain as before. Mao smiled broadly and responded: "What are you going to do with all that food? On second thought, it's not too bad to have too much food, really. The state doesn't want it. Everybody else has plenty of their own. But the farmers here can just eat and eat. You can eat five meals a day!" Mao was intoxicated, indulging in the eternal dream of the Chinese peasant—surplus food. After these remarks, the villagers further stoked the desires of their Great Leader by claiming that they were producing more than a million pounds of potatoes per *mu* (one *mu* is one-sixth of an acre), over 130,000 pounds of wheat per *mu*, and cabbages weighing 500 pounds each.

It was a time when telling fantasies to oneself as well as others, and believing them, was practiced to an incredible degree. Peasants moved crops from several plots of land to one plot to show Party officials that they had produced a miracle harvest. Similar "Potemkin fields" were shown off to gullible—or self-blinded—agricultural scientists, reporters, visitors from other regions, and foreigners. Although these crops generally died within a few days because of untimely transplantation and harmful density, the visitors did not know that, or did not want to know. A large part of the population was swept into this confused, crazy world. "Self-deception while deceiving others" (*zi-qi-qi-ren*) gripped the nation. Many people—including agricultural scientists and senior Party leaders—said they saw the miracles themselves. Those who failed to match other people's fantastic claims began to doubt and blame themselves. Under a dictatorship like Mao's, where information was withheld and fabricated, it was very difficult for ordinary people to have confidence in their own experience or knowledge. Not to mention that they were now facing a nationwide tidal wave of fervor which promised to swamp any individual coolheadedness. It was easy to start ignoring reality and simply put one's faith in Mao. To go along with the frenzy was by far the easiest course. To pause and think and be circumspect meant trouble.

An official cartoon portrayed a mouselike scientist whining, "A stove like yours can only boil water to make tea." Next to him stood a giant worker, lifting a huge sluice gate releasing a flood of molten steel, who retorted, "How much can you drink?" Most who saw the absurdity of the situation were too frightened to speak their minds, particularly after the Anti-Rightist Campaign of 1957. Those who did voice doubts were immediately silenced, or sacked, which also meant discrimination against their family and a bleak prospect for their children.

In many places, people who refused to boast of massive increases in output were beaten up until they gave in. In Yibin, some leaders of production units were trussed up with their arms behind their backs in the village square while questions were hurled at them:

"How much wheat can you produce per *mu*?"

"Four hundred *jin*" (about 450 pounds—a realistic amount).

Then, beating him: "How much wheat can you produce per *mu*?"

"Eight hundred *jin*."

Even this impossible figure was not enough. The unfortunate man would be beaten, or simply left hanging, until he finally said: "Ten thousand *jin*." Sometimes the man died hanging there because he refused to increase the figure, or simply before he could raise the figure high enough.

Many grass-roots officials and peasants involved in scenes like this did not believe in the ridiculous boasting, but fear of being accused themselves drove them on. They were carrying out the orders of the Party, and they were safe as long as they followed Mao. The totalitarian system in which they had been immersed had sapped and warped their sense of responsibility. Even doctors would boast about miraculously healing incurable diseases.

Trucks used to turn up at our compound carrying grinning peasants coming to report on some fantastic, record-breaking achievement. One day it was a monster cucumber half as long as the truck. Another time it was a tomato carried with difficulty by two children. On another occasion there was a giant pig squeezed into a truck. The peasants claimed they had bred an actual pig this size. The pig was only made of papier-mâché, but as a child I imagined that it was real. Maybe I was confused by the adults around me, who behaved as though all this were true. People had learned to defy reason and to live with acting.

The whole nation slid into doublespeak. Words became divorced from reality, responsibility, and people's real thoughts. Lies were told with ease because words had lost their meanings—and had ceased to be taken seriously by others.

This was entrenched by the further regimentation of society. When he first set up the communes, Mao said their main advantage was that "they are easy to control," because the peasants would now be in an organized system rather than being, to a certain extent, left alone. They were given detailed orders from the very top about how to till their land. Mao summed up the whole of agriculture in eight characters: "soil, fertilizer, water, seeds, dense planting, protection, tending, technology." The Party Central Committee in Peking was handing out two-page instructions on how peasants all over China should improve their fields, another page on how to use fertilizers, another on planting crops densely. Their incredibly simplistic instructions had to be strictly followed: the peasants were ordered to replant their crops more densely in one mini-campaign after another.

Another means of regimentation, setting up canteens in the communes, was an obsession with Mao at the time. In his airy way, he defined communism as "public canteens with free meals." The fact that the canteens themselves did not produce food did not concern him. In 1958 the regime effectively banned eating at home. Every peasant had to eat in the commune canteen. Kitchen utensils like woks—and, in some places, money—were outlawed. Everybody was going to be looked after by the commune and the state. The peasants filed into the canteens everyday after work and ate to their heart's content, which they had never been able to do before, even in the best years and in the most fertile areas. They consumed and wasted the entire food reserve in the countryside. They filed into the fields, too. But how much work was done did not matter, because the produce now belonged to the state, and was completely unrelated to the peasants' lives. Mao put forward the prediction that China was reaching a society of communism, which in Chinese means "sharing material goods," and the peasants took this to mean that they would get a share anyway, regardless of how much work they did. With no incentive to work, they just went to the fields and had a good snooze.

Agriculture was also neglected because of the priority given to steel. Many of the peasants were exhausted from having to spend long hours finding fuel, scrap iron, and iron ore and keeping the furnaces going. The fields were often left to the women and children, who had to do everything by hand, as the animals were busy making their contribution to steel production. When harvest time came in autumn 1958, few people were in the fields.

The failure to get in the harvest in 1958 flashed a warning that a food shortage was on its way, even though official statistics showed a double-digit increase in agricultural output. It was officially announced that in 1958 China's wheat output had overtaken that of the United States. The Party newspaper, the *People's Daily*, started a discussion on the topic "How do we cope with the problem of producing too much food?"

My father's department was in charge of the press in Sichuan, which printed outlandish claims, as did every publication in China. The press was the voice of the Party, and when it came to Party policies, neither my father nor anyone else in the media had any say. They were part of a huge conveyor belt. My father watched the turn of events with alarm. His only option was to appeal to the top leaders.

At the end of 1958 he wrote a letter to the Central Committee in Peking stating that producing steel like this was pointless and a waste of resources; the peasants were exhausted, their labor was being squandered, and there was a food shortage. He appealed for urgent action. He gave the letter to the governor to pass on. The governor, Lee Da-zhang, was the number-two man in the province. He had given my father his first job when he had come to Chengdu from Yibin, and treated him like a friend.

Governor Lee told my father he was not going to forward the letter. Nothing in it was new, he said. "The Party knows everything. Have faith in it." Mao had said that under no circumstances must the people's morale be dampened. The Great Leap Forward had changed the psychological attitude of the Chinese from passivity to a can-do, get-up-and-go spirit, he said, which must not be imperiled.

Governor Lee also told my father that he had been given the dangerous nickname "Opposition" among the provincial leaders, to whom he had voiced disagreements. It was only because of his other qualities, his absolute loyalty to the Party and his stern sense of discipline, that my father was still all right. "The good thing," the governor said, "is that you only voiced your doubts to the Party, and not to the public." He warned my father he could get into serious trouble if he insisted on raising these concerns, as could his family and "others," clearly meaning himself, my father's friend. My father did not insist. He was half convinced by the argument, and the stakes were too high. He had reached a stage where he was not insusceptible to compromise.

But my father and the people working in the departments of Public Affairs collected a great number of complaints, as part of their jobs, and forwarded them to Peking. There was general discontent among the people and officials alike. In fact, the Great Leap Forward triggered off the most serious split in the leadership since the Communists had taken power a decade before. Mao had to step down from the less important of his two main posts, president of the state, in favor of Liu Shaoqi. Liu became the number-two man in China, but his prestige was only a fraction of that of Mao, who kept his key post as chairman of the Party.

The voices of dissent grew so strong that the Party had to convene a special conference, which was held at the end of June 1959 in the mountain resort of Lushan, in central China. At the conference the defense minister, Marshal Peng Dehuai, wrote a letter to Mao criticizing what had happened in the Great Leap Forward and recommending a realistic approach to the economy. The letter was actually rather restrained, and ended on the obligatory note of optimism (in this case, catching up with Britain in four years). But although Peng was one of Mao's oldest comrades, and one of the people closest to him, Mao could not take even this slight criticism, particularly at a time when he was on the defensive, because he knew he was wrong. Using the aggrieved language of which he was enamored, Mao called the letter "a bombardment intended to level Lushan." He dug in his heels and dragged the conference out for over a month, fiercely attacking Marshal Peng. Peng and the few who openly supported him were branded "rightist opportunists." Peng was dismissed as defense minister, placed under house arrest, and later sent into premature retirement in Sichuan, where he was assigned a lowly post.

Mao had had to scheme hard to preserve his power. In this he was a supreme master. His favorite reading, which he recommended to other Party leaders, was a classic multi-volume collection about court power and intrigues. In fact, Mao's rule was best understood in terms of a medieval court, in which he exercised spellbinding power over his courtiers and subjects. He was also a maestro at "divide and rule," and at manipulating men's inclination to throw others to the wolves. In the end, few top officials stood up for Marshal Peng, in spite of their private disenchantment with Mao's policies. The only one who avoided having to show his hand was the general secretary of the Party, Deng Xiaoping, who had broken his leg. Deng's stepmother had been grumbling at home, "I was a farmer all my life and I have never heard of such a nonsensical way of farming!" When Mao heard how Deng had broken his leg—playing billiards—he commented, "How very convenient."

Commissar Li, the Sichuan first secretary, returned to Chengdu from the conference with a document containing the remarks Peng had made at Lushan. This was distributed to officials of Grade 17 and above; they were asked to state formally whether they agreed with it.

My father had heard something about the Lushan dispute from the governor of Sichuan. At his "exam" meeting my father made some vague remarks about Peng's letter. Then he did something he had never done before: he warned my mother that it was a trap. She was greatly moved. This was the first time he had ever put her interests before the rules of the Party.

She was surprised to see that a lot of other people seemed to have been tipped off as well. At her collective "exam," half of her colleagues showed flaming indignation against Peng's letter, and claimed the criticisms in it were "totally untrue." Others looked as though they had lost their ability to speak, and mumbled something evasive. One man managed to straddle the fence, saying, "I am not in a position to agree or disagree because I do not know whether the evidence given by Marshal Peng is factual or not. If it is, I would support him. Of course, I would not if it were not true."

The chief of the grain bureau for Chengdu and the chief of the Chengdu post office were Red Army veterans who had fought under

Marshal Peng. They both said they agreed with what their old and much-revered commander had said, adding their own experiences in the countryside to back up Peng's observations. My mother wondered whether these old soldiers knew about the trap. If so, the way they spoke their minds was heroic. She wished she had their courage. But she thought of her children—what would happen to them? She was no longer the free spirit she had been as a student. When her turn came she said, "The views in the letter are not in keeping with the policies of the Party over the last couple of years."

She was told by her boss, Mr. Guo, that her remarks were thoroughly unsatisfactory because she had failed to state her attitude. For days she lived in a state of acute anxiety. The Red Army veterans who had supported Peng were denounced as "rightist opportunists," sacked, and sent to do manual labor. My mother was called to a meeting to have her "right-wing tendencies" criticized. At the meeting, Mr. Guo described another of her "serious errors." In 1959 a sort of black market had sprung up in Chengdu selling chickens and eggs. Because the communes had taken over chickens from individual peasants, and were incapable of raising them, chickens and eggs had disappeared from the shops, which were state owned. A few peasants had somehow managed to keep one or two chickens at home under their beds, and were now surreptitiously selling them and their eggs in the back alleys at about twenty times their previous price. Officials were sent out every day to try to catch the peasants. Once, when my mother was asked by Mr. Guo to go on one of these raids, she said, "What's wrong with supplying things people need? If there is demand, there should be supply." Because of this remark, my mother was given a warning about her "right-wing tendencies."

The purge of "rightist opportunists" rocked the Party once again, as a great many officials agreed with Peng. The lesson was that Mao's authority was unchallengeable—even though he was clearly in the wrong. Officials could see that no matter how high up you were— Peng, after all, was the defense minister—and no matter what your standing—Peng had reputedly been Mao's favorite—if you offended Mao you would fall into disgrace. They also knew that you could not speak your mind and resign, or even resign quietly: resignation was seen as an unacceptable protest. There was no opting out. The mouths of the Party as well as the people were now tightly sealed. After this, the Great Leap Forward went into further, madder excesses. More impossible economic goals were imposed from on high.

More peasants were mobilized to make steel. And more arbitrary orders rained down, causing chaos in the countryside.

At the end of 1958, at the height of the Great Leap Forward, a massive construction project was begun: ten great buildings in the capital, Peking, to be completed in ten months to mark the tenth anniversary, 1 October 1959, of the founding of the People's Republic.

One of the ten buildings was the Great Hall of the People, a Soviet-style columned edifice on the west side of Tiananmen Square. Its marbled front was a good quarter of a mile long, and its chandeliered main banqueting hall could seat several thousand people. This was where important meetings were to be held and the leaders were to receive foreign visitors. The rooms, all to be on a grand scale, were named after the provinces of China. My father was put in charge of the decoration of the Sichuan Room, and when the work was completed he invited Party leaders who had been connected with Sichuan to inspect it. Deng Xiaoping, who was from Sichuan, came, as did Marshal Ho Lung, a famous Robin Hood figure who had been one of the founders of the Red Army, and was a close friend of Deng's.

At one point my father was called away, leaving these two and another old colleague of theirs—actually Deng's brother—chatting among themselves. As he came back into the room he heard Marshal Ho saying to Deng's brother, while pointing at Deng: "It really should be him on the throne." At that moment they spotted my father and immediately stopped talking.

My father was in a state of intense apprehension after this. He knew he had accidentally overheard hints of disagreements at the top of the regime. Any conceivable action, or inaction, could get him into deadly trouble. In fact, nothing happened to him, but when he told me about the incident almost ten years later he said he had lived with the fear of disaster ever since. "Just to have heard that amounts to treason," he said, using a phrase which means "a crime bringing decapitation."

What he had overheard was nothing but an indication of some disenchantment with Mao. This sentiment was shared by many top leaders, not least by the new president, Liu Shaoqi.

In autumn 1959 Liu came to Chengdu to inspect a commune called "Red Splendor." The previous year, Mao had been highly enthusiastic about the astronomical rice output there. Before Liu arrived the local officials rounded up anyone they thought might expose them, and locked them up in a temple. But Liu had a "mole," and as he was walking past the temple he stopped and asked to have a look inside.

The officials made various excuses, even claiming that the temple was about to collapse, but Liu refused to take no for an answer. Eventually the big, rusty lock was clicked open, and a group of shabby peasants stumbled out into the daylight. The embarrassed local officials tried to explain to Liu that these were "troublemakers" who had been locked up because they might harm the distinguished visitor. The peasants themselves were silent. Commune officials, though completely impotent regarding policies, held awesome power over people's lives. If they wanted to punish someone, they could give him the worst job to do, the least food, and invent an excuse to have him harassed, denounced, even arrested.

President Liu asked some questions, but the peasants just smiled and mumbled. From their point of view it was better to offend the president than the local bosses. The president would be leaving for Peking in a few minutes, but the commune bosses would be with them for the rest of their lives.

Shortly afterward another senior leader also came to Chengdu—Marshal Zhu De—accompanied by one of Mao's private secretaries. Zhu De was from Sichuan and had been the commander of the Red Army, and military architect of the Communists' victory. Since 1949 he had kept a low profile. He visited several communes near Chengdu, and afterward, as he strolled by the Silk River looking at the pavilions, bamboo groves, and willow-embraced teahouses along the riverbank, he waxed emotional: "Sichuan is indeed a heavenly place. . . ." He spoke the words in the style of a line of poetry. Mao's secretary added the matching line, in the traditional poet's fashion: "Pity that damning gales of lie telling and false communism are destroying it!" My mother was with them, and thought to herself: I agree wholeheartedly.

Suspicious of his colleagues, and still angry about being attacked at Lushan, Mao obstinately stuck to his crazy economic policies. Although he was not unaware of the disasters they had been causing, and was discreetly allowing some of the most impracticable ones to be revised, his "face" would not allow him to give up completely. Meanwhile, as the sixties began, a great famine spread across the whole of China.

In Chengdu, the monthly food ration for each adult was reduced to 19 pounds of rice, 3.5 ounces of cooking oil, and 3.5 ounces of meat, when there was any. Scarcely anything else was available, not even cabbage. Many people were afflicted by edema, a condition in which fluid accumulates under the skin because of malnutrition. The patient turns yellow and swells up. The most popular remedy was eating chlorella, which was supposed to be rich in protein. Chlorella fed on human urine, so people stopped going to the toilet and peed into spittoons instead, then dropped the chlorella seeds in; they grew into something looking like green fish roe in a couple of days, and were scooped out of the urine, washed, and cooked with rice. They were truly disgusting to eat, but did reduce the swelling.

Like everybody else, my father was entitled only to a limited food ration. But as a senior official he had some privileges. In our compound there were two canteens, a small one for departmental directors and their wives and children, and a big one for everyone else, which included my grandmother, my aunt Jun-ying, and the maid. Most of the time we collected our food at the canteens and took it home to eat. There was more food in the canteens than on the streets. The provincial government had its own farm, and there were also "presents" from county governments. These valuable supplies were divided between the canteens, and the small one got preferential treatment.

As Party officials, my parents also had special food coupons. I used to go with my grandmother to a special store outside the compound to buy food with them. My mother's coupons were blue. She was entitled to five eggs, almost an ounce of soybeans, and the same amount of sugar per month. My father's coupons were yellow. He was entitled to twice as much as my mother because of his higher rank. My family pooled the food from the canteens and the other sources and ate together. The adults always gave the children more, so I did not go hungry. But the adults all suffered from malnutrition, and my grandmother developed slight edema. She grew chlorella at home, and I was aware that the adults were eating it, although they would not tell me what it was for. Once I tried a little, and immediately spat it out as it tasted revolting. I never had it again.

I had little idea that famine was raging all around me. One day on my way to school, as I was eating a small steamed roll, someone rushed up and snatched it from my hands. As I was recovering from the shock, I caught a glimpse of a very thin, dark back in shorts and bare feet running down the mud alley with his hand to his mouth, devouring the roll. When I told my parents what had happened, my father's eyes were terribly sad. He stroked my head and said, "You are lucky. Other children like you are starving."

I often had to visit the hospital for my teeth at that time. Whenever I went there I had an attack of nausea at the horrible sight of dozens of people with shiny, almost transparent swollen limbs, as big as barrels. The patients were carried to the hospital on flat carts, there were so many of them. When I asked my dentist what was wrong with them, she said with a sigh, "Edema." I asked her what that meant, and she mumbled something which I vaguely linked with food.

These people with edema were mostly peasants. Starvation was much worse in the countryside because there were no guaranteed rations. Government policy was to provide food for the cities first, and commune officials were having to seize grain from the peasants by force. In many areas, peasants who tried to hide food were arrested, or beaten and tortured. Commune officials who were reluctant to take food from the hungry peasants were themselves dismissed, and some were physically maltreated. As a result, the peasants who had actually grown the food died in the millions all over China.

I learned later that several of my relatives from Sichuan to Manchuria had died in this famine. Among them was my father's retarded brother. His mother had died in 1958, and when the famine struck he was unable to cope as he would not listen to anyone else's advice. Rations were allotted on a monthly basis, and he ate his within days, leaving nothing for the rest of the month. He soon starved to death. My grandmother's sister, Lan, and her husband, "Loyalty" Pei-o, who had been sent to the inhospitable countryside in the far north of Manchuria because of his old connection with Kuomintang intelligence, both died too. As food began to run out, the village authorities allocated supplies according to their own, unwritten priorities. Pei-o's outcast status meant that he and his wife were among the first to be denied food. Their children survived because their parents gave their food to them. The father of Yu-lin's wife also died. At the end, he had eaten the stuffing in his pillow and the braids of garlic plants.

One night, when I was about eight, a tiny, very old-looking woman, her face a mass of wrinkles, walked into our house. She looked so thin and feeble it seemed a puff of wind would blow her down. She dropped to the ground in front of my mother and banged her forehead on the floor, calling her "the savior of my daughter." She was our maid's mother. "If it wasn't for you," she said, "my daughter would not survive. . . ." I did not grasp the full meaning of this until a month later, when a letter came for our maid. It said that her mother had died soon after visiting our house, where she had passed on the news that her husband and her younger son were dead. I will never forget the heart-rending sobs of our maid as she stood on the terrace, leaning against a wooden pillar and stifling her moans in her handkerchief. My grandmother sat cross-legged on her bed, weeping as well. I hid myself in a corner outside my grandmother's mosquito net. I could hear my grandmother saying to herself: "The Communists are good, but all these people are dead. . . ." Years later, I heard that our maid's other brother and her sister-in-law died soon after this. Landlords' families were placed at the bottom of the list for food in a starving commune.

In 1989 an official who had been working in famine relief told me that he believed that the total number of people who had died in Sichuan was seven million. This would be 10 percent of the entire population of a rich province. An accepted estimate for the death toll for the whole country is around thirty million.

One day in 1960, the three-year-old daughter of my aunt Jun-ying's next-door neighbor in Yibin went missing. A few weeks later the neighbor saw a young girl playing in the street wearing a dress that looked like her daughter's. She went up and examined it: it had a mark which identified it as her daughter's. She reported this to the police. It turned out that the parents of the young girl were selling wind-dried meat. They had abducted and murdered a number of babies and sold them as rabbit meat at exorbitant prices. The couple were executed and the case was hushed up, but it was widely known that baby killing did go on at the time.

Years later I met an old colleague of my father's, a very kind and capable man, not given to exaggeration. He told me with great emotion what he had seen during the famine in one particular commune. Thirty-five percent of the peasants had died, in an area where the harvest had been good—although little was collected, since the men had been pulled out to produce steel, and the commune canteen had wasted a large proportion of what there was. One day a peasant burst into his room and threw himself on the floor, screaming that he had committed a terrible crime and begging to be punished. Eventually it came out that he had killed his own baby and eaten it. Hunger had been like an uncontrollable force driving him to take up the knife. With tears rolling down his cheeks, the official ordered the peasant to be arrested. Later he was shot as a warning to baby killers.

One official explanation for the famine was that Khrushchev had suddenly forced China to pay back a large debt it had incurred during the Korean War in order to come to the aid of North Korea. The regime played on the experience of much of the population, who had been landless peasants and could remember being hounded by heartless creditors to pay rent or reimburse loans. By identifying the Soviet Union, Mao also created an external enemy to take the blame and to rally the population.

Another cause mentioned was "unprecedented natural calamities." China is a vast country, and bad weather causes food shortages somewhere every year. No one but the highest leaders had access to nationwide information about the weather. In fact, given the immobility of the population, few knew what happened in the next region, or even over the next mountain. Many thought then, and still think today, that the famine was caused by natural disasters. I have no full picture, but of all the people I have talked to from different parts of China, few knew of natural calamities in their regions. They only have stories to tell about deaths from starvation.

At a conference for 7,000 top-ranking officials at the beginning of 1962, Mao said that the famine was caused 70 percent by natural disasters and 30 percent by human error. President Liu Shaoqi chipped in, apparently on the spur of the moment, that it was caused 30 percent by natural disasters and 70 percent by human error. My father was at the conference, and when he returned he said to my mother: "I fear Comrade Shaoqi is going to be in trouble."

When the speeches were relayed to lower-rank officials like my mother, President Liu's assessment was cut out. The population at large was not even told about Mao's figures. This concealing of information did help keep the people quiet, and there were no audible complaints against the Communist Party. Quite apart from the fact that most dissenters had been killed off or otherwise suppressed in the past few years, whether the Communist Party was to blame was far from clear to the general population. There was no corruption in the sense of officials hoarding grain. Party officials were only marginally better off than the ordinary people. In fact, in some villages they themselves starved first—and died first. The famine was worse than anything under the Kuomintang, but it *looked* different: in the Kuomintang days, starvation took place alongside blatant unchecked extravagance.

Before the famine, many Communist officials from landlords' families had brought their parents to stay with them in the cities. When the famine hit, the Party gave orders for these elderly men and women to be sent back to their villages to share the hard life—meaning starvation—with the local peasants. The idea was that Communist officials should not be seen to be using their privileges to benefit their "class-enemy" parents. Some grandparents of friends of mine had to leave Chengdu and died in the famine.

Most peasants lived in a world where they did not look much beyond the boundary of the village, and they blamed the famine on their immediate bosses for giving them all the catastrophic orders. There were popular rhymes to the effect that the Party leadership was good, only the grass-roots officials were rotten.

The Great Leap Forward and the appalling famine shook my parents deeply. Although they did not have the full picture, they did not believe that "natural calamities" were the explanation. But their overwhelming feeling was one of guilt. Working in the field of propaganda, they were right in the center of the misinformation machine. To salve his conscience, and to avoid the dishonest daily routine, my father volunteered to help with famine relief in the communes. This meant staying—and starving—with the peasants. In doing so, he was "sharing weal and woe with the masses," in line with Mao's instructions, but it was resented by his staff. They had to take turns going with him, which they hated, because it meant going hungry.

From late 1959 to 1961, in the worst period of the famine, I seldom saw my father. In the countryside he ate the leaves of sweet potatoes, herbs, and tree bark like the peasants. One day he was walking along a bank between the paddy fields when he saw a skeletal peasant moving extremely slowly, and with obvious difficulty, in the distance. Then the man suddenly disappeared. When my father rushed over, he was lying in the field, dead of starvation.

Every day my father was devastated by what he saw, although he hardly saw the worst, because in the customary manner local officials surrounded him everywhere he went. But he suffered bad hepatomegaly and edema—and deep depression. Several times when he came back from his trips he went straight into the hospital. In the summer of 1961, he stayed there for months. He had changed. He was no longer the assured puritan of yesteryear. The Party was not pleased with him. He was criticized for "letting his revolutionary will wane" and ordered out of the hospital.

He took to spending a lot of time fishing. Across from the hospital there was a lovely river called the Jade Brook. Willows bent over to stroke its surface with their curving shoots, and clouds melted and solidified in their many reflections. I used to sit on its sloping bank gazing at the clouds and watching my father fish. The smell was of human manure. On top of the bank were the hospital grounds, which had once been flowerbeds, but had now been turned into vegetable fields to supply the staff and patients with additional food. When I close my eyes now, I can still see the larvae of the butterflies eating away at the cabbage leaves. My brothers caught them for my father to use as bait. The fields had a pathetic look. The doctors and nurses were obviously no experts on farming.

Throughout history Chinese scholars and mandarins had traditionally taken up fishing when they were disillusioned with what the emperor was doing. Fishing suggested a retreat to nature, an escape from the politics of the day. It was a kind of symbol for disenchantment and noncooperation.

My father seldom caught any fish, and once wrote a poem with the line: "Not for the fish I go fishing." But his angling companion, another deputy director of his department, always gave him part of his catch. This was because in 1961, in the middle of the famine, my mother was pregnant again, and the Chinese regard fish as essential for the development of a baby's hair. She had not wanted another child. Among other things, she and my father were on salaries, which meant the state no longer provided them with wet-nurses or nannies. With four children, my grandmother, and part of my father's family to support, they did not have a lot of money to spare. A large chunk of my father's salary went for buying books, particularly huge volumes of classical works, one set of which could cost two months' salary. Sometimes my mother grumbled slightly: other people in his position dropped hints to the publishing houses and got their copies free, "for work purposes." My father insisted on paying for everything.

Sterilization, abortion, and even contraception were difficult. The Communists had started promoting family planning in 1954, and my mother was in charge of the program in her district. She was then in an advanced stage of pregnancy with Xiao-hei, and often started her meetings with a good-humored self-criticism. But Mao turned against birth control. He wanted a big, powerful China, based on a large population. He said that if the Americans dropped atomic bombs on China, the Chinese would "just go on reproducing" and reconstitute their numbers at great speed. He also shared the traditional Chinese peasant's attitude toward children: the more hands the better. In 1957, he personally named a famous Peking University professor who had advocated birth control as a rightist. After that, family planning was seldom mentioned.

My mother had become pregnant in 1959, and had written to the Party asking for permission to have an abortion. This was the standard procedure. One reason the Party had to give its consent was that the operation was a dangerous one at the time. My mother had said that she was busy working for the revolution, and could serve the people better if she did not have another baby. She was granted an abortion, which was dreadfully painful because the method used was primitive. When she became pregnant again in 1961, another abortion was out of the question in the opinion of the doctors, my mother herself, and the Party, which stipulated a minimum three-year gap between abortions.

Our maid was also pregnant. She had married my father's former manservant, who was now working in a factory. My grandmother cooked both of them the eggs and soybeans which could be obtained with my parents' coupons, as well as the fish which my father and his colleague caught.

Our maid gave birth to a boy at the end of 1961 and left to set up her own home with her husband. When she was still with us, she would go to the canteens to fetch our food. One day my father saw her walking along a garden path stuffing some meat into her mouth and chewing voraciously. He turned and walked away in case she saw him and was embarrassed. He did not tell anyone until years later when he was ruminating over how differently things had turned out from the dreams of his youth, the main one of which had been putting an end to hunger.

When the maid left, my family could not afford another one, because of the food situation. Those who wanted the job—women from the countryside—were not entitled to a food allocation. So my grandmother and my aunt had to look after the five of us.

My youngest brother, Xiao-fang, was born on 17 January 1962. He was the only one of us who was breast-fed by my mother. Before he was born, my mother had wanted to give him away, but by the time he arrived she had become deeply attached to him, and he became the favorite. We all played with him as though he were a big toy. He grew up surrounded by loving crowds, which, my mother believed, accounted for his ease and confidence. My father spent a lot of time with him, which he had never done with his other children. When Xiao-fang was old enough to play with toys, my father carried him every Saturday to the department store at the top of the street and bought him a new toy. The moment Xiao-fang started to cry, for any reason, my father would drop everything and rush to comfort him.

By the beginning of 1961, tens of millions of deaths had finally forced Mao to give up his economic policies. Reluctantly, he allowed the pragmatic President Liu and Deng Xiaoping, general secretary of the Party, more control over the country. Mao was forced to make self-criticisms, but they were full of self-pity, and were always phrased in such a way that it sounded as if he was carrying the cross for incompetent officials all over China. He further magnanimously instructed the Party to "draw lessons" from the disastrous experience, but what the lessons were was not left to the judgment of the lowly officials: Mao told them they had become divorced from the people, and had made decisions which did not reflect ordinary people's feelings. Starting from Mao, the endless self-criticisms masked the real responsibility, which no one pursued.

Nevertheless, things began to improve. The pragmatists put through a succession of major reforms. It was in this context that Deng Xiaoping made the remark: "It doesn't matter whether the cat is white or black, as long as it catches mice." There was to be no more mass production of steel. A stop was put to crazy economic goals, and realistic policies were introduced. Public canteens were abolished, and peasants' income was now related to their work. They were given back household property, which had been confiscated by the communes, including farm implements and domestic animals. They were also allowed small plots of land to till privately. In some areas, land was effectively leased out to peasant households. In industry and commerce, elements of a market economy were officially sanctioned, and within a couple of years the economy was flourishing again.

Hand in hand with the loosening up of the economy, there was also political liberalization. Many landlords had the label of "class enemy" removed. A large number of people who had been purged in the various political campaigns were "rehabilitated." These included the "counterrevolutionaries" from 1955, "rightists" from 1957, and "rightist opportunists" from 1959. Because my mother had received a warning for her "right-wing tendencies" in 1959, in 1962 she was raised from Grade 17 to Grade 16 in her civil service rank as compensation. There was greater literary and artistic freedom. A more relaxed general atmosphere prevailed. For my father and mother, as for many others, the regime seemed to be showing it could correct and learn from its mistakes and that it could work—and this restored their confidence in it.

While all this was going on I lived in a cocoon behind the high walls of the government compound. I had no direct contact with tragedy. It was with these "noises off" that I embarked on my teens.

13. "Thousand-Gold Little Precious"— In a Privileged Cocoon

(1958–1965)

When my mother took me to register at primary school in 1958, I was wearing a new pink cord jacket and green flannel trousers with a huge pink ribbon in my hair. We went straight into the office of the headmistress, who was waiting for us with the academic supervisor and one of the teachers. They were all smiling, and they addressed my mother respectfully as "Director Xia" and treated her like a VIP. Later I learned that the school came under my mother's department.

I had this special interview because I was six, and normally they only took children from the age of seven, as there was a shortage of schools. But even my father did not mind the rules being bent this time, as he and my mother both wanted me to start school early. My fluent recitation of classical poems and my handsome calligraphy convinced the school I was advanced enough. After I had satisfied the headmistress and her colleagues in the standard entrance test, I was accepted as a special case. My parents were tremendously proud of me. Many of their colleagues' children had been turned down by this school.

Everyone wanted to get their children into this school because it was the best in Chengdu, and the top "key" school for the whole province. It was very difficult to get into the key schools and universities. Entrance was strictly on merit, and children from officials' families were not given priority.

Whenever I was introduced to a new teacher, it was always as "the daughter of Director Chang and Director Xia." My mother often came to the school on her bicycle as part of her job, to check on how it was being run. One day the weather suddenly turned cold, and she brought a warm green cord jacket with flowers embroidered on the front for me. The headmistress herself came to my classroom to give it to me. I was terribly embarrassed with all my classmates staring at me. Like most children, I just wanted to belong and to be accepted as part of my peer group.

We had exams every week and the results were put up on the notice board. I was always at the top of the class, which was rather resented by those behind me. They sometimes took their bitterness out on me by calling me "thousand-gold little precious" (*qian-jin xiao-jie*), doing things like putting a frog in my desk drawer, and tying the ends of my plaits to the back of my seat. They said I had no "collective spirit" and looked down on others. But I knew I simply liked being on my own.

The curriculum was like that in a Western school, except during the period when we had to produce steel. There was no political education, but we did have to do a lot of sports: running, high jump and long jump, as well as compulsory gym and swimming. We each had one after-school sport: I was selected for tennis. At first my father was against the prospect of my becoming a sportswoman, which was the purpose of the training, but the tennis coach, a very pretty young woman, came to see him, dressed in her fetching shorts. Among his other jobs, my father was in charge of sports for the province. The coach gave him her most charming smile and told him that since tennis, the most elegant of sports, was not played much in China at the time, it would be good if his daughter set an example—"for the nation," as she put it. My father had to give in.

I loved my teachers, who were excellent and had the gift of making their subjects fascinating and exciting. I remember the science teacher, a Mr. Da-li, who taught us the theory behind putting a satellite into orbit (the Russians had just launched the first Sputnik) and the possibility of visiting other planets. Even the most unruly boys were glued to their seats during his lessons. I overheard some pupils saying that he had been a rightist, but none of us knew what this meant, and it did not make any difference to us.

My mother told me years later that Mr. Da-li had been a writer of children's science fiction. He was named a rightist in 1957 because he had written an article about mice stealing food and fattening themselves up, which was alleged to be a covert attack on Party officials. He was banned from writing, and was about to be sent to the countryside when my mother managed to get him relocated to my school. Few officials were brave enough to reemploy a rightist.

My mother was, and this was the very reason she was in charge of my school. According to its location, it should have come under the Western District of Chengdu. But the city authorities assigned it to my mother's district in the east because they wanted it to have the best teachers, even if they came from "undesirable" backgrounds, and the head of the Public Affairs Department of the Western District would not dare to give such people jobs. The academic supervisor in my school was the wife of a former Kuomintang officer who was in a labor camp. Usually people with a background like hers would not have been able to occupy a job like this, but my mother refused to transfer them, and even gave them honorary grades. Her superiors approved, but they wanted her to take the responsibility for this unorthodox behavior. She did not mind. With the implicit additional protection which my father's position brought her, she felt more secure than her colleagues.

In 1962 my father was invited to send his children to a new school that had just been set up next to the compound where we lived. It was called "Plane Tree" after the trees which formed an avenue on the grounds. The school was set up by the Western District with the express purpose of making it into a key school, since there was no key school under the jurisdiction of this district. Good teachers were transferred to Plane Tree from other schools in the district. The school soon acquired a reputation as the "aristocratic school" for the children of VIPs in the provincial government.

Before Plane Tree was set up there had been one boarding school in Chengdu, for the children of top army officers. A few senior civilian officials also sent their children there. Its academic level was poor, and it earned a reputation for snobbery, as the children were highly competitive about their parents. They could often be heard saying things like: "My father is a division commander. Yours is only a brigadier!" At weekends there were long lines of cars outside, with nannies, bodyguards, and chauffeurs waiting to take the children home. Many people thought the atmosphere was poisoning the children, and my parents had always been totally averse to this school.

Plane Tree was not set up as an exclusive school, and after meeting the headmaster and some of the teachers, my parents felt that it was committed to high ethical standards and discipline. There were only about twenty-five pupils in each year. Even in my previous school there had been fifty pupils in my class. The advantages of Plane Tree were, of course, partly intended for the benefit of the top officials who lived next door, but my newly mellowed father overlooked this fact.

Most of my new classmates were children of officials in the provincial government. Some lived in the compound with me. Apart from school, the compound was my entire world. The gardens were filled with flowers and luxuriant plants. There were palm trees, sisal hemps, oleanders, magnolias, camellias, roses, hibiscus, and even a pair of rare Chinese aspens which had grown toward each other and intertwined their arms, like lovers. They were very sensitive, too. If we scratched one of the trunks even ever so gently the two trees would tremble and their leaves would start to flutter. During the summer lunch breaks I would sit on a drum-shaped stone stool under a trellis of wisteria, my elbows resting on a stone table reading a book or playing chess. Around me were the blazing colors of the grounds and not far away a rare coconut tree thrust arrogantly into the sky. My favorite, though, was a heavily scented jasmine, also climbing on a big trellis. When it was in blossom, my room was filled with its fragrance. I loved to sit by the window gazing at it and soaking up the delicious smell.

When we first moved into the compound we lived in a lovely detached one-story house set in its own courtyard. It was built in traditional Chinese style, with no modern facilities: no running water indoors, no flush toilet, no ceramic bath. In 1962, some modern Western-type apartments with all these amenities were built in one corner of the compound, and my family was assigned one of them. Before we moved in, I visited this wonderland and examined all the novel and magical taps and flush toilets and mirrored cupboards on the walls. I ran my hand along the shiny white tiles on the walls of the bathrooms. They felt cool and pleasant to the touch.

There were thirteen apartment blocks in the compound. Four were for the directors of departments, the rest for bureau chiefs. Our apartment occupied a whole floor, whereas the bureau chiefs had to share a floor between two families. Our rooms were more spacious. We had anti-mosquito screens on our inner windows, which they did not, and two bathrooms, while they had only one. We had hot water three days a week, whereas they had none. We had a telephone, which was extremely rare in China, and they did not. Lesser officials occupied blocks in a smaller compound on the other side of the street, and their amenities were one grade lower still. The half-dozen Party secretaries who formed the core of the provincial leadership had their own inner compound within our compound. This inner sanctum lay behind two gates, which were guarded around-the-clock by army guards with guns, and only specially authorized personnel were allowed through. Inside these gates were detached two-story houses, one for each Party secretary. On the doorstep of the first secretary, Li Jing-quan, stood yet another armed guard. I grew up taking hierarchy and privilege for granted.

All adults working in the main compound had to show their passes when they came through the main gate. We children had no passes, but the guards recognized us. Things became complicated if we had visitors. They had to fill out forms, then the porter's lodge would ring our apartment and someone had to go all the way down to the front gate to collect them. The staff did not welcome other children. They said they did not want the grounds messed up. This discouraged us from bringing friends home, and during the whole of my four years in the top key school I invited girlfriends home only a very few times.

I hardly ever went outside the compound except to go to school. A few times I went to a department store with my grandmother, but I never felt the need to buy anything. Shopping was an alien concept to me, and my parents gave me pocket money only on special occasions. Our canteen was like a restaurant, and served excellent food. Except during the famine, there were always at least seven or eight dishes from which to choose. The chefs were handpicked, and were all either "grade one" or "special grade." Top chefs were graded like teachers. At home, there were always sweets and fruit. There was nothing else I wanted to eat except ice lollies. Once, on Children's Day, 1 June, when I was given some pocket money, I ate twenty-six in one go.

Life in the compound was self-contained. It had its own shops, hairdressers, cinemas, and dance halls, as well as plumbers and engineers. Dancing was very popular. On weekends there were different dancing parties for the different levels of staff in the provincial government. The one in the former U.S. servicemen's ballroom was for families at and above the level of bureau chief. It always had an orchestra, and actors and actresses from the Provincial Song and Dance Troupe to make it more colorful and elegant. Some of the actresses used to come to our apartment to chat with my parents, and then they would take me for a walk around the compound. I was terribly proud to be seen in their company, as actors and actresses were endowed with tremendous glamour in China. They enjoyed special tolerance and were allowed to dress more flamboyantly than other people, and even to have affairs. Since the troupe came under his department, my father was their boss. But they did not defer to him like other people. They used to tease him and call him "the star dancer." My father just smiled and looked shy. The dancing was a kind of casual ballroom dancing, and the couples glided up and down rather demurely on the highly polished floor. My father was indeed a good dancer, and he obviously enjoyed himself. My mother was no good at it—she could not get the rhythm right, so she did not like it. During the intervals, the children were allowed onto the dance floor, and we pulled each other by the hands and did a kind of floor skiing. The atmosphere, the heat, the perfume, the glamorously dressed ladies and beaming gentlemen formed a dreamy, magical world for me.

There were films every Saturday evening. In 1962, with the more relaxed atmosphere, there were even some from Hong Kong, mostly love stories. They gave a glimpse of the outside world, and were very popular. There were also, of course, uplifting revolutionary films. The screenings were held in two different places, according to status. The elite one was in a spacious hall with big, comfortable seats. The other was in a large auditorium in a separate compound and was jam-packed. I went there once because it was showing a film I wanted to see. The seats had all been taken long before the film started. Late-comers had to bring their own stools. Lots of people were standing. If you were stuck at the back, you had to stand on a chair to see anything. I had no idea it was going to be like this, and had not brought a stool. I was caught in the crush at the back, unable to see a thing. I glimpsed a chef I knew who was standing on a short bench which could seat two people. When he saw me squeezing past, he asked me to get on it with him. It was very narrow and I felt terribly unsteady. People kept pushing by, and soon one of them knocked me off. I fell quite hard and cut my eyebrow on the edge of a stool. The scar is still there today.

In our elite hall there were more restricted films which were not shown to anyone else, even the staff in the big auditorium. These were called "reference films" and were made up mostly of clips of films from the West. This was the first time I ever saw a miniskirt—or the Beatles. I remember one film showed a Peeping Tom at the seaside; the women he had been peeping at poured a bucket of water over him. Another extract from a documentary showed abstract painters using a chimpanzee to daub ink on a sheet of paper and a man playing the piano with his bottom.

I suppose these must have been selected to show how decadent the West was. They were only for high Party officials, and even they were denied access to most information about the West. Occasionally, a film from the West was shown in a small screening room where children were not allowed. I was intensely curious and begged my parents to take me. They agreed a couple of times. By then my father had become quite soft with us. There was a guard at the door, but because I was with my parents, he did not object. The films were totally beyond me. One seemed to be about an American pilot going mad after dropping an atom bomb on Japan. The other was a black-and-white feature film. In one scene a trade union leader was punched by two thugs in a car: blood trickled out of the corner of his mouth. I was absolutely horrified. This was the first time in my life I had ever seen an act of violence with blood being shed (corporal punishment in schools had been abolished by the Communists). Chinese films in those days were gentle, sentimental, and uplifting; if there was even a hint of violence it was stylized, as in Chinese opera.

I was baffled by the way the Western workers were dressed—in neat suits that were not even patched, a far cry from my idea of what the oppressed masses in a capitalist country ought to be wearing. After the film I asked my mother about this and she said something about "relative living standards." I did not understand what she meant, and the question remained with me.

As a child, my idea of the West was that it was a miasma of poverty and misery, like that of the homeless "Little Match Girl" in the Hans Christian Andersen story. When I was in the boarding nursery and did not want to finish my food, the teacher would say: "Think of all the starving children in the capitalist world!" In school, when they were trying to make us work harder, the teachers often said: "You are lucky to have a school to go to and books to read. In the capitalist countries children have to work to support their hungry families." Often when adults wanted us to accept something they would say that people in the West wanted it, but could not get it, and therefore we should appreciate our good fortune. I came to think this way automatically. When I saw a girl in my class wearing a new kind of pink translucent raincoat I had never seen, I thought how nice it would be to swap my commonplace old wax-paper umbrella for one. But I immediately castigated myself for this "bourgeois" tendency, and wrote in my diary: "Think of all the children in the capitalist world—they can't even think of owning an umbrella!"

In my mind foreigners were terrifying. All Chinese have black hair and brown eyes, so they regard differently colored hair and eyes as strange. My image of a foreigner was more or less the official stereotype: a man with red, unkempt hair, strange-colored eyes, very, very long nose, stumbling around drunk, pouring Coca-Cola into his mouth from a bottle, with his legs splayed out in a most inelegant position. Foreigners said "hello" all the time, with an odd intonation. I did not know what "hello" meant; I thought it was a swear word. When boys played "guerrilla warfare," which was their version of cowboys and Indians, the enemy side would have thorns glued onto their noses and say "hello" all the time.

During my third year in primary school, when I was nine, my classmates and I decided to decorate our classroom with plants. One of the girls suggested she could get some unusual ones from a garden which her father looked after at a Catholic church on Safe Bridge Street. There had once been an orphanage attached to the church, but it had been closed down. The church was still functioning, under the control of the government, which had forced Catholics to break with the Vatican and join a "patriotic" organization. The idea of a church was both mysterious and frightening, because of the propaganda about religion. The first time I ever heard about rape was reading about one attributed to a foreign priest in a novel. Priests also invariably appeared as imperialist spies and evil people who used babies from orphanages for medical experiments.

Every day on my way to and from school, I used to walk past the top of scholar-tree-lined Safe Bridge Street and see the profile of the church gate. To my Chinese eye, it had the most alien-looking pillars: they were made of white marble, and were fluted in the Greek style, whereas Chinese pillars were always made of painted wood. I was dying to look inside, and had asked the girl to let me visit her home, but she said her father did not want her to bring any visitors. This only increased the mystery. When this girl offered to get some plants from her garden I eagerly volunteered to go with her.

As we approached the church gate I tensed up and my heart almost stopped beating. It seemed to be the most imposing gate I had ever seen. My friend stood on tiptoe and reached up to bang a metal ring on the gate. A small door creaked open in the gate, revealing a wrinkled old man, bent almost double. To me he seemed like a witch in one of the illustrations in a fairy tale. Although I could not see his face clearly, I imagined that he had a long hooked nose and pointed hat and was about to ride up into the sky on a broomstick. The fact that he was of a different sex from a witch was irrelevant to me. Avoiding looking at him, I hurried through the doorway. Immediately in front of me was a garden in a small, neat courtyard. I was so nervous I could not see what was in it. My eyes could only register a proliferation of colors and shapes, and a small fountain trickling in the middle of a rockery. My friend took my hand and led me along the arcade around the courtyard. On the far side, she opened a door and told me that that was where the priest delivered his sermons. Sermons! I had come across this word in a book in which the priest used his "sermon" to pass state secrets to another imperialist spy. I tensed up even more when I crossed the threshold into a large, dark room, which seemed to be a hall; for a moment I could not see anything. Then I saw a statue at the end of the hall. This was my first encounter with a crucifix. As I got nearer, the figure on the cross seemed to be hovering over me, enormous and crushing. The blood, the posture, and the expression on the face combined to produce an utterly terrifying sensation. I turned and dashed out of the church. Outside, I nearly collided with a man in a black robe. He stretched out a hand to steady me; I thought he was trying to grab me, and dodged and rushed away. Somewhere behind me a heavy door creaked. The next moment it was terrifyingly still except for the murmuring of the fountain. I opened the small door in the front gate and ran all the way to the end of the street without stopping. My heart was pounding and my head was spinning.

Unlike me, my brother Jin-ming, who was born a year after me, was independent-minded from a young age. He loved science and read a lot of popular scientific magazines. Although these, like all other publications, carried the inevitable propaganda, they did report advances in science and technology in the West, and these impressed Jin-ming enormously. He was fascinated by photographs of lasers, Hovercraft, helicopters, electronics, and cars in these magazines, in addition to the glimpses he got of the West in the "reference films." He began to feel that school, the media, and adults in general could not be trusted when they said that the capitalist world was hell and China was paradise.

The United States in particular caught Jin-ming's imagination as the country with the most highly developed technology. One day when he was eleven and was excitedly describing new developments in lasers in America over the dinner table, he said to my father that he adored America. My father was at a loss about how to respond, and looked deeply worried. Eventually he stroked Jin-ming's head and said to my mother, "What can we do? This child is going to grow up to become a rightist!"

Before he was twelve, Jin-ming had made a number of "inventions" based on illustrations in children's science books, including a telescope with which he tried to observe Halley's Comet and a microscope using glass from a light bulb. One day he was trying to improve a repeating rubber-band "gun" which fired small stones and yew nuts.

In order to create the right sound effect he asked a classmate of his, whose father was an army officer, to find him some empty bullet casings. His friend got hold of some bullets, took off the ends, emptied out the gunpowder, and gave them to Jin-ming without realizing that the detonators were still inside. Jin-ming filled a shell with a cut-up toothpaste tube and held it over the coal stove in the kitchen with tongs to bake it. There was a kettle sitting on a grill over the coal, and Jin-ming was holding the tongs under it when suddenly there was an enormous bang, and a big hole in the bottom of the kettle. Everyone rushed in to see what had happened. Jin-ming was terrified. Not because of the explosion, but because of my father, who was a very intimidating figure.

But my father did not hit Jin-ming, or even scold him. He just looked at him hard for a while, then said he was already scared enough, and should go outside and take a walk. Jin-ming was so relieved he could hardly keep from jumping up and down. He never thought he would get off so easily. After his walk, my father said he was not to do any more experiments without being supervised by an adult. But he did not enforce this order for long, and soon Jin-ming was carrying on as before.

I helped him with a couple of his projects. Once we made a model pulverizer powered by tap water which could crush chalk into powder. Jin-ming provided the brains and the skill, of course. My interest never lasted.

Jin-ming went to the same key primary school as I did. Mr. Da-li, the science teacher who had been condemned as a rightist, also taught him, and played a crucial role in opening up the world of science to him. Jin-ming has remained deeply grateful to him all his life.

My second brother, Xiao-hei, who was born in 1954, was my grandmother's favorite, but he did not get much attention from my father and mother. One of the reasons was that they thought he got enough affection from my grandmother. Sensing he was not in favor, Xiao-hei became defensive toward my parents. This irritated them, especially my father, who could not stand anything he considered unstraightforward.

Sometimes he was so enraged by Xiao-hei that he beat him. But he would regret it afterward, and at the first opportunity he would stroke Xiao-hei on the head and tell him he was sorry he had lost control of his temper. My grandmother would have a tearful row with my father, and he would accuse her of spoiling Xiao-hei. This was a constant source of tension between them. Inevitably, my grandmother grew even more attached to Xiao-hei and spoiled him even more.

My parents thought that only their sons should be scolded and hit, and not their daughters. One of the only two times when my sister, Xiao-hong, was hit was when she was five. She had insisted on eating sweets before a meal, and when the food came she complained that she could not taste anything because of the sweet taste in her mouth. My father said she had only gotten what she wanted. Xiao-hong took umbrage at this and started yelling and threw her chopsticks across the dining room. My father smacked her and she grabbed a feather duster to hit him. He snatched the duster away from her, so she got hold of a broom. After some scuffling, my father locked her in our bedroom and kept saying, "Too spoiled! Too spoiled!" My sister missed her lunch.

Xiao-hong was quite willful as a child. For some reason, she absolutely refused to watch films or plays, or to travel. And there were a lot of things she hated eating: she would scream her head off when she was fed milk, beef, or lamb. When I was a child, I followed her example, and missed out on many films and a lot of delicious food.

My character was very different, and people said I was both sensible and sensitive (dong-shi) well before my teens. My parents never laid a hand on me or said a harsh word to me. Even their rare criticisms were delivered extremely delicately, as if I were a grown-up and easily wounded. They gave me plenty of love, particularly my father, who always took his after-supper walk with me, and often took me with him when he visited his friends. Most of his closest friends were veteran revolutionaries, intelligent and able, and they all seemed to have something "wrong" in their pasts in the eyes of the Party, and so had been given only lowly posts. One had been in the branch of the Red Army led by Mao's challenger Zhang Guo-tao. Another was a Don Juan—his wife, a Party official whom my father always tried to avoid, was insufferably stern. I enjoyed these adult gatherings, but I liked nothing better than to be alone with my books, which I sat reading all day during my school holidays, chewing the ends of my hair. Apart from literature, including some reasonably simple classical poems, I loved science fiction and adventure stories. I remember one book about a man spending what seemed to him to be a few days on another planet and coming back to earth in the twenty-first century, finding everything had changed. People ate food capsules, traveled by Hovercraft, and had telephones with video screens. I longed to be living in the twenty-first century with all these magic gadgets.

I spent my childhood racing toward the future, hurrying to be an adult, and was always daydreaming about what I would do when I was older. From the moment I could read and write, I preferred books with substantial amounts of words to picture books. I was also impatient in every other way: when I had a sweet, I would never suck it, but bit into it and chewed it at once. I even chewed my cough lozenges.

My siblings and I got on unusually well. Traditionally, boys and girls seldom played together, but we were good friends and cared about each other. There was little jealousy or competitiveness, and we rarely had rows. Whenever my sister saw me crying, she would burst into tears herself. She did not mind hearing people praising me. The good relationship between us was much commented on, and parents of other children were constantly asking my parents how they did it.

Between them my parents and my grandmother provided a loving family atmosphere. We saw only affection between our parents, never their quarrels. My mother never showed us her disenchantment with my father. After the famine, my parents, like most officials, were no longer as passionately devoted to their work as they had been in the 1950s. Family life took a more prominent place, and was no longer equated with disloyalty. My father, now over forty, mellowed and became closer to my mother. My parents spent more time together, and as I was growing up I often saw evidence of their love for each other.

One day I heard my father telling my mother about a compliment paid to her by one of his colleagues, whose wife had the reputation of being a beauty. "The two of us are lucky to have such outstanding wives," he had said to my father. "Look around: they stand out from everyone else." My father was beaming, recalling the scene with restrained delight. "I smiled politely, of course," he said. "But I was really thinking, How can you compare your wife with mine? My wife is in a class of her own!"

Once my father went away on a three-week sight-seeing tour for the directors of the Public Affairs departments of every province in China, which was to take them all over the country. It was the only such tour ever given in the whole of my father's career and was supposed to be a special treat. The group enjoyed VIP treatment all the way, and a photographer traveled with them, recording their progress. But my father was restless. By the start of the third week, when the tour had reached Shanghai, he missed home so much that he said he did not feel well, and flew back to Chengdu. Forever afterward, my mother would call him a "silly old thing." "Your home wouldn't have flown away. I wouldn't have disappeared. Not in that week, anyway. What a chance you missed to have fun!" I always had a feeling when she said this that she was really quite pleased about my father's "silly homesickness."

In their relationship with their children, my parents seemed to be concerned above all with two things. One was our academic education. No matter how preoccupied they were with their jobs, they always went through our homework with us. They were in constant touch with our teachers, and firmly established in our heads that our goal in life was academic excellence. Their involvement in our studies increased after the famine, when they had more spare time. Most evenings, they took turns giving us extra lessons.

My mother was our math teacher, and my father tutored us in Chinese language and literature. These evenings were solemn occasions for us, when we were allowed to read my father's books in his study, which was lined from floor to ceiling with thick hardbacks and thread-bound Chinese classics. We had to wash our hands before we turned the leaves of his books. We read Lu Xun, the great modern Chinese writer, and poems from the golden ages of Chinese poetry, which were considered difficult even for adults.

My parents' attention to our studies was matched only by their concern for our education in ethics. My father wanted us to grow up to be honorable and principled citizens, which was what he believed the Communist revolution was all about. In keeping with Chinese tradition, he gave a name to each of my brothers which represented his ideals: *Zhi*, meaning "honest," to Jin-ming; *Pu*, "unpretentious," to Xiao-hei; and *Fang*, "incorruptible," was part of Xiao-fang's name. My father believed that these were the qualities which had been lacking in the old China and which the Communists were going to restore. Corruption, in particular, had sapped the old China. Once he rebuked Jin-ming for making a paper airplane out of a sheet of paper with his department letterhead on it. If we ever wanted to use the telephone at home we had to get his permission. As his job covered the media, he was supplied with a lot of newspapers and periodicals. He encouraged us to read them, but they could not be taken out of his study. At the end of the month he took them back to his department, as old newspapers were sold for recycling. I spent many tedious Sundays helping him check that not one was missing.

My father was always very strict with us, which was a constant source of tension between him and my grandmother, and between him and us. In 1965 one of the daughters of Prince Sihanouk of Cambodia came to Chengdu to give a ballet performance. This was a great novelty in a society which was almost totally isolated. I was dying to see the ballet. Because of his job, my father was given complimentary tickets, the best, for all new performances, and he often took me. This time, for some reason, he could not go. He gave me a ticket but said I had to exchange it with somebody with a seat at the back so that I would not be in the best seat.

That evening I stood by the door of the theater, holding my ticket in my hand, while the audience crowded in—all, in fact, with complimentary tickets, allocated according to their rank. A good quarter of an hour passed and I was still by the door. I was too embarrassed to ask anyone to swap. Eventually the number of people going in thinned out; the performance was about to start. I was on the verge of tears, wishing I had a different father. At that moment I saw a junior official from my father's department. I summoned up my courage and pulled the edge of his jacket from behind. He smiled and immediately agreed to let me have his seat, which was right at the back. He was not surprised. My father's strictness to his children was legendary in our compound.

For Chinese New Year, 1965, a special performance was organized for schoolteachers. This time my father went to the performance with me, but instead of letting me sit with him, he exchanged my ticket for one at the very back. He said it was inappropriate for me to sit in front of the teachers. I could hardly see the stage, and felt miserable. Later I heard from the teachers how much they appreciated his sensitivity. They had been annoyed at seeing other high officials' children lounging on the front seats in a manner which they regarded as disrespectful.

Throughout China's history there was a tradition of official's children being arrogant and abusing their privileges. This caused widespread resentment. Once a new guard in the compound did not recognize a teenage girl who lived there and refused to let her in. She screamed at him and hit him with her satchel. Some children talked to the chefs, chauffeurs, and other staff in a rude and imperious manner. They would call them by their names, which a younger person should never do in China—it is supremely disrespectful. I will never forget the pained look in the eyes of a chef in our canteen when the son of one of my father's colleagues took some food back and said it was no good, and shouted out his name. The chef was deeply wounded, but said nothing. He did not want to displease the boy's father. Some parents did nothing about this kind of behavior by their children, but my father was outraged. Often he said: "These officials are no Communists."

My parents regarded it as very important that their children should be brought up to be courteous and respectful to everyone. We called the service staff "Uncle" or "Aunt" So-and-so, which was the traditional polite form for a child addressing an adult. After we had finished our meal, we always took the dirty bowls and chopsticks back to the kitchen. My father told us we should do this as a courtesy to the chefs, as otherwise they would have to clear the tables themselves. These small things earned us immense affection from the compound staff. The chefs would keep food warm for us if we were late. The gardeners used to give me flowers or fruit. And the chauffeur happily made detours to pick me up and drop me home—this was strictly behind my father's back, as he would never let us use the car without him being there.

Our modern apartment was on the third floor, and our balcony looked down on a narrow alley of mud and cobbles outside the compound wall. One side of the alley was the brick wall of the compound; the other was a row of thin wooden one-story terraced houses, typical of poor people's dwellings in Chengdu. The houses had mud floors and no toilets or running water. Their facades were made out of vertical planks, two of which served as the door. The front room led directly into another room, which led to another, and a row of several such rooms formed the house. The back room opened onto another street. Since the side walls of the house were shared with neighbors, these houses had no windows. The inhabitants had to leave the doors at both ends open to let in light or air. Often, especially on hot summer evenings, they would sit on the narrow pavement, reading, sewing, or chatting. From the pavement they could look straight up at the spacious balconies of our apartments with their shiny glass windows. My father said we must not offend the feelings of the people living in the alley, and so he forbade us to play on the balcony.

On summer evenings, boys from the huts in the alley often used to walk through the streets peddling anti-mosquito incense. They sang a special tune to attract attention to their wares. My evening reading used to be punctuated by this lingering, sad tune. Through my father's constant reminding, I knew that being able to study undisturbed in a big, cool room with a parquet floor and mosquito-netted open windows was an enormous privilege. "You must not think you are superior to them," he would say. "You are just lucky to be here. You know why we need communism? So that everyone can live in a good house like ours, and in much better ones."

My father said things like this so often that I grew up feeling ashamed of my privileges. Sometimes boys from the compound would stand on their balconies and mimic the tune the young peddlers sang. I felt ashamed when they did this. When I went out with my father in his car, I was always embarrassed when the car honked through the crowds. If people stared into the car, I would sink down in my seat and try to avoid their gaze.

In my early teens I was a very serious girl. I liked to be on my own, thinking, often about moral issues that confused me. I had become rather lukewarm about games and fairgrounds and playing with other children, and rarely gossiped with other girls. Although I was sociable and popular, there always seemed to be a certain distance between me and the others. In China people easily become familiar with one another, particularly women. But ever since I was a child, I have always wanted to be left alone.

My father noticed this side of my character, and would comment on it with approval. While my teachers constantly said I should have more "collective spirit," he told me that familiarity and living on top of each other could be a destructive thing. With this encouragement, I kept my privacy and my space. There are no exact words for these two concepts in the Chinese language, but they were instinctively yearned for by many, certainly by my siblings as well as me. Jin-ming, for instance, insisted so strongly on being allowed to lead his own life that he was sometimes thought by those who did not know him to be antisocial; in fact he was gregarious and extremely popular with his peers.

My father often said to us, "I think it is marvelous that your mother has this policy of 'letting you roam free on the pasture.' " Our parents left us alone and respected our need to keep our separate worlds.

14. "Father Is Close, Mother Is Close, but Neither Is as Close as Chairman Mao"— The Cult of Mao

(1964–1965)

"Chairman Mao," as we always called him, began to impinge directly on my life in 1964, when I was twelve. Having been in retreat for some time after the famine, he was starting his comeback, and in March of the previous year he had issued a call to the whole country, particularly the young, to "learn from Lei Feng."

Lei Feng was a soldier who, we were told, had died at the age of twenty-two in 1962. He had done an awful lot of good deeds—going out of his way to help the elderly, the sick, and the needy. He had donated his savings to disaster relief funds and given up his food rations to comrades in the hospital.

Lei Feng soon began to dominate my life. Every afternoon we left school to "do good deeds like Lei Feng." We went down to the railway station to try to help old ladies with their luggage, as Lei Feng had done. We sometimes had to grab their bundles from them forcibly because some countrywomen thought we were thieves. On rainy days, I stood on the street with an umbrella, anxiously hoping that an old lady would pass by and give me an opportunity to escort her home— as Lei Feng had done. If I saw someone carrying water buckets on a shoulder pole—old houses still did not have running water—I would try unsuccessfully to summon up the courage to offer my help, although I had no idea how heavy a load of water was.

Gradually, during the course of 1964, the emphasis began to shift from boy scoutish good deeds to the cult of Mao. The essence of Lei Feng, the teachers told us, was his "boundless love and devotion to Chairman Mao." Before he took any action, Lei Feng always thought of some words of Mao's. His diary was published and became our moral textbook. On almost every page there was a pledge like: "I must study Chairman Mao's works, heed Chairman Mao's words, follow Chairman Mao's instructions, and be a good soldier of Chairman Mao's." We vowed to follow Lei Feng, and be ready to "go up mountains of knives and down seas of flames," to "have our bodies smashed to powder and our bones crushed to smithereens," to "submit ourselves unquestioningly to the control of the Great Leader"—Mao. The cult of Mao and the cult of Lei Feng were two sides of the same coin: one was the cult of personality; the other, its essential corollary, was the cult of impersonality.

I read my first article by Mao in 1964, at a time when two slogans of Mao's—"Serve the People" and "Never Forget Class Struggle"—dominated our lives. The essence of these two complementary slogans was illustrated in Lei Feng's poem "The Four Seasons," which we all learned by heart:

Like spring, I treat my comrades warmly.
Like summer, I am full of ardor for my revolutionary work.
I eliminate my individualism as an autumn gale sweeps away fallen leaves,
And to the class enemy, I am cruel and ruthless like harsh winter.

In line with this, our teacher said we had to be careful whom we helped on our do-good errands. We must not help "class enemies." But I did not understand who they were, and when I asked, neither the teachers nor my parents were keen to elaborate. One common answer was: "like the baddies in the movies." But I could not see anyone around me who looked like the highly stylized enemy characters in the movies. This posed a big problem. I no longer felt sure about seizing bags from old ladies. I could not possibly ask, "Are you a class enemy?"

We sometimes went to clean the houses in an alley next to our school. In one house there was a young man who used to lounge on a bamboo chair watching us with a cynical smile as we toiled away on his windows. Not only did he not offer to help, he even wheeled his bicycle out of the shed and suggested we clean that for him as well.

"What a pity," he once said, "that you are not the real Lei Feng, and that there are no photographers on hand to take your pictures for the newspapers." (Lei Feng's good deeds were miraculously recorded by an official photographer.) We all hated the lounger with the dirty bicycle. Could he be a class enemy? But we knew he worked at a machinery factory, and workers, we had been repeatedly told, were the best, the leading class in our revolution. I was confused.

One of the things I had been doing was helping to push carts on the streets after school. The carts were often piled high with cement blocks or chunks of sandstone. They were terribly heavy, and every step was an enormous effort for the men who pulled them. Even in cold weather, some would be bare-chested, and shiny beads of sweat trickled down their faces and backs. If the road was even slightly uphill, it was very hard for some of them to keep going. Whenever I saw them, I was attacked by a wave of sadness. Since the campaign to learn from Lei Feng had started, I had stood by a ramp waiting for carts to pass. I would be exhausted after helping to push just one of them. As I left off, the man pulling would give me an almost imperceptible sideways smile, trying not to break his stride and lose momentum.

One day a classmate said to me in a very serious tone of voice that most of the people pulling carts were class enemies who had been assigned to do hard labor. Therefore, she told me, it was wrong to help them. I asked my teacher, since I, in accordance with Chinese tradition, always turned to teachers for authority. But instead of her normal air of confidence, she looked unsettled and said she did not know the answer, which puzzled me. In fact, it was actually true that people pulling carts had often been assigned the job because they had Kuomintang links, or because they were victims of one of the political purges. My teacher obviously did not want to tell me this, but she did ask me to stop helping to push carts. From then on, every time I happened on a cart in the street, I averted my eyes from the bent figure trudging along and quickly walked away with a heavy heart.

To fill us with hatred for class enemies, the schools started regular sessions of "recalling bitterness and reflecting on happiness," at which older people would tell us about the miseries of pre-Communist China. Our generation had been born "under the red flag" in new China, and had no idea what life was like under the Kuomintang. Lei Feng had, we were taught, which was why he could hate the class enemies so deeply and love Chairman Mao with all his heart. When he was seven, his mother was supposed to have hanged herself after being raped by a landlord.

Workers and peasants came to give talks at our school: we heard of childhoods dominated by starvation, freezing winters with no shoes, and premature, painful deaths. They told us how boundlessly grateful they were to Chairman Mao for saving their lives and giving them food and clothing. One speaker was a member of an ethnic group called the Yi, who had a system of slavery until the late 1950s. He had been a slave and showed us scars from appalling beatings under his previous masters. Every time the speakers described the hardships they had endured the packed hall was shaken by sobs. I came out of these sessions feeling devastated at what the Kuomintang had done, and passionately devoted to Mao.

To show us what life without Mao would be like, every now and then the school canteen cooked something called a "bitterness meal," which was supposed to be what poor people had to eat under the Kuomintang. It was composed of strange herbs, and I secretly wondered whether the cooks were playing a practical joke on us—it was truly unspeakable. The first couple of times I vomited.

One day we were taken to an exhibition of "class education" about Tibet: on display were photos of dungeons crawling with scorpions, and horrific instruments of torture, including a tool for scooping out eyes and knives for cutting the tendons in the ankles. A man in a wheelchair who came to our school to give a talk told us he was a former serf from Tibet who had had his ankle tendons severed for some trivial offense.

Since 1964, large houses had also been opened as "museums of class education" to show how class enemies like landlords had lived in luxury on the sweat and blood of the peasants before Mao came. During the holiday for Chinese New Year in 1965, my father took us to a famous mansion two and a half hours' drive from home. Underneath the political justification, the journey was really an excuse for an outing to the countryside in early spring, in accordance with the Chinese tradition of "walking on the tender green" (*ta-qing*) to welcome the season. This was one of the few occasions that my family ever went on a trip out to the country.

As the car drove across the green Chengdu Plain along the eucalyptus-lined asphalt road, I looked intently out of the window at the lovely bamboo groves embracing the farmhouses, and the curving smoke lingering above the thatched cottages peeping between the bamboo leaves. Occasionally, a branch of early plum blossom was reflected in the streams that meandered around almost every thicket. My father had asked us all to write an essay after the trip, describing the scenery, and I observed everything with great care. There was one sight which puzzled me: the few trees dotted around the fields were completely stripped of their branches and leaves except for the very top, and looked like bare flagpoles with a cap of green. My father explained that firewood was scarce on the densely cultivated Chengdu Plain, and that the peasants had cut off as many branches as they could reach. What he did not tell me was that there had been many more trees until a few years before, but most of them had been cut down to feed the furnaces to produce steel during the Great Leap Forward.

The countryside seemed extremely prosperous. The market town where we stopped for lunch was teeming with peasants in bright new clothes, the older ones wearing shiny white turbans and clean dark-blue aprons. Golden roast ducks glowed in the windows of the packed restaurants. Deliciously scented clouds burst out of the lids of huge bamboo steamers in the stalls on the crowded streets. Our car crawled through the market to the local government offices, which were in a mansion with two stone lions squatting outside the gate. My father had lived in this county during the famine in 1961, and now, four years later, the local officials wanted to show him how much had changed. They took us to a restaurant where a private room had been reserved for us. As we squeezed through the crowded restaurant the peasants stared at us, obvious outsiders ushered in respectfully by the local bosses. I saw that the tables were covered with strange, mouth-watering dishes. I had hardly ever eaten anything except what we were given in our canteen, and the food in this market town was full of lovely surprises. It had novel names too: "Pearl Balls," "Three Gunshots," "Lions' Heads." Afterward the manager of the restaurant said goodbye to us on the pavement while the local peasants gawked at our entourage.

On the way to the museum, our car overtook an open truck with some boys and girls from my school in it. They were obviously going to the "class-education" mansion as well. One of my teachers was standing on the back. She smiled at me, and I shrank down in my seat with embarrassment at the difference between our chauffeur-driven car and the open truck on the bumpy road in the cold early spring air. My father was sitting in front with my youngest brother on his lap. He recognized my teacher and smiled back at her. When he turned around to attract my attention, he saw that I had completely disappeared. He beamed with pleasure. My embarrassment showed my good qualities, he said; it was good that I felt ashamed of privilege rather than flaunting it.

I found the museum incredibly shocking. There were sculptures of landless peasants having to pay exorbitant rent. One showed how the landlord used two different measures: a big one for collecting grain and a small one for lending it out—at crippling interest, too. There were also a torture chamber and a dungeon with an iron cage sitting in filthy water. The cage was too small for a man to be able to stand up straight, and too narrow for him to sit down. We were told the landlord used it to punish peasants who could not pay their rent. One room was said to have housed three wet-nurses who provided him with human milk, which he believed was the most nutritious kind. His number-five concubine was said to have eaten thirty ducks a day— not the meat, only the feet, which were considered a great delicacy.

We were not told that the brother of this allegedly inhuman land- lord was now a minister in the government in Peking, having been given the post as a reward for surrendering Chengdu to the Commu- nists in 1949. Throughout, while we were being instructed about the "man-eating days of the Kuomintang," we were reminded that we should be grateful to Mao.

The cult of Mao went hand in hand with the manipulation of people's unhappy memories of their past. Class enemies were pre- sented as vicious malefactors who wanted to drag China back to the days of the Kuomintang, which would mean that we children would lose our schools, our winter shoes, and our food. That was why we had to smash these enemies, we were told. Chiang Kai-shek was said to have launched assaults on the mainland and tried to stage a come- back in 1962 during the "difficult period"—the regime's euphemism for the famine.

In spite of all this talk and activity, class enemies for me, and for much of my generation, remained abstract, unreal shadows. They were a thing of the past, too far away. Mao had not been able to give them an everyday material form. One reason, paradoxically, was that he had smashed the past so thoroughly. However, the expectation of an enemy figure was planted in us.

At the same time, Mao was sowing the seeds for his own deification, and my contemporaries and I were immersed in this crude yet effec- tive indoctrination. It worked partly because Mao adroitly occupied the moral high ground: just as harshness to class enemies was pre- sented as loyalty to the people, so total submission to him was cloaked in a deceptive appeal to be selfless. It was very hard to get behind the rhetoric, particularly when there was no alternative viewpoint from the adult population. In fact, the adults positively colluded in enhanc- ing Mao's cult.

For two thousand years China had an emperor figure who was state power and spiritual authority rolled into one. The religious feelings which people in other parts of the world have toward a god have in China always been directed toward the emperor. My parents, like hundreds of millions of Chinese, were influenced by this tradition.

Mao made himself more godlike by shrouding himself in mystery. He always appeared remote, beyond human approach. He eschewed radio, and there was no television. Few people, except his court staff, ever had any contact with him. Even his colleagues at the very top only met him in a sort of formal audience. After Yan'an, my father only set eyes on him a few times, and then only at large-scale meetings. My mother only ever saw him once, when he came to Chengdu in 1958 and summoned all officials above Grade 18 to have a group photo taken with him. After the fiasco of the Great Leap Forward, he had disappeared almost completely.

Mao, the emperor, fitted one of the patterns of Chinese history: the leader of a nationwide peasant uprising who swept away a rotten dynasty and became a wise new emperor exercising absolute authority. And, in a sense, Mao could be said to have earned his god-emperor status. He *was* responsible for ending the civil war and bringing peace and stability, which the Chinese always yearned for—so much that they said "It's better to be a dog in peacetime than a human being in war." It was under Mao that China became a power to be reckoned with in the world, and many Chinese stopped feeling ashamed and humiliated at being Chinese, which meant a tremendous amount to them. In reality, Mao turned China back to the days of the Middle Kingdom and, with the help of the United States, to isolation from the world. He enabled the Chinese to feel great and superior again, by blinding them to the world outside. Nonetheless, national pride was so important to the Chinese that much of the population was genuinely grateful to Mao, and did not find the cult of his personality offensive, certainly not at first. The near total lack of access to information and the systematic feeding of disinformation meant that most Chinese had no way to discriminate between Mao's successes and his failures, or to identify the relative role of Mao and other leaders in the Communists' achievements.

Fear was never absent in the building up of Mao's cult. Many people had been reduced to a state where they did not dare even to think, in case their thoughts came out involuntarily. Even if they did entertain unorthodox ideas, few mentioned them to their children, as they might blurt out something to other children, which could bring disaster to themselves as well as their parents. In the learn-from-Lei Feng years it was hammered into children that our first and only loyalty should be to Mao. A popular song went: "Father is close,

Mother is close, but neither is as close as Chairman Mao." We were drilled to think that anyone, including our parents, who was not totally for Mao was our enemy. Many parents encouraged their children to grow up as conformists, as this would be safest for their future.

Self-censorship covered even basic information. I never heard of Yu-lin, or my grandmother's other relatives. Nor was I told about my mother's detention in 1955, or about the famine—in fact, anything that might sow a grain of doubt in me about the regime, or Mao. My parents, like virtually every parent in China, never said anything unorthodox to their children.

In 1965, my New Year resolution was "I will obey my grandmother" —a traditional Chinese way of promising to behave well. My father shook his head: "You should not say that. You should only say 'I obey Chairman Mao.' " On my thirteenth birthday, in March that year, my father's present was not his usual books of science fiction, but a volume containing the four philosophical works of Mao.

Only one adult ever said anything to me which conflicted with the official propaganda, and that was the stepmother of Deng Xiaoping, who lived some of the time in the apartment block next to ours, with her daughter, who worked in the provincial government. She liked children, and I was constantly in and out of her apartment. When my friends and I stole pickles from the canteen, or picked melon flowers and herbs from the compound garden, we did not dare to take them home for fear of being scolded, so we used to go to her apartment, where she would wash and fry them for us. This was all the more exciting because we were eating something illicit. She was about seventy then, but looked much younger, with tiny feet and a gentle, smooth, but strong face. She always wore a gray cotton jacket and black cotton shoes, which she made herself. She was very relaxed and treated us like equals. I liked sitting in her kitchen chatting with her. On one occasion, when I was about thirteen, I went to see her straight after an emotional "speak-bitterness" session. I was bursting with compassion for anyone who had had to live under the Kuomintang, and I said: "Grandma Deng, how you must have suffered under the evil Kuomintang! How the soldiers must have looted you! And the blood-sucking landlords! What did they do to you?" "Well," she answered, "they didn't always loot . . . and they were not always evil. . . ." Her words hit me like a bombshell. I was so shocked that I never told anyone what she had said.

At the time, none of us had any idea that the cult of Mao and the emphasis on class struggle were part of Mao's plans for a showdown with the president, Liu Shaoqi, and Deng Xiaoping, the general secretary of the Party. Mao was unhappy about what Liu and Deng were doing. Since the famine they had been liberalizing both the economy and the society. To Mao, their approach smacked of capitalism rather than socialism. It especially galled him that what he called "the capitalist road" was proving successful, while his chosen way, the "correct" way, had turned out to be a disaster. As a practical man, Mao recognized this, and had to allow them to have their way. But he planned to impose his ideas again as soon as the country was in good enough shape to stand the experiment, and as soon as he could build up enough momentum to dislodge his powerful enemies in the Party.

Mao found the idea of peaceful progress suffocating. A restless military leader, a warrior-poet, he needed action—violent action— and regarded permanent human struggle as necessary for social development. His own Communists had become too tolerant and soft for his taste, seeking to bring harmony rather than conflict. There had been no political campaigns, in which people fought each other, since 1959!

And Mao was sore. He felt that his opponents had humiliated him by showing him up as incompetent. He had to take revenge, and, being aware that his opponents had widespread support, he needed to increase his authority hugely. To achieve this, he needed to be deified.

Mao bided his time while the economy was recovering. But as it improved, especially after 1964, he began to prepare the grand opening of his confrontation. The relative liberalization of the early 1960s began to fade.

The weekly dances in the compound stopped in 1964. So did the films from Hong Kong. Out went my mother's fluffy bobs; in came short, straight hair. Her blouses and jackets were no longer colorful or figure-hugging. They were made of plain quiet colors and looked like tubes. I was particularly sorry to see her skirts go. I remembered how, a short time before, I had watched her getting off her bicycle, gracefully lifting her blue-and-white check skirt with her knee. I was leaning against the mottled trunk of a plane tree that formed part of the glade covering the street outside the compound. Her skirt had been flowing like a fan as she rode toward me. On summer evenings, I had often pushed Xiao-fang there in his bamboo pram and waited for her to come home.

My grandmother, now in her mid-fifties, kept more signs of her femininity than my mother. Although her jackets—still in the traditional style—all became the same color of pale gray, she took particular care of her long, thick black hair. According to Chinese tradition, which the Communists inherited, hair had to be well above the shoulder for women of middle age, meaning over thirty. My grandmother kept her hair tied up in a neat bun at the back of her head, but she always had flowers there, sometimes a pair of ivory-colored magnolias, and sometimes a white Cape jasmine cupped by two dark-green leaves, which set off her lustrous hair. She never used shampoo from the shops, which she thought would make her hair dull and dry, but would boil the fruit of the Chinese honey locust and use the liquid from that. She would rub the fruit to produce a perfumed lather, and slowly let her mass of black hair drop into the shiny, white, slithery liquid. She soaked her wooden combs in the juice of pomelo seeds, so that the comb ran smoothly through her hair, and gave it a faint aroma. She added a final touch by putting on a little water of osmanthus flowers which she made herself, as perfume had begun to disappear from the shops. I remember watching her combing her hair. It was the only thing over which she took her time. She did everything else very swiftly. She would also paint her eyebrows lightly with a black charcoal pencil and dab a little powder on her nose. Seeing her eyes smiling into the mirror with a particular kind of intense concentration, I think these must have been among her most pleasurable moments.

Watching her doing her face was strange, even though I had been watching her do it since I was a baby. The women in books and films who made themselves up now were invariably wicked characters, like concubines. I vaguely knew something about my beloved grandmother having been a concubine, but I was learning to live with contradictory thoughts and realities, and getting used to compartmentalizing them. When I went out shopping with my grandmother, I began to realize that she was different from other people, with her makeup, no matter how discreet, and the flowers in her hair. People noticed her. She walked proudly, her figure erect, with a restrained self-consciousness.

She could get away with it because she lived in the compound. If she had been living outside, she would have fallen under one of the residents' committees, which supervised the lives of any adult who did not have a job and so did not belong to a work unit. The committees usually contained retired men and old housewives, and some of them became notorious for minding other people's business and throwing their weight around. Had my grandmother been under one of these, she would have received disapproving hints or open criticism. But the compound had no committee. She did have to go to a meeting once a week with other parents-in-law and maids and nannies from the compound, to be told about Party policies, but she was mainly left alone. Actually, she enjoyed the meetings; they were a chance to chat with the other women and she always came home beaming with the latest gossip.

Politics invaded my life more and more after I went to middle school in the autumn of 1964. On our first day we were told we should thank Chairman Mao for being there, because his "class line" had been applied to our year's enrollment. Mao had accused schools and universities of having taken in too many children of the bourgeoisie. Now, he had instructed, priority should be given to sons and daughters of "good backgrounds" (chu-shen hao). This meant having workers, peasants, soldiers, or Party officials as parents, particularly as fathers. The application of this "class-line" criterion to the whole society meant that one's lot was more than ever determined by one's family and the accident of birth.

However, the status of a family was often ambiguous: a worker might once have been employed in a Kuomintang office; a clerk did not belong to any category; an intellectual was an "undesirable," but what if he was a Party member? How should the children of such parents be classified? Many enrollment officers decided to play it safe, which meant giving preference to children whose parents were Party officials. They constituted half the pupils in my class.

My new school, the Number Four Middle School, was the leading key school for the whole province and took students with the highest marks in the all-Sichuan entrance exams. In previous years, entrance had been decided solely on the basis of exam results. In my year, exam marks and family background were equally important.

In the two exam papers, I got 100 percent for math and an unusual 100 percent "plus" for Chinese. My father had constantly drummed it into me that I should not rely on my parents' name, and I did not like the suggestion that the "class line" had helped me get into the school. But I soon thought no more about it. If this was what Chairman Mao said, it must be good.

It was in this period that "high officials' children" (gao-gan zi-di) became almost a stratum of their own. They developed an air which identified them unmistakably as members of an elite group, exuding an awareness of powerful backing and untouchability. Many high officials' children now grew more arrogant and haughty than ever, and from Mao downward concern was constantly being expressed about their behavior. It became a recurrent theme in the press. All this only reinforced the idea that they were a special group.

My father frequently warned us against this air and against forming cliques with other children of high officials. The result was that I had few friends, as I seldom met children from any other background. When I did come into contact with them, I found we had been so conditioned by the importance of family background and the lack of shared experience that we seemed to have little in common with each other.

When I entered the new school two teachers came to see my parents to ask which foreign language they wanted me to learn. They chose English rather than Russian, which was the only other option. The teachers also wanted to know whether I was going to take physics or chemistry in my first year. My parents said they would leave that up to the school.

I loved the school from the moment I walked in. It had an imposing gate with a broad roof of blue tiles and carved eaves. A flight of stone stairs led up to it, and the loggia was supported by six red-timber columns. Symmetrical rows of dark-green cypresses enhanced the atmosphere of solemnity leading into the interior.

The school had been founded in 141 B.C. It was the first school set up by a local government in China. At its center was a magnificent temple, formerly dedicated to Confucius. It was well preserved, but was not functioning as a temple any longer. Inside were half a dozen Ping-Pong tables, separated by the massive columns. In front of the carved doors, down a long flight of stairs, lay extensive grounds designed to provide a majestic approach to the temple. A two-story teaching block had been erected, which cut off the grounds from a brook crossed by three little arched bridges, with sculptures of miniature lions and other animals sitting on their sandstone edges. Beyond the bridges was a beautiful garden surrounded by peaches and plane trees. Two giant bronze incense burners were set at the bottom of the stairs in front of the temple, although there was no longer any blue smoke curling up and lingering in the air above them. The grounds on the sides of the temple had been converted into basketball and volleyball courts. Farther along were two lawns where we used to sit or lie in spring and enjoy the sun during lunch breaks. Behind the temple was another lawn, beyond which lay a big orchard at the foot of a small hill covered with trees, vines, and herbs.

Dotted around were laboratories where we studied biology and chemistry, learned to use microscopes, and dissected dead animals. In the lecture theaters, we watched teaching films. For after-school activities, I joined the biology group which strolled around the hill and the back garden with the teacher learning the names and characteristics of the different plants. There were temperature-controlled breeding cases for us to observe how tadpoles and ducklings broke out of their eggs. In spring, the school was a sea of pink because of all the peach trees. But what I liked most was the two-story library, built in the traditional Chinese style. The building was encircled on both floors by loggias, and the outside of these was enclosed by a row of gorgeously painted seats which were shaped like wings. I had a favorite corner in these "wing seats" (fei-lai-yi) where I used to sit for hours reading, occasionally stretching my arm out to touch the fan-shaped leaves of a rare ginkgo tree. There was a pair of them outside the front gate of the library, towering and elegant. They were the only sight that could distract me from my books.

My clearest memory is of my teachers. They were the best in their field; many were grade one, or special grade. Their classes were sheer joy, and I could never have enough of them.

But more and more political indoctrination was creeping into school life. Gradually, morning assembly became devoted to Mao's teachings, and special sessions were instituted in which we read Party documents. Our Chinese-language textbook now contained more propaganda and less classical literature, and politics, which mainly consisted of works by Mao, became part of the curriculum.

Almost every activity became politicized. One day at morning assembly the headmaster told us we were going to do eye exercises. He said Chairman Mao had observed that there were too many schoolchildren wearing spectacles, a sign that they had hurt their eyes by working too hard. He had ordered something to be done about it. We were all terribly moved by his concern. Some of us wept in gratitude. We started doing eye exercises for fifteen minutes every morning. A set of movements had been devised by doctors and set to music. After rubbing various points around our eyes, we all stared intently at the rows of poplars and willows outside the window. Green was supposed to be a restful color. As I enjoyed the comfort the exercises and the leaves brought me, I thought of Mao and repledged my loyalty to him.

A repeated theme was that we must not allow China to "change color," which meant going from Communist to capitalist. The split between China and the Soviet Union, which had been kept secret at first, had burst into the open in early 1963. We were told that since Khrushchev had come to power after the death of Stalin in 1953 the Soviet Union had surrendered to international capitalism, and that Russian children had been reduced to suffering and misery again, just like Chinese children under the Kuomintang. One day, after warning us for the umpteenth time against the road taken by Russia, our politics teacher said: "If you aren't careful, our country will change color gradually, first from bright red to faded red, then to gray, then to black." It so happened that the Sichuan expression "faded red" had exactly the same pronunciation *(er-hong)* as my name. My classmates giggled, and I could see them stealing glances at me. I felt I must get rid of my name immediately. That evening I begged my father to give me another name. He suggested *Zhang*, meaning both "prose" and "coming into one's own early," which expressed his desire for me to become a good writer at a young age. But I did not want the name. I told my father that I wanted "something with a military ring to it." Many of my friends had changed their names to incorporate the characters meaning "army" or "soldier." My father's choice reflected his classical learning. My new name, Jung (pronounced "Yung"), was a very old and recondite word for "martial affairs" which appeared only in classical poetry and a few antiquated phrases. It evoked an image of bygone battles between knights in shining armor, with tasseled spears and neighing steeds. When I turned up at school with my new name even some teachers could not recognize the character 戎.

At this time Mao had called on the country to go from learning from Lei Feng to learning from the army. Under the defense minister, Lin Biao, who had succeeded Marshal Peng Dehuai in 1959, the army had become the trailblazer for the cult of Mao. Mao also wanted to regimentalize the nation even more. He had just written a well-publicized poem exhorting women to "doff femininity and don military attire." We were told that the Americans were waiting for a chance to invade and reinstate the Kuomintang, and that in order to defeat an invasion by them Lei Feng had trained day and night to overcome his weak physique and become a champion hand-grenade thrower. Physical training suddenly assumed vital importance. There was compulsory running, swimming, high jumping, working out on parallel bars, shot-putting, and throwing wooden hand grenades. In addition to the two hours of sports per week, forty-five minutes of after-school sports now became obligatory.

I had always been hopeless at sports, and hated them, except tennis. Previously this had not mattered, but now it took on a political connotation, with slogans like: "Build up a strong physique to defend our motherland." Unfortunately, my aversion to sports was increased by this pressure. When I tried to swim, I always had a mental picture of being pursued by invading Americans to the bank of a surging river. As I could not swim, my only choice was between being drowned or being captured and tortured by the Americans. Fear gave me frequent cramps in the water, and once I thought I was drowning in the swimming pool. In spite of compulsory swimming every week during the summer, I never managed to learn to swim all the time I lived in China.

Hand-grenade throwing was also regarded as very important, for obvious reasons. I was always at the bottom of the class. I could only throw the wooden hand grenades we practiced with a couple of yards. I felt that my classmates were questioning my resolve to fight the U.S. imperialists. Once at our weekly political meeting somebody commented on my persistent failure at hand-grenade throwing. I could feel the eyes of the class boring into me like needles, as if to say: "You are a lackey of the Americans!" The next morning I went and stood in a corner of the sports field, with my arms held out in front of me and a couple of bricks in each hand. In Lei Feng's diary, which I had learned by heart, I had read that this was how he had toughened up his muscles to throw hand grenades. After a few days, by which time my upper arms were red and swollen, I gave up, and whenever I was handed the wooden chunk, I became so nervous that my hands shook uncontrollably.

One day in 1965, we were suddenly told to go out and start removing all the grass from the lawns. Mao had instructed that grass, flowers, and pets were bourgeois habits and were to be eliminated. The grass in the lawns at our school was of a type I have not seen anywhere outside China. Its name in Chinese means "bound to the ground." It crawls all over the hard surface of the earth and spreads thousands of roots which drill down into the soil like claws of steel. Underground they open up and produce further roots which shoot out in every direction. In no time there are two networks, one aboveground and one belowground, which intertwine and cling to the earth, like knotted metal wires that have been nailed into the ground. Often the only casualties were my fingers, which always ended up with deep, long cuts. It was only when they were attacked with hoes and spades that some of the root systems went, reluctantly. But any fragment left behind would make a triumphant comeback after even a slight rise in temperature or a gentle drizzle, and we would have to go into battle all over again.

Flowers were much easier to deal with, but they went with even more difficulty, because no one wanted to remove them. Mao had attacked flowers and grass several times before, saying that they should be replaced by cabbages and cotton. But only now was he able to generate enough pressure to get his order implemented—but only up to a point. People loved their plants, and some flowerbeds survived Mao's campaign.

I was extremely sad to see the lovely plants go. But I did not resent Mao. On the contrary, I hated myself for feeling miserable. By then I had grown into the habit of "self-criticism" and automatically blamed myself for any instincts that went against Mao's instructions. In fact, such feelings frightened me. It was out of the question to discuss them with anyone. Instead, I tried to suppress them and acquire the correct way of thinking. I lived in a state of constant self-accusation.

Such self-examination and self-criticism were a feature of Mao's China. You would become a new and better person, we were told. But all this introspection was really designed to serve no other purpose than to create a people who had no thoughts of their own.

The religious aspect of the Mao cult would not have been possible in a traditionally secular society like China had there not been impressive economic achievements. The country had made a stunning recovery from the famine, and the standard of living was improving dramatically. In Chengdu, although rice was still rationed, there was plenty of meat, poultry, and vegetables. Winter melons, turnips, and eggplants were piled up on the pavements outside the shops because there was not enough space to store them. They were left outside overnight, and almost nobody took them; the shops were giving them away for a pittance. Eggs, once so precious, sat rotting in large baskets —there were too many of them. Only a few years before it had been hard to find a single peach—now peach eating was being promoted as "patriotic," and officials went around to people's homes and tried to persuade them to take peaches for next to nothing.

There were a number of success stories which boosted the nation's pride. In October 1964 China exploded its first atomic bomb. This was given huge publicity and touted as a demonstration of the country's scientific and industrial achievement, particularly in relation to "standing up to imperialist bullies." The explosion of the atomic bomb coincided with the ousting of Khrushchev, which was presented as proof that Mao was right again. In 1964 France recognized China at full ambassadorial level, the first leading Western nation to do so. This was received with rapture inside China as a major victory over the United States, which was refusing to acknowledge China's rightful place in the world.

In addition, there was no general political persecution, and people were relatively content. All the credit was given to Mao. Although the very top leaders knew what Mao's real contribution was, the people were kept completely in the dark. Over the years I composed passionate eulogies thanking Mao for all his achievements and pledging my undying loyalty to him.

I was thirteen in 1965. On the evening of 1 October that year, the sixteenth anniversary of the founding of the People's Republic, there was a big fireworks display on the square in the center of Chengdu. To the north of the square was the gate to an ancient imperial palace, which had recently been restored to its third-century grandeur, when Chengdu was the capital of a kingdom and a prosperous walled city. The gate was very similar to the Gate of Heavenly Peace in Peking, now the entrance to the Forbidden City, except for its color: it had sweeping green-tiled roofs and gray walls. Under the glazed roof of the pavilion stood enormous dark-red pillars. The balustrades were made of white marble. I was standing behind them with my family and the Sichuan dignitaries on a reviewing stand enjoying the festival atmosphere and waiting for the fireworks to begin. Below in the square 50,000 people were singing and dancing. *Bang! Bang!* The signals for the fireworks went off a few yards from where I stood. In an instant, the sky was a garden of spectacular shapes and colors, a sea of wave after wave of brilliance. The music and noise rose from below the imperial gate to join in the sumptuousness. After a while, the sky was clear for a few seconds. Then a sudden explosion brought out a gorgeous blossom, followed by the unfurling of a long, vast, silky hanging. It stretched itself in the middle of the sky, swaying gently in the autumn breeze. In the light over the square, the characters on the hanging were shining: "Long Live Our Great Leader Chairman Mao!" Tears sprang to my eyes. "How lucky, how incredibly lucky I am to be living in the great era of Mao Zedong!" I kept saying to myself. "How can children in the capitalist world go on living without being near Chairman Mao, and without the hope of ever seeing him in person?" I wanted to do something for them, to rescue them from their plight. I made a pledge to myself there and then to work hard to build a stronger China, in order to support a world revolution. I needed to work hard to be entitled to see Chairman Mao, too. That was the purpose of my life.

My grandfather General Xue Zhi-heng,
chief of police in the warlord government in Peking, 1922–1924.

My mother (left) with her mother and stepfather, Dr. Xia; Jinzhou, c. 1939.
Standing center is Dr. Xia's second son, De-gui, the only member of his family
who approved of Dr. Xia's marriage to my grandmother. Dr. Xia's eldest son shot
himself in protest. Standing far right is De-gui's son.

Dr. Xia.

My mother as a schoolgirl, age thirteen, in Manchukuo, 1944.

Cousin Hu, my mother's first boyfriend. On the back of the photo is a poem he wrote:

> Wind and dust are my companions,/The end of the earth is my home.

—The Exile

After Cousin Hu was bought out of prison by his father in 1947, he gave this photograph to a friend and asked him to give it to my mother, so that she would know that he was alive. Because of the siege, the friend did not see my mother until after the Communists had taken Jinzhou; seeing her in love with my father, he decided not to give her the photo. He only passed it to her after a chance meeting in 1985; it was then she learned that Cousin Hu had died in the Cultural Revolution.

My grandmother's sister Lan and her husband, "Loyalty," with their baby son shortly after "Loyalty" joined Kuomintang intelligence, Jinzhou, 1946.

Communist soldiers walking below Kuomintang slogans on one of the city gates which survived the siege of Jinzhou, 1948.

Painting slogans on the soles of "liberation shoes" during the civil war—
"Safeguard Our Land" (left) and "Beat Chiang Kai-shek."

Communist forces attacking Jinzhou, October 1948.

My parents in Nanjing, the former Kuomintang capital, en route from Manchuria to Sichuan, a few days before my mother's miscarriage of her first child, September 1949. They are both wearing Communist army uniforms.

Farewell party for my mother before she left Yibin, June 1953. From left (back): my father's youngest sister and my mother; (front): my paternal grandmother, me, my maternal grandmother, Xiao-hong, Jin-ming, Aunt Jun-ying.

My parents (back), with my grandmother (left) holding Xiao-hong and my wet nurse (holding me), shortly after we arrived in Chengdu, fall 1953.

My grandmother holding me (aged 2 with ribbons in hair) and Jin-ming; my mother holding Xiao-hei; Xiao-hong standing; Chengdu, late 1954.

My father, in a photograph which I think catches his mood particularly well, during the journey from Manchuria to Sichuan, late 1949.

My mother making a speech, Chengdu, 1958.

Age six.

My mother with (from left) Xiao-hong, Jin-ming, Xiao-hei, and me, Chengdu, early 1958. This photograph was taken in a hurry for my father to bring with him to Yibin to show his mother, who was gravely ill. Signs of haste show in my mother's hair, which has not been brushed down, and in the handkerchief still pinned (as was customary for young children) to Jin-ming's sailor suit.

With Xiao-hong (left), Xiao-hei (behind), and Jin-ming (right) at the annual Chengdu flower show, 1958.

Soon after this photo was taken, famine struck. My father was constantly away in the countryside, so for several years there were no family photographs.

On Tiananmen Square, Peking, as a Red Guard (front, second from left), with friends and air force officers (including one woman) assigned to train us. I am wearing a Red Guard armband, my mother's "Lenin jacket," and patched trousers to look "proletarian." We are all holding the Little Red Book in a standard posture of the time. November 1966.

The last photograph of my father before the Cultural Revolution, spring 1966.

My father in the camp at Miyi, with Jin-ming, late 1971, just after the death of Lin Baio.

My mother in her camp at Buffalo Boy Flatland, in front of a field of corn she helped plant, 1971.

My grandmother's brother Yu-lin with his wife and children in front of the house they had just built for themselves after ten years' exile in the country, in 1976. It was then they decided to get in touch with my grandmother after a decade of silence. They sent this photo to tell her they were all right, not knowing she had died seven years earlier.

On the eve of being expelled to the edge of the Himalayas (standing, second from right) with (standing from left) Jin-ming, Xiao-hong, and Xiao-hei; (front row, from left): my grandmother, Xiao-fang, and Aunt Jun-ying; Chengdu, January 1969. The last photograph of my grandmother and my aunt.

With the electricians' work team in the machinery factory, Chengdu (front row, center). The Chinese characters read "Seeing Off Comrade Jung Chang to University, 27 September 1973, Electricians' Work Team."

Army training as an undergraduate at Sichuan University (back row, second from right). The Chinese characters read "Fish-Water Link (a slogan describing the relationship between the army and the people), English Class 1, Foreign Languages Department, Sichuan University, 27 November 1974."

With male comrades and Filipino sailor (center) on trip to practice English, Zhanjiang, October 1975. The sailors were the only foreigners I ever talked to before I left China in 1978.

With my class (front row, third from left) outside the gate of Sichuan University, Chengdu, January 1975.

Before my father's cremation, supporting my mother with Jin-ming. Opposite us (from left): Cheng-yi, Xiao-fang, Xiao-hei (in air force uniform), Xiao-hong. Chengdu, April 1975.

At the memorial service for my father (I am standing with my family, fourth from right). An official is reading the Party's valedictory. Chengdu, 21 April 1975. This speech was extremely important, as it was the Party's assessment of my father, and would determine his children's future even though he himself was dead. Because my father had criticized Mao, who was still alive, the original version was ominously negative. My mother fought for changes and won a much improved compromise. The memorial service was organized by a "funeral committee" of my father's former colleagues, including people who had helped to persecute him. It was carefully staged down to the last detail, and was attended by about five hundred people, according to a prescribed formula. Even the size of the wreaths was specified.

In Peking, September 1978,
just before leaving China for
Britain.

In Italy, summer 1990.
(Jon Halliday)

15. "Destroy First, and Construction Will Look After Itself"— The Cultural Revolution Begins

(1965–1966)

At the beginning of the 1960s, in spite of all the disasters Mao had caused, he was still China's supreme leader, idolized by the population. But because the pragmatists were actually running the country, there was relative literary and artistic freedom. A host of plays, operas, films, and novels emerged after long hibernation. None attacked the Party openly, and contemporary themes were rare. At this time Mao was on the defensive, and he turned more and more to his wife, Jiang Qing, who had been an actress in the 1930s. They decided that historical themes were being used to convey insinuations against the regime and against Mao himself.

In China, there was a strong tradition of using historical allusion to voice opposition, and even apparently esoteric allusions were widely understood as coded references to the present day. In April 1963 Mao banned all "Ghost Dramas," a genre rich in ancient tales of revenge by dead victims' spirits on those who had persecuted them. To him, these ghost avengers were uncomfortably close to the class enemies who had perished under his rule.

The Maos also turned their attention to another genre, the "Dramas of the Ming Mandarin," the protagonist of which was Hai Rui, a mandarin from the Ming dynasty (1368–1644). A famous personification of justice and courage, the Ming Mandarin remonstrated with the emperor on behalf of the suffering ordinary people, at the risk of his own life. He was dismissed and exiled. The Maos suspected that the Ming Mandarin was being used to represent Marshal Peng Dehuai, the former defense minister who in 1959 had spoken out against Mao's disastrous policies which had caused the famine. Almost immediately after Peng's dismissal, there was a noticeable resurgence of the Ming Mandarin genre. Mme. Mao tried to get the plays denounced, but when she approached the writers and ministers in charge of the arts they turned a deaf ear.

In 1964, Mao drew up a list of thirty-nine artists, writers, and scholars for denunciation. He branded them "reactionary bourgeois authorities," a new category of class enemies. Prominent names on the list included the most famous playwright in the Ming Mandarin genre, Wu Han, and Professor Ma Yin-chu, who had been the first leading economist to advocate birth control. For this he had already been named a rightist in 1957. Mao had subsequently realized that birth control was necessary, but he resented Professor Ma for showing him up and making it clear that he was wrong.

The list was not made public, and the thirty-nine people were not purged by their Party organizations. Mao had the list circulated to officials down to my mother's level with instructions to catch other "reactionary bourgeois authorities." In the winter of 1964–65, my mother was sent as the head of a work team to a school named "Ox Market." She was told to look for suspects among prominent teachers and those who had written books or articles.

My mother was appalled, particularly as the purge threatened the very people she most admired. Besides, she could plainly see that even if she were to look for "enemies" she would not find any. Apart from anything else, with the memory of all the recent persecutions few had dared to open their mouths at all. She told her superior, Mr. Pao, who was in charge of the campaign in Chengdu, how she felt.

Nineteen sixty-five passed, and my mother did nothing. Mr. Pao did not exert any pressure on her. Their inaction reflected the general mood among Party officials. Most of them were fed up with persecutions, and wanted to get on with improving living standards and building a normal life. But they did not openly oppose Mao, and indeed went on promoting his personality cult. The few who watched Mao's deification with apprehension knew there was nothing they could do to stop it: Mao had such power and prestige that his cult was irresistible. The most they could do was engage in some kind of passive resistance.

Mao interpreted the reaction from the Party officials to his call for a witch-hunt as an indication that their loyalty to him was weakening and that their hearts were with the policies being pursued by President Liu and Deng. His suspicion was confirmed when the Party newspapers refused to publish an article he had authorized denouncing Wu Han and his play about the Ming Mandarin. Mao's purpose in getting the article published was to involve the population in the witch-hunt. Now he found he was cut off from his subjects by the Party system, which had been the intermediary between himself and the people. He had, in effect, lost control. The Party Committee of Peking, where Wu Han was deputy mayor, and the Central Department of Public Affairs, which looked after the media and the arts, stood up to Mao, refusing either to denounce Wu Han or to dismiss him.

Mao felt threatened. He saw himself as a Stalin figure, about to be denounced by a Khrushchev while he was still alive. He wanted to make a preemptive strike and destroy the man he regarded as "China's Khrushchev," Liu Shaoqi, and his colleague Deng, as well as their followers in the Party. This he deceptively termed the "Cultural Revolution." He knew his would be a lone battle, but this gave him the majestic satisfaction of feeling that he was challenging nothing less than the whole world, and maneuvering on a grand scale. There was even a tinge of self-pity as he portrayed himself as the tragic hero taking on a mighty enemy—the huge Party machine.

On 10 November 1965, having repeatedly failed to have the article condemning Wu Han's play published in Peking, Mao was at last able to get it printed in Shanghai, where his followers were in charge. It was in this article that the term "Cultural Revolution" first appeared. The Party's own newspaper, the *People's Daily*, refused to reprint the article, as did the *Peking Daily*, the voice of the Party organization in the capital. In the provinces, some papers did carry the article. At the time, my father was overseeing the provincial Party newspaper, the *Sichuan Daily*, and was against reprinting the article, which he could sense was an attack on Marshal Peng and a call for a witch-hunt. He went to see the man in charge of cultural affairs for the province, who suggested they telephone Deng Xiaoping. Deng was not in his office, and the call was taken by Marshal Ho Lung, a close friend of Deng's, and a member of the Politburo. It was he whom my father had overheard saying in 1959: "It really should be him [Deng] on the throne." Ho said not to reprint the article.

Sichuan was one of the last provinces to run the article, doing so only on 18 December, well after the *People's Daily* finally printed it on 30 November. The article appeared in the *People's Daily* only after

Zhou Enlai, the premier, who had emerged as the peacekeeper in the power struggle, added a note to it, in the name of "the editor," saying that the Cultural Revolution was to be an "academic" discussion, meaning that it should be nonpolitical and should not lead to political condemnations.

Over the next three months there was intense maneuvering, with Mao's opponents, as well as Zhou, trying to head off Mao's witch-hunt. In February 1966, while Mao was away from Peking, the Politburo passed a resolution that "academic discussions" must not degenerate into persecutions. Mao had objected to this resolution, but he was ignored.

In April my father was asked to prepare a document in the spirit of the Politburo's February resolution to guide the Cultural Revolution in Sichuan. What he wrote became known as the "April Document." It said: The debates must be strictly academic. No wild accusations should be allowed. Everyone is equal before the truth. The Party must not use force to suppress intellectuals.

Just as this document was about to be published in May, it was suddenly blocked. There was a new Politburo decision. This time, Mao had been present and had got the upper hand, with Zhou Enlai's complicity. Mao tore up the February resolution and declared that all dissident scholars and their ideas must be "eliminated." He emphasized that it was officials in the Communist Party who had been protecting the dissident scholars and other class enemies. He termed these officials "those in power following the capitalist road," and declared war on them. They became known as "capitalist-roaders." The mammoth Cultural Revolution was formally launched.

Who exactly were these "capitalist-roaders"? Mao himself was not sure. He knew he wanted to replace the whole of the Peking Party Committee, which he did. He also knew he wanted to get rid of Liu Shaoqi and Deng Xiaoping, and "the bourgeois headquarters in the Party." But he did not know who in the vast Party system were loyal to him and who were followers of Liu and Deng and their "capitalist road." He calculated that he controlled only a third of the Party. In order not to let a single one of his enemies escape, he resolved to overthrow the entire Communist Party. Those faithful to him would survive the upheaval. In his own words: "Destroy first, and construction will look after itself." Mao was not worried about the possible destruction of the Party: Mao the Emperor always overrode Mao the Communist. Nor was he fainthearted about hurting anyone unduly, even those most loyal to him. One of his great heroes, General Tsao Tsao of the first century, had spoken an immortal line which Mao openly admired: "I would rather wrong all people under Heaven; and no one under Heaven must ever wrong me." The general proclaimed this when he discovered that he had murdered an elderly couple by mistake—the old man and woman, whom he had suspected of betraying him, had in fact saved his life.

Mao's vague battle calls threw the population and the majority of Party officials into profound confusion. Few knew what he was driving at, or who exactly were the enemies this time. My father and mother, like other senior Party people, could see that Mao had decided to punish some officials. But they had no idea who these would be. It could well be themselves. Apprehension and bewilderment overwhelmed them.

Meanwhile, Mao made his single most important organizational move: he set up his own personal chain of command that operated outside the Party apparatus, although—by formally claiming it was under the Politburo and the Central Committee—he was able to pretend it was acting on Party orders.

First, he picked as his deputy Marshal Lin Biao, who had succeeded Peng Dehuai as defense minister in 1959 and had greatly boosted Mao's personality cult in the armed forces. He also set up a new body, the Cultural Revolution Authority, under his former secretary Chen Boda, with his intelligence chief Kang Sheng and Mme. Mao as its *de facto* leaders. It became the core of the leadership of the Cultural Revolution.

Next, Mao moved in on the media, primarily the *People's Daily*, which carried the most authority as it was the official Party newspaper and the population had become accustomed to it being the voice of the regime. He appointed Chen Boda to take it over on 31 May, thus securing a channel through which he could speak directly to hundreds of millions of Chinese.

Starting in June 1966, the *People's Daily* showered the country with one strident editorial after another, calling for "establishing Chairman Mao's absolute authority," "sweeping away all the ox devils and snake demons" (class enemies), and exhorting people to follow Mao and join the vast, unprecedented undertaking of a Cultural Revolution.

In my school, teaching stopped completely from the beginning of June, though we had to continue to go there. Loudspeakers blasted out *People's Daily* editorials, and the front page of the newspaper, which we had to study every day, was frequently taken up entirely by a full-page portrait of Mao. There was a daily column of Mao's quotations. I still remember the slogans in bold type, which, through reading in class over and over again, were engraved into the deepest folds of my brain: "Chairman Mao is the red sun in our hearts!" "Mao Zedong Thought is our lifeline!" "We will smash whoever opposes Chairman Mao!" "People all over the world love our Great Leader Chairman Mao!" There were pages of worshipping comments from foreigners, and pictures of European crowds trying to grab Mao's works. Chinese national pride was being mobilized to enhance his cult.

The daily newspaper reading soon gave way to the recitation and memorizing of *The Quotations of Chairman Mao*, which were collected together in a pocket-size book with a red plastic cover, known as "The Little Red Book." Everyone was given a copy and told to cherish it "like our eyes." Every day we chanted passages from it over and over again in unison. I still remember many verbatim.

One day, we read in the *People's Daily* that an old peasant had stuck thirty-two portraits of Mao on his bedroom walls, "so that he can see Chairman Mao's face as soon as he opens his eyes, whatever direction he looks in." So we covered the walls of our classroom with pictures of Mao's face beaming his most benign smile. But we soon had to take them down, and quickly, too. Word circulated that the peasant had really used the pictures as wallpaper, because Mao's portraits were printed on the best-quality paper and were free. Rumor had it that the reporter who had written up the story had been found to be a class enemy for advocating "abuse of Chairman Mao." For the first time, fear of Chairman Mao entered my subconscious.

Like "Ox Market," my school had a work team stationed in it. The team had halfheartedly branded several of the school's best teachers as "reactionary bourgeois authorities," but had kept this from the pupils. In June 1966, however, panicked at the tide of the Cultural Revolution and feeling the need to create some victims, the work team suddenly announced the names of the accused to the whole school.

The work team organized pupils and the teachers who had not been accused to write denunciation posters and slogans, which soon covered the grounds. Teachers became active for a variety of reasons: conformity, loyalty to the Party's orders, envy of the prestige and privileges of other teachers—and fear.

Among the victims was my Chinese language and literature teacher, Mr. Chi, whom I adored. According to one of the wall posters, he had said in the early 1960s: "Shouting 'Long live the Great Leap Forward!' will not fill our stomachs, will it?" Having no idea that the Great Leap had caused the famine, I did not understand his alleged remark, although I could catch its irreverent tone.

There was something about Mr. Chi which set him apart. At the time I could not put my finger on it, but now I think it was that he had an air of irony about him. He had a way of making dry, short half-cough, half-laughs which suggested he had kept something unsaid. He once made this noise in response to a question I asked him. One lesson in our textbook was an extract from the memoirs of Lu Dingyi, the then head of Central Public Affairs, about his experience on the Long March. Mr. Chi drew our attention to a vivid description of the troops marching along a zigzagging mountain path, the whole procession lit up by pine torches carried by the marchers, the flames glowing against a moonless black sky. When they reached their night's destination, they all "rushed to grab a bowlful of food to pour down their stomachs." This puzzled me profoundly, as Red Army soldiers had always been described as offering their last mouthful to their comrades and going starving themselves. It was impossible to imagine them "grabbing." I went to Mr. Chi for an answer. He cough-laughed, said I did not know what being hungry meant, and quickly changed the subject. I was unconvinced.

In spite of this, I felt the greatest respect for Mr. Chi. It broke my heart to see him, and other teachers I admired, being wildly condemned and called ugly names. I hated it when the work team asked everyone in the school to write wall posters "exposing and denouncing" them.

I was fourteen at the time, instinctively averse to all militant activities, and I did not know what to write. I was frightened of the wall posters' overwhelming black ink on giant white sheets of paper, and the outlandish and violent language, such as "Smash So-and-so's dog's head" and "Annihilate So-and-so if he does not surrender." I began to play truant and stay at home. For this I was constantly criticized for "putting family first" at the endless meetings that now made up almost our entire school life. I dreaded these meetings. A sense of unpredictable danger haunted me.

One day my deputy headmaster, Mr. Kan, a jolly, energetic man, was accused of being a capitalist-roader and of protecting the condemned teachers. Everything he had done in the school over the years was said to be "capitalist," even studying Mao's works—as fewer hours had been devoted to this than to academic studies.

I was equally shocked to see the cheerful secretary of the Communist Youth League in the school, Mr. Shan, being accused of being "anti-Chairman Mao." He was a dashing-looking young man whose attention I had been eager to attract, as he might help me join the Youth League when I reached the minimum age, fifteen.

He had been teaching a course on Marxist philosophy to the sixteen- to eighteen-year-olds, and had given them some essay-writing assignments. He had underlined bits of the essays which he thought were particularly well written. Now these disconnected parts were joined together by his pupils to form an obviously nonsensical passage which the wall posters claimed was anti-Mao. I learned years later that this method of concocting an accusation through the arbitrary linking of unconnected sentences had started as early as 1955, the year my mother suffered her first detention under the Communists, when some writers had used it to attack their fellow writers.

Mr. Shan told me years later that the real reason he and the deputy headmaster were picked out as victims was that they were not around at the time—they had been absent as members of another work team —which made them convenient scapegoats. The fact that they did not get on with the headmaster, who had stayed behind, made things worse. "If we'd been there and he'd been away, that son of a turtle wouldn't have been able to pull his pants up, he would have had so much shit on his arse," Mr. Shan told me ruefully.

The deputy headmaster, Mr. Kan, had been devoted to the Party, and felt terribly wronged. One evening he wrote a suicide note and then slashed his throat with a razor. He was rushed to hospital by his wife, who had come home earlier than usual. The work team hushed up his suicide attempt. For a Party member like Mr. Kan to commit suicide was regarded as a betrayal. It was seen as a loss of faith in the Party and an attempt at blackmail. Therefore, no mercy should be shown to the unfortunate person. But the work team was nervous. They knew very well that they had been inventing victims without the slightest justification.

When my mother was told about Mr. Kan she cried. She liked him very much, and knew that as he was a man of immense optimism he must have been under inhuman pressure to have acted in this way.

In her own school, my mother refused to be swept into any panic victimizing. But the teenagers in the school, stirred up by the articles in the *People's Daily*, began to move against their teachers. The *People's Daily* called for "smashing up" the examination system which "treated pupils like enemies" (quoting Mao) and was part of the vicious designs of the "bourgeois intellectuals," meaning the majority of the teachers (again quoting Mao). The paper also denounced "bourgeois intellectuals" for poisoning the minds of the young with capitalist rubbish in preparation for a Kuomintang comeback. "We cannot allow bourgeois intellectuals to dominate our schools anymore!" said Mao.

One day my mother bicycled to the school to find that the pupils had rounded up the headmaster, the academic supervisor, the graded teachers, whom they understood from the official press to be "reactionary bourgeois authorities," and any other teachers they disliked. They had shut them all up in a classroom and put a notice on the door saying "demons' class." The teachers had let them do it because the Cultural Revolution had thrown them into bewilderment. The pupils now seemed to have some sort of authorization, undefined but nonetheless real. The grounds were covered with giant slogans, mostly headlines from the *People's Daily*.

As my mother was shown to the classroom now turned "prison," she passed through a crowd of pupils. Some looked fierce, some ashamed, some worried, and others uncertain. More pupils had been following her from the moment she arrived. As the leader of the work team, she had supreme authority, and was identified with the Party. The pupils looked to her for orders. Having set up the "prison," they had no idea what to do next.

My mother announced forcefully that the "demons' class" was dismissed. There was a stir among the pupils, but nobody challenged her order. A few boys muttered to one another, but lapsed into silence when my mother asked them to speak out. She went on to tell them that it was illegal to detain anyone without authorization, and that they should not ill-treat their teachers, who deserved their gratitude and respect. The door to the classroom was opened and the "prisoners" set free.

My mother was very brave to go against the tide. Many other work teams engaged in victimizing completely innocent people to save their own skins. In fact, she had more cause than most to worry. The provincial authorities had already punished several scapegoats, and my father had a strong presentiment that he was going to be the next in line. A couple of his colleagues had told him discreetly that the word was going around in some organizations under him that they should turn their suspicion on him.

My parents never said anything to me or my siblings. The restraints which had kept them silent about politics before still prevented them from opening their minds to us. Now it was even less possible for them to speak. The situation was so complex and confusing that they could not understand it themselves. What could they possibly say to us that would make us understand? And what use would it have been anyway? There was nothing anyone could do. What was more, knowledge itself was dangerous. As a result, my siblings and I were totally unprepared for the Cultural Revolution, although we had a vague feeling of impending catastrophe.

In this atmosphere, August came. All of a sudden, like a storm sweeping across China, millions of Red Guards emerged.

16. "Soar to Heaven, and Pierce the Earth"— Mao's Red Guards

(June–August 1966)

Under Mao a generation of teenagers grew up expecting to fight class enemies, and the vague calls in the press for a Cultural Revolution had stoked the feeling that a "war" was imminent. Some politically well-attuned youngsters sensed that their idol, Mao, was directly involved, and their indoctrination gave them no alternative but to take his side. By the beginning of June a few activists from a middle school attached to one of China's most renowned universities, Qinghua in Peking, had got together several times to discuss their strategies for the forthcoming battle and had decided to call themselves "the Red Guards of Chairman Mao." They adopted a quotation by Mao that had appeared in the *People's Daily*, "Rebellion is justified," as their motto.

These early Red Guards were "high officials' children." Only they could feel sufficiently secure to engage in activities of this kind. In addition, they had been brought up in a political environment, and were more interested in political intrigues than most Chinese. Mme. Mao noticed them, and gave them an audience in July. On 1 August, Mao made the unusual gesture of writing them an open letter to offer his "most warm and fiery support." In the letter he subtly modified his earlier saying to "Rebellion *against reactionaries* is justified." To the teenage zealots, this was like being addressed by God. After this,

Red Guard groups sprang up all over Peking, and then throughout China.

Mao wanted the Red Guards to be his shock troops. He could see that the people were not responding to his repeated calls to attack the capitalist-roaders. The Communist Party had a sizable constituency, and, moreover, the lesson of 1957 was also still fresh in people's minds. Then, too, Mao had called on the population to criticize Party officials, but those who had taken up his invitation had ended up being labeled as rightists and had been damned. Most people suspected the same tactic again—"enticing the snake out of its haunt in order to cut off its head."

If he was to get the population to act, Mao would have to remove authority from the Party and establish absolute loyalty and obedience to himself alone. To achieve this he needed terror—an intense terror that would block all other considerations and crush all other fears. He saw boys and girls in their teens and early twenties as his ideal agents. They had been brought up in the fanatical personality cult of Mao and the militant doctrine of "class struggle." They were endowed with the qualities of youth—they were rebellious, fearless, eager to fight for a "just cause," thirsty for adventure and action. They were also irresponsible, ignorant, and easy to manipulate—and prone to violence. Only they could give Mao the immense force that he needed to terrorize the whole society, and to create a chaos that would shake, and then shatter, the foundation of the Party. One slogan summed up the Red Guards' mission: "We vow to launch a bloody war against anyone who dares to resist the Cultural Revolution, who dares to oppose Chairman Mao!"

All policies and orders had hitherto been conveyed through a tightly controlled system which was entirely in the hands of the Party. Mao now discarded this channel and turned directly to the masses of the youth. He did this by combining two quite different methods: vague, high-flown rhetoric carried openly in the press; and conspiratorial manipulation and agitation conducted by the Cultural Revolution Authority, particularly his wife. It was they who filled out the real meaning of the rhetoric. Phrases like "rebellion against authority," "revolution in education," "destroying an old world so a new one could be born," and "creating new man"—all of which attracted many in the West in the 1960s—were interpreted as calls for violent action. Mao understood the latent violence of the young, and said that since they were well fed and had had their lessons stopped, they could easily be stirred up and use their boundless energy to go out and wreak havoc.

To arouse the young to controlled mob violence, victims were nec-essary. The most conspicuous targets in any school were the teachers, some of whom had already been victimized by work teams and school authorities in the last few months. Now the rebellious children set upon them. Teachers were better targets than parents, who could only have been attacked in an atomized and isolated manner. They were also more important figures of authority than parents in Chinese cul-ture. In practically every school in China, teachers were abused and beaten, sometimes fatally. Some schoolchildren set up prisons in which teachers were tortured.

But this was not enough on its own to generate the kind of terror that Mao wanted. On 18 August, a mammoth rally was held in Tian-anmen Square in the center of Peking, with over a million young participants. Lin Biao appeared in public as Mao's deputy and spokes-man for the first time. He made a speech calling on the Red Guards to charge out of their schools and "smash up the four olds"—defined as "old ideas, old culture, old customs, and old habits."

Following this obscure call, Red Guards all over China took to the streets, giving full vent to their vandalism, ignorance, and fanaticism. They raided people's houses, smashed their antiques, tore up paint-ings and works of calligraphy. Bonfires were lit to consume books. Very soon nearly all treasures in private collections were destroyed. Many writers and artists committed suicide after being cruelly beaten and humiliated, and being forced to witness their work being burned to ashes. Museums were raided. Palaces, temples, ancient tombs, stat-ues, pagodas, city walls—anything "old" was pillaged. The few things that survived, such as the Forbidden City, did so only because Premier Zhou Enlai sent the army to guard them, and issued specific orders that they should be protected. The Red Guards only pressed on when they were encouraged.

Mao hailed the Red Guards' actions as "Very good indeed!" and ordered the nation to support them.

He encouraged the Red Guards to pick on a wider range of victims in order to increase the terror. Prominent writers, artists, scholars, and most other top professionals, who had been privileged under the Communist regime, were now categorically condemned as "reaction-ary bourgeois authorities." With the help of some of these people's colleagues who hated them for various reasons, ranging from fanati-cism to envy, the Red Guards began to abuse them. Then there were the old "class enemies": former landlords and capitalists, people with Kuomintang connections, those condemned in previous political campaigns like the "rightists"—and their children.

Quite a number of "class enemies" had not been executed or sent to labor camps, but had been kept "under surveillance." Before the Cultural Revolution, the police were allowed to release information about them only to authorized personnel. Now that policy changed. The police chief, one of Mao's own liegemen, Xie Fuzhi, ordered his men to offer the "class enemies" to the Red Guards, and to tell the Red Guards about their crimes, such as their "intention to overthrow the Communist government."

Up till the beginning of the Cultural Revolution torture, as distinct from torment, had been forbidden. Now Xie ordered policemen "not to be bound by the old rules, no matter if they had been set by the police authorities or by the state." After saying "I'm not in favor of beating people to death," he continued: "But if some [Red Guards] hate the class enemies so much that they want to kill them, you don't have to force them to stop."

A wave of beating and torture swept the country, mainly during house raids. Almost invariably, the families would be ordered to kneel on the floor and kowtow to the Red Guards; they were then beaten with the brass buckles of the Guards' leather belts. They were kicked around, and one side of their head was shaved, a humiliating style called the "yin and yang head," because it resembled the classic Chinese symbol of a dark side (*yin*) and a light side (*yang*). Most of their possessions were either smashed or taken away.

It was worst in Peking, where the Cultural Revolution Authority was on hand to incite the young people. In the city center some theaters and cinemas were turned into torture chambers. Victims were dragged in from all over Peking. Pedestrians avoided the spots because the streets around echoed with the screams of the victims.

The earliest Red Guard groups were made up of high officials' children. Soon, when more people from other backgrounds joined, some of the high officials' children managed to keep their own special groups, like the "Pickets." Mao and his camarilla took a number of steps calculated to increase their sense of power. At the second mass Red Guards rally, Lin Biao wore their armband, to signify that he was one of them. Mme. Mao made them the guards of honor in front of the Gate of Heavenly Peace in Tiananmen Square on National Day, 1 October. As a result, some of them developed an outrageous "theory of the bloodline," summed up in the words of a song: "The son of a hero father is always a great man; a reactionary father produces nothing but a bastard!" Armed with this "theory," some high officials' children tyrannized and even tortured children from "undesirable" backgrounds.

Mao let all this happen in order to generate the terror and chaos he wanted. He was not scrupulous about either who was hit or who were the agents of violence. These early victims were not his real targets, and Mao did not particularly like or trust his young Red Guards. He was simply using them. For their part, the vandals and torturers were not always devoted to Mao. They were just having a wild time, having been licensed to indulge their worst instincts.

Only a small proportion of the Red Guards was actually involved in cruelty or violence. Many were able to avoid taking part because the Red Guard was a loose organization which, by and large, did not physically force its members to do evil. As a matter of fact, Mao himself never ordered the Red Guards to kill, and his instructions regarding violence were contradictory. One could feel devoted to Mao without perpetrating violence or evil. Those who chose to do so could not simply blame Mao.

But Mao's insidious encouragement of atrocities was undeniable. On 18 August, at the first of the eight gigantic rallies which altogether were attended by thirteen million people, he asked a female Red Guard what her name was. When she answered "Bin-bin," which means "gentle," he said disapprovingly, "Be violent" (yao-wu-ma). Mao rarely spoke in public, and this remark, well publicized, was naturally followed like the gospel. At the third mammoth rally, on 15 September, when the Red Guards' atrocities were reaching their zenith, Mao's recognized spokesman, Lin Biao, announced, with Mao standing next to him: "Red Guard fighters: The direction of your battles has always been correct. You have soundly, heartily battered the capitalist-roaders, the reactionary bourgeois authorities, the bloodsuckers and parasites. You have done the right thing! And you have done marvelously!" At that, hysterical cheers, deafening screams of "Long live Chairman Mao," uncontrollable tears, and howled pledges of loyalty took possession of the crowds filling the enormous Tiananmen Square. Mao waved paternally, generating more frenzy.

Through his Cultural Revolution Authority, Mao kept control over the Peking Red Guards. He then sent them to the provinces to tell the local young people what to do. In Jinzhou, in Manchuria, my grandmother's brother Yu-lin and his wife were beaten up, and they and their two children were exiled to a barren part of the country. Yu-lin had come under suspicion when the Communists first arrived, because of his possession of a Kuomintang intelligence card, but nothing had happened to him or his family until now. My family did not know about this at the time. People avoided exchanging news. With accusations so willfully concocted, and the consequences so horrific, you never knew what catastrophe you might bring to your correspondents, or they to you.

People in Sichuan had little idea of the extent of the terror in Peking. There were fewer atrocities in Sichuan, partly because the Red Guards there were not directly incited by the Cultural Revolution Authority. In addition, the police in Sichuan turned a deaf ear to their minister in Peking, Mr. Xie, and refused to offer up the "class enemies" under their control to the Red Guards. However, the Red Guards in Sichuan, as in other provinces, copied the actions of those in Peking. There was the same kind of chaos as everywhere in China —controlled chaos. The Red Guards may have looted the houses which they were authorized to raid, but they rarely stole from shops. Most sectors, including commerce, the postal services and transport, worked normally.

In my school, a Red Guard organization was formed on 16 August, with the help of some Red Guards from Peking. I had been staying at home feigning illness to escape the political meetings and frightening slogans, and was unaware that the organization had been set up until a couple of days later, when a phone call summoned me back "to participate in the Great Proletarian Cultural Revolution." When I got to the school, I noticed that many pupils were proudly wearing red armbands with gold characters saying "Red Guards."

In these early days, the newborn Red Guards had the immense prestige of being Mao's babies. It went without saying that I should join, and I immediately submitted my application to the Red Guard leader in my form—a fifteen-year-old boy named Geng who had been constantly seeking my company, but became shy and gauche the moment he was with me.

I could not help wondering how Geng had become a Red Guard, and he was mysterious about his activities. But it was very clear to me that the Red Guards were mostly high officials' children. The head of the school Red Guards was one of the sons of Commissar Li, the Party first secretary for Sichuan. I ought to have been a natural; few pupils had fathers in higher positions than mine. But Geng privately told me that I was considered soft and "too inactive," and must be toughened up before they could consider accepting me.

Since June, there had been an unwritten rule that everyone should remain in school around-the-clock to devote themselves entirely to the Cultural Revolution. I was one of the few who did not. But now the thought of playing truant somehow gave me a sense of danger, and I felt compelled to stay. The boys slept in the classrooms so we girls could occupy the dormitories. Non–Red Guards were attached to Red Guard groups and taken with them on their various activities.

The day after I returned to school, I was taken out with several dozen other children to change street names to make them more "revolutionary." The street where I lived was called Commerce Street, and we debated what it should be renamed. Some proposed "Beacon Road," to signify the role of our provincial Party leaders. Others said "Public Servants' Street," as that was what officials should be, according to a quote of Mao's. Eventually we left without settling on anything because a preliminary problem could not be solved: the name plate was too high up on the wall to reach. As far as I knew, no one ever went back.

In Peking the Red Guards were much more zealous. We heard about their successes: the British mission was now on "Anti-Imperialism Road," the Russian embassy on "Anti-Revisionism Road."

In Chengdu, streets were shedding their old names like "Five Generations under One Roof" (a Confucian virtue), "The Poplar and Willow Are Green" (green was not a revolutionary color), and "Jade Dragon" (a symbol of feudal power). They became "Destroy the Old," "The East Is Red," and "Revolution" streets. A famous restaurant called "The Fragrance of Sweet Wind" had its plaque broken to bits. It was renamed "The Whiff of Gunpowder."

Traffic was in confusion for several days. For red to mean "stop" was considered impossibly counterrevolutionary. It should of course mean "go." And traffic should not keep to the right, as was the practice, it should be on the left. For a few days we ordered the traffic policemen aside and controlled the traffic ourselves. I was stationed at a street corner telling cyclists to ride on the left. In Chengdu there were not many cars or traffic lights, but at the few big crossroads there was chaos. In the end, the old rules reasserted themselves, owing to Zhou Enlai, who managed to convince the Peking Red Guard leaders. But the youngsters found justifications for this: I was told by a Red Guard in my school that in Britain traffic kept to the left, so ours had to keep to the right to show our anti-imperialist spirit. She did not mention America.

As a child I had always shied away from collective activity. Now, at fourteen, I felt even more averse to it. I suppressed this dread because of the constant sense of guilt I had come to feel, through my education, when I was out of step with Mao. I kept telling myself that I must train my thoughts according to the new revolutionary theories and practices. If there was anything I did not understand, I must reform myself and adapt. However, I found myself trying very hard to avoid militant acts such as stopping passersby and cutting their long hair, or narrow trouser legs, or skirts, or breaking their semi-high-heeled shoes. These things had now become signs of bourgeois decadence, according to the Peking Red Guards.

My own hair came to the critical attention of my schoolmates. I had to have it cut to the level of my earlobes. Secretly, though much ashamed of myself for being so "petty bourgeois," I shed tears over losing my long plaits. As a young child, my nurse had a way of doing my hair which made it stand up on top of my head like a willow branch. She called it "fireworks shooting up to the sky." Until the early 1960s I wore my hair in two coils, with rings of little silk flowers wound around them. In the mornings, while I hurried through my breakfast, my grandmother or our maid would be doing my hair with loving hands. Of all the colors for the silk flowers, my favorite was pink.

After 1964, following Mao's calls for an austere life-style, more suited to the atmosphere of class struggle, I put patches on my trousers to try to look "proletarian" and wore my hair in the uniform style of two plaits with no colors, but long hair had not been condemned as yet. My grandmother cut it for me, muttering all the while. Her hair survived, because she never went out at that time.

The famous teahouses in Chengdu also came under attack as "decadent." I did not understand why, but did not ask. In the summer of 1966 I learned to suppress my sense of reason. Most Chinese had been doing that for a long time.

A Sichuan teahouse is a unique place. It usually sits in the embrace of a bamboo grove or under the canopy of a large tree. Around the low, square wooden tables are bamboo armchairs which give out a faint aroma even after years of use. To prepare the tea a pinch of tea leaves is dropped into a cup and boiling water is poured on top. Then a lid is sunk loosely onto the cup, allowing the steam to seep through the gap, bringing out the fragrance of the jasmine or other blossoms. Sichuan has many kinds of tea. Jasmine alone has five grades.

Teahouses are as important to the Sichuanese as pubs are to the British. Older men, in particular, spend a lot of time there, puffing their long-stemmed pipes over a cup of tea and a plateful of nuts and melon seeds. The waiter shuttles between the seats with a kettle of hot water which he pours from a couple of feet away with pinpoint accuracy. A skillful waiter makes the water level higher than the edge of the cup without it spilling over. As a child I was always mesmerized watching the water fall from the spout. I was rarely taken to a teahouse, though. It had an air of indulgence of which my parents disapproved.

Like European cafés, a Sichuan teahouse provides newspapers on bamboo frames. Some customers go there to read, but it is primarily a place to meet and chat, exchanging news and gossip. There is often entertainment—storytelling punctuated with wooden clappers.

Perhaps because they had an aura of leisure, and if people were sitting in one they were not out making revolution, teahouses had to be closed. I went with a couple of dozen pupils between thirteen and sixteen years old, most of whom were Red Guards, to a small one on the bank of the Silk River. Chairs and tables were spread outside under a Chinese scholar tree. The summer evening breeze from the river fanned out a heavy scent from the clusters of white blossoms. The customers, mostly men, raised their heads from their chessboards as we approached along the uneven cobblestones that paved the bank. We stopped under the tree. A few voices from our group started to shout: "Pack up! Pack up! Don't linger in this bourgeois place!" A boy from my form snatched a corner of the paper chessboard on the nearest table and jerked it away. The wooden pieces scattered on the ground.

The men who had been playing were quite young. One of them lunged forward, his fists clenched, but his friend quickly pulled the corner of his jacket. Silently they began to pick up the chess pieces. The boy who had jerked away their board shouted: "No more chess playing! Don't you know it is a bourgeois habit?" He stooped to sweep up a handful of pieces and threw them toward the river.

I had been brought up to be courteous and respectful to anyone older than I, but now to be revolutionary meant being aggressive and militant. Gentleness was considered "bourgeois." I was repeatedly criticized for it, and it was one reason given for not allowing me into the Red Guards. Over the years of the Cultural Revolution, I was to witness people being attacked for saying "thank you" too often, which was branded as "bourgeois hypocrisy"; courtesy was on the brink of extinction.

But now, outside the teahouse, I could see that most of us, including the Red Guards, were uneasy about the new style of speaking and lording it over others. Not many of us opened our mouths. Quietly, a few started to paste rectangular slogans onto the walls of the teahouse and the trunk of the scholar tree.

The customers silently began to walk away along the bank. Watching their disappearing figures, a feeling of loss overwhelmed me. A couple of months before, these adults probably would have told us to get lost. But now they knew that Mao's backing had given the Red Guards power. Thinking back, I can see the thrill some children must have felt at demonstrating their power over adults. A popular Red Guard slogan went: "We can soar to heaven, and pierce the earth, because our Great Leader Chairman Mao is our supreme commander!" As this declaration reveals, the Red Guards were not enjoying genuine freedom of self-expression. From the start they were nothing but the tool of a tyrant.

Standing on the riverbank in August 1966, though, I was just confused. I went into the teahouse with my fellow pupils. Some asked the manager to close down. Others started pasting slogans on the walls. Many customers were getting up to go, but in a far corner one old man was still sitting at his table, calmly sipping his tea. I stood beside him, feeling embarrassed that I was supposed to assume the voice of authority. He looked at me, and resumed his noisy sipping. He had a deeply lined face that was almost stereotypical "working class" as shown in propaganda pictures. His hands reminded me of one of my textbook stories which described the hands of an old peasant: they could bundle thorny firewood without feeling any pain.

Perhaps this old man was very sure of his unquestionable background, or his advanced age, which had hitherto been the object of respect, or perhaps he simply did not think I was very impressive. Anyway, he remained in his seat taking no notice of me. I summoned up my courage and pleaded in a low voice, "Please, could you leave?" Without looking at me, he said, "Where to?" "Home, of course," I replied.

He turned to face me. There was emotion in his voice, though he spoke quietly. "Home? What home? I share a tiny room with my two grandsons. I have a corner surrounded by a bamboo curtain. Just for the bed. That's all. When the kids are home I come here for some peace and quiet. Why do you have to take this away from me?"

His words filled me with shock and shame. This was the first time I had heard a firsthand account of such miserable living conditions. I turned and walked away.

This teahouse, like all the others in Sichuan, was shut for fifteen years—until 1981, when Deng Xiaoping's reforms decreed it could be reopened. In 1985 I went back there with a British friend. We sat under the scholar tree. An old waitress came to fill our cups with a kettle from two feet away. Around us, people were playing chess. It was one of the happiest moments of that trip back.

When Lin Biao called for everything that represented the old culture to be destroyed, some pupils in my school started to smash things up. Being more than 2,000 years old, the school had a lot of antiques and was therefore a prime site for action. The school gateway had an old tiled roof with carved eaves. These were hammered to pieces. The same happened to the sweeping blue-glazed roof of the big temple which had been used as a Ping-Pong hall. The pair of giant bronze incense burners in front of the temple were toppled, and some boys urinated into them. In the back garden, pupils with big hammers and iron rods went along the sandstone bridges casually breaking the little statues. On one side of the sports field was a pair of towering rectangular tablets made of red sandstone, each twenty feet high. Some lines about Confucius were carved on them in beautiful calligraphy. A huge rope was tied around them, and two gangs pulled. It took them a couple of days, as the foundations were deep. They had to get some workers from outside to dig a hole around the tablets. When the monuments finally crashed down amidst cheers, they lifted part of the path that ran behind them.

All the things I loved were disappearing. The saddest thing of all for me was the ransacking of the library: the golden tiled roof, the delicately sculpted windows, the blue painted chairs. . . . Bookshelves were turned upside down, and some pupils tore books to pieces just for the hell of it. Afterward, X-shaped white paper strips with black characters were stuck on what was left of the doors and windows to signal that the building was sealed.

Books were major targets of Mao's order to destroy. Because they had not been written within the last few months, and therefore did not quote Mao on every page, some Red Guards declared that they were all "poisonous weeds." With the exception of Marxist classics and the works of Stalin, Mao, and the late Lu Xun, whose name Mme. Mao was using for her personal vendettas, books were burning all across China. The country lost most of its written heritage. Many of the books which survived later went into people's stoves as fuel.

But there was no bonfire at my school. The head of the school Red Guards had been a very conscientious student. A rather feminine-looking seventeen-year-old, he had been made the Red Guard leader because his father was the Party chief for the province, rather than because of his own ambition. While he could not prevent the general vandalism, he did manage to stop the books from being burned.

Like everyone else, I was supposed to join in the "revolutionary actions." But I, like most pupils, was able to avoid them, because the destruction was not organized, and no one made sure we took part. I could see that many pupils hated the whole thing, but nobody tried to stop it. Like myself, many boys and girls may well have been telling themselves that they were wrong to feel sorry about the destruction and needed to reform. But subconsciously we all knew we would have been crushed instantly had we raised any objection.

By then "denunciation meetings" were becoming a major feature of the Cultural Revolution. They involved a hysterical crowd and were seldom without physical brutality. Peking University had taken the lead, under the personal supervision of Mao. At its first denunciation meeting, on 18 June, over sixty professors and heads of departments, including the chancellor, were beaten, kicked, and forced to kneel for hours. Dunce caps with humiliating slogans were forced onto their heads. Ink was poured over their faces to make them black, the color of evil, and slogans were pasted all over their bodies. Two students gripped the arms of each victim, twisting them around behind his back and pushing them up with such ferocity as almost to dislocate them. This posture was called the "jet plane," and soon became a feature of most denunciation meetings all over the country.

I was once called by the Red Guards in my form to attend such a meeting. Horror made me feel very chilly in the hot summer afternoon when I saw a dozen or so teachers standing on the platform on the sports ground, with their heads bent and their arms twisted into the "jet plane" position. Then, some were kicked on the back of their knees and forced to kneel, while others, including my English-language teacher, an elderly man with the fine manner of a classical gentleman, were forced to stand on long, narrow benches. He found it hard to keep his balance, and swayed and fell, cutting his forehead on the sharp corner of a bench. A Red Guard standing next to him instinctively stooped and extended his hands to help, but immediately straightened up and assumed an exaggeratedly harsh posture, with his fists clenched, yelling: "Get back onto the bench!" He did not want to be seen as soft on a "class enemy." Blood trickled down the teacher's forehead and coagulated on the side of his face.

He, like the other teachers, was accused of all sorts of outlandish crimes; but they were really there because they were graded, and therefore the best, or because some pupils had grudges against them.

I learned in later years that the pupils in my school behaved relatively mildly because, being in the most prestigious school, they were successful and academically inclined. In the schools which took in wilder boys, there were teachers who were beaten to death. I witnessed only one beating in my school. My philosophy teacher had been somewhat dismissive to those who had not done well in her classes, and some of them hated her and now started to accuse her of being "decadent." The "evidence," which reflected the extreme conservatism of the Cultural Revolution, was that she had met her husband on a bus. They got to chatting, and fell in love. Love arising out of a chance meeting was regarded as a sign of immorality. The boys took her to an office and "took revolutionary actions over her"—the euphemism for beating somebody up. Before they started, they called for me especially and made me attend. "What will she think when she sees you, her pet pupil, there!"

I was considered her favorite because she had praised my work often. But I was also told that I should be there because I had been too soft, and needed "a lesson in revolution."

When the beating started, I shrank at the back of the ring of pupils who crowded into the small office. A couple of classmates nudged me to go to the front and join in the hitting. I ignored them. In the center my teacher was being kicked around, rolling in agony on the floor, her hair askew. As she cried out, begging them to stop, the boys who had set upon her said in cold voices, "Now you beg! Haven't you been ferocious? Now beg properly!" They kicked her again, and ordered her to kowtow to them and say "Please spare my life, masters!" To make someone kowtow and beg was an extreme humiliation. She sat up and stared blankly ahead: I met her eyes through her knotted hair. In them I saw agony, desperation, and emptiness. She was gasping for breath, and her face was ashen gray. I sneaked out of the room. Several pupils followed me. Behind us I could hear people shouting slogans, but their voices were tentative and uncertain. Many pupils must have been scared. I walked away swiftly, my heart pounding. I was afraid I might be caught and beaten myself. But no one came after me, and I was not condemned afterward.

I did not get into trouble in those days, in spite of my obvious lack of enthusiasm. Apart from the fact that the Red Guards were loosely organized, I was, according to the "theory of bloodlines," born bright red, because my father was a high official. Although I was disapproved of, nobody did anything drastic, except criticize me.

At the time, the Red Guards divided pupils into three categories: "reds," "blacks," and "grays." The "reds" were from the families of "workers, peasants, revolutionary officials, revolutionary officers, and revolutionary martyrs." The "blacks" were those with parents classified as "landlords, rich peasants, counterrevolutionaries, bad elements, and rightists." The "grays" came from ambiguous families such as shop assistants and clerks. In my year, all pupils ought to have been "reds" because of the screening in the enrollment. But the pressure of the Cultural Revolution meant that some villains had to be found. As a result, more than half a dozen became "grays" or "blacks."

There was a girl named Ai-ling in my year. We were old friends, and I had often been to her house and knew her family well. Her grandfather had been a prominent economist, and her family had been enjoying a very privileged life under the Communists. Their house was large, elegant, and luxurious, with an exquisite garden— much better than my family's apartment. I was especially attracted by their collection of antiques, in particular the snuff bottles which Ai-ling's grandfather had brought back from England where he had studied at Oxford in the 1920s.

Now, suddenly, Ai-ling became a "black." I heard that pupils from her form had raided her house, smashed all the antiques, including the snuff bottles, and beaten her parents and grandfather with the brass buckles of their belts. The next day when I saw her she was wearing a scarf. Her classmates had given her a "yin and yang head." She had had to have it completely shaved. She wept with me. I felt terribly inadequate because I could not find any words to comfort her.

In my own form a meeting was organized by the Red Guards at which we all had to give our family backgrounds so we could be categorized. I announced "revolutionary official" with great relief. Three or four pupils said "office staff." In the jargon of the day, this was different from "officials," who held more senior positions. The division was unclear, as there was no definition of what "senior" meant. Nevertheless, these vague labels had to be used on various forms, all of which had a space for "family background." Together with a girl whose father was a shop assistant, the children of "office staff" were branded as "grays." It was announced that they were to be kept under surveillance, sweep the school grounds and clean toilets, bow their heads at all times, and be prepared to be lectured by any Red Guard who cared to address them. They also had to report their thoughts and behavior every day.

These pupils suddenly looked subdued and shrunken. Their vigor and enthusiasm, which they had had in abundance up to now, had deserted them. One girl bent her head and tears streamed down her cheeks. We had been friends. After the meeting I went over to her to say something comforting, but when she raised her head I saw resentment, almost hatred, in her eyes. I walked away without a word, and wandered listlessly through the grounds. It was the end of August. The Cape jasmine bushes spread their rich fragrance. It seemed strange there should be any scent at all.

As dusk was descending I was walking back to the dormitory when I saw something flash by a second-floor window of a classroom block about forty yards away. There was a muffled bang at the foot of the building. The hazy branches of some orange trees prevented me from seeing what was happening, but people started to run in the direction of the noise. Out of the confused, suppressed exclamations I made out the message: "Someone has jumped out of the window!"

I instinctively raised my hands to cover my eyes, and ran to my room. I was terribly scared. My mind's eye fixated on the blurry crooked figure in midair. Hurriedly I shut the windows, but the noise of people talking nervously about what had happened filtered through the thin glass.

A seventeen-year-old girl had attempted suicide. Before the Cultural Revolution, she had been one of the leaders of the Communist Youth League, and had been a model in studying Chairman Mao's works and learning from Lei Feng. She had done many good deeds like washing her comrades' clothes and cleaning out toilets, and frequently gave talks to the school about how loyally she followed Mao's teachings. She was often to be seen strolling deep in conversation with a fellow pupil, with a conscientious and purposeful look on her face, carrying out "heart-to-heart" duties with someone who wanted to join the Youth League. But now, suddenly, she had been categorized as a "black." Her father was "office staff." He worked for the municipal government, and was a Party member. But some of her classmates who found her a "pain," and whose fathers were in higher posts, decided she should be a "black." In the last couple of days, she had been put under guard with other "blacks" and "grays" and forced to pull grass out of the sports ground. To humiliate her, her classmates had shaved her beautiful black hair, leaving her head grotesquely bald. On that evening, the "reds" in her form had been giving her and the other victims an insulting lecture. She retorted that she was more loyal to Chairman Mao than they were. The "reds" slapped her and told her she was not fit to talk about her loyalty to Mao because she was a class enemy. She ran to the window and threw herself out.

Stunned and scared, the Red Guards rushed her to a hospital. She did not die, but she was crippled for life. When I saw her many months later on the street, she was bent over on crutches, her eyes blank.

On the night of her attempted suicide, I could not sleep. The moment I closed my eyes, an indistinct figure loomed over me, smeared with blood. I was terrified and shaking. The next day I asked for sick leave, which was granted. Home seemed to be the only escape from the horror at school. I desperately wished I would never have to go out again.

17. "Do You Want Our Children to Become 'Blacks'?"— My Parents' Dilemma

(August–October 1966)

Home was no relief this time. My parents seemed distracted, and hardly noticed me. When Father was not pacing up and down the apartment, he was shut in his study. Mother threw one wastebasketful of crushed paper balls after another into the kitchen stove. My grandmother also looked as though she was expecting disaster. Her intense eyes were fixed on my parents, full of anxiety. Timorously, I watched their moods, too afraid to ask what was wrong.

My parents did not tell me about a conversation they had had some evenings before. They had been sitting by an open window, outside which a loudspeaker tied to a street lamp was blasting out endless quotations of Mao's, particularly one about all revolutions being violent by definition—"the savage tumult of one class overthrowing another." The quotations were chanted again and again in a high-pitched shriek that roused fear and, for some, excitement. Every now and then there were announcements of "victories" achieved by Red Guards: they had raided more homes of "class enemies" and "smashed their dogs' heads."

My father had been looking out at the blazing sunset. He turned to my mother and said slowly: "I don't understand the Cultural Revolution. But I am certain that what is happening is terribly wrong. This revolution cannot be justified by any Marxist or Communist principles. People have lost their basic rights and protection. This is unspeakable. I am a Communist, and I have a duty to stop a worse disaster. I must write to the Party leadership, to Chairman Mao."

In China there was virtually no channel through which people could voice a grievance, or influence policy, except appealing to the leaders. In this particular case, only Mao could change the situation. Whatever Father thought, or guessed, about Mao's role, the only thing he could do was to petition him.

My mother's experience told her that complaining was extremely dangerous. People who had done it, and their families, had suffered vicious retribution. She was silent for a long time, staring out over the distant burning sky, trying to control her worry, anger, and frustration. "Why do you want to be a moth that throws itself into the fire?" she said at last.

My father replied, "This is no ordinary fire. It concerns the life and death of so many people. I must do something this time."

My mother said, with exasperation, "All right, you don't care about yourself. You have no concern for your wife. I accept that. But what about our children? You know what will happen to them once you get into trouble. Do you want our children to become 'blacks'?"

My father said thoughtfully, as though he were trying to persuade himself, "Every man loves his children. You know that before a tiger is about to jump and kill, he always looks back and makes sure that his cub is all right. Even a man-eating beast feels that way, let alone a human being. But a Communist has to be more than that. He has to think about other children. What about the children of the victims?"

My mother stood up and walked away. It was no use. Once she was on her own, she wept bitterly.

Father began to write his letter, tearing up draft after draft. He had always been a perfectionist, and a letter to Chairman Mao was no small matter. Not only did he have to formulate exactly what he wanted to say, he had to try to minimize the potential consequences, particularly to his family. In other words, his criticism must not be seen as a criticism. He could not afford to offend Mao.

Father had begun thinking about his letter in June. Waves of scapegoating had claimed several of his colleagues, and he wanted to speak up for them. But events had kept overtaking his plans. Among other things, there had been more and more signs that he was about to become a victim himself. One day, my mother saw a prominent wall poster in the center of Chengdu attacking him by name, calling him "the number-one opponent of the Cultural Revolution in Sichuan." This was based on two accusations: the previous winter he had resisted printing the article denouncing the Dramas of the Ming Mandarin, which was Mao's original summons for the Cultural Revolution; and he had drafted the "April Document," which opposed persecution and attempted to limit the Cultural Revolution to nonpolitical debate.

When my mother told my father about the poster, he said at once that it was the doing of the provincial Party leaders. The two things it accused him of were known only to a small circle at the top. Father felt convinced that they had now made up their minds to scapegoat him, and he knew why. Students from universities in Chengdu were beginning to direct their offensive at the provincial leaders. University students were entrusted with more information by the Cultural Revolution Authority than middle-school pupils, and had been told that Mao's real intention was to destroy the "capitalist-roaders"—that is, Communist officials. The students were generally not high officials' children, as most Communist officials had married only after the founding of the People's Republic in 1949 and so did not have children of university age. Having no vested interest in the status quo, the students were happy to turn on the officials.

The Sichuan authorities were outraged by the violence committed by middle-school children, but the university students really made them panic. They felt they had to find a prominent scapegoat to placate the students. My father was one of the top officials in the field of "culture," which was a major target of the Cultural Revolution. He had a reputation for insisting on his principles. At a time when they needed unanimity and obedience, they felt they could do without him.

Father's predicament was soon confirmed. On 26 August he was asked to attend a meeting for the students of Sichuan University, the most prestigious university in the province. They had been attacking the chancellor and the senior staff, and were now raising their sights toward the provincial Party officials. The meeting was nominally for the provincial leaders to hear the students' complaints. Commissar Li sat on the platform, together with the whole panoply of top Party officials. The huge auditorium, the biggest in Chengdu, was packed.

The students came to the meeting intending to make trouble, and the hall was soon in pandemonium. Students, shouting slogans and waving flags, began jumping onto the stage to try to grab the microphone. Although my father was not the chairman, it was he who was asked to bring the situation under control. While he was confronting the students, the other Party officials left.

My father shouted: "Are you intelligent students, or are you hooligans? Will you talk reason?" In general, officials in China maintain an impassive manner, in keeping with their status, but my father was yelling like one of the students. Unfortunately, his genuineness did not impress them, and he left amid much screaming of slogans. Immediately afterward, huge wall posters appeared calling him "the most obstinate capitalist-roader, the diehard who opposes the Cultural Revolution."

This meeting became a milestone. It was from it that the Red Guard group at Sichuan University took its name—"26 August." This organization was to become the core of a provincewide bloc, incorporating millions of people, and the major force in the Cultural Revolution in Sichuan.

After the meeting, the provincial authorities ordered my father not to leave our apartment under any circumstances—for his own "protection." My father could see that he had first been deliberately exposed to the students as a target, and then put under virtual house arrest. He added his own anticipated victimization to his letter to Mao. One night, with tears in his eyes, he asked my mother to take the letter to Peking now that he had lost his freedom.

My mother had never wanted him to write the letter, but now she changed her mind. What tipped the balance was the fact that he was being turned into a victim. This meant that her children would become "blacks"—and she knew what that meant. Going to Peking and appealing to the top leaders was her only chance, however remote, of saving her husband and her children. She promised to take the letter.

On the last day of August I was awakened from an uneasy nap by a noise from my parents' quarters. I tiptoed to the half-opened door of my father's study. My father was standing in the middle of the room. Several people were crowding around him. I recognized them: they were from his department. They all looked stern, devoid of their usual eager-to-please smiles. My father was saying, "Would you please thank the provincial authorities for me? I'm very grateful for their concern. But I prefer not to go into hiding. A Communist should not be afraid of students."

His voice was calm, but it contained a hint of emotion which made me afraid. Then I heard a rather important-sounding man's voice saying threateningly, "But Director Chang, surely the Party knows best. The university students are attacking you, and they can be violent. The Party thinks you should be placed under protection. This is the decision of the Party. You must know that a Communist has to obey Party decisions unconditionally."

After a silence, my father said quietly, "I obey the decision of the Party. I will go with you." "But where to?" I heard my mother asking.

Then an impatient man's voice: "The Party's instructions are: no one is to know." When he came out of the study my father saw me and took my hand. "Father is going away for a while," he said. "Be a good girl to your mother."

My mother and I walked with him to the side gate of the compound. The long path was lined with members of his department. My heart was pounding and my legs seemed to be made of cotton wool. Father appeared very agitated. His hand was shaking in mine. I stroked it with my other hand.

A car was parked outside the gate. The door was held open for him. There were two men in the car, one in front and one in the back. Mother's face was taut, but she was calm. She looked into my father's eyes and said, "Don't worry. I will do it." Without hugging me or my mother, my father was gone. The Chinese show little physical affection in public, even at extraordinary times.

I did not realize that my father was being taken into custody, because the act was dressed up as "protection." Being fourteen, I had not learned to decipher the regime's hypocritical style; deviousness was involved here because the authorities had not made up their minds what to do with my father. As in most such cases, the police played no role. The people who came to take my father away were members of his department with a verbal authorization from the Provincial Party Committee.

As soon as Father was gone, my mother threw a few clothes into a bag and told us she was going to Peking. My father's letter was still in draft form, with scribbles and alterations. The minute he saw the staff posse coming he had pushed it into her hand.

My grandmother hugged my four-year-old brother Xiao-fang and wept. I said I wanted to go with my mother to the station. There was no time to wait for a bus, so we jumped into a tricycle taxi.

I was fearful and confused. My mother did not explain what was happening. She looked strained and preoccupied, deep in her thoughts. When I asked her what was going on, she said briefly that I would know in time, and left it at that. I assumed she thought it was too complicated to explain, and I was used to being told I was too young to know certain things. I could also tell that my mother was busy sizing up the situation and planning her next moves, and I did not want to distract her. What I did not know was that she was battling to comprehend the confused situation herself.

We sat in the tricycle taxi silent and tense, my hand in hers. My mother kept glancing over her shoulder: she knew the authorities would not want her to get to Peking, and had only let me come with her so I could be a witness in case anything happened. At the station she bought a "hard-seat" ticket for the next train to Peking. It was not due until dawn, so we sat down on a bench in the waiting room, a kind of shed with no walls.

I huddled up against her to wait for the long hours to pass. Silently, we gazed at the darkness descending over the cement ground of the square in front of the station. A few feeble bare bulbs on top of wooden lampposts were shedding a pale light, reflected in the puddles of water left over from a heavy thunderstorm that morning. I felt chilly in my summer blouse. My mother wrapped her raincoat around me. As the night dragged on, she told me to go to sleep. Exhausted, I dozed off with my head on her lap.

I was awakened by a movement of her knees. I lifted my head and saw two people in hooded raincoats standing in front of us. They were arguing about something in low voices. In my muddled state, I could not work out what they were saying. I could not even tell whether they were men or women. I vaguely heard my mother say, in a calm, restrained voice, "I will shout for the Red Guards." The gray-hooded raincoats fell silent. They whispered to each other and then walked away, obviously not wanting to attract attention.

At dawn, my mother got on the train to Peking.

Years later she told me that the two people were women she knew, junior officials from my father's department. They told her the authorities had ruled that her going to Peking was an "anti-Party" act. She quoted the Party charter, which said that it was the right of any Party member to appeal to the leaders. When the emissaries indicated that they had men waiting in a car who could seize her by force, my mother said that if they did she would shout for help from the Red Guards around the station and tell them they were trying to stop her going to Peking to see Chairman Mao. I asked her how she could be sure the Red Guards would help her rather than the pursuers. "Suppose they denounced you to the Red Guards as a class enemy who was trying to escape?" Mother smiled and said, "I calculated that they would not take the risk. I was prepared to gamble everything. I had no alternative."

In Peking my mother took my father's letter to a "grievance office." Chinese rulers throughout history, having never permitted an independent legal system, had set up offices where ordinary people could lodge grievances against their bosses, and the Communists inherited this tradition. When during the Cultural Revolution it began to look as though Communist bosses were losing their power, many people who had been persecuted by them in the past flooded into Peking to appeal. But the Cultural Revolution Authority soon made it clear that "class enemies" were not allowed to complain, even against "capitalist-roaders." If they tried to do so they would be doubly punished.

Few cases concerning senior officials like my father were presented to the grievance office, so my mother received special attention. She was also one of the very few spouses of victims who had the courage to go and appeal in Peking, as they were under pressure to "draw a line" between themselves and those accused rather than invite trouble by speaking up for the victims. My mother was received almost immediately by Vice-Premier Tao Zhu, who was the head of the Central Department of Public Affairs and one of the leaders of the Cultural Revolution at the time. She gave him my father's letter, and pleaded with him to order the Sichuan authorities to release my father.

A couple of weeks later, Tao Zhu saw her again. He gave her a letter which said my father had acted in a perfectly constitutional manner and in concert with the Sichuan party leadership, and should be released at once. Tao had not investigated the case. He took my mother's word, because what had happened to my father was a common occurrence: Party officials all over China were choosing scapegoats in their panic to save their own skins. Tao gave her the letter directly rather than sending it through normal Party channels, knowing they were in disarray.

Tao Zhu showed he understood and agreed with the other concerns in my father's letter: the epidemic of scapegoating, and the widespread random violence. My mother could see he wanted to control the situation. As it happened, because of this, he himself was soon to be condemned as "the third biggest capitalist-roader," after Liu Shaoqi and Deng Xiaoping.

Meanwhile, my mother hand-copied Tao Zhu's letter, mailed the copy to my grandmother, and asked her to show it to my father's department and to tell them that she would return only after they released my father. My mother was worried that if she returned to Sichuan the authorities there might arrest her, seize the letter—and not release my father. She felt that, on balance, her best bet was to stay in Peking, where she could continue to exercise pressure.

My grandmother passed on my mother's hand-copied text of Tao Zhu's letter. But the provincial authorities said the whole thing was a misunderstanding, and that they were just protecting my father. They insisted that my mother must come back and stop her individualistic meddling.

Officials came to our apartment several times to try to persuade my grandmother to go to Peking and bring my mother back. One said to her, "I'm really thinking of your daughter. Why persist in misunderstanding the Party? The Party was only trying to protect your son-in-law. Your daughter would not listen to the Party and went to Peking. I'm worried for her that if she does not come back, she will be regarded as anti-Party. And you know how serious that is. Being her mother, you must do what is best for her. The Party has promised that as long as she comes back and makes a self-criticism, she will be forgiven."

The thought that her daughter was in trouble brought my grandmother to the verge of collapse. After several such sessions, she was wavering. Then one day her mind was made up for her: she was told that my father was having a nervous breakdown, and only when my mother came home would they send him to a hospital.

The Party gave my grandmother two tickets, one for herself and one for Xiao-fang, and they set off to Peking, thirty-six hours away by train. As soon as my mother heard the news, she sent a telegram to tell my father's department she was on her way, and started making arrangements to return home. She arrived back with my grandmother and Xiao-fang in the second week of October.

During her absence, the whole of September, I had stayed at home to keep my grandmother company. I could see that she was consumed by worry, but I did not know what was going on. Where was my father? Was he under arrest, or was he being protected? Was my family in trouble or not? I did not know—no one said anything.

I could stay at home because the Red Guards never exercised the rigorous control the Party did. Besides, I had a sort of "patron" in the Red Guards, Geng, my gauche fifteen-year-old boss, who had made no effort to summon me back to the school. But at the end of September he telephoned to urge me to get back before 1 October, National Day, or I would never be able to join the Red Guards.

I was not forced to join the Red Guards. I was keen to do so. In spite of what was happening around me, my aversion and fear had no clear object, and it never occurred to me to question the Cultural Revolution or the Red Guards explicitly. They were Mao's creations, and Mao was beyond contemplation.

Like many Chinese, I was incapable of rational thinking in those days. We were so cowed and contorted by fear and indoctrination that to deviate from the path laid down by Mao would have been inconceivable. Besides, we had been overwhelmed by deceptive rhetoric, disinformation, and hypocrisy, which made it virtually impossible to see through the situation and to form an intelligent judgment.

Back at school, I heard that there had been many complaints from "reds" demanding to know why they had not been admitted to the Red Guards. That was why it was important to be there on National Day, as there was going to be a big enrollment, incorporating all the rest of the "reds." So, at the very time the Cultural Revolution had brought disaster on my family, I became a Red Guard.

I was thrilled by my red armband with its gold characters. It was the fashion of the day for Red Guards to wear old army uniforms with leather belts, like the one Mao was seen wearing at the beginning of the Cultural Revolution. I was keen to follow the fashion, so as soon as I was enrolled I rushed home, and from the bottom of an old trunk I dug out a pale-gray Lenin jacket which had been my mother's uniform in the early 1950s. It was a little too big, so I got my grandmother to take it in. With a leather belt from a pair of my father's trousers my costume was complete. But out on the streets I felt very uncomfortable. I found my image too aggressive. Still, I kept the outfit on.

Soon after this my grandmother went to Peking. I had to stay in the school, having just joined the Red Guards. Because of what had happened at home, the school frightened and startled me all the time. When I saw the "blacks" and "grays" having to clean the toilets and the grounds, their heads bowed, a creeping dread came over me, as though I were one of them. When the Red Guards went off at night on house raids, my legs went weak, as if they were heading for my family. When I noticed pupils whispering near me, my heart started to palpitate frantically: were they saying that I had become a "black," or that my father had been arrested?

But I found a refuge: the Red Guard reception office.

There were a lot of visitors to the school. Since September 1966, more and more young people were on the road, traveling all over the country. To encourage them to travel around and stir things up, transport, food, and accommodations were provided free.

The reception office was in what had once been a lecture hall. The wandering—and often aimless—visitors would be given cups of tea and chatted to. If they claimed to have serious business, the office would make an appointment for them to see one of the school Red Guard leaders. I zeroed in on this office because the people in it did not have to participate in actions like guarding the "blacks" and "grays," or go on house raids. I also liked it because of the five girls working there. There was an air of warmth and lack of zealotry around them which made me feel soothed the moment I met them.

A lot of people used to come to the office, and many would hang around to chat with us. There was often a line at the door, and some returned again and again. Looking back now, I can see that the young

men really wanted some female company. They were not that engrossed in the revolution. But I remember being extremely earnest. I
never avoided their gazes or returned their winks, and I conscientiously took notes of all the nonsense they spouted.

One hot night two rather coarse middle-aged women turned up at
the reception office, which was boisterous as usual. They introduced
themselves as the director and deputy director of a residents' committee near the school. They talked in a very mysterious and grave manner, as though they were on some grand mission. I had always disliked
this kind of affectation, so I turned my back. But soon I could tell that
an explosive piece of information had been delivered. The people who
had been hanging around started shouting, "Get a truck! Get a truck!
Let's all go there!" Before I knew what was happening, I was swept out
of the room by the crowd and into a truck. As Mao had ordered the
workers to support the Red Guards, trucks and drivers were permanently at our service. In the truck, I was squeezed next to one of the
women. She was retelling her story, her eyes full of eagerness to
ingratiate herself with us. She said that a woman in her neighborhood
was the wife of a Kuomintang officer who had fled to Taiwan, and that
she had hidden a portrait of Chiang Kai-shek in her apartment.

I did not like the woman, especially her toadying smile. And I
resented her for making me go on my first house raid. Soon the truck
stopped in front of a narrow alley. We all got out and followed the two
women down the cobbled path. It was pitch-dark, the only light coming from the crevices between the planks of wood that formed the
walls of the houses. I staggered and slipped, trying to fall behind. The
apartment of the accused woman consisted of two rooms, and was so
small that it could not hold our truckful of people. I was only too
happy to stay outside. But before long someone shouted that space
had been made for those outside to come in and "receive an education
in class struggle."

As soon as I was pressed into the room with the others, my nostrils
were filled with the stench of feces, urine, and unwashed bodies. The
room had been turned upside down. Then I saw the accused woman.
She was perhaps in her forties, kneeling in the middle of the room,
partly naked. The room was lit by a bare fifteen-watt bulb. In its
shadows, the kneeling figure on the floor looked grotesque. Her hair
was in a mess, and part of it seemed to be matted with blood. Her eyes
were bulging out in desperation as she shrieked: "Red Guard masters!
I do not have a portrait of Chiang Kai-shek! I swear I do not!" She was
banging her head on the floor so hard there were loud thuds and blood
oozed from her forehead. The flesh on her back was covered with cuts

and bloodstains. When she lifted her bottom in a kowtow, murky patches were visible and the smell of excrement filled the air. I was so frightened that I quickly averted my eyes. Then I saw her tormentor, a seventeen-year-old boy named Chian, whom up to now I had rather liked. He was lounging in a chair with a leather belt in his hand, playing with its brass buckle. "Tell the truth, or I'll hit you again," he said languidly.

Chian's father was an army officer in Tibet. Most officers sent to Tibet left their families in Chengdu, the nearest big city in China proper, because Tibet was considered an uninhabitable and barbaric place. Previously I had been rather attracted by Chian's languorous manner, which had given an impression of gentleness. Now I murmured, trying to control the quaking in my voice, "Didn't Chairman Mao teach us to use verbal struggle [*wen-dou*] rather than violent struggle [*wu-dou*]? Maybe we shouldn't . . . ?"

My feeble protest was echoed by several voices in the room. But Chian cast us a disgusted sideways glance and said emphatically: "Draw a line between yourselves and the class enemy. Chairman Mao says, 'Mercy to the enemy is cruelty to the people!' If you are afraid of blood, don't be Red Guards!" His face was twisted into ugliness by fanaticism. The rest of us fell silent. Although it was impossible to feel anything but revulsion at what he was doing, we could not argue with him. We had been taught to be ruthless to class enemies. Failure to do so would make us class enemies ourselves. I turned and walked quickly into the garden at the back. It was crammed with Red Guards with shovels. From inside the house the sound of lashes started again, accompanied by screams that made my hair stand on end. The yelling must have been unbearable for the others too, because many swiftly straightened up from their digging: "There is nothing here. Let's go! Let's go!" As we passed through the room, I caught sight of Chian standing casually over his victim. Outside the door, I saw the woman informer with the ingratiating eyes. Now there was a cringing and frightened look there. She opened her mouth as if to say something, but no words came out. As I glanced at her face, it dawned on me that there was no portrait of Chiang Kai-shek. She had denounced the poor woman out of vindictiveness. The Red Guards were being used to settle old scores. I climbed back into the truck full of disgust and rage.

18. "More Than Gigantic Wonderful News"— Pilgrimage to Peking

(October–December 1966)

I found an excuse to get out of school, and was home again the next morning. The apartment was empty. My father was in detention. My mother, grandmother, and Xiao-fang were in Peking. My teenage siblings were living their own, separate lives elsewhere.

Jin-ming had resented the Cultural Revolution from the very beginning. He was in the same school as me, and was in his first year. He wanted to become a scientist, but this was denounced by the Cultural Revolution as "bourgeois." He and some boys in his form had formed a gang before the Cultural Revolution. They loved adventure and mystery, and had called themselves the "Iron-Wrought Brotherhood." Jin-ming was their number-one brother. He was tall, and brilliant at his studies. He had been giving his form weekly magic shows using his chemistry knowledge, and had been openly skipping lessons which he was not interested in or which he had already gone beyond. And he was fair and generous to the other boys.

When the school Red Guard organization was set up on 16 August, Jin-ming's "brotherhood" was merged into it. He and his gang were given the job of printing leaflets and distributing them on the streets. The leaflets had been written by older Red Guards in their mid-teens and typically had titles like "Founding Declaration of the First Brigade of the First Army Division of the Red Guards of the Number Four

School" (all Red Guard organizations had grand names), "Solemn Statement" (a pupil announced he was changing his name to "Huang the Guard for Chairman Mao"), "More Than Gigantic Wonderful News" (a member of the Cultural Revolution Authority had just given an audience to some Red Guards), and "The Latest Most Supreme Instructions" (a word or two by Mao had just been leaked out).

Jin-ming was soon bored stiff by this gibberish. He started to absent himself from his missions, and became interested in a girl of his age, thirteen. She seemed to him the perfect lady—beautiful, gentle, and slightly aloof, with a touch of shyness. He did not approach her, but was content to admire her from afar.

One day the pupils in his form were summoned to go on a house raid. The older Red Guards said something about "bourgeois intellectuals." All members of the family were declared prisoners and ordered to gather in one room while the Red Guards searched the rest of the house. Jin-ming was appointed to watch the family. To his delight, the girl was the other "jailer."

There were three "prisoners": a middle-aged man and his son and daughter-in-law. They had obviously been expecting the raid, and sat with resigned expressions on their faces, staring into Jin-ming's eyes as though into space. Jin-ming felt very awkward under their gaze, and he was also uneasy because of the presence of the girl, who looked bored and kept glancing toward the door. When she saw several boys carrying a huge wooden case full of porcelain, she mumbled to Jin-ming that she was going to have a look, and left the room.

Facing his captives alone, Jin-ming felt his discomfort growing. Then the woman prisoner stood up and said she wanted to go and breast-feed her baby in the next room. Jin-ming readily agreed.

The moment she left the room, the object of Jin-ming's affection rushed in. Sternly, she asked him why a prisoner was at large. When Jin-ming said he had given permission, she yelled at him for being "soft on class enemies." She was wearing a leather belt on what Jin-ming had thought of as her "willowy" waist. Now she pulled it off and pointed it at his nose—a stylized Red Guard posture—while she screamed at him. Jin-ming was struck dumb. The girl was unrecognizable. All of a sudden she was far from gentle, shy, or lovely. She was all hysterical ugliness. Thus was Jin-ming's first love extinguished.

But he shouted back. The girl left the room and returned with an older Red Guard, the leader of the group. He started yelling so much his spittle splashed on Jin-ming, and he too pointed his rolled-up belt at him. Then he stopped, realizing that they should not be washing their dirty linen in front of class enemies. He ordered Jin-ming to go back to the school to "wait for adjudication."

That evening, the Red Guards in Jin-ming's form held a meeting without him. When the boys came back to the dormitory, their eyes avoided his. They behaved distantly for a couple of days. Then they told Jin-ming they had been arguing with the militant girl. She had reported Jin-ming's "surrender to the class enemies" and had insisted that he be given a severe punishment. But the Iron-Wrought Brotherhood defended him. Some of them resented the girl, who had been terribly aggressive toward other boys and girls too.

Still, Jin-ming was punished: he was ordered to pull out grass alongside the "blacks" and "grays." Mao's instruction to exterminate grass had led to a constant demand for manpower because of the grass's obstinate nature. This fortuitously offered a form of punishment for the newly created "class enemies."

Jin-ming pulled up grass only for a few days. His Iron-Wrought Brotherhood could not bear to see him suffer. But he had been classified as a "sympathizer with class enemies," and was never sent on any more raids, which suited him fine. He soon embarked on a journey with his brotherhood sight-seeing all over the country, taking in China's rivers and mountains, but, unlike most Red Guards, Jin-ming never made the pilgrimage to Peking to see Mao. He did not come home until the end of 1966.

My sister Xiao-hong, at fifteen, was a founding member of the Red Guards at her school. But she was only one among hundreds, as the school was crammed with officials' children, many of them competing to be active. She hated and feared the atmosphere of militancy and violence so much that she was soon on the verge of a nervous collapse. She came home to ask my parents for help at the beginning of September, only to find they were not there: my father was in detention and my mother had gone to Peking. My grandmother's anxiety made her even more scared, so she returned to her school. She volunteered to help "guard" the school library, which had been ransacked and sealed, like the one at my school. She spent her days and nights reading, devouring all the forbidden fruits she could. It was this that held her together. In mid-September, she set out on a long tour around the country with her friends and like Jin-ming she did not come home until the end of the year.

My brother Xiao-hei was almost twelve, and was at the same key primary school I had attended. When the Red Guards were formed in the middle schools, Xiao-hei and his friends were eager to join. To them the Red Guards meant freedom to live away from home, staying up all night, and power over adults. They went to my school and begged to be allowed into the Red Guards. To get rid of them, one Red Guard said offhandedly, "You can form the First Army Division of Unit 4969." So Xiao-hei became the head of the Propaganda Department of a troop of twenty boys, all the others being "commander," "chief of staff," and so on. There were no privates.

Xiao-hei joined in hitting teachers twice. One of the victims was a sports teacher, who had been condemned as a "bad element." Some girls of Xiao-hei's age had accused the teacher of touching their breasts and thighs during gym lessons. So the boys set upon him, not least to impress the girls. The other teacher was the moral tutor. As corporal punishment was banned in schools, she would complain to the parents, who would beat their sons.

One day, the boys set out on a house raid, and were assigned to go to a household which was rumored to be that of an ex-Kuomintang family. They did not know what exactly they were supposed to do there. Their heads had been filled with vague notions of finding something like a diary saying how the family longed for Chiang Kai-shek's comeback and hated the Communist Party.

The family had five sons, all well-built and tough-looking. They stood by the door, arms akimbo, and looked down at the boys with their most intimidating stares. Only one boy attempted to tiptoe in. One of the sons picked him up by the scruff of his neck and threw him out with one hand. This put an end to any further such "revolutionary actions" by Xiao-hei's "division."

So, in the second week of October, while Xiao-hei was living at his school and enjoying his freedom, Jin-ming and my sister were away traveling, and my mother and grandmother were in Peking, I was alone at home when one day, without warning, my father appeared on the doorstep.

It was an eerily quiet homecoming. My father was a changed person. He was abstracted and sunk deep in thought, and did not say where he had been or what had been happening to him. I listened to him pacing his room through sleepless nights, too frightened and worried to sleep myself. Two days later, to my tremendous relief, my mother returned from Peking with my grandmother and Xiao-fang.

My mother immediately went to my father's department and handed Tao Zhu's letter to a deputy director. Straight away, my father was sent to a health clinic. My mother was allowed to go with him.

I went there to see them. It was a lovely place in the country, bordered on two sides by a beautiful green brook. My father had a suite with a sitting room in which there was a row of empty book-shelves, a bedroom with a large double bed, and a bathroom with shiny white tiles. Outside his balcony, several osmanthus trees spread an intoxicating scent. When the breeze blew, tiny golden blossoms floated softly down to the grassless earth.

Both my parents seemed peaceful. My mother told me they went fishing in the brook every day. I felt they were safe, so I told them I was planning to leave for Peking to see Chairman Mao. I had longed to make this trip, like almost everybody else. But I had not gone because I felt I should be around to give my parents support.

Making the pilgrimage to Peking was very much encouraged—and food, accommodations, and transport were all free. But it was not organized. I left Chengdu two days later with the five other girls from the reception office. As the train whistled north, my feelings were a mixture of excitement and nagging disquiet about my father. Outside the window, on the Chengdu Plain, some rice fields had been har-vested, and squares of black soil shone among the gold, forming a rich patchwork. The countryside had been only marginally affected by the upheavals, in spite of repeated instigations by the Cultural Revolution Authority led by Mme. Mao. Mao wanted the population fed so that they could "make revolution," so he did not give his wife his full backing. The peasants knew that if they got involved and stopped producing food, they would be the first to starve, as they had learned in the famine only a few years before. The cottages among the green bamboo groves seemed as peaceful and idyllic as ever. The wind gently swayed the lingering smoke to form a crown over the graceful bamboo tips and the concealed chimneys. It was less than five months since the beginning of the Cultural Revolution, but my world had changed completely. I gazed out at the quiet beauty of the plain, and let a wistful mood envelop me. Fortunately, I did not have to worry about being criticized for being "nostalgic," which was considered bourgeois, as none of the other girls had an accusing turn of mind. With them, I felt I could relax.

The prosperous Chengdu Plain soon gave way to low hills. The snowy mountains of west Sichuan glistened in the distance. Before very long we were traveling in and out of the tunnels through the towering Qin Mountains, the wild range that cuts Sichuan off from the north of China. With Tibet to the west, the hazardous Yangtze Gorges to the east, and the southern neighbors considered barbarians, Sichuan had always been rather self-contained, and the Sichuanese were known for their independent spirit. Mao had been concerned about their legendary inclination to seek some margin of independence, and had always made sure the province was in the firm grip of Peking.

After the Qin Mountains, the scenery became dramatically different. The soft greenness gave way to harsh yellow earth, and the thatched cottages of the Chengdu Plain were replaced by rows of dry mud cave-huts. It was in caves like these that my father had spent five years as a young man. We were only a hundred miles from Yan'an, where Mao had set up his headquarters after the Long March. It was there that my father dreamed his youthful dreams and became a devoted Communist. Thinking of him, my eyes became moist.

The journey took two days and a night. The attendants came to talk to us often and told us how envious they were that we would be seeing Chairman Mao soon.

At Peking Station huge slogans welcomed us as "Chairman Mao's guests." It was after midnight, yet the square in front of the station was lit up like daytime. Searchlights swept through the thousands and thousands of young people, all wearing red armbands and speaking often mutually unintelligible dialects. They were talking, shouting, giggling, and quarreling against the background of a gigantic chunk of stolid Soviet-style architecture—the station itself. The only Chinese features were the pastiche pavilionlike roofs on the two clock towers at each end.

As I stumbled drowsily out into the searchlights, I was enormously impressed by the building, its ostentatious grandeur and its shiny marbled modernity. I had been used to traditional dark timber columns and rough brick walls. I looked back, and with a surge of emotion saw a huge portrait of Mao hanging in the center, under three golden characters, "Peking Station," in his calligraphy.

Loudspeakers directed us to the reception rooms in a corner of the station. In Peking, as in every other city in China, administrators were appointed to arrange food and accommodations for the traveling youngsters. Dormitories in universities, schools, hotels, and even offices were pressed into service. After waiting on line for hours, we were assigned to Qinghua University, one of the most prestigious in the country. We were taken there by coach and told that food would be provided in the canteen. The running of the gigantic machine for the millions of traveling youngsters was overseen by Zhou Enlai, who dealt with the daily chores with which Mao could not be bothered. Without Zhou or somebody like him, the country—and with it the Cultural Revolution—would have collapsed, and Mao let it be known that Zhou was not to be attacked.

We were a very serious group, and all we wanted to do was to see

Chairman Mao. Unfortunately, we had just missed his fifth review of Red Guards in Tiananmen Square. What were we to do? Leisure activities and sight-seeing were out—irrelevant to the revolution. So we spent all our time on the campus copying wall posters. Mao had said that one purpose of traveling was to "exchange information about the Cultural Revolution." That was what we would do: bring the slogans of the Peking Red Guards back to Chengdu.

Actually, there was another reason for not going out: transport was impossibly crowded and the university was out in the suburbs, about ten miles from the city center. Still, we had to tell ourselves that our disinclination to move was correctly motivated.

Staying on the campus was intensely uncomfortable. Even today I can still smell the latrines down the corridor from our room, which were so blocked that the water from the washbasins and urine and loosened excrement from the toilets flooded the tiled floor. Fortunately, the doorway to the latrines had a ridge, which prevented the stinking overflow from invading the corridor. The university administration was paralyzed, so there was nobody to get repairs done. But children from the countryside were still using the toilets: manure was not considered untouchable by peasants. When they trudged out, their shoes left highly odorous stains along the corridor and in the rooms.

A week passed, and still there was no news of another rally at which we could see Mao. Subconsciously desperate to get away from our discomfort, we decided to go to Shanghai to visit the site where the Communist Party had been founded in 1921, and then on to Mao's birthplace in Hunan, in south-central China.

These pilgrimages turned out to be hell: the trains were unbelievably packed. The dominance of the Red Guards by high officials' children was coming to an end, because their parents were beginning to come under attack as capitalist-roaders. The oppressed "blacks" and "grays" began to organize their own Red Guard groups and to travel. The color codes were beginning to lose their meaning. I remember meeting on one train a very beautiful, slim girl of about eighteen, with unusually big, velvet black eyes and long, thick eyelashes. As was the custom, we started by asking each other what "family background" we were from. I was amazed at the unembarrassed manner with which this lovely girl replied that she was a "black." And she seemed confidently to be expecting us "red" girls to be friendly with her.

The six of us were very unmilitant in our behavior, and our seats were always the center of boisterous chatting. The oldest member of our group was eighteen, and she was particularly popular. Everyone called her "Plumpie," as she was very well padded all around. She laughed a lot, with a deep, chesty, operatic sound. She sang a lot too, but, of course, only songs of Chairman Mao's quotations. All songs except these and a few in praise of Mao were banned, like all other forms of entertainment, and remained so for the ten years of the Cultural Revolution.

This was the happiest I had been since the start of the Cultural Revolution, in spite of the persistent worry about my father and the agony involved in traveling. Every inch of space in the trains was occupied, even the luggage racks. The toilet was jam-packed: no one could get in. Only our determination to see the holy sites of China sustained us.

Once, I desperately needed to relieve myself. I was sitting squeezed up next to a window, because five people were crammed onto a narrow seat made for three. With an incredible struggle I reached the toilet— but when I got there I decided it was impossible to use it. Even if the boy who sat on the lid of the tank with his feet on the toilet seat cover could lift his legs for one moment, even if the girl who sat between his feet could somehow manage to be held up briefly by the others filling every usable space around her, I could not bring myself to do it in front of all these boys and girls. I returned to my seat on the verge of tears. Panic worsened the bursting sensation, and my legs were shaking. I resolved to use the toilet at the next stop. After what seemed an interminable time, the train stopped at a small, dusk-enveloped station. The window was opened and I clambered out, but when I came back I found I could not get in.

I was perhaps the least athletic of us six. Previously, whenever I had had to climb into a train through the window, one of my friends had always lifted me from the platform while others pulled me from inside. This time, although I was being helped by about four people from inside, I could not hoist my body high enough to get my head and elbows in. I was sweating like mad, even though it was freezing cold. At this point, the train started to pull away. Panicking, I looked around to see if there was anyone who could help. My eyes fell on the thin, dark face of a boy who had sidled up beside me. But his intention was not to lend me a hand.

I had my purse in a pocket of my jacket, and because of my climbing position it was quite visible. With two fingers, the boy picked it out. He had presumably chosen the moment of departure to snatch it. I burst out crying. The boy paused. He looked at me, hesitated, and put the purse back. Then he took hold of my right leg and hoisted me up. I landed on the table as the train was beginning to pick up speed.

Because of this incident, I developed a soft spot for adolescent pickpockets. In the coming years of the Cultural Revolution, when the economy was in a shambles, theft was widespread, and I once lost a whole year's food coupons. But whenever I heard that policemen or other custodians of "law and order" had beaten a pickpocket, I always felt a pang. Perhaps the boy on that winter platform had shown more humanity than the hypocritical pillars of society.

Altogether we traveled about 2,000 miles on this trip, in a state of exhaustion such as I had never experienced in my life. We visited Mao's old house, which had been turned into a museum-cum-shrine. It was rather grand—quite different from my idea of a lodging for exploited peasants, as I had expected it to be. A caption underneath an enormous photograph of Mao's mother said that she had been a very kind person and, because her family was relatively well off, had often given food to the poor. So our Great Leader's parents had been rich peasants! But rich peasants were class enemies! Why were Chairman Mao's parents heroes when other class enemies were objects of hate? The question frightened me so much that I immediately suppressed it.

When we got back to Peking in mid-November, the capital was freezing. The reception offices were no longer at the station, because the area was too small for the huge number of youngsters now pouring in. A truck took us to a park where we spent the whole night waiting for accommodations to be allocated. We could not sit down because the ground was covered with frost and it was unbearably cold. I dozed off for a second or two standing up. I was not used to the harsh Peking winter and, having left home in the autumn, had not brought any winter clothes with me. The wind cut through my bones, and the night seemed never-ending. So did the line. It meandered around and around the ice-covered lake in the middle of the park.

Dawn came and went and we were still in line, absolutely exhausted. It was not until dusk fell that we reached our accommodations: the Central Drama School. Our room had once been used for singing classes. Now there were two rows of straw mattresses on the floor, no sheets or pillows. We were met by some air force officers, who said they had been sent by Chairman Mao to look after us and give us military training. We all felt very moved by the concern Chairman Mao showed us.

Military training for the Red Guards was a new development. Mao had decided to put a brake on the random destruction which he had unleashed. The hundreds of Red Guards lodged in the Drama School were organized into a "regiment" by the air force officers. We struck up a good relationship with them, and liked two officers in particular, whose family backgrounds we learned at once, as was customary. The company commander had been a peasant from the north, while the political commissar came from an intellectual's family in the famous garden city of Suzhou. One day they proposed taking the six of us to the zoo, but asked us not to tell the others because their jeep could not hold any more people. Besides, they implied, they were not supposed to divert us to activities irrelevant to the Cultural Revolution. Not wanting to get them into trouble we declined, saying we wanted to "stick to making revolution." The two officers brought us bagfuls of big ripe apples, which were seldom seen in Chengdu, and bunches of toffee-coated water chestnuts, which we had all heard of as a great Peking specialty. To repay their kindness, we sneaked into their bedroom and collected their dirty clothes, then washed them with great enthusiasm. I remember struggling with the big khaki uniforms, which were extremely heavy and hard in the icy water. Mao had told the people to learn from the armed forces, because he wanted everyone to be as regimented and indoctrinated with loyalty to him alone as the army was. Learning from servicemen had gone hand in hand with the promotion of affection for them, and numerous books, articles, songs, and dances featured girls helping soldiers by washing their clothes.

I even washed their underpants, but nothing sexual ever entered my mind. I suppose many Chinese girls of my generation were too dominated by the crushing political upheavals to develop adolescent sexual feelings. But not all. The disappearance of parental control meant it was a time of promiscuity for some. When I got back home I heard about a former classmate of mine, a pretty girl of fifteen, who went off traveling with some Red Guards from Peking. She had an affair on the way and came back pregnant. She was beaten by her father, followed by the accusing eyes of the neighbors, and enthusiastically gossiped about by her comrades. She hanged herself, leaving a note saying she was "too ashamed to live." No one challenged this medieval concept of shame, which might have been a target of a genuine cultural revolution. But it was never one of Mao's concerns, and was not among the "olds" which the Red Guards were encouraged to destroy.

The Cultural Revolution also produced a large number of militant puritans, mostly young women. Another girl from my form once received a love letter from a boy of sixteen. She wrote back calling him "a traitor to the revolution": "How dare you think about such shameless things when the class enemies are still rampant, and people in the capitalist world still live in an abyss of misery!" Such a style was affected by many of the girls I knew. Because Mao called for girls to be militant, femininity was condemned in the years when my generation was growing up. Many girls tried to talk, walk, and act like aggressive, crude men, and ridiculed those who did not. There was not much possibility of expressing femininity anyway. To start with, we were not allowed to wear anything but the shapeless blue, grey or green trousers and jackets.

Our air force officers drilled us round and round the Drama School's basketball courts every day. Next to the courts was the canteen. My eyes used to steal toward it as soon as we formed up, even if I had just finished breakfast. I was obsessed with food, although I was not sure whether this was due to the lack of meat, or the cold, or the boredom of the drilling. I dreamed of the variety of Sichuan cuisine, of crispy duckling, sweet-and-sour fish, "Drunken Chicken," and dozens of other succulent delicacies.

None of us six girls was used to having money. We also thought that buying things was somehow "capitalist." So, in spite of my obsession with food, I only bought one bunch of toffee-coated water chestnuts, after my appetite for them had been whetted by the ones our officers gave us. I resolved to give myself this treat after a great deal of agonizing and consultation with the other girls. When I got home after the trip I immediately devoured some stale biscuits, while handing my grandmother the almost untouched money she had given me. She pulled me into her arms and kept saying, "What a silly girl!"

I also returned home with rheumatism. Peking was so cold that water froze in the taps. Yet I was drilling, in the open, without an overcoat. There was no hot water to warm up our icy feet. When we first arrived, we were given a blanket each. Some days later, more girls arrived, but there were no more blankets. We decided to give them three and share the other three between us six. Our upbringing had taught us to help comrades in need. We had been informed that our blankets had come from stores reserved for wartime. Chairman Mao had ordered them to be taken out for the comfort of his Red Guards. We expressed our heartfelt gratitude to Mao. Now, when we ended up with hardly any blankets, we were told to be even more grateful to Mao, because he had given us all China had.

The blankets were small, and could not cover two people unless they slept close together. The shapeless nightmares which had started after I had seen the attempted suicide had become worse after my father was taken away and my mother left for Peking; and since I slept badly, I often twisted out from under the blanket. The room was poorly heated, and once I fell asleep, an icy chill invaded me. By the time we left Peking the joints in my knees were so inflamed that I could hardly bend them.

My discomfort did not stop there. Some children from the country-side had fleas and lice. One day I came into our room and saw one of my friends crying. She had just discovered a blot of tiny white eggs in the armpit seam of her underwear—lice eggs. This threw me into a panic, because lice caused unbearable itchiness and were associated with dirtiness. From then on, I felt itchy all the time, and examined my underwear several times a day. How I longed for Chairman Mao to see us soon so I could go home!

On the afternoon of 24 November, I was in one of our usual Mao quotation studying sessions in one of the boys' rooms (officers and boys would not come into the girls' rooms, out of modesty). Our nice company commander came in with an unusually light gait and pro-posed conducting us in the most famous song of the Cultural Revo-lution: "When Sailing the Seas, We Need the Helmsman." He had never done this before, and we were all pleasantly surprised. He waved his arms beating time, his eyes shining, his cheeks flushed. When he finished, and announced with restrained excitement that he had some good news, we knew immediately what it was.

"We're going to see Chairman Mao tomorrow!" he exclaimed. The rest of his words were drowned out by our cheers. After the initial wordless yelling, our excitement took the form of shouting slogans: "Long live Chairman Mao!" "We will follow Chairman Mao forever!"

The company commander told us that no one could leave the campus from that minute on, and that we should watch one another to make sure of this. To be asked to watch one another was quite normal. Besides, these were safety measures for Chairman Mao, which we were only too glad to apply. After dinner, the officer ap-proached my five companions and me, and said in a hushed and solemn voice: "Would you like to do something to ensure Chairman Mao's safety?" "Of course!" He signaled for us to keep quiet, and continued in a whisper: "Would you propose before we leave tomor-row morning that we all search each other to make sure that no one is carrying anything they shouldn't? You know, young people might forget about the rules. . . ." He had announced the rules earlier—that we must not bring anything metal, not even keys, to the rally.

Most of us could not sleep, and excitedly talked the night away. At four o'clock in the morning we got up and gathered in disciplined ranks for the hour-and-a-half walk to Tiananmen Square. Before our "company" set off, at a wink from the officer, Plumpie stood up and proposed a search. I could see that some of the others thought she was wasting our time, but our company commander cheerfully seconded her proposal. He suggested we search him first. A boy was called to do this, and found a big bunch of keys on him. Our commander acted as though he had been genuinely careless, and gave Plumpie a victorious smile. The rest of us searched each other. This roundabout way of doing things reflected a Maoist practice: things had to look as though they were the wish of the people, rather than commands from above. Hypocrisy and playacting were taken for granted.

The early-morning streets were bursting with activity. Red Guards were marching toward Tiananmen Square from all over the capital. Deafening slogans surged like roaring waves. As we chanted, we raised our hands and our Little Red Books formed a dramatic red line against the darkness. We reached the square at dawn. I was placed in the seventh row from the front on the wide northern pavement of the Avenue of Eternal Peace to the east side of Tiananmen Square. Behind me were many more rows. After lining us up tidily, our officers ordered us to sit down on the hard ground cross-legged. With my inflamed joints, this was agony, and I soon got pins and needles in my bottom. I was deadly cold and drowsy—and exhausted because I could not fall asleep. The officers conducted nonstop singing, making different groups challenge each other, to keep up our spirits.

Shortly before noon, hysterical waves of "Long live Chairman Mao!" roared from the east. I had been flagging and was slow to realize that Mao was about to pass by in an open car. Suddenly thunderous yelling exploded all around me. "Long live Chairman Mao! Long live Chairman Mao!" People sitting in front of me shot up and hopped in delirious excitement, their raised hands frantically waving their Little Red Books. "Sit down! Sit down!" I cried, in vain. Our company commander had said that we all had to remain seated throughout. But few seemed to be observing the rules, possessed by their urge to set eyes on Mao.

Having been sitting for so long, my legs had gone numb. For some seconds, all I could see was a boiling sea of the backs of heads. When I finally managed to totter to my feet, I caught only the very end of the motorcade. Liu Shaoqi, the president, had his face turned in my direction.

Wall posters had already started attacking Liu as "China's Khrushchev" and the leading opponent of Mao. Although he had not been officially denounced, it was clear that his downfall was imminent. In press reports of the Red Guard rallies, he was always given a very undistinguished place. In this procession, instead of standing next to Mao, as the number-two man should have done, he was right at the back, in one of the last cars.

Liu looked subdued and weary. But I did not have any feelings for him. Although he was the president, he did not mean anything to my generation. We had grown up imbued with the cult of Mao alone. And if Liu was against Mao, it seemed to us natural that he should go.

At that moment, with the sea of youngsters screaming their loyalty to Mao, Liu must have felt how utterly hopeless his situation was. The irony was that he himself had been instrumental in promoting Mao's deification, which had led to this explosion of fanaticism in the youth of a nation which was largely unreligious. Liu and his colleagues may have helped deify Mao in order to appease him, thinking that he would be satisfied with abstract glory and leave them to get on with the mundane work, but Mao wanted absolute power both on earth and in heaven. And perhaps there was nothing they could have done: the cult of Mao may have been unstoppable.

These reflections did not occur to me on the morning of 25 November 1966. All I cared about then was catching a glimpse of Chairman Mao. I turned my eyes quickly away from Liu to the front of the motorcade. I spotted Mao's stalwart back, his right arm steadily waving. In an instant, he had disappeared. My heart sank. Was that all I would see of Chairman Mao? Only a fleeting glimpse of his back? The sun seemed suddenly to have turned gray. All around me the Red Guards were making a huge din. The girl standing next to me had just pierced the index finger of her right hand and was squeezing blood out of it to write something on a neatly folded handkerchief. I knew exactly the words she was going to use. It had been done many times by other Red Guards and had been publicized *ad nauseam:* "I am the happiest person in the world today. I have seen our Great Leader Chairman Mao!" Watching her, my despair grew. Life seemed pointless. A thought flickered into my mind: perhaps I should commit suicide?

It vanished almost the next instant. Looking back, I suppose the idea was really a subconscious attempt to quantify my devastation at having my dream smashed, especially after all the hardships I had suffered on my journey. The bursting trains, the inflamed knees, the hunger and cold, the itchiness, the blocked toilets, the exhaustion— all in the end unrewarded.

Our pilgrimage was over and a few days later we headed home. I had had enough of the trip, and I longed for warmth and comfort, and a hot bath. But the thought of home was tinged with apprehension. No matter how uncomfortable, the journey had never been frightening, as my life immediately prior to it had been. Living in close contact with thousands and thousands of Red Guards for well over a month, I had never seen any violence, or felt terror. The gigantic crowds, hysterical though they were, were well disciplined and peaceful. The people I met were friendly.

Just before I left Peking, a letter came from my mother. It said my father had fully recovered and everyone in Chengdu was fine. But she added at the end that both she and my father were being criticized as capitalist-roaders. My heart sank. By now it had become clear to me that capitalist-roaders—Communist officials—were the main targets of the Cultural Revolution. I was soon to see what this meant for my family and for me.

19. "Where There Is a Will to Condemn, There Is Evidence"— My Parents Tormented

(December 1966–1967)

A capitalist-roader was supposed to be a powerful official who was pursuing capitalist policies. But in reality no officials had any choice about which policies they pursued. The orders of Mao and those of his opponents were all presented as coming from the Party, and the officials had to obey all of them—even though in doing so they were obliged to carry out many zigzags and even U-turns. If they really disliked a particular order, the most they could do was engage in passive resistance, which they had to try hard to disguise. It was therefore impossible to determine whether officials were capitalist-roaders or not on the basis of their work.

Many officials had their own views, but the Party rule was that they must not reveal them to the public. Nor did they dare to. So whatever the officials' sympathies were, they were unknown to the general public.

But ordinary people were the very force Mao now ordered to attack capitalist-roaders—without, of course, the benefit of either information or the right to exercise any independent judgment. So what happened was that officials came under attack as capitalist-roaders because of the positions they held. Seniority alone was not the criterion. The decisive factor was whether a person was the leader of a relatively self-contained unit or not. The whole population was organized into units, and the people who represented power to ordinary people were their immediate bosses—unit leaders. In designating these people for attack, Mao was tapping into the most obvious pool of resentment, in the same way that he had incited pupils against teachers. Unit leaders were also the key links in the chain of the Communist power structure which Mao wanted to get rid of.

It was because they were leaders of departments that both my parents were denounced as capitalist-roaders. "Where there is a will to condemn, there is evidence," as the Chinese saying has it. On this basis, all unit leaders across China, big and small, were summarily denounced by people under them as capitalist-roaders for implementing policies that were alleged to be "capitalist" and "anti–Chairman Mao." These included allowing free markets in the countryside, advocating better professional skills for workers, permitting relative literary and artistic freedom, and encouraging competitiveness in sports —now termed "bourgeois cups-and-medals mania." Until now most officials had had no idea that Mao had disliked these policies—after all, the directives had all come from the Party, which was led by him. Now they were told, out of the blue, that all these policies had come from the "bourgeois headquarters" within the Party.

In every unit there were people who became activists. They were called Rebel Red Guards, or "Rebels" for short. They wrote wall posters and slogans proclaiming "Down with the capitalist-roaders," and held denunciation meetings against their bosses. The denunciations often sounded hollow, because the accused simply said that they had been carrying out Party orders—Mao had always told them to obey Party orders unconditionally, and had never told them of the existence of the "bourgeois headquarters." How were they to know? And how could they have acted otherwise? The officials had many supporters, some of whom rallied to their defense. They were called the "Loyalists." Verbal and physical battles broke out between them and the Rebels. Because Mao never said explicitly that all Party bosses should be condemned, some militants became hesitant: what if the bosses they attacked turned out not to be capitalist-roaders? Beyond the posters and slogans and denunciation meetings, ordinary people did not know what they were expected to do.

So when I returned to Chengdu in December 1966 I sensed a distinct uncertainty in the air.

My parents were living at home. The health clinic where my father had been staying had asked them to leave in November because capitalist-roaders were supposed to go back to their units to be denounced. The small canteen in the compound had been closed down, and we all had to get our food from the big canteen, which went on working normally. My parents continued to receive their salaries every month, in spite of the fact that the Party system was paralyzed and they did not go to work. Since their departments dealt with culture, and their bosses in Peking were particularly hated by the Maos and had been purged at the start of the Cultural Revolution, my parents were in the direct line of fire. They were attacked in wall posters with standard abuse like "Bombard Chang Shou-yu" and "Burn Xia De-hong." The accusations against them were the same as those made against almost every director of every Department of Public Affairs up and down the country.

Meetings were convened in my father's department to denounce him. He was yelled at. As with most political struggles in China, the real impetus came from personal animosity. Father's foremost accuser was a Mrs. Shau, a prim and fiercely self-righteous deputy section chief who had long been aspiring to get rid of the prefix "deputy." She considered that her promotion had been blocked by my father, and was determined to take revenge. Once she spat in his face and slapped him. But in general the anger was limited. Many of the staff liked and respected my father and were not fierce to him. Outside his department, some organizations for which he had been responsible, like the *Sichuan Daily*, also held denunciation meetings against him. But the staff there bore no personal grudges against him, and the meetings were formalities.

Against my mother there were no denunciation meetings at all. As a grass-roots official, she had looked after more individual units than my father—schools, hospitals, and entertainment groups. Normally, someone in her position would have been denounced by people from these organizations. But she was left alone by all of them. She had been responsible for solving their personal problems, such as housing, transfers, and pensions. And she had done her job with unfailing helpfulness and efficiency. She had tried her best in previous campaigns not to victimize anyone, and had in fact managed to protect many. People knew the risks she had run, and repaid her by refusing to turn on her.

On my first evening back home my grandmother made "cloud-swallowing" dumplings and steamed rice in palm leaves filled with "eight treasures." My mother gave me a cheerful account of what had been happening to her and my father. She said they had agreed they did not want to be officials anymore after the Cultural Revolution. They were going to apply to be ordinary citizens, and enjoy a normal family life. As I was to realize later, this was no more than a self-deluding fantasy, because the Communist Party allowed no opting out; but at the time they needed something to hold on to.

My father also said: "Even a capitalist president can become an ordinary citizen overnight. It's a good thing not to be given permanent power. Otherwise officials will tend to abuse their power." He then apologized to me for having been dictatorial with the family. "You are like singing cicadas silenced by chilling winter," he said, "and it is good that you young people should rebel against us, the older generation." Then he said, half to me, half to himself, "I think there is nothing wrong with officials like me being subject to criticism—even a bit of hardship and loss of face."

This was another confused attempt by my parents to try to cope with the Cultural Revolution. They did not resent the prospect of losing their privileged positions—in fact, they were trying to see this as something positive.

Nineteen sixty-seven came. Suddenly, the Cultural Revolution switched into high gear. In its first stage, with the Red Guard movement, an atmosphere of terror had been created. Now Mao turned to his major goal: to replace the "bourgeois headquarters" and the existing Party hierarchy with his personal power system. Liu Shaoqi and Deng Xiaoping were formally denounced and detained, as was Tao Zhu.

On 9 January, the *People's Daily* and the radio announced that a "January Storm" had started from Shanghai, where Rebels had taken control. Mao called on people throughout China to emulate them and seize power from the capitalist-roaders.

"Seize power" *(duo-quan)*! This was a magic phrase in China. Power did not mean influence over policies—it meant license over people. In addition to money, it brought privilege, awe, and fawning, and the opportunity to take revenge. In China, there were virtually no safety valves for ordinary people. The whole country was like a pressure cooker in which a gigantic head of compressed steam had built up. There were no football matches, pressure groups, law suits, or even violent films. It was impossible to voice any kind of protest about the system and its injustices, unthinkable to stage a demonstration. Even talking about politics—an important form of relieving pressure in most societies—was taboo. Subordinates had very little chance of redress against their bosses. But if you were a boss of some kind, you had a chance to vent your frustration. So when Mao launched his call to "seize power," he found a huge constituency of people who wanted to take revenge on somebody. Although power was dangerous, it was more desirable than powerlessness, particularly to people who had never had it. Now it looked to the general public as if Mao was saying that power was up for grabs.

In practically every unit in China, the morale of the Rebels was immensely boosted. So were their numbers. All sorts of people—workers, teachers, shop assistants, even the staff of government offices—started calling themselves "Rebels." Following the example of Shanghai, they physically beat the now disorientated "Loyalists" into surrender. The earlier Red Guard groups, like the one in my school, were disintegrating, because they had been organized around the children of high officials, who were under attack. Some early Red Guards who opposed the new phase of the Cultural Revolution were arrested. One of the sons of Commissar Li was beaten to death by Rebels who accused him of having let slip a remark against Mme. Mao.

The people in my father's department who had been in the posse which had taken him away to be detained were now Rebels. Mrs. Shau was chief of a Rebel group for all the Sichuan government offices, in addition to being its branch leader in my father's department.

No sooner were the Rebels formed than they split into factions and fought for power in almost every work unit in China. All sides accused their opponents of being "anti–Cultural Revolution," or of being loyal to the old Party system. In Chengdu, the numerous groups quickly coalesced into two opposing blocs, headed by two university Rebel groups: the more militant "26 August" from Sichuan University, and the relatively moderate "Red Chengdu" from Chengdu University. Each commanded a following of millions of people throughout the province. In my father's department, Mrs. Shau's group was affiliated with the 26 August, and the opposing group—mainly consisting of more moderate people whom my father had liked and promoted, and who liked him—with the Red Chengdu.

Outside our apartment, beyond the compound walls, 26 August and Red Chengdu each rigged up loudspeakers to trees and electricity poles, which blasted out abuse of each other day and night. One night, I heard that 26 August had gathered hundreds of supporters and attacked a factory which was a stronghold of Red Chengdu. They captured the workers and tortured them, using methods including "singing fountains" (splitting their skulls open so the blood burst out) and "landscape paintings" (slashing their faces into patterns). Red Chengdu's broadcasts said several workers had become martyrs by jumping from the top of the building. I gathered they had killed themselves because they were unable to stand the torture.

One major target of the Rebels was the professional elite in every unit, not only prominent doctors, artists, writers, and scientists, but also engineers and graded workers, even model night-soil collectors (people who collect human waste, which was extremely valuable to the peasants). They were accused of having been promoted by capitalist-roaders, but were really the object of their colleagues' jealousy. Other personal scores were also settled in the name of the revolution.

The "January Storm" triggered brutal violence against the capitalist-roaders. Power was now being seized from Party officials, and people were spurred on to abuse them. Those who had hated their Party bosses grabbed the opportunity to take revenge, although the victims of previous persecutions were not allowed to act. It was some time before Mao got around to making new appointments, as he did not know whom to appoint at this stage, so ambitious careerists were eager to show their militancy in the hope that this would get them chosen as the new holders of power. Rival factions competed to outdo each other in brutality. Much of the population colluded, driven by intimidation, conformism, devotion to Mao, desire to settle personal scores, or just the releasing of frustration.

Physical abuse finally caught up with my mother. It did not come from people working under her, but mainly from ex-convicts who were working in street workshops in her Eastern District—robbers, rapists, drug smugglers, and pimps. Unlike "political criminals," who were on the receiving end of the Cultural Revolution, these common criminals were encouraged to attack designated victims. They had nothing against my mother personally, but she had been one of the top leaders in her district, and that was enough.

At meetings held to denounce her, these ex-convicts were particularly active. One day she came home with her face twisted in pain. She had been ordered to kneel on broken glass. My grandmother spent the evening picking fragments of glass from her knees with tweezers and a needle. The next day she made my mother a pair of thick kneepads. She also made her a padded waist protector, because the tender structure of the waist was where the assailants always aimed their punches.

Several times my mother was paraded through the streets with a dunce cap on her head, and a heavy placard hanging from her neck on which her name was written with a big cross over it to show her humiliation and her demise. Every few steps, she and her colleagues were forced to go down on their knees and kowtow to the crowds. Children would be jeering at her. Some would shout that their kowtowing did not make enough noise and demand that they do it again. My mother and her colleagues then had to bang their foreheads loudly on the stone pavement.

One day that winter there was a denunciation meeting at a street workshop. Before the meeting, while the participants had lunch in the canteen, my mother and her colleagues were ordered to kneel for one and a half hours on grit-covered ground in the open. It was raining and she got soaked to the skin; the biting wind sent icy chills through her wet clothes and into her bones. When the meeting started, she had to stand bent double on the platform, trying to control her shivers. As the wild, empty screaming went on, her waist and neck became unbearably painful. She twisted herself slightly, and tried to lift her head a bit to ease the aching. Suddenly she felt a heavy blow across the back of her head, which knocked her to the ground.

It was only some time later that she learned what had happened. A woman sitting in the front row, a brothel owner who had been imprisoned when the Communists clamped down on prostitution, had fixated on my mother, perhaps because she was the only woman on the platform. The moment my mother lifted her head, this woman jumped up and thrust an awl straight at her left eye. The Rebel guard standing behind my mother saw it coming and struck her to the ground. Had it not been for him, my mother would have lost her eye.

My mother did not tell us about this incident at the time. She seldom referred to what happened to her at all. When she had to mention something like the broken glass she said it casually, trying to make it sound as undramatic as possible. She never showed the bruises on her body, and she was always composed, even cheerful. She did not want us to worry about her. But my grandmother could tell how much she was suffering. She would follow my mother anxiously with her eyes, trying to hide her own pain.

One day our former maid came to see us. She and her husband were among the few who never broke off with our family through the whole of the Cultural Revolution. I felt immensely grateful for the warmth they brought us, especially as they ran the risk of being accused as "sympathizers of capitalist-roaders." Awkwardly, she mentioned to my grandmother that she had just seen my mother being paraded through the streets. My grandmother pressed her to say more, then suddenly collapsed, the back of her head hitting the floor with a loud bang. She had lost consciousness. Gradually, she came to. With tears rolling down her cheeks, she said, "What has my daughter done to deserve this?"

My mother developed a hemorrhage from her womb, and for the next six years, until she had a hysterectomy in 1973, she bled most days. Sometimes it was so severe she would faint and had to be taken to a hospital. Doctors prescribed hormones to control the flow of blood, and my sister and I gave her the injections. My mother knew it was dangerous to depend on hormones, but there was no alternative. It was the only way she could get through the denunciation meetings.

In the meantime, the Rebels in my father's department stepped up their assaults on him. Being one of the most important in the provincial government, the department had more than its share of opportunists. Formerly obedient instruments of the old Party system, many now became fiercely militant Rebels, led by Mrs. Shau under the banner of 26 August.

One day, a group of them barged into our apartment and marched into my father's study. They looked at the bookshelves, and declared him a real "diehard" because he still had his "reactionary books." Earlier, in the wake of the book burning by the teenage Red Guards, many people had set fire to their collections. But not my father. Now he made a faint attempt to protect his books by pointing at the sets of Marxist hardbacks. "Don't try to fool us Red Guards!" yelled Mrs. Shau. "You have plenty of 'poisonous weeds'!" She picked up some Chinese classics printed on flimsy rice paper.

"What do you mean, 'us Red Guards'?" my father retorted. "You are old enough to be their mother—and you ought to have more sense, too."

Mrs. Shau slapped my father hard. The crowd barked at him indignantly, although a few tried to hide their giggles. Then they pulled out his books and threw them into huge jute sacks they had brought with them. When all the bags were full, they carried them downstairs, telling my father they were going to burn them on the grounds of the department the next day after a denunciation meeting against him. They ordered him to watch the bonfire "to be taught a lesson." In the meantime, they said, he must burn the rest of his collection.

When I came home that afternoon, I found my father in the kitchen. He had lit a fire in the big cement sink, and was hurling his books into the flames.

This was the first time in my life I had seen him weeping. It was agonized, broken, and wild, the weeping of a man who was not used to shedding tears. Every now and then, in fits of violent sobs, he stamped his feet on the floor and banged his head against the wall.

I was so frightened that for some time I did not dare to do anything to comfort him. Eventually I put my arms around him and held him from the back, but I did not know what to say. He did not utter a word either. My father had spent every spare penny on his books. They were his life. After the bonfire, I could tell that something had happened to his mind.

He had to go to many denunciation meetings. Mrs. Shau and her group usually got a large number of Rebels from outside to increase the size of the crowd and to lend a hand in the violence. A standard opening was to chant: "Ten thousand years, another ten thousand years, and yet another ten thousand years to our Great Teacher, Great Leader, Great Commander, and Great Helmsman Chairman Mao!" Each time the three "ten thousand"s and four "great"s were shouted out, everyone raised their Little Red Books in unison. My father would not do this. He said that the "ten thousand years" was how emperors used to be addressed, and it was unfitting for Chairman Mao, a Communist.

This brought down a torrent of hysterical yells and slaps. At one meeting, all the targets were ordered to kneel and kowtow to a huge portrait of Mao at the back of the platform. While the others did as they were told, my father refused. He said that kneeling and kowtowing were undignified feudal practices which the Communists were committed to eliminating. The Rebels screamed, kicked his knees, and struck him on the head, but he still struggled to stand upright. "I will not kneel! I will not kowtow!" he said furiously. The enraged crowd demanded, "Bow your head and admit your crimes!" He replied, "I have committed no crime. I will not bend my head!"

Several large young men jumped on him to try to force him down, but as soon as they let go he stood up straight, raised his head, and stared defiantly at the audience. His assailants yanked his hair and pulled his neck. My father struggled fiercely. As the hysterical crowd screamed that he was "anti–Cultural Revolution," he shouted angrily, "What kind of Cultural Revolution is this? There is nothing 'cultural' about it! There is only brutality!"

The men who were beating him howled, "The Cultural Revolution is led by Chairman Mao! How dare you oppose it?" My father raised his voice higher: "I do oppose it, even if it is led by Chairman Mao!"

There was total silence. "Opposing Chairman Mao" was a crime punishable by death. Many people had died simply because they had been accused of it, without any evidence. The Rebels were stunned to see that my father did not seem to be afraid. After they recovered from their initial shock, they began to beat him again, calling on him to withdraw his blasphemous words. He refused. Enraged, they tied him up and dragged him to the local police, demanding that they arrest him. But the policemen there would not take him. They liked law and order and Party officials, and hated the Rebels. They said they needed permission to arrest an official as senior as my father, and no one had given such an order.

My father was to be beaten up repeatedly. But he stuck to his guns. He was the only person in the compound to behave like this, indeed the only one I knew of at all, and many people, including Rebels, secretly admired him. Every now and then a complete stranger passing us in the street would murmur stealthily how my father had impressed them. Some boys told my brothers they wanted to have bones as strong as my father's.

After their day's torment, both my parents would come home to my grandmother's nursing hand. By then, she had set aside her resentment of my father, and he had also mellowed toward her. She applied ointment to his wounds, stuck on special poultices to reduce his bruising, and got him to drink potions made with a white powder called *bai-yao* to help cure his internal injuries.

My parents were under permanent orders to stay at home and wait to be summoned to the next meeting. Going into hiding was out of the question. The whole of China was like a prison. Every house, every street was watched by the people themselves. In this vast land, there was nowhere anyone could hide.

My parents could not go out for relaxation either. "Relaxation" had become an obsolete concept: books, paintings, musical instruments, sports, cards, chess, teahouses, bars—all had disappeared. The parks were desolate, vandalized wastelands in which the flowers and the grass had been uprooted and the tame birds and goldfish killed. Films, plays, and concerts had all been banned: Mme. Mao had cleared the stages and the screens for the eight "revolutionary operas" which she had had a hand in producing, and which were all anyone was allowed to put on. In the provinces, people did not dare to perform even these. One director had been condemned because the makeup he had put on the tortured hero of one of the operas was considered by Mme. Mao to be excessive. He was thrown into prison for "exaggerating the hardship in the revolutionary struggle." We hardly even thought of going out for a walk. The atmosphere outside was terrifying, with the violent street-corner denunciation meetings and all the sinister wall posters and slogans; people were walking around like zombies, with harsh or cowed expressions on their faces. What was more, my parents' bruised faces marked them as condemned, and if they went out they ran the risk of being abused.

As an indication of the terror of the day, no one dared to burn or throw away any newspapers. Every front page carried Mao's portrait, and every few lines featured Mao's quotations. These papers had to be treasured and it would bring disaster if anyone saw you disposing of them. Keeping them was also a problem: mice might gnaw into Mao's portrait, or the papers might simply rot—either of these would be interpreted as a crime against Mao. Indeed, the first large-scale factional fighting in Chengdu was triggered by some Red Guards accidentally sitting on old newspapers which had Mao's face on them. A schoolfriend of my mother's was hounded to suicide because she wrote "Heartily love Chairman Mao" on a wall poster with one brush stroke inadvertently shorter, making the character "heartily" look like the one meaning "sadly."

One day in February 1967, in the depths of this overwhelming terror, my parents had a long conversation which I only came to know about years later. My mother was sitting on the edge of their bed, and my father was in a wicker chair opposite. He told her that he now knew what the Cultural Revolution was really about, and the realization had shattered his whole world. He could see clearly that it had nothing to do with democratization, or with giving ordinary people more say. It was a bloody purge to increase Mao's personal power.

My father talked slowly and deliberately, choosing his words carefully. "But Chairman Mao has always been so magnanimous," my mother said. "He even spared Pu Yi. Why can't he tolerate his comrades-in-arms who fought for a new China with him? How can he be so harsh on them?"

My father said quietly, but intensely, "What was Pu Yi? He was a war criminal, with no support from the people. He couldn't do anything. But . . ." He fell into a meaningful silence. My mother understood him: Mao would not tolerate any possible challenge. Then she asked, "But why all of us, who after all only carry out orders? And why incriminate all these innocent people? And so much destruction and suffering?"

My father replied, "Maybe Chairman Mao feels he could not achieve his goal without turning the whole place upside down. He has always been thorough—and he has never been fainthearted about casualties."

After a charged pause, my father went on: "This cannot be a revolution in any sense of the term. To secure personal power at such cost to the country and the people has to be wrong. In fact, I think it is criminal."

My mother scented disaster. After reasoning like this, her husband had to act. As she expected, he said, "I am going to write a letter to Chairman Mao."

My mother dropped her head into her hands. "What's the use?" she burst out. "How could you possibly imagine Chairman Mao would listen to you? Why do you want to destroy yourself—and for nothing? Don't count on me to take it to Peking this time!"

My father leaned over and kissed her. "I wasn't thinking about your delivering it. I'm going to post it." Then he lifted her head and looked into her eyes. In a tone of despair he said, "What else can I do? What alternatives do I have? I must speak up. It might help. And I must do it even if just for my conscience."

"Why is your conscience so important?" my mother said. "More than your children? Do you want them to become 'blacks'?"

There was a long pause. Then my father said hesitantly, "I suppose you must divorce me and bring up the children your way." Silence fell between them again, making her think that perhaps he had not made up his mind about writing the letter, because he was aware of its consequences. It would surely be catastrophic.

Days passed. In late February, an airplane flew low over Chengdu spreading thousands of sparkling sheets which floated down out of the leaden sky. On them was printed a copy of a letter dated 17 February and signed by the Central Military Committee, the top body of senior army men. The letter told the Rebels to desist from their violent actions. Although it did not condemn the Cultural Revolution directly, it was obviously trying to halt it. A colleague showed the leaflet to my mother. My parents had a surge of hope. Perhaps China's old and much-respected marshals were going to intervene. There was a big demonstration through the streets of central Chengdu in support of the marshals' call.

The leaflets were the result of upheavals behind closed doors in Peking. In late January Mao had for the first time called on the army to support the Rebels. Most of the top military leaders—except Defense Minister Lin Biao—were furious. On 14 and 16 February, they held two long meetings with political leaders. Mao himself stayed away, as did Lin Biao, his deputy. Zhou Enlai presided. The marshals joined forces with Politburo members who had not yet been purged. These marshals had been the commanders of the Communist army, veterans of the Long March, and heroes of the revolution. They condemned the Cultural Revolution for persecuting innocent people and destabilizing the country. One of the vice-premiers, Tan Zhenlin, burst out in a fury, "I've followed Chairman Mao all my life. Now I'm not following him anymore!" Immediately after these meetings the marshals began to take steps to try to stop the violence. Because it was particularly bad in Sichuan, they issued the letter of 17 February especially for the province.

Zhou Enlai declined to throw his weight behind the majority, and stuck with Mao. The personality cult had endowed Mao with demonic power. Retribution against the opposition was swift. Mao stage-managed mob attacks on the dissident Politburo members and military commanders, who were subjected to house raids and brutal denunciation meetings. When Mao gave the word to punish the marshals, the army did not make a move to support them.

This single feeble attempt to stand up to Mao and his Cultural Revolution was termed the "February Adverse Current." The regime released a selective account of it to generate more intense violence against the capitalist-roaders.

The February meetings were a turning point for Mao. He saw that virtually everyone opposed his policies. This led to the total discarding —in all but name—of the Party. The Politburo was effectively replaced by the Cultural Revolution Authority. Lin Biao soon began to purge commanders loyal to the marshals, and the role of the Central Military Committee was taken over by his personal office, which he controlled through his wife. Mao's cabal now was like a medieval court, structured around wives, cousins, and fawning courtiers. Mao sent delegates to the provinces to organize "Revolutionary Committees," which were to be the new instruments of his personal power, replacing the Party system all the way down to the grass roots.

In Sichuan, Mao's delegates turned out to be my parents' old acquaintances, the Tings. After my family had left Yibin, the Tings had practically taken control of the region. Mr. Ting had become its Party secretary; Mrs. Ting was Party chief of the city of Yibin, the capital.

The Tings had used their positions to engage in endless persecutions and personal vendettas. One involved a man who had been Mrs. Ting's bodyguard in the early 1950s. She had tried to seduce him several times, and one day she complained about having stomach trouble and got the young man to massage her abdomen. Then she guided his hand down to her private parts. The bodyguard immediately pulled his hand back and walked away. Mrs. Ting accused him of trying to rape her and had him sentenced to three years in a labor camp.

An anonymous letter exposing the whole affair reached the Sichuan Party Committee, which ordered an investigation. Being the defendants, the Tings were not supposed to see this letter, but a crony of theirs showed it to them. They got every member of the Yibin government to write a report on some issue or other in order to check their handwriting. They were never able to identify the author, but the investigation came to nothing.

In Yibin, officials and ordinary people alike were terrified of the Tings. The recurrent political campaigns and the quota system provided ideal opportunities for them to engage in victimization.

In 1959 the Tings got rid of the governor of Yibin, the man who had succeeded my father in 1953. He was a veteran of the Long March, and was very popular, which made the Tings envious. He was called "Straw Sandal Li" because he always wore peasant's sandals—a sign that he wanted to keep close to his roots in the soil. Indeed, during the Great Leap Forward, he showed little alacrity in forcing the peasants to produce steel, and in 1959 he spoke up about the famine. The Tings denounced him as a "rightist opportunist" and had him demoted to purchasing agent for the canteen of a brewery. He died in the famine, although his job should have meant he had a better opportunity to fill his stomach than most. The autopsy showed there was only straw in his stomach. He had remained an honest man to his death.

Another case, also in 1959, involved a doctor whom the Tings condemned as a class enemy because he made a truthful diagnosis of hunger victims—and the famine was officially unmentionable.

There were scores of cases like these—so many that people risked their lives to write to the provincial authorities to denounce the Tings. In 1962, when the moderates had the upper hand in the central government, they launched a nationwide investigation into the previous campaigns and rehabilitated many of the victims. A team was formed by the Sichuan government to investigate the Tings, who were found guilty of gross abuse of power. They were sacked and detained, and in 1965 General Secretary Deng Xiaoping signed an order expelling them from the Party.

When the Cultural Revolution started, the Tings somehow escaped and got to Peking, where they appealed to the Cultural Revolution Authority. They presented themselves as heroes upholding "class struggle," for which, they claimed, they had been persecuted by the old Party authorities. My mother actually bumped into them once at the grievance office. They asked her warmly for her address in Peking. She declined to give it to them.

The Tings were picked up by Chen Boda, one of the leaders of the Cultural Revolution Authority, and my father's old boss in Yan'an. Through him, Mme. Mao received them, and immediately recognized them as kindred spirits. Mme. Mao's motivation for the Cultural Revolution had much less to do with policy than with settling personal scores—some of the pettiest kind. She had a hand in the persecution of Mme. Liu Shaoqi because, as she herself told the Red Guards, she was furious about Mme. Liu's overseas trips with her husband, the president. Mao only went abroad twice, both times to Russia, and both times without Mme. Mao. What was worse, on her trips abroad Mme. Liu was seen wearing smart clothes and jewelry that no one could wear in Mao's austere China. Mme. Liu was accused of being a CIA agent and thrown into prison, barely escaping death.

Back in the 1930s, before she had met Mao, Mme. Mao had been a minor actress in Shanghai, and had felt cold-shouldered by the literati there. Some of them were Communist underground leaders, who after 1949 became leading figures in the Central Department of Public Affairs. Partly to avenge her real or imagined humiliation in Shanghai thirty years before, Mme. Mao went to extreme lengths to find "anti–Chairman Mao, anti-socialist" elements in their work. As Mao went into retreat during the famine, she managed to get closer to him and whispered much venomous pillow talk in his ear. In order to bring her foes down, she condemned the entire system under them, which meant the departments of Public Affairs all over the country.

She also took revenge on actors and actresses from the Shanghai period who had aroused her jealousy. An actress called Wang Ying had played a role which Mme. Mao had coveted. Thirty years later, in 1966, Mme. Mao had her and her husband imprisoned for life. Wang Ying committed suicide in prison in 1974.

Another well-known actress, Sun Wei-shi, had once appeared decades before with Mme. Mao in a play in Yan'an in front of Mao. Sun's performance was apparently more of a hit than Mme. Mao's, and she became a very popular figure among the top leaders, including Mao. Being Zhou Enlai's adopted daughter, she did not feel the need to butter up Mme. Mao. In 1968, Mme. Mao had her and her brother arrested and tortured to death. Even Zhou Enlai's power could not protect her.

Mme. Mao's vendettas gradually became known to the general public by word of mouth; her character also revealed itself in her speeches, which were reproduced on wall posters. She was to become almost universally hated, but at the beginning of 1967 her evils were still little known.

Mme. Mao and the Tings belonged to the same breed, who had a name in Mao's China—*zheng-ren*, "people-persecuting officials." The tirelessness and single-mindedness with which they engaged in persecution, and the bloodthirsty methods they used, were on a truly horrific scale. In March 1967, a document signed by Mao announced that the Tings had been rehabilitated and empowered to organize the Sichuan Revolutionary Committee.

A transitional authority called the Sichuan Preparatory Revolutionary Committee was set up. It was composed of two generals—the chief political commissar and the commander of the Chengdu Military Region (one of China's eight military regions)—and the Tings. Mao had decreed that every Revolutionary Committee should have three components: the local army, representatives of the Rebels, and "revolutionary officials." The latter were to be chosen from among former officials, and this was at the discretion of the Tings, who were in effect running the committee.

In late March 1967 the Tings came to see my father. They wanted to include him in their committee. My father enjoyed high prestige among his colleagues for being honest and fair. Even the Tings appreciated his qualities, particularly as they knew that when they had been in disgrace my father had not, like some, added his personal denunciations. Besides, they needed someone with his abilities.

My father greeted them as courtesy required, but my grandmother welcomed them with enthusiasm. She had heard little about their vendettas, and she knew that it was Mrs. Ting who had authorized the precious American medicines which had cured my mother of TB when she was pregnant with me.

When the Tings went into my father's quarters, my grandmother quickly rolled out some dough, and soon the loud rhythmic melody of chopping filled the kitchen. She minced pork, cut a bundle of tender young chives, hashed an assortment of spices, and poured hot rapeseed oil onto chili powder to make the sauce for the traditional welcoming meal of dumplings.

In my father's study, the Tings told him about their rehabilitation and their new status. They said they had been to his department and been briefed by the Rebels there about the trouble he had gotten himself into. However, they said, they had always liked him in those early years in Yibin, still had high regard for him, and wanted to work with him again. They promised that all the incriminating things he had said and done could be forgotten if he cooperated. Not only that, he could rise again in the new power structure, taking charge of all cultural affairs in Sichuan, for example. They made it clear it was an offer he could not afford to refuse.

My father had heard about the Tings' appointment from my mother, who had read it on wall posters. He had said to my mother at the time: "We mustn't believe in rumors. This is impossible!" It was incredible to him to see this couple placed in vital positions by Mao. Now he tried to restrain his disgust, and said, "I'm sorry, I can't accept your offer."

Mrs. Ting snapped, "We are doing you a big favor. Other people would have begged for this on their knees. Do you realize what a spot you are in, and who we are now?"

My father's anger rose. He said, "Whatever I have said or done I

take responsibility for myself. I do not want to get mixed up with you."
In the heated exchanges that followed, he went on to say that he
thought their punishment had been just, and they should never have
been trusted with important jobs. Stunned, they told him to be careful
what he said: it was Chairman Mao himself who had rehabilitated
them and had called them "good officials."

My father's outrage spurred him on. "But Chairman Mao could not
have known all the facts about you. What sort of 'good officials' are
you? You have committed unforgivable mistakes." He checked himself from saying "crimes."

"How dare you challenge Chairman Mao's words!" exclaimed Mrs.
Ting. "Deputy Commander Lin Biao said: 'Every word of Chairman
Mao's is universal absolute truth, and every word equals ten thousand
words'!"

"If a word means one word," my father said, "it is already a man's
supreme achievement. It is not humanly possible for one word to
mean ten thousand. What Deputy Commander Lin Biao said was
rhetorical, and should not be taken literally."

The Tings could not believe their ears, according to their account
afterward. They warned my father that his way of thinking, talking,
and behaving was against the Cultural Revolution, which was led by
Chairman Mao. To this my father said he would like a chance to
debate with Chairman Mao about the whole thing. These words were
so suicidal that the Tings were speechless. After a silence, they stood
up to leave.

My grandmother heard angry footsteps and rushed out of the
kitchen, her hands dusted with wheat flour into which she had been
dipping the dumplings. She collided with Mrs. Ting and asked the
couple to stay for lunch. Mrs. Ting ignored her, stormed out of the
apartment, and started to tramp downstairs. At the landing she
stopped, turned around, and said furiously to my father, who had
come out with them, "Are you crazy? I'm asking you for the last time:
Do you still refuse my help? You realize I can do anything to you
now."

"I want nothing to do with you," my father said. "You and I are
different species."

Leaving my startled and fearful grandmother at the top of the stairs,
my father went into his study. He came out almost at once, and
carried an inkstone to the bathroom. He dripped a few drops of water
onto the stone and walked thoughtfully back into the study. Then he
sat down at his desk, and started grinding a stick of ink round and
round the stone, forming a thick black liquid. He spread a blank sheet

of paper in front of him. In no time, he had finished his second letter to Mao. He started by saying: "Chairman Mao, I appeal to you, as one Communist to another, to stop the Cultural Revolution." He went on to describe the disasters into which it had thrown China. The letter ended with the words: "I fear the worst for our Party and our country if people like Liu Jie-ting and Zhang Xi-ting are given power over the lives of tens of millions of people."

He addressed the envelope to "Chairman Mao, Peking," and took it to the post office at the top of the street. He sent it by registered airmail. The clerk behind the counter took the envelope and glanced at it, maintaining an expression of total blankness. Then my father walked home—to wait.

20. "I Will Not Sell My Soul"— My Father Arrested

(1967–1968)

On the afternoon of the third day after my father posted his letter to Mao, my mother answered a knock on the door of our apartment. Three men came in, all wearing the same baggy blue uniformlike clothes as every other man in China. My father knew one of them: he had been a caretaker in his department and was a militant Rebel. One of the others, a tall man with boils on his thin face, announced that they were Rebels from the police and that they had come to arrest him, "a counterrevolutionary in action bombarding Chairman Mao and the Cultural Revolution." Then he and the third man, who was shorter and stouter, gripped my father by the arms, and gestured to him to go.

They did not show any identity cards, much less an arrest warrant. But there was no doubt that they were Rebel plainclothes policemen. Their authority was unquestionable, because they came with a Rebel from my father's department.

Although they did not mention his letter to Mao, my father knew it must have been intercepted, as was almost inevitable. He had known that he would probably be arrested, because not only had he committed his blasphemy to paper, but there was now an authority— the Tings—to sanction his arrest. Even so, he had wanted to take the only chance there was, however slight. He was silent and tense, but did not protest. As he was walking out of the apartment, he paused and said softly to my mother: "Don't bear a grudge against our Party.

Have faith that it will correct its mistakes, however grave they may be. Divorce me and give my love to our children. Don't alarm them."

When I came home later that afternoon, I found both of my parents gone. My grandmother told me my mother had gone to Peking to appeal for my father, who had been taken away by Rebels from his department. She did not say "the police," because that would have been too frightening, being more disastrous and final than detention by Rebels.

I rushed to my father's department to ask where he was. I got no answer except assorted barks, led by Mrs. Shau, of "You must draw a line from your stinking capitalist-roader father" and "Wherever he is, it serves him right." I forced back my furious tears. I was filled with loathing for these supposedly intelligent adults. They did not have to be so merciless, so brutal. A kinder look, a gentler tone, or even silence would have been perfectly possible, even in those days.

It was from this time that I developed my way of judging the Chinese by dividing them into two kinds: one humane, and one not. It took an upheaval like the Cultural Revolution to bring out these characteristics in people, whether they were teenage Red Guards, adult Rebels, or capitalist-roaders.

Meanwhile, my mother was waiting at the station for the train that was to take her to Peking a second time. She felt much more despondent now than six months before. There had still been a chance for some justice then, but it was virtually hopeless now. My mother did not give in to despair. She was determined to fight.

She had decided that the one person she had to see was Premier Zhou Enlai. No one else would do. If she saw anyone else it would only hasten the demise of her husband, herself, and her family. She knew that Zhou was far more moderate than Mme. Mao and the Cultural Revolution Authority—and that he exercised considerable power over the Rebels, to whom he gave orders almost every day.

But getting to see him was like trying to walk into the White House, or see the Pope alone. Even if she reached Peking without being caught, and got to the right grievance office, she could not specify whom she wanted to see, as that would be taken as an insult to, even an attack on, other leaders. Her anxiety grew, and she did not know whether her absence from home had already been discovered by the Rebels. She was meant to be waiting to be summoned to her next denunciation meeting, but there was a possible loophole. One Rebel group might think she was in the hands of another.

As she waited, she saw a huge banner with the words "The Red Chengdu Petition Delegation to Peking." Clustered around it was a crowd of about 200 people in their early twenties. Their other banners made it clear they were university students, going to Peking to protest against the Tings. What was more, the banners proclaimed that they had secured a meeting with Premier Zhou.

Compared with its rival Rebel group, 26 August, Red Chengdu was relatively moderate. The Tings had thrown their weight behind 26 August, but Red Chengdu did not surrender. The power of the Tings was never absolute, even though they were backed by Mao and the Cultural Revolution Authority.

At this time, the Cultural Revolution was dominated by intense factional fighting between Rebel groups. This had begun almost as soon as Mao had given the signal to seize power from the capitalist-roaders; now, three months later, most of the Rebel leaders were emerging as something very different from the ousted Communist officials: they were undisciplined opportunists, and were not even fanatical Maoists. Mao had instructed them to unite and share power, but they only paid lip service to this injunction. They verbally attacked each other with Mao's quotations, making cynical use of his guru-like elusiveness—it was easy to select a quotation of Mao's to suit any situation, or even both sides of the same argument. Mao knew that his vapid "philosophy" was boomeranging on him, but he could not intervene explicitly without losing his mystical remoteness.

In order to destroy 26 August, Red Chengdu knew it had to bring down the Tings. They knew the Tings' reputation for vindictiveness and their lust for power, which were widely discussed, in hushed tones by some, more openly by others. Even Mao's endorsement of the couple was not enough to get Red Chengdu to fall into line. It was against this background that Red Chengdu was sending the students to Peking. Zhou Enlai had promised to receive them because Red Chengdu, as one of the two Rebel camps in Sichuan, had millions of supporters.

My mother followed the Red Chengdu crowd as they were waved through the ticket barrier onto the platform where the Peking express was puffing. She was trying to climb into a carriage with them when she was stopped by a male student. "Who are you?" he shouted. My mother, at thirty-five, hardly looked like a student. "You're not one of us. Get off!"

My mother clung tightly to the handle of the door. "I am going to Peking, too, to appeal against the Tings!" she cried. "I know them from the past." The man looked at her in disbelief. But from behind him came two voices, a man's and a woman's: "Let her in! Let's hear what she has to say!"

My mother squeezed into the packed compartment, and was seated between the man and the woman. They introduced themselves as staff officers of Red Chengdu. The man was called Yong, and the woman Yan. They were both students at Chengdu University.

From what they said, my mother could see that the students did not know very much about the Tings. She told them what she could remember about some of the many cases of persecution in Yibin before the Cultural Revolution; about Mrs. Ting's attempt to seduce my father in 1953; the couple's recent visit to my father, and his refusal to collaborate with them. She said the Tings had had my father arrested because he had written to Chairman Mao to oppose their appointment as the new leaders of Sichuan.

Yan and Yong promised they would take her to their meeting with Zhou Enlai. All night, my mother sat wide-awake planning what she should say to him, and how.

When the delegation arrived at Peking Station, a representative of the premier was waiting for them. They were taken to a government guesthouse, and told that Zhou would see them the next evening.

The next day, while the students were out, my mother prepared a written plea to Zhou. She might not get a chance to talk to him, and in any case it was better to petition him in writing. At 9 P.M. she went with the students to the Great Hall of the People on the west side of Tiananmen Square. The meeting was in the Sichuan Room, which my father had helped decorate in 1959. The students sat in an arc facing the premier. There were not enough seats, so some sat on the carpeted floor. My mother sat in the back row.

She knew her speech had to be succinct and effective, and she rehearsed it again in her head as the meeting got under way. She was too preoccupied to hear what the students were saying. She only noted how the premier reacted. Every now and then he nodded acknowledgment. He never indicated approval or disagreement. He just listened, and occasionally made general remarks about "following Chairman Mao" and "the need to unite." An aide took notes.

Suddenly she heard the premier saying, as though in conclusion: "Anything else?" She shot up from her seat. "Premier, I have something to say."

Zhou raised his eyes. My mother was obviously not a student. "Who are you?" he asked. My mother gave her name and position, and followed immediately with: "My husband has been arrested as a 'counterrevolutionary in action.' I am here to seek justice for him." She then gave my father's name and position.

Zhou's eyes became intent. My father had an important position. "The students can go," he said. "I'll talk to you privately."

My mother longed to talk to Zhou alone, but she had decided to sacrifice this chance for a more important goal. "Premier, I would like the students to stay to be my witnesses." While saying this, she handed her petition to the student in front, who passed it on to Zhou.

The premier nodded: "All right. Go ahead."

Quickly but clearly, my mother said my father had been arrested for what he had written in a letter to Chairman Mao. My father disagreed with the Tings' appointment as the new leaders of Sichuan, because of their record of abuse of power which he had witnessed in Yibin. Apart from that, she said briefly: "My husband's letter also contained serious mistakes about the Cultural Revolution."

She had thought carefully about how she would put this. She had to give a true account to Zhou, but she could not repeat my father's exact words for fear of the Rebels. She had to be as abstract as possible: "My husband held some seriously erroneous views. However, he did not spread his views in public. He was following the charter of the Communist Party and speaking his mind to Chairman Mao. According to the charter, this is the legitimate right of a Party member, and should not be used as an excuse to arrest him. I am here to appeal for justice for him."

When my mother's eyes met Zhou Enlai's, she saw that he had fully understood the real content of my father's letter, and her dilemma of not being able to spell it out. He glanced at my mother's petition, then turned to an aide sitting behind him and whispered something. The hall was deadly quiet. All eyes were on the premier.

The aide handed Zhou some sheets of paper with the letterhead of the State Council (the cabinet). Zhou started writing in his slightly strained way—his right arm had been broken years before when he fell from a horse in Yan'an. When he finished, he gave the paper to the aide, who read it out.

" 'One: As a Communist Party member, Chang Shou-yu is entitled to write to the Party leadership. No matter what serious mistakes the letter contains, it may not be used to accuse him of being a counter-revolutionary. Two: As Deputy Director of the Department of Public Affairs of Sichuan Province, Chang Shou-yu has to submit himself to investigation and criticism by the people. Three: Any final adjudication on Chang Shou-yu must wait till the end of the Cultural Revolution. Zhou Enlai.' "

My mother was speechless with relief. The note was not addressed to the new leaders in Sichuan, which would normally have been the case, so she was not bound to hand it in to them, or to anyone. Zhou intended her to keep it and show it to whoever might prove useful.

Yan and Yong were sitting on my mother's left. When she turned to them, she saw they were beaming with joy.

She caught the train back to Chengdu two days later, keeping with Yan and Yong all the time, as she was worried the Tings might get wind of the note and send their henchmen to grab it and her. Yan and Yong also thought it was vital for her to stick with them, "In case 26 August abducts you." They insisted on accompanying her to our apartment from the station. My grandmother gave them pork-and-chive pancakes, which they devoured in no time.

I immediately took to Yan and Yong. Rebels, and yet so kind, so friendly and warm to my family! It was unbelievable. I could also tell at once that they were in love: the way they glanced at each other, the way they teased and touched each other, was very unusual in company. I heard my grandmother sigh to my mother that it would be nice to give them some presents for their wedding. My mother said this would be impossible, and would get them into trouble if it became known. Accepting "bribes" from a capitalist-roader was no small offense.

Yan was twenty-four, and had been in her third year studying accounting at Chengdu University. Her lively face was dominated by a pair of thick-rimmed spectacles. She laughed frequently, throwing her head back. It was a very heart-warming laugh. In China in those days, dark-blue or gray jacket and trousers were the standard gear for men, women, and children. No patterns were allowed. In spite of the uniformity, some women managed to wear their clothes with signs of care and thoughtfulness. But not Yan. She always looked as though she had put her buttons in the wrong holes, and her short hair was pulled back impatiently into an untidy tail. It seemed that not even being in love could induce her to pay attention to her looks.

Yong looked more fashion conscious. He wore a pair of straw sandals, which were set off by rolled-up trouser legs. Straw sandals were a sort of fashion among some students because of their association with the peasants. Yong seemed exceedingly intelligent and sensitive. I was fascinated by him.

After a happy meal, Yan and Yong took their leave. My mother walked downstairs with them, and they whispered to her that she must keep Zhou Enlai's note in a safe place. My mother said nothing to me or my siblings about her meeting with Zhou.

That evening, my mother went to see an old colleague of hers and showed him Zhou's note. Chen Mo had worked with my parents in

Yibin in the early 1950s, and got on well with both of them. He had also managed to maintain a good relationship with the Tings, and when they were rehabilitated he threw in his lot with them. My mother asked him, in tears, to help secure my father's release for old times' sake, and he promised to have a word with the Tings.

Time passed, and then, in April, my father suddenly reappeared. I was tremendously relieved and happy to see him, but almost immediately my joy turned to horror. There was a strange light in his eyes. He would not say where he had been, and when he did speak, I could hardly understand his words. He was sleepless for days and nights on end, and paced up and down the apartment, talking to himself. One day he forced the whole family to go and stand in the pouring rain, telling us this was "to experience the revolutionary storm." Another day, after collecting his salary packet, he threw it into the kitchen stove, saying that this was "to break with private property." The dreadful truth dawned on us: my father had gone insane.

My mother became the focus of his madness. He raged at her, calling her "shameless," "a coward," and accusing her of "selling her soul." Then, without warning, he would become embarrassingly loving toward her in front of the rest of us—saying over and over again how much he loved her, how he had been an unworthy husband, and begging her to "forgive me and come back to me."

On his first day back he had looked at my mother suspiciously and asked her what she had been doing. She told him she had been to Peking to appeal for his release. He shook his head incredulously, and asked her to produce evidence. She decided not to tell him about the note from Zhou Enlai. She could see he was not himself, and was worried he might hand in the note, even to the Tings, if "the Party" ordered him to. She could not even name Yan and Yong as her witnesses: my father would think it was wrong to get involved with a Red Guard faction.

He kept coming back to the issue obsessively. Every day he would cross-examine my mother, and apparent inconsistencies emerged in her story. My father's suspicion and confusion grew. His rage toward my mother began to verge on violence. My siblings and I wanted to help my mother, and tried to make her story, about which we were vague ourselves, sound more convincing. Of course, when my father started to question us, it became even more muddled.

What had happened was that while my father was in prison, his interrogators had constantly told him he would be deserted by his wife and family if he did not write his "confession." Insisting on confessions was a standard practice. Forcing victims to admit their "guilt" was vital in crushing their morale. But my father said he had nothing to confess, and would not write anything.

His interrogators then told him that my mother had denounced him. When he asked for her to be allowed to visit him, he was told she had been given permission, but had refused, to show that she was "drawing a line" between herself and him. When the interrogators realized that my father was beginning to hear things—a sign of schizophrenia—they drew his attention to a faint buzz of conversation from the next room, saying that my mother was in there, but would not see him unless he wrote his confession. The interrogators play-acted so vividly that my father thought he really heard my mother's voice. His mind began to collapse. Still he would not write the confession.

As he was being released, one of his interrogators told him he was being allowed home to be kept under the eyes of his wife, "who has been assigned by the Party to watch you." Home, he was told, was to be his new prison. He did not know the reason for his sudden release, and in his confusion he latched onto this explanation.

My mother knew nothing about what had happened to him in prison. When my father asked her why he had been released, she could not give him a satisfactory answer. Not only could she not tell him about Zhou Enlai's note, she could not mention going to see Chen Mo, who was the right-hand man of the Tings. My father would not have tolerated his wife's "begging for a favor" from the Tings. In this vicious circle, both my mother's dilemma and my father's insanity grew, and fed off each other.

My mother tried to get medical treatment for him. She went to the clinic that had been attached to the old provincial government. She tried the mental hospitals. But as soon as the people at the registration desks heard my father's name, they shook their heads. They could not take him without sanction from the authorities—and they were not prepared to ask for that themselves.

My mother went to the dominant Rebel group in my father's department and asked them to authorize hospitalization. This was the group led by Mrs. Shau, and firmly in the hands of the Tings. Mrs. Shau snarled at my mother that my father was faking mental illness in order to escape his punishment, and that my mother was helping him, using her own medical background (her stepfather, Dr. Xia, having been a doctor). My father was "a dog that has fallen into the water, and must be flogged and beaten with absolutely no charity," said one Rebel, quoting a current slogan vaunting the mercilessness of the Cultural Revolution.

Under instructions from the Tings, the Rebels hounded my father with a wall-poster campaign. Apparently, the Tings had reported to Mme. Mao the "criminal words" my father had used at the denunciation meeting, in his conversation with them, and in his letter to Mao. According to the posters, Mme. Mao had risen to her feet in indignation and said, "For the man who dares to attack the Great Leader so blatantly, imprisonment, even the death sentence, is too kind! He must be thoroughly punished before we have done with him!"

The terror such wall posters induced in me was immense. Mme. Mao had denounced my father! This was surely the end for him. But, paradoxically, one of Mme. Mao's evil traits was actually to help us: Mme. Mao was more dedicated to her personal vendettas than to real issues, and because she did not know my father and had no personal grudge against him, she did not pursue him. We were not to know this, however, and I tried to take comfort in the thought that her reported comment might only be a rumor. In theory, wall posters were unofficial, since they were written by the "masses" and not part of the official media. But, deep down, I knew that what they said was true.

With the Tings' venom and Mme. Mao's condemnation, the Rebels' denunciation meetings became more brutal, even though my father was still allowed to live at home. One day he came back with one of his eyes badly damaged. Another day I saw him standing on a slow-moving truck, being paraded through the streets. A huge placard hung from a thin wire that was eating into his neck, and his arms were twisted ferociously behind his back. He was struggling to keep his head up under the forceful pushing of some Rebels. What made me saddest of all was that he appeared indifferent to his physical pain. In his insanity, his mind seemed to be detached from his body.

He tore to pieces any photographs in the family album which had the Tings in them. He burned his quilt covers and sheets, and much of the family's clothing. He broke the legs of chairs and tables and burned them, too.

One afternoon my mother was having a rest on their bed and Father was reclining on his favorite bamboo armchair in his study, when he suddenly jumped up and stamped into the bedroom. We heard the banging and dashed after him and found him gripping my mother's neck. We screamed and tried to pull him away. It looked as if my mother was going to be strangled. But then he let go with a jerk, and strode out of the room.

My mother sat up slowly, her face ashen. She cupped her left ear in her hand. My father had awakened her by striking her on the side of the head. Her voice was weak, but she was calm. "Don't worry, I'm all right," she said to my sobbing grandmother. Then she turned to us and said, "See how your father is. Then go to your rooms." She leaned back against the oval mirror framed in camphorwood which formed the headboard of the bed. In the mirror I saw her right hand clutching the pillow. My grandmother sat by my parents' door all night. I could not sleep either. What would happen if my father attacked my mother with their door locked?

My mother's left ear was permanently damaged, and became almost totally deaf. She decided it was too dangerous for her to stay at home, and the next day she went to her department to find a place to move to. The Rebels there were very sympathetic. They gave her a room in the gardener's lodge in the corner of the garden. It was terribly small, about eight feet by ten. Only a bed and a desk could be squeezed in, with no space even to walk between them.

That night, I slept there with my mother, my grandmother, and Xiao-fang, all crammed together on the bed. We could not stretch our legs or turn. The bleeding from my mother's womb worsened. We were very frightened because, having just moved to this new place, we had no stove and could not sterilize the syringe and needle, and therefore could not give her an injection. In the end, I was so exhausted I dropped into a fitful sleep. But I knew that neither my grandmother nor my mother closed their eyes.

Over the next few days, while Jin-ming went on living with Father, I stayed at my mother's new place helping to look after her. Living in the next room was a young Rebel leader from my mother's district. I had not said hello to him because I was not sure whether he would want to be spoken to by someone from the family of a capitalist-roader, but to my surprise he greeted us normally when we ran into each other. He treated my mother with courtesy, although he was a bit stiff. This was a great relief after the ostentatious frostiness of the Rebels in my father's department.

One morning a couple of days after we moved in, my mother was washing her face under the eaves because there was no space inside when this man called out to her and asked if she would like to swap rooms. His was twice as big as ours. We moved that afternoon. He also helped us to get another bed so we could sleep in relative comfort. We were very touched.

This young man had a severe squint—and a very pretty girlfriend who stayed overnight with him, which was almost unheard of in those days. They did not seem to mind us knowing. Of course, capitalist-roaders were in no position to tell tales. When I bumped into them in the mornings, they always gave me a very kind smile which told me they were happy. I realized then that when people are happy they become kind.

When my mother's health improved, I went back to Father. The apartment was in a dreadful state: the windows were broken, and there were bits of burned furniture and clothing all over the floor. My father seemed indifferent to whether I was there or not; he just paced incessantly around and around. At night I locked my bedroom door, because he could not sleep and would insist on talking to me, endlessly, without making sense. But there was a small window over the door which could not be locked. One night I woke up to see him slithering through the tiny aperture and jumping nimbly to the floor. But he paid no attention to me. He aimlessly picked up various pieces of heavy mahogany furniture and let them drop with seemingly little effort. In his insanity he had become superhumanly agile and powerful. Staying with him was a nightmare. Many times, I wanted to run away to my mother, but I could not bring myself to leave him.

A couple of times he slapped me, which he had never done before, and I would go and hide in the back garden under the balcony of the apartment. In the chill of the spring nights I listened desperately for the silence upstairs which meant he had gone to sleep.

One day, I missed his presence. I was seized by a presentiment and rushed out of the door. A neighbor who lived on the top floor was walking down the stairs. We had stopped greeting each other some time before in order to avoid trouble, but this time he said: "I saw your father going out onto the roof."

Our apartment block had five stories. I raced to the top floor. On the landing to the left a small window gave onto the flat, shingled roof of the four-story block next door. The roof had low iron rails around the edge. As I was trying to climb through the window, I saw my father at the edge of the roof. I thought I saw him lifting his left leg over the railing.

"Father," I called, in a voice which was trembling, although I was trying to force it to sound normal. My instinct told me I must not alarm him.

He paused, and turned toward me: "What are you doing here?"

"Please come and help me get through the window."

Somehow, I coaxed him away from the edge of the roof. I grabbed his hand and led him onto the landing. I was shaking. Something seemed to have touched him, and an almost normal expression replaced his usual blank indifference or the intense introspective rolling of his eyes. He carried me downstairs to a sofa and even fetched a towel to wipe away my tears. But the signs of normality were short-lived. Before I had recovered from the shock, I had to scramble up and run because he raised his hand and was about to hit me.

Instead of allowing my father medical treatment, the Rebels found his insanity a source of entertainment. A poster serial appeared every other day entitled "The Inside Story of Madman Chang." Its authors, from my father's department, ridiculed and lavished sarcasm on my father. The posters were pasted up in a prime site just outside the department, and drew large, appreciative crowds. I forced myself to read them, although I was aware of the stares from other readers, many of whom knew who I was. I heard them whispering to those who did not know my identity. My heart would tremble with rage and unbearable pain for my father, but I knew that reports of my reactions would reach my father's persecutors. I wanted to look calm, and to let them know that they could not demoralize us. I had no fear or sense of humiliation, only contempt for them.

What had turned people into monsters? What was the reason for all this pointless brutality? It was in this period that my devotion to Mao began to wane. Before when people had been persecuted I could not be absolutely sure of their innocence; but I knew my parents. Doubts about Mao's infallibility crept into my mind, but at that stage, like many people, I mainly blamed his wife and the Cultural Revolution Authority. Mao himself, the godlike Emperor, was still beyond questioning.

We watched my father deteriorate mentally and physically with each passing day. My mother went to ask Chen Mo for help again. He promised to see what he could do. We waited, but nothing happened: his silence meant he must have failed to get the Tings to allow my father to have treatment. In desperation, my mother went to the Red Chengdu headquarters to see Yan and Yong.

The dominant group at Sichuan Medical College was part of Red Chengdu. The college had a psychiatric hospital attached to it, and a word from Red Chengdu headquarters could get my father in. Yan and Yong were very sympathetic, but they would have to convince their comrades.

Humanitarian considerations had been condemned by Mao as "bourgeois hypocrisy," and it went without saying that there should be no mercy for "class enemies." Yan and Yong had to give a political reason for treating my father. They had a good one: he was being persecuted by the Tings. He could supply ammunition against them, perhaps even help to bring them down. This, in turn, could bring about the collapse of 26 August.

There was another reason. Mao had said the new Revolutionary Committees must contain "revolutionary officials" as well as Rebels and members of the armed forces. Both Red Chengdu and 26 August were trying to find officials to represent them on the Sichuan Revolutionary Committee. Besides, the Rebels were beginning to find out how complex politics was, and how daunting a task it was actually to run an administration. They needed competent politicians as advisers. Red Chengdu thought my father was an ideal candidate, and sanctioned medical treatment.

Red Chengdu knew that my father had been denounced for saying blasphemous things against Mao and the Cultural Revolution, and that Mme. Mao had condemned him. But these claims had only been made by their enemies in wall posters, where truth and lies were often mixed up. They could, therefore, dismiss them.

My father was admitted to the mental hospital of Sichuan Medical College. It was in the suburbs of Chengdu, surrounded by rice fields. Bamboo leaves swayed over the brick walls and the iron main gate. A second gate shut off a walled courtyard green with moss—the residential area for the doctors and nurses. At the end of the courtyard, a flight of red sandstone stairs led into the windowless side of a two-story building flanked by solid, high walls. The stairs were the only access to the inside—the psychiatric wards.

The two male nurses who came for my father were dressed in ordinary clothes, and told him they were taking him to another denunciation meeting. When they reached the hospital my father struggled to get away. They dragged him upstairs into a small empty room, shutting the door behind them so my mother and I would not have to see them putting him into a straitjacket. I was heartbroken to see him being so roughly handled, but I knew it was for his own good.

The psychiatrist, Dr. Su, was in his thirties, with a gentle face and professional manner. He told my mother he would spend a week observing my father before he gave a diagnosis. At the end of the week, he reached his conclusion: schizophrenia. My father was given electric shocks and insulin injections, for which he had to be tied tight onto the bed. In a few days, he began to recover his sanity. With tears in his eyes, he begged my mother to ask the doctor to change the treatment. "It is so painful." His voice broke. "It feels worse than death." But Dr. Su said there was no other way.

The next time I saw my father, he was sitting on his bed chatting to my mother and Yan and Yong. They were all smiling. My father was even laughing. He looked well again. I had to pretend to go to the toilet to wipe away my tears.

On the orders of Red Chengdu, my father received special food and a full-time nurse. Yan and Yong visited him often, with members of his department who were sympathetic to him and who had themselves been subjected to denunciation meetings by Mrs. Shau's group.

My father liked Yan and Yong very much, and although he could be unobservant, he realized they were in love, and teased them charmingly. I could see they enjoyed this greatly. At last, I felt, the nightmare was over; now that my father was well, we could face any disasters together.

The treatment lasted about forty days. By mid-July he was back to normal. He was discharged, and he and my mother were taken to Chengdu University, where they were given a suite in a small self-contained courtyard. Student guards were placed on the gate. My father was provided with a pseudonym and told that he should not go out of the courtyard during the day, for his safety. My mother fetched their meals from a special kitchen. Yan and Yong came to see him every day, as did the Red Chengdu leaders, who were all very courteous to him.

I visited my parents there often, riding a borrowed bicycle for an hour on potholed country roads. My father seemed peaceful. He would say over and over again how grateful he felt to these students for enabling him to get treatment.

When it was dark, he was allowed out, and we went for long, quiet strolls on the campus, followed at a distance by a couple of guards. We wandered along the lanes lined with hedges of Cape jasmine. The fist-sized white flowers gave off a strong fragrance in the summer breeze. It seemed like a dream of serenity, so far away from the terror and violence. I knew this was my father's prison, but I wished he would never have to come out.

In the summer of 1967, factional fighting among the Rebels was escalating into mini–civil war all over China. The antagonism between the Rebel factions was far greater than their supposed anger toward the capitalist-roaders, because they were fighting tooth and nail for power. Kang Sheng, Mao's intelligence chief, and Mme. Mao led the Cultural Revolution Authority in stirring up more animosity by calling the factional fighting "an extension of the struggle between the Communists and the Kuomintang"—without specifying which group was which. The Cultural Revolution Authority ordered the army to "arm the Rebels for self-defense," without telling them which factions to support. Inevitably, different army units armed different factions on the basis of their own preferences.

The armed forces were in great upheaval already, because Lin Biao was busy trying to purge his opponents and replace them with his own men. Eventually Mao realized that he could not afford instability in the army, and reined in Lin Biao. However, he appeared to be in two minds about the factional fighting among the Rebels. On the one hand, he wanted the factions to unite so that his personal power structure could be established. On the other hand, he seemed incapable of repressing his love of fighting: as bloody wars spread across China he said, "It is not a bad thing to let the young have some practice in using arms—we haven't had a war for so long."

In Sichuan, the battles were especially fierce, partly because the province was the center of China's arms industry. Tanks, armored cars, and artillery were taken from the production lines and warehouses by both sides. Another cause was the Tings, who set out to eliminate their opponents. In Yibin there was brutal fighting with guns, hand grenades, mortars, and machine guns. Over a hundred people died in the city of Yibin alone. In the end Red Chengdu was forced to abandon the city.

Many went to the nearby city of Luzhou, which was held by Red Chengdu. The Tings dispatched over 5,000 members of 26 August to attack the city, and eventually seized it, killing nearly 300 and wounding many more.

In Chengdu, the fighting was sporadic, and only the most fanatical joined in. Even so, I saw parades of tens of thousands of Rebels carrying the blood-soaked corpses of people killed in battles, and people shooting rifles in the streets.

It was under these circumstances that Red Chengdu made three requests of my father: to announce his support for them; to tell them about the Tings; and to become an adviser and eventually represent them on the Sichuan Revolution Committee.

He refused. He said he could not back one group against another, nor could he provide information against the Tings, as that might aggravate the situation and create more animosity. He also said he would not represent a faction on the Sichuan Revolutionary Committee—indeed, he had no desire to be on it at all.

Eventually, the friendly atmosphere turned ugly. The chiefs of Red Chengdu were split. One group said they had never encountered anyone so incredibly obstinate and perverse. My father had been persecuted to the brink of death, yet he refused to let other people avenge him. He dared to oppose the powerful Rebels who had saved his life. He turned down an offer to be rehabilitated and return to power. In anger and exasperation, some shouted: "Let's give him a good beating. We should at least break a couple of his bones to teach him a lesson!"

But Yan and Yong spoke up for him, as did a few others. "It is rare to see a character like him," said Yong. "It is not right to punish him. He would not bend even if he were beaten to death. And to torture him is to bring shame on us all. Here is a man of principle!"

Despite the threat of beating, and his gratitude to these Rebels, my father would not go against his principles. One night at the end of September 1967 a car brought him and my mother home. Yan and Yong could no longer protect him. They accompanied my parents home, and said goodbye.

My parents immediately fell into the hands of the Tings and Mrs. Shau's group. The Tings made it clear that the attitude staff members took toward my father would determine their future. Mrs. Shau was promised the equivalent of my father's job in the forthcoming Sichuan Revolutionary Committee, provided my father was "thoroughly smashed." Those who showed sympathy to my father were themselves condemned.

One day two men from Mrs. Shau's group came to our apartment to take my father away to a "meeting." Later they returned and told me and my brothers to go to his department to bring him back.

My father was leaning against a wall in the courtyard of the department, in a position which showed that he had been trying to stand up. His face was black and blue, and unbelievably swollen. His head had been half shaved, clearly in a very rough manner.

There had been no denunciation meeting. When he arrived at the office, he was immediately yanked into a small room, where half a dozen large strangers set upon him. They punched and kicked the lower part of his body, especially his genitals. They forced water down his mouth and nose and then stamped on his stomach. Water, blood, and excreta were pressed out. My father fainted.

When he came to, the thugs had disappeared. My father felt terribly thirsty. He dragged himself out of the room, and scooped some water from a puddle in the courtyard. He tried to stand up, but was unable to stay on his feet. Members of Mrs. Shau's group were in the courtyard, but no one lifted a finger to help him.

The thugs came from the 26 August faction in Chongqing, about 150 miles from Chengdu. There had been large-scale battles there, with heavy artillery lobbing shells across the Yangtze. 26 August was driven out of the city, and many members fled to Chengdu, where some were accommodated in our compound. They were restless and frustrated, and told Mrs. Shau's group that their fists "itched to put an end to their vegetarian life and to taste some blood and meat." My father was offered up to them.

That night, my father, who had never once moaned after his previous beatings, cried out in agony. The next morning, my fourteen-year-old brother Jin-ming raced to the compound kitchen as soon as it was open to borrow a cart to take him to the hospital. Xiao-hei, then thirteen, went out and bought a hair clipper, and cut the remaining hair from my father's half-shaved head. When he saw his bald head in the mirror, my father gave a wry smile. "This is good. I won't have to worry about my hair being pulled next time I'm at a denunciation meeting."

We put my father on the cart and pulled him to a nearby orthopedic hospital. This time we did not need authorization to get him looked at, as his ailment had nothing to do with the mind. Mental illness was a very sensitive area. Bones had no ideological color. The doctor was very warm. When I saw how carefully he touched my father, a lump rose in my throat. I had seen so much shoving, slapping, and hitting, and so little gentleness.

The doctor said two of my father's ribs were broken. But he could not be hospitalized. That needed authorization. Besides, there were far too many severe injuries for the hospital to accommodate. It was crammed with people who had been wounded in the denunciation meetings and the factional fighting. I saw a young man on a stretcher with a third of his head gone. His companion told us he had been hit by a hand grenade.

My mother went to see Chen Mo again, and asked him to put in a word with the Tings to stop my father's beatings. A few days later Chen told my mother the Tings were prepared to "forgive" my father if he would write a wall poster singing the praises of "good officials" Liu Jie-ting and Zhang Xi-ting. He emphasized that they had just been given renewed full, explicit backing by the Cultural Revolution Authority, and Zhou Enlai had specifically stated that he regarded the Tings as "good officials." To continue to oppose them, Chen told my mother, was tantamount to "throwing an egg against a rock." When my mother told my father, he said, "There's nothing good to say about them." "But," she implored him tearfully, "this is not to get your job back, or even for rehabilitation, it's for your life! What is a poster compared to a life?" "I will not sell my soul," answered my father.

For over a year, until the end of 1968, my father was in and out of detention, along with most of the former leading officials in the provincial government. Our apartment was constantly raided and turned upside down. Detention was now called "Mao Zedong Thought Study Courses." The pressure in these "courses" was such that many groveled to the Tings; some committed suicide. But my father never gave in to the Tings' demands to work with them. He would say later how much having a loving family had helped him. Most of those who committed suicide did so after their families had disowned them. We visited my father in detention whenever we were allowed, which was seldom, and surrounded him with affection whenever he was home for a fleeting stay.

The Tings knew that my father loved my mother very much, and tried to break him through her. Intense pressure was put on her to denounce him. She had many reasons to resent my father. He had not invited her mother to their wedding. He had let her walk hundreds of agonizing miles, and had not given her much sympathy in her crises. In Yibin he had refused to let her go to a better hospital for a dangerous birth. He had always given the Party and the revolution priority over her. But my mother had understood and respected my father—and had above all never ceased to love him. She would particularly stand by him now that he was in trouble. No amount of suffering could bring her to denounce him.

My mother's own department turned a deaf ear to the Tings' orders to torment her, but Mrs. Shau's group was happy to oblige, and so were some other organizations which had nothing to do with her. Altogether, she had to go through about a hundred denunciation meetings. Once she was taken to a rally of tens of thousands of people in the People's Park in the center of Chengdu to be denounced. Most of the participants had no idea who she was. She was not nearly important enough to merit such a mass event.

My mother was condemned for all sorts of things, not least for having a warlord general as a father. The fact that General Xue had died when she was barely two made no difference.

In those days, every capitalist-roader had one or more teams investigating his or her past in minute detail, because Mao wanted the history of everyone working for him thoroughly checked. At different times my mother had four different teams investigating her, the last of which contained about fifteen people. They were sent to various parts of China. It was through these investigations that my mother came to know the whereabouts of her old friends and relatives with whom she had lost contact for years. Most of the investigators just went sight-seeing and returned with nothing incriminating, but one group came back with a "scoop."

Back in Jinzhou in the late 1940s, Dr. Xia had let a room to the Communist agent Yu-wu, who had been my mother's boss, in charge of collecting military information and smuggling it out of the city. Yu-wu's own controller, who was unknown to my mother then, had been pretending to work for the Kuomintang. During the Cultural Revolution, he was put under intense pressure to confess to being a Kuomintang spy, and was tortured atrociously. In the end, he "confessed," inventing a spy ring which included Yu-wu.

Yu-wu was tortured ferociously as well. In order to avoid incriminating other people, he killed himself by slashing his wrists. He did not mention my mother. But the investigation team found out about their connection and claimed that she was a member of the "spy ring."

Her teenage contact with the Kuomintang was dragged up. All the questions that had come up in 1955 were gone over again. This time they were not asked in order to get an answer. My mother was simply ordered to admit that she was a Kuomintang spy. She argued that the investigation in 1955 had cleared her, but she was told that the chief investigator then, Mr. Kuang, was a "traitor and Kuomintang spy" himself.

Mr. Kuang had been imprisoned by the Kuomintang in his youth. The Kuomintang had promised to release underground Communists if they signed a recantation for publication in the local newspaper. At first he and his comrades had refused, but the Party instructed them to accept. They were told the Party needed them, and did not mind "anti-Communist statements" which were not sincere. Mr. Kuang followed orders and was duly released.

Many others had done the same thing. In one famous case in 1936, sixty-one imprisoned Communists were released this way. The order to "recant" was given by the Party Central Committee and delivered by Liu Shaoqi. Some of these sixty-one subsequently became top officials in the Communist government, including vice-premiers, ministers, and first secretaries of provinces. During the Cultural Revolution, Mme. Mao and Kang Sheng announced that they were "sixty-one big traitors and spies." The verdict was endorsed by Mao personally, and these people were subjected to the cruelest tortures. Even people remotely connected with them got into deadly trouble.

Following this precedent, hundreds of thousands of former underground workers and their contacts, some of the bravest men and women who had fought for a Communist China, were charged with being "traitors and spies" and suffered detention, brutal denunciation meetings, and torture. According to a later official account, in the province next to Sichuan, Yunnan, over 14,000 people died. In Hebei province, which surrounds Peking, 84,000 were detained and tortured; thousands died. My mother learned years later that her first boyfriend, Cousin Hu, was among them. She had thought he had been executed by the Kuomintang, but his father had in fact bought him out of prison with gold bars. No one would ever tell my mother how he died.

Mr. Kuang fell under the same accusation. Under torture, he attempted suicide, unsuccessfully. The fact that he had cleared my mother in 1956 was alleged to prove her "guilt." She was kept in various forms of detention on and off for nearly two years—from late 1967 to October 1969. Her conditions depended largely on her guards. Some were kind to her—when they were alone. One of them, the wife of an army officer, got medicine for her hemorrhage. She also asked her husband, who had access to privileged food supplies, to bring my mother milk, eggs, and chicken every week.

Thanks to kindhearted guards like her, my mother was allowed home several times for a few days. The Tings learned of this, and the kind guards were replaced by a sour-faced woman whom my mother did not know, who tormented and tortured her for pleasure. When the fancy took her, she would make my mother stand bent over in the courtyard for hours. In the winter, she would make her kneel in cold water until she passed out. Twice she put my mother on what was called a "tiger bench." My mother had to sit on a narrow bench with her legs stretched out in front of her. Her torso was tied to a pillar and her thighs to the bench so she could not move or bend her legs. Then bricks were forced under her heels. The intention was to break the knees or the hipbones. Twenty years before, in Jinzhou, she had been threatened with this in the Kuomintang torture chamber. The "tiger bench" had to stop because the guard needed men to help her push in the bricks; they helped reluctantly a couple of times, but then refused to have any more to do with it. Years later the woman was diagnosed as a psychopath, and today is in a psychiatric hospital.

My mother signed many "confessions," admitting that she had sympathized with a "capitalist road." But she refused to denounce my father, and she denied all "spy" charges, which she knew would inevitably lead to the incrimination of others.

During her detention we were often not allowed to see her, and even had no idea where she was. I would wander the streets outside the possible places in the hope of catching sight of her.

There was a period when she was detained in a deserted cinema on the main shopping street. There we were occasionally permitted to deliver a parcel for her to a warden, or to see her for a few minutes, although never on her own. When a fierce guard was on duty, we had to sit under freezing eyes. One day in autumn 1968 I went there to deliver a food parcel and was told it could not be accepted. No reason was given, and I was told not to send things anymore. When my grandmother heard the news she passed out. She thought my mother must be dead.

It was unbearable not knowing what had happened to my mother. I took my six-year-old brother Xiao-fang by the hand and went to the cinema. We walked up and down the street in front of the gate. We searched the rows of windows on the second floor. In desperation we screamed "Mother! Mother!" at the top of our voices again and again. Passersby stared at us, but I took no notice. I just wanted to see her. My brother cried. But my mother did not appear.

Years later, she told me that she had heard us. In fact, her psychopath guard had opened the window slightly so our voices would be louder. My mother was told that if she agreed to denounce my father, and to confess to being a Kuomintang spy, she could see us immediately. "Otherwise," said the guard, "you may never get out of this building alive." My mother said no. All the time, she dug her nails into her palms to stop her tears from falling.

21. "Giving Charcoal in Snow"— My Siblings and My Friends

(1967–1968)

Throughout 1967 and 1968, while Mao struggled to set up his personal power system, he kept his victims, like my parents, in a state of uncertainty and suffering. Human anguish did not concern Mao. People existed only to help him realize his strategic plans. But his purpose was not genocide, and my family, like many other victims, were not deliberately starved. My parents still received their salaries every month in spite of the fact that not only were they doing no work, they were also being denounced and tormented. The main compound canteen was working normally to enable the Rebels to carry on with their "revolution," and we, like the families of other capitalist-roaders, were fed. We also got the same rations from the state as everyone else in the cities.

Much of the urban population was kept "on hold" for the revolution. Mao wanted the population to fight, but to live. He protected the extremely capable premier, Zhou Enlai, so that he could keep the economy going. He knew he needed another first-class administrator in reserve in case anything happened to Zhou, so he kept Deng Xiaoping in relative security. The country was not allowed to collapse totally.

But, as the revolution dragged on, large parts of the economy slipped into paralysis. The urban population increased by several tens of millions, but virtually no new housing or other service facilities were built in the towns. Nearly everything, from salt, toothpaste, and toilet paper to every kind of food and clothing, either was rationed or disappeared completely. In Chengdu there was no sugar for a year, and six months passed without a single bar of soap.

Starting from June 1966, there was no schooling. The teachers either had been denounced or were organizing their own Rebel groups. No school meant no control. But what could we do with our freedom? There were virtually no books, no music, no films, no theater, no museums, no teahouses, almost no way of keeping oneself occupied—except cards, which, though not officially sanctioned, made a stealthy comeback. Unlike most revolutions, in Mao's there was nothing to do. Naturally, "Red Guardship" became many youngsters' full-time occupation. The only ways they could release their energy and frustration were in violent denunciations and in physical and verbal battles with each other.

Joining the Red Guards was not compulsory. With the disintegration of the Party system, control over individuals loosened, and most of the population was left alone. Many people just stayed idle at home, and one result was an explosion of petty fights. Surliness replaced the good service and polite behavior of the pre–Cultural Revolution days. It became extremely common to see people quarreling on the streets —with shop assistants, with bus conductors, with passersby. Another result was that, since no one was looking after birth control, there was a baby boom. The population increased during the Cultural Revolution by two hundred million.

By the end of 1966 my teenage siblings and I had decided that we had had enough of being Red Guards. Children in condemned families were supposed to "draw a line" between themselves and their parents, and many did so. One of President Liu Shaoqi's daughters wrote wall posters "exposing" her father. I knew children who changed their surnames to demonstrate that they were disowning their fathers, others who never visited their parents in detention, and some who even took part in denunciation meetings against their parents.

Once, when my mother was under tremendous pressure to divorce my father, she asked us what we thought. Standing by him meant we could become "blacks"; we had all seen the discrimination and torment such people suffered. But we said we would stick by him, come what may. My mother said she was pleased and proud of us. Our devotion to our parents was increased by our empathy for their suffering, our admiration for their integrity and courage, and our loathing for their tormentors. We came to feel a new degree of respect, and love, for our parents.

We grew up fast. We had no rivalries, no squabbles, and no resentment of each other, none of the usual problems—or pleasures—of teenagers. The Cultural Revolution destroyed normal adolescence, with all its pitfalls, and threw us straight into sensible adulthood in our early teens.

At the age of fourteen, my love for my parents had an intensity that could not have existed under normal circumstances. My life revolved entirely around them. Whenever they were briefly at home, I would watch their moods, trying to provide amusing company. When they were in detention, I would repeatedly go to the disdainful-looking Rebels and demand a visit. Sometimes I would be allowed a few minutes to sit and talk with one of my parents, in the company of a guard. I would tell them how much I loved them. I became well known among the former staff of the Sichuan government and the Eastern District of Chengdu, and an irritation to my parents' tormentors, who also hated me for refusing to show fear of them. Once Mrs. Shau screamed that I "looked straight through" her. Their fury led them to invent the accusation, printed on one of their wall posters, that Red Chengdu had given my father treatment because I had used my body to seduce Yong.

Apart from being with my parents, I spent most of my abundant free time with friends. After I came back from Peking in December 1966, I went for a month to an airplane maintenance factory on the outskirts of Chengdu with Plumpie and Ching-ching, a friend of hers. We needed something to occupy ourselves, and the most important thing we could do, according to Mao, was to go to factories to stir up rebellious actions against capitalist-roaders. Upheaval was invading industry too slowly for Mao's liking.

The only action the three of us stirred up was the attention of some young men from the now defunct factory basketball team. We spent a lot of time strolling on the country roads together, enjoying the rich evening scent of the early bean blossoms. But soon, as my parents' suffering worsened, I went home, leaving Mao's orders and my participation in the Cultural Revolution behind once and for all.

My friendship with Plumpie, Ching-ching, and the basketball players lasted. Also in our circle were my sister Xiao-hong and several other girls from my school. They were all older than I. We would meet frequently in the home of one or another of us, and linger there for the whole day, and often the night as well, having nothing else to do.

We had endless discussions about which of the basketball players fancied whom. The captain of the team, a handsome nineteen-year-old called Sai, was the center of speculation. The girls wondered whether he liked me or Ching-ching more. He was reticent and reserved, and Ching-ching was very keen on him. Every time we were going to see him, she would meticulously wash and comb her shoulder-length hair, carefully iron and adjust her clothes to look stylish, and even put on a little powder and rouge and pencil her eyebrows. We all teased her gently.

I was also drawn to Sai. I could feel my heart pound whenever I thought of him, and would wake up at night seeing his face and feeling feverishly hot. I often murmured his name and talked to him in my mind whenever I felt fear or worry. But I never revealed anything to him, or to my friends, or even to myself explicitly. I only timidly fantasized about him. My parents dominated my life and my conscious thoughts. Any indulgence in my own affairs was immediately suppressed as being disloyal. The Cultural Revolution had deprived me of, or spared me, a normal girlhood with tantrums, bickerings, and boyfriends.

But I was not without vanity. I sewed big blue wax-dyed, abstract-patterned patches on the knees and seat of my trousers, which had faded to pale gray. My friends would laugh at the sight of them. My grandmother was scandalized, and complained, "No other girls dress like you." But I insisted. I was not trying to make myself look beautiful, just different.

One day one of my friends told us that her parents, both distinguished actors, had just committed suicide, unable to stand the denunciations. Not long after, news came that the brother of another girl had killed himself. He had been a student at the Peking Aeronautical College, and he and some fellow students had been denounced for trying to organize an anti-Mao party. He threw himself out of a third-floor window when the police came to arrest him. Some of his fellow "conspirators" were executed; others were given life sentences, the normal punishment for anyone attempting to organize an opposition, which was rare. Tragedies like this were part of our everyday life.

The families of Plumpie, Ching-ching, and some others were not hit. And they remained my friends. They were not harassed by my parents' persecutors, who could not extend their power to that degree. But they still ran risks by not swimming with the tide. My friends were among the millions who held sacred the traditional Chinese code of loyalty—"giving charcoal in snow." The fact that they were there helped me through the worst years of the Cultural Revolution.

They gave me a lot of practical help, too. Toward the end of 1967 Red Chengdu began to attack our compound, which was controlled by 26 August, and our block was turned into a fortress. We were ordered to move from our third-floor apartment into some ground-floor rooms in the next block.

My parents were in detention at the time. My father's department, which would normally have looked after the move, now only gave us our marching orders. As there were no furniture-removal companies, without the help of our friends my family would have ended up without a bed. Still, we moved only the most essential furniture, leaving things like my father's heavy bookcases behind; we could not lift them, let alone cart them down several flights of stairs.

Our new quarters were in an apartment already occupied by the family of another capitalist-roader, who were now ordered to vacate half of it. Apartments were being reorganized like this all over the compound so the top floors could be used as command posts. My sister and I shared a room. We kept the window facing the now deserted back garden permanently shut, because the moment it was opened, a strong stench would flood in from the blocked drains outside. At night, we heard cries for surrender from outside the compound wall, and sporadic shooting. One night I was awakened by the sound of shattering glass: a bullet had come through the window and embedded itself in the wall opposite. Strangely, I was not frightened. After the horrors I had been through, bullets had lost their effect.

To occupy myself, I began writing poetry in classical styles. The first poem with which I felt satisfied was written on my sixteenth birthday, 25 March 1968. There was no birthday celebration. Both my parents were in detention. That night, as I lay in bed listening to the gunshots and the Rebels' loudspeakers blaring out bloodcurdling diatribes, I reached a turning point. I had always been told, and had believed, that I was living in a paradise on earth, socialist China, whereas the capitalist world was hell. Now I asked myself: If this is paradise, what then is hell? I decided that I would like to see for myself whether there was indeed a place more full of pain. For the first time, I consciously hated the regime I lived under, and craved an alternative.

Still, I subconsciously avoided Mao. He had been part of my life ever since I was a child. He was the idol, the god, the inspiration. The purpose of my life had been formulated in his name. A couple of years before, I would happily have died for him. Although his magic power had vanished from inside me, he was still sacred and undoubtable. Even now, I did not challenge him.

It was in this mood that I composed my poem. I wrote about the death of my indoctrinated and innocent past as dead leaves being swept from a tree by the whirlwind and carried to a world of no return. I described my bewilderment at the new world, at not knowing what and how to think. It was a poem of groping in the dark, searching.

I wrote the poem down, and was lying in bed going over it in my head when I heard banging on the door. From the sound, I knew it was a house raid. Mrs. Shau's Rebels had raided our apartment several times. They had taken away "bourgeois luxury items" like my grandmother's elegant clothes from the pre-Communist days, my mother's fur-lined Manchurian coat, and my father's suits—even though they were Mao-style. They even confiscated my woolen trousers. They kept coming back to try to find "evidence" against my father. I had grown used to our quarters being turned upside down.

I was seized with anxiety about what would happen if they saw my poem. When my father first came under attack he asked my mother to burn his poems; he knew how writing, any writing, could be twisted against its author. But my mother could not bring herself to destroy them all. She kept a few which he had written for her. These cost him several brutal denunciation meetings.

In one poem my father poked fun at himself for failing to climb to the top of a scenic mountain. Mrs. Shau and her comrades accused him of "lamenting his frustrated ambition to usurp China's supreme leadership."

In another, he described working at night:

The light shines whiter when the night grows darker,
My pen races to meet the dawn . . .

The Rebels claimed he was referring to socialist China as "dark night," and that he was working with his pen to welcome a "white dawn"—a Kuomintang comeback (white was the color of counterrevolution). In those days it was commonplace for such ridiculous interpretations to be forced upon someone's writings. Mao, who was a lover of classical poetry, did not think of making it an exception to this ghastly rule. Writing poetry became a highly dangerous occupation.

When the pounding on the door began, I quickly ran to the toilet, and locked the door while my grandmother answered Mrs. Shau and her posse. My hands trembling, I managed to tear the poem into tiny pieces, throw them into the bowl, and flush the toilet. I searched the floor carefully to make sure no pieces had fallen out. But the paper did not all disappear the first time. I had to wait and flush again. By now the Rebels were banging on the door of the toilet, curtly ordering me to come out immediately. I did not answer.

My brother Jin-ming also got a fright that night. Ever since the Cultural Revolution had started, he had been frequenting a black market specializing in books. The commercial instinct of the Chinese is so strong that black markets, Mao's greatest capitalist *bête noire*, existed right through the crushing pressure of the Cultural Revolution.

In the center of Chengdu, in the middle of the main shopping street, was a bronze statue of Sun Yat-sen, who had led the 1911 republican revolution which had overthrown 2,000 years of imperial rule. The statue had been erected before the Communists came to power. Mao was not particularly keen on any revolutionary leaders before himself, including Sun. But it was politic to lay claim to his tradition, so the statue was allowed to stay, and the patch of ground around it became a plant nursery. When the Cultural Revolution broke out, Red Guards attacked emblems of Sun Yat-sen until Zhou Enlai slapped a protection order on them. The statue survived, but the plant nursery was abandoned as "bourgeois decadence." When Red Guards began raiding people's houses and burning their books, a small crowd started to gather on this deserted ground to deal in the volumes which had escaped the bonfires. All manner of people were to be found there: Red Guards who wanted to make some cash from the books they had confiscated; frustrated entrepreneurs who smelled money; scholars who did not want their books to be burned but were afraid of keeping them; and book lovers. The books being traded had all been published or sanctioned under the Communist regime before the Cultural Revolution. Apart from Chinese classics, they included Shakespeare, Dickens, Byron, Shelley, Shaw, Thackeray, Tolstoy, Dostoyevsky, Turgenev, Chekhov, Ibsen, Balzac, Maupassant, Flaubert, Dumas, Zola, and many other world classics. Even Conan Doyle's Sherlock Holmes, who had been a great favorite in China.

The price of the books depended on a variety of factors. If they had a library stamp in them, most people shunned them. The Communist government had such a reputation for control and order that people did not want to risk being caught with illegally gotten state property, for which they would be severely punished. They were much happier buying privately owned books with no identification marks. Novels with erotic passages commanded the highest prices, and also carried the greatest danger. Stendhal's *Le Rouge et le Noir*, considered erotic, cost the equivalent of two weeks' wages for an average person.

Jin-ming went to this black market every day. His initial capital came from books which he had obtained from a paper recycling shop, to which frightened citizens were selling their collections as scrap paper. Jin-ming had chatted up a shop assistant and bought a lot of these books, which he resold at much higher prices. He then bought more books at the black market, read them, sold them, and bought more.

Between the start of the Cultural Revolution and the end of 1968, at least a thousand books passed through his hands. He read at the rate of one or two a day. He only dared to keep a dozen or so at any one time, and had to hide them carefully. One of his hiding places was under an abandoned water tower in the compound, until a downpour destroyed a stock of his favorites, including Jack London's *The Call of the Wild*. He kept a few at home stashed in the mattresses and the corners of our storeroom. On the night of the house raid he had *Le Rouge et le Noir* hidden in his bed. But, as always, he had torn the cover off and replaced it with that of *The Selected Works of Mao Zedong*, and Mrs. Shau and her comrades did not examine it.

Jin-ming dealt in other black-market goods as well. His enthusiasm for science had not waned. At the time, the only black market dealing in scientific goods in Chengdu traded in semi-conductor radio parts: this branch of industry was in favor because it "spread Chairman Mao's words." Jin-ming bought parts and made his own radios, which he sold at good prices. He bought more parts for his real purpose: testing various theories in physics which had been nagging him.

To get money for his experiments, he even dealt in Mao badges. Many factories had stopped normal production to produce aluminum badges with Mao's head on them. Collecting of any kind, including stamps and paintings, had been banned as a "bourgeois habit." So people's instinct for collecting turned to this sanctioned object— although they could only deal in it clandestinely. Jin-ming made a small fortune. Little did the Great Helmsman know that even the image of his head had become a piece of property for capitalist speculation, the very activity he had tried so hard to stamp out.

There were repeated clampdowns. Often truckloads of Rebels would arrive, seal off the streets, and grab anyone who looked suspicious. Sometimes they sent spies who pretended to be browsing. Then a whistle would blow and they would swoop on the dealers. Those who were caught had their belongings confiscated. They were usually beaten. One regular punishment was "bloodletting"—stabbing them in the buttocks. Some were tortured, and all were threatened with double punishment if they did not stop. But most came back, again and again.

My second brother, Xiao-hei, was twelve at the beginning of 1967. Having nothing to do, he soon found himself involved in a street gang. Virtually nonexistent before the Cultural Revolution, these were now flourishing. A gang was called a "dock," and its leader the "helmsman." Everyone else was a "brother," and had a nickname, usually with some connection with animals: "Thin Dog" if a boy was thin; "Gray Wolf" if he had a lock of gray hair. Xiao-hei was called "Black Hoof" because part of his name, *hei*, means "black," and also because he was dark, and was swift at running errands, which was one of his duties, as he was younger than most of the gang members.

At first the gangsters treated him as a revered guest, because they had rarely known any high officials' children. Gang members tended to come from poor families, and had often been school dropouts before the Cultural Revolution. Their families were not targets of the revolution, and they were not interested in it, either.

Some boys sought to imitate the ways of the high officials' children, disregarding the fact that the high officials had been toppled. In their Red Guard days, the high officials' children favored old Communist army uniforms, as they were the only people who had access to these through their parents. Some street boys got the old gear through black-market trading, or dyed their clothes green. But they lacked the haughty air of the elite, and their green was often not quite the right shade. They were sneered at by high officials' children, as well as by their own friends, as "pseuds."

Later the high officials' children switched to wearing dark-blue jackets and trousers. Although most of the population was wearing blue at the time, theirs was a particular shade, and it was also unusual to wear the same color top and bottom. After they had made this their distinguishing sign, boys and girls from other backgrounds had to avoid it, if they did not want to be treated as pseuds. The same went for a certain kind of shoes: black cord uppers with white plastic soles and a white plastic band showing in between.

Some gang members invented their own style. They wore many layers of shirts under an outer garment, and turned out all their collars. The more collars you turned out, the smarter you were considered to be. Often Xiao-hei wore six or seven shirts under his jacket —and two even in the boiling summer heat. Jogging pants always had to show under their shortened trousers. They also wore white sneakers without laces, and sported army caps, with cardboard strips tucked inside to make the peaks stick up so they looked imposing.

One of the main ways in which Xiao-hei's "brothers" occupied their empty days was stealing. Whatever they got, their haul had to be handed over to the helmsman to be divided up evenly among them. Xiao-hei was too afraid to steal anything, but his brothers gave him his share without demur.

Theft was extremely widespread during the Cultural Revolution, particularly pickpocketing and stealing bicycles. Most people I knew had their pockets picked at least once. For me, shopping trips often involved either losing my own purse or seeing someone yelling because their purse had been stolen. The police, who had split into factions, exercised only token surveillance.

When foreigners first came to China in large numbers in the 1970s, many were impressed by the "moral cleanliness" of the society: a discarded sock would follow its owner a thousand miles from Peking to Guangzhou, cleaned and folded and placed in his hotel room. The visitors did not realize that only foreigners and Chinese under close surveillance received such attention, or that no one would dare to steal from foreigners, because taking even a handkerchief was likely to be punished by death. The clean folded sock bore no relation to the real state of society: it was just part of the regime's theater.

Xiao-hei's brothers were also obsessed with chasing girls. The twelve- and thirteen-year-olds like Xiao-hei were often too shy to go after girls themselves, so they became the older boys' messengers, delivering their error-riddled love letters. Xiao-hei would knock on a door, praying that it would be opened by the girl herself and not her father or brother, who was sure to slap him across the head. Sometimes, when fear got the upper hand, he would slip the letter under the door.

When a girl rejected a proposal, Xiao-hei and other younger boys became the tool of revenge of the spurned lover, making noises outside her house and firing catapults at her window. When the girl came out, they spat at her, swore at her, shook their middle fingers at her, and yelled dirty words which they did not fully understand. Abusive Chinese terms for women are rather graphic: "shuttle" (for the shape of her genitals), "horse saddle" (for the image of being mounted), "overspilling oil lamp" ("too frequent" discharge), and "worn-out shoes" (much "used").

Some girls tried to find protectors in the gangs, and the more capable ones became helmswomen themselves. The girls who became involved in this male world sported their own picturesque sobriquets, like "Dewy Black Peony," "Broken Wine Vessel," "Snake Enchantress."

The third major occupation of the gangs was fighting, at the slightest provocation. Xiao-hei was very excited by the fights, but much to his regret, he was endowed with what he called "a cowardly disposition." He would run away at the first sign that a battle was turning ugly. Thanks to his lack of bravado, he survived intact while many boys were injured, even killed, in these pointless exchanges.

One afternoon, he and some of his brothers were loitering about as usual when a member of the gang rushed over and said the home of a brother had just been raided by another dock, and this brother had been subjected to a "bloodletting." They went back to their own "dockyard" to collect their weapons—sticks, bricks, knives, wire whips, and cudgels. Xiao-hei tucked a three-section cudgel into his leather belt. They ran to the house where the incident had occurred, but found that their enemies had gone and their wounded brother had been taken to a hospital by his family. Xiao-hei's helmsman wrote a letter, peppered with errors, throwing down the gauntlet to the other gang, and Xiao-hei was charged with delivering it.

The letter demanded a formal fight in the People's Sports Stadium, where there was plenty of space. The stadium no longer hosted any kind of sport now, competitive games having been condemned by Mao. Athletes had to devote themselves to the Cultural Revolution.

On the appointed day, Xiao-hei's gang of several dozen boys waited on the running track. Two slow hours passed, then a man in his early twenties limped into the stadium. It was "Lame Man" Tang, a famous figure in the Chengdu underworld. In spite of his relative youth, he was treated with the respect normally reserved for the old.

Lame Man Tang had become lame from polio. His father had been a Kuomintang official, and so the son was allocated an undesirable job in a small workshop located in his old family house, which the Communists had confiscated. Employees in small units like this did not enjoy the benefits available to workers in big factories, such as guaranteed employment, free health services, and a pension.

His background had prevented Tang from going on to higher education, but he was extremely bright, and became the *de facto* chief of the Chengdu underworld. Now he had come at the request of the other dock, to ask for a truce. He produced several cartons of the best cigarettes and handed them around. He delivered apologies from the other dock, and their promise to foot the bills for the damaged house and the medical care. Xiao-hei's helmsman accepted: it was impossible to say no to Lame Man Tang.

Lame Man Tang was soon arrested. By the beginning of 1968, a new, fourth stage of the Cultural Revolution had started. Phase One had been the teenage Red Guards; then came the Rebels and the attacks on capitalist-roaders; the third phase had been the factional wars among the Rebels. Mao now decided to halt the factional fighting. To bring about obedience, he spread terror to show that no one was immune. A sizable part of the hitherto unaffected population, including some Rebels, now became victims. New political campaigns were cranked up one after another to consume new class enemies. The largest of these witch-hunts, "Clean Up the Class Ranks," claimed Lame Man Tang. He was released after the end of the Cultural Revolution in 1976, and in the early 1980s he became an entrepreneur and a millionaire, one of the richest men in Chengdu. His dilapidated family house was returned to him. He tore it down and built a grand two-story edifice. When the craze for discos hit China he was often to be seen sitting in the most prominent spot, benignly watching the young boys and girls of his entourage dancing while he slowly counted out a thick wad of bank notes with emphatic, deliberate nonchalance, paying for the whole crowd and reveling in his newfound power—money.

The "Clean Up the Class Ranks" campaign ruined the lives of millions. In one single case, the so-called Inner Mongolia People's Party affair, some ten percent of the adult Mongolian population were subjected to torture or physical maltreatment; at least twenty thousand died. This particular campaign was modeled on pilot studies of six factories and two universities in Peking, which were under Mao's personal supervision. In a report on one of the six factories, the Xinhua Printing Unit, there was a passage which read: "After this woman was labeled a counterrevolutionary, one day when she was doing forced labor and the guard turned his eyes away, she rushed up to the fourth floor of the women's dormitory, jumped out of a window, and killed herself. Of course, it is inevitable that counterrevolutionaries should kill themselves. But it is a pity that we now have one less 'negative example.' " Mao wrote on this report: "This is the best written of all the similar reports I have read."

This and other campaigns were managed by the Revolutionary Committees which were being set up all over the country. The Sichuan Provincial Revolutionary Committee was established on 2 June 1968. Its leaders were the same four people who had headed the Preparatory Committee—the two army chiefs and the Tings. The committee included the chiefs of the two major Rebel camps, Red Chengdu and 26 August, and some of "revolutionary officials."

This consolidation of Mao's new power system had profound effects on my family. One of the first results was a decision to withhold part of the salaries of the capitalist-roaders and only to leave each dependent a small monthly cash allowance. Our family income was cut by more than half. Although we were not starving, we could no longer afford to buy from the black market, and the state supply of food was deteriorating fast. The meat ration, for instance, was half a pound per person per month. My grandmother worried and planned day and night to enable us children to eat better, and to produce food parcels for our parents in detention.

The next decision of the Revolutionary Committee was to order all the capitalist-roaders out of the compound to make room for the new leaders. My family was assigned some rooms at the top of a three-story house which had been the office of a now defunct magazine. There was no running water or toilet on the top floor. We had to go downstairs even to brush our teeth, or to pour away a cup of leftover tea. But I did not mind, because the house was so elegant, and I was thirsty for beautiful things.

Unlike our apartment in the compound, which was in a featureless cement block, our new residence was a splendid brick-and-timber double-fronted mansion with exquisitely framed reddish brown-colored windows under gracefully curving eaves. The back garden was dense with mulberry trees, and the front garden had a thick vine trellis, a grove of oleander, a paper mulberry, and a huge nameless tree whose pepperlike fruit grew in little clusters inside the folds of its boat-shaped brown and crispy leaves. I particularly loved the ornamental bananas and their long arc of leaves, an unusual sight in a nontropical climate.

In those days, beauty was so despised that my family was sent to this lovely house as a punishment. The main room was big and rectangular, with a parquet floor. Three sides were glass, which made it brilliantly light and on a clear day offered a panoramic view of the distant snowy mountains of west Sichuan. The balcony was not made of the usual cement, but of wood painted a reddish brown color, with "Greek key" patterned railings. Another room which opened onto the balcony had an unusually high, pointed ceiling—about twenty feet in height—with exposed, faded scarlet beams. I fell in love with our new residence at once. Later I realized that in winter the rectangular room was a battlefield of bitter winds from all directions through the thin glass, and dust fell like rain from the high ceiling when the wind blew. Still, on a calm night, lying in bed with the moonlight filtering through the windows, and the shadow of the tall paper mulberry tree dancing on the wall, I was filled with joy. I was so relieved to be out of the compound and all its dirty politics that I hoped my family would never go near it again.

I loved our new street as well. It was called Meteorite Street, because hundreds of years before a meteorite had fallen there. The street was paved with crushed cobblestones, which I much preferred to the asphalt surface of the street outside the compound.

The only thing that reminded me of the compound was some of our neighbors, who worked in my father's department and belonged to Mrs. Shau's Rebels. When they looked at us it was with expressions of steely rigidity, and on the rare, unavoidable occasions when we had to communicate, they spoke to us in barks. One of them had been the editor of the closed-down magazine, and his wife had been a schoolteacher. They had a boy of six called Jo-jo, the same age as my brother Xiao-fang. A minor government official, with a five-year-old daughter, came to stay with them, and the three children often played together in the garden. My grandmother was anxious about Xiao-fang playing with them, but she dared not forbid him—our neighbors might interpret this as hostility toward Chairman Mao's Rebels.

At the foot of the wine-red spiral staircase which led to our rooms was a big half-moon-shaped table. In the old days, a huge porcelain vase would have been placed on it with a bouquet of winter jasmine or peach blossom. Now it was bare, and the three children often played on it. One day, they were playing "doctor": Jo-jo was the doctor, Xiao-fang a nurse, and the five-year-old girl the patient. She lay on her stomach on the table and pulled her skirt up for an injection. Xiao-fang held a piece of wood from the back of a broken chair as his "needle." At this moment, the girl's mother came up the sandstone steps onto the landing. She screamed and snatched her daughter off the table.

She found a few scratches on the child's inner thigh. Instead of taking her to a hospital, she fetched some Rebels from my father's office a couple of streets away. A crowd soon marched into the front garden. My mother, who happened to be home for a few days from detention, was immediately seized. Xiao-fang was grabbed and yelled at by the adults. They told him they would "beat him to death" if he refused to say who had taught him to "rape the girl." They tried to force him to say it was his elder brothers. Xiao-fang was unable to say a word, even to cry. Jo-jo looked badly scared. He cried and said it was he who had asked Xiao-fang to give the injection. The little girl cried, too, saying she had not had her injection. But the adults shouted at them to shut up, and continued to hector Xiao-fang. Eventually, at my mother's suggestion, the crowd, jostling my mother and dragging Xiao-fang, stormed off to the Sichuan People's Hospital.

As soon as they entered the outpatients' department, the angry mother of the girl and the dramatically heated crowd started to make accusations to the doctors, nurses, and the other patients: "The son of a capitalist-roader has raped the daughter of a Rebel! The capitalist-roader parents must be made to pay!" While the girl was being examined in the doctor's room a young man in the corridor, a complete stranger, shouted, "Why don't you grab the capitalist-roader parents and beat them to death?"

When the doctor finished examining the girl, she came out and announced that there was absolutely no sign that the girl had been raped. The scratches on her legs were not recent, and they could not have been caused by Xiao-fang's piece of wood which, as she showed the crowd, was painted and smooth. They were probably caused by climbing a tree. The crowd dispersed, reluctantly.

That evening, Xiao-fang was delirious. His face was dark red and he screamed and raved incoherently. The next day, my mother carried him to a hospital, where a doctor gave him a large dose of tranquilizers. After a few days he was well again, but he stopped playing with other children. With this incident, he practically said goodbye to his childhood at the age of six.

Our move to Meteorite Street had been left to the resources of my grandmother and us five children. But by then we had the help of my sister Xiao-hong's boyfriend, Cheng-yi.

Cheng-yi's father had been a minor official under the Kuomintang and had not been able to get a proper job after 1949, partly because of his undesirable past and partly because he had TB and a gastric ulcer. He did odd jobs like street cleaning and collecting the fees at a communal water tap. During the famine he and his wife, who were living in Chongqing, died from illnesses aggravated by starvation.

Cheng-yi was a worker in an airplane engine factory, and had met my sister at the beginning of 1968. Like most people in the factory, he was an inactive member of its major Rebel group, which was affiliated with 26 August. In those days, there was no entertainment, so most Rebel groups set up their own song-and-dance troupes, which performed the few sanctioned songs of Mao quotations and eulogies. Cheng-yi, who was a good musician, was a member of one such troupe. Though she was not in the factory, my sister, who loved dancing, joined it, together with Plumpie and Ching-ching. She and Cheng-yi soon fell in love. The relationship came under pressure from all sides: from his sister and his fellow workers, who were worried that a liaison with a capitalist-roader family would jeopardize his future; from our circle of high officials' children, who scorned him for not being "one of us," and from the unreasonable me, who regarded my sister's desire to live her own life as deserting our parents. But their love survived, and sustained my sister through the following difficult years. I soon came to like and respect Cheng-yi very much, as did all my family. Because he wore glasses, we took to calling him "Specs."

Another musician from the troupe, a friend of Specs, was a carpenter and the son of a truck driver. He was a jolly young man with a spectacularly large nose which made him look somewhat un-Chinese. In those days the only foreigners whose pictures we saw often were Albanians, because tiny, faraway Albania was China's only ally—even the North Koreans were considered to be too decadent. His friends nicknamed him "Al," short for "Albanian."

Al came with a cart to help us move to Meteorite Street. Not wanting to overtax him, I suggested we leave some things behind. But he wanted us to take everything. With a nonchalant smile, he clenched his fists and proudly flexed his taut, bulging muscles. My brothers poked the hard lumps with great admiration.

Al was very keen on Plumpie. The day after the move, he invited her, Ching-ching, and me to lunch at his home, one of the common windowless Chengdu houses with mud floors, which opened directly onto the pavement. This was the first time I had been in one of these houses. When we reached Al's street, I saw a group of young men hanging about on the corner. Their eyes followed us as they said a pointed hello to Al. He flushed with pride, and went over to talk to them. He came back with an animated smile on his face. In a casual tone he said, "I told them you were high officials' children, and that I had made friends with you so I could lay my hands on privileged goods when the Cultural Revolution is over."

I was stunned. First, what he said seemed to suggest that people thought officials' children had access to consumer goods, which was not the case. Second, I was amazed at his obvious pleasure at being associated with us, and the prestige this clearly gave him in the eyes of his friends. At the moment when my parents were in detention and we had just been thrown out of the compound, when the Sichuan Revolutionary Committee had been established and the capitalist-roaders had been ousted, when the Cultural Revolution seemed to have won, Al and his friends still apparently took it for granted that officials like my parents would come back.

I was to encounter a similar attitude again and again. Whenever I went out of the imposing gate of our courtyard, I was always aware of the stares from people on Meteorite Street, stares which were a mixture of curiosity and awe. It was clear to me that the general public regarded the Revolutionary Committees, rather than the capitalist-roaders, as transient.

In the autumn of 1968 a new type of team came to take over my school; they were called "Mao Zedong Thought Propaganda Teams." Made up of soldiers or workers who had not been involved in factional fighting, their task was to restore order. In my school, as in all others, the team recalled all the pupils who had been in the school when the Cultural Revolution started two years before, so they could be kept under control. Those few who were out of the city were tracked down and summoned back by telegram. Few dared to stay away.

Back at school, the teachers who had not fallen victim did no teaching. They did not dare. The old textbooks had all been condemned as "bourgeois poison," and nobody was brave enough to write new ones.

So we just sat in classes reciting Mao's articles and reading *People's Daily* editorials. We sang songs of Mao's quotations, or gathered to dance "loyalty dances," gyrating and waving our Little Red Books.

Making "loyalty dances" compulsory was one of the major orders issued by the Revolutionary Committees throughout China. This absurd twisting was mandatory everywhere: in schools and factories, on the streets, in shops, on railway platforms, even in hospitals for the patients who could still move.

On the whole, the propaganda team sent to my school was fairly benign. Others were not. The one at Chengdu University was hand-picked by the Tings because the university had been the headquarters of their enemy Red Chengdu. Yan and Yong suffered more than most. The Tings instructed the propaganda team to put pressure on them to condemn my father. They refused. They later told my mother that they so admired my father's courage that they decided to take a stand.

By the end of 1968, all university students in China had been summarily "graduated" *en masse*, without any exam, assigned jobs, and dispersed to every corner of the land. Yan and Yong were warned that if they did not denounce my father, they would have no future. But they stuck to their guns. Yan was sent to a small coal mine in the mountains of east Sichuan. This was just about the worst job possible; the work conditions were extremely primitive and there were virtually no safety measures. Women, like men, had to crawl down the pit on all fours to drag the coal baskets out. Yan's fate was partly the result of the twisted rhetoric of the time: Mme. Mao had been insisting on women doing the same kind of work as men, and one of the slogans of the day was Mao's saying "Women can hold up half the sky." But women knew that when they were given the privilege of this equality they were in for hard physical labor.

Immediately after the expulsion of university students, middle-school pupils like me discovered that we were to be exiled to faraway rural and mountainous areas, to do backbreaking farm labor. Mao intended me to spend the rest of my life as a peasant.

22. "Thought Reform through Labor"—
To the Edge of the Himalayas

(January–June 1969)

In 1969 my parents, my sister, my brother Jin-ming, and I were expelled from Chengdu one after another, and sent to distant parts of the Sichuan wilderness. We were among millions of urban dwellers to be exiled to the countryside. In this way, young people would not be roaming the cities with nothing to do, creating trouble out of sheer boredom, and adults like my parents would have a "future." They were part of the old administration which had been replaced by Mao's Revolutionary Committees, and packing them off to the sticks to do hard labor was a convenient solution.

According to Mao's rhetoric, we were sent to the countryside "to be reformed." Mao advocated "thought reform through labor" for everyone, but never explained the relationship between the two. Of course, no one asked for clarification. Merely to contemplate such a question was tantamount to treason. In reality, everyone in China knew that hard labor, particularly in the countryside, was always punishment. It was noticeable that none of Mao's henchmen, the members of the newly established Revolutionary Committees, army officers —and very few of their children—had to do it.

The first of us to be expelled was my father. Just after New Year 1969 he was sent to Miyi County in the region of Xichang, on the eastern edge of the Himalayas, an area so remote that it is China's satellite launch base today. It lies about 300 miles from Chengdu, four days' journey by truck, as there was no railway. In ancient times, the area was used for dumping exiles, because its mountains and waters were said to be permeated with a mysterious "evil air." In today's terms, the "evil air" was subtropical diseases.

A camp was set up there to accommodate the former staff of the provincial government. There were thousands of such camps throughout China. They were called "cadres' schools," but apart from the fact that they were not schools, they were not just for officials either. Writers, scholars, scientists, teachers, doctors, and actors who had become "useless" in Mao's know-nothing new order were also dispatched there.

Among officials, it was not only capitalist-roaders like my father and other class enemies who were packed off to the camps. Most of their Rebel colleagues were also expelled, as the new Sichuan Revolutionary Committee could not accommodate anything like all of them, having filled its posts with Rebels from other backgrounds like workers and students, and with army men. "Thought reform through labor" became a handy way of dealing with the surplus Rebels. In my father's department only a few stayed in Chengdu. Mrs. Shau became deputy director of Public Affairs on the Sichuan Revolutionary Committee. All Rebel organizations were now disbanded.

The "cadres' schools" were not concentration camps or gulags, but they were isolated places of detention where the inmates had restricted freedom and had to do hard labor under strict supervision. Because every cultivable area in China is densely populated, only in arid or mountainous areas was there space to contain the exiles from the cities. The inmates were supposed to produce food and be self-supporting. Although they were still paid salaries, there was little for them to buy. Life was very harsh.

In order to prepare for his trip, my father was released from his place of detention in Chengdu a few days before his departure. The only thing he wanted to do was to see my mother. She was still being detained, and he thought he might never see her again. He wrote to the Revolutionary Committee, as humbly as he could, begging to be allowed to see her. His request was turned down.

The cinema in which my mother was being kept was on what used to be the busiest shopping street in Chengdu. Now the shops were half empty, but the black market for semiconductor parts which my brother Jin-ming frequented was nearby, and he sometimes saw my mother walking along the street in a line of detainees, carrying a bowl and a pair of chopsticks. The canteen in the cinema did not operate every day, so the detainees had to go out for their meals from time to time. Jin-ming's discovery meant we could sometimes see our mother by waiting on the street. Occasionally she did not appear with the other detainees, and we would be consumed by anxiety. We did not know that those were the times when her psychopath guard was punishing her by denying her permission to go and eat. But perhaps the next day we would catch sight of her, one among a dozen or so silent and grim-looking men and women, their heads bowed, all wearing white armbands with four sinister black characters: "ox devil, snake demon."

I took my father to the street for several days running, and we waited there from dawn till lunchtime. But there was no sign of her. We would walk up and down, stamping our feet on the frost-covered pavement to keep warm. One morning, we were again watching the thick fog lift to reveal the lifeless cement buildings, when my mother appeared. Having seen her children many times on the street, she looked up quickly to see whether we were there this time. Her eyes met my father's. Their lips quivered, but no sounds came out. They just locked eyes until the guard shouted at my mother to lower her head. Long after she had turned the corner, my father stood gazing after her.

A couple of days later, my father was gone. Despite his calm and reserve, I detected signs his nerves were on the verge of snapping. I was desperately worried that he might go out of his mind again, particularly now that he had to suffer his physical and mental torment in solitude, without his family nearby. I resolved to go and keep him company soon, but it was extremely difficult to find transport to Miyi, as public services to such remote areas were paralyzed. So when I was told some days later that my school was being dispatched to a place called Ningnan, which was only about fifty miles from his camp, I was delighted.

In January 1969, every middle school in Chengdu was sent to a rural area somewhere in Sichuan. We were to live in villages among the peasants and be "reeducated" by them. What exactly they were supposed to educate us in was not made specific, but Mao always maintained that people with some education were inferior to illiterate peasants, and needed to reform to be more like them. One of his sayings was: "Peasants have dirty hands and cowshit-sodden feet, but they are much cleaner than intellectuals."

My school and my sister's were full of children of capitalist-roaders, so they were sent to particularly godforsaken places. None of the children of members of the Revolutionary Committees went. They joined the armed services, which was the only, and much cushier, alternative to the countryside. Starting at this time, one of the clearest signs of power was for one's children to be in the army.

Altogether, some fifteen million young people were sent to the country in what was one of the largest population movements in history. It was an indication of the order within the chaos that this was swiftly and supremely well organized. Everyone was given a subsidy to help buy extra clothes, quilts, sheets, suitcases, mosquito nets, and plastic sheets for wrapping up bedrolls. Minute attention was paid to such details as providing us with sneakers, water cans, and torches. Most of these things had to be manufactured specially, as they were not available in the poorly stocked shops. Those from poor families could apply for extra financial help. For the first year we were to be provided by the state with pocket money and food rations, including rice, cooking oil, and meat. These were to be collected from the village to which we were assigned.

Since the Great Leap Forward, the countryside had been organized into communes, each of which grouped together a number of villages and could contain anywhere from 2,000 to 20,000 households. Under the commune came production brigades which, in turn, governed several production teams. A production team was roughly equivalent to a village, and was the basic unit of rural life. In my school, up to eight pupils were assigned to each production team, and we were allowed to choose with whom we wanted to form a group. I chose my friends from Plumpie's form. My sister chose to go with me instead of with her school: we were allowed to opt to go to a place with a relative. My brother Jin-ming, though he was in the same school as I, stayed in Chengdu because he was not yet sixteen, which was the cutoff age. Plumpie did not go either, because she was an only child.

I looked forward to Ningnan. I had had no real experience of physical hardship and little appreciated what it meant. I imagined an idyllic environment where there was no politics. An official had come from Ningnan to talk to us, and he had described the subtropical climate with its high blue sky, huge red hibiscus flowers, foot-long bananas, and the Golden Sand River—the upper part of the Yangtze—shining in the bright sun, rippled by gentle breezes.

I was living in a world of gray mist and black wall slogans, and sunshine and tropical vegetation were like a dream to me. Listening to the official, I pictured myself in a mountain of blossoms with a golden river at my feet. He mentioned the mysterious "evil air" which I had read about in classical literature, but even that added a touch of ancient exoticism. Danger existed for me only in political campaigns.

I was also eager to go because I thought it would be easy to visit my father. But I failed to notice that between us lay pathless mountains 10,000 feet high. I have never been much good at maps.

On 27 January 1969, my school set off for Ningnan. Each pupil was allowed to take one suitcase and a bedroll. We were loaded into trucks, about three dozen of us in each. There were only a few seats; most of us sat on our bedrolls or on the floor. The column of trucks bumped up and down country roads for three days before we reached the border of Xichang. We passed through the Chengdu Plain and the mountains along the eastern edge of the Himalayas, where the trucks had to put on chains. I tried to sit near the back so I could watch the dramatic snow showers and hail which whitened the universe, and which almost instantly cleared into turquoise sky and dazzling sunshine. This tempestuous beauty left me speechless. In the distance to the west rose a peak almost 25,000 feet high, beyond which lay the ancient wilderness in which were born many of the world's flora. I only realized when I came to the West that such everyday sights as rhododendrons, chrysanthemums, most roses, and many other flowers came from here. It was still inhabited by pandas.

The second evening we entered a place called Asbestos County, named after its major product. Somewhere in the mountains, our convoy stopped so we could use the toilets—two mud huts containing round communal pits covered with maggots. But if the sight inside the toilet was revolting, the one outside was horrifying. The faces of the workers were ashen, the color of lead, and devoid of any animation. Terrified, I asked a nice propaganda team man, Dong-an, who was taking us to our destination, who these zombielike people were. Convicts from a *lao-gai* ("reform through labor") camp, he replied. Because asbestos mining was highly noxious, it was mainly done by forced labor, with few safety or health precautions. This was my first, and only, encounter with China's gulag.

On the fifth day, the truck unloaded us at a granary at the top of a mountain. Propaganda publicity had led me to expect a ceremony with people beating drums and pinning red paper flowers on the new arrivals with great fanfare, but all that happened was that a commune official came to meet us at the grain station. He made a speech of welcome in the stilted jargon of the newspapers. A couple of dozen peasants were there to help us with our bedrolls and suitcases. Their faces were blank and inscrutable, and their speech was unintelligible to me.

My sister and I walked to our new home with the two other girls and four boys who made up our group. The four peasants who carried some of our luggage walked in complete silence, and did not seem to understand the questions we put to them. We fell into silence, too. For hours we trekked in single file, deeper and deeper into the great universe of dark-green mountains. But I was far too exhausted to notice their beauty. Once, after I had been struggling to support myself against a rock to catch my breath, I looked around, into the distance. Our group seemed so insignificant amid the vast, boundless mountain world, with no roads, no houses, and no other human beings in sight, only the wind soughing through the forests, and the purling of hidden streams. I felt I was disappearing into a hushed, alien wilderness.

At dusk, we arrived at the lightless village. There was no electricity, and oil was too precious to be wasted if it was not completely dark. People stood by their doors and stared at us with open-mouthed blankness; I did not know if it denoted interest or indifference. It was stares like these which many foreigners encountered in China after it was first opened in the 1970s. Indeed, we were like foreigners to the peasants—and they to us.

The village had prepared a residence for us, made of timber and mud and comprising two big rooms—one for the four boys, and one for the four girls. A corridor led to the village hall, where a brick stove had been built for us to cook on.

I fell exhausted onto the hard plank of wood that was the bed I was to share with my sister. Some children followed us, making excited noises. They now started banging on our door, but when we opened it they would scamper away, only to reappear to rap on the door again. They peeped into our window, which was just a square hole in the wall, with no shutter, and screamed odd noises. At first we smiled and invited them in, but our friendliness met no response. I was desperate for a wash. We nailed an old shirt onto the window frame as a curtain and began to dip our towels into the freezing water in our washbasins. I tried to ignore the children's giggles as they repeatedly flipped up the "curtain." We had to keep our padded jackets on while we washed.

One of the boys in our group acted as leader and liaison with the villagers. We had a few days, he told us, to get all our daily necessities like water, kerosene, and firewood organized; after that we would have to start working in the fields.

Everything at Ningnan was done manually, the way it had been for at least 2,000 years. There was no machinery—and no draft animals, either. The peasants were too short of food to be able to afford any for horses or donkeys. For our arrival the villagers had filled a round earthenware water tank for us. The next day I realized how precious every drop was. To get water, we had to climb for thirty minutes up narrow paths to the well, carrying a pair of wooden barrels on a shoulder pole. They weighed ninety pounds when they were full. My shoulders ached agonizingly even when they were empty. I was vastly relieved when the boys gallantly declared that fetching water was their job.

They cooked, too, as three out of us four girls, me included, had never cooked in our lives, having come from the kind of families we did. Now I began to learn to cook the hard way. The grain came unhusked, and had to be put into a stone mortar and beaten with all one's might with a heavy pestle. Then the mixture had to be poured into a big shallow bamboo basket, which was swung with a particular movement of the arms so that the light shells gathered on top and could be scooped away, leaving the rice behind. After a couple of minutes my arms became unbearably sore and soon were shaking so much I could not pick up the basket. It was an exhausting battle for every meal.

Then we had to collect fuel. It was two hours' walk to the woods designated by the forest protection regulations as the area where we could collect firewood. We were only allowed to chop small branches, so we climbed up the short pines and slashed ferociously with our knives. The logs were bundled together and carried on our backs. I was the youngest in our group, so I only had to carry a basket of feathery pine needles. The journey home was another couple of hours, up and down mountain paths. I was so exhausted when I got back that I felt my load must weigh 140 pounds at least. I could not believe my eyes when I put my basket on the scales: it came to only five pounds. This would burn up in no time: it was not enough even to boil a wok of water.

On one of the first trips to gather fuel, I tore the seat of my trousers getting down from a tree. I was so embarrassed I hid in the woods and came out last so no one could walk behind me and see. The boys, who were all perfect gentlemen, kept insisting I should go in front so they would not walk too fast for me. I had to repeat many times that I was happy to go last, and that I was not just being polite.

Even going to the toilet was no easy job. It involved climbing down a steep, slippery slope to a deep pit next to the goatfold. One always had either one's bottom or one's head toward the goats, who were keen to butt at intruders. I was so nervous I could not move my bowels for days. Once out of the goatfold, it was a struggle to clamber up the slope again. Every time I came back I had new bruises on me somewhere.

On our first day working with the peasants, I was assigned to carry goat droppings and manure from our toilet up to the tiny fields which had just been burned free of bushes and grass. The ground was now covered by a layer of plant ash that, together with the goat and human excrement, was to fertilize the soil for the spring plowing, which was done manually.

I loaded the heavy basket on my back and desperately crawled up the slope on all fours. The manure was fairly dry, but still some of it began to soak through onto my cotton jacket and through to my underwear—and my back. It also slopped over the top of the basket and seeped into my hair. When I finally arrived at the field I saw the peasant women skillfully unloading by bending their waists sideways and tilting the baskets in such a way that the contents poured out. But I could not make mine pour. In my desperation to get rid of the weight on my back I tried to take the basket off. I slipped my right arm out of its strap, and suddenly the basket lurched with a tremendous pull to the left, taking my left shoulder with it. I fell to the ground into the manure. Some time later, a friend dislocated her knee like this. I only strained my waist slightly.

Hardship was part of the "thought reform." In theory, it was to be relished, as it brought one closer to becoming a new person, more like the peasants. Before the Cultural Revolution, I had subscribed whole-heartedly to this naive attitude, and had deliberately done hard work in order to make myself a better person. Once in the spring of 1966 my form was helping with some roadwork. The girls were asked to do light jobs like separating out stones which were then broken up by the boys. I offered to do the boys' work and ended up with horribly swollen arms from crushing stones with a huge sledgehammer which I could hardly lift. Now, scarcely three years later, my indoctrination was collapsing. With the psychological support of blind belief gone, I found myself hating the hardship in the mountains of Ningnan. It seemed utterly pointless.

I developed a serious skin rash as soon as I arrived. For over three years this rash recurred the moment I was in the country, and no medicine seemed able to cure it. I was tormented by itchiness day and night, and could not stop myself from scratching. Within three weeks of starting my new life I had several sores running with pus, and my legs were swollen from infections. I was also hit by diarrhea and vomiting. I was hatefully weak and sick all the time when I needed physical strength most, and the commune clinic was thirty-odd miles away.

I soon came to the conclusion that I had little chance of visiting my father from Ningnan. The nearest proper road was a day's hard walk away, and even when one got there, there was no public transport. Trucks were few and far between, and they were extremely unlikely to be going from where I was to Miyi. Fortunately, the propaganda team man, Dong-an, came to our village to check that we were settled in all right, and when he saw I was ill he kindly suggested I should go back to Chengdu for treatment. He was returning with the last of the trucks which had brought us to Ningnan. Twenty-six days after I had arrived, I set off back to Chengdu.

As I was leaving I realized that I had hardly got to know the peasants in our village. My only acquaintance was the village accountant who, being the most educated man around, came to see us often to claim some intellectual kinship. His home was the only one I had been in, and what I remember most were the suspicious stares on his young wife's weather-beaten face. She was cleaning the bloody intestines of a pig, and had a silent baby on her back. When I said hello, she shot me an indifferent look and did not return my greeting. I felt alien and awkward, and soon left.

In the few days I actually worked with the villagers, I had little spare energy and did not talk to them properly. They seemed remote, uninterested, separated from me by the impenetrable Ningnan mountains. I knew we were supposed to make the effort to visit them, as my friends and my sister, who were in better shape, were doing in the evenings, but I was exhausted, sick, and itchy all the time. Besides, visiting them would have meant that I was resigned to making the best of my life there. And I subconsciously refused to settle for a life as a peasant. Without spelling it out to myself, I rejected the life Mao had assigned to me.

When the time came for me to leave, I suddenly missed the extraordinary beauty of Ningnan. I had not appreciated the mountains properly when I was struggling with life there. Spring had come early, in February, and golden winter jasmines shone beside the icicles hanging from the pines. The brooks in the valleys formed one crystal-clear pool after another, dotted around which were fancifully shaped rocks. The reflections in the water were of gorgeous clouds, canopies of stately trees, and the nameless blossoms that elegantly wriggled out of the cracks in the rocks. We washed clothes in those heavenly pools, and spread them on the rocks to dry in the sunshine and the crisp air. Then we would lie down on the grass and listen to the vibration of the pine forests in the breeze. I would marvel at the slopes of distant mountains opposite us, covered with wild peach trees, and imagine the masses of pink in a few weeks' time.

. . .

When I reached Chengdu, after four interminable days of being thrown about in the back of an empty truck, with constant stomach pains and diarrhea, I went straight to the clinic attached to the compound. Injections and tablets cured me in no time. Like the canteen, the clinic was still open to my family. The Sichuan Revolutionary Committee was split—and second-rate: it had not managed to organize a functioning administration. It had not even got around to issuing regulations concrning many aspects of everyday life. As a result, the system was full of holes; many of the old ways continued, and people were largely left to their own devices. The managements of the canteen and the clinic did not refuse to serve us, so we went on enjoying the facilities.

In addition to the Western injections and pills prescribed at the clinic, my grandmother said I needed Chinese medicines. One day she came home with a chicken and some roots of membranous milk vetch and Chinese angelica, which were considered very *bu* (healing), and made a soup for me into which she sprinkled finely chopped spring onions. These ingredients were unavailable in the shops, and she had hobbled for miles to buy them in a country black market.

My grandmother was unwell herself. Sometimes I saw her lying on her bed, which was extremely unusual for her; she had always been so energetic I had hardly ever seen her sit still for a minute. Now her eyes were shut tight and she bit her lips hard, which made me feel she must be in great pain. But when I asked her what the matter was, she would say it was nothing, and she continued collecting medicines and standing in line to get food for me.

I was soon much better. As there was no authority to order me to return to Ningnan, I began to plan a trip to see my father. But then a telegram came from Yibin saying that my aunt Jun-ying, who had been looking after my youngest brother, Xiao-fang, was seriously ill. I thought I should go and take care of them.

Aunt Jun-ying and my father's other relations in Yibin had been very kind to my family, in spite of the fact that my father had broken the deep-rooted Chinese tradition of looking after one's relatives. By tradition, it was considered the filial duty of a son to prepare for his mother a heavy wooden coffin with many layers of paint, and to provide a grand—and often financially crippling—funeral. But the government strongly encouraged cremation—to save land—and simpler funerals. When his mother died in 1958, my father was not told until after the funeral, because his family was worried that he would object to the burial and the elaborate service. After we moved to Chengdu his family hardly ever visited us.

However, when my father fell into trouble in the Cultural Revolution, they came to see us and offered their help. Aunt Jun-ying, who had been traveling frequently between Chengdu and Yibin, eventually took Xiao-fang under her care to relieve my grandmother of some of her burden. She shared a house with my father's youngest sister, but had also selflessly given up half of her part to the family of a distant relative who had had to abandon their own dilapidated lodgings.

When I arrived, my aunt was sitting in a wicker easy chair by the front door to the hall, which served as the sitting room. In the place of honor lay a huge coffin made of heavy, dark-red wood. This coffin, her own, was her only indulgence. The sight of my aunt overwhelmed me with sadness. She had just had a stroke, and her legs were half-paralyzed. Hospitals were working only sporadically. With no one to repair them, facilities had broken down and the supply of medicine was erratic. The hospitals had told Aunt Jun-ying there was nothing they could do for her, so she stayed at home.

What my aunt found most traumatic were her bowel movements. After eating, she felt unbearably bloated, but she could not relieve herself without great agony. Her relatives' formulas helped sometimes, but more often failed. I massaged her stomach frequently, and once, when she felt desperate and asked me to, I even put my finger into her anus to try to scratch out the excrement. All these remedies only gave her momentary relief. As a result, she did not dare to eat much. She was terribly weak, and would sit in the wicker chair in the hall for hours, gazing at the papaya and banana trees in the back garden. She never complained. Only once did she say to me in a gentle whisper, "I'm so very hungry. I wish I could eat . . ."

She could no longer walk without help, and even sitting up required a great effort. To prevent her getting bedsores, I would sit beside her so she could lean on me. She said I was a good nurse and that I must be tired and bored sitting there. No matter how much I insisted, she would only sit for a brief period every day, so that I could "go out and have some fun."

Of course, there was no fun outside. I longed for something to read. But apart from the four volumes of *The Selected Works of Mao Zedong*, all I discovered in the house was a dictionary. Everything else had been burned. I occupied myself with studying the 15,000 characters in it, learning the ones I did not know by heart.

I spent the rest of my time looking after my seven-year-old brother, Xiao-fang, and took long walks with him. Sometimes he got bored and demanded things like a toy gun or the charcoal-colored sweets that were on lonely display in the shops. But I had no money—our basic allowance was small. Xiao-fang, at seven, could not understand this, and would throw himself on the dusty ground, kicking, yelling, and tearing my jacket. I would crouch and coax and eventually, at my wits' end, start crying as well. At this, he would stop and make up with me. We would both go home exhausted.

Yibin was a very atmospheric town, even in the middle of the Cultural Revolution. The waving rivers and serene hills, and the hazy horizon beyond, produced a sense of eternity in me, and soothed me temporarily from the miseries all around. When dusk fell, the posters and loudspeakers all over the city were obscured, and the unlit back lanes were enveloped in mist, broken only by the flickering of oil lamps seeping through the cracks between the frames of the doors and the windows. From time to time, there was a bright patch: a small food stall was open. There was not much for sale, but there would be a square wooden table on the pavement, with four long narrow benches around it, all dark brown and shiny from years of rubbing and sitting. On the table would be a tiny pea-shaped spark—a lamp that burned rapeseed oil. There was never anyone sitting at these tables chatting, but the owner kept the stall open. In the old days, it would have been crowded with people gossiping and drinking the local "five-grained liquor," accompanied by marinated beef, soy-stewed pig's tongue, and salt-and-pepper roasted peanuts. The empty stalls evoked for me a Yibin in the days when life had not been completely taken over by politics.

Once out of the back lanes, my ears were assaulted by loudspeakers. For up to eighteen hours a day the town center was a perpetual hubbub of chanting and denouncing. Quite apart from the content, the noise level was unbearable, and I had to develop a technique of forcing myself to hear nothing to preserve my sanity.

One evening in April, a broadcast suddenly caught my attention. A Party Congress had been convened in Peking. As usual, the Chinese people were not told what this most important assembly of their "representatives" was actually doing. A new top leadership team was announced. My heart sank as I heard that the new organization of the Cultural Revolution was confirmed.

This Congress, the Ninth, marked the formal establishment of Mao's personal power system. Few senior leaders from the previous Congress, in 1956, had made it to this one. Out of seventeen Politburo members, only four—Mao, Lin Biao, Zhou Enlai, and Li Xiannian— were still in office. All the rest, apart from those already dead, had been denounced and ousted. Some of these were soon to die.

President Liu Shaoqi, the number-two man at the Eighth Congress, had been under detention since 1967, and was ferociously beaten at denunciation meetings. He was denied medicine for both his long-term illness, diabetes, and his newly caught pneumonia, and was given treatment only when he was on the brink of death because Mme. Mao explicitly ordered that he be kept alive so the Ninth Congress would "have a living target." At the Congress the verdict that he was "a criminal traitor, enemy agent, and scab in the service of the imperialists, modern revisionists [Russians], and the Kuomintang reactionaries" was read by Zhou Enlai. After the Congress, Liu was allowed to die, in agony.

Marshal Ho Lung, another former Politburo member and a founder of the Communist army, died scarcely two months after the Congress. Because he had wielded power in the army, he was subjected to two and a half years of slow torture, which, he said to his wife, was "intended to destroy my health so they can murder me without spilling my blood." The torment included allowing him only a small can of water every day during the boiling summer, cutting off all heating during the winter, when the temperature remained well below zero for months on end, and denying him medicine for his diabetes. In the end, he died after a large dose of glucose was administered when his diabetes got worse.

Tao Zhu, the Politburo member who had helped my mother at the start of the Cultural Revolution, was detained under inhuman conditions for nearly three years, which destroyed his health. He was denied proper treatment until his gallbladder cancer was far advanced and Zhou Enlai sanctioned an operation. But the windows in his hospital room were permanently blacked out with newspapers, and his family was not allowed to see him at his deathbed or after his death.

Marshal Peng Dehuai died of the same kind of drawn-out torment, which in his case lasted eight years, until 1974. His last request was to see the trees and the daylight outside his newspaper-covered hospital windows, and it was turned down.

These and many similar persecutions were typical of Mao's methods in the Cultural Revolution. Instead of signing death warrants Mao would simply indicate his intentions, and some people would volunteer to carry out the tormenting and improvise the gruesome details. Their methods included mental pressure, physical brutality, and denial of medical care—or even the use of medicine to kill. Death caused in this way came to have a special term in Chinese: *po-hai zhi-si*—"persecuted to death." Mao was fully aware of what was happening, and would encourage the perpetrators by giving his "silent consent" (mo-xu). This enabled him to get rid of his enemies without attracting blame. The responsibility was inescapably his, but not his alone. The tormentors took some initiative. Mao's subordinates were always on the lookout for ways to please him by anticipating his wishes and, of course, to indulge their own sadistic tendencies.

The horrible details of the persecutions of many top leaders were not revealed until years later. When they came out, they surprised no one in China. We knew all too many similar cases from our own experience.

As I stood in the crowded square listening to the broadcast, the new Central Committee was read out. With dread I waited for the names of the Tings. And there they were—Liu Jie-ting and Zhang Xi-ting. Now I felt there was to be no end to my family's suffering.

Shortly afterward a telegram came saying my grandmother had collapsed and taken to her bed. She had never done anything like this before. Aunt Jun-ying urged me to go home and look after her. Xiao-fang and I took the next train back to Chengdu.

My grandmother was approaching her sixtieth birthday, and her stoicism had at last been conquered by pain. She felt it piercing and moving all over her body, then concentrating in her ears. The doctors at the compound clinic said it might be nerves, and that they had no cure for it except that she should maintain a cheerful mood. I took her to a hospital half an hour's walk from Meteorite Street.

Ensconced in their chauffeur-driven cars, the new holders of power felt little concern for how ordinary people had to live. Buses were not running in Chengdu, as they were not considered vital to the revolution, and pedicabs had been banned, on the grounds that they exploited labor. My grandmother could not walk because of the intense pain. She had to sit on the luggage rack of a bicycle, with a cushion on it, holding on to the seat. I pushed the bicycle, Xiao-hei propped her up, and Xiao-fang sat on the crossbar.

The hospital was still working, thanks to the professionalism and dedication of some of the staff. On its brick walls, I saw huge slogans from their more militant colleagues accusing them of "using work to suppress revolution"—a standard accusation for people sticking to their jobs. The doctor we saw had twitching eyelids and black rings under her eyes, and I guessed she must be exhausted by the throngs of patients, in addition to the political attacks she was having to endure. The hospital was bursting at the seams with grim-looking men and women, some with bruised faces, others with broken ribs lying on stretchers—victims of denunciation meetings.

None of the doctors could diagnose what was wrong with my grandmother. There was no X-ray machine or any other instrument to examine her properly. They were all broken. My grandmother was given various painkillers. When these failed to work, she was admitted to the hospital. The wards were crowded, the beds jammed right up against each other. Even the corridors were lined with beds. The few nurses rushing from ward to ward could not manage to look after all the patients, so I decided to stay with my grandmother.

I went home and got some utensils so I could cook for her there. I also brought a bamboo mattress which I spread under her bed. At night I was constantly awakened by her groaning, and I would climb out from under my thin quilt and massage her, which soothed her temporarily. From under the bed, the room smelled intensely of urine. Everyone's chamberpot was placed next to the bed. My grandmother was very fussy about cleanliness, and she would insist on getting up and going to the toilet down the corridor even at night. But the other patients did not bother, and often the chamberpots were not emptied for days. The nurses were too busy to attend to such details.

The window by my grandmother's bed looked out over the front garden. It was overgrown with weeds, and its wooden benches were collapsing. The first time I looked out at it, several children were busy trying to break off the few branches of a small magnolia tree that still had one or two flowers on them. Adults walked by indifferently. Vandalism against trees had become too much a part of everyday life to attract any attention.

One day, from the open window, I saw Bing, a friend of mine, getting off his bicycle. My heart started to leap, and my face suddenly felt hot. I quickly checked in the windowpane. To look into a real mirror in public was to invite condemnation as a "bourgeois element." I was wearing a pink-and-white checked jacket, a pattern that had just been allowed for young women's clothing. Long hair was permissible again, but only in two plaits, and I would dither for hours over how I should do mine: Should they be close together or far apart? Straight, or curved a little at the ends? Should the plaited part be longer than the loose part, or vice versa? The decisions, all minute, were endless. There were no state regulations about hairstyles or clothes. It was what everyone else was wearing that determined the rules of the day. And because the range was so narrow, people were always looking out for the tiniest variations. It was a real test of ingenuity to look different and attractive, and yet similar enough to everybody else so that nobody with an accusing finger could pinpoint what exactly was heretical.

I was still wondering how I looked when Bing walked into the ward. His appearance was nothing out of the ordinary, but a certain air set him apart. He had a touch of cynicism, which was rare in those humorless years. I was very much drawn to him. His father had been a departmental director in the pre–Cultural Revolution provincial government, but Bing was different from most other high officials' children. "Why should I be sent to the countryside?" he said, and actually succeeded in not going by obtaining an "incurable illness" certificate. He was the first person to show me a free intelligence, an ironic, inquisitive mind which did not take anything for granted. It was he who first opened up the taboo areas in my mind.

Up to now, I had shunned any love relationship. My devotion to my family, which had been intensified by adversity, overshadowed every other emotion. Although within me there had always been another being, a sexual being, yearning to get out, I had succeeded in keeping it locked in. Knowing Bing pulled me to the brink of an entanglement.

On this day, Bing turned up at my grandmother's ward with a black eye. He said he had just been hit by Wen, a young man who had come back from Ningnan as the escort for a girl who had broken her leg there. Bing described the fight with deliberate nonchalance, saying with a great deal of satisfaction that Wen was jealous of him for enjoying more of my attention and company. Later, I heard Wen's story: he had hit Bing because he could not stand "that conceited grin of his."

Wen was short and stout, with big hands and feet and buck teeth. Like Bing, he was the son of high officials. He took to rolling up his sleeves and trouser legs and wearing a pair of straw sandals like a peasant, in the spirit of a model youth in the propaganda posters. One day he told me he was going back to Ningnan to continue "reforming" himself. When I asked why, he said casually, "To follow Chairman Mao. Why else? I'm Chairman Mao's Red Guard." For a moment I was speechless. I had begun to assume that people only spouted this sort of jargon on official occasions. What was more, he had not put on the obligatory solemn face that was part of the act. The offhanded way he spoke made me feel he was sincere.

Wen's way of thinking did not make me want to avoid him. The Cultural Revolution had taught me not to divide people by their beliefs, but by whether they were capable of cruelty and viciousness or not. I knew Wen was a decent person, and when I wanted to get out of Ningnan permanently, it was to him that I turned for help.

I had been away from Ningnan for over two months. There was no rule that forbade this, but the regime had a powerful weapon to make sure I would have to go back to the mountains sooner or later: my residence registration had been moved there from Chengdu, and as long as I stayed in the city, I was entitled to no food or any other rations. For the time being I was living off my family's rations, but that could not last forever. I realized that I had to get my registration moved to somewhere near Chengdu.

Chengdu itself was out of the question, because no one was allowed to move a country registration to a city. Moving one's registration from a harsh mountainous place to a richer area like the plain around Chengdu was also forbidden. But there was a loophole: we could move if we had relatives who were willing to accept us. It was possible to invent such a relative, as no one could keep track of the numerous relatives a Chinese might have.

I planned the transfer with Nana, a good friend of mine who was just back from Ningnan to try to find a way to get out of there. We included my sister, who was still in Ningnan, in our plan. To get our registrations moved, we first of all needed three letters: one from a commune saying it would accept us, on the recommendation of a relative in that commune; a second from the county to which the commune belonged, endorsing the first; and a third from the Sichuan Bureau for City Youth, sanctioning the transfer. When we had all three, we had to go back to our production teams in Ningnan to obtain their approval before the registrar at Ningnan county would give us the final release. Only then could we be given the crucial document, which was essential for every citizen in China—our registration books —which we had to hand in to the authorities at our next place of residence.

Life was always as daunting and complex as this whenever one took even the smallest step outside the authorities' rigid plan. And in most cases there were unexpected complications. While I was planning how to arrange the transfer, out of the blue the central government issued a regulation freezing all registration transfers as of 21 June. It was already the third week in May. It would be impossible to locate a real relative who would accept us and go through all the procedures in time.

I turned to Wen. Without hesitating for a moment, he offered to "create" the three letters. Forging official documents was a serious offense, punishable by a long prison sentence. But Mao's devoted Red Guard shrugged off my words of caution.

The crucial elements in the forgery were the seals. In China, all documents are made official by the stamps on them. Wen was good at calligraphy, and could carve in the style of official stamps. He used cakes of soap. In one evening all three letters for the three of us, which would have taken months to obtain, if we were lucky, were ready. Wen offered to go back to Ningnan with Nana and me to help with the rest of the procedure.

When the time came to go, I was agonizingly torn, because it meant leaving my grandmother in the hospital. She urged me to go, saying she would return home and keep an eye on my younger brothers. I did not try to dissuade her: the hospital was a terribly depressing place. Apart from the revolting smell, it was also incredibly noisy, with moaning and clattering and loud conversations in the corridors day and night. Loudspeakers woke everyone up at six in the morning, and there were often deaths in full view of other patients.

On the evening she was discharged, my grandmother felt a sharp pain at the base of her spine. She could not sit on the luggage rack of the bicycle, so Xiao-hei rode it home with her clothes, towels, washbowls, thermos flasks, and the cooking utensils, and I walked with her, supporting her. The evening was sultry. Walking even very slowly hurt her, as I could see from her tightly pursed lips and her trembling as she tried to suppress her moans. I told her stories and gossip to divert her. The plane trees that used to shade the pavements now produced only a few pathetic branches with leaves on them—they had not been pruned in the three years of the Cultural Revolution. Here and there, buildings were scarred, the result of the fierce fighting between Rebel factions.

It took us nearly an hour to get halfway. Suddenly the sky turned dark. A violent gale swept up the dust and the torn fragments of wall posters. My grandmother staggered. I held her tight. It started to pour with rain, and in an instant we were drenched. There was nowhere to take cover, so we struggled on. Our clothes were clinging to us and impeding our movements. I was panting for breath. My grandmother's tiny, thin figure felt heavier and heavier in my arms. The rain was hissing and splashing, the wind slashed against our soaked bodies, and I felt very cold. My grandmother sobbed, "Oh heaven, let me die! Let me die!" I wanted to cry too, but I only said, "Grandma, we'll soon be home. . . ."

Then I heard a bell tinkling. "Hey, do you want a lift?" A pedal-cart had pulled over; a young man in an open shirt was straddling it, rain running down his cheeks. He came over and carried my grandmother onto the open cart on which an old man was crouching. He nodded to us. The young man said this was his father whom he was taking home from the hospital. He dropped us at our door, waving off my profuse thanks with a cheerful "No trouble at all," before disappearing into the sodden darkness. Because of the pressure of the downpour, I never learned his name.

Two days later my grandmother was up and about in the kitchen, rolling out dumpling wrappings to give us a treat. She started to tidy up the rooms, too, in her usual nonstop way. I could see she was overdoing things and asked her to stay in bed, but she would not listen.

By now it was the beginning of June. She kept telling me I should leave, and insisted that Jin-ming should go as well, to look after me, since I had been so sick last time in Ningnan. Though he had just turned sixteen, Jin-ming had not yet been assigned a commune. I sent a telegram asking my sister to come back from Ningnan and look after our grandmother. Xiao-hei, fourteen at the time, promised that he could be depended on, and seven-year-old Xiao-fang solemnly made the same announcement.

When I went to say goodbye to her, my grandmother wept. She said she did not know whether she would ever see me again. I stroked the back of her hand, which was now bony, with bulging veins, and pressed it to my cheek. I suppressed the surge of tears and said I would be back very soon.

After a long search, I had finally found a truck going to the Xichang region. Since the mid-1960s Mao had ordered many important factories (including the one where my sister's boyfriend Specs worked) to be moved to Sichuan, particularly to Xichang, where a new industrial base was being built. Mao's theory was that the mountains of Sichuan provided the best deterrent in case the Americans or the Russians attacked. Trucks from five different provinces were busy delivering goods to the base. Through a friend, a driver from Peking agreed to take us—Jin-ming, Nana, Wen, and me. We had to sit on the back of the open truck because the cabin was reserved for the relief driver. Every truck belonged to a convoy which met up in the evening.

These drivers had the reputation of being happy to take girls but not boys—much the same as their brotherhood the world over. Since they were almost the only source of transport, this angered some boys. Along the way I saw slogans pasted on the trunks of trees: "Strongly protest the truckers who only take females and not males!" Some bolder boys stood in the middle of the road to try to force the trucks to stop. One boy from my school did not manage to leap away in time and was killed.

From the lucky female hitchhikers, there were a few reports of rape, but many more of romance. Quite a few marriages resulted from these journeys. A truck driver who took part in the construction of the strategic base enjoyed certain privileges, one being the right to transfer his wife's country registration to the city where he lived. Some girls jumped at this opportunity.

Our drivers were very kind, and behaved impeccably. When we stopped for the night, they would help us secure a hotel bed before going to their guesthouse, and they would invite us to have supper with them so we could share their special food, free.

Only once did I feel there was something faintly sexual on their minds. At one stop another pair of drivers invited Nana and me to go on their truck for the next leg. When we told our driver, his face fell a mile, and he said in a sulky voice, "Go ahead then, go ahead with those nice guys of yours if you like them better." Nana and I looked at each other and mumbled in embarrassment, "We didn't say we liked them better. You are all very nice to us. . . ." We did not go.

Wen kept an eye on Nana and me. He constantly warned us about drivers, about men in general, about thieves, about what to eat and what not to eat, and about going out after dark. He also carried our bags and fetched hot water for us. At dinnertime, he would tell Nana, Jin-ming, and me to join the drivers to eat while he stayed behind in the hotel to look after our bags, as theft was rampant. We brought food back for him.

There was never any sexual advance from Wen. On the evening we crossed the border into Xichang, Nana and I wanted to wash in the river, because the weather was so hot and the evening so beautiful. Wen found us a quiet bend in the river where we bathed in the company of wild ducks and twirling reeds. The rays of the moon were pouring onto the river, the image scattering into masses of sparkling silver rings. Wen sat near the road with his back studiously to us, keeping guard. Like many other young men, he had been brought up in the pre–Cultural Revolution days to be chivalrous.

To get into a hotel, we needed to produce a letter from our unit. Wen, Nana, and I had each secured a letter from our production teams in Ningnan, and Jin-ming had a letter from his school. The hotels were inexpensive, but we did not have much money, since our parents' salaries had been drastically reduced. Nana and I would get a single bed between us in a dormitory and the boys would do the same. The hotels were filthy, and very basic. Before going to bed, Nana and I would turn the quilt over and over looking for fleas and lice. The hotel washbowls usually had rings of dark-gray or yellow dirt on them. Trachoma and fungal infections were commonplace, so we used our own.

One night we were awakened about twelve o'clock by loud bangs on the door: everyone in the hotel had to get up to make an "evening report" to Chairman Mao. This farcical activity was in the same package as the "loyalty dances." It involved gathering in front of a statue or portrait of Mao, chanting quotations from the Little Red Book, and shouting "Long live Chairman Mao, long long live Chairman Mao, and long long long live Chairman Mao!" while waving the Little Red Book rhythmically.

Half awake, Nana and I staggered out of our room. Other travelers were emerging in twos and threes, rubbing their eyes, buttoning their jackets, and pulling up the cotton backs of their shoes. There was not a single complaint. No one dared. At five in the morning we had to go through the same thing again. This was called "morning request for instructions" from Mao. Later, when we were on our way, Jin-ming said, "The head of the Revolutionary Committee in this town must be an insomniac."

Grotesque forms of worshipping Mao had been part of our lives for some time—chanting, wearing Mao badges, waving the Little Red Book. But the idolatry had escalated when the Revolutionary Committees were formally established nationwide by late 1968. The committee members reckoned that the safest and most rewarding course of action was to do nothing, except promote the worship of Mao—and, of course, continue to engage in political persecutions. Once, in a pharmacy in Chengdu, an old shop assistant with a pair of impassive eyes behind gray-rimmed spectacles murmured without looking at me, "When sailing the seas we need a helmsman . . ." There was a pregnant pause. It took me a moment to realize I was supposed to complete the sentence, which was a fawning quotation from Lin Biao about Mao. Such exchanges had just been enforced as a standard greeting. I had to mumble, "When making revolution we need Mao Zedong Thought."

Revolutionary Committees all over China ordered statues of Mao to be built. A huge white marble figure was planned for the center of Chengdu. To accommodate it, the elegant ancient palace gate, on which I had stood so happily only a few years before, was dynamited. The white marble was to come from Xichang, and special trucks, called "loyalty trucks," were shipping the marble out from the mountains. These trucks were decorated like floats in a parade, festooned with red silk ribbons and a huge silk flower in front. They made the journey from Chengdu empty, as they were devoted exclusively to carrying the marble. The trucks which supplied Xichang returned to Chengdu empty: they were not allowed to sully the material that was going to form Mao's body.

After we said goodbye to the driver who had brought us from

Chengdu we hitched a lift on one of these "loyalty trucks" for the last stretch to Ningnan. On the way we stopped at a marble quarry for a rest. A group of sweating workers, naked to the waist, were drinking tea and smoking their yard-long pipes. One of them told us they were not using any machinery, as only working with their bare hands could express their loyalty to Mao. I was horrified to see a badge of Mao pinned to his bare chest. When we were back in the truck, Jin-ming observed that the badge might have been stuck on with a plaster. And, as for their devoted quarrying by hand: "They probably don't have any machines in the first place."

Jin-ming often made skeptical comments like this which kept us laughing. This was unusual in those days, when humor was dangerous. Mao, hypocritically calling for "rebellion," wanted no genuine inquiry or skepticism. To be able to think in a skeptical way was my first step toward enlightenment. Like Bing, Jin-ming helped to destroy my rigid habits of thinking.

As soon as we entered Ningnan, which was about 5,000 feet above sea level, I was hit by stomach trouble again. I vomited up everything I had eaten and the world seemed to be spinning around me. But we could not afford to stop. We had to get to our production teams and complete the rest of the transfer procedure by 21 June. Since Nana's team was nearer, we decided to go there first. It was a day's walk through wild mountains. The summer torrents roared down ravines across which there were often no bridges. While Wen waded ahead to test the depth of the water, Jin-ming carried me on his bony back. Often we had to walk on goat trails about two feet wide at the edges of cliffs with sheer drops of thousands of feet. Several of my school friends had been killed walking home along them at night. The sun was blazing down, and my skin began to peel. I became obsessed with thirst, and drank all the water from everybody's water cans. When we came to a gully, I threw myself on the ground and gulped down the cool liquid. Nana tried to stop me. She said even the peasants would not drink this water unboiled. But I was too wild with thirst to care. Of course, this was followed by more violent vomiting.

Eventually we came to a house. It had several gigantic chestnut trees in front, stretching out their majestic canopies. The peasants invited us in. I licked my cracked lips and immediately made for the stove where I could see a big earthenware bowl, probably containing rice fluid. Here in the mountains this was considered the most delicious drink, and the owner of the house kindly offered it to us. Rice fluid is normally white, but what I saw was black. A whine burst out from it, and a mass of flies lifted off from the jellied surface. I stared into the bowl and saw a few casualties drowning. I had always been very squeamish about flies, but now I picked up the bowl, flicked aside the corpses, and downed the liquid in great gulps.

It was dark when we reached Nana's village. The next day, her production team leader was only too glad to stamp her three letters and get rid of her. In the last few months the peasants had learned that what they had acquired were not extra hands, but extra mouths to feed. They could not throw the city youths out, and were delighted when anyone offered to leave.

I was too sick to go on to my own team, so Wen set off alone to try to secure the release of my sister and myself. Nana and the other girls in her team tried their best to nurse me. I ate and drank only things which had been boiled and reboiled many times, but I lay there feeling miserable, missing my grandmother and her chicken soup. Chicken was considered a great delicacy in those days, and Nana joked that I somehow managed to combine turmoil in my stomach with an appetite for the best food. Nevertheless, she and the other girls and Jin-ming went all out to try to purchase a chicken. But the local peasants did not eat or sell chickens, which they raised only for eggs. They put this custom down to their ancestors' rules, but we were told by friends that chickens here were infested with leprosy, which was widespread in these mountains. So we shunned eggs as well.

Jin-ming was determined to make me some soup like my grandmother's, and put his bent for invention to practical use. On the open platform in front of the house, he propped up a big round bamboo lid with a stick and spread some grain underneath. He tied a piece of string to the stick and hid behind a door, holding the other end of the string, and placed a mirror in such a position that he could monitor what went on under the half-open lid. Crowds of sparrows landed to fight for the grain, and sometimes a turtledove swaggered in. Jin-ming would choose the best moment to pull the string and bring down the lid. Thanks to his ingenuity, I had delicious game soup.

The mountains at the back of the house were covered with peach trees now bearing ripe fruit, and Jin-ming and the girls came back every day with baskets full of peaches. Jin-ming said I must not eat them uncooked, and made me jam.

I felt pampered, and spent my days in the hall, gazing at the faraway mountains and reading Turgenev and Chekhov, which Jin-ming had brought for the journey. I was deeply affected by the mood in Turgenev, and learned many passages from "First Love" by heart.

In the evenings, the serpentine curve of some distant mountains burned like a dramatic fire dragon silhouetted against the dark sky.

Xichang had a very dry climate, and forest protection rules were not being enforced, nor were the fire services working. As a result, the mountains were burning day after day, only stopping when a gorge blocked the way, or a storm doused the flames.

After a few days Wen returned with the permission from my production team for my sister and me to leave. We set off immediately to find the registrar, although I was still weak, and could walk only a few yards before my eyes became dazzled by a mass of sparkling stars. There was only a week left before 21 June.

We reached the county town of Ningnan, and found the atmosphere there like wartime. In most parts of China heavy factional fighting had stopped by now, but in remote areas like this local battles continued. The losing side was hiding in the mountains, and had been launching frequent lightning attacks. There were armed guards everywhere, mostly members of an ethnic group, the Yi, a lot of whom lived in the deeper recesses of the Xichang wilderness. Legend had it that when they slept, the Yi did not lie down, but squatted, burying their heads in the folds of their arms. The faction leaders, who were all Han, talked them into doing the dangerous jobs like fighting in the front line and keeping guard. As we searched the county offices for the registrar, we often had to engage in long, involved explanations with the Yi guards, using hand gestures, as we had no language in common. When we approached, they lifted their guns and aimed them at us, their fingers on the triggers, and their left eyes narrowed. We were scared to death, but had to look nonchalant. We had been advised that they would regard any demonstration of fear as a sign of guilt, and react accordingly.

We finally found the registrar's office, but he was not there. Then we bumped into a friend who told us that he had gone into hiding because of the hordes of city youth besieging him to sort out their problems. Our friend did not know where the registrar was, but he told us about a group of "old city youth" who might.

"Old city youth" were ones who had gone to the countryside before the Cultural Revolution. The Party had been trying to persuade those who had failed exams for high schools and universities to go and "build a splendid new socialist countryside" which would benefit from their education. In their romantic enthusiasm, a number of young people followed the Party's call. The harsh reality of rural life, with no chance to escape, and the realization of the regime's hypocrisy—because no officials' children ever went, even if they had failed their exams—had turned many of them into cynics.

This group of "old city youth" was very friendly. They gave us an excellent meal of game and offered to find out where the registrar was. While a couple of them went to look for him, we chatted with the others, sitting on their spacious pine veranda facing a roaring river called the Black Water. On the high rocks above, egrets were balancing on one long slender leg, raising the other in various balletic postures. Others were flying, fanning their gorgeous snow-white wings with panache. I had never seen these stylish dancers wild and free.

Our hosts pointed out a dark cave across the river. From its ceiling hung a rusty-looking bronze sword. The cave was inaccessible because it was right next to the turbulent river. Legend had it that the sword had been left there by the famous, wise prime minister of the ancient kingdom of Sichuan, Marquis Zhuge Liang, in the third century. He had led seven expeditions from Chengdu to try to conquer the barbarian tribes here in the Xichang area. I knew the story well, and was thrilled to see evidence of it before my eyes. He captured the chieftain of the tribes seven times, and each time he released him, hoping to win him over by his magnanimity. Six times, the chieftain was unmoved and continued his rebellion, but after the seventh time he became wholeheartedly loyal to the Sichuanese king. The moral of this legend was that to conquer a people, one must conquer their hearts and minds—a strategy to which Mao and the Communists subscribed. I vaguely mused that this was why we had to go through "thought reform"—so that we would follow orders willingly. That was why peasants were set up as models: they were the most unquestioning and submissive subjects. On reflection today, I think the variant of Nixon's adviser Charles Colson spelled out the hidden agenda: When you have them by the balls, their hearts and minds will follow.

My train of thought was interrupted by our hosts. What we should do, they enthusiastically advised, was drop a hint to the registrar about our fathers' positions. "He will slap the seal on in no time," declared one jolly-looking young man. They knew we were high officials' children because of the reputation of my school. I felt dubious about their advice. "But our parents no longer hold these positions. They have been labeled capitalist-roaders," I pointed out hesitantly.

"What does that matter?" Several voices brushed aside my worry. "Your father is a Communist veteran, right?"

"Right," I murmured.

"A high official, right?"

"Sort of," I mumbled. "But that was before the Cultural Revolution. Now . . ."

"Never mind that. Has anyone announced his dismissal? No? That's all right, then. You see, it's as clear as daylight that the mandate of

Party officials is not over. *He* will tell you that"—the jolly young man pointed in the direction of the sword of the wise old prime minister. I did not realize at the time that, consciously or subconsciously, people regarded Mao's personal power structure as no alternative to the old Communist administration. The ousted officials would come back. Meanwhile, the jolly young man was continuing, shaking his head for emphasis: "No official here would dare to offend you and create problems for himself in the future." I thought of the appalling vendettas of the Tings. Of course, people in China would always be alert to the possibility of revenge by those with power.

As we left, I asked how I should drop the hint to the registrar about my father's position without sounding vulgar. They laughed heartily. "He is just like a peasant! They don't have that kind of sensibility. They won't be able to tell the difference anyway. Just tell him straight out: 'My father is the head of—' " I was struck by the scornful tone in their voices. Later I discovered that most city youth, old or new, developed a strong contempt for the peasants after they had settled down among them. Mao, of course, had expected the opposite reaction.

On 20 June, after days of desperately searching the mountains, we found the registrar. My rehearsal of how to drop the hint about my parents' positions proved completely unnecessary. The registrar himself took the initiative by asking me: "What did your father do before the Cultural Revolution?" After many personal questions, put from curiosity rather than necessity, he took a dirty handkerchief out of his jacket pocket and unfolded it to reveal a wooden seal and a flat tin box containing a sponge in red ink. Solemnly he pressed the seal into the sponge and then stamped our letters.

With that vital seal and by the skin of our teeth—with less than twenty-four hours to spare—we had accomplished our mission. We still had to find the clerk in charge of our registration books, but we knew that that was not going to be a big problem. The authorization had been obtained. I relaxed immediately—into stomach pains and diarrhea.

I struggled back with the others to the county town. It was dark by the time we arrived. We made for the government guesthouse, a drab two-story building standing in the middle of a walled enclosure. The porter's lodge was empty, and there was no one visible on the grounds either. Most of the rooms were shut, but on the top floor some bedroom doors were half open.

I entered one, after making sure there was no one in it. An open window looked out on some fields beyond a dilapidated brick wall.

Across the corridor was another row of rooms. There was not a soul around. From some personal things in the room and a half-drunk mug of tea, I gathered that someone had been staying here very recently. But I was too tired to wonder why he or she—and everyone else—had deserted the building. Without even the energy to close the door, I threw myself onto the bed and fell asleep fully dressed.

I was jolted awake by a loudspeaker chanting some quotations by Mao, one being: "If the enemy won't surrender, we will eliminate them!" I was suddenly wide awake. I realized our building was under attack.

The next thing I heard was the whine of bullets very close by, and windows breaking. The loudspeaker yelled out the name of some Rebel organization, urging it to surrender. Otherwise, it screeched, the attackers would dynamite the building.

Jin-ming burst in. Several armed men wearing rattan helmets were rushing into the rooms opposite mine, which overlooked the front gate. One of them was a young boy shouldering a gun taller than himself. Without a word, they raced to the windows, smashed the glass with the butts of their rifles, and started shooting. A man who seemed to be their commander told us hurriedly that the building had been the headquarters of his faction, and was now being attacked by the opposition. We had better get out quickly—but not down the stairs, which led to the front. How then?

We frantically tore the sheets and quilt covers off the bed and made a sort of rope. We tied one end of it to a window frame and scrambled down the two stories. As we landed, bullets whistled and hissed into the hard mud around us. We bent double and ran for the collapsed wall. Once over it, we kept running for a long time before we felt safe enough to stop. The sky and the maize fields were beginning to show their pale features. We made for a friend's place in a nearby commune to catch our breath and decide what to do next. On the way, we heard from some peasants that the guesthouse had been blown up.

At our friend's place, a message was waiting for me. A telegram from my sister in Chengdu had arrived just after we had left Nana's village in search of the registrar. As no one knew where I was, my friends had opened it and passed the message around so that whoever saw me could let me know.

This was how I learned that my grandmother was dead.

23. "The More Books You Read, the More Stupid You Become"— I Work as a Peasant and a Barefoot Doctor

(June 1969–1971)

Jin-ming and I sat on the bank of the Golden Sand River, waiting for a ferry. I rested my head on my hands and stared at the unruly river tumbling past me on its long journey from the Himalayas to the sea. It was to become the longest river in China—the Yangtze, after joining the Min River at Yibin, 300 miles downstream. Toward the end of its journey, the Yangtze spreads and meanders, irrigating vast areas of flat farmland. But here, in the mountains, it was too violent to build a bridge across it. Only ferries linked Sichuan province with Yunnan to the east. Every summer, when the torrent was high and fierce with the melted snow, the river claimed lives. Only a few days before, it had swallowed a ferry with three of my schoolmates in it.

Dusk was descending. I felt very ill. Jin-ming had spread his jacket on the ground for me so I would not have to sit on the damp grass. Our aim was to cross over to Yunnan and try to hitch a lift to Chengdu. The roads through Xichang were cut off by fighting between Rebel factions, so we had to try a roundabout route. Nana and Wen had offered to get my registration book and luggage, and those of Xiao-hong, to Chengdu.

A dozen strong men rowed the ferry against the current, chanting a song in unison. When they reached the middle of the river, they stopped and let the ferry be carried downstream toward the Yunnan side. Huge waves broke over us several times. I had to hold on tight to the side while the boat listed helplessly. Normally I would have been terrified, but now I felt only numbness. I was too preoccupied with the death of my grandmother.

A solitary truck stood on a basketball court in the town on the Yunnan bank, Qiaojia. The driver readily agreed to give us a lift in the back. All the time, I kept turning over in my head what I could have done to save my grandmother. As the truck jolted along, we passed banana groves at the back of mud houses in the embrace of cloud-capped mountains. Seeing the gigantic banana leaves, I remembered the small, potted, fruitless banana by the door of my grandmother's hospital ward in Chengdu. When Bing came to see me, I used to sit beside it with him, chatting deep into the night. My grandmother did not like him because of his cynical grin and the casualness with which he treated adults, which she considered disrespectful. Twice she came staggering downstairs to call me back. I had hated myself for making her anxious, but I could not help it. I could not control my desire to see Bing. Now how I wished I could start all over again! I would not do anything to upset her. I would just make sure she got better—although how I did not know.

We passed through Yibin. The road wound down Emerald Screen Hill on the edge of the city. Staring at the elegant redwoods and bamboo groves, I thought back to April, when I had just returned home to Meteorite Street from Yibin. I was telling my grandmother how I had gone to sweep Dr. Xia's tomb, which was on the side of this hill, on a sunny spring day. Aunt Jun-ying had given me some special "silver money" to burn at the tomb. God knows where she had got it from, as it had been condemned as "feudal." I searched up and down for hours, but could not find the tomb. The hillside was a battered mess. The Red Guards had leveled the cemetery and smashed the tombstones, as they considered burial an "old" practice. I can never forget the intense flame of hope in my grandmother's eyes when I mentioned the visit, and how it darkened almost immediately when I stupidly added that the tomb was lost. Her look of disappointment had been haunting me. Now I kicked myself for not telling her a white lie. But it was too late.

When Jin-ming and I got home, after more than a week on the road, there was only her empty bed. I remembered seeing her stretched out on it, her hair loose but still tidy, biting her lips hard, her cheeks sunken. She had suffered her murderous pains in silence and composure, never screaming, never writhing. Because of her stoicism, I had failed to realize how serious her illness was.

My mother was in detention. What Xiao-hei and Xiao-hong told me about Grandmother's last days caused me such anguish that I had to ask them to stop. It was only years later that I learned what had happened after I left. She would do some housework, then go back to bed and lie there with her face taut, trying to fight back the pain. She constantly murmured that she was anxious about my trip, and worried about my younger brothers. "What will become of the boys, with no schools?" she would sigh.

Then one day she could not get out of bed. No doctor would come to the house, so my sister's boyfriend, Specs, carried her to the hospital on his back. My sister walked by his side, propping her up. After a couple of journeys, the doctors asked them not to come anymore. They said they could find nothing wrong with her and there was nothing they could do.

So she lay in bed, waiting for death. Her body became lifeless bit by bit. Her lips moved from time to time, but my sister and brothers could hear nothing. Many times they went to my mother's place of detention to beg for her to be permitted to come home. Each time, they were turned away without being able to see her.

My grandmother's entire body seemed to be dead. But her eyes were still open, looking around expectantly. She would not close them until she had seen her daughter.

At last my mother was allowed home. Over the next two days, she did not leave my grandmother's bedside. Every now and then, my grandmother would whisper something to her. Her last words were about how she had fallen into this pain.

She said the neighbors belonging to Mrs. Shau's group had held a denunciation meeting against her in the courtyard. The receipt for the jewelry she had donated during the Korean War had been confiscated by some Rebels in a house raid. They said she was "a stinking member of the exploiting class," otherwise how could she have acquired all that jewelry in the first place?

My grandmother said she had had to stand on a small table. The ground was uneven and the table wobbled, and she felt dizzy. The neighbors were yelling at her. The woman who had accused Xiao-fang of raping her daughter hit one leg of the table ferociously with a club. My grandmother could not keep her balance and fell backwards onto the hard ground. She said she had felt a sharp pain ever since.

In fact, there had been no denunciation meeting. But that was the image that haunted my grandmother to her last breath.

On the third day after my mother came home, my grandmother died. Two days later, immediately after my grandmother was cremated, my mother had to return to detention.

I have often dreamed of my grandmother since, and awakened sobbing. She was a great character—vivacious, talented, and immensely capable. Yet she had no outlet for her abilities. The daughter of an ambitious small-town policeman, concubine to a warlord, stepmother to an extended but divided family, and mother and mother-in-law to two Communist officials—in all these circumstances she had little happiness. The days with Dr. Xia were lived under the shadow of their past, and together they endured poverty, Japanese occupation, and the civil war. She might have found happiness in looking after her grandchildren, but she was rarely free from anxiety about us. Most of her life she had lived in fear, and she faced death many times. She was a strong woman, but in the end the disasters which hit my parents, the worries about her grandchildren, the tide of ugly human hostility—all conspired to crush her. But the most unbearable thing for her was what happened to her daughter. It was as though she felt in her own body and soul every bit of the pain that my mother suffered, and she was finally killed by the accumulation of anguish.

There was another, more immediate factor in her death: she was denied proper medical care—and could not be looked after, or even seen, by her daughter when she was fatally ill. Because of the Cultural Revolution. How could the revolution be good, I asked myself, when it brought such human destruction, for nothing? Over and over again, I told myself I hated the Cultural Revolution, and I felt even worse because there was nothing I could do.

I blamed myself for not looking after my grandmother as well as I might have. She was in the hospital at the time when I had come to know Bing and Wen. My friendships with them had cushioned and insulated me, and had blunted my awareness of her suffering. I told myself it was despicable to have had any happy feelings at all, by the side of what I now realized was my grandmother's deathbed. I resolved never to have a boyfriend again. Only by self-denial, I thought, could I expiate some of my guilt.

The next two months I stayed in Chengdu, desperately looking, with Nana and my sister, for a "relative" nearby whose commune would accept us. We had to find one by the end of the autumn harvest when food was distributed, otherwise we would have nothing to eat for the following year—our state supply ran out in January.

When Bing came to see me, I was very cold to him, and told him never to come again. He wrote me letters but I threw them into the stove without opening them—a gesture I had perhaps picked up from Russian novels. Wen came back from Ningnan with my registration book and luggage, but I refused to see him. Once I passed him on the street, and looked straight through him, catching only a glimpse of his eyes, in which I saw confusion and hurt.

Wen returned to Ningnan. One summer day in 1970, a forest fire broke out near his village. He and a friend rushed out with a couple of brooms to try to put it out. A gust of wind threw a ball of flames into his friend's face, leaving him permanently disfigured. The two of them left Ningnan and crossed into Laos, where there was a war going on between left-wing guerrillas and the United States. At the time a number of high officials' children were going to Laos and Vietnam to fight the Americans secretly, as it was forbidden by the government. These young people had become disillusioned with the Cultural Revolution, and hoped they could get back their youthful adrenaline by taking on the "U.S. imperialists."

One day soon after they got to Laos, Wen heard the alarm which signaled that American planes were coming. He was the first to leap up and charge out, but in his inexperience he stepped on a mine which his comrades had planted themselves. He was blown to smithereens. My last memory of him is his perplexed and wounded eyes watching me from a muddy street corner in Chengdu.

Meanwhile, my family was scattered. On 17 October 1969 Lin Biao ordered the country into a state of war, using as a pretext clashes which had broken out earlier that year on the border with the Soviet Union. In the name of "evacuation," he sent his opponents in the army and the disgraced top leaders out of the capital and placed them under house arrest or detention in different parts of China. The Revolutionary Committees used this opportunity to speed up the deportation of "undesirables." The 500 members of my mother's Eastern District staff were ordered out of Chengdu to a place in the Xichang hinterland called Buffalo Boy Flatland. My mother was allowed ten days at home from detention to make arrangements. She put Xiao-hei and Xiao-fang on a train to Yibin. Although Aunt Jun-ying was half-paralyzed, there were other aunts and uncles there who could look after them. Jin-ming had been sent by his school to a commune fifty miles northeast of Chengdu.

At the same time Nana, my sister, and I finally found a commune that would take us in a county called Deyang, not far from where Jin-ming was. Specs, my sister's boyfriend, had a colleague from the county who was prepared to claim we were his cousins. Some communes in the area needed more farmhands. Although we had no proof of kinship, no one asked any questions. The only thing that mattered was that we were—or at least seemed to be—extra labor.

We were allocated to two different production teams, because two extra people was the maximum any one team could accommodate. Nana and I went to one team and my sister to another, three miles away. The railway station was about five hours' walk away, much of it along eighteen-inch-wide ridges between rice paddies.

My family of seven was now dispersed in six different places. Xiao-hei was happy to leave Chengdu, where the new Chinese-language textbook at his school, compiled by some teachers and members of the propaganda team there, contained a condemnation of my father by name, and Xiao-hei was ostracized and bullied.

In the early summer of 1969, his school had been sent to the countryside on the outskirts of Chengdu to help with the harvest. The boys and girls camped separately in two large halls. In the evenings, under the starry vault of the sky, the paths between the paddy fields were frequented by young couples. Romance bloomed, not least in the heart of my fourteen-year-old brother, who started to fancy a girl in his group. After days of summoning up his courage, he nervously approached her one afternoon when they were cutting wheat, and invited her to go for a walk that evening. The girl bent her head and said nothing. Xiao-hei thought this was a sign of "silent consent," *mo-xu*.

He leaned on a haystack in the moonlight, and waited with all the anxieties and longings of first love. Suddenly, he heard a whistle. A gang of boys from his form appeared. They shoved him around and called him names, then they threw a jacket over his head and started to hit and kick him. He managed to break free, and staggered to the door of one of the teachers and shouted for help. The teacher opened the door, but pushed him away, saying, "I can't help you! Don't you dare come back!"

Xiao-hei was too frightened to return to his camp, and spent the night hiding in a haystack. He realized it was his "sweetheart" who had called in the bullies: she had felt insulted that the son of a "counterrevolutionary capitalist-roader" should have the audacity to fancy her.

When they returned to Chengdu, Xiao-hei went to his street gang for help. They appeared at his school with much flaunting of muscles, and a gigantic wolfhound, and hauled the leading bully out of the classroom. He was shaking, his face ashen. But before the gang set upon him, Xiao-hei was overtaken by pity, and asked his helmsman to let the boy go.

Pity had become an alien concept, and was seen as a sign of stupidity. Xiao-hei was bullied even more than before. He made a feeble attempt at enlisting the help of his gang again, but they told him they would not help a "shrimp."

Xiao-hei approached his new school in Yibin dreading more bullying. To his amazement, he received a warm, almost emotional welcome. The teachers, the propaganda team members who were running the school, the children—all seemed to have heard of my father and referred to him with open admiration. Xiao-hei immediately acquired a certain prestige. The prettiest girl in the school became his girlfriend. Even the most thuggish boys treated him with respect. It was clear to him that my father was a revered figure in Yibin, in spite of the fact that everyone knew he was in disgrace, and the Tings were in power. The population of Yibin had suffered horribly under the Tings. Thousands had died or been injured in the factional fighting or under torture. One family friend escaped death because when his children went to collect his corpse in the morgue, they found he was still breathing.

People in Yibin had developed a great yearning for the days of peace, for officials who did not abuse their power, for a government that was dedicated to getting things to work. The focus of this nostalgia was the early 1950s, when my father was the governor. It was then that the Communists were at their most popular—just after they had replaced the Kuomintang, put an end to starvation, and established law and order, but before their incessant political campaigns (and their own, Mao-induced famine). My father became identified in the folk memory with the good old days. He was seen as the legendary good official, in stark contrast with the Tings.

Because of him, Xiao-hei enjoyed his stay in Yibin—although he learned little at school. Teaching materials still consisted of Mao's works and People's Daily articles, and no one had any authority over the pupils—since Mao had not retracted his blanket dismissal of formal learning.

The teachers and the workers' propaganda team tried to enlist Xiao-hei's help to enforce discipline in his class. But here even my father's reputation failed, and Xiao-hei was eventually ostracized by some of the boys for being the teacher's "lackey." A whispering campaign began claiming that he had embraced his girlfriend under lampposts in the street, which was a "bourgeois crime." Xiao-hei lost his privileged position and was told to write self-criticisms and to pledge to carry out thought reform. The girl's mother turned up one day insisting on a surgical examination to prove her daughter's chastity. After a big scene, she took her daughter out of the school.

Xiao-hei had one close friend in his class, a popular boy of seventeen who had one sensitive spot: his mother had never married, but had five children—all with different and unknown fathers, which was extremely unusual in a society where "illegitimacy" was heavily stigmatized, in spite of having been formally abolished. Now, in one of the witch-hunting tides, she was publicly humiliated as a "bad element." The boy felt very ashamed of his mother, and told Xiao-hei in private that he hated her. One day the school was awarding a best-swimmer prize (because Mao liked swimming), and Xiao-hei's friend was unanimously nominated by the pupils; but when the award was announced, it was not to him. Apparently one young woman teacher had objected: "We can't give it to him: his mother is a 'worn shoe.' "

When the boy heard this, he grabbed a kitchen chopper and stormed into the teacher's office. Someone stopped him while the teacher scuttled off and hid. Xiao-hei knew how much this incident had hurt his friend: for the first time, the boy was seen weeping bitterly. That night, Xiao-hei and some of the other boys sat up with him, trying to comfort him. The next day, he disappeared. His corpse was washed up on the bank of the Golden Sand River. He had tied his hands together before he jumped.

The Cultural Revolution not only did nothing to modernize the medieval elements in China's culture, it actually gave them political respectability. "Modern" dictatorship and ancient intolerance fed on each other. Anyone who fell foul of the age-old conservative attitudes could now become a political victim.

My new commune in Deyang was in an area of low hills dotted with shrubs and eucalyptus trees. Most of the farmland was good, producing two major harvests a year, one of wheat and one of rice. Vegetables, rapeseed, and sweet potatoes grew in abundance. After Ningnan, the biggest relief for me was that we did not have to do any climbing, and I could breathe normally instead of panting for breath all the time. I did not mind the fact that walking here meant staggering along narrow, muddy ridges between paddy fields. I often fell on my bottom, and sometimes in a grab for support I would push the person in front—usually Nana—into a rice paddy. Nor did I mind another peril of walking at night: the possibility of being bitten by dogs, quite a few of which had rabies.

When we first arrived, we stayed next to a pigsty. At night, we fell asleep to a symphony of pigs grunting, mosquitoes whining, and dogs barking. The room smelled permanently of pig manure and anti-mosquito incense. After a while the production team built Nana and me a two-room cottage on a plot of land which had been used for cutting mud bricks. The land was lower than the rice paddy which lay just across a narrow footpath, and in spring and summer, when the paddy fields were filled with water, or after heavy rain, marshy water would ooze up from the mud floor. Nana and I had to take off our shoes, roll up our trouser legs, and wade into the cottage. Fortunately the double bed we shared had tall legs, so we slept about two feet above the muddy water. Getting into bed involved putting a bowl of clean water on a stool, climbing up onto the stool, and washing our feet. Living in these damp conditions, my bones and muscles ached all the time.

But the cottage was also fun. When the flood receded, mushrooms would spring up under the bed and in the corners of the rooms. With a little imagination, the floor looked like something out of a fairy tale. Once I dropped a spoonful of peas on the ground. After the water had come and gone, a cluster of delicate petals unfolded from slender stems, as though they had just awakened to the rays of the sun, which brimmed through the wood-framed opening in the wall which was our window.

The view was perpetually magical to me. Beyond our door lay the village pond, overgrown with water lilies and lotuses. The path in front of the cottage led up to a pass in the hill about 350 feet above us. The sun set behind it, framed by black rocks. Before darkness fell, silver mist would hang over the fields at the foot of the hills. Men, women, and children walked back to the village after their day's work in the evening haze, carrying baskets, hoes, and sickles, and were met by their dogs who yapped and leaped about them. They looked as though they were sailing in clouds. Smoke curved out from the thatched cottages. Wooden barrels clicked at the stone well, as people fetched water for the evening meal. Loud voices were heard as people chatted by the bamboo groves, the men squatting and puffing their long, slender pipes. Women neither smoked nor squatted: these were traditionally considered unbecoming for women, and no one in "revolutionary" China had talked about changing these attitudes.

It was in Deyang that I came to know how China's peasants really lived. Each day started with the production team leader allocating jobs. All the peasants had to work, and they each earned a fixed number of "work points" (gong-fen) for their day's work. The number of work points accumulated was an important element in the distribution at the end of the year. The peasants got food, fuel, and other daily necessities, plus a tiny sum of cash, from the production team. After the harvest, the production team paid part of it over as tax to the state. Then the rest was divided up. First, a basic quantity was meted out equally to every male, and about a quarter less to every female. Children under three received a half portion. Since a child just over three obviously could not eat an adult's share, it was desirable to have more children. The system functioned as a positive disincentive to birth control.

The remainder of the crop was then distributed according to how many work points each person had earned. Twice a year, the peasants would all assemble to fix the daily work points for each person. No one missed these meetings. In the end, most young and middle-aged men would be allocated ten points a day, and women eight. One or two whom the whole village acknowledged to be exceptionally strong got an extra point. "Class enemies" like the former village landlord and his family got a couple of points less than the others, in spite of the fact that they worked no less hard and were usually given the toughest jobs. Nana and I, being inexperienced "city youth," got four —the same number as children barely in their teens; we were told this was "to start with," though mine were never raised.

Since there was little variation from individual to individual of the same gender in terms of daily points, the number of work points accumulated depended mainly on how many days one worked, rather than how one worked. This was a constant source of resentment among the villagers—in addition to being a massive discouragement to efficiency. Every day, the peasants would screw up their eyes to watch how the others were working in case they themselves were being taken advantage of. No one wanted to work harder than others who earned the same number of work points. Women felt bitter about men who sometimes did the same kind of job as they, but earned two points more. There were constant arguments.

We frequently spent ten hours in the fields doing a job which could have been done in five. But we had to be out there for ten hours for it to be counted as a full day. We worked in slow motion, and I stared at the sun impatiently willing it to go down, and counted the minutes until the whistle blew, signaling an end to work. I soon discovered that boredom was as exhausting as backbreaking labor.

Here, as in Ningnan, and much of Sichuan, there were no machines at all. Farming methods were more or less the same as 2,000 years ago, except for some chemical fertilizers, which the team received from the government in exchange for grain. There were practically no work animals except water buffaloes for plowing. Everything else, including the transport of water, manure, fuel, vegetables, and grain, was done entirely by hand, and shoulders, using bamboo baskets or wooden barrels on a shoulder pole. My biggest problem was carrying loads. My right shoulder was perpetually swollen and sore from having to carry water from the well to the house. Whenever a young man who fancied me came to visit I displayed such helplessness that he never failed to offer to fill the water tank for me. And not only the water tank—jugs, bowls, and even cups too.

The team leader considerately stopped assigning me to carry things, and sent me to do "light" jobs with the children and the older and pregnant women. But they were not always light to me. Ladling out manure soon made my arms sore, not to mention churning up my stomach when I saw the fat maggots swimming on the surface. Picking cotton in a sea of brilliant whiteness might have made an idyllic picture, but I quickly realized how demanding it was directly under the relentless sun, in temperatures well over 85°F, with high humidity, among prickly branches that left scratches all over me.

I preferred transplanting rice shoots. This was considered a hard job because one had to bend so much. Often at the end of the day, even the toughest men complained about not being able to stand up straight. But I loved the cool water on my legs in the otherwise unbearable heat, the sight of the neat rows of tender green, and the soft mud under my bare feet, which gave me a sensuous pleasure. The only thing that really bothered me was the leeches. My first encounter was when I felt something ticklish on my leg. I lifted it to scratch and saw a fat, slithery creature bending its head into my skin, busily trying to squeeze in. I let out a mighty scream. A peasant girl next to me giggled. She found my squeamishness funny. Nevertheless, she trudged over and slapped my leg just above the leech. It fell into the water with a plop.

On winter mornings, in the two-hour work period before breakfast, I climbed up the hills with the "weaker" women to collect firewood. There were scarcely any trees on the hills, and even the bushes were few and far between. We often had to walk a long way. We cut with a sickle, grabbing the plants with our free hand. The shrubs were covered with thorns, quite a few of which would always manage to embed themselves in my left palm and wrist. At first I spent a long time trying to pick them out, but eventually I got used to leaving them to come out on their own, after the spots became inflamed.

We gathered what the peasants called "feather fuel." This was pretty useless, and burned up in no time. Once I voiced my regret about the lack of proper trees. The women with me said it had not always been like this. Before the Great Leap Forward, they told me, the hills had been covered with pine, eucalyptus, and cypress. They had all been felled to feed the "backyard furnaces" to produce steel.

The women told me this placidly, with no bitterness, as though it were not the cause of their daily battle for fuel. They seemed to treat it as something which life had thrust on them, like many other misfortunes. I was shocked to come face-to-face, for the first time, with the disastrous consequences of the Great Leap, which I had known only as a "glorious success."

I found out a lot of other things. A "speak-bitterness" session was organized for the peasants to describe how they had suffered under the Kuomintang, and to generate gratitude to Mao, particularly among the younger generation. Some peasants talked about childhoods of unrelieved hunger, and lamented that their own children were so spoiled that they often had to be coaxed to finish their food.

Then their conversation turned to a particular famine. They described having to eat sweet potato leaves and digging into the ridges between the fields in the hope of finding some roots. They mentioned the many deaths in the village. Their stories reduced me to tears. After saying how they hated the Kuomintang and how they loved Chairman Mao, the peasants referred to this famine as taking place at "the time of forming the communes." Suddenly it struck me that the famine they were talking about was under the Communists. They had confused the two regimes. I asked: "Were there unprecedented natural calamities in this period? Wasn't that the cause of the problem?" "Oh no," they said. "The weather could not have been better and there was plenty of grain in the fields. But that man"—they pointed to a cringing forty-year-old—"ordered the men away to make steel, and half the harvest was lost in the fields. But he told us: no matter, we were in the paradise of Communism now and did not have to worry about food. Before, we had always had to control our stomachs, but then we ate our fill in the commune canteen; we threw away the leftovers; we even fed the pigs with precious rice. Then the canteen had no more food, but he placed guards outside the store. The rest of the grain was to be shipped to Peking and Shanghai—there were foreigners there."

Bit by bit, the full picture came out. The cringing man had been the leader of the production team during the Great Leap. He and his cronies had smashed the peasants' woks and stoves so they could not cook at home, and so the woks could be fed into the furnaces. He had reported vastly exaggerated harvests, with the result that the taxes were so high they took every morsel of grain the peasants had left. The villagers had died in scores. After the famine, he was blamed for all the wrongs in the village. The commune allowed the villagers to vote him out of office, and labeled him a "class enemy."

Like most class enemies, he was not put in prison but kept "under surveillance" by his fellow villagers. This was Mao's way: to keep "enemy" figures among the people so they always had someone visible and at hand to hate. Whenever a new campaign came along, this man would be one of the "usual suspects" to be rounded up and attacked afresh. He was always assigned the hardest jobs, and was allocated only seven work points a day, three fewer than most of the other men. I never saw anyone talking to him. Several times I spotted village children throwing stones at his sons.

The peasants thanked Chairman Mao for punishing him. No one questioned his guilt, or the degree of his responsibility. I sought him out, on my own, and asked him his story.

He seemed pathetically grateful to be asked. "I was carrying out orders," he kept saying. "I had to carry out orders. . . ." Then he sighed: "Of course, I didn't want to lose my post. Somebody else would have taken my place. Then what would have happened to me and my kids? We probably would have died of hunger. A production team leader is small, but at least he can die after everyone else in the village."

His words and the peasants' stories shook me to the core. It was the first time I had come across the ugly side of Communist China before the Cultural Revolution. The picture was vastly different from the rosy official version. In the hills and fields of Deyang my doubts about the Communist regime deepened.

I have sometimes wondered whether Mao knew what he was doing putting the sheltered urban youth of China in touch with reality. But then he was confident that much of the population would not be able to make rational deductions with the fragmentary information available to them. Indeed, at the age of eighteen I was still only capable of vague doubts, not explicit analysis of the regime. No matter how much I hated the Cultural Revolution, to doubt Mao still did not enter my mind.

In Deyang, as in Ningnan, few peasants could read the simplest article in a newspaper or write a rudimentary letter. Many could not even write their own name. The Communists' early drive to tackle illiteracy had been pushed aside by incessant witch-hunts. There had once been an elementary school in the village, subsidized by the commune, but at the beginning of the Cultural Revolution the children abused the teacher to their hearts' content. They paraded him around the village with heavy cast-iron woks piled up on his head and his face blackened with soot. Once they almost fractured his skull. Since then, no one could be persuaded to teach.

Most peasants did not miss the school. "What's the point?" they would say. "You pay fees and read for years, and in the end you are still a peasant, earning your food with your sweat. You don't get a grain of rice more for being able to read books. Why waste time and money? Might as well start earning your work points right away." The virtual absence of any chance of a better future and the near total immobility for anyone born a peasant took the incentive out of the pursuit of knowledge. Children of school age would stay at home to help their families with their work or look after younger brothers and sisters. They would be out in the fields when they were barely in their teens. As for girls, the peasants considered it a complete waste of time for them to go to school. "They get married and belong to other people. It's like pouring water on the ground."

The Cultural Revolution was trumpeted as having brought education to the peasants through "evening classes." One day my production team announced it was starting evening classes and asked Nana and me to be the teachers. I was delighted. However, as soon as the first "class" began, I realized that this was no education.

The classes invariably started with Nana and me being asked by the production team leader to read out articles by Mao or other items from the *People's Daily*. Then he would make an hour-long speech consisting of all the latest political jargon strung together in undigested and largely unintelligible hunks. Now and then he would give specific orders, all solemnly delivered in the name of Mao. "Chairman Mao says we must eat two meals of rice porridge and only one meal of solid rice a day." "Chairman Mao says we mustn't waste sweet potatoes on pigs."

After a hard day's work in the fields, the peasants' minds were on their household chores. Their evenings were valuable to them, but no one dared to skip the "classes." They just sat there, and eventually dozed off. I was not sorry to see this form of "education," designed to stupefy rather than enlighten, gradually wither away.

Without education, the peasants' world was painfully narrow. Their conversations usually centered on minute details of daily living. One woman would spend a whole morning complaining that her sister-in-law had used ten bundles of feather fuel for cooking breakfast when she could have made do with nine (fuel, like everything else, was pooled). Another would grumble for hours that her mother-in-law put too many sweet potatoes in the rice (rice being more precious and desirable than sweet potatoes). I knew their restricted horizon was not their fault, but nonetheless I found their conversations unbearable.

One unfailing topic of gossip was, of course, sex. A twenty-year-old woman called Mei from the Deyang county town had been assigned to the village next to mine. She had allegedly slept with a lot of city youths as well as peasants, and every now and then in the fields someone would come up with a lewd story about her. It was rumored that she was pregnant, and had been binding her waist to hide it. In an effort to prove that she was not carrying a "bastard," Mei deliberately did all the things a pregnant woman was not supposed to do, like carrying heavy loads. Eventually a dead baby was discovered in the bushes next to a stream in her village. People said it was hers. Nobody knew whether it had been born dead. Her production team leader ordered a hole dug and buried the baby. And that was that, apart from the gossip, which became even more virulent.

The whole story appalled me, but there were other shocks. One of my neighbors had four daughters—four dark-skinned, round-eyed beauties. But the villagers did not think they were pretty. Too dark, they said. Pale skin was the main criterion for beauty in much of the Chinese countryside. When it was time for the eldest daughter to get married, the father decided to look for a son-in-law who would come and live in their house. That way, he would not only keep his daughter's work points, but would also get an extra pair of hands. Normally, women married into men's families, and it was considered a great humiliation for a man to marry into a woman's family. But our neighbor eventually found a young man from a very poor mountain area who was desperate to get out—and could never do so except through marriage. The young man thus had a very low status. I often heard his father-in-law shouting abuse at him at the top of his voice. To torment the young man, he made his daughter sleep alone when the whim took him. She did not dare to refuse because "filial piety," which was deep-rooted in Confucian ethics, enjoined that children must obey their parents—and because she must not be seen as being keen to sleep with a man, even her husband: for a woman to enjoy sex was considered shameful. I was awakened one morning by a commotion outside my window. The young man had somehow got hold of a few bottles of alcohol made from sweet potatoes and had poured them down his throat. His father-in-law had been kicking his bedroom door to get him to start working. When he finally broke the door down, the son-in-law was dead.

One day my production team was making pea noodles, and borrowed my enamel washbowl to carry water. That day, the noodles collapsed into a shapeless mess. The crowd that had gathered excitedly and expectantly around the noodle-making barrel started muttering loudly when they saw me approaching, and glared at me with disgust. I was scared. Later I was told by some women that the villagers blamed the sagging noodles on me. They said I must have used the bowl to wash when I was menstruating. The women told me I was lucky to be a "city youth." If it had been one of them, their menfolk would have given them "a really good hiding."

On another occasion, a group of young men passing through our village carrying baskets of sweet potatoes were taking a break on a narrow road. Their shoulder poles were lying on the ground, blocking the way. I stepped over one of them. All of a sudden, one of the young men jumped to his feet, picked up his pole, and stood in front of me, with fiery eyes. He looked as though he was going to strike me. From the other peasants, I learned that he believed he would develop shoulder sores if a woman stepped over his pole. I was made to cross back over it "to undo the poison." During the whole time I was in the countryside, I never saw any attempt to tackle such warped thinking —in fact, it was never even mentioned.

The most educated person in my production team was the former landlord. I had been conditioned to regard landlords as evil, and now, to my initial uneasiness, I found that I got on best with this family. They bore no resemblance to the stereotypes that had been drilled into my mind. The husband did not have cruel, vicious eyes, and his wife did not wiggle her bottom, or make her voice sugary, to appear seductive.

Sometimes, when we were alone, he would talk about his grievances. "Chang Jung," he once said, "I know you are a kind person. You must be a reasonable person as well, since you have read books. You can judge whether this is fair." Then he told me why he had been classified as a landlord. He had been a waiter in Chengdu in 1948, and had saved up some money by watching every penny. At the time, some farsighted landlords were selling their land cheap, as they could see land reform coming if the Communists reached Sichuan. The waiter was not politically astute, and bought some land, thinking he had got a bargain. He not only soon lost most of it in the land reform, but became a class enemy to boot. "Alas," he said, with resignation, quoting a classic line, "one single slip has caused a thousand years of sorrow."

The villagers seemed to feel no hostility toward the landlord and his family, although they kept their distance. But, like all "class enemies," they were always given the jobs no one else wanted. And the two sons got one work point less than other men, in spite of the fact that they were the hardest-working men in the village. They seemed to me to be highly intelligent, and also the most refined young men around. Their gentleness and gracefulness set them apart, and I found that I felt closer to them than to any other young people in the village. However, in spite of their qualities, no girls wanted to marry them. Their mother told me how much money she had spent buying presents for the few girls whom the go-betweens had introduced. The girls would accept the clothes and money and then walk off. Other peasants could have demanded the presents back, but a landlord's family could do nothing. She would sigh long and loud about the fact that her sons had little prospect of decent marriages. But, she told me, they bore their misfortune lightly: after each disappointment, they would try to cheer her up. They would offer to work on market days to earn back the cost of her lost presents.

All these misfortunes were told to me without much drama or emotion. Here it seemed that even shocking deaths were like a stone being dropped into a pond where the splash and the ripple closed over into stillness in no time.

In the placidity of the village, in the hushed depth of the nights in my damp home, I did a lot of reading and thinking. When I first came to Deyang, Jin-ming gave me several big cases of his black-market books, which he had been able to accumulate because the house raiders had now mostly been packed off to the "cadres' school" at Miyi, together with my father. All day while I was out in the fields, I itched to get back to them.

I devoured what had survived the burning of my father's library. There were the complete works of Lu Xun, the great Chinese writer of the 1920s and 1930s. Because he died in 1936, before the Communists came to power, he escaped being persecuted by Mao, and even became a great hero of his—whereas Lu Xun's favorite pupil and closest associate, Hu Feng, was personally named by Mao as a counterrevolutionary, and was imprisoned for decades. It was the persecution of Hu Feng that led to the witch-hunt in which my mother was detained in 1955.

Lu Xun had been my father's great favorite. When I was a child, he often read us essays by Lu. I had not understood them at the time, even with my father's explanations, but now I was engrossed. I found that their satirical edge could be applied to the Communists as well as to the Kuomintang. Lu Xun had no ideology, only enlightened humanitarianism. His skeptical genius challenged all assumptions. He was another whose free intelligence helped liberate me from my indoctrination.

My father's collection of Marxist classics was also useful to me. I read randomly, following the obscure words with my finger, and wondering what on earth those nineteenth-century German controversies had to do with Mao's China. But I was attracted by something I had rarely come across in China—the logic that ran through an argument. Reading Marx helped me to think rationally and analytically.

I enjoyed these new ways of organizing my thoughts. At other times I would let my mind slip into more nebulous moods and wrote poetry, in classical styles. While I was working in the fields I was often absorbed in composing poems, which made working bearable, at times even agreeable. Because of this, I preferred solitude, and positively discouraged conversation.

One day I had been working all morning, cutting cane with a sickle and eating the juiciest parts near the roots. The cane went to the commune sugar factory, in exchange for sugar. We had to fill a quota in quantity, but not in quality, so we ate the best parts. When lunch break came, and someone had to stay in the field to keep watch for thieves, I offered my services so I would have some time alone. I would go for my lunch when the peasants came back—and so have even more time to myself.

I lay on my back on a stack of canes, a straw hat partly shading my face. Through the hat I could see the vast turquoise sky. A leaf protruded from the stack above my head, looking disproportionately enormous against the sky. I half-closed my eyes, feeling soothed by the cool greenness.

The leaf reminded me of the swaying leaves of a grove of bamboo on a similar hot summer afternoon many years before. Sitting in its shade fishing, my father had written a forlorn poem. In the same *ge-lu*—pattern of tones, rhymes, and types of words—as his poem, I began to compose one of my own. The universe seemed to be standing still, apart from the light rustle of the refreshing breeze in the cane leaves. Life felt beautiful to me at that moment.

In this period, I snatched at the chance for solitude, and ostentatiously showed that I wanted nothing to do with the world around me, which must have made me seem rather arrogant. And because the peasants were the model I was meant to emulate, I reacted by concentrating on their negative qualities. I did not try to get to know them, or to get on with them.

I was not very popular in the village, although the peasants largely left me alone. They disapproved of me for failing to work as hard as they thought I should. Work was their whole life, and the major criterion by which they judged anyone. Their eye for hard work was both uncompromising and fair, and it was clear to them that I hated physical labor and took every opportunity to stay at home and read my books. The stomach trouble and skin rash I had suffered in Ningnan hit me again as soon as I came to Deyang. Virtually every day I had some sort of diarrhea, and my legs broke out in infected sores. I constantly felt weak and dizzy, but it was no good complaining to the peasants; their harsh life had made them regard all nonfatal illnesses as trivial.

The thing that made me most unpopular, though, was that I was often away. I spent about two-thirds of the time that I should have been in Deyang visiting my parents in their camps, or looking after Aunt Jun-ying in Yibin. Each trip lasted several months, and there was no law forbidding it. But although I did not work nearly enough to earn my keep, I still took food from the village. The peasants were stuck with their egalitarian distribution system, and they were stuck with me—they could not throw me out. Naturally, they blamed me, and I felt sorry for them. But I was stuck with them, too. I could not get out.

In spite of their resentment, my production team allowed me to come and go as I liked, which was partly because I had kept my distance from them. I learned that the best way to get by was to be regarded as an unobtrusively aloof outsider. Once you became "one of the masses," you immediately let yourself in for intrusion and control.

Meanwhile, my sister Xiao-hong was doing well in the neighboring village. Although, like me, she was perpetually bitten by fleas and poisoned by manure so that her legs were sometimes so swollen she got fever, she continued to work hard, and was awarded eight work points a day. Specs often came from Chengdu to help her. His factory, like most others, was at a virtual standstill. The management had been "smashed," and the new Revolutionary Committee was only concerned with getting the workers to take part in the revolution rather than in production, and most just came and went as they pleased. Sometimes Specs worked in the fields in my sister's place to give her a break. At other times, he worked with her, which delighted the villagers, who said: "This is a bargain. We took in one young girl, but we've ended up with two pairs of hands!"

Nana, my sister, and I used to go to the country market together on market day, which was once a week. I loved the boisterous alleys lined with baskets and shoulder poles. The peasants would walk for hours to sell a single chicken or a dozen eggs, or a bundle of bamboo. Most money-making activities, such as growing cash crops, making baskets, or raising pigs for sale, were banned for individual households, on the grounds that they were "capitalist." As a result, peasants had very little to exchange for cash. Without money, it was impossible for them to travel to cities, and market day was almost their only source of entertainment. They would meet up with their relatives and friends, the men squatting on the muddy pavements puffing on their pipes.

In spring 1970 my sister and Specs were married. There was no ceremony. In the atmosphere of the day, it did not cross their minds to have one. They just collected their marriage certificate from the commune headquarters and then went back to my sister's village with sweets and cigarettes with which to entertain the villagers. The peasants were thrilled: they could rarely afford these precious treats.

For the peasants, a wedding was a big thing. As soon as the news broke, they crowded into my sister's thatched cottage to offer their congratulations. They brought presents like a handful of dried noodles, a pound of soybeans, and a few eggs, wrapped carefully in red straw paper and tied with straw in a fancy knot. These were no ordinary gifts. The peasants had deprived themselves of valuable items. My sister and Specs were very touched. When Nana and I went to see the new couple, they were teaching the village children how to do "loyalty dances"—for fun.

Marriage did not get my sister out of the countryside, as couples were not automatically granted residence together. Of course, if Specs had been willing to relinquish his city registration, he could easily have settled with my sister, but she could not move to Chengdu with him because she had a country registration. Like tens of millions of couples in China, they lived separately, entitled by regulation to twelve days a year together. Luckily for them, Specs's factory was not working normally, so he could spend a lot of time in Deyang.

After a year in Deyang there was a change in my life: I entered the medical profession. The production brigade to which my team belonged ran a clinic which dealt with simple illnesses. It was funded by all the production teams under the brigade, and treatment was free, but very limited. There were two doctors. One of them, a young man with a fine, intelligent face, had graduated from the medical school of Deyang County in the fifties, and had come back to work in his native village. The other was middle-aged with a goatee. He had started out as an apprentice to an old country doctor practicing Chinese medicine, and in 1964 he had been sent by the commune to attend a crash course in Western medicine.

At the beginning of 1971, the commune authorities ordered the clinic to take on a "barefoot doctor." The name came about because the "doctor" was supposed to live like the peasants, who treasured their shoes too much to wear them in the muddy fields. At the time, there was a big propaganda campaign hailing barefoot doctors as an invention of the Cultural Revolution. My production team jumped at this opportunity to get rid of me: if I worked in the clinic, the brigade, rather than my team, would be responsible for my food and other income.

I had always wanted to be a doctor. The illnesses in my family, particularly the death of my grandmother, had driven home to me how important doctors were. Before I went to Deyang, I had started learning acupuncture from a friend, and I had been studying a book called A *Barefoot Doctor's Manual*, one of the few printed items allowed in those days.

The propaganda about barefoot doctors was one of Mao's political maneuvers. He had condemned the pre–Cultural Revolution Health Ministry for not looking after peasants and concerning itself only with city dwellers, especially Party officials. He also condemned doctors for not wanting to work in the countryside, particularly in the remote areas. But Mao took no responsibility as head of the regime, nor did he order any practical steps to remedy the situation, such as giving instructions to build more hospitals or train more proper doctors, and during the Cultural Revolution the medical situation got worse. The propaganda line about peasants having no doctors was really intended to generate hatred against the pre–Cultural Revolution Party system, and against intellectuals (this category included doctors and nurses).

Mao offered a magic cure to the peasants: "doctors" who could be turned out *en masse*—barefoot doctors. "It is not at all necessary to have so much formal training," he said. "They should mainly learn and raise their standard in practice." On 26 June 1965 he made the remark which became a guideline for health and education: "The more books you read, the more stupid you become." I went to work with absolutely no training.

The clinic was in a large hall on top of a hill about an hour's walk from my cottage. Next door was a shop selling matches, salt, and soy sauce—which were all rationed. One of the surgery rooms became my bedroom. My professional duties were left vague.

The only medical book I had ever set eyes on was A *Barefoot Doctor's Manual*. I studied it avidly. There was no theory in it, just a summary of symptoms, followed by suggested prescriptions. When I sat at my desk, with the other two doctors behind me, all wearing our dusty everyday clothes, it was clear that the sick peasants who came in very sensibly wanted nothing to do with me, an inexperienced eighteen-year-old with some sort of book they could not read, and which was not even very thick. They went straight past me to the other two desks. I felt more relieved than offended. It was not my idea of being a doctor to have to consult a book every time patients described their symptoms, and then to copy down the recommended prescription. Sometimes, in an ironic mood, I would contemplate whether our new leaders—Chairman Mao was still beyond questioning—would want me as their personal doctor, barefoot or not. But then, I told myself, of course not: barefoot doctors were supposed to "serve the people, not the officials" in the first place. I settled happily for just being a nurse, doling out medicines on prescription and giving injections, which I had learned to give to my mother for her hemorrhage.

The young doctor who had been to medical school was the one everybody wanted. His prescriptions of Chinese herbs cured many ailments. He was very conscientious, too, visiting patients in their villages and collecting and growing herbs in his spare time. The other doctor, with the goatee, terrified me with his medical nonchalance. He would use the same needle to inject several different patients without any sterilization. And he injected penicillin without testing whether the person was allergic to it, which was extremely dangerous because Chinese penicillin was not pure and could cause serious reactions, even death. Politely, I offered to do it for him. He smiled, not offended by my interference, and said there had never been any accidents: "The peasants are not like delicate city folk."

I liked the doctors, and they were very kind to me, always helpful when I asked questions. Not surprisingly, they did not see me as a threat. Out in the countryside, it was one's professional skills, rather than political rhetoric, that counted.

I enjoyed living on that hilltop, far away from any village. Every morning I got up early, strolled along the edge of the hill, and to the rising sun recited lines from an ancient book of verse about acupuncture. Beneath my feet, the fields and cottages began to wake up to the cocks' crowing. A lonely Venus watched with a pale glow from a sky that was getting brighter every minute. I loved the fragrance of the honeysuckle in the morning breeze, and the big petals of nightshade shaking off pearls of dew. Birds chirped all around, distracting me from my recitations. I would linger for a bit, and then walk back to light my stove for breakfast.

With the help of an anatomical chart and my acupuncture verses, I had a fairly clear idea where on the body I should stick my needles to cure what. I was eager for patients. And I had some enthusiastic volunteers—boys from Chengdu who were now living in other villages and who were keen on me. They would walk for hours for an acupuncture session. One young man, rolling up his sleeve to expose an acupuncture point near his elbow, declared with a brave face, "What are men friends for?"

I did not fall in love with any of them, although my resolution to deny myself a boyfriend in order to dedicate myself to my parents and appease my guilt over my grandmother's death was weakening. But I found it difficult to let my heart go, and my upbringing prevented me from having any physical relationship without surrendering my heart. All around me, other boys and girls from the city were leading rather freer lives. But I sat, lonely, on a pedestal. Word got out that I wrote poetry, and that helped keep me there.

The young men all behaved most chivalrously. One gave me a musical instrument called a *san-xian*, made of a snakeskin bowl with a long handle and three silk strings, which were plucked, and spent days teaching me how to play it. The permitted tunes were all in praise of Mao, and were very limited. But that did not make much difference to me: my ability was even more limited.

In the warm evenings, I sat by the fragrant medicinal garden encircled by Chinese trumpet creepers, and thrummed to myself. Once the shop next door closed for the night, I was entirely alone. It was dark except for the gently shining moon and the twinkling of lights from distant cottages. Sometimes fireflies glowed and floated by like torches carried by tiny, invisible flying men. The scents from the garden made me dizzy with pleasure. My music hardly matched the enthusiastic chorus of the thundering frogs and the wistful croon of the crickets. But I found solace in it.

24. "Please Accept My Apologies That Come a Lifetime Too Late"— My Parents in Camps

(1969–1972)

Three days' truck journey from Chengdu, in northern Xichang, is Buffalo Boy Flatland. There the road forks, one branch heading southwest to Miyi, where my father's camp was, the other southeast to Ningnan.

A famous legend gave the Flatland its name. The Goddess Weaver, daughter of the Celestial Queen Mother, used to descend from the Celestial Court to bathe in a lake there. (The meteor which fell on Meteorite Street is supposed to have been a stone that propped up her loom.) A boy living by the lake who looks after buffaloes sees the goddess, and they fall in love. They marry, and have a son and a daughter. The Celestial Queen Mother is jealous of their happiness, and sends some gods down to kidnap the goddess. They carry her off, and the buffalo boy rushes after them. Just as he is about to catch them, the Celestial Queen Mother pulls a hairpin from her coil and draws a huge river between them. The Silver River separates the couple permanently, except on the seventh day of the seventh moon, when magpies fly from all over China to form a bridge for the family to meet.

The Silver River is the Chinese name for the Milky Way. Over Xichang it looks vast, with a mass of stars, the bright Vega, the Goddess Weaver, on one side, and Altair, the Buffalo Boy, with his two children, on the other. This legend has appealed to the Chinese for centuries because their families have often been broken up by wars, bandits, poverty, and heartless governments. Ironically, it was to this place that my mother was sent.

She arrived there in November 1969, with her 500 former colleagues from the Eastern District—Rebels as well as capitalist-roaders. Because they had been ordered out of Chengdu in a hurry there was nowhere for them to live, except for a few shacks left by army engineers who had been building a railway from Chengdu to Kunming, the capital of Yunnan. Some squeezed into these. Others had to cram their bedrolls into the houses of local peasants.

There were no building materials except cogon grass and mud, which had to be dug out and carried down from the mountains. The mud for the walls was mixed with water and made into bricks. There were no machines, no electricity, not even any work animals. On the Flatland, which is about 5,000 feet above sea level, it is the day, rather than the year, that is divided into four seasons. At seven in the morning, when my mother started working, the temperature was around freezing. By midday, it could reach the high 80s. At about 4 P.M. hot winds swirled through the mountains and literally swept people off their feet. At seven in the evening, when they finished work, the temperature plummeted again. In these harsh extremes my mother and the other inmates worked twelve hours a day, breaking only for a brief lunch. For the first few months, all they had to eat was rice and boiled cabbage.

The camp was organized like an army, run by army officers, and came under the control of the Chengdu Revolutionary Committee. At first my mother was treated as a class enemy and was forced to stand for the whole of every lunch break with her head bowed. This form of punishment, called "fieldside denunciation," was recommended by the media as a way to remind the others, who were able to rest, that they should save some energy for hatred. My mother protested to her company commander that she could not work all day without resting her legs. The officer had been in the Military Department of the Eastern District before the Cultural Revolution, and had got on well with her; he put a stop to the practice. Still, my mother was given the hardest jobs, and she did not have Sundays off, unlike the other inmates. The bleeding from her womb worsened. Then she was struck down with hepatitis. Her whole body was yellow and swollen, and she could hardly stand up.

One thing the camp did have was doctors, as half the hospital staff in the Eastern District had been packed off there. Only those who were most in demand by the bosses of the Revolutionary Committees remained in Chengdu. The doctor who treated my mother told her how grateful he and the other hospital staff were to her for protecting them before the Cultural Revolution, and said that had it not been for her he would probably have been labeled a rightist back in 1957. There was no Western medicine available, so he went miles to gather herbs like Asiatic plantain and sun plants which the Chinese consider good for hepatitis.

He also exaggerated the infectiousness of her illness to the camp authorities, who then moved her to a place entirely on her own, half a mile away. Her tormentors left her alone, for fear of infection, but the doctor came to see her every day, and secretly ordered a daily supply of goat's milk from a local peasant. My mother's new residence was a deserted pigsty. Sympathetic inmates cleaned it for her and put a thick layer of hay on the ground. It felt to her like a luxurious mattress. A friendly cook volunteered to deliver meals. When no one was looking, she would include a couple of eggs. When meat became available, my mother had it every day, while the others got it only once a week. She also had fresh fruit—pears and peaches—provided by friends who bought them at markets. As far as she was concerned, her hepatitis was a godsend.

After about forty days, much to her regret, she recovered and was moved back into the camp, now housed in new mud huts. The Flatland is an odd place in that it attracts lightning and thunder but not rain, which falls on the surrounding mountains. The local peasants did not plant crops on the plains, because the soil was too dry and it was dangerous during the frequent dry thunderstorms. But this land was the only resource available to the camp, so they planted a special strain of drought-resistant corn and carried water from the lower slopes of the mountains. In order to get a future supply of rice, they offered to help the local peasants harvest theirs.

The peasants agreed, but it was the local custom that women were forbidden to carry water and men were barred from planting rice, which could only be done by married women with children, particularly sons. The more sons a woman had, the more she was in demand for this backbreaking job. The belief was that a woman who had produced a lot of sons would produce more grains in the rice she planted ("sons" and "seeds" have the same sound, zi, in Chinese). My mother was the prime "beneficiary" of this ancient custom. As she had three sons, more than most of her women colleagues, she had to spend up to fifteen hours a day bent double in the paddy fields, with an inflamed lower abdomen, and bleeding.

At night, she joined everyone else in taking turns to guard the pigs from wolves. The mud-and-grass shacks backed on to a range of mountains aptly called "Wolves' Lair." The wolves were very clever, the locals told the new arrivals. When one got into a pigsty, it would gently scratch and lick a pig, particularly behind its ears, to get the animal into a kind of pleasurable trance, so it would not make a noise. Then the wolf would lightly bite the pig on one ear and lead it out of the sty, all the time rubbing its body with its fluffy tail. The pig would still be dreaming of being caressed by a lover when the wolf pounced.

The peasants told the city folk that the wolves—and occasional leopards—were afraid of fires. So every night a fire was lit outside the pigsty. My mother spent many sleepless nights watching meteors shooting across the starlit vault of the sky, with the silhouette of the Wolves' Lair against it, listening to the distant howling of the wolves.

One evening she was washing her clothes in a small pond. When she straightened up from her squatting position she found she was staring straight into the red eyes of a wolf standing about twenty yards away across the pond. Her hair stood on end, but she remembered that her childhood friend Big Old Lee had told her that the way to deal with a wolf was to walk backwards, slowly, never showing any sign of panic, and not to turn and run. So she backed away from the pond and walked as calmly as she could toward the camp, all the time facing the wolf, who followed her. When she reached the edge of the camp, the wolf stopped. The fire was in sight, and voices could be heard. She swung around and raced into a doorway.

The fire was almost the only light in the depth of the nights in Xichang. There was no electricity. Candles, when available at all, were prohibitively expensive, and there was very little kerosene. But there was not much to read anyway. Unlike Deyang, where I had relative freedom to read Jin-ming's black-market books, a cadres' school was tightly controlled. The only printed materials allowed were the selected works of Mao and the *People's Daily*. Occasionally, a new film was shown in an army barracks a few miles away: it was invariably one of Mme. Mao's model operas.

As the days, then months went by, the harsh work and lack of relaxation became unbearable. Everyone missed their families and children, the Rebels included. Their resentment was perhaps more intense because they now felt that all their past zealotry had turned out to be for nothing, and that whatever they did, they would never get back to power in Chengdu. The Revolutionary Committees had been filled in their absence. Within months of reaching the Flatland, depression replaced denunciations, and the Rebels sometimes had to

be cheered up by my mother. She was given the nickname "Kuanyin"
—the goddess of kindness.

At night, lying on her straw mattress, she thought back over her
children's early years. She realized that there was not an awful lot of
family life to remember. She had been an absentee mother when we
were growing up, having submitted herself to the cause at the cost of
her family. Now she reflected with remorse on the pointlessness of
her devotion. She found she missed her children with a pain which
was almost unendurable.

Ten days before Chinese New Year, in February 1970, after over
three months on the Flatland, my mother's company was lined up in
front of their camp to welcome an army commander who was coming
for an inspection. After waiting for a long time, the crowd spotted a
small figure approaching along the dirt track which climbed up from
the distant road. They all stared at the moving figure, and decided it
could not be the big shot: he would be in a car with an entourage. But
it could not be a local peasant, either: the way the long black wool
scarf was wrapped around the bent head was too stylish. It was a young
woman with a large basket on her back. Watching her slowly coming
nearer and nearer, my mother's heart started pounding. She felt it
looked like me, and then she thought she might be imagining it. "How
wonderful it would be if it was Er-hong!" she said to herself. Suddenly,
people were nudging her excitedly: "It's your daughter! Your daughter's here to see you! Er-hong's here!"

This was my mother's account of how she saw me coming after
what seemed to her a lifetime. I was the first visitor to the camp, and
was received with a mixture of warmth and envy. I had come on the
same truck which had taken me to Ningnan to get my registration
moved in June the year before. The big basket on my back was full of
sausages, eggs, sweets, cakes, noodles, sugar, and tinned meats. All
five of us children and Specs had pooled things from our rations, or
our shares from our production teams, to give our parents a treat. I
was practically dragged down by the weight.

Two things immediately struck me. My mother looked well—she
was just over her convalescence from hepatitis, as she told me later.
And the atmosphere around her was not hostile. In fact, some people
were already calling her "Kuanyin," which was absolutely incredible
to me since she was officially a class enemy.

A dark-blue scarf covered her hair and was knotted under her chin.
Her cheeks were no longer fine and delicate. They had turned rough
and deep red under the fierce sun and harsh wind, and her skin looked
very much like that of a Xichang peasant. She appeared at least ten

years older than her thirty-eight years. When she stroked my face, her hands felt like cracked old tree bark.

I stayed ten days, and was to depart for my father's camp on New Year's Day. My nice truck driver was to pick me up where he had dropped me off. My mother's eyes moistened because, although his camp was not far away, she and my father were forbidden to visit each other. I put the food basket on my back untouched—my mother insisted I take the whole lot to my father. Saving precious food for others has always been a major way of expressing love and concern in China. My mother was very sad that I was going, and kept saying she was sorry I had to miss the traditional Chinese New Year breakfast which her camp was going to serve: tang-yuan, round dumplings, symbolizing family union. But I could not wait for it for fear of missing the truck.

My mother walked half an hour with me to the roadside and we sat down in the high grass to wait. The sweep of the landscape undulated with the gentle waves of the thick cogon grass. The sun was already bright and warm. My mother hugged me, her whole body seeming to say that she did not want to let me go, that she was afraid she would never see me again. At the time, we did not know whether her camp and my commune would ever come to an end. We had been told we would be there for life. There were hundreds of reasons why we might die before we saw each other again. My mother's sadness infected me, and I thought of my grandmother dying before I was able to get back from Ningnan.

The sun rose higher and higher. There was no trace of my truck. As the large rings of smoke that had been pouring out of the chimney of her camp in the distance thinned down, my mother was seized by regret that she had not been able to give me the New Year's breakfast. She insisted on going back to get some for me.

While she was away the truck came. I looked toward the camp and saw her running toward me, the white-golden grass surging around her blue scarf. In her right hand she carried a big colorful enamel bowl. She was running with the kind of carefulness that told me she did not want the soup with the dumplings to spill. She was still a good way off, and I could see she would not reach me for another twenty minutes or so. I did not feel I could ask the driver to wait that long, as he was already doing me a big favor. I clambered onto the back of the truck. I could see my mother still running toward me in the distance. But she no longer seemed to be carrying the bowl.

Years later, she told me the bowl had fallen from her hand when she saw me climbing onto the truck. But she still ran to the spot where we had been sitting, just to make sure I had really gone, although it could not have been anyone else getting onto the truck. There was not a single person around in that vast yellowness. For the next few days she walked around the camp as though in a trance, feeling blank and lost.

After many hours of being bounced around on the back of the truck, I arrived at my father's camp. It was deep in the mountains, and had been a forced labor camp—a gulag. The prisoners had hacked a farm out of the wild mountains and had since been moved on to open up more harsh virgin land, leaving this relatively cultivated site for those one rung better off on China's punishment ladder, the deported officials. The camp was huge: it held thousands of former employees of the provincial government.

I had to walk for a couple of hours from the road to reach my father's "company." A rope suspension bridge wobbled over a deep chasm as I stepped onto it, almost making me lose my balance. Exhausted as I was, with the load on my back, I still managed to be amazed by the stunning beauty of the mountains. Although it was only early spring, bright flowers were everywhere, next to kapok trees and bushes of papayas. When I finally got to my father's dormitory, I saw a couple of colorful pheasants swaggering majestically under a glade of early pear, plum, and almond blossoms. Weeks later, the fallen petals, pink and white, were to bury the mud path.

My first sight of my father after over a year was harrowing. He was trotting into the courtyard carrying two baskets full of bricks on a shoulder pole. His old blue jacket hung loose on him, and his rolled-up trouser legs revealed a pair of very thin legs with prominent sinews. His sun-beaten face was wrinkled, and his hair was almost gray. Then he saw me. He put down his load with a fumbling movement, the result of overexcitement, as I rushed over to him. Because the Chinese tradition permitted little physical contact between fathers and daughters, he told me how happy he was through his eyes. They were so full of love and tenderness. In them I also saw traces of the ordeal he had been going through. His youthful energy and spark had given way to an air of aged confusion with a hint of quiet determination. Yet he was still in his prime, only forty-eight years old. A lump rose in my throat. I searched his eyes for signs of my worst fear, the return of his insanity. But he looked all right. A heavy load lifted from my heart.

He was sharing a room with seven other people, all from his department. There was only one tiny window, so the door had to be left open all day to let in some light. The people in the room seldom spoke to each other, and no one greeted me at all. I felt immediately that the atmosphere was much more severe than in my mother's camp. The reason was that this camp was under the direct control of the Sichuan Revolutionary Committee, and therefore of the Tings. On the walls of the courtyard there were still layers of posters and slogans reading "Down with So-and-so" or "Eliminate So-and-so," against which were propped scarred hoes and spades. As I soon discovered, my father was still being subjected to frequent denunciation meetings in the evenings after a hard day's work. Since one way to get out of the camp was to be invited back to work for the Revolutionary Committee, and the way to do that was to please the Tings, some Rebels competed with each other to demonstrate their militancy, and my father was their natural victim.

He was not allowed into the kitchen. As an "anti-Mao criminal," he was alleged to be so dangerous he might poison the food. It did not matter whether anyone believed this. The point was in the insult.

My father bore this and other cruelties with fortitude. Only once did he allow his anger to show. When he first came to the camp, he was ordered to wear a white armband with black characters saying "counterrevolutionary element in action." He pushed away the armband violently and said from between clenched teeth, "Come on and beat me to death. I will not wear this!" The Rebels backed away. They knew he meant it—and they had no order from above to kill him.

Here in the camp, the Tings were able to revenge themselves on their enemies. Among them was a man who had been involved in the investigation into them in 1962. He had worked in the underground before 1949, and had been imprisoned and tortured by the Kuomintang, which had destroyed his health. In the camp he soon fell gravely ill, but he had to go on working, and was not allowed a single day off. Because he was slow, he was ordered to make it up in the evenings. Wall posters denounced him for his laziness. One of the posters I saw opened with the words: "Have you, Comrade, noticed this grotesque living skeleton with hideous facial features?" Under Xichang's relentless sun, his skin had become scorched and withered, and was peeling off in great chunks. Also, he was starved out of human shape: he had had two-thirds of his stomach cut out, and could digest only a small amount of food at a time. Because he could not have frequent meals, as he needed to, he was permanently starving. One day, in desperation, he went into the kitchen to look for some pickle juice. He was accused of trying to poison the food. Knowing he was on the verge of total collapse, he wrote to the camp authorities saying that he was dying and requesting to be spared some heavy jobs. The only answer was a venomous poster campaign. Soon afterward he fainted in a field under the blazing sun, as he was spreading manure. He was taken to the camp hospital and died the next day. He had no family at his deathbed. His wife had committed suicide.

The capitalist-roaders were not the only ones who suffered in the cadres' school. People who had had any connection, however remote, with the Kuomintang, anyone who had by some misfortune become the target of some personal revenge, or the object of jealousy—even leaders of the unsuccessful Rebel factions—had been dying in the camp in scores. Many had thrown themselves into the roaring river that sliced through the valley. The river was called "Tranquillity" (*An-ning-he*). In the dead of night, its echoes spread many miles, and sent chills up the spines of the inmates, who said it sounded like the sobbing of ghosts.

Hearing about these suicides increased my determination to help relieve the mental and physical pressure on my father as a matter of urgency. I had to make him feel life was worth living, and that he was loved. At his denunciation meetings, which were now largely nonviolent, as the inmates had run out of steam, I would sit where he could see me, so that he could feel reassured by my being with him. As soon as the meeting was over, we would go off together on our own. I would tell him cheerful things to make him forget the ugliness of the meeting, and massage his head, neck, and shoulders. And he would recite classical poems for me. During the day, I helped him with his jobs, which, naturally, were the hardest and dirtiest. Sometimes I would carry his loads, which weighed over a hundred pounds. I managed to show him a nonchalant face, although I could hardly stand under the weight.

I stayed over three months. The authorities allowed me to eat in the canteen, and gave me a bed in a room with five other women, who only spoke to me briefly and coldly, if at all. Most of the inmates immediately assumed an air of hostility whenever they saw me. I just looked through them. But there were kind people as well, or people who were more courageous than others in showing their kindness.

One was a man in his late twenties with a sensitive face and big ears. His name was Young, and he was a university graduate who had come to work in my father's department just before the Cultural Revolution. He was the "commander" of the "squad" to which my father belonged. Although he was obliged to assign the hardest jobs to my father, whenever he could he would unobtrusively reduce his workload. In one of my fleeting conversations with him, I told him that I could not cook the food I had brought with me, as there was no kerosene for my small stove.

A couple of days later, Young sauntered past me with a blank expression on his face. I felt something metal thrust into my hand: it was a wire burner about eight inches high and four inches in diameter, which he had made himself. It burned paper balls made out of old newspapers—they could be torn up now because Mao's portrait had disappeared from the pages. (Mao himself had stopped the practice, as he considered that its purpose—"to greatly and especially establish" his "absolute supreme authority"—had been achieved, and to go on with it would only result in overkill.) On the burner's blue-and-orange flames I produced food that was far superior to the camp fare. When the delicious steam seeped through the saucepan, I could see the jaws of my father's seven roommates involuntarily masticating. I regretted that I could not offer any of it to Young: we would both be in trouble if his militant colleagues got wind of it.

It was thanks to Young and other decent people like him that my father was allowed to have visits from his children. It was also Young who gave my father permission to leave the camp premises on rainy days, which were his only days off, since, unlike other inmates, he had to work on Sundays, just like my mother. As soon as it stopped raining, my father and I would go into the forests and collect wild mushrooms under the pine trees, or search for wild peas, which I would cook with a tin of duck or some other meat back in the camp. We would enjoy a heavenly meal.

After supper we often strolled to my favorite spot, which I called my "zoological garden"—a group of fantastically shaped rocks in a grassy clearing in the woods. They looked like a herd of bizarre animals lazing in the sun. Some of them had hollows that fitted our bodies, and we would lie back and gaze into the distance. Down the slope from us was a row of gigantic kapok trees, their leafless scarlet flowers, bigger versions of magnolia, growing directly from the stark black branches, which all grew uncompromisingly straight up. During my months in the camp, I had watched these giant flowers open, a mass of crimson against black. Then they bore fruit as big as figs, and each burst into silky wool, which was blown all over the mountains like feathery snow by the warm winds. Beyond the kapok trees lay the River of Tranquillity, and beyond it stretched endless mountains.

One day when we were relaxing in our "zoological garden," a peasant passed by who was so gnarled and dwarfish he gave me a fright. My father told me that in this isolated region inbreeding was common. Then he said, "There is so much to be done in these mountains! It is such a beautiful place with great potential. I'd love to come and live here to look after a commune, or maybe a production brigade, and do some real work. Something useful. Or maybe just be an ordinary peasant. I am so fed up with being an official. How nice it would be if our family could come here and enjoy the simple life of the farmers." In his eyes, I saw the frustration of an energetic, talented man who was desperate to work. I also recognized the traditional idyllic dream of the Chinese scholar disillusioned with his mandarin career. Above all, I could see that an alternative life had become a fantasy for my father, something wonderful and unobtainable, because there was no opting out once you were a Communist official.

I visited the camp three times, staying each time for several months. My siblings did the same, so that my father would have warmth around him all the time. He often said proudly that he was the envy of the camp because no one else had so much company from their children. Indeed, few had any visitors at all: the Cultural Revolution had brutalized human relationships, and alienated countless families.

My family became closer as time went by. My brother Xiao-hei, who had been beaten by my father when he was a child, now came to love him. On his first visit to the camp, he and my father had to sleep on a single bed because the camp leaders were jealous that my father had so much family company. In order to let my father have a good night's sleep—which was particularly important for his mental condition—Xiao-hei would never allow himself to fall into a deep sleep lest he stretch out and disturb him.

For his part, my father reproached himself for having been harsh to Xiao-hei, and would stroke his head and apologize. "It seems inconceivable I could have hit you so hard. I was too tough on you," he would say. "I've been thinking a lot about the past, and I feel very guilty toward you. Funny the Cultural Revolution should turn me into a better person."

The camp fare was mainly boiled cabbage, and the lack of protein made people feel hungry all the time. Every meat-eating day was eagerly anticipated, and celebrated with an air almost of exhilaration. Even the most militant Rebels seemed to be in a better humor. On these occasions, my father would pick the meat from his bowl and force it into his children's. There would always be a kind of fight with chopsticks and bowls.

My father was in a constant state of remorse. He told me how he had not invited my grandmother to his wedding, and had sent her on the perilous journey back to Manchuria from Yibin only a month after she had arrived. I heard him reproach himself many times for not showing his own mother enough affection, and for being so rigid that he was not even told about her funeral. He would shake his head: "It's too late now!" He also blamed himself for his treatment of his sister Jun-ying in the 1950s, when he had tried to persuade her to give up her Buddhist beliefs, and even to get her, a vegetarian by conviction, to eat meat.

Aunt Jun-ying died in the summer of 1970. Her paralysis had gradually invaded her whole body, and she had received no proper treatment. She died in the same state of quiet composure as she had shown all her life. My family kept the news from my father. We all knew how deeply he loved and respected her.

That autumn my brothers Xiao-hei and Xiao-fang were staying with my father. One day they were having a walk after supper, when eight-year-old Xiao-fang let slip the news that Aunt Jun-ying had died. Suddenly, my father's face changed. He stood still, looking blank for a long time, then turned to the side of the path, sagged onto his haunches, and covered his face with both hands. His shoulders shook with sobs. Never having seen my father cry, my brothers were dumbfounded.

At the beginning of 1971 news filtered through that the Tings had been sacked. For my parents, particularly my father, there was some improvement in their lives. They began to have Sundays off and lighter jobs. The other detainees started to speak to my father, though still coldly. Proof that things really were changing came when a new inmate arrived at the camp early in 1971—Mrs. Shau, my father's old tormentor, who had fallen from grace together with the Tings. Then my mother was allowed to spend two weeks with my father—the first chance for them to be together for several years, in fact the first time they had even glimpsed each other since the winter morning on the street in Chengdu just before my father's departure for the camp, over two years before.

But my parents' misery was far from over. The Cultural Revolution continued. The Tings had not been purged because of all the evil they had done, but because they were suspected by Mao of being closely linked to Chen Boda, one of the leaders of the Cultural Revolution Authority, who had fallen foul of Mao. In this purge, more victims were generated. Chen Mo, the Tings' right-hand man, who had helped secure my father's release from prison, committed suicide.

One day in the summer of 1971 my mother had a severe hemorrhage from her womb; she passed out and had to be taken to a hospital. My father was not permitted to visit her, although they were both in Xichang. When her condition stabilized, she was allowed to go back to Chengdu for treatment. There, the bleeding was finally stopped; but the doctors discovered that she had developed a skin disease called scleroderma. A patch of skin behind her right ear had turned hard and had begun to contract. The right side of her jaw had become considerably smaller than the left, and the hearing in her right ear was going. The right side of her neck was stiff, and her right hand and arm felt rigid and numb. Dermatologists told her the hardening of the skin could eventually spread to the internal organs and, if so, she would shrink and die in three or four years. They said there was nothing Western medicine could do. All they could suggest was cortisone, which my mother took in the form of tablets—and injections in her neck.

I was in the camp with my father when a letter came from Mother with the news. Immediately my father went to ask for permission to go home and see her. Young was very sympathetic, but the camp authorities refused. My father burst out crying in front of a whole courtyard of inmates. The people from his department were taken aback. They knew him as a "man of iron." Early the next morning, he went to the post office and waited outside for hours until it opened. He sent a three-page telegram to my mother. It began: "Please accept my apologies that come a lifetime too late. It is for my guilt toward you that I am happy for any punishment. I have not been a decent husband. Please get well and give me another chance."

On 25 October 1971, Specs came to see me in Deyang with a dynamite piece of news: Lin Biao had been killed. Specs had been officially told in his factory that Lin had attempted to assassinate Mao and that, having failed, he had tried to flee to the Soviet Union, and his plane had crashed in Mongolia.

Lin Biao's death was shrouded in mystery. It was linked with the downfall of Chen Boda a year before. Mao grew suspicious of both of them when they went too far with their over-the-top deification of him, which he suspected was part of a scheme to kick him upstairs to abstract glory and deprive him of earthly power. Mao particularly smelled a rat with Lin Biao, his chosen successor, who was known for "never letting the Little Red Book leave his hand, nor 'Long live Mao!' leave his lips," as a later rhyme put it. Mao decided that Lin, being next in line to the throne, was up to no good. Either Mao or Lin, or both, took action to save their own power and life.

My village was given the official version of events by the commune soon afterward. The news meant nothing to the peasants. They hardly even knew Lin's name, but I received the news with blinding joy. Not having been able to challenge Mao in my mind, I blamed Lin for the Cultural Revolution. The evident rift between him and Mao meant, I thought, that Mao had repudiated the Cultural Revolution, and would put an end to all the misery and destruction. The demise of Lin in a way reaffirmed my faith in Mao. Many people shared my optimism because there were signs that the Cultural Revolution was going to be reversed. Almost immediately some capitalist-roaders started to be rehabilitated and released from the camps.

My father was told the news about Lin in mid-November. At once, the occasional smile appeared on the faces of some Rebels. At the meetings, he was asked to sit down, which was unprecedented, and "expose Yeh Chun"—Mme. Lin Biao, who had been a colleague of his in Yan'an in the early 1940s. My father said nothing.

But although his colleagues were being rehabilitated, and leaving the camp in droves, my father was told by the camp commandant: "Don't you assume you can get off the hook now." His offense against Mao was considered too serious.

His health had been deteriorating under the combination of intolerable mental and physical pressure, with years of brutal beatings followed by hard physical labor under atrocious conditions. For nearly five years he had been taking large doses of tranquilizers in order to keep himself under control. Sometimes he consumed up to twenty times the normal dose, and this had worn out his system. He felt crippling pains somewhere in his body all the time; he began to cough blood, and was frequently short of breath, accompanied by severe dizzy spells. At the age of fifty, he looked like a seventy-year-old. The doctors in the camp always greeted him with cold faces and impatient prescriptions of more tranquilizers; they refused to give him a checkup, or even to hear him out. And each trip to the clinic would be followed by a barked lecture from some of the Rebels: "Don't imagine you can get away with faking illness!"

Jin-ming was in the camp at the end of 1971. He was so worried about Father that he stayed on until the spring of 1972. Then he got a letter from his production team ordering him to return immediately, or he would not be allocated any food at harvest time. The day he was leaving, my father went with him to the train—a railway line had just come to Miyi because of the strategic industries relocated to Xichang. During the long walk, they were both silent. Then Father had a sudden attack of breathlessness, and Jin-ming had to help him sit down by the side of the road. For a long time Father struggled to catch his breath. Then Jin-ming heard him sigh deeply and say, "It looks as though I probably don't have long to live. Life seems to be a dream."

Jin-ming had never heard him talk about death. Startled, he tried to comfort him. But Father said slowly, "I ask myself whether I am afraid of death. I don't think I am. My life as it is now is worse. And it looks as if there is not going to be any ending. Sometimes I feel weak: I stand by Tranquillity River and think, Just one leap and I can get it over with. Then I tell myself I must not. If I die without being cleared, there will be no end of trouble for all of you. . . . I have been thinking a lot lately. I had a hard childhood, and society was full of injustice. It was for a fair society that I joined the Communists. I've tried my best through the years. But what good has it done for the people? As for myself, why is it that in the end I have come to be the ruin of my family? People who believe in retribution say that to end badly you must have something on your conscience. I have been thinking hard about the things I've done in my life. I have given orders to execute some people . . ."

Father went on to tell Jin-ming about the death sentences he had signed, the names and stories of the *e-ba* ("ferocious despots") in the land reform in Chaoyang, and the bandit chiefs in Yibin. "But these people had done so much evil that God himself would have had them killed. What, then, have I done wrong to deserve all this?"

After a long pause, Father said, "If I die like this, don't believe in the Communist Party anymore."

25. "The Fragrance of Sweet Wind"—
A New Life with *The Electricians'*
Manual and *Six Crises*
(1972–1973)

It was with deaths, love, torment, and respite that 1969, 1970, and 1971 passed. In Miyi, the dry and rainy seasons followed hard on each other's heels. On Buffalo Boy Flatland the moon waxed and waned, the wind roared and hushed, the wolves howled and fell silent. In the medicinal garden in Deyang, the herbs flowered once, and then again —and again. I rushed between my parents' camps, my aunt's death-bed, and my village. I spread manure in the paddy fields and composed poems to water lilies.

My mother was at home in Chengdu when she heard of Lin Biao's demise. She was rehabilitated in November 1971 and told that she did not have to return to her camp. But although she received her full salary, she was not given back her old job, which had been filled by someone else. Her department in the Eastern District now had no fewer than seven directors—the existing members of the Revolutionary Committees and the newly rehabilitated officials who had just returned from the camp. Poor health was one reason Mother did not go back to work, but the most important reason was that my father had not been rehabilitated, unlike most capitalist-roaders.

Mao had sanctioned the mass rehabilitation not because he had at last come to his senses, but because, with the death of Lin Biao and the inevitable purge of his men, Mao had lost the hand with which he had controlled the army. He had removed and alienated virtually all the other marshals, who opposed the Cultural Revolution, and had had to rely almost solely on Lin. He had put his wife, relatives, and stars of the Cultural Revolution in important army posts, but these people had no military record, and therefore received no allegiance from the army. With Lin gone, Mao had to turn to those purged leaders who still commanded the loyalty of the army, including Deng Xiaoping, who was soon to reemerge. The first concession Mao had to make was to bring back most of the denounced officials.

Mao also knew that his power depended on a functioning economy. His Revolutionary Committees were hopelessly divided and second-rate, and could not get the country moving. He had no choice but to turn to the old, disgraced officials again.

My father was still in Miyi, but the part of his salary which had been held back since June 1968 was returned to him, and we suddenly found ourselves with what seemed to us an astronomical sum in the bank. Our personal belongings that had been taken away by the Rebels in the house raids were all returned, the only exception being two bottles of *mao-tai*, the most sought-after liquor in China. There were other encouraging signs. Zhou Enlai, who now had increased power, set about getting the economy going. The old administration was largely restored, and production and order were emphasized. Incentives were reintroduced. Peasants were allowed some cash sidelines. Scientific research began again. Schools started proper teaching, after a gap of six years; and my youngest brother, Xiao-fang, belatedly started his schooling at the age of ten.

With the economy reviving, factories began to recruit new workers. As part of the incentive system, they were allowed to give priority to their employees' children who had been sent to the country. Though my parents were not factory employees, my mother spoke to the managers of a machinery factory that had formerly come under her Eastern District, and now belonged to the Second Bureau of Light Industry in Chengdu. They readily agreed to take me on. So, a few months before my twentieth birthday, I left Deyang for good. My sister had to stay, because young people from the cities who married after going to the country were banned from returning, even if their spouses had city registrations.

Becoming a worker was my only option. Most universities were still shut, and there were no other careers available. Being in a factory meant working only eight hours a day compared with the peasant's dawn-to-dusk day. There were no heavy loads to carry, and I could live with my family. But the most important thing was getting back my city registration, which meant guaranteed food and other basics from the state.

The factory was in the eastern suburbs of Chengdu, about forty-five minutes by bicycle from home. For much of the way I rode along the bank of the Silk River, then along muddy country roads through fields of rapeseed and wheat. Finally I reached a shabby-looking enclosure dotted with piles of bricks and rusting rolled steel. This was my factory. It was a rather primitive enterprise, with some machines dating back to the turn of the century. After five years of denunciation meetings, wall slogans, and physical battles between the factions in the factory, the managers and engineers had just been put back to work and it had begun to resume producing machine tools. The workers gave me a special welcome, largely on account of my parents: the destructiveness of the Cultural Revolution had made them hanker for the old administration, under which there had been order and stability.

I was assigned as an apprentice in the foundry, under a woman whom everyone called "Auntie Wei." She had been very poor as a child, and had not even had a decent pair of trousers when she was a teenager. Her life had changed when the Communists came, and she was immensely grateful to them. She joined the Party, and at the beginning of the Cultural Revolution she was among the Loyalists who defended the old Party officials. When Mao openly backed the Rebels, her group was beaten into surrender and she was tortured. A good friend of hers, an old worker who also owed much to the Communists, died after being hung horizontally by his wrists and ankles (a torture called "duck swimming"). Auntie Wei told me the story of her life in tears, and said that her fate was tied to that of the Party, which she considered had been wrecked by "anti-Party elements" like Lin Biao. She treated me like a daughter, primarily because I came from a Communist family. I felt uneasy with her because I could not match her faith in the Party.

There were about thirty men and women doing the same job as me, ramming earth into molds. The incandescent, bubbling molten iron was lifted and poured into the molds, generating a mass of sparkling white-hot stars. The hoist over our workshop creaked so alarmingly that I was always worried it might drop the crucible of boiling liquid iron onto the people ramming away underneath.

My job as a caster was dirty and hard. I had swollen arms from pounding the earth into the molds, but I was in high spirits, as I naively believed that the Cultural Revolution was coming to an end. I threw myself into my work with an ardor that would have surprised the peasants in Deyang.

In spite of my newfound enthusiasm, I was relieved to hear after a month that I was going to be transferred. I could not have sustained ramming eight hours a day for long. Owing to the goodwill toward my parents, I was given several jobs to choose from—lathe operator, hoist operator, telephone operator, carpenter, or electrician. I dithered between the last two. I liked the idea of being able to create lovely wooden things, but decided that I did not have talented hands. As an electrician, I would have the glamour of being the only woman in the factory doing the job. There had been one woman in the electricians' team, but she was leaving for another post. She had always attracted great admiration. When she climbed to the top of the electric poles people would stop to marvel. I struck up an immediate friendship with this woman, who told me something which made up my mind for me: electricians did not have to stand by a machine eight hours a day. They could stay in their quarters waiting to be called out on a job. That meant I would have time to myself to read.

I received five electric shocks in the first month. Like being a barefoot doctor, there was no formal training: the result of Mao's disdain for education. The six men in the team taught me patiently, but I started at an abysmally low level. I did not even know what a fuse was. The woman electrician gave me her copy of *The Electricians' Manual*, and I plunged into it, but still came out confusing electric current with voltage. In the end, I felt ashamed of wasting the other electricians' time, and tried to copy what they did without understanding much of the theory. I managed fairly well, and gradually was able to do some repairs on my own.

One day a worker reported a faulty switch on a power distribution board. I went to the back of the board to examine the wiring, and decided a screw must have come loose. Instead of switching off the electric supply first, I impetuously poked my mains-tester cum screwdriver at the screw. The back of the board was a net of wires, connections, and joints carrying 380 volts of power. Once inside this minefield, I had to push my screwdriver extremely carefully through a gap. I reached the screw, only to find it was not loose after all. By then my arm had started to shake slightly from being taut and nervous. I began to pull it back, holding my breath. Right at the very edge, just as I was about to relax, a series of colossal jolts shot through my right hand and down to my feet. I leaped in the air, and the screwdriver sprang out of my hand. It had touched a joint at the entrance to the power distribution network. I sagged onto the floor, thinking I could have been killed if the screwdriver had slipped a little earlier. I did not tell the other electricians, as I did not want them to feel they had to go on calls with me.

I got used to the shocks. No one else made a fuss about them, either. One old electrician told me that before 1949, when the factory was privately owned, he had had to use the back of his hand to test the current. It was only under the Communists that the factory was obliged to buy the electricians mains-testers.

There were two rooms in our quarters, and when they were not out on a call, most of the electricians would play cards in the outer room while I read in the inner room. In Mao's China, failure to join the people around you was criticized as "cutting oneself off from the masses," and at first I was nervous about going off on my own to read. I would put my book down as soon as one of the other electricians came inside, and would try to chat with him in a somewhat awkward manner. As a result they seldom came in. I was enormously relieved that they did not object to my eccentricity. Rather, they went out of their way not to disturb me. Because they were so nice to me I volunteered to do as many repairs as possible.

One young electrician in the team, Day, had been in a high school until the start of the Cultural Revolution, and was considered very well educated. He was a good calligrapher and played several musical instruments beautifully. I was very attracted to him, and in the mornings I would always find him leaning against the door to the electricians' quarters, waiting to greet me. I found myself doing a lot of calls with him. One early spring day, after finishing a maintenance job, we spent the lunch break leaning against a haystack at the back of the foundry, enjoying the first sunny day of the year. Sparrows were chirping over our heads, fighting for the grains left on the rice plants. The hay gave off an aroma of sunshine and earth. I was overjoyed to discover that Day shared my interest in classical Chinese poetry, and that we could compose poems to each other using the same rhyme sequence, as ancient Chinese poets had done. In my generation, few people understood or liked classical poetry. We were very late back to work that afternoon, but there were no criticisms. The other electricians only gave us meaningful smiles.

Soon Day and I were counting the minutes during our days off from the factory, eager to be back together. We sought every opportunity to be near each other, to brush each other's fingers, to feel the excitement of being close, to smell the smell of each other, and to look for reasons to be hurt—or pleased—by each other's half-spoken words.

Then I began to hear gossip that Day was unworthy of me. The disapproval was partly caused by the fact that I was considered special. One of the reasons was that I was the only offspring of high officials in the factory, and indeed the only one most of the workers had ever come into contact with. There had been many stories about high officials' children being arrogant and spoiled. I apparently came as a nice surprise, and some workers seemed to feel that no one in the factory could possibly be worthy of me.

They held it against Day that his father had been a Kuomintang officer, and had been in a labor camp. The workers were convinced I had a bright future, and should not be "dragged into misfortune" by being associated with Day.

Actually, it was purely by chance that Day's father had become a Kuomintang officer. In 1937, he and two friends were on their way to Yan'an to join up with the Communists to fight the Japanese. They had almost reached Yan'an when they were stopped at a Kuomintang roadblock where the officers urged them to join the Kuomintang instead. While the two friends insisted on pressing on to Yan'an, Day's father settled for the Kuomintang, thinking it did not matter which Chinese army he joined, as long as it fought the Japanese. When the civil war restarted he and his two friends ended up on opposite sides. After 1949, he was sent to a labor camp, while his companions became high-ranking officers in the Communist army.

Because of this accident of history, Day was sniped at in the factory for not knowing his place by "pestering" me, and even for being a social climber. I could see from his drained face and bitter smiles that he was stung by the snide gossip, but he said nothing to me. We had only hinted at our feelings in allusions in our poems. Now he stopped writing poems to me. The confidence with which he had begun our friendship disappeared, and he adopted a subdued and humbled manner toward me in private. In public, he tried to appease the people who disapproved of him by awkwardly trying to show them he really thought nothing of me. At times I felt that he behaved in such an undignified way that I could not help being irritated as well as saddened. Having been brought up in a privileged position, I did not realize that in China dignity was a luxury scarcely available to those who were not privileged. I did not appreciate Day's dilemma, and the fact that he could not show his love for me, for fear of ruining me. Gradually we became alienated.

During the four months of our acquaintance, the word "love" had never been mentioned by either of us. I had even suppressed it in my mind. One could never let oneself go, because consideration of the vital factor, family background, was ingrained in one's mind. The consequences of being tied to the family of a "class enemy" like Day's were too serious. Because of the subconscious self-censorship, I never quite fell in love with Day.

During this period my mother had come off the cortisone, and had been receiving treatment with Chinese medicines for her scleroderma. We had been scouring country markets for the weird ingredients prescribed for her—tortoiseshell, snake gallbladder, and anteater scales. The doctors recommended that as soon as the weather turned warmer, she should go to see some top-class specialists in Peking for both her womb and the scleroderma. As part compensation for what she had suffered, the authorities offered to send a companion with her. My mother asked if I could go.

We left in April 1972, staying with family friends, whom it was now safe to contact. My mother saw several gynecologists in Peking and Tianjin, who diagnosed a benign tumor in her womb and recommended a hysterectomy. Meanwhile, they said her bleeding could be controlled if she had plenty of rest and tried to keep cheerful. The dermatologists thought that the scleroderma might be localized, in which case it would not be fatal. My mother followed the doctors' advice and had a hysterectomy the following year. The scleroderma remained localized.

We visited many friends of my parents. Everywhere we went, they were being rehabilitated. Some had just come out of prison. *Mao-tai* and other treasured liquors flowed freely, as did tears. In almost every family, one or more members had died as a result of the Cultural Revolution. The eighty-year-old mother of an old friend died after falling off a landing where she had had to sleep, her family having been driven out of their apartment. Another friend struggled to hold back his tears when he set eyes on me. I reminded him of his daughter, who would have been my age. She had been sent with her school to a godforsaken place on the border with Siberia, where she had become pregnant. Frightened, she consulted a back-street midwife who tied musk around her waist and told her to jump off a wall to get rid of the baby. She died of a violent hemorrhage. Tragic stories cropped up in every household. But we also talked about hope, and looked forward to happier times ahead.

One day we went to see Tung, an old friend of my parents who had just been released from prison. He had been my mother's boss on her march from Manchuria to Sichuan, and had become a bureau chief in the Ministry of Public Security. At the beginning of the Cultural Revolution he was accused of being a Russian spy, and of having supervised the installation of tape recorders in Mao's quarters—which he had apparently done, under orders. Every word of Mao's was supposed to be so precious it had to be preserved, but Mao spoke a dialect which his secretaries found hard to understand, and in addition they were sometimes sent out of the room. In early 1967 Tung was arrested and sent to the special prison for top people, Qincheng. He spent five years in chains, in solitary confinement. His legs were like matchsticks, while from the hips up he was terribly bloated. His wife had been forced to denounce him, and had changed the surname of their children from his to hers to demonstrate that they were cutting him off forever. Most of their household things, including his clothes, had been taken away in house raids. As a result of Lin Biao's downfall, Tung's patron, a foe of Lin Biao's, was back in power, and Tung was released from prison. His wife was summoned back from her camp in the northern border region to be reunited with him.

On the day of his release, she brought him new clothes. His first words to her were, "You shouldn't have just brought me material goods. You should have brought me spiritual food [meaning Mao's works]." Tung had been reading nothing but these during his five years in solitary. I was staying with his family at the time, and saw him making them study Mao's articles every day, with a seriousness which I found more tragic than ridiculous.

A few months after our visit Tung was sent to supervise a case in a port in the south. His long confinement had left him unfit for a demanding job, and he soon had a heart attack. The government dispatched a special plane to take him to a hospital in Guangzhou. The lift in the hospital was not working, and he insisted on walking up four floors because he considered being carried upstairs against Communist morality. He died on the operating table. His family was not with him because he had left word that "they should not interrupt their work."

It was while we were staying with Tung and his family at the end of May 1972 that my mother and I received a telegram saying my father had been allowed to leave his camp. After the fall of Lin Biao, the camp doctors had at last given my father a diagnosis, saying that he was suffering from dangerously high blood pressure, serious heart and liver trouble, and vascular sclerosis. They recommended a complete checkup in Peking.

He took a train to Chengdu, and then flew to Peking. Because there was no public transport to the airport for nonpassengers, my mother and I had to wait to meet him at the city terminal. He was thin and burned almost black by the sun. It was the first time in three and a half years that he had been out of the mountains of Miyi. For the first few days he seemed at a loss in the big city, and would refer to crossing the road as "crossing the river" and taking a bus as "taking a boat." He walked hesitantly on the crowded streets and looked somewhat baffled by all the traffic. I assumed the role of his guide. We stayed with an old friend of his from Yibin who had also suffered atrociously in the Cultural Revolution.

Apart from this man and Tung, my father did not visit anyone—because he had not been rehabilitated. Unlike me, who was full of optimism, he was heavy-hearted most of the time. To try to cheer him up, I dragged him and my mother out sight-seeing in temperatures sometimes exceeding 100°F. Once I half-forced him to go to the Great Wall with me in a crowded coach, choking with dust and sweat. As I babbled away, he listened with pensive smiles. A baby in the arms of a peasant woman sitting in front of us started crying, and she smacked it hard. My father shot up from his seat and yelled at her, "Don't you hit the baby!" I hurriedly pulled his sleeve and made him sit down. The whole coach stared at us. It was most unusual for a Chinese to interfere in a matter like this. I thought with a sigh of how my father had changed from the days when he had beaten Jin-ming and Xiao-hei.

In Peking I also read books which opened new horizons for me. President Nixon had visited China in February that year. The official line was that he had come "with a white flag." The idea that America was the number-one enemy had by now vanished from my mind, together with much of my indoctrination. I was overjoyed that Nixon had come because his visit helped generate a new climate in which some translations of foreign books were becoming available. They were marked "for internal circulation," which meant in theory that they were to be read only by authorized personnel, but there were no rules specifying to whom they should be circulated, and they passed freely between friends if one of them had privileged access through their job.

I was able to lay my hands on some of these publications. It was with unimaginable pleasure that I read Nixon's own *Six Crises* (somewhat expurgated, of course, given his anti-Communist past), David Halberstam's *The Best and the Brightest*, William L. Shirer's *The Rise and Fall of the Third Reich*, and *The Winds of War* by Herman Wouk, with their (to me) up-to-date picture of the outside world. The descriptions of the Kennedy administration in *The Best and the Brightest* made me marvel at the relaxed atmosphere of the American government, in contrast with my own—so remote, frightening, and secretive. I was captivated by the style of writing in the nonfiction works. How cool and detached it was! Even Nixon's *Six Crises* seemed a model of calmness compared with the sledgehammer style of the Chinese media, full of hectoring, denunciations, and assertions. In *The Winds of War* I was less impressed by its majestic descriptions of the times than by its vignettes showing the uninhibited fuss that Western women could make about their clothing, by their easy access to it and by the range of colors and styles available. At twenty, I had only a few clothes, in the same style as everybody else, almost every piece blue, gray, or white. I closed my eyes and caressed in my imagination all the beautiful dresses I had never seen or worn.

The increased availability of information from abroad was, of course, part of the general liberalization after the downfall of Lin Biao, but Nixon's visit gave it a convenient pretext—the Chinese must not lose face by showing themselves to be totally ignorant of America. In those days, every step in the process of relaxation had to be given some farfetched political justification. Learning English was now a worthy cause—for "winning friends from all over the world"—and was therefore no longer a crime. So as not to alarm or frighten our distinguished guest, streets and restaurants lost the militant names that had been imposed on them at the beginning of the Cultural Revolution by the Red Guards. In Chengdu, although it was not visited by Nixon, the restaurant The Whiff of Gunpowder switched back to its old name, The Fragrance of Sweet Wind.

I was in Peking for five months. Whenever I was alone, I thought of Day. We did not write to each other. I composed poems to him, but kept them to myself. Eventually, my hope for the future conquered my regrets about the past. One piece of news in particular overshadowed all my other thoughts—for the first time since I was fourteen I saw the possibility of a future I had not dared to dream about: I might be able to go to college. In Peking, small numbers of students had been enrolled in the previous couple of years, and it looked as though universities all over the country would be opening soon. Zhou Enlai was emphasizing a quote by Mao to the effect that universities were still needed, particularly for science and technology. I could not wait to get back to Chengdu to start studying to try to get in.

I returned to the factory in September 1972, and saw Day without too much pain. He had also become calm, only occasionally revealing a glimpse of melancholy. We were good friends again, but we no longer talked about poetry. I buried myself in my preparations for a university course, although I had no idea which. It was not up to me to choose, as Mao had said that "education must be thoroughly revolutionized." This meant, among other things, that university students were to be assigned to courses with no consideration for what they were interested in—that would be individualism, a capitalist vice. I began to study all the major subjects: Chinese, math, physics, chemistry, biology, and English.

Mao had also decreed that students were not to come from the traditional source—middle-school graduates—but had to be workers or peasants. This suited me, as I had been a genuine peasant and was now a worker.

There was to be an entrance exam, Zhou Enlai had decided, although he had to change the term "exam" *(kao-shi)* to "an investigation into the candidates' situation of handling some basic knowledge, and their ability to analyze and solve concrete problems," a criterion based on another Mao quote. Mao did not like exams. The new procedure was that first one had to be recommended by one's work unit, then came entrance examinations, then the enrollment authorities weighed the exam results and the applicant's "political behavior."

For nearly ten months I spent all my evenings and weekends, and much of my time at the factory as well, poring over textbooks that had survived the flames of the Red Guards. They came from many friends. I also had a network of tutors who gave up their evenings and holidays happily and enthusiastically. People who loved learning felt a rapport which bound them together. This was the reaction from a nation with a highly sophisticated civilization which had been subjected to virtual extinction.

In spring 1973, Deng Xiaoping was rehabilitated and appointed vice-premier, the *de facto* deputy to the ailing Zhou Enlai. I was thrilled. Deng's comeback seemed to me a sure sign that the Cultural Revolution was being reversed. He was known to be dedicated to construction rather than destruction, and was an excellent administrator. Mao had sent him away to a tractor factory in relative security to keep him in reserve in case of Zhou Enlai's demise. No matter how power-crazed, Mao was always careful not to burn his bridges.

I was delighted at Deng's rehabilitation for personal reasons as well. I had known his stepmother very well when I was a child, and his half-sister was our neighbor for years in the compound—we all called her "Auntie Deng." She and her husband had been denounced simply because they were related to Deng, and the compound residents who had fawned over her before the Cultural Revolution shunned her. But my family greeted her as usual. At the same time, she was one of the very few people in the compound who would tell my family how they admired my father at the height of his persecution. In those days even a nod, or a fleeting smile, was rare and precious, and our two families developed very warm feelings for each other.

In the summer of 1973, university enrollment started. I felt as if I was awaiting a sentence of life or death. One place in the Foreign Languages Department at Sichuan University was allocated to the Second Bureau of Light Industry in Chengdu, which had twenty-three factories under it, mine being one of them. Each of the factories had to nominate one candidate to sit for exams. In my factory there were several hundred workers, and six people applied, including me. An election was held to select the candidate, and I was chosen by four of the factory's five workshops.

In my own workshop there was another candidate, a friend of mine who was nineteen. Both of us were popular, but our workmates could only vote for one of us. Her name was read out first; there was an awkward stirring—it was clear that people could not decide what to do. I was miserable in the extreme—if there were a lot of votes for her, there would be fewer for me. Suddenly she stood up and said with a smile, "I'd like to forgo my candidacy and vote for Chang Jung. I'm two years younger than she is. I'll try next year." The workers burst out in relieved laughter, and promised to vote for her next year. And they did. She went to the university in 1974.

I was hugely moved by her gesture, and also by the outcome of the vote. It was as if the workers were helping me to achieve my dreams. My family background did not hurt, either. Day did not apply: he knew he had no chance.

I took the Chinese, math, and English exams. I was so nervous the night before that I could not sleep. When I came home for the lunch break, my sister was waiting for me. She massaged my head gently, and I fell into a light snooze. The papers were very elementary, and scarcely touched on my assiduously imbibed geometry, trigonometry, physics, and chemistry. I got honors in all my papers, and for my English oral I got the highest mark of all the candidates in Chengdu.

Before I could relax, there came a crushing blow. On 20 July an article appeared in the *People's Daily* about a "blank exam paper." Unable to answer the questions in his university entrance papers, an applicant called Zhang Tie-sheng, who had been sent to the countryside near Jinzhou, had handed in a blank sheet, along with a letter complaining that the exams were tantamount to a "capitalist restoration." His letter was seized on by Mao's nephew and personal aide, Mao Yuanxin, who was running the province. Mme. Mao and her cohorts condemned the emphasis on academic standards as "bourgeois dictatorship." "What does it matter even if the whole country becomes illiterate?" they declared. "What matters is that the Cultural Revolution achieves the greatest triumph!"

The exams I had taken were declared void. Entrance to universities was now to be decided solely by "political behavior." How that should be measured became a big question. The recommendation from my factory had been written after a "collective appraisal meeting" of the electricians' team. Day had drafted it and my former female electrician master had polished it. It made me out to be an absolute paragon, the most model worker that ever existed. I had no doubt that the other twenty-two candidates had exactly the same credentials. There was therefore no way to differentiate between us.

The official propaganda was not much help. One widely publicized "hero" shouted, "You ask me for my qualification for university? My qualification is this!"—at which he raised his hands and pointed at his calluses. But we all had calluses on our hands. We had all been in factories, and most had worked on farms.

There was only one alternative: the back door.

Most directors of the Sichuan Enrollment Committee were old colleagues of my father's who had been rehabilitated, and they admired his courage and integrity. But, much though he wanted me to have a university education, my father would not ask them to help. "It would not be fair to people with no power," he said. "What would our country become if things had to be done this way?" I started to argue with him, and ended up in tears. I must have looked truly heartbroken, because eventually he said, with a pained face. "All right, I'll do it."

I took his arm and we walked to a hospital about a mile away where one of the directors of the Enrollment Committee was having a checkup: nearly all victims of the Cultural Revolution suffered appalling health as a result of their ordeals. My father walked slowly, with the help of a stick. His old energy and sharpness had disappeared. Watching him shuffling along, stopping to rest every now and then, battling with his mind as well as his legs, I wanted to say "Let's go back." But I also desperately wanted to get into the university.

On the hospital grounds we sat on the edge of a low stone bridge to rest. My father looked in torment. Eventually he said, "Would you forgive me? I really find it very difficult to do this. . . ." For a second I felt a surge of resentment, and wanted to cry out at him that there was no fairer alternative. I wanted to tell him how much I had dreamed of going to the university, and that I deserved it—for my hard work, for my exam results, and because I had been elected. But

I knew my father knew all this. And it was he who had given me my thirst for knowledge. Still, he had his principles, and because I loved him I had to accept him as he was, and understand his dilemma of being a moral man living in a land which was a moral void. I held back my tears and said, "Of course." We trudged back home in silence.

How lucky I was to have my resourceful mother! She went to the wife of the head of the Enrollment Committee, who then spoke to her husband. My mother also went to see the other chiefs, and got them to back me. She emphasized my exam results, which she knew would be the clincher for these former capitalist-roaders. In October 1973, I entered the Foreign Languages Department of Sichuan University in Chengdu to study English.

26. "Sniffing after Foreigners' Farts and Calling Them Sweet"— Learning English in Mao's Wake

(1972–1974)

Since her return from Peking in autumn 1972, helping her five children had been my mother's major occupation. My youngest brother, Xiao-fang, then aged ten, needed daily coaching to make up for his missed school years, and the future of her other children depended largely on her.

With the society half paralyzed for over six years, an enormous number of social problems had been created, and simply left unsolved. One of the most serious was the many millions of young people who had been sent to the countryside and who were desperate to come back to the cities. After the demise of Lin Biao it began to be possible for some to get back, partly because the state needed labor for the urban economy, which it was now trying to revitalize. But the government also had to put strict limits on the number who could return because it was state policy in China to control the population of the cities: the state took it on itself to guarantee the urban population food, housing, and jobs.

So competition for the limited "return tickets" was fierce. The state created regulations to keep the number down. Marriage was one criterion for exclusion. Once married, no organization in the city would take you. It was on these grounds that my sister was disqualified from applying for a job in the city, or to a university, which were the only legitimate ways to get back to Chengdu. She was extremely miserable, as she wanted to join her husband; his factory had started working normally again, and as a result he could not go to Deyang and live with her, except for the official "marriage leave" of just twelve days a year. Her only chance of getting to Chengdu was to obtain a certificate that said she had an incurable disease—which was what many like her were doing. So my mother had to help her get one from a doctor friend which said Xiao-hong suffered from cirrhosis of the liver. She came back to Chengdu at the end of 1972.

The way to get things done now was through personal connections. There were people coming to see my mother every day—schoolteachers, doctors, nurses, actors, and minor officials—appealing for help to get their children out of the countryside. Often she was their only hope, although she had no job, and she pulled strings on their behalf with unflagging energy. My father would not help; he was too set in his ways to start "fixing."

Even when the official channel worked, the personal connection was still essential to make sure things went smoothly and to avoid potential disaster. My brother Jin-ming got out of his village in March 1972. Two organizations were recruiting new workers from his commune: one was a factory in his county town making electrical appliances, the other an unspecified enterprise in the Western District of Chengdu. Jin-ming wanted to get back to Chengdu, but my mother made inquiries among her friends in the Western District and found out that the job was in a slaughterhouse. Jin-ming immediately withdrew his application and went to work in the local factory instead.

It was in fact a large plant which had relocated from Shanghai in 1966 as part of Mao's plan to conceal industry in the mountains of Sichuan against an American or Soviet attack. Jin-ming impressed his fellow workers with his hard work and fairness, and in 1973 he was one of four young people elected by the factory to attend a university, out of 200 applicants. He passed his exam papers brilliantly and effortlessly. But because Father had not been rehabilitated, my mother had to make sure that when the university came to do the obligatory "political investigation" they would not be scared off, and would instead get the impression that he was about to be cleared. She also had to ensure that Jin-ming was not pushed out by some failed applicant with powerful connections. In October 1973, when I went to Sichuan University, Jin-ming was admitted to the Engineering College of Central China at Wuhan to study casting. He would have preferred to do physics, but he was in seventh heaven anyway.

While Jin-ming and I had been preparing to try to get into a university, my second brother, Xiao-hei, was living in a state of despondency. The basic qualification for university entrance was that one had to have been either a worker, a peasant, or a soldier, and he had been none of these. The government was still expelling urban youth *en masse* to the rural areas, and this was the only future facing him—except joining the armed forces. Dozens applied for every place, and the only way in was via connections.

My mother got Xiao-hei in in December 1972, against almost impossible odds, as my father had not been cleared. Xiao-hei was assigned to an air force college in northern China, and after three months' basic training became a radio operator. He worked five hours a day, in a supremely leisurely manner, and spent the rest of the time in "political studies" and producing food.

In the "studies" sessions everyone claimed they had joined the armed forces "to follow the Party's command, to protect the people, to safeguard the motherland." But there were more pertinent reasons. The young men from the cities wanted to avoid being sent to the countryside, and those from the country hoped to use the army as a springboard to leap into the city. For peasants from poor areas, being in the armed forces meant at least a better-filled stomach.

As the 1970s unfolded, joining the Party, like joining the army, became increasingly unrelated to ideological commitment. Everyone said in their applications that the Party was "great, glorious, and correct," and that "to join the Party means to devote my life to the most splendid cause of mankind—the liberation of the world proletariat." But for most the real reason was personal advantage. This was the obligatory step to becoming an officer; and when an officer was discharged he automatically became a "state official," with a secure salary, prestige, and power, not to mention a city registration. A private had to go back to his village and become a peasant again. Every year before discharge time there would be stories of suicides, breakdowns, and depressions.

One evening Xiao-hei was sitting with about a thousand soldiers and officers, and the officers' families, watching an open-air movie. Suddenly submachine-gun fire crackled out, followed by a huge explosion. The audience scattered, screaming. The shots came from a guard who was about to be discharged and sent back to his village, having failed to get into the Party and thus to be promoted to officer grade. First he shot dead the commissar of his company, whom he held responsible for blocking his promotion, and then he fired at random into the crowd, tossing a hand grenade. Five more people were killed, all women and children from officers' families. Over a dozen were wounded. He then fled into a residential block, where he was besieged by fellow soldiers, who shouted at him through megaphones to surrender. But the moment the guard fired out of the window, they broke and ran, to the amusement of the hundreds of excited onlookers. Finally, a special unit arrived. After a fierce exchange of fire, they broke into the apartment and found the guard had committed suicide.

Like everyone else around him, Xiao-hei wanted to get into the Party. It was not such a matter of life and death for him as for the peasant soldiers, since he knew he would not have to go to the countryside after his military career. The rule was that you went back to where you came from, so he would automatically be given a job in Chengdu whether he was a Party member or not. But the job would be better if he was a Party member. He would also have more access to information, which was important to him, since China at the time was an intellectual desert, with almost nothing to read apart from the crudest propaganda.

Besides these practical considerations, *fear* was never absent. For many people, joining the Party was rather like taking out an insurance policy. Party membership meant you were less distrusted, and this sense of relative security was very comforting. What was more, in an extremely political environment like the one Xiao-hei was in, if he did not want to join the Party it would be noted in his personal file and suspicion would follow him: "Why does he not want to join the Party?" To apply and not be accepted was also likely to give rise to suspicion: "Why was he not accepted? There must be something wrong with him."

Xiao-hei had been reading Marxist classics with genuine interest— they were the only books available, and he needed something to satisfy his intellectual thirst. Because the Communist Party charter stated that studying Marxism-Leninism was the first qualification for being a Party member, he thought he could combine his interest with practical gain. But neither his bosses nor his comrades were impressed. In fact, they felt shown up because, coming mostly from peasant backgrounds and being semiliterate, they could not understand Marx. Xiao-hei was criticized for being arrogant and cutting himself off from the masses. If he wanted to join the Party, he would have to find another way.

The most important thing, he soon realized, was to please his immediate bosses. The next was to please his comrades. In addition to being popular and working hard at his job, he had to "serve the people" in the most literal sense.

Unlike most armies, which assign unpleasant and menial tasks to the lower ranks, the Chinese army operated by waiting for people to volunteer for jobs like fetching water for morning ablutions and sweeping the grounds. Reveille was at 6:30 A.M.; the "honored task" of getting up before this fell to those who aspired to join the Party. And there were so many of them they fought each other for the brooms. In order to secure a broom, people got up earlier and earlier. One morning Xiao-hei heard someone sweeping the grounds just after 4 A.M.

There were other important chores, and the one which counted most was helping to produce food. The basic food allowance was very small, even for officers. There was meat only once a week. So every company had to grow its own grain and vegetables and raise its own pigs. At harvest time the company commissar would often deliver pep talks: "Comrades, now is the time of testing by the Party! We must finish the whole field by this evening! Yes, the work needs ten times the manpower we have. But every one of us revolutionary fighters can do the job of ten men! Communist Party members must take a leading role. For those who want to join the Party, this is the best time to prove yourselves! Those who have passed the test will be able to join the Party on the battlefield at the end of the day!"

Party members did have to work hard to fulfill their "leading role," but it was the aspiring applicants who really had to exert themselves. On one occasion, Xiao-hei became so exhausted that he collapsed in the middle of a field. While the new members who had earned "battle-field enrollment" raised their right fists and gave the standard pledge "to fight all my life for the glorious Communist cause," Xiao-hei was taken to a hospital, where he had to stay for days.

The most direct path to the Party was raising pigs. The company had several dozen of these, and they occupied an unequaled place in the hearts of the soldiers; officers and men alike would hang around the pigsty, observing, commenting, and willing the animals to grow. If the pigs were doing well, the swineherds were the darlings of the company, and there were many contestants for this profession.

Xiao-hei became a full-time swineherd. It was hard, filthy work, not to mention the psychological pressure. Every night he and his colleagues took turns to get up in the small hours to give the pigs an extra feed. When a sow produced piglets they kept watch night after night in case she crushed them. Precious soybeans were carefully picked, washed, ground, strained, made into "soybean milk," and lov-ingly fed to the mother to stimulate her milk. Life in the air force was very unlike what Xiao-hei had imagined. Producing food took up more than a third of the entire time he was in the military. At the end of a year's arduous pig raising, Xiao-hei was accepted into the Party. Like many others, he put his feet up and began to take it easy.

After membership in the Party, everyone's ambition was to become an officer; whatever advantage the former brought, the latter doubled it. Getting to be an officer depended on being picked by one's superiors, so the key was never to displease them. One day Xiao-hei was summoned to see one of the college's political commissars. Xiao-hei was on tenterhooks, not knowing whether he was in for some unexpected good fortune or total disaster. The commissar, a plump man in his fifties with puffy eyes and a loud, commanding voice, looked exceedingly benign as he lit up a cigarette and asked Xiao-hei about his family background, age, and state of health. He also asked whether he had a fiancée—to which Xiao-hei replied that he did not. It struck Xiao-hei as a good sign that the man was being so personal. The commissar went on to praise him: "You have studied Marxism–Leninism–Mao Zedong Thought conscientiously. You have worked hard. The masses have a good impression of you. Of course, you must keep on being modest; modesty makes you progress," and so on. By the time the commissar stubbed out his cigarette, Xiao-hei thought his promotion was in his pocket.

The commissar lit a second cigarette and began to tell a story about a fire in a cotton mill, and about a woman spinner who had been severely burned dashing back in to rescue "state property." In fact, all her limbs had had to be amputated, so that there was only a head and a torso left, although, the commissar stressed, her face had not been destroyed, or—more important—her ability to produce babies. She was, said the commissar, a heroine, and was going to be publicized on a grand scale in the press. The Party would like to grant all her wishes, and she had said that she wanted to marry an air force officer. Xiao-hei was young, handsome, unattached, and could be made an officer at any time. . . .

Xiao-hei sympathized with the lady, but marrying her was another matter. But how could he refuse the commissar? He could not produce any convincing reasons. Love? Love was supposed to be bound up with "class feelings," and who could deserve more class feelings than a Communist heroine? Saying he did not know her would not get him off the hook either. Many marriages in China had been the result of an arrangement by the Party. As a Party member, particularly one hoping to become an officer, Xiao-hei was supposed to say: "I resolutely obey the Party's decision!" He bitterly regretted having said he had no fiancée. His mind was racing to think of a way to say no tactfully as the commissar went on about the advantages: immediate promotion to officer, publicity as a hero, a full-time nurse, and a large allowance for life.

The commissar lit yet another cigarette, and paused. Xiao-hei weighed his words. Taking a calculated risk, he asked if this was already an irreversible Party decision. He knew the Party always preferred people to "volunteer." As he expected, the commissar said no: it was up to Xiao-hei. Xiao-hei decided to bluff his way through: he "confessed" that although he did not have a fiancée, his mother had arranged a girlfriend for him. He knew this girlfriend had to be good enough to knock out the heroine, and this meant possessing two attributes: the right class background and good works—in that order. So she became the daughter of the commander of a big army region, and worked in an army hospital. They had just begun "talking about love."

The commissar backed off, saying he had only wanted to see how Xiao-hei felt, and had no intention of forcing a match on him. Xiao-hei was not punished, and not long afterward he became an officer and was put in charge of a ground radio communications unit. A young man from a peasant background came forward to marry the disabled heroine.

Meanwhile, Mme. Mao and her cohorts were renewing their efforts to prevent the country from working. In industry, their slogan was: "To stop production is revolution itself." In agriculture, in which they now began to meddle seriously: "We would rather have socialist weeds than capitalist crops." Acquiring foreign technology became "sniffing after foreigners' farts and calling them sweet." In education: "We want illiterate working people, not educated spiritual aristocrats." They called for schoolchildren to rebel against their teachers again; in January 1974, classroom windows, tables, and chairs in schools in Peking were smashed, as in 1966. Mme. Mao claimed this was like "the revolutionary action of English workers destroying machines in the eighteenth century." All this demagoguery had one purpose: to create trouble for Zhou Enlai and Deng Xiaoping and generate chaos. It was only in persecuting people and in *destruction* that Mme. Mao and the other luminaries of the Cultural Revolution had a chance to "shine." In *construction* they had no place.

Zhou and Deng had been making tentative efforts to open the country up, so Mme. Mao launched a fresh attack on foreign culture. In early 1974 there was a big media campaign denouncing the Italian director Michelangelo Antonioni for a film he had made about China, although no one in China had seen the film, and few had even heard of it—or of Antonioni. This xenophobia was extended to Beethoven after a visit by the Philadelphia Orchestra.

In the two years since the fall of Lin Biao, my mood had changed from hope to despair and fury. The only source of comfort was that there was a fight going on at all, and that the lunacy was not reigning supreme, as it had in the earlier years of the Cultural Revolution. During this period, Mao was not giving his full backing to either side. He hated the efforts of Zhou and Deng to reverse the Cultural Revolution, but he knew that his wife and her acolytes could not make the country work.

Mao let Zhou carry on with the administration of the country, but set his wife upon Zhou, particularly in a new campaign—to "criticize Confucius." The slogans ostensibly denounced Lin Biao, but were really aimed at Zhou, who, it was widely held, epitomized the virtues advocated by the ancient sage. Even though Zhou had been unwaveringly loyal, Mao still could not leave him alone. Not even now, when Zhou was fatally ill with cancer of the gastrointestinal tract.

It was in this period that I started to realize that it was Mao who was really responsible for the Cultural Revolution. But I still did not condemn him explicitly, even in my own mind. It was so difficult to destroy a god! But, psychologically, I was ripe for his name to be spelled out for me.

Education became the front line of the sabotage by Mme. Mao and her cabal, because it was not immediately vital to the economy and because every attempt at learning and teaching involved a reversal of the glorified ignorance of the Cultural Revolution. When I entered the university, I found myself in a battlefield.

Sichuan University had been the headquarters of 26 August, the Rebel group that had been the task force of the Tings, and the buildings were pockmarked with scars from the seven years of the Cultural Revolution. Scarcely a window was intact. The pond in the middle of the campus, once renowned for its elegant lotuses and goldfish, was now a stinking, mosquito-breeding swamp. The French plane trees which lined the avenue leading from the main gate had been mutilated.

The moment I entered the university a political campaign started up against "going through the back door." Of course, there was no mention of the fact that it was the Cultural Revolution leaders themselves who had blocked the "front door." I could see that there were a lot of high officials' children among the new "worker-peasant-soldier" students, and that virtually all the rest had connections—the peasants with their production team leaders or commune secretaries, the workers with their factory bosses, if they were not petty officials themselves. The "back door" was the only way in. My fellow students demonstrated little vigor in this campaign.

Every afternoon, and some evenings, we had to "study" turgid *People's Daily* articles denouncing one thing or another, and hold nonsensical "discussions" at which everyone repeated the newspaper's overblown, vapid language. We had to stay on the campus all the time, except Saturday evening and Sunday, and had to return by Sunday evening.

I shared a bedroom with five other girls. There were two tiers of three bunk beds on opposite walls. In between was a table and six chairs where we did our work. There was scarcely room for our washbasins. The window opened onto a stinking open sewer.

English was my subject, but there was almost no way to learn it. There were no native English speakers around, indeed no foreigners at all. The whole of Sichuan was closed to foreigners. Occasionally the odd one was let in, always a "friend of China," but even to speak to them without authorization was a criminal offense. We could be put into prison for listening to the BBC or the Voice of America. No foreign publications were available except *The Worker*, the paper of the minuscule Maoist Communist Party of Britain, and even this was locked up in a special room. I remember the thrill of being given permission once, just once, to look at a copy. My excitement wilted when my eyes fell on the front-page article echoing the campaign to criticize Confucius. As I was sitting there nonplussed, a lecturer whom I liked walked past and said with a smile, "That paper is probably read only in China."

Our textbooks were ridiculous propaganda. The first English sentence we learned was "Long live Chairman Mao!" But no one dared to explain the sentence grammatically. In Chinese the term for the optative mood, expressing a wish or desire, means "something unreal." In 1966 a lecturer at Sichuan University had been beaten up for "having the audacity to suggest that 'Long live Chairman Mao!' was unreal!" One chapter was about a model youth hero who had drowned after jumping into a flood to save an electricity pole because the pole would be used to carry the word of Mao.

With great difficulty, I managed to borrow some English-language textbooks published before the Cultural Revolution from lecturers in my department and from Jin-ming, who sent me books from his university by post. These contained extracts from writers like Jane Austen, Charles Dickens, and Oscar Wilde, and stories from European and American history. They were a joy to read, but much of my energy went toward finding them and then trying to keep them.

Whenever someone approached, I would quickly cover the books with a newspaper. This was only partly because of their "bourgeois" content. It was also important not to appear to be studying too conscientiously, and not to arouse my fellow students' jealousy by reading something far beyond them. Although we were studying English, and were paid—partly for our propaganda value—by the government to do this, we must not be seen to be too devoted to our subject: that was considered being "white and expert." In the mad logic of the day, being good at one's profession ("expert") was automatically equated with being politically unreliable ("white").

I had the misfortune to be better at English than my classmates, and was therefore resented by some of the "student officials," the lowest-level controllers, who supervised political indoctrination sessions and checked the "thought conditions" of their fellow students. The student officials in my course had mostly come from the countryside. They were keen to learn English, but most of them were semiliterate, and had little aptitude. I sympathized with their anxiety and frustration, and understood their jealousy of me. But Mao's concept of "white and expert" made them feel virtuous about their inadequacies, and gave their envy political respectability, and them a malicious opportunity to vent their exasperation.

Every now and then a student official would require a "heart-to-heart" with me. The leader of the Party cell in my course was a former peasant named Ming who had joined the army and then become a production team leader. He was a very poor student, and would give me long, righteous lectures about the latest developments in the Cultural Revolution, the "glorious tasks of us worker-peasant-soldier students," and the need for "thought reform." I needed these heart-to-hearts because of my "shortcomings," but Ming would never come straight to the point. He would let a criticism hang in midair—"The masses have a complaint about you. Do you know what it is?"—and watch the effect on me. He would eventually disclose some allegation. One day it was the inevitable charge that I was "white and expert." Another day I was "bourgeois" because I failed to fight for the chance to clean the toilet, or to wash my comrades' clothes—all obligatory good deeds. And yet another time he would attribute a despicable motive: that I did not spend most of my time tutoring my classmates because I did not want them to catch up with me.

One criticism that Ming would put to me with trembling lips (he obviously felt strongly about it) was "The masses have reported that you are aloof. You cut yourself off from the masses." It was common in China for people to assert that you were looking down on them if you failed to hide your desire for some solitude.

One level up from the student officials were the political supervisors, who also knew little or no English. They did not like me. Nor I them. From time to time I had to report my thoughts to the one in charge of my year, and before every session I would wander around the campus for hours summoning up the courage to knock on his door. Although he was not, I believed, an evil person, I feared him. But most of all I dreaded the inevitable tedious, ambiguous diatribe. Like many others, he loved playing cat and mouse to indulge his feeling of power. I had to look humble and earnest, and promise things I did not mean and had no intention of doing.

I began to feel nostalgia for my years in the countryside and the factory, when I had been left relatively alone. Universities were much more tightly controlled, being of particular interest to Mme. Mao. Now I was among people who had benefited from the Cultural Revolution. Without it, many of them would never have been here.

Once some students in my year were given the project of compiling a dictionary of English abbreviations. The department had decided that the existing one was "reactionary" because, not surprisingly, it had far more "capitalist" abbreviations than ones with an approved origin. "Why should Roosevelt have an abbreviation—FDR—and not Chairman Mao?" some students asked indignantly. With tremendous solemnity they searched for acceptable entries, but eventually had to give up their "historic mission" as there simply were not enough of the right kinds.

I found this environment unbearable. I could understand ignorance, but I could not accept its glorification, still less its right to rule.

We often had to leave the university to do things that were irrelevant to our subjects. Mao had said that we should "learn things in factories, the countryside, and army units." What exactly we were meant to learn was, typically, unspecified. We started with "learning in the countryside." One week into the first term of my first year, in October 1973, the whole university was packed off to a place on the outskirts of Chengdu called Mount Dragon Spring, which had been the victim of a visit by one of China's vice-premiers, Chen Yonggui. He was previously the leader of a farming brigade called Dazhai in the mountainous northern province of Shanxi, which had become Mao's model in agriculture, ostensibly because it relied more on the peasants' revolutionary zeal than on material incentives. Mao did not notice, or did not care, that Dazhai's claims were largely fraudulent.

When Vice-Premier Chen visited Mount Dragon Spring he had re-marked, "Ah, you have mountains here! Imagine how many fields you could create!" as if the fertile hills covered in orchards were like the barren mountains of his native village. But his remarks had the force of law. The crowds of university students dynamited the orchards that had provided Chengdu with apples, plums, peaches, and flowers. We transported stones from afar with pull carts and shoulder poles, for the construction of terraced rice paddies.

It was compulsory to demonstrate zeal in this, as in all actions called for by Mao. Many of my fellow students worked in a manner that screamed out for notice. I was regarded as lacking in enthusiasm, partly because I had difficulty hiding my aversion to this activity, and partly because I did not sweat easily, no matter how much energy I expended. Those students whose sweat poured out in streams were invariably praised at the summing-up sessions every evening.

My university colleagues were certainly more eager than proficient. The sticks of dynamite they shoved into the ground usually failed to go off, which was just as well, as there were no safety precautions. The stone walls we built around the terraced edges soon collapsed, and by the time we left, after two weeks, the mountain slope was a wasteland of blast holes, cement solidified into shapeless masses, and piles of stones. Few seemed concerned about this. The whole episode was ultimately a show, a piece of theater—a pointless means to a pointless end.

I loathed these expeditions and hated the fact that our labor, and our whole existence, was being used for a shoddy political game. To my intense irritation, I was sent off to an army unit, again with the whole university, in late 1974.

The camp, a couple of hours' truck journey from Chengdu, was in a beautiful spot, surrounded by rice paddies, peach blossoms, and bamboo groves. But our seventeen days there felt like a year. I was perpetually breathless from the long runs every morning, bruised from falling and crawling under the imaginary gunfire of "enemy" tanks, and exhausted from hours of aiming a rifle at a target or throwing wooden hand grenades. I was expected to demonstrate my passion for, and my excellence at, all these activities, at which I was hopeless. It was unforgivable for me to be good only at English, my subject. These army tasks were *political* assignments, and I had to prove myself in them. Ironically, in the army itself, good marksmanship and other military skills would lead to a soldier being condemned as "white and expert."

I was one of the handful of students who threw the wooden hand grenades such a dangerously short distance that we were banned from the grand occasion of throwing the real thing. As our pathetic group sat on the top of a hill listening to the distant explosions, one girl burst into sobs. I felt deeply apprehensive too, at the thought of having given apparent proof of being "white."

Our second test was shooting. As we marched onto the firing range, I thought to myself: I cannot afford to fail this, I absolutely have to pass. When my name was called and I lay on the ground, gazing at the target through the gunsight, I saw complete blackness. No target, no ground, nothing. I was trembling so much my whole body felt powerless. The order to fire sounded faint, as though it was floating from a great distance through clouds. I pulled the trigger, but I did not hear any noise, or see anything. When the results were checked, the instructors were puzzled: none of my ten bullets had even hit the board, let alone the target.

I could not believe it. My eyesight was perfect. I told the instructor the gun barrel must be bent. He seemed to believe me: the result was too spectacularly bad to be entirely my fault. I was given another gun, provoking complaints from others who had asked, unsuccessfully, for a second chance. My second go was slightly better: two of the ten bullets hit the outer rings. Even so, my name was still at the bottom of the whole university. Seeing the results stuck on the wall like a propaganda poster, I knew that my "whiteness" was further bleached. I heard snide remarks from one student official: "Humph! Getting a second chance! As if that would do her any good! If she has no class feelings, or class hatred, a hundred goes won't save her!"

In my misery, I retreated into my own thoughts, and hardly noticed the soldiers, young peasants in their early twenties, who instructed us. Only one incident drew my attention to them. One evening when some girls collected their clothes from the line on which they had hung them to dry, their knickers were unmistakably stained with semen.

In the university I found refuge in the homes of the professors and lecturers who had obtained their jobs before the Cultural Revolution, on academic merit. Several of the professors had been to Britain or the United States before the Communists took power, and I felt I could relax and speak the same language with them. Even so, they were cautious. Most intellectuals were, as the result of years of repression. We avoided dangerous topics. Those who had been to the West rarely talked about their time there. Although I was dying to ask, I checked myself, not wanting to place them in a difficult position.

Partly for the same reason, I never discussed my thoughts with my parents. How could they have responded—with dangerous truths or safe lies? Besides, I did not want them to worry about my heretical ideas. I wanted them to be genuinely in the dark, so that if anything happened to me they could truthfully say they did not know.

The people to whom I did communicate my thoughts were friends of my own generation. Actually, there was little else to do except talk, particularly with men friends. To "go out" with a man—being seen alone together in public—was tantamount to an engagement. There was still virtually no entertainment to go to anyway. Cinemas showed only the handful of works approved by Mme. Mao. Occasionally a rare foreign movie, perhaps from Albania, would be screened, but most of the tickets disappeared into the pockets of people with connections. A ferocious crowd would swamp the box office and try to tear each other away from the window to get the remaining few tickets. Scalpers made a killing.

So, we just sat at home and talked. We sat very properly, as in Victorian England. For women to have friendships with men was unusual in those days, and a girlfriend once said to me, "I've never known a girl who has so many men friends. Girls normally have girlfriends." She was right. I knew many girls who married the first man who came near them. From my own men friends, the only demonstrations of interest I got were some rather sentimental poems and restrained letters, one of which, admittedly, was written in blood—from the goalkeeper on the college football team.

My friends and I often talked about the West. By then I had come to the conclusion that it was a wonderful place. Paradoxically, the first people to put this idea into my head were Mao and his regime. For years, the things to which I was naturally inclined had been condemned as evils of the West: pretty clothes, flowers, books, entertainment, politeness, gentleness, spontaneity, mercy, kindness, liberty, aversion to cruelty and violence, love instead of "class hatred," respect for human lives, the desire to be left alone, professional competence. . . . As I sometimes wondered to myself, how could anyone not desire the West?

I was extremely curious about the alternatives to the kind of life I had been leading, and my friends and I exchanged rumors and scraps of information we dug from official publications. I was struck less by the West's technological developments and high living standards than by the absence of political witch-hunts, the lack of consuming suspicion, the dignity of the individual, and the incredible amount of liberty. To me, the ultimate proof of freedom in the West was that there seemed to be so many people there attacking the West and praising China. Almost every other day the front page of *Reference*, the newspaper which carried foreign press items, would feature some eulogy of Mao and the Cultural Revolution. At first I was angered by these, but they soon made me see how tolerant another society could be. I realized that this was the kind of society I wanted to live in: where people were allowed to hold different, even outrageous views. I began to see that it was the very tolerance of oppositions, of protesters, that kept the West progressing.

Still, I could not help being irritated by some observations. Once I read an article by a Westerner who came to China to see some old friends, university professors, who told him cheerfully how they had enjoyed being denounced and sent to the back end of beyond, and how much they had relished being reformed. The author concluded that Mao had indeed made the Chinese into "new people" who would regard what was misery to a Westerner as pleasure. I was aghast. Did he not know that repression was at its worst when there was no complaint? A hundred times more so when the victim actually presented a smiling face? Could he not see to what a pathetic condition these professors had been reduced, and what horror must have been involved to degrade them so? I did not realize that the acting that the Chinese were putting on was something to which Westerners were unaccustomed, and which they could not always decode.

I did not appreciate either that information about China was not easily available, or was largely misunderstood, in the West, and that people with no experience of a regime like China's could take its propaganda and rhetoric at face value. As a result, I assumed that these eulogies were dishonest. My friends and I would joke that they had been bought by our government's "hospitality." When foreigners were allowed into certain restricted places in China following Nixon's visit, wherever they went the authorities immediately cordoned off enclaves even within these enclaves. The best transport facilities, shops, restaurants, guesthouses, and scenic spots were reserved for them, with signs reading "For Foreign Guests Only." *Mao-tai*, the most sought-after liquor, was totally unavailable to ordinary Chinese, but freely available to foreigners. The best food was saved for foreigners. The newspapers proudly reported that Henry Kissinger had said his waistline had expanded as a result of the many twelve-course banquets he enjoyed during his visits to China. This was at a time when in Sichuan, "Heaven's Granary," our meat ration was half a pound per month, and the streets of Chengdu were full of homeless peasants who had fled there from famine in the north, and were living as beggars. There was great resentment among the population about how the foreigners were treated like lords. My friends and I began saying among ourselves: "Why do we attack the Kuomintang for allowing signs saying 'No Chinese or Dogs'—aren't we doing the same?"

Getting hold of information became an obsession. I benefited enormously from my ability to read English, as although the university library had been looted during the Cultural Revolution, most of the books it had lost had been in Chinese. Its extensive English-language collection had been turned upside down, but was still largely intact.

The librarians were delighted that these books were being read, especially by a student, and were extremely helpful. The index system had been thrown into chaos, and they dug through piles of books to find the ones I wanted. It was through the efforts of these kind young men and women that I laid my hands on some English classics. Louisa May Alcott's *Little Women* was the first novel I read in English. I found women writers like her, Jane Austen, and the Brontë sisters much easier to read than male authors like Dickens, and I also felt more empathy with their characters. I read a brief history of European and American literature, and was enormously impressed by the Greek tradition of democracy, Renaissance humanism, and the Enlightenment's questioning of everything. When I read in *Gulliver's Travels* about the emperor who "published an Edict, commanding all his Subjects, upon great Penalties, to break the smaller End of their Eggs," I wondered if Swift had been to China. My joy at the sensation of my mind opening up and expanding was beyond description.

Being alone in the library was heaven for me. My heart would leap as I approached it, usually at dusk, anticipating the pleasure of solitude with my books, the outside world ceasing to exist. As I hurried up the flight of stairs, into the pastiche classical-style building, the smell of old books long stored in airless rooms would give me tremors of excitement, and I would hate the stairs for being too long.

With the help of dictionaries which some professors lent me, I became acquainted with Longfellow, Walt Whitman, and American history. I memorized the whole of the Declaration of Independence, and my heart swelled at the words "We hold these truths to be self-evident, that all men are created equal," and those about men's "unalienable Rights," among them "Liberty and the pursuit of Happiness." These concepts were unheard of in China, and opened up a marvelous new world for me. My notebooks, which I kept with me at all times, were full of passages like these, passionately and tearfully copied out.

One autumn day in 1974, with an air of extreme secrecy, a friend of mine showed me a copy of *Newsweek* with pictures of Mao and Mme. Mao in it. She could not read English, and was keen to know what the article said. This was the first genuine foreign magazine I had ever set eyes on. One sentence in the article struck me like a flash of lightning. It said that Mme. Mao was Mao's "eyes, ears, and voice." Up till that moment, I had never allowed myself to contemplate the obvious connection between Mme. Mao's deeds and her husband. But now Mao's name was spelled out for me. My blurred perceptions surrounding his image came sharply into focus. It was Mao who had been behind the destruction and suffering. Without him, Mme. Mao and her second-rate coterie could not have lasted a single day. I experienced the thrill of challenging Mao openly in my mind for the first time.

27. "If This Is Paradise, What Then Is Hell?"— The Death of My Father
(1974–1976)

All this time, unlike most of his former colleagues, my father had not been rehabilitated or given a job. He had been sitting at home in Meteorite Street doing nothing since he came back from Peking with my mother and me in autumn 1972. The problem was that he had criticized Mao by name. The team investigating him was sympathetic and tried to ascribe some of what he had said against Mao to his mental illness. But the team came up against fierce opposition amongst the higher authorities, who wanted to give him a severe condemnation. Many of my father's colleagues sympathized with him and indeed admired him. But they had to think about their own necks. Besides, my father did not belong to any clique and had no powerful patron—which might have helped get him cleared. Instead, he had well-placed enemies.

One day back in 1968, my mother, who was briefly out from detention, saw an old friend of my father's at a roadside food stall. This man had thrown in his lot with the Tings. He was with his wife, who had actually been introduced to him by my mother and Mrs. Ting when they were working together in Yibin. In spite of the couple's obvious reluctance to have anything to do with her beyond a brief nod, my mother marched up to their table and joined them. She asked them to appeal to the Tings to spare my father. After hearing my mother out, the man shook his head and said, "It's not so simple. . . ." Then he dipped a finger into his tea and wrote the character Zuo on the table. He gave my mother a meaningful look, got up with his wife, and left without another word.

Zuo was a former close colleague of my father's, and was one of the few senior officials who did not suffer at all in the Cultural Revolution. He became the darling of Mrs. Shau's Rebels and a friend of the Tings, but survived their demise and that of Lin Biao and remained in power.

My father would not withdraw his words against Mao. But when the team investigating him suggested putting them down to his mental illness, he acquiesced, with great anguish.

Meanwhile, the general situation made him despondent. There were no principles governing either the behavior of the people or the conduct of the Party. Corruption began to come back in a big way. Officials looked after their families and friends first. For fear of being beaten up, teachers gave all pupils top marks irrespective of the quality of their work, and bus conductors would not collect fares. Dedication to public good was openly sneered at. Mao's Cultural Revolution had destroyed both Party discipline and civic morality.

My father found it difficult to control himself so that he would not speak his mind and say things that would incriminate him and his family further.

He had to rely on tranquilizers. When the political climate was more relaxed, he took less; when the campaigns intensified, he took more. Every time the psychiatrists renewed his supply, they shook their heads, saying it was extremely dangerous for him to continue taking such large doses. But he could only manage short periods off the pills. In May 1974 he sensed that he was on the verge of a breakdown, and asked to be given psychiatric treatment. This time he was hospitalized swiftly, thanks to his former colleagues who were now back in charge of the health service.

I got leave from the university and went to stay with him in the hospital to keep him company. Dr. Su, the psychiatrist who had treated him before, was looking after him again. Under the Tings, Dr. Su had been condemned for giving a true diagnosis about my father, and had been ordered to write a confession saying my father had been faking madness. He refused, for which he was subjected to denunciation meetings, beaten up, and thrown out of the medical profession. I saw him one day in 1968, emptying rubbish bins and cleaning the hospital spittoons. His hair had turned gray, though he was only in his thirties. After the downfall of the Tings he was rehabilitated. He was very friendly to my father and me, as were all the doctors and nurses. They told me they would take good care of my father, and that I did not have to stay with him. But I wanted to. I thought he needed love more than anything else. And I was anxious about what might happen if he fell down with no one around. His blood pressure was dangerously high, and he had already had several minor heart attacks, which had left him with a walking impediment. He looked as though he might slip at any time. Doctors warned that a fall could be fatal. I moved into the men's ward with him, into the same room he had occupied in summer 1967. Each room could accommodate two patients, but my father had the room to himself, and I slept in the spare bed.

I was with him every moment in case he fell over. When he went to the toilet, I waited outside. If he stayed in there for what I thought was too long, I would start to imagine he had had a heart attack, and would make a fool of myself by calling out to him. Every day I took long walks with him in the back garden, which was full of other psychiatric patients in gray-striped pajamas walking incessantly, with spiritless eyes. The sight of them always made me scared and intensely sad.

The garden itself was full of vivid colors. White butterflies fluttered among yellow dandelions on the lawn. In the surrounding flowerbeds were a Chinese aspen, graceful swaying bamboos, and a few garnet flowers of pomegranates behind a thicket of oleanders. As we walked, I composed my poems.

At one end of the garden was a large entertainment room where the inmates went to play cards and chess and to flip through the few newspapers and sanctioned books. One nurse told me that earlier in the Cultural Revolution the room had been used for the inmates to study Chairman Mao's works because his nephew, Mao Yuanxin, had "discovered" that Mao's Little Red Book, rather than medical treatment, was the cure for mental patients. The study sessions did not last long, the nurse told me, because "whenever a patient opened his mouth, we were all scared to death. Who knew what he was going to say?"

The patients were not violent, as their treatment had sapped their physical and mental vitality. Even so, living among them was frightening, particularly at night, when my father's pills had sent him into a sound sleep and the whole building had become quiet. Like all the rooms, ours had no lock, and several times I woke with a start to find a man standing by my bed, holding the mosquito net open and staring at me with the intensity of the insane. I would break into a cold sweat and pull up the quilt to stifle a scream: the last thing I wanted was to wake my father—sleep was vital to his recovery. Eventually, the patient would shuffle away.

After a month, my father went home. But he was not completely cured—his mind had been under too much pressure for too long, and the political environment was still too repressive for him to relax. He had to keep taking tranquilizers. There was nothing the psychiatrists could do. His nervous system was wearing out, and so were his body and mind.

Eventually, a draft verdict on him was drawn up by the team investigating him. It said that he had "committed serious political errors" —which was one step away from being labeled a "class enemy." In line with Party regulations, the draft verdict was given to my father to sign as confirmation that he accepted it. When he read it, he wept. But he signed.

The verdict was not accepted by the higher authorities. They wanted a harsher one.

In March 1975, my brother-in-law Specs was up for promotion in his factory, and the personnel officers of the factory came to my father's department for the obligatory political investigation. A former Rebel from Mrs. Shau's group received the visitors and told them my father was "anti-Mao." Specs did not get his promotion. He did not mention it to my parents for fear of upsetting them, but a friend from my father's department came to the house and my father overheard him whispering the news to my mother. The pain he showed was harrowing when he apologized to Specs for jeopardizing his future. In tears of despair he said to my mother, "What have I done for even my son-in-law to be dragged down like this? What do I have to do to save you?"

In spite of taking a large number of tranquilizers, my father hardly slept over the following days and nights. On the afternoon of 9 April he said he was going to have a nap.

When my mother finished cooking supper in our small ground-floor kitchen, she thought she would leave him to sleep a little longer. Eventually she went upstairs to the bedroom and found she could not wake him. She realized he had had a heart attack. We had no telephone, so she rushed to the provincial government clinic one street away and found its head, Dr. Jen.

Dr. Jen was extremely able, and before the Cultural Revolution he had been in charge of the health of the elite in the compound. He had often come to our apartment, and would discuss the health of all my family, with great concern. But when the Cultural Revolution started and we were out of favor, he became cold and disdainful toward us. I saw many people like Dr. Jen, and their behavior never ceased to shock me.

When my mother found him, Dr. Jen was clearly irritated, and said he would come when he had finished what he was doing. She told him a heart attack could not wait, but he looked at her as if to say that impatience would not help her. It was an hour before he deigned to come to our house with a nurse, but without any first-aid equipment. The nurse had to walk back to fetch it. Dr. Jen turned Father over a few times, and then just sat and waited. Another half an hour passed, by which time my father was dead.

That night I was in my dormitory at the university, working by candlelight during one of the frequent blackouts. Some people from my father's department arrived and drove me home without explanation.

Father lay sideways in his bed, his face unusually peaceful, as though he had gone to a restful sleep. He no longer looked senescent, but youthful, even younger than his age of fifty-four. I felt as if my heart was torn into fragments, and I wept uncontrollably.

For days I wept in silence. I thought of my father's life, his wasted dedication and crushed dreams. He need not have died. Yet his death seemed so inevitable. There was no place for him in Mao's China, because he had tried to be an honest man. He had been betrayed by something to which he had given his whole life, and the betrayal had destroyed him.

My mother demanded that Dr. Jen be punished. If it had not been for his negligence, my father might not have died. Her request was dismissed as a "widow's emotionalism." She decided not to pursue the matter. She wanted to concentrate on a more important battle: getting an acceptable memorial speech for my father.

This speech was extremely important, because it would be understood by everyone to be the Party's assessment of my father. It would be put into his personal file and continue to determine his children's future, even though he was dead. There were set patterns and fixed formulations for such a speech. Any deviation from the standard expressions used for an official who had been cleared would be interpreted as the Party having reservations about, or condemning, the dead person. A draft speech was drawn up and shown to my mother. It was full of damning deviations. My mother knew that with this valedictory my family would never be free of suspicion. At best we would live in a state of permanent insecurity; more likely, we would be discriminated against for generation after generation. She turned down several drafts.

The odds were heavily against her, but she knew that there was a lot of sympathy for my father. This was the traditional time for a Chinese family to engage in a bit of emotional blackmail. After my father's death she had had a collapse, but she battled with undiminished determination from her sickbed. She threatened to denounce the authorities at the memorial service if she did not get an acceptable valedictory. She summoned my father's friends and colleagues to her bedside, and told them she was putting the future of her children in their hands. They promised to speak up for my father. In the end, the authorities relented. Although no one yet dared to treat him as rehabilitated, the assessment was modified to one that was fairly innocuous.

The service was held on 21 April. Following the standard practice, it was organized by a "funeral committee" of my father's former colleagues, including people who had helped to persecute him, like Zuo. It was carefully staged down to the last detail, and was attended by about 500 people, according to the prescribed formula. These were apportioned between the several dozen departments and bureaus of the provincial government and the offices that came under my father's department. Even the odious Mrs. Shau was there. Each organization was asked to send a wreath, made of paper flowers, the size of which was specified. In a way, my family welcomed the fact that the occasion was official. A private ceremony was unheard of for someone of my father's position, and would be taken as a repudiation by the Party. I did not recognize most of the people there, but all my close friends who knew about my father's death came, including Plumpie, Nana, and the electricians from my old factory. My classmates from Sichuan University came as well, including the student official Ming. My old friend Bing, whom I had refused to see after my grandmother's death, turned up and our friendship immediately picked up where it had left off six years before.

The ritual prescribed that one "representative of the family of the deceased" should speak, and this role fell to me. I recalled my father's character, his moral principles, his faith in his Party, and his passionate dedication to the people. I hoped that the tragedy of his death would leave the participants with plenty to mull over.

At the end, when everyone filed past and shook hands with us, I saw tears on the faces of many former Rebels. Even Mrs. Shau looked lugubrious. They had a mask for every occasion. Some of the Rebels murmured to me, "We are all very sorry about what your father went through." Maybe they were. But what difference did that make? My father was dead—and they had had a big hand in killing him. Would they do the same thing to somebody else in the next campaign, I wondered.

A young woman I did not know laid her head on my shoulder and sobbed violently. I felt a note being tucked into my hand. I read it afterward. On it was scribbled: "I was deeply moved by the character of your father. We must learn from him and be worthy successors to the cause he has left behind—the great proletarian revolutionary cause." Did my speech really give rise to this, I pondered. It seemed there was no escape from the Communists' appropriation of moral principles and noble sentiments.

Some weeks before my father's death, I had been sitting in the Chengdu railway station with him waiting for a friend of his to arrive. We were in the same half-open waiting area where my mother and I had sat nearly a decade before when she was going to Peking to appeal for him. The waiting area had not changed much, except that it looked shabbier, and was much more crowded. Still more people thronged the large square out in front. Some were sleeping there, some just sitting, others breast-feeding their babies; quite a few were begging. These were peasants from the north, where there was a local famine—the result of bad weather and, in some cases, sabotage by Mme. Mao's coterie. They had come down on trains, crammed onto the roofs of the carriages. There were many stories about people being swept off, or decapitated going through tunnels.

On our way to the station, I had asked my father if I could go down the Yangtze during the summer vacation. "The priority in my life," I had declared, "is to have fun." He had shaken his head disapprovingly. "When you are young, you should make your priority study and work."

I brought up the subject again in the waiting area. A cleaner was sweeping the ground. At one point her path was partly blocked by a northern peasant woman who was sitting on the cement floor with a tattered bundle next to her and two toddlers in rags. A third child was suckling her breast, which she had bared without a trace of shyness, and which was black with dirt. The cleaner swept the dust right over them, as though they were not there. The peasant woman did not move a muscle.

My father turned to me and said, "With people living like this all around you, how can you possibly have fun?" I was silent. I did not say, "But what can I, a mere individual, do? Must I live miserably for nothing?" That would have sounded shockingly selfish. I had been brought up in the tradition of "regarding the interest of the whole nation as my own duty" (yi tian-xia wei ji-ren).

Now, in the emptiness I felt after my father's death, I began to question all such precepts. I wanted no grand mission, no "causes," just a life—a quiet, perhaps a frivolous life—of my own. I told my mother that when the summer vacation came I wanted to travel down the Yangtze.

She urged me to go. So did my sister, who, along with Specs, had been living with my family since she had returned to Chengdu. Specs's factory, which should normally have been responsible for providing him with housing, had built no new apartments during the Cultural Revolution. Then many employees, like Specs, had been single, and lived in dormitories eight to a room. Now, ten years later, most of them were married and had children. There was nowhere for them to live, so they had to stay with their parents or parents-in-law, and it was commonplace for three generations to live in one room.

My sister had not been given a job, as the fact that she had got married before she had a job in the city excluded her from employment. Now, thanks to a regulation which said that when a state employee died one of their offspring could take their place, my sister was given a post in the administration of the Chengdu College of Chinese Medicine.

In July I set off on my journey with Jin-ming, who was studying in Wuhan, a big city on the Yangtze. Our first stop was the nearby mountain of Lushan, which had luxuriant vegetation and an excellent climate. Important Party conferences had been held there, including the one in 1959 at which Marshal Peng Dehuai was denounced, and the site was designated as a place of interest "for people to receive a revolutionary education." When I suggested going there to have a look, Jin-ming said incredulously, "You don't want a break from 'revolutionary education'?"

We took a lot of photographs on the mountain, and had finished a whole roll of thirty-six exposures except for one. On our way down, we passed a two-story villa, hidden in a thicket of Chinese parasol trees, magnolia, and pines. It looked almost like a random pile of stones against the background of the rocks. It struck me as an unusually lovely place, and I snapped my last shot. Suddenly a man materialized out of nowhere and asked me in a low but commanding voice to hand over my camera. He wore civilian clothes, but I noticed he had a pistol. He opened the camera and exposed my entire roll of film. Then he disappeared, as if into the earth. Some tourists standing next to me whispered that this was one of Mao's summer villas. I felt another pang of revulsion toward Mao, not so much for his privilege, but for the hypocrisy of allowing himself luxury while telling his people that even comfort was bad for them. After we were safely out of earshot of the invisible guard, and I was bemoaning the loss of my thirty-six pictures, Jin-ming gave me a grin: "See where goggling at holy places gets you!"

We left Lushan by bus. Like every bus in China, it was packed, and we had to crane our necks desperately trying to breathe. Virtually no new buses had been built since the beginning of the Cultural Revolution, during which time the urban population had increased by several tens of millions. After a few minutes, we suddenly stopped. The front door was forced open, and an authoritative-looking man in plainclothes squeezed in. "Get down! Get down!" he barked. "Some American guests are coming this way. It is harmful to the prestige of our motherland for them to see all these messy heads!" We tried to crouch down, but the bus was too crowded. The man shouted, "It is the duty of everyone to safeguard the honor of our motherland! We must present an orderly and dignified appearance! Get down! Bend your knees!"

Suddenly I heard Jin-ming's booming voice: "Doesn't Chairman Mao instruct us never to bend our knees to American imperialists?" This was asking for trouble. Humor was not appreciated. The man shot a stern glance in our direction, but said nothing. He gave the bus another quick scan, and hurried off. He did not want the "American guests" to witness a scene. Any sign of discord had to be hidden from foreigners.

Wherever we went as we traveled down the Yangtze we saw the aftermath of the Cultural Revolution: temples smashed, statues toppled, and old towns wrecked. Little evidence remained of China's ancient civilization. But the loss went even deeper than this. Not only had China destroyed most of its beautiful things, it had lost its appreciation of them, and was unable to make new ones. Except for the much-scarred but still stunning landscape, China had become an ugly country.

At the end of the vacation, I took a steamer alone from Wuhan back up through the Yangtze Gorges. The journey took three days. One morning, as I was leaning over the side, a gust of wind blew my hair loose and my hairpin fell into the river. A passenger with whom I had been chatting pointed to a tributary which joined the Yangtze just where we were passing, and told me a story.

In 33 B.C., the emperor of China, in an attempt to appease the country's powerful northern neighbors, the Huns, decided to send a woman to marry the barbarian king. He made his selection from the portraits of the 3,000 concubines in his court, many of whom he had never seen. As she was for a barbarian, he selected the ugliest portrait, but on the day of her departure he discovered that the woman was in fact extremely beautiful. Her portrait was ugly because she had refused to bribe the court painter. The emperor ordered the artist to be executed, while the lady wept, sitting by a river, at having to leave her country to live among the barbarians. The wind carried away her hairpin and dropped it into the river as though it wanted to keep something of hers in her homeland. Later on, she killed herself.

Legend had it that where her hairpin dropped, the river turned crystal clear, and became known as the Crystal River. My fellow passenger told me this was the tributary we were passing. With a grin, he declared: "Ah, bad omen! You might end up living in a foreign land and marrying a barbarian!" I smiled faintly at the traditional Chinese obsession about other races being "barbarians," and wondered whether this lady of antiquity might not actually have been better off marrying the "barbarian" king. She would at least be in daily contact with the grassland, the horses, and nature. With the Chinese emperor, she was living in a luxurious prison, without even a proper tree, which might enable the concubines to climb a wall and escape. I thought how we were like the frogs at the bottom of the well in the Chinese legend, who claimed that the sky was only as big as the round opening at the top of their well. I felt an intense and urgent desire to see the world.

At the time I had never spoken with a foreigner, even though I was twenty-three, and had been an English-language student for nearly two years. The only foreigners I had ever even set eyes on had been in Peking in 1972. A foreigner, one of the few "friends of China," had come to my university once. It was a hot summer day and I was having a nap when a fellow student burst into our room and woke us all by shrieking: "A foreigner is here! Let's go and look at the foreigner!" Some of the others went, but I decided to stay and continue my snooze. I found the whole idea of gazing, zombielike, rather ridiculous. Anyway, what was the point of staring if we were forbidden to open our mouths to him, even though he was a "friend of China"?

I had never even heard a foreigner speaking, except on one single Linguaphone record. When I started learning the language, I had borrowed the record and a phonograph, and listened to it at home in Meteorite Street. Some neighbors gathered in the courtyard, and said with their eyes wide open and their heads shaking, "What funny sounds!" They asked me to play the record over and over again.

Speaking to a foreigner was the dream of every student, and my opportunity came at last. When I got back from my trip down the Yangtze, I learned that my year was being sent in October to a port in the south called Zhanjiang to practice our English with foreign sailors. I was thrilled.

Zhanjiang was about 750 miles from Chengdu, a journey of two days and two nights by rail. It was the southernmost large port in China, and quite near the Vietnamese border. It felt like a foreign country, with turn-of-the-century colonial-style buildings, pastiche Romanesque arches, rose windows, and large verandas with colorful parasols. The local people spoke Cantonese, which was almost a foreign language. The air smelled of the unfamiliar sea, exotic tropical vegetation, and an altogether bigger world.

But my excitement at being there was constantly doused by frustration. We were accompanied by a political supervisor and three lecturers, who decided that, although we were staying only a mile from the sea, we were not to be allowed anywhere near it. The harbor itself was closed to outsiders, for fear of "sabotage" or defection. We were told that a student from Guangzhou had managed to stow away once in a cargo steamer, not realizing that the hold would be sealed for weeks, by which time he had perished. We had to restrict our movements to a clearly defined area of a few blocks around our residence.

Regulations like these were part of our daily life, but they never failed to infuriate me. One day I was seized by an absolute compulsion to get out. I faked illness and got permission to go to a hospital in the middle of the city. I wandered the streets desperately trying to spot the sea, without success. The local people were unhelpful: they did not like non-Cantonese speakers, and refused to understand me. We stayed in the port for three weeks, and only once were we allowed, as a special treat, to go to an island to see the ocean.

As the point of being there was to talk to the sailors, we were organized into small groups to take turns working in the two places they were allowed to frequent: the Friendship Store, which sold goods for hard currency, and the Sailors' Club, which had a bar, a restaurant, a billiards room, and a ping-pong room.

There were strict rules about how we could talk to the sailors. We were not allowed to speak to them alone, except for brief exchanges over the counter of the Friendship Store. If we were asked our names and addresses, under no circumstances were we to give our real ones. We all prepared a false name and a nonexistent address. After every conversation, we had to write a detailed report of what had been said, which was standard practice for anyone who had contact with foreigners. We were warned over and over again about the importance of observing "discipline in foreign contacts" *(she wai ji-lu)*. Otherwise, we were told, not only would we get into serious trouble, other students would be banned from coming.

Actually, our opportunities for practicing English were few and far between. The ships did not come every day, and not all sailors came on shore. Most of the sailors were not native English speakers: there were Greeks, Japanese, Yugoslavs, Africans, and many Filipinos, most of whom spoke only a little English, although there was also a Scottish captain and his wife, as well as some Scandinavians whose English was excellent.

While we waited in the club for our precious sailors, I often sat on the veranda at the back, reading and gazing at the groves of coconut and palm trees, silhouetted against a sapphire-blue sky. The moment the sailors sauntered in, we would leap up and virtually grab them, while trying to appear as dignified as possible, so eager were we to engage them in conversation. I often saw a puzzled look in their eyes when we declined their offers of a drink. We were forbidden to accept drinks from them. In fact, we were not allowed to drink at all: the fancy foreign bottles and cans on display were exclusively for the foreigners. We just sat there, four or five intimidatingly serious-looking young men and women. I had no idea how odd it must have seemed to the sailors—and how far from their expectations of port life.

When the first black sailors arrived, our teachers gently warned the women students to watch out: "They are less developed and haven't learned to control their instincts, so they are given to displaying their feelings whenever they like: touching, embracing, even kissing." To a roomful of shocked and disgusted faces, our teachers told us that one woman in the last group had burst out screaming in the middle of a conversation when a Gambian sailor had tried to hug her. She thought she was going to be raped (in the middle of a crowd, a Chinese crowd!), and was so scared that she could not bring herself to talk to another foreigner for the rest of her stay.

The male students, particularly the student officials, assumed responsibility for safeguarding us women. Whenever a black sailor started talking to one of us, they would eye each other and hurry to our rescue by taking over the conversation and positioning themselves between us and the sailors. Their precautions may not have been noticed by the black sailors, especially as the students would immediately start talking about "the friendship between China and the peoples of Asia, Africa, and Latin America." "China is a developing country," they would intone, reciting from our textbook, "and will stand forever by the side of the oppressed and exploited masses in the third world in their struggle against the American imperialists and the Soviet revisionists." The blacks would look baffled but touched. Sometimes they embraced the Chinese men, who returned comradely hugs.

Much was being made by the regime about China being one of the developing countries, part of the third world, according to Mao's "glorious theory." But Mao made it sound as if this was not the acknowledgment of a fact, but that China was magnanimously lowering itself to their level. The way he said it left no doubt that we had joined the ranks of the third world in order to lead it and protect it, and the world regarded our rightful place to be somewhat grander.

I was extremely irritated by this self-styled superiority. What had we got to be superior about? Our population? Our size? In Zhanjiang, I saw that the third world sailors, with their flashy watches, cameras, and drinks—none of which we had ever seen before—were immeasurably better off, and incomparably freer, than all but a very few Chinese.

I was terribly curious about foreigners, and was eager to discover what they were really like. How similar to the Chinese were they, and how different? But I had to try to conceal my inquisitiveness which, apart from being politically dangerous, would be regarded as losing face. Under Mao, as in the days of the Middle Kingdom, the Chinese placed great importance on holding themselves with "dignity" in front of foreigners, by which was meant appearing aloof, or inscrutable. A common form this took was to show no interest in the outside world, and many of my fellow students never asked any questions.

Perhaps partly due to my uncontrollable curiosity, and partly due to my better English, the sailors all seemed keen to talk to me in spite of the fact that I took care to speak as little as possible so that my fellow students had more chance to practice. Some sailors would even refuse to talk to the other students. I was also very popular with the director of the Sailors' Club, an enormous, burly man called Long. This aroused the ire of Ming and some of the minders. Our political meetings now included an examination of how we were observing "the disciplines in foreign contact." It was stated that I had violated these because my eyes looked "too interested," I "smiled too often," and when I did so I opened my mouth "too wide." I was also criticized for using hand gestures: we women students were supposed to keep our hands under the table and sit motionless.

Much of Chinese society still expected its women to hold themselves in a sedate manner, lower their eyelids in response to men's stares, and restrict their smile to a faint curve of the lips which did not expose their teeth. They were not meant to use hand gestures at all. If they contravened any of these canons of behavior they would be considered "flirtatious." Under Mao, flirting with *foreigners* was an unspeakable crime.

I was furious at the innuendo against me. It had been my Communist parents who had given me a liberal upbringing. They had regarded the restrictions on women as precisely the sort of thing a Communist revolution should put an end to. But now oppression of women joined hands with political repression, and served resentment and petty jealousy.

One day, a Pakistani ship arrived. The Pakistani military attaché came down from Peking. Long ordered us all to spring-clean the club from top to bottom, and laid on a banquet, for which he asked me to be his interpreter, which made some of the other students extremely envious. A few days later the Pakistanis gave a farewell dinner on their ship, and I was invited. The military attaché had been to Sichuan, and they had prepared a special Sichuan dish for me. Long was delighted by the invitation, as was I.

But despite a personal appeal from the captain and even a threat from Long to bar future students, my teachers said that no one was allowed on board a foreign ship. "Who would take the responsibility if someone sailed away on the ship?" they asked. I was told to say I was busy that evening. As far as I knew, I was turning down the only chance I would ever have of a trip out to sea, a foreign meal, a proper conversation in English, and an experience of the outside world.

Even so, I could not silence the whispers. Ming asked pointedly, "Why do foreigners like her so much?" as though there was something suspicious in that. The report filed on me at the end of the trip said my behavior was "politically dubious."

In this lovely port, with its sunshine, sea breezes, and coconut trees, every occasion that should have been joyous was turned into misery. I had a good friend in the group who tried to cheer me up by putting my distress into perspective. Of course, what I encountered was no more than minor unpleasantness compared with what victims of jealousy suffered in the earlier years of the Cultural Revolution. But the thought that this was what my life at its best would be like depressed me even more.

This friend was the son of a colleague of my father's. The other students from cities were also friendly to me. It was easy to distinguish them from the students of peasant backgrounds, who provided most of the student officials. The city students were much more secure and confident when confronted with the novel world of the port and they therefore did not feel the same anxiety and the urge to be aggressive toward me. Zhanjiang was a severe culture shock to the former peasants, and their feelings of inferiority were at the core of their compulsion to make life a misery for others.

After three weeks, I was both sorry and relieved to say goodbye to Zhanjiang. On the way back to Chengdu, some friends and I went to the legendary Guilin, where the mountains and waters looked as though they had sprung from a classical Chinese painting. There were foreign tourists there, and we saw one couple with a baby in the man's arms. We smiled at each other, and said "Good morning" and "Goodbye." As soon as they disappeared, a plainclothes policeman stopped us and questioned us.

I returned to Chengdu in December, to find the city seething with emotion against Mme. Mao and three men from Shanghai, Zhang Chunqiao, Yao Wenyuan, and Wang Hongwen, who had banded together to hold the fort of the Cultural Revolution. They had become so close that Mao had warned them against forming a "Gang of Four" in July 1974, although we did not know this at the time. By now the eighty-one-year-old Mao had begun to give them his full backing, having had enough of the pragmatic approach of Zhou Enlai and then of Deng Xiaoping, who had been running the day-to-day work of the government since January 1975, when Zhou had gone into a hospital with cancer. The Gang's endless and pointless minicampaigns had driven the population to the end of their tether, and people had started circulating rumors privately, as almost the only outlet for their intense frustration.

Highly charged speculation was particularly directed against Mme. Mao. Since she was frequently seen together with one particular opera actor, one ping-pong player, and one ballet dancer, each of whom had been promoted by her to head their fields, and since they all happened to be handsome young men, people said she had taken them as "male concubines," something she had openly and airily said women should do. But everyone knew this did not apply to the general public. In fact, it was under Mme. Mao in the Cultural Revolution that the Chinese suffered extreme sexual repression. With her controlling the media and the arts for nearly ten years, any reference to love was deleted from the hearing and sight of the population. When a Vietnamese army song-and-dance troupe came to China, those few who were lucky enough to see it were told by the announcer that a song which mentioned love "is about the comradely affection between two comrades." In the few European films which were allowed—

mainly from Albania and Romania—all scenes of men and women standing close to each other, let alone kissing, were cut out.

Frequently in crowded buses, trains, and shops I would hear women yelling abuse at men and slapping their faces. Sometimes the man would shout a denial and an exchange of insults would ensue. I experienced many attempted molestations. When it happened, I would just sneak away from the trembling hands or knees. I felt sorry for these men. They lived in a world where there could be no outlet for their sexuality unless they were lucky enough to have a happy marriage, the chances of which were slim. The deputy Party secretary of my university, an elderly man, was caught in a department store with sperm oozing through his trousers. The crowds had pressed him against a woman in front of him. He was taken to the police station, and subsequently expelled from the Party. Women had just as tough a time. In every organization, one or two of them would be condemned as "worn-out shoes" for having had extramarital affairs.

These standards were not applied to the rulers. The octogenarian Mao surrounded himself with pretty young women. Although the stories about him were whispered and cautious, those about his wife and her cronies, the Gang of Four, were open and uninhibited. By the end of 1975, China was boiling with incensed rumors. In the mini-campaign called "Our Socialist Motherland Is Paradise," many openly hinted at the question which I had asked myself for the first time eight years before: "If this is paradise, what then is hell?"

On 8 January 1976, Premier Zhou Enlai died. To me and many other Chinese, Zhou had represented a comparatively sane and liberal government that believed in making the country work. In the dark years of the Cultural Revolution, Zhou was our meager hope. I was grief-stricken at his death, as were all my friends. Our mourning for him and our loathing of the Cultural Revolution and of Mao and his coterie became inseparably interwoven.

But Zhou had collaborated with Mao in the Cultural Revolution. It was he who delivered the denunciation of Liu Shaoqi as an "American spy." He met almost daily with the Red Guards and the Rebels and issued orders to them. When a majority of the Politburo and the country's marshals tried to put a halt to the Cultural Revolution in February 1967 Zhou did not give them his support. He was Mao's faithful servant. But perhaps he had acted as he did in order to prevent an even more horrendous disaster, like a civil war, which an open challenge to Mao could have brought on. By keeping China running, he made it possible for Mao to wreak havoc on it, but probably also saved the country from total collapse. He protected a number of people as far as he judged safe, including, for a time, my father, as well as some of China's most important cultural monuments. It seemed that he had been caught up in an insoluble moral dilemma, although this does not exclude the possibility that survival was his priority. He must have known that if he had tried to stand up to Mao, he would have been crushed.

The campus became a spectacular sea of white paper wreaths and mourning posters and couplets. Everyone wore a black armband, a white paper flower on their chest, and a sorrowful expression. The mourning was partly spontaneous and partly organized. Because it was generally known that at the time of his death Zhou had been under attack from the Gang of Four, and because the Gang had ordered the mourning for him to be played down, showing grief at his death was a way for both the general public and the local authorities to show their disapproval of the Gang. But there were many who mourned Zhou for very different reasons. Ming and other student officials from my course extolled Zhou's alleged contribution to "suppressing the counterrevolutionary Hungarian uprising in 1956," his hand in establishing Mao's prestige as a world leader, and his absolute loyalty to Mao.

Outside the campus, there were more encouraging sparks of dissent. In the streets of Chengdu, graffiti appeared on the margins of the wall posters—and large crowds gathered, craning their necks to read the tiny handwriting. One poster read,

The sky is now dark,
A great star is fallen . . .

Scribbled in the margin were the words: "How could the sky be dark: what about 'the red, red sun'?" (meaning Mao). Another graffito appeared on a wall slogan reading "Deep-fry the persecutors of Premier Zhou!" It said: "Your monthly ration of cooking oil is only two *liang* [3.2 ounces]. What would you use to fry these persecutors with?" For the first time in ten years, I saw irony and humor publicly displayed, which sent my spirits soaring.

Mao appointed an ineffectual nobody called Hua Guofeng to succeed Zhou, and launched a campaign to "denounce Deng and hit back against a right-wing comeback." The Gang of Four published Deng Xiaoping's speeches as targets for denunciation. In one speech in 1975, Deng had admitted that peasants in Yan'an were worse off than when the Communists first arrived there after the Long March forty years before. In another, he had said that a Party boss should say to the professionals, "I follow, you lead." In yet another, he had outlined his plans for improving living standards, for allowing more free-dom, and for ending political victimization. Comparing these documents to the Gang of Four's actions made Deng a folk hero and brought people's loathing of the Gang to the boiling point. I thought incredulously: they seem to hold the Chinese population in such con-tempt that they assume we will hate Deng rather than admire him after reading these speeches, and what is more, that we will love *them!*

In the university, we were ordered to denounce Deng in endless mass meetings. But most people showed passive resistance, and wan-dered around the auditorium, or chatted, knitted, read, or even slept during the ritual theatrics. The speakers read their prepared scripts in flat, expressionless, almost inaudible voices.

Because Deng came from Sichuan, there were numerous rumors about him having been sent back to Chengdu for exile. I often saw crowds lining the streets because they had heard he was about to pass by. On some occasions the crowds numbered tens of thousands.

At the same time, there was more and more public animosity to-ward the Gang of Four, also known as the Gang from Shanghai. Suddenly bicycles and other goods made in Shanghai stopped selling. When the Shanghai football team came to Chengdu they were booed all the way through the game. Crowds gathered outside the stadium and shouted abuse at them as they went in and came out.

Acts of protest broke out all over China, and reached their peak during the Tomb-Sweeping Festival in spring 1976, when the Chinese traditionally pay their respects to the dead. In Peking, hundreds of thousands of citizens gathered for days on end in Tiananmen Square to mourn Zhou with specially crafted weaths, passionate poetry read-ings, and speeches. In symbolism and language which, though coded, everyone understood, they poured out their hatred of the Gang of Four, and even of Mao. The protest was crushed on the night of 5 April, when the police attacked the crowds, arresting hundreds. Mao and the Gang of Four called this a "Hungarian-type counterrevolu-tionary rebellion." Deng Xiaoping, who was being held incommuni-cado, was accused of stage-managing the demonstrations, and was labeled "China's Nagy" (Nagy was the Hungarian prime minister in 1956). Mao officially fired Deng, and intensified the campaign against him.

The demonstration may have been suppressed and ritually con-demned in the media, but the fact that it had taken place at all changed the mood of China. This was the first large-scale open chal-lenge to the regime since it was founded in 1949.

In June 1976 my class was packed off for a month to a factory in the mountains to "learn from the workers." When the month was up, I went with some friends to climb the lovely Mount Emei, "Beauty's Eyebrow," to the west of Chengdu. On our way down the mountain, on 28 July, we heard a loud transistor radio which a tourist was carrying. I had always felt intensely annoyed by some people's insatiable love for this propaganda machine. And in a scenic spot! As though our ears had not suffered enough with all the blaring nonsense from the ever-present loudspeakers. But this time something caught my attention. There had been an earthquake at a coal-mining city near Peking called Tangshan. I realized it must be an unprecedented disaster, because the media normally did not report bad news. The official figure was 242,000 dead and 164,000 badly injured.

Although they filled the press with propaganda about their concern for the victims, the Gang of Four warned that the nation must not be diverted by the earthquake and forget the priority: to "denounce Deng." Mme. Mao said publicly, "There were merely several hundred thousand deaths. So what? Denouncing Deng Xiaoping concerns eight hundred million people." Even from Mme. Mao, this sounded too outrageous to be true, but it was officially relayed to us.

There were numerous earthquake alerts in the Chengdu area, and when I returned from Mount Emei I went with my mother and Xiaofang to Chongqing, which was considered safer. My sister, who remained in Chengdu, slept under a massive thick oak table covered in blankets and quilts. Officials organized people to erect makeshift shacks, and detailed teams to keep a round-the-clock watch on the behavior of various animals which were thought to possess earthquake-predicting powers. But followers of the Gang of Four put up wall slogans barking "Be alert to Deng Xiaoping's criminal attempt to exploit earthquake phobia to suppress revolution!" and held a rally to "solemnly condemn the capitalist-roaders who use the fear of an earthquake to sabotage the denunciation of Deng." The rally was a flop.

I returned to Chengdu at the beginning of September, by which time the earthquake scare was subsiding. On the afternoon of 9 September 1976 I was attending an English class. At about 2:40 we were told that there would be an important broadcast at three o'clock, and that we were all to assemble in the courtyard to listen. We had had to do such things before, and I walked outside in a state of irritation. It was a typically cloudy autumn Chengdu day. I heard the rustling of bamboo leaves along the walls. Just before three, while the loudspeaker was making scratching noises as it tuned up, the Party secretary of our department took up a position in front of the assembly.

She looked at us sadly, and in a low, halting voice, choked out the words: "Our Great Leader Chairman Mao, His Venerable Reverence [*ta-lao-ren-jia*], has . . ."

Suddenly, I realized that Mao was dead.

28. Fighting to Take Wing

(1976–1978)

The news filled me with such euphoria that for an instant I was numb. My ingrained self-censorship immediately started working: I registered the fact that there was an orgy of weeping going on around me, and that I had to come up with some suitable performance. There seemed nowhere to hide my lack of correct emotion except the shoulder of the woman in front of me, one of the student officials, who was apparently heartbroken. I swiftly buried my head in her shoulder and heaved appropriately. As so often in China, a bit of ritual did the trick. Sniveling heartily, she made a movement as though she was going to turn around and embrace me. I pressed my whole weight on her from behind to keep her in her place, hoping to give the impression that I was in a state of abandoned grief.

In the days after Mao's death, I did a lot of thinking. I knew he was considered a philosopher, and I tried to think what his "philosophy" really was. It seemed to me that its central principle was the need—or the desire?—for perpetual conflict. The core of his thinking seemed to be that human struggles were the motivating force of history, and that in order to make history "class enemies" had to be continuously created *en masse*. I wondered whether there were any other philosophers whose theories had led to the suffering and death of so many. I thought of the terror and misery to which the Chinese population had been subjected. For what?

But Mao's theory might just be the extension of his personality. He was, it seemed to me, really a restless fight promoter by nature, and good at it. He understood ugly human instincts such as envy and resentment, and knew how to mobilize them for his ends. He ruled by getting people to hate each other. In doing so, he got ordinary Chinese to carry out many of the tasks undertaken in other dictatorships by professional elites. Mao had managed to turn the people into the ultimate weapon of dictatorship. That was why under him there was no real equivalent of the KGB in China. There was no need. In bringing out and nourishing the worst in people, Mao had created a moral wasteland and a land of hatred. But how much individual responsibility ordinary people should share, I could not decide.

The other hallmark of Maoism, it seemed to me, was the reign of ignorance. Because of his calculation that the cultured class were an easy target for a population that was largely illiterate, because of his own deep resentment of formal education and the educated, because of his megalomania, which led to his scorn for the great figures of Chinese culture, and because of his contempt for the areas of Chinese civilization that he did not understand, such as architecture, art, and music, Mao destroyed much of the country's cultural heritage. He left behind not only a brutalized nation, but also an ugly land with little of its past glory remaining or appreciated.

The Chinese seemed to be mourning Mao in a heartfelt fashion. But I wondered how many of their tears were genuine. People had practiced acting to such a degree that they confused it with their true feelings. Weeping for Mao was perhaps just another programmed act in their programmed lives.

Yet the mood of the nation was unmistakably against continuing Mao's policies. Less than a month after his death, on 6 October, Mme. Mao was arrested, along with the other members of the Gang of Four. They had no support from anyone—not the army, not the police, not even their own guards. They had had only Mao. The Gang of Four had held power only because it was really a Gang of Five.

When I heard about the ease with which the Four had been removed, I felt a wave of sadness. How could such a small group of second-rate tyrants ravage 900 million people for so long? But my main feeling was joy. The last tyrants of the Cultural Revolution were finally gone. My rapture was widely shared. Like many of my countrymen, I went out to buy the best liquors for a celebration with my family and friends, only to find the shops out of stock—there was so much spontaneous rejoicing.

There were official celebrations as well—exactly the same kinds of rallies as during the Cultural Revolution, which infuriated me. I was particularly angered by the fact that in my department, the political supervisors and the student officials were now arranging the whole show, with unperturbed self-righteousness.

The new leadership was headed by Mao's chosen successor, Hua Guofeng, whose only qualification, I believed, was his mediocrity. One of his first acts was to announce the construction of a huge mausoleum for Mao on Tiananmen Square. I was outraged: hundreds of thousands of people were still homeless after the earthquake in Tangshan, living in temporary shacks on the pavements.

With her experience, my mother had immediately seen that a new era was beginning. On the day after Mao's death she had reported for work at her department. She had been at home for five years, and now she wanted to put her energy to use again. She was given a job as the number-seven deputy director in her department, of which she had been the director before the Cultural Revolution. But she did not mind.

To me in my impatient mood, things seemed to go on as before. In January 1977, my university course came to an end. We were given neither examinations nor degrees. Although Mao and the Gang of Four were gone, Mao's rule that we had to return to where we had come from still applied. For me, this meant the machinery factory. The idea that a university education should make a difference to one's job had been condemned by Mao as "training spiritual aristocrats."

I was desperate to avoid being sent back to the factory. If that happened, I would lose any chance of using my English: there would be nothing to translate, and no one to speak the language with. Once again, I turned to my mother. She said there was only one way out: the factory had to refuse to take me back. My friends at the factory persuaded the management to write a report to the Second Bureau of Light Industry saying that, although I was a good worker, they realized they should sacrifice their own interests for a greater cause: our motherland would benefit from my English.

After this florid letter went off, my mother sent me to see the chief manager of the bureau, a Mr. Hui. He had been a colleague of hers, and had been very fond me when I was a baby. My mother knew he still had a soft spot for me. The day after I went to see him, a board meeting of his bureau was convened to discuss my case. The board consisted of some twenty directors, all of whom had to meet to make any decision, however trivial. Mr. Hui managed to convince them that I should be given a chance to use my English, and they wrote a formal letter to my university.

Although my department had given me a hard time, they needed teachers, and in January 1977 I became an assistant lecturer in English at Sichuan University. I had mixed feelings about working there, as I would have to live on the campus, under the eyes of political supervisors and ambitious and jealous colleagues. Worse, I soon learned that I was not to have anything to do with my profession for a year. A week after my appointment I was sent to the countryside on the outskirts of Chengdu, as part of my "reeducation" program.

I labored in the fields and sat through endless tedious meetings. Boredom, dissatisfaction, and the pressure put on me for not having a fiancé at the advanced age of twenty-five helped push me into infatuations with a couple of men. One of them I had never met, but he wrote me beautiful letters. I fell out of love the moment I set eyes on him. The other, Hou, had actually been a Rebel leader. He was a kind of product of the times: brilliant and unscrupulous. I was dazzled by his charm.

Hou was detained in the summer of 1977 when a campaign started to apprehend "the followers of the Gang of Four." These were defined as the "heads of the Rebels" and anyone who had engaged in criminal violence, which was vaguely described as including torture, murder, and destruction or looting of state property. The campaign petered out within months. The main reason was that Mao was not repudiated, nor was the Cultural Revolution as such. Anyone who had done evil simply claimed that they had acted out of loyalty to Mao. There were no clear criteria to judge criminality either, except in the case of the most blatant murderers and torturers. So many had been involved in house raids, in destroying historical sites, antiques, and books, and in the factional fighting. The greatest horror of the Cultural Revolution—the crushing repression which had driven hundreds of thousands of people to mental breakdown, suicide, and death—was carried out by the population collectively. Almost everyone, including young children, had participated in brutal denunciation meetings. Many had lent a hand in beating the victims. What was more, victims had often become victimizers, and vice versa.

There was also no independent legal system to investigate and to judge. Party officials decided who was to be punished and who was not. Personal feelings were often the decisive factor. Some Rebels were rightly punished. Some got rough justice. Others were let off lightly. Of my father's main persecutors, nothing happened to Zuo, and Mrs. Shau was simply transferred to a slightly less desirable job.

The Tings had been detained since 1970, but were not now brought to justice—because the Party had not issued criteria by which they could be judged. The only thing that happened to them was having to sit through nonviolent meetings at which victims could "speak bitterness" against them. My mother spoke at one such mass meeting about how the couple had persecuted my father. The Tings were to remain in detention without trial until 1982, when Mr. Ting was given twenty years' imprisonment and Mrs. Ting seventeen.

Hou, over whose detention I had lost much sleep, was soon set free. But the bitter emotions reawakened in those brief days of reckoning had killed whatever feeling I had for him. Although I was never to know his exact responsibility, it was clear that as a mass Red Guard leader in the most savage years he could not possibly have been guiltless. I still could not make myself hate him personally, but I was no longer sorry for him. I hoped that justice would be done to him, and to all those who deserved it.

When would that day come? Could justice ever be done? And could this be achieved without more bitterness and animosity being stirred up, given that there was so much steam already? All around me, factions that had fought bloody wars against each other now cohabited under the same roof. Capitalist-roaders were obliged to work side by side with former Rebels who had denounced and tormented them. The country was still in a state of extreme tension. When, if ever, would we be rid of the nightmare cast by Mao?

In July 1977 Deng Xiaoping was rehabilitated again and made deputy to Hua Guofeng. Every speech by Deng was a blast of fresh air. Political campaigns were to end. Political "studies" were "exorbitant taxes and levies" and must be stopped. Party policies must be based on reality, not dogma. And most importantly, it was wrong to follow every word of Mao's to the letter. Deng was changing China's course. Then I started to suffer from anxiety: I so feared that this new future might never come to pass.

In the new spirit of Deng, the end of my sentence in the commune came in December 1977, one month short of the original one-year schedule. This difference of a mere month thrilled me beyond reason. When I got back to Chengdu, the university was about to hold belated entrance examinations for 1977, the first proper examinations since 1966. Deng had declared that university entrance must be through academic exams, not the back door. The autumn term had had to be postponed because of the need to prepare the population for the change from Mao's policies.

I was sent to the mountains of northern Sichuan to interview applicants for my department. I went willingly. It was on this trip, traveling from county to county on the meandering dusty roads, all on my own, that a thought first occurred to me: how wonderful it would be to go and study in the West!

A few years before, a friend of mine had told me a story. He had originally come to "the motherland" from Hong Kong in 1964, but had not been allowed out again until 1973, when, in the openness following Nixon's visit, he was permitted to go and see his family. On his first night in Hong Kong, he heard his niece on the phone to Tokyo arranging a weekend there. His apparently inconsequential story had become a permanent source of perturbation to me. This freedom to see the world, a freedom I could not dream of, tormented me. Because it had been impossible, my desire to go abroad had always remained firmly imprisoned in my subconscious. There had been odd scholarships to the West at some other universities in the past, but, of course, the candidates had all been chosen by the authorities, and Party membership was a prerequisite. I had no chance, being neither a Party member nor trusted by my department, even if a scholarship were to fall from heaven onto my university. But now it began to bud somewhere in my mind that since exams were back, and China was shedding its Maoist straitjacket, I might have a chance. Hardly had I begun to dream this than I forced myself to kill the idea, I was so afraid of the inevitable disappointment.

When I came back from my trip, I heard that my department had been given a scholarship for a young or middle-aged teacher to go to the West. And they had decided on someone else.

It was Professor Lo who told me the devastating news. She was in her early seventies and walked unsteadily with a stick, but was nonetheless perky and almost impetuously quick in every other way. She spoke English rapidly, as if she was impatient to get out all the things she knew. She had lived in the United States for about thirty years. Her father had been a Kuomintang high court judge, and had wanted to give her a Western upbringing. In America she had taken the name Lucy, and had fallen in love with an American student called Luke. They planned to get married, but when they told Luke's mother, she said, "Lucy, I like you very much. But what would your children look like? It would be very difficult. . . ."

Lucy broke with Luke because she was too proud to be accepted into his family with reluctance. At the beginning of the 1950s, after the Communists took over, she went back to China, thinking that at last the dignity of the Chinese would be restored. She never got over Luke, and entered into a very late marriage with a Chinese professor of English, whom she did not love, and they quarreled nonstop. They had been thrown out of their apartment during the Cultural Revolution and were living in a tiny room, about ten feet by eight, crammed with fading old papers and dusty books. It was heart-rending to see this frail white-haired couple, unable to bear each other, one sitting on the edge of their double bed, the other on the only chair that could be squeezed into the room.

Professor Lo became very fond of me. She said she saw in me her own vanished youth of fifty years before when she had also been restless, wanting happiness out of life. She had failed to find it, she told me, but she wanted me to succeed. When she heard about the scholarship to go abroad, probably to America, she was terribly excited, but also anxious because I was away and could not stake my claim. The place went to a Miss Yee, who had been one year ahead of me and was now a Party official. She and the other young teachers in my department who had been graduated since the Cultural Revolution had been put in a training scheme to improve their English while I was in the countryside. Professor Lo was one of their tutors; she taught partly by using articles from English-language publications she had procured from friends in the more open cities like Peking and Shanghai (Sichuan was still completely closed to foreigners). Whenever I was back from the country, I sat in on her classes.

One day the text was about the use of atomic energy in U.S. industry. After Professor Lo explained the meaning of the article, Miss Yee looked up, straightened her back, and said with great indignation, "This article has to be read critically! How can the American imperialists use atomic energy peacefully?" I felt my irritation flaring up at Miss Yee's parroting of the propaganda line. Impulsively I retorted, "But how do you know they can't?" Miss Yee and most of the class stared at me incredulously. To them, a question like mine was still inconceivable, even blasphemous. Then I saw the sparkle in Professor Lo's eyes, the smile of appreciation that only I could detect. I felt understood and fortified.

Besides Professor Lo, some other professors and lecturers wanted me, not Miss Yee, to go to the West. But although they had begun to be respected in the new climate, none of them had any say. If anyone could help, it had to be my mother. Following her advice, I went to see my father's former colleagues, who were now in charge of universities, and told them I had a complaint: since Comrade Deng Xiaoping had said that university entrance was to be based on merit, not the back door, surely it was wrong not to follow this procedure for studying overseas. I begged them to allow me a fair competition, which meant an exam.

While my mother and I were lobbying, an order suddenly came from Peking: for the first time since 1949, scholarships for studying in the West were to be awarded on the basis of a national academic examination, and it was soon to be held simultaneously in Peking,

Shanghai, and Xi'an, the ancient capital where the terra-cotta army was later excavated.

My department had to send three candidates to Xi'an. It withdrew Miss Yee's scholarship and chose two candidates, both excellent lecturers around the age of forty, who had been teaching since before the Cultural Revolution. Partly because of Peking's order to base selection on professional ability, and partly because of the pressure from my mother's campaign, the department decided that the third candidate, a younger one, should be chosen from among the two dozen people who were graduated during the Cultural Revolution, through a written and an oral examination on 18 March.

I received the highest marks in both, although I won the oral test somewhat irregularly. We had to go one at a time into a room where two examiners, Professor Lo and another elderly professor, were seated. On a table in front of them were some paper balls: we had to pick one and answer the question on it in English. Mine read: "What are the main points in the communiqué of the recent Second Plenary Session of the Eleventh Congress of the Communist Party of China?" Of course I had no idea, and stood there stupefied. Professor Lo looked into my face and stretched out her hand for the slip of paper. She glanced at it and showed it to the other professor. Silently she put it in her pocket and motioned with her eyes for me to pick another. This time the question was: "Say something about the glorious situation of our socialist motherland."

Years of compulsory exaltation of the glorious situation of my socialist motherland had bored me sick, but this time I had plenty to say. In fact, I had just written a rapturous poem about the spring of 1978. Deng Xiaoping's right-hand man, Hu Yaobang, had become head of the Party's Organization Department, and had begun the process of clearing all sorts of "class enemies" *en masse*. The country was palpably shaking off Maoism. Industry was going at full blast and there were many more goods in the shops. Schools, hospitals, and other public services were working properly. Long-banned books were being published, and people sometimes waited outside bookshops for two days to obtain them. There was laughter, on the streets and in people's homes.

I began to prepare frantically for the examinations in Xi'an, which were not quite three weeks away. Several professors offered their help. Professor Lo gave me a reading list and a dozen English books, but then decided I would not have time to read them all. So she briskly cleared a space on her crowded desk for her portable typewriter, and spent the next two weeks typing out summaries of them in English.

This, she said with a mischievous wink, was how Luke had helped her with her examinations fifty years before, as she had preferred dancing and parties.

The two lecturers and I, accompanied by the deputy Party secretary, took a train to Xi'an, a day and a night's journey away. For most of the journey I lay on my stomach on my "hard sleeper," busily annotating Professor Lo's pile of notes. No one knew the exact number of scholarships or the countries for which the winners were destined, as most information in China was a state secret. But when we arrived in Xi'an we heard that there were twenty-two people taking the exams there, mostly senior lecturers from four provinces in western China. The sealed exam paper had been flown in from Peking the day before. There were three parts to the written exam, which took up the morning; one was a long passage from *Roots*, which we had to translate into Chinese. Outside the windows of the examination hall, white showers of willow flowers swept across the April city as if in a magnificent rhapsodic dance. At the end of the morning, our papers were collected, sealed, and sent straight to Peking to be marked together with the ones done there and in Shanghai. In the afternoon there was an oral exam.

At the end of May I was told unofficially that I had come through both exams with distinction. As soon as she heard the news, my mother stepped up her campaign to get my father's name cleared. Although he was dead, his file still continued to decide the future of his children. It contained the draft verdict which said he had committed "serious political errors." My mother knew that even though China was beginning to become more liberal, this would still disqualify me from going abroad.

She lobbied my father's former colleagues, who were now back in power in the provincial government, backing up her case with the note from Zhou Enlai which said that my father had the right to petition Mao. This note had been hidden with great ingenuity by my grandmother, stitched into the cotton upper of one of her shoes. Now, eleven years after Zhou had given it to her, my mother decided to hand it to the provincial authorities, who were now headed by Zhao Ziyang.

It was a propitious time—Mao's spell was beginning to lose its paralyzing power, with considerable help from Hu Yaobang, who was in charge of rehabilitations. On 12 June, a senior official turned up at Meteorite Street bearing the Party's verdict on my father. He handed my mother a flimsy piece of paper on which it was written that Father had been "a good official and a good Party member." This marked his official rehabilitation. It was only after this that my scholarship was finally endorsed by the Education Ministry in Peking.

The news that I was to go to Britain reached me through excited friends in the department before the authorities told me. People who barely knew me felt hugely pleased for me, and I received many letters and telegrams of congratulations. Celebration parties were thrown, and many tears of joy were shed. It was a gigantic thing to go to the West. China had been closed for decades, and everyone felt stifled by the airlessness. I was the first person from my university and, as far as I know, the first person from the whole of Sichuan (which then had a population of about ninety million) to be allowed to study in the West since 1949. And I had earned this on professional merit—I was not even a Party member. It was another sign of the dramatic changes sweeping the country. People saw hope and opportunities opening up.

But I was not entirely overwhelmed with excitement. I had achieved something so desirable and so unobtainable for everyone else around me that I felt guilty toward my friends. To show elation seemed embarrassing or even cruel to them, but to conceal it would have been dishonest. So subconsciously I opted for a subdued mood. I also felt sad when I thought about how narrow and monolithic China was—so many people had been denied opportunities and their talents had had no outlet. I knew that I was lucky to come from a privileged family, much though it had suffered. Now that a more open and fair China was on its way, I was impatient for change to come faster and transform the whole society.

Wrapped up in my own thoughts, I went through the inescapable rigmarole connected with leaving China in those days. First I had to go to Peking for a special training course for people going abroad. We had a month of indoctrination sessions, followed by a month traveling around China. The point was to impress us with the beauty of the motherland so we would not contemplate defecting. All the arrangements for going abroad were made for us, and we were given a clothing allowance. We had to look smart for the foreigners.

The Silk River meandered past the campus, and I often wandered along its banks on my last evenings. Its surface glimmered in the moonlight and the hazy mist of the summer night. I contemplated my twenty-six years. I had experienced privilege as well as denunciation, courage as well as fear, seen kindness and loyalty as well as the depths of human ugliness. Amid suffering, ruin, and death, I had above all known love and the indestructible human capacity to survive and to pursue happiness.

` All sorts of emotions swept over me, particularly when I thought of my father, as well as my grandmother and Aunt Jun-ying. Until then I had tried to suppress my memories of them, as their deaths had remained the most painful spot in my heart. Now I pictured how delighted and proud they would be for me.

I flew to Peking and was to travel with thirteen other university teachers, one of whom was the political supervisor. Our plane was due to leave at 8 P.M. on 12 September 1978, and I almost missed it, because some friends had come to say goodbye at Peking Airport and I did not feel I should keep looking at my watch. When I was finally slumped in my seat, I realized I had hardly given my mother a proper hug. She had come to see me off at Chengdu Airport, almost casually, with no trace of tears, as though my going half a globe away was just one more episode in our eventful lives.

As I left China farther and farther behind, I looked out of the window and saw a great universe beyond the plane's silver wing. I took one more glance over my past life, then turned to the future. I was eager to embrace the world.

Epilogue

I have made London my home. For ten years, I avoided thinking about the China I had left behind. Then in 1988, my mother came to England to visit me. For the first time, she told me the story of her life and that of my grandmother. When she returned to Chengdu, I sat down and let my own memory surge out and the unshed tears flood my mind. I decided to write *Wild Swans*. The past was no longer too painful to recall because I had found love and fulfillment and therefore tranquillity.

China has become an altogether different place since I left. At the end of 1978, the Communist Party dumped Mao's "class struggle." Social outcasts, including the "class enemies" in my book, were rehabilitated; among them were my mother's friends from Manchuria who had been branded "counterrevolutionaries" in 1955. Official discrimination against them and their families stopped. They were able to leave their hard physical labor, and were given much better jobs. Many were invited into the Communist Party and made officials. Yulin, my great-uncle, and his wife and children were allowed back to Jinzhou from the countryside in 1980. He became the chief accountant in a medicine company, and she the headmistress of a kindergarten.

Verdicts clearing the victims were drawn up and lodged in their files. The old incriminating records were taken out and burned. In every organization across China, bonfires were lit to consume these flimsy pieces of paper that had ruined countless lives.

My mother's file was thick with suspicion about her teenage connections with the Kuomintang. Now all the damning words went up in flames. In their place was a two-page verdict dated 20 December 1978, which said in unambiguous terms that the accusations against her were false. As a bonus, it redefined her family background: rather than the undesirable "warlord," it now became the more innocuous "doctor."

In 1982, when I decided to stay in Britain, it was still a very unusual choice. Thinking it might cause dilemmas in her job, my mother applied for early retirement, and was granted it, in 1983. But a daughter living in the West did not bring her trouble, as would certainly have been the case under Mao.

The door of China has been opening wider and wider. My three brothers are all in the West now. Jin-ming, who is an internationally recognized scientist in a branch of solid-state physics, is carrying out research at Southampton University in England. Xiao-hei, who became a journalist after leaving the air force, works in London. Both of them are married, with a child each. Xiao-fang obtained a master's degree in international trade from Strasbourg University in France, and is now a businessman with a French company.

My sister, Xiao-hong, is the only one of us still in China. She works in the administration of the Chengdu College of Chinese Medicine. When a private sector was first allowed in the 1980s, she took a two-year leave of absence to help set up a clothes design company, which was something she had set her heart on. When her leave was up, she had to choose between the excitement and risk of private business and the routine and security of her state post. She chose the latter. Her husband, Specs, is an executive in a local bank.

Communication with the outside world has become part of everyday life. A letter gets from Chengdu to London in a week. My mother can send me faxes from a downtown post office. I phone her at home, direct dial, from wherever I am in the world. There is filtered foreign-media news on television every day, side by side with official propaganda. Major world events, including the revolutions and upheavals in Eastern Europe and the Soviet Union, are reported.

Between 1983 and 1989, I went back to visit my mother every year, and each time I was overwhelmed by the dramatic diminution of the one thing that had most characterized life under Mao: fear.

In spring 1989 I traveled around China researching this book. I saw the buildup of demonstrations from Chengdu to Tiananmen Square. It struck me that fear had been forgotten to such an extent that few of the millions of demonstrators perceived danger. Most seemed to be taken by surprise when the army opened fire. Back in London, I could hardly believe my eyes when I saw the killing on television. Was it really ordered by the same man who had been to me and to so many others a liberator?

Fear made a tentative comeback, but without the all-pervasive and crushing force of the Maoist days. In political meetings today, people openly criticize Party leaders by name. The course of liberalization is irreversible. Yet Mao's face still stares down on Tiananmen Square.

The economic reforms of the 1980s brought an unprecedented rise in the standard of living, partly thanks to foreign trade and investment. Everywhere in China officials and citizens greet businessmen from abroad with overflowing eagerness. In 1988, on a trip to Jinzhou, my mother was staying at Yu-lin's small, dark, primitive apartment, which was next to a rubbish dump. Across the street stands the best hotel in Jinzhou, where lavish feasts are laid on every day for potential investors from overseas. One day, my mother spotted one such visitor coming out of a banquet, surrounded by a flattering crowd to whom he was showing off photographs of his luxury house and cars in Taiwan. It was Yao-han, the Kuomintang political supervisor at her school who, forty years earlier, had been responsible for her arrest.

May 1991

Index

ABOUT THE AUTHOR

Jung Chang was born in Yibin, Sichuan Province, China, in 1952. She was a Red Guard briefly at the age of fourteen and then worked as a peasant, a "barefoot doctor," a steelworker, and an electrician before becoming an English-language student and, later, an assistant lecturer at Sichuan University. She left China for Britain in 1978 and was subsequently awarded a scholarship by York University (UK), where she obtained a Ph.D. in Linguistics in 1982—the first person from the People's Republic of China to receive a doctorate from a British university.

Jung Chang lives in London and is writing a biography of Mao.

Wild Swans

by Jung Chang

1. All three of the women at the center of *Wild Swans* display great courage, often to a stunning extent—speaking out in times of enforced unanimity, facing firing squads, risking their lives for the sake of others. Compare the kinds of bravery they exemplified. Does one stand out as particularly courageous?

2. The twentieth century could rightly be called an era of violence in China, and the lives of these three women were touched by brutality. Although none was violent by nature, all were witnesses to—and sometimes victims of—naked savagery, to the extent that it may have begun to seem almost mundane. How did this affect their lives and specifically their political feelings?

3. The women of *Wild Swans* lived through an era during which they were constantly being called upon to swear loyalty to a new regime or a new leading figure, each one distant from their day-to-day lives, and each usually claiming to be more "revolutionary" or diehard than the one before. What was the effect of this disorientation? Did the women ever show a sense of political or spiritual homelessness?

4. In twentieth-century China, romantic love was strictly controlled and radically circumscribed—and yet such feelings played a powerful role in the lives of the principal figures in this book. How did the politicization of the deeply personal affect them? At what cost did these men and women pursue love?

5. Familial love was also the object of close government scrutiny and control in the last century, despite the historical importance of the clan in Chinese tradition. Particularly watchful was the Communist regime, which stipulated heavy penalties for "putting family first."

The key players in *Wild Swans* often found themselves caught between concern for their loved ones and the social and political demands placed on them. Discuss the range of ways in which they reacted to this.

6. Ceremony, pageantry, and ritual have been important elements of Chinese culture for millennia. As the author notes, it was not uncommon even in the twentieth century for a family to bankrupt itself to put on an impressive wedding or funeral. Did prevailing attitudes about ceremony seem to change over the course of the narrative in *Wild Swans*? What attitudes did the individual women appear to hold on the subject?

7. After the Kuomintang era and the brief occupations in the north by the Soviets and Japanese, the advent of Communism was embraced by the author's parents. Soon Jung Chang herself, born during the early years of the Chinese Communist Party's rule, was swept up in the widespread fervor for the party. But seeds of doubt slowly begin to appear in her mind. What do you think were the key moments in Jung Chang's and her parents' changes of heart? Why?

8. For obvious reasons, Jung Chang's narrative of her own life contains the most details, reported feelings, and other personal touches. Describe her psychological growth or transformation during the course of her young life. Did you feel she reported her thoughts honestly? Did you ever applaud her choices? Did you ever disapprove?

9. *Wild Swans* is a work of biography and autobiography with many novelistic elements. It is also a valuable work of twentieth-century Chinese history. What did you learn about the country from reading it? If you knew the basic outline of the history, was anything especially striking because of the personal narrative approach?